Student Resources

The printed text is not all that you have to rely on in your study of macroeconomics. The following Web-based resources are also available to help you learn faster and more effectively:

Text Home Page

http://macro.swcollege.com

- **Before the Test Interactive Quizzes:** At the text's home page, you can take interactive quizzes on concepts covered in each chapter of the text.

- **Chapter-Ending *Online Applications*:** Each *Online Application* problem is an extensive Internet exercise that takes you to a particular URL to engage in an application. Every *Online Application* also includes a section entitled "For Group Study and Analysis."

- **"*Link to...*" Web Resources:** Each *Link to...* feature includes Internet resources relating to the subject of the feature and the proposed research project. These are maintained and updated on the home page.

- **On the Web Margin URLs:** These margin URLs are also included and updated at the text home page.

Macro Xtra! Site

http://macroxtra.swcollege.com

- **Interactive Key Graphs:** You can access Web-based *Key Graphs* to experiment with factors that shift schedules and to work through guided interactive exercises illustrating fundamental ideas of alternative macroeconomic theories.

- **Online Perspectives:** Readings on topics covered in each chapter, which are referenced in the margin of the book beside the most relevant text, are available at this site. Each *Online Perspective* reading includes quiz questions covering the reading's key points.

- **Economic Applications Margin Features:** These features appear in margins alongside related text and direct you to the Macro Xtra! site for links to *EconData* and *EconDebate* sites of South-Western that closely relate to concepts discussed in the text.

Macro   xtra!

CONGRATULATIONS!

Your purchase of this new textbook includes complimentary access to the Macro Xtra! Web Site (http://macroxtra.swcollege.com). Macro Xtra! offers a variety of online learning enhancements, including:

INTERACTIVE KEY GRAPHS

Interactive Key Graphs provide you with hands-on interaction with many of the important graphs in the text. You can access an interactive version of a diagram, work through guided exercises, and experiment with changes in macroeconomic variables that induce shifts in schedules.

ONLINE PERSPECTIVES

Online Perspectives provide readings on topics covered in each chapter with associated quiz questions to test your comprehension of the reading.

ECONOMIC APPLICATIONS (e-con @pps)

EconNews Online, EconDebate Online, and EconData Online features help to deepen your understanding of theoretical concepts through hands-on exploration and analysis of the latest economic news stories, policy debates, and data.

XTRA! QUIZZING

You can create and take randomly-generated quizzes on whichever chapter(s) you wish to test yourself, and endlessly practice for exams.

Tear Out Card Missing?

If you did not buy a new textbook, the tear-out portion of this card may be missing, or the Access Code may not be valid. Access Codes can be used only once to register for access to Macro Xtra!, and are not transferable. You can choose to either buy a new book or purchase access to the Macro Xtra! site at http://macroxtra.swcollege.com.

HOW TO REGISTER YOUR SERIAL NUMBER

STEP 1   Launch a Web browser and go to http://macroxtra.swcollege.com

STEP 2   Click the "Register" button to enter your serial number.

STEP 3   Enter your serial number exactly as it appears here and create a unique User ID, or enter an existing User ID if you have previously registered for a different product via a serial number.

SERIAL NUMBER: SC-0001K4GA-MAXT

STEP 4   When prompted, create a password (or enter an existing password, if you have previously registered for a different product via a serial number). Submit the necessary information when prompted. Record your User ID and password in a secure location.

STEP 5   Once registered, follow the link to enter the product, or return to the URL above and select the "Enter" button. Note that the duration of your access

xtra

THOMSON
SOUTH-WESTERN

For technical support, 1-800-423-0563 or en support@thomsonlea

Macroeconomics
Theories, Policies, and International Applications
Third Edition

Roger LeRoy Miller
Institute for University Studies
Arlington, Texas

David VanHoose
Department of Economics
Baylor University

THOMSON
SOUTH-WESTERN

Australia · Canada · Mexico · Singapore · Spain · United Kingdom · United States

SOUTH-WESTERN
™
THOMSON LEARNING

Macroeconomics: Theories, Policies, and International Applications, Third Edition
Roger LeRoy Miller, David VanHoose

Editor-in-Chief
Jack Calhoun

Team Leader
Michael P. Roche

Publisher of Economics
Michael B Mercier

Senior Acquisitions Editor
Michael W. Worls

Senior Developmental Editor Jan Lamar

Marketing Manager
Lisa L. Lysne

Senior Production Editor
Ann Borman

Manufacturing Coordinator
Sandee Milewski

Compositor
Parkwood Composition,
New Richmond, WI

Printer
Transcontinental

Internal Designer
Ann Borman

Cover Designer
Tippy McIntosh

Cover Photo
Artville

Copyeditor
Pat Lewis

Indexer
Bob Marsh

Library of Congress Control Number: 2002115371

ISBN: 0-324-15992-7

Dedications

To Sandra, Jeff, and Remi,
May your growing family
enjoy growing wealth,
health, and happiness
forever.
From your friend

RLM

For Carol.

DDV

Contents in Brief

Contents

Unit II: Classical Macroeconomic Theory and Economic Growth 49

Chapter 3 *The Self-Adjusting Economy—Classical Macroeconomic Theory: Employment, Output, and Prices* 51

Chapter 4 *Classical Macroeconomic Theory: Interest Rates and Exchange Rates* 78

Chapter 5   *Utopia Just Beyond the Horizon or Future Shock?*—The Theory of Economic Growth   98

Unit III   Keynesian and Monetarist Macroeconomic Perspectives   131

Chapter 6   *Business Cycles and Short-Run Macroeconomics*—Essentials of the Keynesian System   133

Chapter 7   *Fiscal Policy*—What Can Government Spending and Taxation Policies Accomplish?   169

Chapter 8   *Do Central Banks Matter?*—Money in the Traditional Keynesian System   197

Unit IV   Rational Expectations and Modern Macroeconomic Theory   307

Chapter 11   *The Pursuit of Self-Interest*—Rational Expectations, New Classical Macroeconomics, and Efficient Markets   309

Management Notebook
Tracking Business
Labor Costs in the United
States 349

LINK to Policy
Indexing Employee
Compensation to Firm
Performance 366

Management Notebook
Taking into Account
Morale Effects When
Weighing Whether to
Eliminate Jobs or Cut
Workers' Pay 384

Global Notebook
Voting to Keep the
Insider-Outsider Model
Relevant to Europe 386

Chapter 16   *Policymaking in the World Economy—* International Dimensions of Macroeconomic Policy   482

To the Instructor

A fact that we kept in mind as we wrote the two previous editions of *Macroeconomics: Theories, Policies, and International Applications* was that intermediate macroeconomics can be a challenging course to teach. In this third edition, we have again made every effort to make this the most pedagogically sound text in the field. Toward this end, we have extensively improved the entire teaching-learning package:

- **Web resources for the text have been significantly enhanced.** In addition to resources available at the text's home page (http://macro.swcollege.com), there is also a Macro Xtra! site (http://macroxtra.swcollege.com) containing a number of learning tools.

- In each chapter following the introductory first unit, we have highlighted a *Key Graph*. Via the Macro Xtra! site, a student can access an interactive version of the identified diagram, work through guided exercises, and experiment with changes in macroeconomic variables that induce shifts in schedules.

- Also available at the Macro Xtra! Web site are *Online Perspective* **readings relevant to each chapter**. References to these readings have been placed in the margin beside relevant text. Accompanying each Internet-based reading are quiz questions that students can use to test their comprehension.

- **Interactive *Before the Test* online quizzes** covering the material in each chapter of the text are now available for students at the text's home page (http://macro.swcollege.com).

- **PowerPoint slides for all figures and tables** are available to instructors.

- **The *Instructor's Manual, Test Bank,* and *Study Guide*** have all been updated and enhanced. Qualified instructors can now download the *Test Bank* via links available at the text's home page.

- We have developed **32 new learning-motivating *Policy Notebook, Global Notebook,* and *Management Notebook* features** that illustrate the applicability of macroeconomics to up-to-date topics of current interest.

- The opening to each chapter now introduces an issue that is addressed in a chapter-concluding **Link to Policy, Link to the Global Economy, or Link to Management feature**. Each *Link to . . .* feature provides an in-depth illustration of policy, international, or management applications of concepts addressed within the chapter. Each of these features includes suggested research topics and Internet resources students can use to explore them.

- Another new feature in this edition is a one-page **Macroeconomics in Perspective feature at the beginning of each unit**, which helps provide the context for the topic areas covered in the unit's chapters.

- Also new to this edition are **Economic Applications margin features** that steer students, via the Macro Xtra! site, to *EconData* and *EconDebate* Web pages provided by South-Western that closely relate to concepts discussed in the text.

Within the text, we have addressed several fundamental issues that have emerged in recent years, including:

- How much information technologies contribute to economic growth (Chapter 5).
- The role of computer and software investment in the recent recession (Chapter 6).
- The upsurge of international tax competition (Chapter 7).
- Possible explanations for the apparent direct relationship between the inflation rate and the unemployment rate from the early 1990s until 2001 (Chapter 10).
- The interplay between the interest-rate-focused monetary policies of the Federal Reserve and the European Central Bank (Chapter 11).
- Adoption of inflation targets in several nations (Chapter 14).
- The macroeconomic effects of international financial crises and the role of the International Monetary Fund (Chapter 16).

Of course, we strengthened the key elements of the original edition of the book in the following ways:

- Even though this edition has been slimmed down by 25 pages, we have expanded the text to 16 chapters to help sharpen our presentations of all macroeconomic fundamentals.
- Chapter 3 now focuses students' attention solely on the determination of wages and prices and of employment and output in the classical model, and Chapter 4 follows up with a detailed consideration of the classical theory's perspective on the determination of real and nominal interest rates and exchange rates.

- We have continued to strive for the fullest possible integration of global macroeconomic issues throughout the text. The new Chapter 9 provides a full exposition of the *IS-LM-BP* framework as applied to both fixed and floating exchange rates, which permits instructors to address a broader range of international issues earlier in the course. Chapter 16 now addresses the macroeconomic implications of international financial flows and surveys the policymaking functions of the International Monetary Fund and the World Bank.

Presentation of Intermediate Macro Theory

In this third edition of *Macroeconomics: Theories, Policies, and International Applications*, we have not lost sight of our central goal, which is to cover all of the essential elements of intermediate macroeconomics within a compact and highly accessible text. **Essential topics we address include:**

- Gross domestic product, price indexes, and the balance of payments.
- The classical theory of output, employment, price-level, and interest-rate determination.
- The essential determinants of economic growth.
- The Keynesian income-expenditure theory, the *IS-LM* model, and trade-balance determination.
- Macroeconomic policymaking with fixed versus floating exchange rates.
- Short-run and long-run Phillips curves, monetarism, and the theory of political monetary cycles.
- Rational expectations, new classical macroeconomics, modern Keynesian contracting theory, and recent developments in new Keynesian and real-business-cycle models.
- Rules versus discretion in monetary, fiscal, and exchange-rate policies.
- The macroeconomic implications of variations in international capital flows and the possible role for policymakers in addressing international financial crises.

Features That Teach and Reinforce

Motivating students is essential. The following learning-motivating features appear throughout the book:

POLICY NOTEBOOKS: A key aspect of macroeconomics that all instructors must use to motivate their students is that macroeconomic policy issues continue to dominate the news. Included among the new features that are appropriately placed and referred to within the text are the following:

- Is Health Care What the U.S. Economy Ordered?

- Interest Rates and Inflation Rates Really Do Tend to Move Together
- Quantifying the Stabilization Gains from the Income Tax
- Gauging the Stock Market's Effect on Consumption
- The Fiscal Theory of the Price Level—A Deep Idea, or a Crazy Notion?
- Meandering Marginal Tax Rates
- Is Central Bank Secrecy Required to Avoid Creating Self-Fulfilling Expectations?

GLOBAL NOTEBOOKS: As in the first and second editions, a key emphasis is that macroeconomics can no longer be regarded as a domestic subject. U.S. economic events affect economies all over the world, but the reverse is also true. Global issues in macroeconomics are not only exciting to read about, but also important to understand. We have included among others the following new features:

- A Global Current Account Deficit—Evidence for Alien Visitations to Planet Earth?
- An Old-Fashioned Explanation for High Unemployment in France
- Inflation and GDP Growth—Is There a Relationship?
- High Tax Rates on Labor and Consumption in Europe
- Were Capital Controls Malaysia's Salvation?
- Voting to Keep the Insider-Outsider Model Relevant to Europe
- Will Expansion of the European Union Lengthen Policy Time Lags?

MANAGEMENT NOTEBOOKS: These features show how macroeconomics directly relates to today's business environment. Included are features such as the following:

- Why Are Wages So Much Higher in Information Technology Industries?
- The Contribution of Information Technology to Productivity Gains in the U.S. Economy
- Investing in Computing Power
- Excess Returns and Uncovered Interest Parity
- Tracking Business Labor Costs in the United States
- Taking into Account Morale Effects when Weighing Whether to Eliminate Jobs or Cut Workers' Pay
- Are Currency Speculators Really the "Bad Guys"?

LINK TO . . . FEATURES: New to this edition are these chapter-ending features. Each feature provides an in-depth analysis of how macroeconomic concepts covered in the chapter relate to a topic in policy, management, or the global economy. Also included in every *Link to . . .* feature is a proposed research topic and Web resources (available at the text's Web site http://macro.swcollege.com) that students can use to explore the topic area.

- **Link to Management:** Does the Stock Market Forecast Business Productivity?
- **Link to The Global Economy:** The Shadow Economy—Implications for Official Economic Statistics
- **Link to Management:** Using Leading Indicators to Predict Recessions
- **Link to The Global Economy:** Tax Competition Sweeps the Globe
- **Link to Policy:** A Different Sort of Phillips Curve—A Long-Run Trade-Off between the Unemployment Rate and the Rate of Price-Level Acceleration?
- **Link to The Global Economy:** Is Japan Stuck in a "Liquidity Trap"?

MACROECONOMICS IN PERSPECTIVE: These one-page features at the beginning of each unit provide context for the chapters contained in the unit, thereby giving students a clear understanding of why they are about to launch into the study of the particular area of macroeconomics the unit addresses.

CRITICAL–THINKING EXERCISES Critical thinking is an important aspect of every college student's education. We make sure that students are introduced to critical-thinking activities by ending each *Policy Notebook, Global Notebook, Management Notebook,* and *Link to* . . . feature with critical-thinking questions called "For Critical Analysis." Suggested answers to these critical-thinking questions are included in the *Instructor's Manual.*

Full Global Integration Throughout

Macroeconomics: Theories, Policies, and International Applications is the only text in this field to fully integrate global economics, starting from Chapter 1. The student is introduced to world macroeconomic facts from the outset in Chapter 1 and then presented with a straightforward explanation of measuring international transactions in Chapter 2. Chapter 4 presents the international dimensions of classical theory, including exchange-rate determination and the purchasing power parity doctrine. By Chapter 6, full integration of the balance of trade in a macroeconomic model is presented. Each chapter that follows continues this integration within whatever model is discussed.

Of course, there is also a text-ending Chapter 16 on "Policymaking in the World Economy—International Dimensions of Macroeconomic Policy."

The Importance of Growth

A chapter on the theory of economic growth appears early in the text. In addition to standard growth theories, we examine population growth and labor-force participation, freedom, immigration, protectionism, government budgetary policies, and supply-side policymaking as these topics relate to economic growth.

Additionally, we examine new growth theory, specifically knowledge, innovation, and the importance of education. We ask the question "Does growth feed on itself?"

Internet Resources

Most students, particularly those taking intermediate-level economics courses, are familiar with how to use the Internet. We provide the following features to help guide students' exploration of resources on the Web:

1. *Interactive Key Graphs:* Unique to this text are interactive diagrams that students can access at the Macro Xtra! Web site (http://macroxtra. swcollege.com). Students can use these Web-based *Key Graphs* to experiment with factors that shift schedules and to work through guided interactive exercises illustrating fundamental ideas of alternative macroeconomic theories.
2. *Before the Test* Interactive Quizzes: At the text's home page (http://macro. swcollege.com), students can take interactive quizzes on concepts covered in each chapter of the text.
3. *Online Perspectives:* Readings on topics covered in each chapter, which are referenced in the margin of the book beside the most relevant text, are available at the Macro Xtra! Web site. Each *Online Perspective* reading includes quiz questions covering the reading's key points.
4. *Economic Applications* Margin Features: These features appear in margins alongside related text and direct students to the Macro Xtra! site for links to *EconData* and *EconDebate* sites of South-Western that closely relate to concepts discussed in the text.
5. *On the Web* Margin URLs: New and updated *On the Web* features appear in the margins throughout the book. Each opens with a question linking the feature to the text material and provides brief guidance for navigating through the Web site. These margin URLs are also included and updated on the text's support site: http://macro.swcollege.com.
6. *Link to . . .* Web Resources: Each *Link to . . .* feature includes Internet resources relating to the subject of the feature and the proposed

research project. The *Link to . . .* features are all included and updated at the text's Web site: **http://macro.swcollege.com**.

7. **Chapter–Ending *Online Applications:*** All *Online Application* problems at the conclusion of each chapter have been updated or replaced. Each problem is an extensive Internet exercise that takes the student to a particular URL and then asks him or her to engage in an application. Every *Online Application* also includes a section entitled "For Group Study and Analysis." The *Online Applications* are included in the textbook's Web site: **http://macro.swcollege.com**.

Special Note on the Graphs

We believe that the more than 150 graphs for this textbook are the best in any text at this level. All of the lines and curves are color coded in a consistent manner to help your students understand the relationships between the various curves. In addition, we have provided full explanations underneath or alongside each graph or set of graphs.

Finally, fourteen graphs in the text are highlighted as ***Interactive Key Graphs.*** Opportunities to experiment with each of these graphs and to work through guided interactive exercises illustrating fundamental aspects of these diagrams are available to students at the Macro Xtra! Web site.

Key Pedagogy

Learning cannot occur in a vacuum. We have made sure that students using this text have an ample number of pedagogical devices that will help them master the material.

FUNDAMENTAL ISSUES AND ANSWERS WITHIN THE TEXT OF EACH CHAPTER

A unique feature of *Macroeconomics: Theories, Policies, and International Applications* is the inclusion of four to seven fundamental issues at the beginning of each chapter. Within the text itself, the fundamental issues are repeated and highlighted with appropriate answers. Students immediately see the relationship between text materials and the key issues of the chapter.

VOCABULARY IS STRESSED

Because vocabulary is often a stumbling block, we have **boldfaced** all important vocabulary terms within the text. Immediately in the margin these boldfaced terms are defined. They are further defined in the end-of-text glossary.

CHAPTER SUMMARY

The chapter summary is presented in a numbered, point-by-point format that corresponds to the chapter-opening fundamental issues, further reinforcing the full circular nature of the learning process for each chapter.

QUESTIONS AND PROBLEMS

Each chapter now has separate sections entitled *Self-Test Questions*, which focus on conceptual issues, and *Problems*, which emphasize analytical and quantitative applications. Answers to all odd-numbered problems are located at http://macro.swcollege.com (within the "Student Resources"). Answers to every problem in the book appear in the *Instructor's Manual*.

SELECTED REFERENCES AND FURTHER READING

Appropriate references for materials in the chapter are given in this section.

STUDY GUIDE

The *Study Guide,* which was written by text co-author David VanHoose, is designed to facilitate active learning by students. It provides summaries of chapter contents, including an application of a key diagram used in each chapter, along with lists of the key terms for students to look for and define in their own words as they read the text. To assist students in testing their understanding of the material, the *Study Guide* also includes 20 multiple-choice and 10 short-answer questions per chapter.

INSTRUCTOR'S MANUAL

The *Instructor's Manual,* written by David Findlay of Colby College, is intended to simplify the teaching tasks that instructors face. For each chapter it offers an overview of key concepts and objectives, a detailed outline built upon chapter headings in the text, and a special "teaching tips" section. Also included are suggested answers to the critical-thinking questions in the *Policy Notebooks, Global Notebooks,* and *Management Notebooks* and answers to chapter questions and problems.

TEST BANK

One of the most challenging aspects of teaching is evaluation of student performance. To assist instructors in this endeavor, a *Test Bank,* written by David Findlay of Colby College, that includes between 30 and 70 multiple-choice questions per chapter, along with correct answers, is available to all adopters *of Macroeconomics: Theories, Policies, and International Applications* via the text's home page (http://macro.swcollege.com).

EXAMVIEW

Computerized Testing Software contains all of the questions in the printed test bank. This program is an easy-to-use test creation software compatible with Microsoft Windows. Instructors can add or edit questions, instructions, and answers, and select questions by previewing them on the screen, selecting them randomly, or selecting them by number. Instructors can also create and administer quizzes online, whether over the Internet, a local area network (LAN), or a wide area network (WAN).

POWERPOINT SLIDES

For many instructors, multimedia presentations have become an indispensable part of the teaching-learning process. A complete set of PowerPoint slides is available for adopters of this text.

MACRO XTRA!

Free access to the Macro Xtra! Web site (a $25 value) is packaged with every new copy of this text (students purchasing a used book can buy access to Macro Xtra! at http://macroxtra.swcollege.com). Macro Xtra! offers a variety of online learning enhancements, including "Interactive Key Graphs" (which allow students hands-on interaction with many of the important graphs in the text); links to "Economic Applications" (*EconData* and *EconDebate* online features that closely relate concepts discussed in the text to the latest contemporary applications); and "Online Perspectives" (reading on topics covered in each chapter with associated quiz questions). Icons throughout each chapter of the book alert students to an associated Macro Xtra! online enrichment activity anytime one is available to enhance the textual material.

Acknowledgments

We benefited from an extremely active and conscientious group of reviewers of the manuscript for this third edition of *Macroeconomics: Theories, Policies, and International Applications*. To the following reviewers, we extend our sincere appreciation for the critical nature of your comments that we think helped make this a better text.

Michael Ellis
Kent State University

Frank Hefner
College of Charleston

Christina M. L. Kelton
The Pennsylvania State
University

Mark Pernecky
St. Olaf College

Shahrokh Shahrokhi
San Diego State University

Mark Wheeler
Western Michigan University

Of course, no textbook project is done by the authors alone. We wish to thank our editor, Mike Worls, for his indispensable assistance. Jan Lamar provided truly outstanding coordination of all reviews and of supplements. Our production team of Bill Stryker and Ann Borman have developed the best design in this market as well as providing consistent guidance throughout the project. The copyeditor, Pat Lewis, who is the best in the business, masterfully rearranged our manuscript to make the book read more smoothly. Peggy Buskey and Vicky True provided indispensable oversight of the process of developing the Internet resources for the text. Sue Jasin of K&M Consulting provided her usual top-notch assistance, and for that we extend our sincere thanks. For all editions, David Findlay, the author of the *Instructor's Manual* and *Test Bank,* essentially served as an additional manuscript reviewer, and we are especially grateful for his comments and suggestions.

We anticipate continuing to revise this text for years to come and therefore welcome all comments and criticism from students and professors alike.

R.L.M.
D.D.V.

Unit I
Introduction

Chapter 1
The Macroeconomy

Chapter 2
How Do We Know How We're Doing—Measuring Macroeconomic Variables

1

The Importance of Predicting Overall Economic Activity

Private economic forecasting is a big business that attracts a number of entrepreneurs from the ranks of trained economists. Independent economic-forecasting consulting firms sell their predictions of future economic performance to big manufacturers and financial firms, and many economic-forecasting firms earn significant revenues. The media particularly like to quote economists at economic-forecasting firms. These economists often face fewer restraints on what they can say to reporters than do government economists who wish to avoid saying anything that might affect markets or economists on firm payrolls who do not want to release internal forecasts to competitors. At the same time, consulting economists like the publicity, because it attracts the attention of potential clients.

Herein lies a potential problem: an alleged bias in economic forecasts. To appear to be a "maverick" with a better forecasting technique, a private economic forecaster could be tempted to inflate (or deflate) his or her true forecasts just to attract attention. Indeed, studies of forecasts indicate that independent forecasters tend to deviate the most from "consensus forecasts," which are based on an average of forecasts by a number of well-known firms. Of course, independent forecasters generally deny that their predictions are biased by a desire to "get their name in the papers." They point out that if they were to go out on a limb just to get attention and turned out to be persistently wrong, their business would quickly dry up. Some do admit, however, that when they think a change is on the way, they may hurry the public release of this prediction in an attempt to "scoop" the competition.

In addition to these private forecasting firms, state governments, the federal government, and central banks such as the Federal Reserve employ sizable staffs of economists—and pay them with taxpayers' funds—to develop forecasts for policymakers to use as a guide to the future. Many multinational corporations also have a number of economists on staff to provide managers with forecasts of the likely pace of domestic and worldwide economic activity during coming months. How well the overall economy is doing has become a critical piece of information for literally millions of citizens, businesspersons, and policymakers around the globe.

Deciding what economic data are important and whether and how individuals and policymakers should respond to changes in an economy's overall performance and forecasts of its future performance are subjects of *macroeconomics*. This is the analysis of aggregate activity within nations and across the globe, and it is the subject of the path of study on which you are about to embark.

The Macroeconomy

FUNDAMENTAL ISSUES

1. What is macroeconomics, and what are its distinguishing features?

2. What are key macroeconomic variables?

3. What are the key issues in macroeconomics?

4. Why is macroeconomics a controversial subject?

It exists in every country. In Switzerland, it accounts for an estimated 7 percent of total economic activity. In Germany and Canada, the percentage is close to 15 percent, and in Greece it is nearly 30 percent. It is the shadow economy, *or the portion of a nation's economy devoted to activities that people intentionally hide from the government.*

In fact, there is no way to know exactly how large any nation's shadow economy really is. Economists at best can try to infer its size from official statistics on the volume of economic activity, the amount of money in circulation, and the average rate at which people use money to purchase goods and services.

Economists know for certain that the existence of the shadow economy creates two fundamental problems. One is that it causes official statistics to understate the actual amount of economic activity taking place within a nation during a given interval. Among other things, this complicates economists' efforts to understand how different macroeconomic variables are interrelated, and it complicates policymakers' assessments of the state of the economy. The other problem is that unreported activity typically is untaxed. The shadow economy undoubtedly costs the world's governments billions of dollars in forgone taxes.

3

In this chapter you will learn about key macroeconomic variables. By the time you have completed the chapter, you will understand why the shadow economy is such a problem for economists and policymakers.

Objectives of This Book and How They Relate to You

Not surprisingly, the key objective of this text is to help you understand how the macroeconomy works and, more specifically, how monetary and fiscal policy might be able to reduce the frequency and severity of nationwide business fluctuations. In this chapter, you will learn some macroeconomic facts for the United States and for the world, as well as why macroeconomics continues to be a controversial subject. In Chapter 2, you will learn how we measure macroeconomic variables, including those associated with international transactions. Indeed, sections dealing with international trade and finance appear in virtually every chapter in this text.

Chapters 14, 15, and 16 discuss what policymakers should be doing, but to participate in that discussion, you need a foundation in macroeconomic theory. Thus, you first will learn about classical and traditional macroeconomic theory and also about the most modern macroeconomic theories that economists use today.

This foundation in macroeconomics will be of value whatever your plans for the future. If you continue your studies in economics, an in-depth knowledge of macroeconomics is critical to understanding monetary theory, international trade and finance, and economic growth and development. If you choose a career in business economics, a knowledge of macroeconomics is also essential. If you are going to study business and management in general, you will face a variety of problems, dilemmas, and issues throughout your studies and your business career, all of which will relate in some way to what you are going to learn in this text.

Finally, even students who go into other fields can benefit from a course in intermediate macroeconomics. Virtually every day, you will encounter macroeconomic issues in the print media as well as on radio and television.

The Subject of Macroeconomics

Macroeconomics is the branch of economics concerned with the study of a nation's total economic activity. In contrast to **microeconomics,** which focuses on studying resource allocation and price determination in *individual* markets for goods and services, macroeconomics seeks to understand the *overall* structure and performance of a nation's economy.

MACROECONOMICS: The branch of economics that focuses on the study of the total economic activity of a nation.

MICROECONOMICS: The branch of economics that focuses on the study of the allocation of resources and the determination of prices and quantities in individual markets.

The Relationship between Macroeconomics and Microeconomics

In 1964 one observer defined macroeconomics as "a laudable attempt to explain how large parts (or the whole) of an economy work, without pretending to know how the component parts work." At that time, there may have been some truth to this observation. Many economists who specialized in macroeconomics, known as *macroeconomists,* regarded their field as very distinct from microeconomics.

Now, however, most macroeconomists view their field of study as inseparable from microeconomics. Even though macroeconomists still do *not* try to understand every aspect of the economy's components—this remains the domain of microeconomists—today macroeconomics is much more closely related to microeconomics than it was in the 1960s. Indeed, many macroeconomists insist that their theories of how the economy works possess **microeconomic foundations.** In other words, they believe that useful theories in macroeconomics should have a basis in a microeconomic understanding of the behavior of the economy's *key* components.

MICROECONOMIC FOUNDATIONS: A basic understanding of the behavior of individual components of the economy that underlies many macroeconomic theories.

AGGREGATION: The act of summing up the individual parts of the economy to obtain total measures of economy-wide performance.

5

CHAPTER 1 The Macroeconomy

The Distinguishing Features of Macroeconomics

Nevertheless, macroeconomics differs from microeconomics in two important ways. First, **aggregation,** the summing of individual economic components to obtain totals for the economy as a whole, is central to macroeconomics. A microeconomist studies individual consumers, workers, and business firms, which by themselves are too small relative to the economy for their individual decisions to affect a nation's overall economic performance. In contrast, a macroeconomist cares about the *aggregate* effects of the sum total of all the individual decisions by these consumers, workers, and firms. Although understanding how individual decisions are reached is often useful to a macroeconomist, the real issue in macroeconomics is the big picture, or how the economy as a whole performs.

For instance, health-care expenses constitute a much larger portion of total spending in the U.S. economy than they did half a century ago. Furthermore, health care is of considerable importance to each of us. Yet a macroeconomist typically does not believe that a detailed analysis of the market for health care is needed to understand the overall determinants of U.S. economic performance. The market for health care is just one of many among which U.S. residents allocate their expenditures. There also are markets for entertainment services, the provision of electricity, and so on. What matters to a macroeconomist is the aggregate spending of U.S. residents, not how they allocate their spending among consumption of health care, entertainment, and electricity.

Nevertheless, one item does stand out as important to understanding the overall performance of the economy. This is *money,* or the item that we typically use to facilitate the exchange of goods and services. As you will discover as you progress through this text, most macroeconomists believe that understanding the role of this particular good is a key aspect of developing a full theory of how the economy functions. After all, people use money in the bulk of their exchanges for goods and services in *all* markets in the economy. Money, therefore, ought to matter for everyone. As we shall discuss, the key issue for many macroeconomists is *how* money matters. Whereas some macroeconomists believe that changes in the total amount of money in circulation exert significant short-run effects on aggregate production of goods and services, others contend that such changes mainly affect the prices of goods and services without influencing actual production.

In sum, aggregation and a consideration of the role that money plays are the two distinguishing features of macroeconomics. As you will see, these key themes will surface throughout this text:

MACROECONOMIC VARIABLES: Aggregate measures of total economic activity.

STANDARD OF LIVING: The capability of an average resident of a nation to consume goods and services.

Any theory of overall economic activity must seek to explain how aggregate economic variables are determined and what role money plays in this process.

FUNDAMENTAL ISSUE #1

What is macroeconomics, and what are its distinguishing features?

Macroeconomics is the study of the economy as a whole. Its two distinguishing features are its focus on the determination of aggregate variables and its need to consider the role of the quantity of money in circulation.

Macroeconomic Facts: The United States

Before we consider the various issues that macroeconomists seek to address, we need to think about some important **macroeconomic variables,** or aggregate measures that summarize various aspects of overall economic activity. There are three broad groupings of macroeconomic variables: (1) aggregate output and employment, (2) money growth and inflation, and (3) measures of international trade and of the U.S. dollar's exchange value relative to other nations' currencies.

Output and Employment

Figure 1–1 displays measures of aggregate output and employment in the U.S. economy for every year since 1959. The output measure is *real gross domestic product,* or *real GDP.* As we shall discuss in detail in Chapter 2, real gross domestic product is a measure of the total amount of production of final goods and services. The employment measure is the annual average of monthly totals of the number of people over the age of sixteen employed in income-generating jobs.

CHANGES IN U.S. PRODUCTIVITY AND LIVING STANDARDS   Figure 1–1 shows that the U.S. economy experienced significant growth during the latter half of the twentieth century. The total number of people employed more than doubled between 1959 and 2003, and the total output of goods and services more than tripled. Because the production of goods and services grew faster than employment, the per worker production of goods and services clearly increased during this interval. This means that a typical worker became *more productive.* Indeed, in 1959 the average output of an employed individual was equal to $34,230 (in 1996 prices) worth of real output of goods and services. By 2003, this amount had increased to more than $65,000 (in 1996 prices), so a typical U.S. worker was almost twice as productive in 2003 as compared with 1959.

An implication of this productivity improvement has been that a typical U.S. resident can consume more goods and services as compared with years past. This means that the overall U.S. **standard of living,** or overall capability of an average employed resident to consume goods and services, has increased considerably.

Figure 1–1   Output and Employment in the United States, 1959–Present

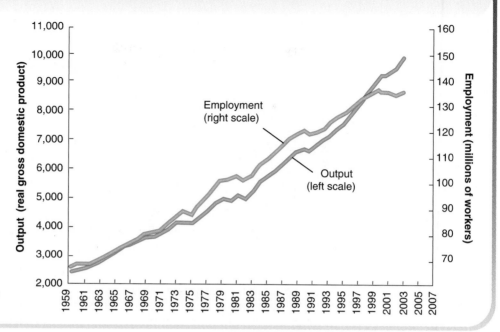

SOURCES: *Economic Report of the President, 2002; Economic Indicators* (various issues).

THE UNEMPLOYMENT RECORD   Of course, not all people who might like to have a job are actually employed. Such people are among the ranks of the unemployed, and the total number of these individuals constitutes the economy's **unemployment,** which is simply the number of people who currently are interested in gainful employment but do not have a job. Figure 1–2 on the following page displays U.S. unemployment since 1959. As you can see, unemployment can vary considerably from year to year.

As we shall discuss, these data on output and employment and unemployment raise a host of questions for macroeconomists. Two questions in particular are obvious: What determines the long-run output and employment performance of an economy such as that of the United States? What causes year-to-year changes in this performance that result in the unemployment variations that we observe?

UNEMPLOYMENT: The number of people who are interested in finding a job but currently do not have one.

Money Growth and Inflation

Figure 1–3 on the next page shows annual growth rates for measures of the quantity of money in circulation and of the overall level of prices in the United States. Money growth is the annual rate of change in a Federal Reserve measure of money called *M2,* which includes currency, checking accounts, savings accounts, and small-denomination savings deposits. The price measure is the *consumer price index (CPI),* which is a weighted average of the prices of goods and services purchased by a typical U.S. resident.

On the Web

How does the United Nations compare national economic performances? To learn the answer to this question, go to the UN's home page at **http://www.un.org/english/**, click on "Economic and Social Development," and then click on "Statistics."

UNIT I Introduction

Figure 1–2   U.S. Unemployment, 1959–Present

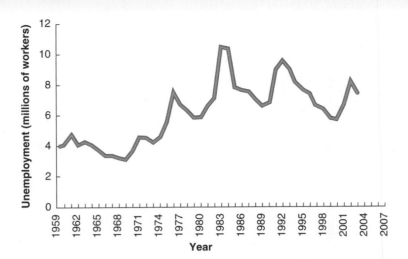

SOURCES: *Economic Report of the President,* 2002; *Economic Indicators* (various issues).

As you can see, money growth rates and inflation rates can exhibit considerable year-to-year variability. These two macroeconomic variables appear to be closely related during some intervals but not during others.

As noted earlier, macroeconomists have good reason to think that, in the long run, the amount of money in circulation affects the overall level of

Figure 1–3   Annual Money Growth Rates and Inflation Rates in the United States, 1960–Present

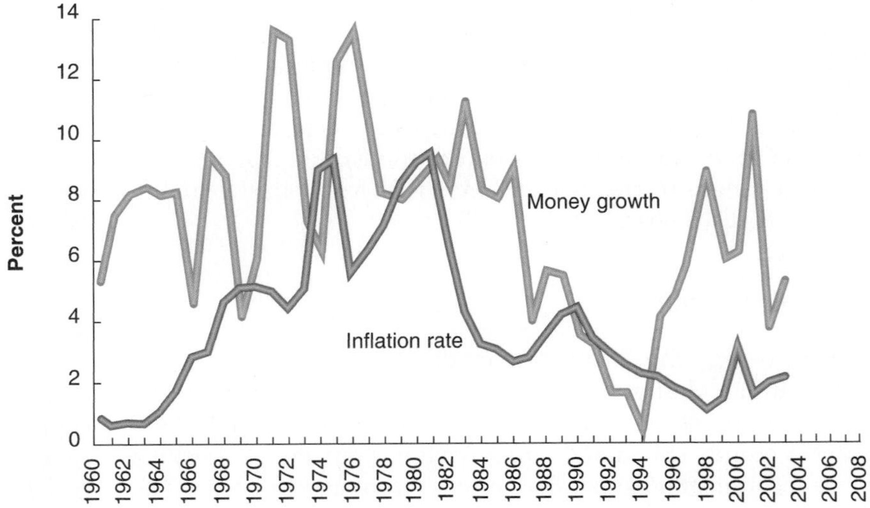

SOURCES: *Economic Report of the President,* 2002; *Economic Indicators* (various issues).

prices that consumers pay for goods and services. Therefore, understanding the changing relationship between money growth and inflation is an important issue in macroeconomics.

International Trade and the Value of the Dollar

The sets of macroeconomic variables we have just considered are known as **domestic variables.** They are aggregate measures of economic activity relating primarily to the U.S. economy in isolation from the rest of the world. Like many other nations today, however, the United States engages in a considerable amount of international exchange of goods, services, and financial assets such as stocks, bonds, and currencies.

INTERNATIONAL TRADE AND THE TRADE DEFICIT   Although nations now exchange more *services* across their borders than in years past, a sizable portion of international exchange still entails transfers of physical goods. *International trade* refers primarily to exchanges of goods. Domestic purchases of goods manufactured and sold by business firms located abroad are **merchandise imports.** Sales of goods manufactured and sold by domestic firms to residents of other nations are **merchandise exports.** The difference between merchandise exports and merchandise imports is a nation's **merchandise balance of trade,** or the *trade balance.* A country with a positive trade balance—merchandise exports exceed merchandise imports—experiences a *trade surplus.* In contrast, a country with a negative trade balance, meaning that its residents import more goods than they export, runs a *trade deficit,* which Figure 1–4 on the following page shows the United States has experienced since the late 1970s.

In Chapter 2 we shall discuss the pros and cons of using the merchandise balance of trade as an indicator of a nation's performance in the world economy. Despite some important shortcomings with this interpretation, many observers use the trade balance as a bellwether for a country's relative standing in the world economy.

EXCHANGE RATES   Another macroeconomic variable that relates to a nation's performance in the world economy is the **exchange rate,** or the value of a nation's currency in terms of the currencies of other nations. There are different rates of exchange among all the currencies of the world. For instance, on a given day one dollar might trade at a market exchange rate of 110 Japanese yen per dollar or 0.60 British pounds per dollar. Nevertheless, Figure 1–5 on the next page displays an overall index measure of the U.S. dollar's value relative to the currencies of its major trading partners around the globe.

As you can see, the dollar's value relative to other currencies rose considerably in the early 1980s. The dollar's value then declined very quickly through the early 1990s before leveling off, rising again, and then leveling off again. Why such movements in exchange rates occur is another important macroeconomic issue.

DOMESTIC VARIABLES: Macroeconomic variables that provide information about a nation's economic activity in isolation from the rest of the world.

MERCHANDISE IMPORTS: Domestic residents' purchases of physical goods manufactured and sold by business firms located abroad.

MERCHANDISE EXPORTS: Domestic firms' sales of physical goods to residents of other nations.

MERCHANDISE BALANCE OF TRADE: Merchandise exports minus merchandise imports.

EXCHANGE RATE: The value of a nation's currency measured in terms of the currency of another nation.

Figure 1–4   The U.S. Balance of Trade, 1949–Present

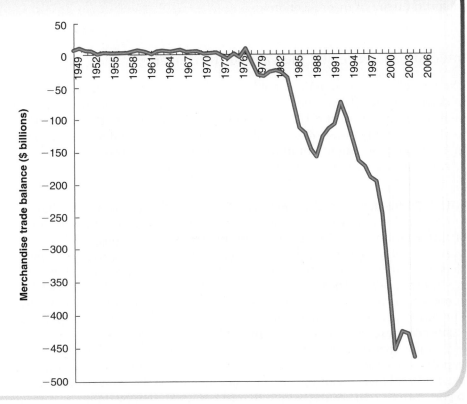

SOURCES: *Economic Report of the
President,* 2002; *Economic Indicators*
(various issues).

Figure 1–5   The Changing Value of the Dollar

Aside from a signifi-
cant increase during
the mid-1980s, in
general the value of
the dollar has been
steady or slightly
falling since the
1970s.

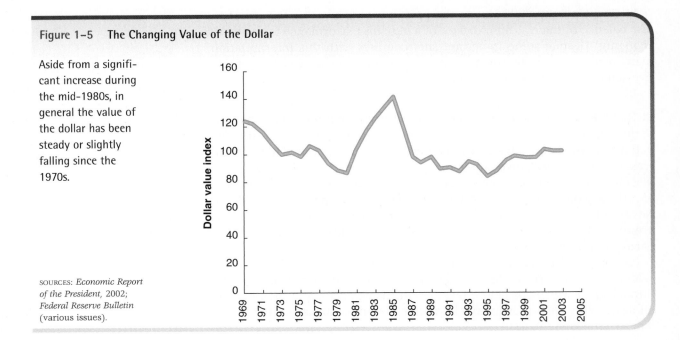

SOURCES: *Economic Report
of the President,* 2002;
Federal Reserve Bulletin
(various issues).

FUNDAMENTAL ISSUE #2

What are key macroeconomic variables?   The field of macroeconomics seeks to explain movements in several macroeconomic variables, or aggregate measures of economic activity. These include domestic variables, such as a nation's total output, employment, and unemployment and its money growth rate and inflation rate, or measure of price changes. Macroeconomics also addresses international variables, such as a nation's trade balance and the rate of exchange between its currency and the currencies of other nations.

Macroeconomic Facts: The World

Levels of economic activity often differ markedly across nations of the world. Standards of living are often higher in small nations than in large nations. Output and employment sometimes grow at very high rates in some countries even as other nations experience little or no growth in output and employment. Likewise, inflation rates may decline in some nations even as they rise in others.

Output and Inflation: International Comparisons

Because nations' populations vary, direct comparisons of total output levels can be misleading. For instance, the population of China is much larger than the population of the United Kingdom, and China's total output of goods and services is also larger. Nevertheless, the standard of living of a typical British resident is much higher than that of a resident of China.

Consequently, economists typically compare nations' output performances by calculating and comparing measures of output per person, called *output per capita.* Figure 1–6 on the next page displays estimates of per capita output for selected nations. Also shown is the estimated average output per capita for the world. As the figure indicates, a few nations such as Germany and the United States, with per capita output levels at six to seven times the world average, have very high living standards as compared with the rest of the world. In contrast, nations such as China, Nigeria, and Bolivia have per capita output levels well below the world average.

Some parts of the world currently are growing quickly, while others are experiencing relatively low output growth. This can be seen in Figure 1–7 on page 13, which compares average annual output growth rates for 1994–2003 of three industrialized nations—the United States, Japan, and Germany—with estimated 1994–2003 growth rates of four less-developed regions of the world. With the exception of the Europe/Middle East area, the less-developed regions generally have grown at a more rapid pace than Japan, Germany, and even the United States. The growth of many emerging economies slowed in 1997 and 1998, but the pace of growth has picked up in the 2000s.

On the Web

Is there a relationship between inequality and a nation's growth? To keep up with some of the most recent research on this issue, visit the World Bank's PovertyNet home page at http://www.worldbank.org/poverty/.

Figure 1–6   Per Capita Output Comparisons for Selected Nations

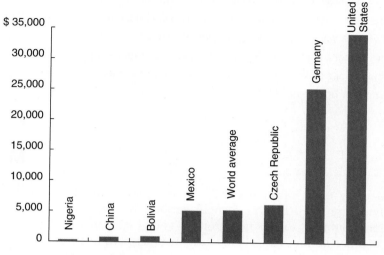

Although some nations have per capita output levels very close to the world average, there also are considerable disparities in per capita output levels.

SOURCE: World Bank, *World Development Indicators,* 2003.

Inflation rates can also differ considerably across countries and regions of the world. Panel (a) of Figure 1–8 shows the recent inflation experiences of the United States, nations of the European Union (including Germany, the Netherlands, and the United Kingdom), Japan, and developing countries of Asia (including China, the Philippines, and Vietnam). Although panel (a) indicates that developing nations in Asia have experienced higher inflation than the United States, the European Union nations, and Japan, panel (b) shows that inflation rates have been even higher in developing countries in Africa (such as Angola, Kenya, and the Sudan), in the Middle East and Eastern Europe (including Iran, Jordan, and Turkey), and in the Western Hemisphere (including Argentina, Brazil, and Nicaragua). Some nations in Asia, including Japan, have even experienced episodes of *deflation* (a declining price level) in recent years.

World Output and Its Changing Distribution

The world is a collection of distinct, though interrelated, national economies. Nevertheless, it is possible to use market exchange rates to measure the total output of all nations of the world in U.S. dollar terms. Panel (a) of Figure 1–9 on page 14 shows how this measure of total world output has changed over time.

macroxtra!
Online
Perspective

To consider the various ways that the world's central banks try to forecast inflation, go to the Chapter 1 reading, entitled "Why Do Central Banks Monitor So Many Inflation Indicators?" by Sharon Kozicki of the Federal Reserve Bank of Kansas City. http://macroxtra.swcollege.com

Figure 1–7 Output Growth Comparisons

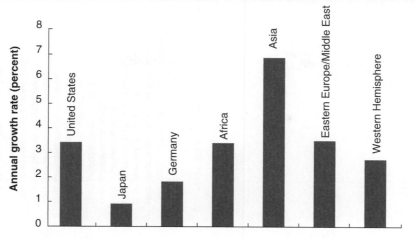

With the exception of the developing nations of the Europe/Middle East area, developing regions have been experiencing output growth rates at least as great as those of the United States, Japan, and Germany.

SOURCE: International Monetary Fund, *World Economic Outlook,* April 2002.

Panel (b) shows how the distribution of world output between the United States and other nations of the world has changed since the late 1980s. The large share of world output accounted for by the U.S. economy in each selected year is striking. Nevertheless, as this panel indicates, the share of total world output produced in the United States has leveled off as other

Figure 1–8 Average Inflation Rates for Selected Nations and Regions of the World

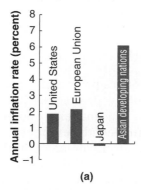

(a)

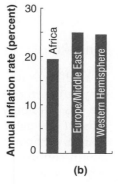

(b)

Although inflation rates in developing nations of Asia are several times higher than those of the United States, countries in the European Union, and Japan [panel (a)], the inflation rates of other developing regions are even higher [panel (b)].

SOURCE: International Monetary Fund, *World Economic Outlook,* April 2002.

Figure 1–9   World Output and the Declining Predominance of the United States

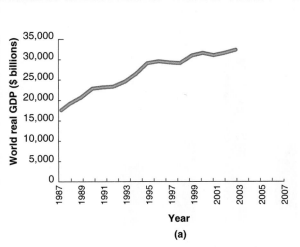

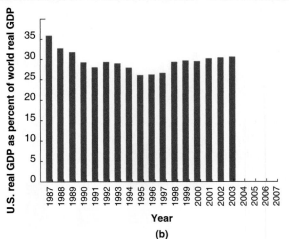

Panel (a) shows how an aggregate world real GDP measure has changed since the late 1980s. Panel (b) displays the ratio of U.S. real GDP to this world real GDP measure: it indicates that U.S. real GDP has leveled off as a share of world real GDP.

SOURCES: International Monetary Fund, *World Economic Outlook,* April 2002; *Economic Report of the President,* 2002; *Economic Indicators* (various issues).

nations have grown. The United States still has the preeminent economy of the world, but other countries are catching up, albeit slowly.

The Key Issues of Macroeconomics

In light of the evidence on macroeconomic variables that we have presented, let's now identify the issues that stand out as important to consider in the study of macroeconomics.

Long-Run Economic Growth

macroxtra!
Economic
Applications

Is more spending on infrastructure the key to economic growth? To review alternative perspectives on this debate and make your own judgment, go to EconDebate Online.
http://macroxtra.swcollege.com

As we have seen, the United States possessed the world's preeminent economy during the twentieth century. Before the eighteenth century, however, the U.S. economy was among the smaller economies of the world. During most of the eighteenth and nineteenth centuries, the economies of Britain, France, Germany, and Austria were all larger. In the sixteenth and seventeenth centuries, Spain and Portugal had been among the economic powerhouses of the world. In earlier centuries, civilizations located in what are now Italy, Greece, Turkey, Egypt, and China had contended for economic preeminence.

What has accounted for the changes in the relative positions of world economies? The answer must be that during certain periods some economies have grown faster than others, which has allowed them ultimately to bypass economies that previously were predominant in output, income, and wealth.

Thus, if we are to sort out the reasons why nations' prospects for world economic leadership rise or fall, we must understand the determinants of economic growth. This is an important subject of macroeconomics. Although the topic of economic growth surfaces at various points throughout this text, Chapter 5 is devoted solely to this subject.

Short-Run Variations in Output and Employment

The determinants of economic growth ultimately explain the performances of national economies over periods of many years. Factors that influence a nation's long-run growth rarely attract bold media headlines, however. For better or worse, most of us find ourselves captivated by news of near-term variations in nationwide economic activity, which, after all, can have an immediate impact on our lives.

Traditionally, therefore, a key objective of macroeconomics is to try to understand why an economy's near-term performance can depart considerably from levels consistent with its long-term potential. For instance, what accounted for the significant economic slowdowns in the United States in the mid-1970s and early 1980s? Why did brief but sharp slowdowns in economic activity occur in the early 1990s and early 2000s? What accounted for the sustained expansion of the U.S. economy throughout the 1990s, even as the pace of activity slowed in many other parts of the world? Looking into the past, what factors caused the great economic contraction of the 1930s? How do international trade and foreign exchange markets influence short-run economic performance? These questions matter, because even short-run variations in economic activity can entail significant social costs in the form of lost jobs and temporarily or even permanently derailed careers. (Among those who are employed around the world, the hours of work can vary widely; see on the next page *Global Notebook: A Hard Day's Work Means Different Things in Different Places.*)

Our basis for thinking about both long-run growth and short-run economic fluctuations is the *classical macroeconomic model* discussed in Chapters 3 and 4. This model of the determination of employment, output, prices, and the exchange rate provides a foundation for Chapter 5's discussion of economic growth as well as for the traditional views of short-run economic performance that are the subject of Chapters 6 through 10.

Money, Expectations, and Inflation

As noted earlier, a key element of any macroeconomic theory is the role of the quantity of money in circulation. You will learn in the chapters that follow that a key division among alternative theories of economic activity relates to this issue. Some theories propose an important role for money as a factor influencing output and employment. In contrast, competing macroeconomic theories hold that the only macroeconomic variables that the quantity of money can affect are prices and exchange rates.

Global NOTEBOOK

A Hard Day's Work Means Different Things in Different Places

Undoubtedly, there have been times in your life—on a full-time or part-time job or even in your efforts as a student—when you have felt that you have put in long hours of work. Exactly what it means to put in "long hours" differs around the world, however.

As you can see in Figure 1–10, the average number of hours that an individual works during an entire year can vary considerably from place to place. In the United States, the average resident works just over 1,978 hours per year. Comparing this figure with the 1,376 hours that a typical resident of Norway spends working each year reveals that on average a U.S. resident devotes the equivalent of more than fifteen additional 40-hour weeks to work each year relative to an individual in Norway.

Although the average U.S. resident spends more time working than a typical individual in any other developed, industrialized nation, people in some countries, such as the Czech Republic and South Korea, allocate even more of their time to work each year. A typical South Korean resident works almost 500 hours more than an average U.S. resident and nearly 1,100 hours more than a resident of Norway. This means that for every hour that an individual in Norway spends on the job, someone in South Korea is at work 50 minutes longer.

For Critical Analysis
Does the fact that a typical individual in Spain works more hours per year than an average German resident necessarily imply that the individual in Spain produces more output of a comparable good or service in that time?

Figure 1–10   **Annual Hours Worked Per Person in Selected Nations**

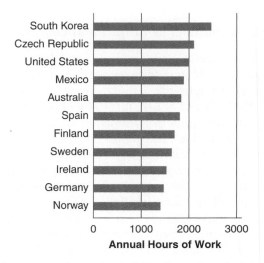

The amount of time that individuals spend on the job can vary considerably across countries.

SOURCE: International Labor Organization.

Chapters 11, 12, and 13 discuss modern perspectives on this issue. You will learn that *expectations* are a key element of current macroeconomic theories. According to these theories, the extent to which people anticipate future events and policies is a crucial determinant of current and future economic activity. Although the proponents of expectation-based macroeconomic theories agree on this fundamental point, they reach different conclusions about how the quantity of money affects the economy and how macroeconomic policymaking should be conducted.

By its nature, macroeconomics is a policy-oriented subject. What, if anything, should policymakers do to try to influence aggregate economic activity? How should they formulate policies? These questions depend in part upon which macroeconomic theory one adopts, which is why the first thirteen chapters of this text focus on theoretical issues in macroeconomics.

Nevertheless, certain questions are specific to *policy* issues alone. Among these are the following: What are appropriate goals for macroeconomic policy? Should policymakers follow explicit rules in policymaking, or should they simply do what seems best at the time? These issues are addressed in Chapters 14 and 15.

International Trade, Exchange Rates, and Macroeconomic Performance and Policy

The extent of international trade increased sharply during the 1970s and has grown gradually since then. Many economists argue that nations' economies have become more interdependent as a result of this increase in trade. Since World War II, variations in U.S. economic performance have affected the economies of Europe and Japan. Now, however, a sharp downturn in economic activity in Japan can have broader effects than in years past, when only a few U.S. export and import industries might have felt the aftershocks.

The structure of this text reflects this changed world environment. Although Chapter 16 focuses solely on issues relating to international macroeconomic policy, such topics as the balance of payments, exchange-rate determination, the role of international trade as a factor in economic growth, and potential conflicts between domestic and international policy objectives surface in nearly every chapter. Today, students of macroeconomics cannot ignore international issues, no matter where they live.

FUNDAMENTAL ISSUE #3

What are the key issues in macroeconomics? One key issue is determining the factors that influence a nation's long-term growth in output and employment. Another is isolating the reasons that output and employment can vary so much from their long-run levels as a result of short-run fluctuations in economic activity. A third important issue is resolving the role that the quantity of money plays in affecting a nation's output, employment, and prices. Fourth, determining the proper goals and implementation of policies is a centerpiece issue of macroeconomics. Finally, macroeconomists recognize that greater interdependence among the world's nations means that it is important to understand how factors such as exchange rates and international trade affect a country's economic performance.

Why Macroeconomics Is a Controversial Subject

Historically, one of the hallmarks of macroeconomics has been that people can disagree sharply about how the economy works and how macroeconomic policies should be conducted. To a student taking an intermediate macroeconomics course, these disagreements can make the study of macroeconomics somewhat frustrating at times. After all, shouldn't macroeconomists be able to develop one single, *correct* theory to explain macroeconomic performance and to guide policymakers?

Unfortunately for macroeconomics students, there is no one macroeconomic theory that economists regard as "truth." Although all macroeconomists work with the same data and use the same basic economics tools to try to understand the functioning of the economy, many of them have reached different conclusions. From a student's perspective, the negative aspect of this state of affairs is that the student must learn more than one approach to macroeconomic theory. The positive aspect, however, is that the current disagreements make macroeconomics an interesting area to study.

The Problem of Aggregation

Traditionally, one of the main sources of contention about macroeconomics has been the issue of aggregation. Just how much can we aggregate before developing a theory of how the economy works?

AN EXAMPLE OF THE AGGREGATION PROBLEM   Consider an example of a property-casualty insurance company with three lines of business: auto insurance, liability insurance, and workers' compensation insurance. All three types of insurance share the common characteristics that the company earns income from selling policies and experiences losses arising from claims of policyholders. Because the company knows that it will experience some losses, it, like other insurers, maintains cash reserves from which it makes payments when losses occur. Hence, a key issue for the company is estimating its policyholders' losses from auto, liability, and workers' compensation insurance so that it can hold the appropriate amount of reserves.

There are at least two basic approaches that the company might use to estimate the losses that its policyholders will experience. One approach is to carefully examine how losses evolve over time in each *separate* line of business. In auto insurance, losses will depend on how safely insured policyholders drive, how safe the roads are in the areas where they live, and so on. In liability insurance, such factors as the legal treatment of claims against policyholders will affect potential losses. Finally, in workers' compensation insurance, the care that employers and employees take in the workplace will determine the magnitude of losses resulting from injuries or deaths on the job. The insurance company's *actuaries,* professionals who specialize in the analysis of statistical data, could analyze past losses in each line of business individually to determine appropriate cash reserves for each type of policy. Then, the company could total these amounts to determine the total cash reserve that it should maintain.

An alternative approach is for the company's actuaries to add up the past losses of all three lines of business *before* doing their statistical analysis and estimating future losses. With this purely aggregative approach, the actuaries could then calculate the company's total cash reserve needs directly. Most insurance company actuaries do not use this alternative approach, however, because the three lines of business are very different. Auto loss experiences of policyholders typically depend on factors that are very different from workers' compensation losses. The same is true of liability losses. Consequently, insurance actuaries rarely use such a purely aggregative approach to calculate a company's needed cash reserves.

HOW MUCH SHOULD MACROECONOMISTS AGGREGATE?   This example illustrates a problem that some have with macroeconomics as a field of study and research. Critics of macroeconomics commonly argue that trying to understand the behavior of aggregate variables of concern to macroeconomists is not unlike summing up three insurance business lines to estimate a company's loss reserves. Just as aggregation is misleading to an insurance company, they argue, it can lead to the wrong answers for economists.

If macroeconomists fully accepted this argument, they would have to give up macroeconomics. If they did, we would be left in a quandary. Economic policymakers would have no guidance when trying to determine how their policies might affect the economy. Business firms would have no theory to guide their efforts to understand the overall business climate that they face. When choosing among potential leaders, individual citizens would have no understanding of the broad macroeconomic issues their nation faces. In short, we would live in a world where people would no longer try to understand aggregate macroeconomic variables, even though those variables are crucial to their welfare.

General Equilibrium Analysis   Another possible reaction would be to decide that the answer might lie in **general equilibrium analysis.** In this approach to economics, the economy is regarded as a collection of many consumers, workers, and firms. Each makes its own choices, and then all these choices interact to determine wages, prices, quantities of output, and incomes in many *individual* markets. A general equilibrium theorist could *then* develop aggregate measures of wages, prices, output, and income to contemplate how these aggregates change when all people in the economy respond to some external event, such as a new policy action.

Returning to our insurance example, this approach would be analogous to insurance actuaries computing a company's cash reserves by estimating losses for *each individual policyholder.* An insurance company would face two problems in such a task. First, if it is a large company, then it might have to analyze thousands and thousands of policyholders. Second, not all policyholders experience losses from auto accidents, liability claims, or workers' compensation losses. Indeed, some policyholders might be loss-free for years before filing a claim. Others by chance might experience a number of losses. The issue for the insurance company, of course, is predicting the *average* losses across all policyholders. In this case, insurance actuaries can actually *benefit* from some aggregation. This is why they study the loss experiences of full *lines of business* instead of individual policyholders.

Aggregating across Markets   Analogously, economists potentially can *gain* from aggregating, as long as they do not overdo it. As you will see in

GENERAL EQUILIBRIUM ANALYSIS: An approach to analyzing the economy by examining the multiple interactions of all individual consumers, workers, and firms.

future chapters, complete macroeconomic models can never really be boiled down to a single diagram or equation. Just as actuaries aggregate the loss experiences of policies in similar lines of business, economists aggregate across similar markets. They consider aggregations of labor markets, financial markets, and markets for goods and services under the assumption that individual behavior in markets for labor, financial assets, and goods and services is essentially the same. Then macroeconomists develop theories about how these various aggregated components function and interact. Ultimately, these theories permit macroeconomists to develop a theory of how fully aggregate variables such as total output and income are determined. (Recently, one sector in particular has helped boost U.S. output and employment even as the rest of the economy lagged behind; see *Policy Notebook: Is Health Care What the U.S. Economy Ordered?*) In the same way, an actuary works out cash reserves for broad lines of business before determining the insurance company's total cash needs.

The key issue, naturally, is how much aggregation is appropriate. Not surprisingly, economists disagree on this point. As you will see in future chapters, this issue is a source of division between alternative approaches to macroeconomics.

Data Problems

Another potential source of division among macroeconomists involves the data that they are able to observe. We shall discuss measures of key macroeconomic variables, such as aggregate output, aggregate income, and the price level, in Chapter 2. All these measures have two important characteristics in common. First, they are artificially constructed measures. As you will learn, for instance, measures of the overall price level are index numbers. In contrast to a market price, which is the actual price at which buyers and sellers agree to exchange a good or service, a measure of the aggregate price level is an index number that economists construct after the fact. This can lead to disagreement about how to interpret changes in the price level or in other macroeconomic variables.

Second, macroeconomic data can rarely be regarded as the result of a *controlled experiment.* Chemists and physicists, for example, can control background conditions to test their theories. Some microeconomists also have developed experimental methods to test various theories of market interactions. Macroeconomists, however, are limited to the aggregate data they observe. Conducting a controlled experiment for the entire economy is not feasible. In this regard, macroeconomics is somewhat like astronomy: Astronomical researchers can observe the planets, stars, quasars, galaxies, and so on but cannot act upon them. Like an astronomer, all a macroeconomist can do is interpret the data as well as possible. Naturally, the end result can be further differences in interpretation among macroeconomists.

As you will learn in this text, there have indeed been wide differences in the ways that macroeconomists have perceived the world that they observe, as revealed to them by data on macroeconomic variables. Although all macroeconomic theories share a number of basic elements, they also differ in many respects. Before we can discuss these issues fur-

Is Health Care What the U.S. Economy Ordered?

As U.S. economic activity began to wane in 2001 and 2002, most people had trouble seeing places where there might be a silver lining. For most businesses, and in particular manufacturing and retailing, things looked bad all over.

For the health-care sector of the economy, however, there was barely a ripple. As panel (a) of Figure 1–11 indicates, during late 2000 and throughout 2001 and into 2003, there was an upsurge in the portion of U.S. economic growth relating to health care—everything from clinics and hospitals to drug manufacturing and biotechnology research firms. Without this sector's contribution, the economic downturn in 2001 and 2002 would have been much more severe.

Panel (b) shows that health care also helped keep job growth from dropping off as much as it would have otherwise. Producing additional health-care-related goods and services required additional employees at clinics, pharmaceutical firms, and the like, which contributed to U.S. employment even as job growth fell off in other parts of the economy.

For Critical Analysis
Does the U.S. experience with diverging economic activity and employment levels for health care versus other industries necessarily imply that aggregation is misguided?

Figure 1–11   The Contribution of Health Care to U.S. Economic Activity and Employment

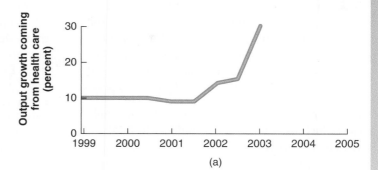

(a)

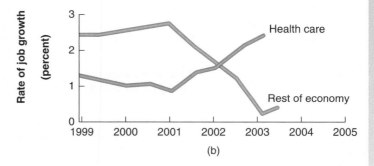

(b)

As economic activity in much of the United States fell off in the early 2000s, health care's contribution to U.S. output and employment was surging.

SOURCE: Bureau of Economic Analysis.

ther, however, it is important that you understand the data with which macroeconomists work. We turn to this issue in the next chapter.

> **FUNDAMENTAL ISSUE #4**
>
> **Why is macroeconomics a controversial subject?**   Two aspects of macroeconomics in particular lead to disagreements among economists. One is that economists may diverge in their views about how much aggregation is appropriate. Another is that macroeconomists work with artificially constructed aggregate measures of economic activity that cannot be manipulated through controlled experiments. These two features of macroeconomics lead to differences in opinion and divergent interpretations, thereby leading to theoretical controversies.

LINK to **The Global Economy**

The Shadow Economy—Implications for Official Economic Statistics

The *shadow economy*—also known as the "underground economy"—is the portion of a nation's economy devoted to hidden endeavors that are not included in official measures of total economic activity. Many of these endeavors keep a number of people gainfully employed and account for significant flows of income. Most of them, however, are also illegal.

Estimating the Size of the Shadow Economy and How Much Official Statistics Understate Total Economic Activity

Friedrich Schneider of the Johannes Kepler University of Linz, Austria, has conducted a detailed study of the relative sizes of the shadow economies within a number of countries. To estimate the amount of economic activity that takes place within a nation, Schneider carefully examined currency holdings in the country. After taking into account all the various factors that might plausibly determine the amount of currency used by the nation's residents, such as their incomes, payment habits, and interest rates, he estimated an "excess" amount of currency used to finance underground economic activities not recorded in official statistics. Then, based on the extent to which people use currency to fund measured transactions, Schneider developed estimates of the total transactions undertaken in the shadow economy.

Panel (a) of Figure 1-12 shows his estimates of the relative size of the shadow economy as a

Figure 1–12   The Relative Size of the Shadow Economy and the Total Tax and Social Security Burden in Selected Nations

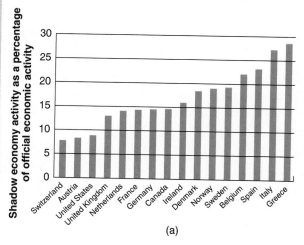

(a)

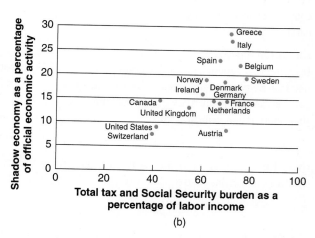

(b)

Panel (a) shows that the relative size of the underground economy differs considerably from country to country. As panel (b) indicates, the relative size of a nation's underground economy tends to increase with the amount of the tax and Social Security burden.

SOURCE: Friedrich Schneider, "The Increase of the Size of the Shadow Economy of Eighteen OECD Countries: Some Preliminary Explanations," CESifo Working Paper no. 306, June 2000.

percentage of officially measured economic activity for sixteen countries. Because these figures are percentages of total economic activity tabulated by national governments, they indicate the fraction by which official statistics may understate aggregate activity in these countries. According to these estimates, in Switzerland official figures understate total activity by about 7.5 percent. In Greece the extent of the understatement is close to 28.5 percent.

Explaining the Shadow Economy

Although people may engage in shadow economy transactions for a variety of reasons, many underground endeavors are aimed at avoiding taxes. Thus, a possible hypothesis is that the relative size of a nation's underground economy is likely to rise as the relative amount of income that people must transfer to the government increases.

Panel (b) displays the figures from panel (a) matched with each nation's average tax and Social Security payments as a percentage of labor income. As you can see, overall there does appear to be a positive relationship between the relative size of a nation's shadow economy and the overall tax and Social Security burden that its government imposes on workers and firms.

Research Project

How might using currency holdings to estimate the size of the shadow economy be prone to produce over- or understatements? In what ways can the existence of a sizable shadow economy affect a nation's government? Make a list of steps that countries might take to try to reduce the size of the shadow economy. Take a stand on which of these steps is likely to do the least harm to the government's interests while simultaneously reducing the size of the shadow economy significantly.

Web Resources

1. What are the implications of the shadow economy? For a detailed examination of how various nations are affected by the shadow economy, read selections in "The Underground Economy: Global Evidence of Its Size and Impact," edited by Owen Lippert and Michael Walker, Fraser Institute, at http://www.oldfraser.lexi.net/publications/books/underground/.

2. Are any pitfalls associated with using currency holdings to estimate the size of the shadow economy? Find out by reading "The Demand for Currency and the Underground Economy," by Thérèse Laflèche, at http://www.bankofcanada.ca/en/res/r944b-ea.htm.

1. Macroeconomics and Its Distinguishing Features: Macroeconomics is the study of the entire economy. One distinguishing feature of macroeconomics is its focus on the aggregate, economy-wide variables. The other is the requirement to explain the role of the quantity of money in circulation, given money's use in all markets in the economy.

2. Key Macroeconomic Variables: The primary measures of overall economic activity include domestic variables, such as the total output, employment, and unemployment of a nation and its money growth and inflation rates, and international variables, including the trade balance and exchange rates of a nation.

3. Key Issues in Macroeconomics: One primary issue is determining the factors that influence a nation's long-term growth in output and employment. Another is identifying the reasons that output and employment fluctuate in the short

run. A third key issue is determining what influence the quantity of money has on a nation's output, employment, and prices. A fourth important issue is identifying the appropriate goals of macroeconomic policies and determining how they should be implemented. Finally, macroeconomics seeks to understand how factors such as exchange rates and international trade affect a country's economic performance.

4. Why Macroeconomics Is a Controversial Subject: Two features of macroeconomics in particular engender conflicting views. One is that macroeconomists may disagree about how much aggregation is optimal. Another is that macroeconomists observe and analyze artificially constructed data on economic activity, which they cannot manipulate via controlled experiments. These features of macroeconomics naturally produce different interpretations and foster controversies.

Self-Test Questions

(Answers to odd-numbered questions may be found on the Web at **http://macro. swcollege.com** under "Student Resources.")

1. Explain in your own words the difference between microeconomics and macroeconomics.

2. Why does the quantity of money in circulation occupy a central role in macroeconomics?

3. Why does it make sense to compare nations' output performances on a per capita basis?

4. As an example of the aggregation problem that macroeconomists face, suppose that you were asked to predict the overall grade point average at your college or university. Discuss the pros and cons of making such a prediction based on an analysis using data at the level of (a) all individual students and professors, (b) departments, and (c) the college or university.

Problems

(Answers to odd-numbered problems may be found on the Web at **http://macro. swcollege.com** under "Student Resources.")

1. Real GDP, the key measure of overall U.S. output of goods and services, was equal to $2,376.7 billion in 1960. In 2003, it was close to $9,900 billion. Using the 1960 level of GDP as a base, what is the implied percentage growth of the nation's total output between 1960 and 2003?

2. To calculate the unemployment rate, the government divides the number of unemployed people seeking work by the civilian labor force. Suppose that throughout 2005, the U.S. civilian labor force—composed of employed people and those unemployed people seeking employment—remains unchanged at 140 million people. Meanwhile the number of unemployed individuals increases from 7.00 million at the beginning of 2005 to 7.84 million at the end of the year. Based on these figures, what is the U.S. unemployment rate at the start of 2005? At the end?

3. The Federal Reserve has two key measures of the quantity of money in circulation. The first of these, M1, is the sum of currency and coins, traveler's checks, and checking deposits; it was equal to $1,137 billion in July 2001. The other, M2, is equal to M1 plus savings deposits, time deposits with denominations less than $100,000, and miscellaneous other financial assets that people can easily convert to spendable cash. M2 was equal to $5,200 billion in July 2001. In July 2002, M1 was equal to $1,195 billion, and M2 was equal to $5,613 billion. Using the starting values as a base, calculate the percentage changes in M1 and M2 during this interval.

4. In 1960, when real GDP was equal to $2,376.7 billion, U.S. exports of goods and services totaled $72.4 billion, and U.S. imports were equal to $106.6 billion. By 2001, when GDP had risen to $9,214.5 billion, exports had increased to $1,076.1 billion, and imports had risen to $1,492.0 billion. For each year, compute the following ratio: the sum of exports and imports divided by GDP. If we were to regard this ratio as an "index measure" of international trade, has the United States become a more or less internationally open economy relative to 1960?

Before the Test

Test your understanding of the material covered in this chapter by taking the Chapter 1 interactive quiz at http://macro.swcollege.com.

Online Application

An excellent resource for information about the economic performances of different regions of the United States is the Federal Reserve's "Beige Book." This publication is compiled by the Federal Reserve's Board of Governors in Washington, D.C., based on contributions from the twelve Federal Reserve Banks.

Internet URL: http://www.federalreserve.gov/fomc/BeigeBook/2003/default.htm

Title: *The Beige Book*

Navigation: Begin with the Federal Reserve's home page (http://federalreserve.gov). Click on *Monetary Policy*. Then click on *Beige Book*. Click on *Report*.

Application: Read the latest Beige Book Summary and answer the following questions:

1. What measures of overall business activity does the Beige Book's analysis consider? According to these measures, do regional variations in business activity exist at present? What is the outlook for overall U.S. business activity?

2. What measures of inflation does the Beige Book's analysis focus on? Are there currently any regional differences in inflation pressures? What is the outlook for overall U.S. inflation?

For Group Study and Analysis: Assign groups of students to individual Federal Reserve districts (or sets of districts grouped by geographic region). Have each group study the portion of the most recent Beige Book relevant to their district or region. Ask each group to summarize the economic performance of their district or region and to identify key factors that appear to have influenced this performance.

macro**xtra!**

Log on to the MacroXtra Web site now http://macroxtra.swcollege.com for additional learning resources such as practice quizzes, Interactive Key Graphs, readings, and additional economic applications.

Selected References and Further Reading

Clayton, Gary, and Martin Gerhard Giesbrecht. *A Guide to Everyday Economic Statistics*. McGraw-Hill: New York, Fifth Edition, 2001.

Economic Report of the President. Washington, D.C.: U.S. Government Printing Office. Published annually.

Frumkin, Norman. *Guide to Economic Indicators*. M. E. Sharpe: Armonk, New York, Third Edition, 2000.

International Monetary Fund. *World Economic Outlook*. Published biannually in May and October.

President's Council of Economic Advisers. *Economic Indicators*. Washington, D.C.: U.S. Government Printing Office. Published monthly.

How Do We Know How We're Doing? —

Measuring Macroeconomic Variables

FUNDAMENTAL ISSUES

1. What is gross domestic product, and how is it calculated?

2. How do economists measure international transactions?

3. What is the difference between nominal GDP and real GDP?

*I*n late 1999 and early 2000, before the U.S. economic downturn of 2001 began, the main source of worry to the Federal Reserve was inflation. Annualized inflation measured using the consumer price index—*a weighted average of the prices of goods and services that the Bureau of Labor Statistics determines a representative individual consumes—had jumped about 3 percent. It appeared that it was time for the Federal Reserve to start tapping the brakes.*

But then another piece of information arrived. Another price index called the personal consumption expenditure price index, which also involves a weighted average of a typical individual's consumption across different years, showed that the annualized inflation rate was closer to 2 percent.

Yet another price index, the producer price index that measures the average prices received by sellers of goods and services, told a different story. Annualized producer price inflation was not much above 1.5 percent.

Suddenly, it was not so apparent to officials at the Federal Reserve what, if anything, they should do to slow down economic activity. As economists debated whether an upswing in inflation was on the horizon, economic activity began to drop off in the latter part of 2000 and into 2001. Then the Federal Reserve's concern was no longer focused on inflation, which by all measures had dropped considerably.

In this chapter you will learn why it is important to develop measures of the overall level of prices in the economy. In addition, you will see how the government keeps track of transactions between U.S. residents and residents of other nations of the world. First, however, you must learn how the government measures the total volume of activity in the U.S. economy.

The Circular Flow of Income and Product

To have any idea how the economy as a whole is doing, economists must have a measure of aggregate performance. Economists have developed several such measures. The most important is the measure of the economy's output. As we noted in Chapter 1, this can give us some idea about how a nation's overall standard of living is changing.

Gross Domestic Product

The key measure of the aggregate output of an economy is **gross domestic product (GDP),** which is the total of all *final* goods and services produced within the nation's borders during a given interval (such as a year) and valued at market prices. GDP is a measure of the flow of aggregate output produced in an economy. To avoid having to add together very different items such as annual fish harvests, the production of diamond rings, and the provision of travel services, economists add up the dollar values of the final goods and services. To construct these dollar values, market prices are multiplied by the quantities produced and sold. To have market prices, however, the final goods and services must be traded in markets. This means that GDP excludes nonmarket transactions such as child-care services provided by husbands or wives who stay at home to care for their young children instead of working outside the home and sending their children to a day-care center. In addition, only the values of final goods and services are part of GDP. Hence, GDP does not include the values of exchanges of stocks, bonds, or other financial assets.

Furthermore, we cannot emphasize too much that GDP counts only the production of goods and services in their *final form* during a given period of time. If an automobile company purchases auto parts from various manufacturers and assembles them into a sport-utility vehicle during 2005 and sells the assembled vehicle that year, then only the sale price of the *vehicle* counts in GDP. The market values of the auto parts that the company purchased before assembling the sport-utility vehicle are not included in GDP separately. Doing so would result in double-counting the production and sale of these parts, because their value is already included in the sale price of the final vehicle.

Suppose, however, that when we compute 2005 GDP at the end of that year, the company still has a stock of unassembled parts and several partially assembled vehicles. Then we would count the market value of the unassembled or partially assembled parts as *inventory investment* in materials used in the production process. What if the auto company also has some fully assembled vehicles that are still unsold at the time of our GDP

GROSS DOMESTIC PRODUCT (GDP): The value of all final goods and services produced during a given period; tabulated using market prices. GDP includes foreign residents' earnings from home production but excludes home residents' earnings abroad.

calculation? Any produced but unsold goods are also included in the inventory investment. GDP includes all inventory investment that takes place during the year to ensure that we total up all production that occurred during that year.

Another item counted in GDP is the **capital consumption allowance,** which is the value of equipment used up or worn out as part of the production process and must be replaced if the existing amount of equipment is to be maintained. Economists refer to the total stock of productive equipment as **capital goods,** or goods that may be used to produce other goods and services in the future. Depreciation expense, therefore, is the allocation of new production to maintaining the current amount of capital. Because depreciation is a part of a year's production of goods, it is counted in GDP.

Income Equals the Value of Product

When thinking about the GDP measure of aggregate economic performance, Figure 2–1 can be helpful. This figure depicts a basic **circular flow diagram,** which is a chart illustrating the aggregate flows of income and product in the economy. Business firms use the total factor services—labor services, the service flow from capital goods, the flow of services from land, and entrepreneurship or business know-how—to produce goods and services. Firms

CAPITAL CONSUMPTION ALLOWANCE: The total value of capital expended during the process of production.

CAPITAL GOOD: A good that may be used in the production of other goods and services in the future.

CIRCULAR FLOW DIAGRAM: A chart that depicts the economy's flows of income and product.

Figure 2–1   The Circular Flow of Income and Product

Business firms make factor payments to households in return for the use of households' factor services. The total value of these factor payments constitutes total household income, which households spend on the goods and services that firms produce. The aggregate value of these goods and services is gross domestic product (GDP).

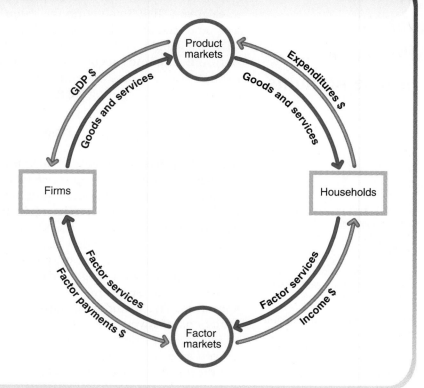

sell these goods and services in *product markets.* In turn, households, which are individuals or families, purchase these goods and services with the income that they earn by providing factor services to firms. The households receive this income in the form of wages and salaries, interest, rents, and profits. The values of these services, in turn, are determined in the *factor markets,* which are the markets for labor, capital, land, and entrepreneurship.

It is easy to see how the circular flow diagram gets its name. The diagram indicates that households purchase the product of firms—their output, or GDP—using the income that they earn from providing the factor services that go into producing GDP. Thus, the value of the circular flow in Figure 2–1 *is* the amount of GDP. This means that:

GDP serves both as a measure of the economy's total output *and* as a measure of the total income of all individuals in that economy.

GDP measures both total output and total income because it is the production of output that generates the income of households.

Throughout this text, therefore, we shall think of GDP as both an overall measure of output and an overall measure of income. As we shall see later, in a purely accounting sense there are slight distinctions between GDP and "national income." In a broader conceptual sense, however, the two are equivalent.

Measuring Domestic Variables: The National Income Accounts

A look at the circular flow diagram suggests that there ought to be two ways to calculate GDP. Totaling up the value of all spending on goods and services produced and sold or counted as inventory investment should give us GDP, as should adding together all the income earnings. Indeed, the **national income accounts,** which are the formal tabulations of the nation's income and product, take into consideration both of these approaches to computing GDP.

The Product Approach to GDP

Because our basic definition of GDP is a measure of output, it makes sense to begin with the *product approach* to accounting for a nation's income and product. This approach entails summing up the aggregate expenditures on final goods and services produced during a given year. You can think of it as determining the size of the upper flow—the flow through the product markets—in the circular flow diagram.

Table 2–1 illustrates this way of computing GDP. There are four basic types of spending on final goods and services during the year. The first is **consumption spending** by households. The second is **investment spending.** This includes business spending on new capital goods, net accumulations of inventories of newly produced goods, and expenditures on residential construction—houses and apartment buildings—by households as well as business firms. *Gross investment* includes all investment spending during the course of a year. A portion of this spending, however, is

NATIONAL INCOME ACCOUNTS: Tabulations of the values of a nation's flows of income and product.

CONSUMPTION SPENDING: Total purchases of goods and services by households.

INVESTMENT SPENDING: The sum of purchases of new capital goods, spending on new residential construction, and inventory investment.

Table 2–1 The Product Approach to Calculating Gross Domestic Product

	1988	1993	1998	2003*
Consumption spending	3,356.6	4,454.7	5,856.0	7,701.1
Investment spending	821.1	955.1	1,538.7	1,831.0
Government spending	1,036.9	1,293.0	1,538.5	2,013.2
Net export spending	−106.3	−60.5	−151.7	−370.5
GROSS DOMESTIC PRODUCT	5,108.3	6,642.3	8,781.5	11,174.8

*Estimates.
NOTE: Amounts are in billions of dollars.
SOURCES: 2002 *Economic Report of the President*; *Economic Indicators* (various issues).

On the Web

Where are the latest data on U.S. GDP and its components? One location is the Federal Reserve Bank of St. Louis's "FRED (Federal Reserve Economic Data)" at http://research.stlouisfed.org/fred/, where you can click on "Gross Domestic Product and Components."

directed to replacement of worn-out capital, or depreciation. Hence, *net investment* is equal to gross investment less depreciation. Economists regard net investment as the best indicator of the addition to the economy's stock of capital goods during a year. Nevertheless, gross investment measures total spending on such goods. For this reason, the full amount of gross investment is included in GDP.

The third form of spending on final goods and services produced in an economy is **government spending.** This is the total expenditures on goods and services by state, local, and federal governments.

The final component of GDP is **net export spending,** which is equal to total spending on domestically produced goods and services by residents of other nations, less expenditures on foreign-produced goods and services by home residents that do not constitute spending on home production. As Table 2–1 indicates, net export spending has been negative, since the 1980s reflecting the fact that spending by U.S. residents on foreign goods and services has exceeded foreign spending on U.S.-produced goods and services. The total of all four types of spending on domestically produced final goods and services during a year is that year's GDP.

The Income Approach to GDP

Table 2–2 on the following page shows the alternative approach to calculating GDP—the *income approach.* This approach attempts to measure the lower flow, through the factor markets, in the circular flow diagram in Figure 2–1. The income approach involves three steps: First, economists add together wages and salaries, interest income, rental income, and business profits. In the national income accounts, this total is called **national income,** or simply the total of all factor earnings in the economy. Second, economists add indirect taxes and transfer payments to businesses, which are sales and excise taxes and government subsidies that artificially reduce reported income flows. The sum of national income and indirect taxes is **net national product.** Next, economists add depreciation to obtain **gross national product (GNP).** Finally, they add net income earned by foreign residents from U.S.-based production to gross national product, and the result is GDP. Hence, GNP and GDP are different measures of a nation's output:

GOVERNMENT SPENDING: Total state, local, and federal government expenditures on goods and services.

NET EXPORT SPENDING: The difference between spending on domestically produced goods and services by residents of other countries and spending on foreign-produced goods and services by residents of the home country.

NATIONAL INCOME: The sum of all factor earnings, or net domestic product minus indirect business taxes.

NET NATIONAL PRODUCT: GNP minus depreciation, or national income plus indirect business taxes.

GROSS NATIONAL PRODUCT (GNP): A measure of a nation's total production that includes home residents' earnings abroad but excludes foreign residents' earnings from home production.

Table 2–2   The Income Approach to Calculating Gross Domestic Product

	1988	1993	1998	2003*
Wages and salaries	2,973.8	3,814.4	4,989.6	6,522.2
Interest income	389.4	374.3	511.9	640.0
Rental income	44.1	90.9	138.6	155.4
Business profits	743.8	972.3	1,401.3	1,662.5
NATIONAL INCOME	4,151.1	5,251.9	7,041.4	8,980.1
Indirect taxes and transfers	348.3	602.0	664.7	847.7
NET NATIONAL PRODUCT	4,499.4	5,853.9	7,706.1	9,827.8
Capital consumption allowance	627.4	812.8	1,072.0	1,367.2
GROSS NATIONAL PRODUCT	5,126.8	6,666.7	8,778.1	11,195.0
Net income payments abroad	−18.5	−24.4	+3.4	−20.2
GROSS DOMESTIC PRODUCT	5,108.3	6,642.3	8,781.5	11,174.8

*Estimates.

NOTE: Amounts are in billions of dollars.

SOURCES: 2002 *Economic Report of the President; Economic Indicators.*

GNP includes earnings of home residents abroad but excludes foreign residents' earnings from home production. In contrast, GDP excludes earnings of home residents abroad but includes foreign residents' earnings from home production. For this reason, GDP measures the value of all goods and services produced within a nation's borders.

What GDP Is and Is Not

Like any statistical measure, gross domestic product is a concept that can be both well used and misused. As already noted, economists find it invaluable as an overall indicator of a nation's economic performance. As discussed in Chapter 1, and as we shall reemphasize in Chapter 5, the ratio of GDP to the number of people in a country, or per capita GDP, is a useful benchmark measure of the standard of living of a typical resident of a nation.

Nevertheless, it is important to realize that GDP has weaknesses. Because it includes only the value of goods and services traded in markets, it excludes *nonmarket* production, such as the household services of home-makers discussed earlier. This omission can cause problems when comparing the GDP of an industrialized country with the GDP of a highly agrarian nation where nonmarket production typically is relatively more important. It also causes problems if nations have different definitions of legal versus illegal activities. For instance, a nation where gambling is legal will count the value of gambling services, which have a reported market value. In a country where gambling is illegal, however, those who provide such services naturally will not report their market value, and they will not be counted in that country's GDP. (The U.S. government is in the process of changing the way it collects and reports the data used to compute GDP; see *Policy Notebook: In the Battle of Acronyms, SIC Gives Way to NAICS in the NIPAs.*)

In the Battle of Acronyms, SIC Gives Way to NAICS in the NIPAs

There is no shortage of acronyms—words formed by combining the first letters of other words—when it comes to the way the U.S. Commerce Department's Bureau of Economic Analysis constructs the National Income and Product Accounts, or NIPAs (pronounced as it appears). Today, however, a new acronym is replacing one that has been around for seventy years.

The Shortcomings of the SIC System

Since the 1930s, economists putting the NIPAs together have relied on the Standard Industrial Classification, or SIC (also pronounced as it appears), system for organizing data on production, employment, and prices. Because the U.S. economy was so heavily oriented toward manufacturing in the 1930s through the 1960s, economists developed the SIC system primarily with measurement of the output of manufacturing firms in mind.

During the past three decades, the U.S. economy has seen a rise in new service industries. Now firms that provide services employ about three-fourths of all workers and produce a growing share of total U.S. GDP. The SIC system traditionally lumped firms providing certain services to manufacturers together with those manufacturers, a categorization that is now inappropriate.

The Transition to NAICS

Because the underlying organizing principles of SIC no longer fit the U.S. economy, economists designed an entirely new reporting system for business data called the North American Industry Classification System, or NAICS (pronounced "nakes"). The Bureau of Economic Analysis is implementing NAICS in stages, with the final phase of the transition planned to occur in 2004. During the transition to NAICS, the process of aggregating data for inclusion in the NIPAs for purposes of tabulating U.S. GDP requires some readjustment. Economists who work with the NIPAs must convert all NAICS data into SIC categories—a very cumbersome process.

In the meantime, the Bureau of Economic Analysis is also converting SIC data back to January 1992 into NAICS. Thus, 1992 will be the farthest back that the NIPAs ultimately will be restated in terms of industry classifications from NAICS. Economists are still unsure just how much of a difference this restating will make in comparisons of output, employment, and prices before and after 1992. Most economists believe, however, that difficulties in making comparisons over time are likely to be more severe for microeconomists who study the entirely restructured industry-level data.

For Critical Analysis
Why are macroeconomic aggregates likely to be less affected by changes in industry classification systems for reporting output, employment, and price data?

Although GDP is often used as a benchmark measure for standard-of-living calculations, it is not necessarily a good measure of the well-being of a nation. As the now-defunct Soviet Union illustrated to the world, the large-scale production of such goods as minerals, electricity, and irrigation for farming can have negative effects on the environment: deforestation from strip mining, air and soil pollution from particulate emissions or accidents at nuclear power plants, and erosion of the natural balance between water and salt in bodies of water such as the Aral Sea. Hence, it is important to recognize the following point:

GDP is a measure of production and an indicator of economic activity. It is not a measure of a nation's overall welfare.

FUNDAMENTAL ISSUE #1

What is gross domestic product, and how is it calculated? Gross domestic product (GDP) is the market value of all final goods and services produced during a given period. Using the product approach, GDP is equal to the sum of consumption spending, investment spending, government expenditures, and net export spending. Under the income approach, GDP is equal to the sum of wages and salaries, net interest, rental income, profits, indirect taxes, and depreciation.

Measuring International Transactions: The Balance of Payments

In addition to keeping track of large domestic flows of income and product, economists must account for sizable flows of payments across nations' borders. To do this, they use a system of accounting known as the **balance of payments accounts.** The U.S. balance of payments accounts consist of a complete tabulation of the exchanges between U.S. residents and residents of all other nations. The accounts include all transactions in goods, services, income earnings and payments, and assets by individuals, businesses, and governments across U.S. borders.

The balance of payments accounts consist of three separate accounts. The first is the **current account.** This account tabulates international trade and transfers of goods and services and flows of income. The second is the **capital account,** which tabulates all nongovernmental international asset transactions. Finally, international asset transactions involving governmental agencies appear in an account called the **official settlements balance.**

In all three accounts, any cross-border exchange entailing a *payment* by a U.S. individual, business, or government agency is a deficit item that appears as a *negative* entry. This accounting convention is used because such a transaction causes funds to flow out of the United States. By way of contrast, any international transaction that leads to a *receipt* by a U.S. resident, company, or government agency appears as a *positive* entry. Such a receipt indicates that funds have flowed into the United States.

Exports, Imports, and the Current Account

The most straightforward balance of payments account is the *current account.* This account also commonly receives the most public notice, because it includes U.S. trade of goods and services. A subtotal of this account is the *merchandise balance of trade,* which tends to be the focus of media attention, as Chapter 1 noted.

THE MERCHANDISE TRADE BALANCE   Recall from Chapter 1 that the merchandise balance of trade refers only to cross-border purchases and sales of *physical goods.* Sales of goods by U.S. firms to residents of other nations are *merchandise exports,* while purchases of goods by U.S. residents from abroad are *merchandise imports.* Table 2–3 gives dollar values of U.S. merchandise

BALANCE OF PAYMENTS ACCOUNTS: A tabulation of all transactions between the residents of a nation and the residents of all other nations in the world.

CURRENT ACCOUNT: The balance of payments account that tabulates international trade and transfers of goods and services and flows of income.

CAPITAL ACCOUNT: The balance of payments account that records all nongovernmental international asset transactions.

OFFICIAL SETTLEMENTS BALANCE: A balance of payments account that records international asset transactions involving agencies of home and foreign governments.

Table 2–3   The U.S. Merchandise Trade Balance ($ Millions)

	1993	1998	2003*
Merchandise exports	+456,943	+670,416	+789,765
Merchandise imports	−589,394	−917,112	−1,252,315
MERCHANDISE TRADE BALANCE	−132,451	−246,696	−462,550

*Estimates.

SOURCES: *Economic Report of the President; Economic Indicators.*

exports and imports for recent years. Note that exports generate receipts by U.S. residents and appear as positive entries in the table. Imports, in contrast, entail payments abroad by U.S. residents. Consequently, these appear in the table as negative entries.

The final row in Table 2–3 displays the *merchandise trade balance* for each year. As we noted in Chapter 1, when the merchandise trade balance is positive, a *trade surplus* exists. In that case, U.S. residents would be exporting more goods than they import. As the table indicates, however, the reverse situation has arisen in recent years. Typically, U.S. merchandise imports have exceeded merchandise exports, so the U.S. merchandise trade balance has been negative, and by wide margins. The United States has experienced significant *trade deficits.*

THE CURRENT ACCOUNT BALANCE   Although the media pay considerable attention to the merchandise balance of trade, a number of economists contend that this balance can be a misleading indicator. Since the 1970s, they point out, the share of total U.S. output produced by service industries has increased, while the output share of industries that produce physical goods has declined. Travel, transportation, and financial services have become conspicuously more important among U.S. producers.

As Table 2–4 indicates, net international exchanges of services are part of the current account in the U.S. balance of payments accounts. In recent years U.S. residents have sold more services to residents of other nations than they have purchased from abroad. Consequently, service transactions on net have generated receipts for U.S. residents. This is reflected by the positive entries for this category in the second row of Table 2–4.

macroxtra!
Economic
Applications

For the latest data on the U.S. current account, take a look at EconData Online. http://macroxtra.swcollege.com

Table 2–4   The U.S. Current Account ($ Millions)

	1993	1998	2003*
Merchandise trade balance	−132,451	−246,696	−462,550
Net service transactions	+63,660	+79,868	+83,895
BALANCE ON GOODS AND SERVICES	−68,791	−166,828	−378,655
Net income flow	+23,905	−6,202	+16,140
Unilateral transfers	−37,637	−44,427	−52,858
CURRENT ACCOUNT BALANCE	−82,523	−217,457	−415,373

*ESTIMATES.

SOURCES: *Economic Report of the President; Economic Indicators.*

If we add together the first and second rows of Table 2–4, we obtain the *balance on goods and services,* which appears in the third row of the table. This balance includes *both* goods *and* services. For this reason, most economists believe that this statistic is a more useful indicator of U.S. trade performance than the merchandise trade balance, even though the latter receives more media attention. Nevertheless, as you can see, the U.S. balance on goods and services has run a deficit for some time. The growth of U.S. service industries that typically generate net receipts of funds has not made up for the net payments that U.S. residents have made on cross-border transactions in physical goods.

The U.S. current account also tabulates international flows of income receipts to U.S. residents and payments abroad by U.S. residents. Individuals and firms that reside in the United States earn income on assets that they hold in other nations. Such income earnings appear as positive entries in the U.S. current account. At the same time, foreign individuals and firms earn income on assets that they own in the United States. These flows of income to foreigners from the United States appear as negative entries in the U.S. current account. The fourth line of Table 2–4 shows the *net* income flow for each period.

The final component of the current account is a tabulation of all *unilateral transfers.* These are gifts that U.S. residents give to residents or governments of other nations or that foreign residents or governments give to U.S. residents. Transfers from foreigners to U.S. residents are receipts by U.S. residents and are positive entries, while transfers from U.S. residents to foreigners are payments by U.S. residents and are negative entries. The fifth line of Table 2–4 shows total *net* unilateral transfers. The U.S. government has provided sizable amounts of foreign aid and military transfers to other countries, so net unilateral transfers typically have been negative.

The final line of Table 2–4 gives the sum of lines 3 through 5. This total is the *current account balance,* which is the sum of all net international flows of goods, services, income, and transfers. The U.S. current account balance has been negative for all recent intervals, so the United States has experienced *current account deficits.* In fact, the U.S. current account balance has consistently been in deficit since 1981. Since that year, U.S. residents have persistently paid out more to the rest of the world than they have received in international transactions of goods and services, income flows, and transfers.

The Capital Account, the Private Payments Balance, and the Overall Balance of Payments

Changes in asset holdings by U.S. residents and residents of other nations take place in international financial markets and are recorded outside the current account. The private *capital account* tabulates asset transactions involving private individuals or companies. Asset transactions involving official governmental entities such as the U.S. Treasury or the Federal Reserve enter a third account called the *official settlements balance.* Economists sometimes combine these two tabulations of asset transactions into a single, overall "capital account." We shall refer to them as separate accounts, however, because this approach can be helpful in understanding the operation of government policies concerning international financial transactions.

THE CAPITAL ACCOUNT AND THE PRIVATE PAYMENTS BALANCE

All changes in private asset holdings by U.S. residents abroad and by foreigners in the United States appear in the capital account. U.S. acquisitions of foreign assets, such as purchases of shares of ownership of plants or equipment or purchases of securities such as bonds, are negative entries in the U.S. capital account. Foreign acquisitions of such assets within U.S. borders are positive entries.

The total of all these asset changes for individuals and businesses is the *capital account balance.* U.S. capital account balances for recent years are shown in the second line of Table 2–5. Since 1981, this balance has been positive, indicating that on net U.S. residents have been acquiring fewer foreign assets relative to acquisitions of U.S. assets by foreigners.

The first line of Table 2–5 shows the current account balances from Table 2–4. The sum of the first and second lines of Table 2–5—that is, the sum of the current account balance and the private capital account balance—is the **private payments balance.** The private payments balance gives the net total of all private exchanges between U.S. individuals and businesses and the rest of the world. Commonly, the private payments balance is referred to as the "balance of payments." Unfortunately, as we shall discuss shortly, this term is misleading. Therefore, we shall be careful to refer to it mainly by its proper name: the *private payments balance.*

Since the early 1980s, private U.S. individuals and businesses have made more payments to foreigners relative to their receipts from foreigners, so the U.S. private payments balance has persistently been negative. This means that the United States has experienced *private payments deficits,* commonly called "balance of payments deficits."

THE OFFICIAL SETTLEMENTS BALANCE

As we noted earlier, governments also make cross-border asset exchanges. Purchases of foreign assets or overseas deposits of funds by the U.S. Treasury, the Federal Reserve, or other agencies of the U.S. government are receipts that appear as negative entries in the *official settlements balance,* the last account of the balance of payments accounts. Acquisitions of U.S. assets or deposits by foreign central banks or governments are recorded as inflows and appear as positive entries in this account.

PRIVATE PAYMENTS BALANCE: The sum of the current account balance and the private capital account balance, or the net total of all private exchanges between U.S. individuals and businesses and the rest of the world.

On the Web

How many international funds are flowing through the Federal Reserve, the U.S. central banking institution? To find out, go to the Federal Reserve's home page, http://www.federalreserve.gov, and click on "Economic Research and Data" and then "Statistics, Releases and Historical Data." Under "Monthly Releases," click on "U.S. Reserve Assets: Foreign Official Assets held at Federal Reserve Banks—Releases."

Table 2–5   The U.S. Private Payments Balance ($ Millions)

	1993	1998	2003*
Current account balance	−82,523	−217,457	−415,373
Capital account balance	+11,465	+ 90,917	+352,111
PRIVATE PAYMENTS BALANCE	−71,058	−126,540	−63,262

*Estimates.

SOURCES: *Economic Report of the President; Economic Indicators.*

Governments and central banks of various nations also keep deposit accounts with other countries' central banks. If the U.S. Treasury or the Federal Reserve deposits additional funds with another nation's central bank, then this outflow of funds from the United States appears as a negative entry in the U.S. official settlements balance. In contrast, if a foreign government or central bank deposits more funds at the Federal Reserve, then the inflow of funds appears as a positive entry in the U.S. official settlements balance.

The total net amount of all governmental and central bank transactions is the final amount of the official settlements balance. The second line of Table 2–6 gives recent values for the U.S. official settlements balance, which typically has been positive.

THE OVERALL BALANCE OF PAYMENTS   The first line of Table 2–6 carries down the private payments balance figures from Table 2–5. If all this accounting goes well, then the sum of the first two lines of Table 2–6 should be the *overall balance of payments,* or the net of *all* transactions of U.S. individuals, businesses, and governmental agencies with all other nations of the world. In the end, however, the accounting rarely works out exactly, and a significant *statistical discrepancy* occurs in each period. The statistical discrepancy for each year appears in the third line of Table 2–6. One reason for this discrepancy is that errors naturally occur during the collection of the large volume of data on international transactions. Another reason is the significant number of illegal exchanges, relating to such activities as illicit drug trade or armaments shipments, that cannot be recorded because those who engage in the transactions go to great lengths to keep them secret.

The final line of Table 2–6 is the overall balance of payments, which *must always equal zero.* The reason is that every transaction between a U.S. resident and a foreign resident involves both a payment and a receipt. As a result, across all the accounts the payments and receipts *must* cancel out. This means that the overall balance of payments must equal zero.

We noted earlier that using the term "balance of payments" to describe the private payments balance is misleading. The reason, as you now can see, is that the *overall balance of payments always is equal to zero.* The private payments balance, in contrast, may be positive (a private payments surplus) or negative (a private payments deficit). The traditional, though misleading, term for a private payments surplus is "balance of payments surplus," and the traditional term for a private payments deficit is "balance of payments deficit." Because these terms are used so widely by the media,

On the Web

When nations encounter significant international imbalances and turn to the International Monetary Fund (IMF) for assistance, how does the IMF determine its appropriate response? For a general overview, go to the IMF's home page at http://www.imf.org and click on "About the IMF." To review the IMF's current assistance to a specific nation, click on "Country Info" and select the country of interest to you.

Table 2–6 The Overall U.S. Balance of Payments ($ Millions)			
	1993	**1998**	**2003***
Private payments balance	−71,058	−126,540	−63,262
Official settlements balance	+69,935	+139,314	+23,050
Statistical discrepancy	+1,123	−12,774	+40,212
OVERALL BALANCE OF PAYMENTS	0	0	0

*ESTIMATES.
SOURCES: *Economic Report of the President* and *Economic Indicators.*

many economists use them as well, while keeping in mind that the *true* balance of payments is the overall figure that must equal zero.

An important point follows from the zero value for the overall balance of payments:

After allowing for the statistical discrepancy, the private payments balance must always be offset by the official settlements balance.

For example, if there is a private payments deficit, the official settlements balance must be positive. If a private payments deficit occurs, U.S. residents pay more to residents of other countries than they receive from foreigners. Eventually, however, other countries' governments and central banks accumulate dollars that the U.S. residents have paid, on net, to those countries. Foreign governments and central banks hold many of these dollars in deposit accounts in the United States. The result is an increase in the U.S. official settlements balance that tends to make its value positive. In the end, in the absence of statistical discrepancies, the two balances offset each other. This leads to a zero value for the overall balance of payments. (In principle, there is also a worldwide balance of payments; see on p. 40 *Global Notebook: A Global Current Account Deficit—Evidence of Alien Visitations to Planet Earth?*)

FUNDAMENTAL ISSUE #2

How do economists measure international transactions?   They use the balance of payments accounts. The balance of payments is composed of three accounts that tabulate exchanges between U.S. residents and residents of other nations. The current account tabulates cross-border exchanges of goods and services, unilateral transfers, and income flows. The capital account records private asset transactions, and the official settlements balance tabulates governmental asset transactions.

Accounting for Inflation: Price Deflators and Real GDP

Figure 2–2 on the following page shows that U.S. GDP has risen each year for the past forty years. Does this mean that the U.S. economy has grown without letup? The answer is no. Annual GDP has increased for two reasons. One, of course, is that in many years the economy really *has* grown. Over the past forty years, U.S. businesses have expanded their resources and developed innovative ways to increase their production and sale of goods and services.

During some years, however, business production has actually declined, even though GDP increased. Statistically, this happened because of inflation. Recall that economists calculate GDP each year using market prices to value the production of firms. Economy-wide price increases, therefore, increase the *measured value* of output.

Thus, we cannot conclude from Figure 2–2 that the true production of goods and services has risen persistently in the United States. The United States has experienced inflation almost every year since World War II, so at least some portion of the general rise in the annual GDP data in the figure occurred simply because of rising prices.

A Global Current Account Deficit—Evidence of Alien Visitations to Planet Earth?

Errors and omissions in data collection typically prevent the debits and credits in a nation's balance of payments from summing exactly to zero. Nevertheless, in principle they should sum to zero for every nation. Furthermore, the sum of all debits and credits across all nations around the world should also sum to zero, because there are no interplanetary transactions.

Or are there? All trade of goods and services and all income flows, when summed across the world's nations, should net to zero. That is, the sum of all current account balances, which amounts to a *global* current account balance, should equal zero. Nevertheless, in the early 2000s the world experienced a global current account deficit of nearly $250 billion. In other words, Earth was operating with a collective trade deficit roughly equal to the total annual output of Sweden. Were aliens elsewhere in the galaxy dumping exports on the Earth while restricting exports of our goods and services to their planetary systems?

Much more likely explanations relate to the difficulty of tracking world trade in full even as reduced trade restrictions in recent years have led to big jumps in its volume. The growing trade in goods and services via Internet transactions also figures into the story. So do deliberate efforts to underreport trade to avoid legal restrictions and tariffs.

For Critical Analysis
What types of cross-border transactions do some individuals and businesses have an incentive to underreport, or even to hide entirely?

Nominal GDP and Real GDP

If we were to use unadjusted calculations of GDP in an inflationary environment, the result would be persistent *overstatements* of the actual volume of economic activity. Therefore, if we are to make year-to-year comparisons of an economy's productive performance, we must somehow adjust GDP data to correct for the bias that inflation creates.

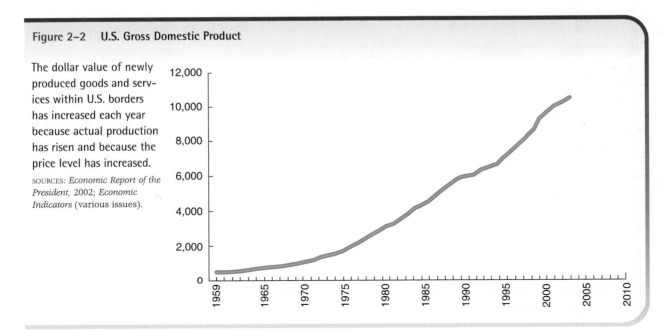

Figure 2–2   U.S. Gross Domestic Product

The dollar value of newly produced goods and services within U.S. borders has increased each year because actual production has risen and because the price level has increased.

SOURCES: *Economic Report of the President, 2002; Economic Indicators* (various issues).

REAL VERSUS NOMINAL GDP   To see clearly why we need to adjust GDP for price changes, suppose that your employer told you that she intended to increase your hourly wage by 100 percent. Ignoring any taxes or other deductions from your pay, this raise would double your hourly income. Suppose, however, that the inflation rate also happened to equal 100 percent, which would imply that the prices you would have to pay to purchase goods and services would also double. In that case, your 100 percent pay raise would merely maintain the purchasing power of your wage. You would be no better off than you were before your wage increase.

Similarly, if measured GDP were to double solely as a result of a 100 percent increase in the overall price level, the total volume of economic activity would not really have changed. Annual GDP changes thus would be vastly distorted measures of the *real* growth in economic activity.

To deal with this potential problem with making year-to-year comparisons of inflation-distorted GDP figures, economists have developed an inflation-adjusted measure of GDP. This is **real gross domestic product,** or *real GDP.* This measure of aggregate output accounts for price changes and thereby more accurately reflects the economy's true volume of productive activity, net of any artificial increases resulting from inflation.

Economists distinguish between real GDP and the unadjusted GDP measure by calling the latter **nominal gross domestic product,** or *nominal GDP.* This means "GDP in name only." In other words, nominal GDP is calculated in current dollars with no adjustment for the effects of price changes.

GDP Price Deflator

If properly calculated, real GDP should measure the economy's actual volume of production of goods and services. This implies that multiplying real GDP by a measure of the overall level of prices should yield the value of real GDP measured in current prices, which in turn is our definition of nominal GDP. If we let y denote real GDP and let P denote a measure of the overall price level, then nominal GDP, denoted Y, must be

$$Y = y \times P.$$

In words, nominal GDP equals real GDP times a measure of the overall price level.

Indeed, the factor P is a standard measure of the price level, which economists call the **GDP price deflator,** or simply the "GDP deflator." P is called a "deflator" because if we solve our expression for nominal GDP, $Y = y \times P$, for y, we get

$$y = Y/P.$$

Thus, real GDP, y, is equal to nominal GDP, Y, adjusted by dividing, or "deflating," by the factor P. For example, suppose that nominal GDP measured in current prices, Y, is equal to $12.3 trillion and the value of the GDP deflator, P, is equal to 3. Then calculating real GDP would entail deflating the $12.3 trillion nominal GDP by a factor of one-third. To do this, we divide $12.3 trillion by 3 to arrive at $4.1 trillion for real GDP.

REAL GROSS DOMESTIC PRODUCT (REAL GDP): A price-adjusted measure of aggregate output, or nominal GDP divided by the GDP price deflator.

NOMINAL GROSS DOMESTIC PRODUCT (NOMINAL GDP): The value of final production of goods and services calculated in current dollars with no adjustment for the effects of price changes.

GDP PRICE DEFLATOR: A flexible-weight measure of the overall price level; equal to nominal GDP divided by real GDP.

macroxtra!
Economic
Applications

What is the current level of real GDP? Take a look at EconData Online. http://macroxtra. swcollege.com

BASE YEAR: A reference year for price-level comparisons, which is a year in which nominal GDP is equal to real GDP, so that the GDP deflator's value is equal to one.

DENOTING A BASE YEAR   Knowing that the GDP deflator P is equal to 3 tells us little, however, unless we have a reference point for interpreting this value. To provide a reference point, economists define a **base year** for the GDP deflator, which is a year in which nominal GDP is equal to real GDP ($Y = y$), so that the GDP deflator's value is one ($P = 1$). Consequently, if the base year were, say, 1965, and the value of P in 2005 were equal to 3, then this would indicate that between 1965 and 2005 the overall level of prices tripled.

At present, the U.S. government uses 1996 as the base year in its real GDP calculations. Panel (a) of Figure 2–3 shows the values of the GDP deflator since 1959. The overall level of prices increased by a factor of about 4.35, from 0.26 to about 1.13, between 1959 and 2003. This means that an item that required \$1 to purchase in 1959 would have cost \$4.35 in 2003. Alternatively stated, \$4.35 in 2003 would have purchased only the equivalent amount of goods and services that \$1 purchased in 1959.

Panel (b) of Figure 2–3 plots real and nominal GDP figures since 1959. Note that in 1996 nominal and real GDP are equal because 1996 is the base year in which $P = 1$, so $Y = y$. Clearly, adjusting for price changes has a significant effect on our interpretation of GDP data. This is why it is so important to convert nominal GDP into real GDP using the GDP price deflator. Thus:

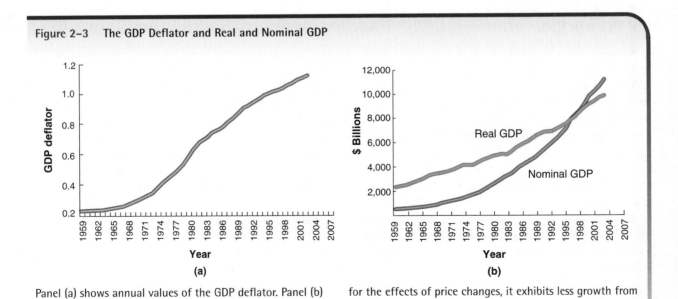

Figure 2–3   The GDP Deflator and Real and Nominal GDP

Panel (a) shows annual values of the GDP deflator. Panel (b) displays nominal GDP (the same chart as Figure 2–2) and real GDP. As panel (b) indicates, because real GDP accounts for the effects of price changes, it exhibits less growth from year to year.

SOURCES: *Economic Report of the President*, 2002; *Economic Indicators* (various issues).

Only real GDP data can provide useful information about true year-to-year changes in the economy's productive performance.

CHAIN-WEIGHT REAL GDP: A method of calculating real GDP for a given year that uses prices for both the year in question and the preceding year as weights.

> ### FUNDAMENTAL ISSUE #3
>
> **What is the difference between nominal GDP and real GDP?**   Nominal GDP is the total value of newly produced goods and services computed using the prices at which they sold during the year they were produced. In contrast, real GDP is the value of final goods and services after adjusting for the effects of year-to-year price changes. The basic approach to calculating real GDP is to divide nominal GDP by the GDP deflator, which is a measure of the level of prices relative to prices for a base year.

macroxtra!
Online
Perspective

Both private and Federal Reserve economists try to forecast output growth and inflation; to consider how closely private forecasts match those of the Fed, go to the Chapter 2 reading, entitled "Forecasting Inflation and Growth: Do Private Forecasts Match Those of Policymakers?" by William Gavin and Rachel Mandal of the Federal Reserve Bank of St. Louis. http://macroxtra.swcollege.com

CHAIN-WEIGHT REAL GDP   In actuality, the real GDP data plotted in panel (b) of Figure 2–3 were not calculated using the simple computation method described above. That method computes real GDP for each year using the prices from the base year only. The government used this simple fixed-base-year approach for nearly fifty years before switching to a new approach at the end of 1995.

The problem with using a fixed base year to calculate real GDP is that as prices change, households and businesses change how they allocate their purchases. They buy fewer of the goods and services whose prices rise the most and more of the goods and services whose prices rise the least. As a result, output increases most for those goods and services whose prices rise the least. Using fixed-base-year GDP, which ignores such changes in the pattern of purchases, tends to produce slightly biased measurements of growth in real output. In an inflationary environment, real output growth tends to be overstated in years after the base year and slightly understated in years before the base year.

For this reason, at the end of 1995 the U.S. government switched to calculating **chain-weight real GDP.** Under this approach, the government computes real GDP using prices for both the year in question and the preceding year as weights. For instance, the calculation of 2001 real GDP that is plotted in panel (b) of Figure 2–3 uses prices in 2000 and 2001 as weights, and the calculation of 2002 real GDP uses prices in 2001 and 2002 as weights. Real GDP for all other years is calculated the same way. Hence, as the calculation procedure moves through time, it forms the "chain" of weights that gives this measure of real GDP its name.

The big drawback of the chain-weight real GDP measure is that it is much more complicated to calculate. Fortunately for students in intermediate macroeconomics, however, inflation rates in the United States typically have been relatively low. Consequently, the differences in U.S. real GDP calculations under the alternative procedures are small enough for us to abstract from in this text. The fixed-base-year approach is much simpler to use, so we shall rely on it to illustrate basic points about nominal versus real GDP.

Stirring the Alphabet Soup of Price Indexes

Even though the basic GDP calculation, $y = Y/P$, produces a slight bias in measured output growth, the GDP price deflator that real GDP calculations imply nonetheless is a *flexible-weight price index*, or a price index whose weights on various goods and services change automatically as the output of goods and services varies over time. Alternatively, the overall price level can be measured using *fixed-weight price indexes*, which are calculated by selecting a fixed set of goods and services and then tracking the prices of those specific goods and services from year to year.

The CPI, PPI, and PCE

The best-known fixed-weight price index is the *consumer price index (CPI)*, which is the weighted sum of the prices of a full set of goods and services that the Bureau of Labor Statistics (BLS) in

the U.S. Department of Labor determines a typical U.S. consumer purchases each year. Categories of expenditures incorporated into the weighting scheme for the CPI include a typical consumer's annual purchases of housing services and utilities, food and beverages, transportation, medical care, apparel, and entertainment. Figure 2–4 shows the current distribution of these expenditures in the computation of the CPI. All told, the BLS samples prices on about 95,000 different items. In addition, the government calculates a number of alternative consumer price indexes, such as CPIs for urban consumers, for rural consumers, and so on.

There are several other fixed-weight price indexes. One is the *producer price index (PPI)*, which is a weighted average of prices of goods that the BLS determines a typical business charges for the goods and services it sells.

Figure 2–4   The Distribution of Expenditures in Computing the Consumer Price Index

The consumer price index is a weighted average of prices of a fixed group of goods and services, which we present here.

SOURCE: Bureau of Labor Statistics.

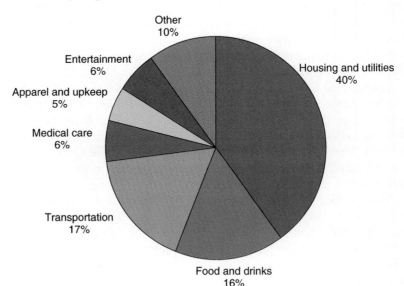

Another is the *personal consumption expenditure (PCE)* price index, which the Bureau of Economic Analysis (BEA) in the U.S. Department of Commerce calculates as an average of two different fixed-weight price indexes based on shifting baskets of goods and services purchased by consumers each year.

Problems with Fixed-Weight Price Indexes

Although the CPI and PPI are popular measures of the overall price level, they suffer from some important drawbacks that relate to the fact that they are fixed-weight indexes. The PCE tries to deal with some of these drawbacks, but it too suffers from problems.

The most glaring problem is that relative prices of goods change over time, so people substitute among goods, changing their spending allocations. This means that the fixed weights that the BLS assigns to a "typical" consumer or producer when computing the CPI and PPI are *artificially* fixed. For any truly representative consumer or producer, the weights surely must change somewhat from year to year. The PCE helps address this problem by calculating year-to-year price changes based on averages of weights in the two years.

Using fixed weights for price indexes also ignores the potential for *quality* changes in the goods and services that consumers buy. Another drawback is that fixed-weight indexes suffer from various data collection problems. To calculate the CPI and PPI, the BLS collects data on *list* prices, which are the prices that businesses formally print in catalogues, price lists, and so on. In fact, however, during times when competition for business is most pressing, consumers often can get bargain prices below those in the formal price lists available to the BLS. The proliferation of discount retailers since the 1980s may have worsened this measurement problem for the CPI and PPI. Data collection problems for the PCE may be even more severe, because the BEA estimates consumer spending on goods and services by subtracting sales to businesses and governments from total sales; thus, it measures consumer spending only indirectly for purposes of constructing the index weights.

Because the government uses the CPI to index Social Security, there have been many studies of the problems with calculating the CPI. Estimates in the mid-1990s indicated that the various problems added as much as 2 percentage points to official CPI inflation figures. Beginning in 1997, the BLS altered its sampling procedure for food and nonfood items and made its treatment of rents and hospital and generic drug prices more accurate, resulting in a drop in the CPI inflation rate of about 0.2 to 0.3 percentage points. Further calculation changes between 1998 and 2003 reduced estimated inflation by nearly 1 percentage point.

Research Project
The government has not changed past published data on the CPI. Why is this fact important to policymaking today?

Web Resources
1. Where is the most information available about the CPI? Go to the "Consumer Price Indexes" home page of the Bureau of Labor Statistics at http://www.bls.gov.

2. What about information about the PPI? In this case, go to the "Producer Price Indexes" home page of the BLS at http://www.bls.gov/ppi/home.htm.

1. **Gross Domestic Product and Its Computation:** By definition, gross domestic product (GDP) is the total of all final goods and services produced during a given period, evaluated at market prices. The product approach totals consumption spending, investment spending, government expenditures, and net export spending to obtain GDP. The income approach yields GDP as the sum of wages and salaries, net interest, rental income, profits, indirect taxes, and depreciation.

2. **How Economists Measure International Transactions:** The balance of payments accounts measure the values of cross-border exchanges. There are three balance of payments accounts. The current account tracks international exchanges of goods and services, unilateral transfers, and income flows. The capital account tabulates private asset transactions. Finally, the official settlements balance accounts for governmental asset transactions.

3. **The Difference between Nominal GDP and Real GDP:** Nominal GDP is the market value of final goods and services evaluated in terms of the prices at which the goods and services traded during the year they were produced. Real GDP, in contrast, is the value of final goods and services after taking into account the effects of price variations. We compute real GDP by dividing nominal GDP by the GDP deflator, which measures the price level relative to the price level of goods and services in a base year.

Self-Test Questions

(Answers to odd-numbered questions may be found on the Web at **http://macro. swcollege.com** under "Student Resources.")

1. In your own words, define GDP. Carefully distinguish between GDP and GNP.
2. Why should the income approach and the product approach to computing GDP both yield the same value? Explain.
3. Explain, in your own words, the distinction between nominal GDP and real GDP.
4. What does the merchandise trade balance measure? Why is it not necessarily a good indicator of a nation's trade position vis-à-vis other countries if the nation has relatively large service-oriented industries?
5. Explain, in your own words, why a nation's overall balance of payments must equal zero.
6. In your own words, explain why an increase in nominal GDP does not necessarily imply a rise in actual output of goods and services.

Problems

(Answers to odd-numbered problems may be found on the Web at **http://macro. swcollege.com** under "Student Resources.")

1. Using the following data ($ billions) for a given year and assuming that GDP equals GNP, calculate (a) gross domestic product, (b) national income, (c) net national product, (d) indirect business taxes:

Consumption spending:	$8,000	Wages and salaries:	$7,000
Interest income:	500	Depreciation:	1,550
Rental income:	200	Government spending:	2,000
Investment spending:	2,500	Net export spending:	−450
Profits:	2,000		

2. Suppose that the GDP deflator for the year considered in question 1 has a value of 1.25. Based on your answer to part (a) in question 1, what is real GDP for this year?

3. Consider a two-good economy. In 2003, firms in this economy produced 25 units of good X, which sold at a market price of $4 per unit, and 15 units of good Y, which sold at a market price of $3 per unit. In 2004, the economy produced the same amounts of both X and Y, but the price of good X rose to $5 per unit, and the price of good Y increased to $4 per unit. What were the values of nominal GDP in 2003 and 2004? If 2003 is the base year, what were the values of real GDP in 2003 and 2004?

4. Using your answers from question 3 and assuming again that 2003 is the base year, what is the value of the GDP price deflator for 2003? What is the approximate value (rounded to the nearest hundredth) of the GDP price deflator for 2004? What is the approximate value (rounded to the nearest percentage point) of inflation between 2003 and 2004?

Before the Test

Test your understanding of the material covered in this chapter by taking the Chapter 2 interactive quiz at http://macro.swcollege.com.

Online Application

To view the most current information concerning the consumer price index (CPI), take a look at the home page of the Bureau of Labor Statistics. As noted in this chapter, the CPI is a fixed-weight index measure of the U.S. price level.

Internet URL: http://www.bls.gov/eag/eag.us.htm

Title: *Bureau of Labor Statistics: Economy at a Glance*

Navigation: Begin at the URL listed above.

Application: Perform the indicated operations, and answer the following questions:

1. On the Bureau of Labor Statistics home page, go to "Inflation and Consumer Spending," and then click on "Consumer Price Index." Scan down the page, and under the heading, "CPI Fact Sheets," click on "How to Use the Consumer Price Index for Escalation." Read the material at this location. Based on this discussion, what exactly does the CPI measure?

2. Return to the BLS home page, and go to the heading "At A Glance Tables," click on "U.S. Economy at a Glance." Then click on the graph box (dinosaur icon) for Consumer Price Index. Take a look at both the graph and the tabular summary. How much does the CPI appear to vary from year to year? Has it varied much in the most recent year?

For Study Group and Analysis: Divide the class into three groups. Assign one group to the producer price index, another to the employment cost index, and the third to the productivity index. Have each group click on the appropriate graph box under *U. S. Economy at a Glance* and compare the behavior of its index with recent behavior of the CPI. Does there appear to be any relationship for any given pairing with the CPI? Should there be a relationship? Why?

macro**xtra!**

Log on to the MacroXtra Web site now http://macroxtra.swcollege.com for additional learning resources such as practice quizzes, Interactive Key Graphs, readings, and additional economic applications.

48 Selected References

and Further Reading

Clayton, Gary E., and Martin Gerhard Giesbrecht. *A Guide to Everyday Economic Statistics.* New York: McGraw-Hill, Fifth Edition, 2001.

Council of Economic Advisers. *Economic Report of the President.* Washington, D.C.: U.S. Government Printing Office, February 2002.

Council of Economic Advisers. *Economic Indicators.* Washington, D.C.: U.S. Government Printing Office, various issues.

International Monetary Fund. *World Economic Outlook.* Washington, D.C.: various issues.

U.S. Department of Commerce. *Survey of Current Business.* Washington, D.C.: various issues.

Unit II
Classical Macroeconomic Theory and Economic Growth

49

The Self-Adjusting Economy

The first systematic and rigorous attempt to explain the determinants of such important economy-wide economic variables as the price level and national levels of output, employment, and expenditures was the classical theory, which attempted to show how these variables were interrelated. Classical economics was the predominant school of thought from the 1770s until the 1930s. Included in the ranks of the classical economists are such intellectual giants as Adam Smith (1723–1790), David Hume (1711–1776), David Ricardo (1772–1823), James Mill (1773–1836) and his son John Stuart Mill (1806–1873), and Thomas Malthus (1766–1834).

By and large, the classical school of thought concluded that capitalism is a self-regulating economic system. Classical economists argued that mechanisms inherent in the capitalist system naturally result in full employment of labor and other resources. They recognized that temporary unemployment might exist when people are between full-time jobs but felt that eventually there is no involuntary labor unemployment. Workers respond to a state of unemployment by offering to work for lower wages, and unemployment disappears as businesses hire more labor services and workers offer fewer of these services at lower wages.

As a result, firms produce the full-employment level of national output and automatically generate income—wages and salaries, rents, interest and dividends, and profits—that households, as owners of all productive factors, use to purchase these items. If households save "too much," so that there is a surplus of saving, then interest rates decline, which induces households to reduce saving and firms to increase investment expenditures. The classical economists summarized their conclusion that firms produce a full-employment level of output that households would purchase in the dictum, "Supply creates its own demand."

Naturally, such an outlook leaves little or no role for government intervention in the economy. Because a capitalistic economy equilibrates at the full-employment output level, monetary policy actions cannot influence this output level. Hence, money is "neutral" in its effects on real economic activity. Only prices adjust to changes in the quantity of money in circulation. Variations in government spending or taxation policies can alter the distribution of output but not the total amount that firms produce.

In the long term and, on average, even in the near term, this output level is determined by technological change and growth in the amounts of available factors of production. Thus, the classical theory also offers a foundation for the theory of how and why the economies of some nations grow faster than others. This naturally makes the classical model the starting point for the theory of economic growth.

The Self-Adjusting Economy—

Classical Macroeconomic Theory: Employment, Output, and Prices

FUNDAMENTAL ISSUES

1. What are the key assumptions of classical macroeconomic theory?

2. According to the classical model, what are the determinants of the demand for labor by firms?

3. How are the aggregate levels of labor employment and real output of goods and services determined in the classical model?

4. What factors determine the price level in the classical framework?

A s the old saying goes, the only things that are certain in life are death and taxes. Those U.S. residents who have been alive since the 1940s might also be tempted to add inflation to this short list of life's certainties. Each year since 1949, the level of prices of goods and services in the United States has risen. During that interval, the average annual rate of increase in overall prices has been 4.1 percent. As a result, the U.S. price level is now more than 10 times higher than it was in 1946.

Something else that has grown considerably during the same period is the quantity of money in circulation. The M1 measure of the quantity of money has increased by a factor of almost 11, or at an annual rate of 4.3 percent, since 1946. The M2 measure is now more than 40 times greater, and its average annual growth rate since 1946 has been 6.6. percent.

The simple fact that both monetary aggregates and prices have increased considerably over the years does not mean that these economic variables are necessarily related. Nevertheless, most economists believe there is good reason to expect a direct relationship between money growth and inflation. In this chapter, you will learn about the classical explanation for this predicted co-movement between the rate of growth of the quantity of money and the rate of inflation.

First, however, you will learn about the classical theory of the aggregate employment of labor. This theory of labor employment is the first step in the classical approach to explaining the level of real GDP. It also provides the underpinning for the theory of economic growth discussed in Chapter 5. Furthermore, it offers a foundation for alternative perspectives on macroeconomics considered in later chapters. Thus, building blocks of the classical model reviewed in this chapter lay the cornerstone for your entire study of macroeconomics.

Key Classical Assumptions

Three fundamental assumptions provide a foundation for classical macroeconomic theory:

1. Workers, consumers, and entrepreneurs are motivated by rational self-interest.
2. People do not experience *money illusion.*
3. Pure competition prevails in the markets for goods and services and for factors of production.

Let's consider each of these assumptions in turn.

Rational Self-Interest

A key tenet of the classical theory is that both households and businesspersons desire to maximize their total satisfaction. This means that in their everyday roles as workers and consumers, members of each household seek to attain the highest possible overall well-being, or utility. Thus, in the classical system, households are *utility maximizers.*

Businesses operate to produce the highest net income for the household entrepreneurs who own them. The net income of any business is its profit flow. Consequently, in the classical theory, businesses are *profit maximizers.*

Absence of Money Illusion

Consider the following example. A college student has a part-time job at a local fast-food establishment. The manager offers to increase her hourly wage rate from $6.00 per hour to $6.60 per hour, or by 10 percent. At the same time, however, prices of the goods and services that the student purchases have also risen by 10 percent, largely because of hefty increases in college tuition and fees. Thus, given the 10 percent rise in her living costs, the student is no better off in real terms than she was before her wage increase.

Suppose, though, that the student nevertheless feels so good about the 10 percent increase in her nominal wages that she offers to work more hours. If she does, she is exhibiting **money illusion.** This is the inclination for a household or business to alter desired trades of goods, services, or factors of production simply because of *nominal* price changes.

A central hypothesis of classical theory is that people do not experience such money illusion. Instead, when they make decisions about how much to produce, sell, or purchase, they pay attention only to *real* variables, which have been adjusted for the price level. In the absence of changes in real quantities, individuals and businesses will not change their market transactions.

Pure Competition

Classical economists recognize that monopoly businesses, such as many electric utilities, exist. Nevertheless, they contend that the predominant mode of interaction among business firms in the aggregate economy is **pure competition.** Under pure competition, there are sufficiently large numbers of buyers and sellers of a typical good, service, or factor of production that no single buyer or seller can affect the market price of the good, service, or factor of production.

As a result, each buyer and seller is a *price taker:* the buyer or seller takes market prices as "given" and incapable of change by means of purchases or sales initiated by the buyer or seller in isolation. Nonetheless, collective— though typically uncoordinated—purchases or sales of a good, service, or factor of production can change market prices. In other words, the forces of demand and supply determine market prices. These prices, in turn, adjust flexibly to variations in demand or supply.

> FUNDAMENTAL ISSUE #1
>
> **What are the key assumptions of classical macroeconomic theory?** The classical macroeconomic model is based on the idea that people pursue their own self-interest. It also presumes that people do not experience money illusion, meaning that people recognize that they are no better off with higher nominal wages if prices also are higher. The third key assumption of the classical model is that there is pure competition throughout the economy, meaning that there are a large number of buyers and sellers of goods and services who individually cannot influence market prices.

MONEY ILLUSION: A situation that exists when economic agents change their behavior in response to changes in nominal values, even though real (adjusted for the price level) values have not changed.

PURE COMPETITION: A situation in which there are large numbers of buyers and sellers in a market for a good, service, or factor of production and in which no single buyer or seller can affect the market price.

The Classical Theory of Production and Employment

Any macroeconomic theory must provide an explanation of how many goods and services businesses produce and how many units of factors of production, such as labor, they utilize. The classical theory is no exception. Indeed, as you will discover in later chapters, the classical theory of production and employment is the benchmark, or starting point of comparison,

PRODUCTION FUNCTION: A relationship between possible quantities of factors of production, such as labor services, and the amount of output of goods and services that firms can produce with current technology.

macroxtra!
**Economic
Applications**

How many hours per week does the average U.S. manufacturing worker spend on the job? Take a look at EconData Online.
http://macroxtra.swcollege.com

for all other macroeconomic theories. Consequently, understanding this topic is crucial to comprehending the subject as a whole.

The Production Function

The aggregate **production function** is a relationship between the quantities of factors of production—labor, capital, land, and entrepreneurship—employed by all firms in the economy and the total production of real output by those firms, given the technology currently available. In this chapter we shall focus on the *short run,* which is a time horizon short enough that firms cannot vary all factors of production. We shall consider the *long run,* in which firms can adjust the amounts of all factors of production, in our discussion of economic growth in Chapter 5.

SHORT-RUN PRODUCTION   In the short run firms cannot adjust the amounts of capital, land, and entrepreneurship. The only variable factor of production for firms is the quantity of labor that they employ on an hourly and weekly basis, which we denote N.

There are three measures of the amount of labor that firms employ. One measure is simply the number of people employed during a given time interval. An alternative measure is the total time worked by all people employed by firms, which is just the total hours of work by all employees during a period. Finally, we can measure employment via a combination of these first two measures, known as *person-hours.*

In the short run firms use labor together with their fixed quantities of other productive factors to produce output. Some firms, such as fast-food restaurants, may use very simple production processes. Others, such as microcomputer manufacturers, may assemble components manufactured at remote points around the world. The aggregate production function sums up the result of these processes as the total quantity of real output of goods and services, y, that results from the use of the total quantity of labor, N, by firms:

$$y = F(N).$$

This expression says that the aggregate amount of real output is a *function* of the amount of labor employed by all firms in the economy.

Panel (a) of Figure 3–1 displays a sample aggregate production function, $F(N)$. Any point along this function tells us how much real output firms can produce for a given quantity of labor employed. For instance, if firms employ an amount of labor equal to N_1, their total output of goods and services, or real GDP, is equal to y_1. If firms employ a larger quantity of labor, N_2, then naturally they are able to produce a larger amount of real output. Real GDP then would be at a higher level, y_2.

The production function in panel (a) of Figure 3–1 is *concave,* meaning that it is bowed downward. This means that the production function's *slope*—the change in output resulting from a change in employment, or "rise" divided by "run"—varies along the function. To see this, note that the slope of the function at the employment level N_1 is given by the slope of the line tangent to the function at this point, or $\Delta y_1 / \Delta N$, where the symbol Δ denotes a change in a quantity. But at the higher employment level N_2, the same change in employment, ΔN, yields a smaller change in output,

Figure 3–1   The Aggregate Production Function and the Marginal-Product-of-Labor (MP_N) Schedule

Given a fixed stock of capital and a current state of technology, higher levels of labor employment are necessary to achieve increased production of real output. The bowed, or concave, shape of the production function in panel (a) reflects the law of diminishing marginal returns, which states that total output increases at a decreasing rate for each additional one-unit rise in employment of labor. Consequently, as shown in panel (b), the marginal product of labor declines as employment rises.

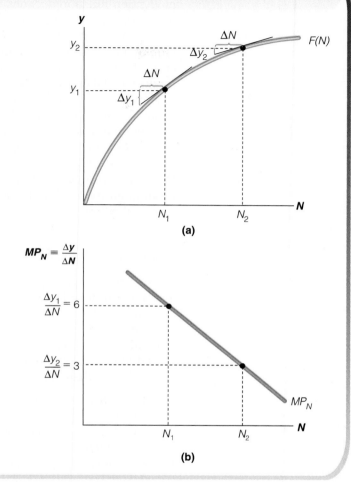

(a)

(b)

Δy_2. This means that the slope of the production function at the employment level N_2, which is equal to $\Delta y_2/\Delta N$, must be smaller than the slope of the production function at the employment level N_1.

THE MARGINAL PRODUCT OF LABOR   The decline in the slope of the production function as the amount of labor employed by firms rises is consistent with the **law of diminishing marginal returns.** This law states that eventually the additional output produced by an additional unit of labor declines as more units of labor are employed by firms. By definition, the slope of the production function, $\Delta y/\Delta N$, is the additional amount of output that firms can produce by employing an additional unit of labor. This is the **marginal product of labor,** or MP_N. In other words, $MP_N \equiv \Delta y/\Delta N$, or the slope of the production function at a given quantity of labor. (The three-barred equals sign $\equiv$ means that a relationship is true by definition; it is an identity.)

Panel (b) of Figure 3–1 graphs the marginal product of labor. At the employment level N_1, the marginal product of labor is equal to $\Delta y_1/\Delta N$, or the slope

LAW OF DIMINISHING MARGINAL RETURNS: The law that states that each successive addition of a unit of a factor of production, such as labor, eventually produces a smaller gain in real output produced, other factors holding constant.

MARGINAL PRODUCT OF LABOR: The change in total output resulting from a one-unit increase in the quantity of labor employed in production.

of the production function at this employment level. The value of this slope is assumed to equal 6. If total employment rises to N_2, then the slope of the production function declines to $\Delta y_2/\Delta N$, which is assumed to equal 3; thus, the marginal product of labor is lower at this higher employment level.

The employment levels N_1 and N_2 are just two examples, of course. At employment levels less than N_1, the marginal product of labor would be larger than $\Delta y_1/\Delta N$. At employment levels greater than N_2, the marginal product of labor would be smaller than $\Delta y_2/\Delta N$. At successively greater employment levels between N_1 and N_2, the marginal product of labor would decline. Consequently, there is a downward-sloping set of values for the marginal product of labor that corresponds to the production function shown in panel (a) of Figure 3–1. This is the *marginal-product-of-labor schedule*, or MP_N *schedule*, displayed in panel (b). The MP_N schedule shows the marginal product of labor, or slope of the production function, at any given quantity of labor. Its downward slope reflects the law of diminishing marginal returns.

The Demand for Labor

Because the marginal product of labor measures how much more output an additional unit of labor produces, it is crucial to any firm's decision about how much labor to employ. Another key factor that a firm must consider, of course, is the expense that it must incur by employing a unit of labor. To maximize its profits, a firm must balance the revenue gain from the sale of the additional production generated by another unit of labor against the cost of hiring that labor unit.

PROFIT MAXIMIZATION   A profit-maximizing firm produces output to the point at which its marginal revenue (*MR*), or additional revenue stemming from production and sale of an additional unit of output, equals its marginal cost (*MC*), or additional production cost that it incurs in this endeavor. If *MR* exceeds *MC* at a given level of production, then the firm would earn a positive net profit from the last unit of production. This would encourage the firm to produce more units. If *MC* exceeds *MR*, however, then the firm's net profit on the last unit produced would be negative, which would induce the firm to cut back on its production. Consequently, when *MR* = *MC*, the firm has produced the output level that ensures positive net profits for every unit of production up to the last unit produced. Thus, the firm has maximized its profit on its total output production.

Recall that a central hypothesis of the classical theory is that pure competition prevails, so prices are market determined. Because no single firm can affect the market price, each unit of output that the firm produces by definition yields the same marginal revenue, which is the market price. Therefore, each purely competitive, profit-maximizing firm produces output up to the point at which

$$MR \equiv P = MC.$$

In words, a purely competitive firm produces output to the point at which price equals marginal cost.

In the short run, however, a firm's marginal cost depends on the expense that it incurs by employing its single variable factor of production, labor. The firm's labor expense is the money wage rate (also called the *nominal* wage rate) that it pays a unit of labor, denoted by W and measured in dollars per labor unit. For instance, suppose that the current market wage rate is $W_1 =$ $30 per unit of labor. A firm's marginal cost is measured in dollars spent per unit of output produced. Suppose that the marginal product of labor at the firm's current output level is $MP_N = \Delta y / \Delta N = 3$ units of output per unit of labor. Then, to calculate the firm's marginal cost of producing output at the money wage $W_1 =$ $30 per unit of labor, we divide W_1 by MP_N, which gives $MC = (\$30 \text{ per unit of labor})/(3 \text{ units of output per unit of labor}) = \$10$ per unit of output. Consequently, marginal cost by definition is equal to W/MP_N.

THE VALUE OF THE MARGINAL PRODUCT OF LABOR   This means that we can rewrite a competitive firm's profit-maximizing condition, $P = MC$, as

$$P = W/MP_N.$$

Now, if we multiply both sides of this equation by MP_N, we get

$$P \times MP_N = (W/MP_N) \times MP_N = W.$$

This tells us that another way to express the firm's profit-maximizing condition is

$$W = P \times MP_N.$$

This is the firm's profit-maximizing rule for employing labor. It says that a purely competitive firm that seeks to maximize its profit should employ labor to the point at which the money wage that the firm pays each unit of labor is equal to the price it receives for each unit of output that labor produces times the marginal product of labor. The price per unit of output times the marginal product of labor is called the **value of the marginal product of labor,** or $VMP_N = P \times MP_N$. For instance, if the market price of a firm's output is $5 per unit of output and the marginal product of labor is 6 units of output per unit of labor, then the value of labor's marginal product is equal to the product of these two figures, or $30 per unit of labor.

Panel (a) of Figure 3–2 on the following page shows how the value of the marginal product of labor typically varies with the amount of labor employed by a firm. We obtain this schedule by multiplying the firm's output price, P, times the MP_N schedule in panel (b) of Figure 3–1. The result is another downward-sloping schedule, called the *value-of-marginal-product-of-labor schedule,* or VMP_N schedule.

As panel (a) of Figure 3–2 indicates, if the market wage that the firm must pay each unit of labor it employs is $W_1 =$ $30, then the firm employs labor to the point at which the value of labor's marginal product is equal to $30 per unit of labor, which in the figure implies employment level N_1. At a lower wage rate of $W_2 =$ $15 per unit of labor, however, the firm requires a smaller value of marginal product to maximize its profit, so it *increases* the amount of labor it employs, to the quantity of labor N_2. A fall in the market wage rate causes the firm to increase the quantity of labor it demands. Hence, the firm decides how many units of labor it desires to employ by moving along its VMP_N schedule. This leads to the following important conclusion:

VALUE OF THE MARGINAL PRODUCT OF LABOR: The marginal product of labor times the price of output.

Figure 3–2   Alternative Labor Demand Schedules for a Purely Competitive Firm

A profit-maximizing firm employs labor to the point at which the value of labor's marginal product is equal to the *money* wage. Thus, a fall in the money wage increases the quantity of labor demanded by a firm, as shown in panel (a). Equivalently, the firm hires labor services to the point at which the marginal product of labor is equal to the *real* wage. Consequently, with an unchanged price level, a fall in the nominal wage induces a decline in the real wage and causes an increase in the quantity of labor demanded by firms, as shown in panel (b).

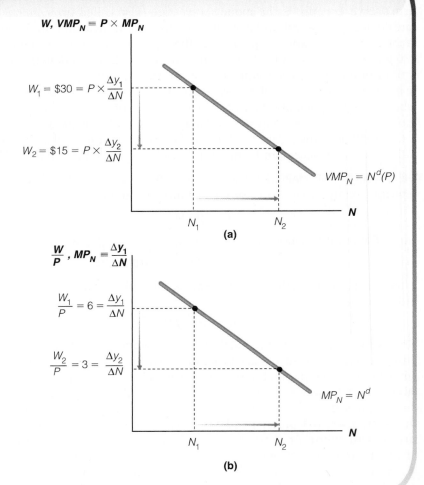

The VMP_N schedule for a purely competitive firm is that firm's labor demand schedule showing how many units of labor, N, the firm demands at any given money wage, W.

Note that we can rearrange the firm's profit-maximizing condition, $W = P \times MP_N$, by dividing both sides of the condition by P, which yields the expression

$$W/P = MP_N.$$

This expression says that another way of stating the firm's profit-maximizing condition is that the firm should hire labor to the point at which W/P, the *real* wage that the firm pays, is equal to the marginal product of labor. Panel (b) of Figure 3–2 illustrates this condition for two examples. One example is for the money wage $W_1 = \$30$ per unit of labor. Because the price of the firm's output, P, is $5 per unit, the real value of this money wage is $30 per unit of labor divided by $5 per unit of output, or 6 units of output per unit of labor.

In other words, the $30 wage that the firm pays each unit of labor is equivalent to a payment of 6 units of the firm's output. This is the real wage that the firm pays. To maximize its profit, the firm therefore employs labor to the point at which the marginal product of labor is equal to 6 units of output per unit of labor and employs a total of N_1 units of labor. Thus, the firm pays the worker an amount equal to the real value of the labor that the worker provides the firm.

THE FIRM'S DEMAND FOR LABOR   If the market wage rate were to fall to $W_2 = \$15$ per unit of labor, then the real wage paid by the firm would decline to $15 per unit of labor divided by $P = \$5$ per unit of output, or 3 units of output per unit of labor. Hence, the firm would require the marginal product of the last unit of labor employed to equal 3 units of output, so it would raise its employment of labor to N_2 units. Thus, the firm would demand more units of labor when the real market wage declines. We conclude:

> The MP_N schedule for a purely competitive firm is that firm's labor demand schedule. This schedule shows how many units of labor, N, the firm wishes to hire at any given real wage, W/P.

In both panels of Figure 3–2, the same money wage decline, from $W_1 = \$30$ per unit of labor to $W_2 = \$15$ per unit of labor, leads to the same increase in desired labor employment by the firm. We may conclude that both schedules depict the same choices by the firm. This makes sense, because in constructing both labor demand schedules, we have worked with the same, single profit-maximizing condition for a purely competitive firm. The only distinction is that the VMP_N schedule in panel (a) is the labor demand schedule if we measure the nominal wage as the factor price of labor, whereas the MP_N schedule in panel (b) is the labor demand schedule if we measure the real wage as the factor price of labor. The labor demand schedule graphed against the money wage, W, in panel (a) depends on the output price P, so we label it $N^d(P)$ to recognize this dependence. The labor demand schedule graphed against the real wage W/P in panel (b) does not depend on the value of P, and so we simply label it N^d.

FUNDAMENTAL ISSUE #2

According to the classical model, what are the determinants of the demand for labor by firms?   The demand for labor stems from the marginal product of labor, which is the slope of the aggregate production function. Profit-maximizing competitive firms hire units of labor to the point where price equals marginal cost, which in turn equals the money wage rate divided by the marginal product of labor. Consequently, firms employ labor to the point where the real wage rate equals the marginal product of labor, or at points along the marginal product schedule, which means that the marginal product schedule is the labor demand schedule when the real wage rate is measured along the vertical axis. Alternatively, firms employ labor to the point where the money wage equals the value of the marginal product of labor, meaning that the value-of-marginal-product schedule is the labor demand schedule when the money wage rate is measured along the vertical axis.

The Supply of Labor

All of us strive to find employment in a field in which we can do work that gives us satisfaction. Nevertheless, the time that we devote to work is time that we could otherwise have devoted to leisure activities that we would enjoy. The value we place on leisure time thereby represents an *opportunity cost* that we incur when we devote our time to work. This is why firms must pay us wages to induce us to devote large chunks of our days to work-related activities.

MEASURING LABOR COMPENSATION: THE REAL WAGE   Classical theorists focus on the *real wage* as the relevant measure of the compensation that laborers receive for time that they spend at work. The reason is that the real wage gives the purchasing power of a worker's earnings.

To see why this is true, consider a simple example. During a full year, an individual works 40 hours per week and earns a weekly money wage of $500. Over the course of the year, however, the level of prices of goods and services that the person consumes *doubles*. By the end of the year, therefore, the $500 weekly wage is worth *half* as much to the worker as it was at the beginning of the year. Consequently, it is not the money wage alone that matters to a worker. What matters is how many goods and services that money wage can be used to buy. This is why the real wage is the appropriate measure of a worker's compensation for labor time.

THE LABOR SUPPLY SCHEDULE   Holding all other factors unchanged, the only way that an individual may be induced to give up some leisure time and work more hours is if the real wage increases. Because the real wage is equal to the money wage divided by the price level, W/P, there are two ways that the real wage can rise. One is if the money wage rises relative to the price level; the other is if the price level falls relative to the money wage.

Figure 3–3 illustrates the effect on an individual's labor supply of a rise in the money wage from an initial value W_1 to a higher value W_2, with the price level unchanged at P_1. As panel (a) shows, this causes the real wage to increase, and the quantity of labor supplied also increases from N_1 to N_2 as workers respond to the higher real wage by giving up leisure time to work. Economists call this the *substitution effect* stemming from a rise in the real wage, because workers substitute labor for leisure. Note that at sufficiently high real wages, theoretically an *income effect* could arise: workers' incomes could be high enough that they would prefer to work less so that they could enjoy more leisure time. Most evidence indicates, however, that the substitution effect predominates in the aggregate. Consequently, the labor supply schedule, N^s, typically slopes upward, as in the figure.

Panel (b) of Figure 3–3 shows another depiction of the labor supply schedule. Here, only the money wage appears on the vertical axis. Again, a rise in the money wage from W_1 to W_2 causes the amount of labor that workers supply to rise from N_1 to N_2. As panel (b) shows, however, this occurs only because the price level has remained unchanged at P_1, so we label this version of labor supply $N^s(P_1)$. In both panels, a rise in the money wage with unchanged prices causes a rightward *movement along* the labor supply schedule.

On the Web

How fast are money wages rising in the United States? Take a look at U.S. employment cost trends by going to the home page of the Bureau of Labor Statistics at http://stats.bls.gov. Under "Wages, Earnings, and Benefits," click on "Employment Costs." Next, click on "Employment Cost Index." Choose desired intervals to display percentage changes in "Civilian Workers, Wages and Salaries," and select desired years.

Figure 3–3 The Labor Supply Effects of a Rise in the Money Wage

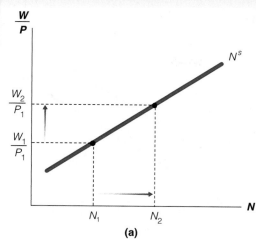

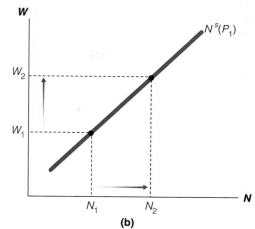

(a)   (b)

An increase in the money wage typically induces a worker to give up leisure time to work. Hence, workers supply more labor as the money wage rises relative to the price level, as shown in panel (a). Therefore the labor supply schedule slopes upward against the real wage. Alternatively, panel (b) displays this effect of a rise in the money wage for a given price level and indicates that the labor supply schedule also slopes upward if the money wage alone is measured along the vertical axis.

Figure 3–4 on the following page examines the labor supply effect of a decline in the price level. Panel (a) shows that a fall in the price level, from an initial value P_1 to a lower level P_2, increases the real wage that an individual earns. The effect is the same as if the money wage had risen with prices unchanged: Individuals work more hours, so the quantity of labor supplied increases from N_1 to N_2.

Panel (b) illustrates the effect of a price-level decrease when we measure only the money wage on the vertical axis of a labor supply diagram. Again the money wage remains unchanged. Nevertheless, the fall in the price level causes the real wage to increase, inducing individuals to work more hours and increase the quantity of labor supplied from N_1 to N_2. Consequently, the labor supply schedule in panel (b) *shifts to the right* as a result of the decline in the price level.

Labor Market Equilibrium and Aggregate Supply

The total demand for labor is the sum of the labor demand schedules for all the firms in the economy. Likewise, the total supply of labor is the sum of the labor supply schedules of all people in the economy who participate in the labor force. In the classical system, the interactions among firms and workers through the forces of demand and supply in the labor market determine the equilibrium wage and the equilibrium level of employment.

Figure 3-4   The Labor Supply Effects of a Fall in the Price Level

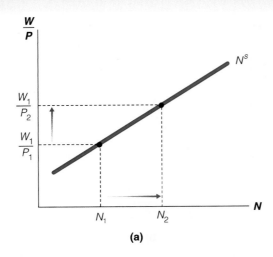

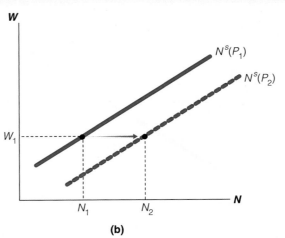

(a)   (b)

A reduction in the price level, from P_1 to P_2, with the money wage unchanged, causes the real wage to rise. As a result, workers choose to supply more labor services, as shown in panel (a). Equivalently, panel (b) shows that with the nomi-nal wage unchanged, the fall in the price level induces workers to increase their supply of labor services, so the labor supply schedule graphed against the money wage alone must shift rightward.

Furthermore, the aggregate production function then yields the aggregate level of real output produced in the economy. (In addition to providing a theory of the aggregate labor market, the classical labor market theory can help to explain why wages are higher in some industries than in others; see *Management Notebook: Why Are Wages So Much Higher in Information Technology Industries?*)

THE PRICE LEVEL, EMPLOYMENT, AND REAL OUTPUT   Figure 3–6 on page 64 depicts the determination of wages, employment, and output in the classical theory. Panels (a) and (b) are alternative illustrations of equilibrium in the labor market. In both panels, an initial equilibrium *money* wage, W_1, arises at which the quantity of labor demanded by firms is equal to the quantity of labor supplied by workers, *given* the prevailing price level, P_1. This equilibrium quantity of labor demanded and supplied is the equilibrium employment level, N_1. The aggregate production function in panel (c) then indicates the equilibrium level of real output, y_1, that is produced with this aggregate amount of labor employed. Finally, panel (d) shows that this yields a price level and real output combination of P_1 and y_1.

The price level ultimately is determined in the aggregate market for goods and services. Nonetheless, we can consider the effects of changes in the price level on money wages, employment, and output via a simple, and rather extreme, example in which the price level doubles from P_1 to $2P_1$. In panel (a), this doubling of the price level causes the real wage, which is measured along the vertical axis, to decline by a factor of two, or to half its

Why Are Wages So Much Higher in Information Technology Industries?

The classical framework applies the theory of perfect competition in labor markets to an aggregate labor market. We can also apply the theory to help understand economy-wide trends in wages across industries. One recent trend has been for workers in occupations that make heavy use of information technology (IT) to earn higher wages than workers in other occupations. As panel (a) of Figure 3–5 indicates, the average real wages earned by workers in IT-intensive occupations have risen since the early 1990s and now are nearly double the average real wages earned by workers throughout the economy as a whole.

According to the classical model, one possible explanation for relatively higher real wages in IT industries might be a boost in labor productivity, which would raise the demand for labor at IT firms. Panel (b) shows that productivity has indeed been higher in firms that produce IT products, as well as in industries that make intensive use of information technologies in their production processes. This higher productivity undoubtedly helps to account for the rise in relative wages earned by workers in IT occupations since the early 1990s.

For Critical Analysis

If numerous workers in other industries were to seek more IT training in hopes of earning the higher wages available in IT occupations, what would likely happen to the wage differential between wages earned by IT workers and wages earned by workers in other industries?

Figure 3–5   Wages and Productivity Growth in Information Technology Industries as Compared with Other U.S. Industries

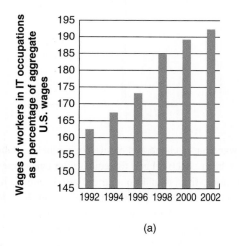

(a)

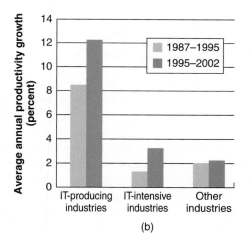

(b)

Panel (a) shows that workers in IT occupations typically earn between one and a half and two times the salaries of workers in other industries. Panel (b) provides one possible explanation: labor productivity is higher in industries that produce or intensively use information technologies.

SOURCE: U.S. Department of Commerce.

original value. The result is an excess quantity of labor demanded, because firms would like to hire more workers at the reduced real wage, but individuals are less willing to supply labor to firms. Firms begin to bid up the money wage to induce individuals to supply more labor, and ultimately

Figure 3–6   The Effects of a Doubling of the Price Level on the Equilibrium Money Wage, Employment, and Real Output

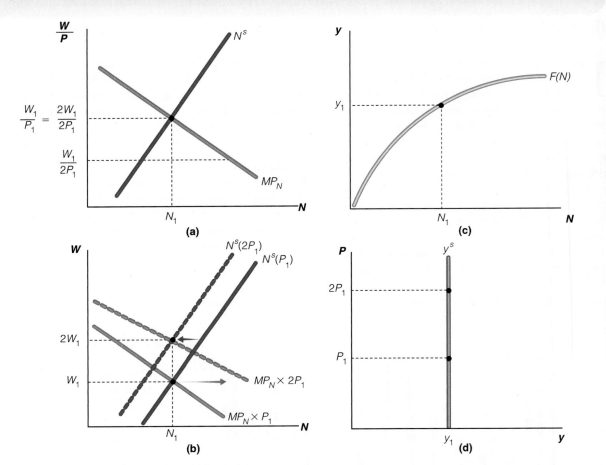

If the price level doubles, then the real wage falls to half its original level in panel (a). At the lower real wage, there is an excess quantity of labor demanded. The money wage is bid upward until labor market equilibrium is reattained. Equivalently, in panel (b) the doubling of the price level doubles the value of the marginal product of labor, and so the demand for labor rises. Workers, however, realize that the real wage has declined and reduce their supply of labor. On net, in both panels (a) and (b), equilibrium employment is unchanged. Thus, equilibrium output also is unchanged, as shown in panel (c). As a result, the increase in the price level has no effect on the production of real output, implying that the aggregate supply schedule in panel (d) is vertical.

the real wage returns to its original level. This happens, however, only after the equilibrium money wage has doubled. Consequently, the end result in response to the doubling of the price level is a doubling of the money wage and no change in the equilibrium employment level.

Panel (b) of Figure 3–6 provides an alternative illustration of these labor market effects of a doubling of the price level. When the price level doubles, so does the value of marginal product at all firms in the economy. Therefore, labor demand increases, as shown by the rightward shift of the labor demand schedule. At the same time, however, workers perceive that the purchasing power of the money wage is half its previous level, inducing them to reduce their supply of labor. Hence, the labor supply schedule shifts leftward. The result, as in panel (a), is a doubling of the equilibrium money wage. Again, equilibrium employment is unaffected by the rise in the price level. (When all wages adjust flexibly, the classical model indicates that no workers should be involuntarily unemployed; the theory does not rule out unemployment induced by factors that prevent the labor market from reaching equilibrium, however; see on the next page *Global Notebook: An Old-Fashioned Explanation for High Unemployment in France.*)

THE CLASSICAL AGGREGATE SUPPLY SCHEDULE Equilibrium employment does not change when the price level doubles, so panel (c) in Figure 3–6 indicates no change in real output. In panel (d), however, there is a new price level–real output combination, $2P_1$ and y_1. This combination, along with the original combination P_1 and y_1, lies along a schedule of price level–real output combinations that is vertical, meaning that any given change in the price level would leave real output unchanged. This vertical schedule is the classical **aggregate supply schedule,** which is the set of combinations of prices and real output at which the labor market is in equilibrium.

Because the aggregate supply schedule is vertical, we can say that the level of real output is "supply determined." Most economists credit Jean Baptiste Say (1767–1832) with first emphasizing this point, which led to the dictum, "Supply creates its own demand." That is:

No matter what shape the economy's demand schedule might take, the classical theory of aggregate supply implies that equilibrium real output is determined solely by factors that influence the position of the vertical aggregate supply schedule.

These factors are discussed in detail in Chapter 5.

> FUNDAMENTAL ISSUE #3
>
> **How are the aggregate levels of labor employment and real output of goods and services determined in the classical model?**   Equilibrium employment occurs at the real wage at which the quantity of labor demanded by firms equals the quantity of labor supplied by households. Equilibrium output then is determined by the aggregate production function. In the classical model, a change in the price level has no effect on equilibrium employment or output, so the classical aggregate supply schedule is vertical.

AGGREGATE SUPPLY SCHEDULE (y^s)**:** Combinations of various price levels and levels of real output that maintain equilibrium in the market for labor services.

65

CHAPTER 3   The Self-Adjusting Economy—Classical Macroeconomic Theory: Employment, Output, and Prices

Money, Aggregate Demand, and Inflation

As we have seen, in the classical system the quantity of real output is determined by the position of the aggregate supply schedule. This feature led to the central classical idea of supply-determined output. Nevertheless, the concept of the aggregate demand for output is crucial to understanding how the price level is determined in the classical theory.

An Old-Fashioned Explanation for High Unemployment in France

Panel (a) of Figure 3-7 compares unemployment rates in France and the United States since the late 1960s. The two countries' unemployment rates began to diverge in the mid-1980s, and since the mid-1990s the French unemployment rate has hovered in ranges nearly double the U.S. rate.

The classical theory offers a very basic explanation for unemployment. Panel (b) of the figure displays the classical demand for labor, the marginal-product-of-labor schedule, and the labor supply schedule. In this diagram, the equilibrium real wage is W_1/P_1, and equilibrium employment is N_1. If the nominal wage rate is artificially high, however, at $\overline{W}$, then the real wage is above its equilibrium value. To maximize their profits, firms will wish to employ a quantity of labor equal to $\overline{N}$, even though workers desire to supply N_2 units of labor. Hence, there is surplus labor, or unemployment.

In the United States, only a little over 13 percent of all workers employed by firms are covered by union contracts that set money wages, often above levels that competitive markets would have determined. In addition, only a small fraction of workers are affected by minimum-wage laws that set floors on money wages. In France, even though less than 10 percent of workers belong to unions, firms are required by law to pay nine out of every ten workers money wages equivalent to those established in union agreements. Minimum wages are also much higher in France than in the United States. According to the classical theory, the fact that less than 20 percent of U.S. workers receive real wages that are above competitive levels while about 95 percent of French workers earn above-

Figure 3-7   U.S. and French Unemployment Rates and Unemployment in the Classical Market for Labor.

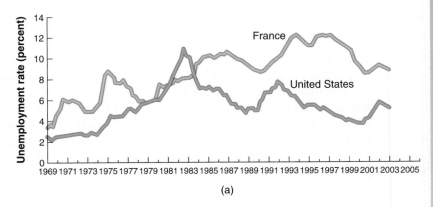

(a)

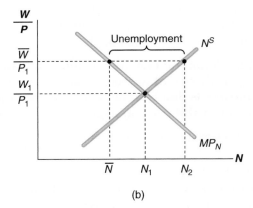

(b)

Panel (a) shows that the French unemployment rate has been much higher than the U.S. unemployment rate since the mid-1980s. According to the classical theory, unemployment occurs when the nominal wage rate is artificially high, as shown in panel (b), which boosts the real wage above its equilibrium level. Firms respond by hiring less labor, even as workers desire to supply more labor, and the result is unemployment.

SOURCES: Erwan Quintin, "Why Is French Unemployment So High?" Federal Reserve Bank of Dallas *Southwest Economy*, September/October 2001, pp. 13–14; Organization for Economic Cooperation and Development.

equilibrium real wages undoubtedly explains much of the differential between U.S. and French unemployment rates.

For Critical Analysis
Unemployed French workers also receive generous government subsidies, including housing allowances. How might this also contribute to relatively high unemployment in France?

The Demand for Money

As you will learn, the classical economists concluded that the primary factor explaining changes in the price level is variability in the amount of money in circulation, which, in turn, induces variations in aggregate demand. Consequently, a prerequisite to understanding the classical theory of aggregate demand for output is ascertaining how households and businesses decide how much money they desire to hold. Therefore, the classical theory of aggregate demand and price-level determination is developed from a theory of the *demand for money.*

THE FUNCTIONS OF MONEY   Although we tend to think of money as coins or dollar bills, the classical economists realized that any item that people are willing to accept in exchange for goods and services is **money.** Modern definitions of money, for instance, include funds that households and businesses hold in accounts in financial institutions such as banks, savings and loan associations, and credit unions.

Money performs four important functions:

1. *Medium of exchange* The fundamental role of money is as a **medium of exchange.** When people trade goods and services, they are willing to accept money in exchange. This saves people from having to engage in **barter,** or the act of exchanging goods and services directly. Barter is a costly process, because it requires locating others willing to exchange items directly. Using money saves on such costs.

2. *Store of value* A second function of money is as a **store of value.** An individual can set money aside for later use in purchasing goods, services, or financial assets. While the funds sit idle, they retain value that the individual can draw upon to make the future purchases. For instance, the individual can hold funds in a checking account for several days and then use the funds to buy groceries as needed.

3. *Unit of account* Money's third function is as a **unit of account.** Households and businesses can value goods and services in terms of money. In addition, people can quote prices of goods and services in money terms. For example, when an individual shops at a U.S. grocery store, the prices of goods are expressed in dollar terms.

4. *Standard of deferred payment* Finally, money also serves as a **standard of deferred payment.** When people reach contractual agreements that require future payments, they specify that the payments will be made with money. Bank loans, for example, specify future dollar repayments.

THE QUANTITY THEORY OF MONEY   Although the original classical theorists recognized that money performs these four functions, they viewed money's property as a medium of exchange as the key to explaining why money exists. After all, they reasoned, if money did not function as a medium of exchange, then people could barter goods, services, and financial assets

---

MONEY: An item that people are willing to accept in exchange for goods and services.

MEDIUM OF EXCHANGE: Money's role as a means of payment for goods and services.

BARTER: The direct exchange of goods and services.

STORE OF VALUE: A function of money in which it is held for future use without loss of value.

UNIT OF ACCOUNT: A function of money in which it is used as a measure of the value of goods, services, and financial assets.

STANDARD OF DEFERRED PAYMENT: Money's role as a means of valuing future receipts in loan contracts.

QUANTITY THEORY OF MONEY: The theory that people hold money for transactions purposes.

EQUATION OF EXCHANGE: An accounting identity that states that the nominal value of all monetary transactions for final goods and services is equal to the nominal value of the output of goods and services purchased.

INCOME VELOCITY OF MONEY: The average number of times that each unit of money is used to purchase final goods and services in a given interval.

CAMBRIDGE EQUATION: An equation developed by economists at Cambridge University, England, which indicates that individuals desire to hold money in proportion to their nominal income.

directly. People would not even use money if it did not perform this key function.

For this reason, the classical theory of the demand for money focuses on money's role as a medium of exchange. To understand how much money people desire to hold, the classical economists concentrated on explaining the demand for money for purchases of newly produced goods and services. The transactions-based theory of money demand that they developed is now known as the **quantity theory of money.**

The starting point for the quantity theory of money is the **equation of exchange:**

$$M \times V \equiv P \times y.$$

In the equation of exchange, M is the nominal quantity of money, or the current-dollar value of currency and checking deposits held by the nonbank public. The term V represents the **income velocity of money,** or the average number of times people spend each unit of money on final goods and services per unit of time. Consequently, the left side of the equation of exchange is the value of current-dollar monetary payments for final goods and services. On the right side of the equation, the price level for final goods and services is multiplied by the quantity of output of goods and services. Note, however, that this quantity is also the current-dollar value of monetary payments for final goods and services. Hence, both sides of the equation of exchange must be identical. The equation of exchange is thus an accounting definition, or identity. It states that the product of the nominal quantity of money times the average number of times that people use money to buy goods and services ($M \times V$) must equal the market value of the goods and services that people use the money to purchase ($P \times y$).

An economic identity is a truism. It is not a theory of how people behave. The basis of the quantity *theory* of money is the **Cambridge equation,** so named because it was first proposed by Alfred Marshall (1842–1924) and other economists at Cambridge University in England. According to the Cambridge equation:

$$M^d = k \times Y,$$

where M^d denotes the total quantity of money all people in the economy wish to hold and k is a fraction ($0 < k < 1$). The Cambridge equation, therefore, says that people desire to hold some fraction of their nominal income as money. Recall from Chapter 2 that the nominal value of real output, $P \times y$, corresponds to the total level of nominal income, Y. This means that the Cambridge equation may also be written as

$$M^d = k \times P \times y.$$

The idea behind this equation is simple. The fraction k represents the public's desired holdings of nominal money balances relative to total nominal income. For instance, if $k = 0.2$, then people wish to hold 20 percent, or one-fifth, of their nominal income as money. They hold this money in anticipation of exchanges they will make during the coming days and weeks. They allocate the rest of their income to immediate consumption of goods and services. It is for this reason that the theory of money demand is directly related to the classical theory of the aggregate demand for real output.

Aggregate Demand and the Price Level

We now have the essential building blocks that we need to see how aggregate demand and the price level are determined in the classical theory.

THE AGGREGATE DEMAND SCHEDULE Suppose that the quantity of nominal money balances supplied through the actions of a central bank is equal to an amount M_1. In equilibrium, all individuals in the economy desire to hold this quantity of money balances, so that

$$M^d = M_1.$$

The Cambridge equation then indicates that

$$M_1 = k \times P \times y.$$

If we divide both sides of this equation by $k \times P$, we obtain

$$M_1/(k \times P) = y.$$

Reversing the two sides of this equation leaves us with

$$y^d = M_1/(k \times P).$$

This is an equation for the economy's **aggregate demand schedule.** The aggregate demand schedule is all combinations of real output and prices for which households are satisfied holding the available quantity of nominal money balances (M_1 in this example), given their average desired ratio of money holdings, k.

Figure 3–8 depicts the aggregate demand schedule. As the equation for the aggregate demand schedule indicates, the quantity of real output of

AGGREGATE DEMAND SCHEDULE (y^d): Combinations of various price levels and levels of real output for which individuals are satisfied with their consumption of output and their holdings of money.

69

CHAPTER 3   The Self-Adjusting Economy—Classical Macroeconomic Theory: Employment, Output, and Prices

---

Figure 3–8   The Classical Aggregate Demand Schedule

The aggregate demand schedule stems from the Cambridge equation. It is negatively sloped, indicating that at higher price levels, with the nominal quantity of money and the Cambridge k unchanged, the quantity of real output demanded declines.

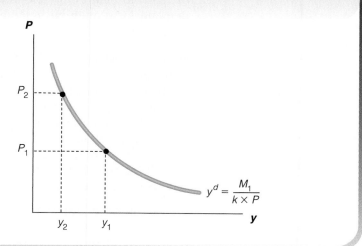

goods and services that people wish to purchase declines as the price level rises. This is so because as the price level increases, so do nominal income earnings. According to the Cambridge equation $M^d = k \times Y = k \times P \times y$, individuals will, as a result, desire to hold more money balances, leaving them with less of their income to purchase real goods and services. As a result, the amount of real output demanded falls from y_1 to y_2 when the price level rises from P_1 to P_2. This is a leftward *movement along* the aggregate demand schedule.

SHIFTS IN THE AGGREGATE DEMAND SCHEDULE   Two factors can cause the aggregate demand schedule's *position* to change. One is a change in the quantity of money supplied by the government or by a central bank. As we can see by referring to the equation for the schedule, $y^d = M_1/(k \times P)$, a rise in the quantity of money to an amount larger than M_1 would increase the right side of the equation. This means that nominal purchasing power available to all individuals in the economy would be higher at any given price level, so people would desire to purchase more real goods and services at any given price level. The aggregate demand schedule would shift to the right, and aggregate demand would *rise*. In contrast, a decline in the quantity of money would shift the aggregate demand schedule to the left, and aggregate demand would *fall*.

The other factor that can alter the position of the aggregate demand schedule is a change in k in the Cambridge equation. For example, a technological change might reduce people's desire to demand as much money—for instance, both debit cards and automated teller machines at banks reduce the desire to keep ready cash on hand. In that case, the value of k would decline. People would hold fewer money balances relative to their nominal income, $Y = P \times y$. This would free up income for purchasing goods and services. Referring once more to the equation for the aggregate demand schedule, $y^d = M_1/(k \times P)$, we can see that a decline in k, because it reduces the denominator of the right-hand side of the equation, increases the total purchasing power available to individuals in the economy. Just as an increase in the quantity of money supplied causes a rise, or rightward shift outward, in aggregate demand, so does a decline in the demand for money by individuals. In contrast, a rise in money demand induces a reduction, or leftward shift inward, in aggregate demand.

PRICE-LEVEL DETERMINATION   Figure 3–9 displays the aggregate demand and aggregate supply schedules together on the same diagram. This is a diagram of the *market for real output,* as visualized in the classical theory. Equilibrium in this market occurs at the point at which the aggregate demand schedule crosses the aggregate supply schedule. At this point on the aggregate demand schedule, the quantity of output demanded equals the amount of output supplied, y_1. The *equilibrium price level* is P_1. At this price level, individuals are satisfied with their current money holdings and with their current purchases of real goods and services.

VELOCITY IN THE CLASSICAL THEORY   In the output-market equilibrium shown in Figure 3–9, the equation of exchange identity tells us that $M_1 \times V \equiv P_1 \times y_1$. We also know that in equilibrium, the aggregate demand equation is

macroxtra!
Interactive Key Graph   The graph below shows how real output and the price level are determined in the classical model. What happens if the money stock changes? What occurs if there is a change in technology? You can discover the answers to these questions by interacting with this graph on the Web.
Go to http://macroxtra.swcollege.com

Figure 3–9   Output–Market Equilibrium in the Classical Model

The equilibrium price level ensures that the amount of real output that individuals wish to purchase, given the quantity of money and the income velocity of money, is equal to the level of real output produced by firms. This price level corresponds to the point where the aggregate demand schedule crosses the aggregate supply schedule.

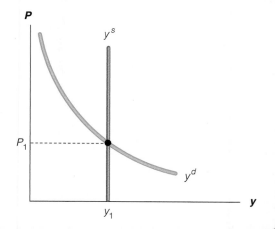

satisfied, so $y_1 = M_1/(k \times P_1)$. If we substitute this value for real output into the equation of exchange identity, we obtain

$$M_1 \times V \equiv P_1 \times M_1/(k \times P_1) = M_1/k.$$

Now, if we divide both sides of this equation by M_1, we obtain

$$V = 1/k.$$

This says that a key assumption of the classical theory is that the income velocity of money, or the average number of times that the quantity of money is used in exchange for real goods and services, is equal to the reciprocal of the k factor of proportionality in the Cambridge equation.

The Cambridge equation assumes that k is constant, so the classical theory of aggregate demand and price-level determination must also implicitly assume that the income velocity of money is constant. Is this a reasonable assumption? Figure 3–10 on page 72 shows the U.S. income velocity of money since 1959. As you can see, it has not been constant over time. The original classical theorists recognized that velocity does change, but they argued that the key factor affecting the ability of their model to explain current and future price-level movements was the *predictability* of velocity. As long as velocity could be predicted fairly accurately, they argued, their theory would provide a reasonable explanation of price-level movements.

Figure 3–10   The Income Velocity of Money in the United States

The U.S. income velocity of money using the Federal Reserve's M2 measure of money has exhibited year-to-year variability. Nevertheless, its value has remained within a relatively narrow range since the late 1950s.

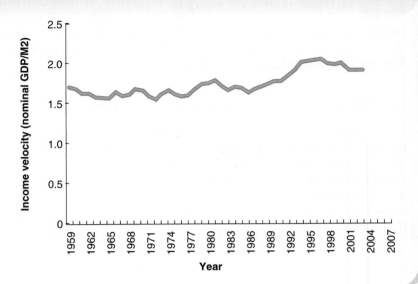

SOURCES: *Economic Report of the President,* 2002; *Federal Reserve Bulletin* (various issues).

macro**xtra!**
Online
Perspective

To understand how economists try to measure long-term trend inflation in the United States, go to the Chapter 3 reading, entitled "Comparing Measures of Core Inflation," by Todd Clark of the Federal Reserve Bank of Kansas City.
http://macroxtra.swcollege.com

FUNDAMENTAL ISSUE #4

What factors determine the price level in the classical framework?   In the classical theory, the equilibrium price level adjusts to equate the quantity of real output demanded with the supply-determined quantity of real output produced. Thus, the equilibrium price level arises at the point of intersection of the aggregate demand and aggregate supply schedules.

Is Inflation Mainly a Monetary Phenomenon?

Panel (c) of Figure 3–11 on page 74 shows that annual U.S. inflation rates for the past few decades have been positive.

Supply-Side Inflation Doesn't Fit the Facts

What accounts for such persistent inflation? The classical theory provides two possible explanations. One is depicted in panel (a) of Figure 3–11, which shows a rise in the price level caused by a *fall in aggregate supply.* Thus, one conceivable rationale for persistent inflation is continual reductions in production of real output.

Consider now the factors that can cause the aggregate supply schedule to shift leftward: (1) lower labor force participation; (2) a decline in labor productivity; (3) higher marginal tax rates on wages; or (4) the provision of government benefits that give households incentives not to supply labor services to firms. Although overall tax rates and government benefits definitely increased during the latter part of the twentieth century, so did the U.S. population. More recently, the government has cut back on the provision of labor-supply-reducing benefits. In addition, although the marginal product of labor has declined for short intervals, labor productivity otherwise has increased since the 1950s. The overall rise in real GDP that has taken place during the past few decades tells us that population growth and productivity gains have dominated other factors. On net, therefore, the aggregate supply schedule actually has shifted *rightward,* not leftward, over time. Thus, the classical approach indicates that this *supply-side* explanation for persistent inflation *cannot* be the *true* explanation.

Money Growth and Demand-Side Inflation

According to classical monetary theory, the only other explanation for the observation of persist-

ent inflation is illustrated in panel (b) of Figure 3–11. If aggregate demand increases for a given level of aggregate supply, then the price level must increase. The reason is that, at an initial price level such as P_1, people desire to purchase more real goods and services (y_2) than firms are willing and able to produce (y_1) given the currently available technology and present labor force participation rates. As a result, the rise in aggregate demand leads only to a general rise in the price level, from P_1 to P_2.

Recall that there are two possible reasons that aggregate demand might shift rightward over time. One is persistent reductions in the demand for money, which would imply year-to-year declines in the factor of proportionality k in the Cambridge equation. Recall that k is equal to the reciprocal of velocity, so Figure 3–10 on page 72 actually plots the reciprocal of k. Despite some periods of general declines or increases in the value of k, overall it has been remarkably stable. Hence, while changes in k have influenced the price level, from a classical perspective this cannot have been the predominant factor explaining U.S. inflation.

The other factor that classical theory indicates could cause persistent increases in aggregate demand is consistent growth of the quantity of money. Panel (d) of Figure 3–11 shows that the Federal Reserve's M2 measure of the quantity of money has exhibited persistent growth since the 1950s. *This,* most classical theorists argue, is the key explanation for the persistence of inflation. Persistent money growth, they contend, has produced persistent inflation.

Research Project

Under what circumstances does classical monetary theory indicate that demand-side inflation could take place without an increase in the quantity of money? How might these

Continued on next page

Link to Policy, continued

circumstances arise in the real world? Would it ever be possible for demand-side inflation to take place, on net, during a period when the quantity of money *declines?*

Web Resource

To evaluate whether there is evidence of international relationships between money growth and inflation, go to the home page of the Federal Reserve Bank of St. Louis (http://www.stlouisfed.org), In the gray bar at the top, click on "Economic Research," and under "Publications," scroll over to "International Economic Trends Quarterly." At the next page, first click on a nation's "Inflation and Prices Charts" to download figures displaying the country's recent inflation performance. Then click on "Monetary Aggregates: Short-Run Charts" to download figures showing growth rates in monetary aggregates. Then compare the charts to see if there is evidence of a direct relationship between money growth rates and inflation in various countries.

Figure 3–11   Assessing Theory and Evidence Concerning U.S. Inflation

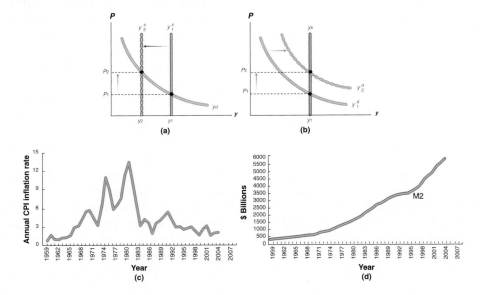

Panels (a) and (b) provide two possible explanations for the persistent U.S. inflation depicted in panel (c). Panel (a) shows the effects of a reduction in aggregate supply. An aggregate supply reduction can bring about a rise in the price level, but the accompanying decline in real output is inconsistent with the significant growth in real output experienced by the United States over the long term. An increase in aggregate demand, which the classical theory indicates could result from the persistent increases in the quantity of money depicted in panel (d), could also bring about a higher price level.

SOURCES: *Economic Report of the President,* various issues: Board of Governors of the Federal Reserve System.

1. **Key Assumptions of Classical Macroeconomic Theory:** One key assumption is that people rationally pursue their own self-interest. A second assumption is that people do not experience money illusion, so they are not fooled by current-dollar changes that make no difference to their real incomes. The final key assumption is that markets for goods, services, and factors of production are purely competitive, meaning that there are large numbers of buyers and sellers, none of whom individually can affect market prices.

2. **Determinants of Firms' Demand for Labor in the Classical Model:** A key determinant of the demand for labor is the marginal product of labor, which is the slope of the aggregate production function. Because profit-maximizing competitive firms hire units of labor to the point where price equals marginal cost, which equals the money wage rate divided by the marginal product of labor, firms employ labor to the point where the real wage rate equals the marginal product of labor. Hence, firms determine how much labor to employ at points along the marginal product schedule, so that when the real wage rate is measured along the vertical axis, the marginal product schedule is the labor demand schedule. When the money wage rate is measured along the vertical axis, firms employ labor to the point

where the nominal wage equals the value of the marginal product of labor, so that the value-of-marginal-product schedule is the labor demand schedule.

3. **The Determination of Employment and Output in the Classical Model:** According to the classical framework, the real and money wages adjust to keep the quantity of labor supplied by workers equal to the quantity of labor demanded by firms. The equilibrium amount of real aggregate output then is the amount that firms can produce with this quantity of labor, given their use of other factors of production and the technology available to them. Because the equilibrium money wage adjusts in equal proportion to changes in prices, employment and output do not change in response to price-level variations. Consequently, the classical aggregate supply schedule is vertical.

4. **The Classical Theory of Prices and Inflation:** The equilibrium price level is the level that ensures that the quantity of real output demanded is equal to the amount supplied by firms. This occurs at the point where the aggregate demand schedule, whose position is determined by the quantity of money in circulation and the income velocity of money, crosses the vertical classical aggregate supply schedule.

Self-Test Questions

1. As we shall discuss in Chapter 5, economists typically measure economic growth using the growth of real GDP as a starting point. Therefore, according to the classical framework, what factors should influence the rate of economic growth? Explain.

2. During the 1970s and 1980s, women entered the U.S. labor force in increasing numbers. Use the classical model to predict the effects that this would have on the equilibrium real wage, equilibrium employment, and equilibrium real GDP.

3. Based on your answer to question 2, determine the effect that a rise in female participation in the labor force would have on the price level in the classical model, holding all other factors constant. Explain your answer.

4. Suppose that a nation becomes involved in a war that results in the destruction of a significant fraction of its capital stock. Use the classical model to predict the effects that this would have on the equilibrium real wage, equilibrium employment, and equilibrium real GDP.

5. Based on your answer to question 4, determine the effect that destruction of part of the nation's capital stock would have on the country's price level in the classical model, holding all other factors constant. Explain your answer.

6. Suppose that the increasing use of the Internet to make transactions without reliance on money causes the income velocity of money to decline substantially. Use the classical model to predict what, if any, effects this would have on the equilibrium price level and equilibrium real GDP.

(Answers to odd-numbered questions may be found on the Web at **http://macro. swcollege.com** under "Student Resources.")

(Answers to odd-numbered problems may be found on the Web at **http://macro. swcollege.com** under "Student Resources.")

1. Suppose that the Cambridge k is equal to 0.25, real GDP is equal to 11 trillion base-year dollars, and the price level is equal to 1.2 current-year dollars per base-year dollar. What is the current-dollar value of the quantity of money in circulation?

2. Verify that the equation for the classical aggregate demand schedule is $y^d = M/Pk$. Next, suppose that at the equilibrium level of real output, the price level is equal to 2 current-year dollars per base-year dollar. The current-year value of the quantity of money in circulation is $1 trillion, and $k = 0.125$ (or one-eighth).

   a. What is the income velocity of money?

   b. What is the equilibrium output level?

   c. Write an equation for the aggregate supply schedule in the form "$y^s = $ ___." (Hint: Your equation will be a very simple one.)

3. Assume that initially Ms. Hansen has an income of $600 per week and that she saves $60 and spends $540 on consumption goods each week. She works 37 hours per week. Now suppose that *all* prices double, so all goods that Ms. Hansen consumes cost twice as much as before. Her wages also are twice as high as before, and nominal interest rates rise by exactly 100 percent. After this event,

   a. Will Ms. Hansen save a larger percentage of her income each week?

   b. Will Ms. Hansen work more than 37 hours per week?

4. Suppose that the total demand for labor in a nation is given by the equation, $W/P = 25 - 2N$. The total supply of labor is given by the equation $W/P = -5 + 2N$.

   a. What is the equilibrium real wage?

   b. What is the equilibrium quantity of labor?

   c. Suppose that the prices of all goods double. Write out the labor demand and labor supply equations after this occurs. Now determine the equilibrium real wage and the equilibrium quantity of labor.

Before the Test

Test your understanding of the material covered in this chapter by taking the Chapter 3 interactive quiz at **http://macro.swcollege.com**.

Online Application

The Federal Reserve's Beige Book (see Chapter 1's *Online Application*) provides a wealth of information about the current status of U.S. labor markets. You can access this Internet locale to keep track of developments in wages, employment, and unemployment in the United States.

Internet URL: http://www.federalreserve.gov/fomc/BeigeBook/2003/

Title: *The Beige Book—Summary*

Navigation: Begin with the Federal Reserve Board's home page (http://federalreserve.gov). Click on Monetary Policy. Then click on *Beige Book* to access the Beige Book home page. Click on the most recent report date.

Application: Read the sections entitled "Labor Markets" and "Prices," and answer the following questions:

1. Has overall employment been rising or falling during the most recent year? According to the classical model, what factors might account for this pattern? Does the Beige Book summary bear out any of these theoretical explanations for changes in aggregate U.S. employment?

2. Have money wages been rising or falling during the most recent year? Does the Beige Book provide any information that permits you to deduce the implications for aggregate real wages?

For Group Study and Analysis: The left-hand margin of the Beige Book site lists the reports for the twelve Federal Reserve districts. Divide the class into twelve groups, and have each group develop brief summaries of the main conclusions of one district's report on the behavior of money wages, prices, employment, and output within that district. Reconvene, and compare the reports. Are there pronounced regional differences?

macro**xtra!**

Log on to the MacroXtra Web site at http://macroxtra.swcollege.com for additional learning resources such as practice quizzes, Interactive Key Graphs, readings, and additional economic applications.

Selected References and Further Reading

Clark, Todd. "Comparing Measures of Inflation." Federal Reserve Bank of Kansas City *Economic Review,* Second Quarter 2001, pp. 5–31.

Dwyer, Gerald, Jr., and R. W. Hafer. "Are Money Growth and Inflation Still Related?" Federal Reserve Bank of Atlanta *Economic Review* 84 (Second Quarter 1999): 32–43.

Hicks, John R. *Theory of Wages.* London: Macmillan, 1932.

Marshall, Alfred. *Principles of Economics.* New York: Macmillan, 1925.

Mill, John S. *Principles of Economics.* New York: Macmillan, 1848.

Say, Jean B. *A Treatise on Political Economy.* London: Longmans, 1821.

4 Classical Macroeconomic Theory: Interest Rates and Exchange Rates

FUNDAMENTAL ISSUES

1. How is the real interest rate determined in the classical theory?

2. How do government spending and taxation policies influence the real interest rate in the classical model?

3. How is the nominal interest rate determined in the classical theory?

4. According to the classical model, how is the value of a nation's currency determined?

*I*t has been the subject of magazine articles. Economic research papers have explored its implications for exchange rates. Ph.D. dissertations have sought to determine whether foreign exchange traders can earn profits using it as a guide to currency exchanges.

It is the Big Mac Index, a guideline for what the rates of exchange of various nations' currencies should be in light of the prices of McDonald's Big Mac sandwiches in those countries. Although the Big Mac Index originally was introduced as a tongue-in-cheek guide to whether current market exchange rates are "too high" or "too low," some evidence indicates that, on average, it can aid in predicting exchange rates. Although economists do not really believe that prices of Big Mac sandwiches influence exchange rates, some suggest that the Big Mac Index may be a rough indicator of whether current market exchange rates are consistent with a broader relationship between exchange rates and national price levels known as purchasing power parity.

As you will learn in this chapter, purchasing power parity is the underpinning of the classical theory of exchange-rate determination. The classical economists also contemplated how interest rates are determined, which is the other key topic of this chapter.

The Real Interest Rate in the Classical Model

Every day, publications such as the *Wall Street Journal* and *The Financial Times* keep their readers abreast of interest rates. Such newspapers list interest rates on Treasury securities issued by the U.S. government, corporate bonds and commercial paper issued by firms, certificates of deposit issued by banks, and money, bond, and equity fund shares issued by mutual funds. In addition, these publications commonly run stories speculating about how changes in interest rates may affect economic activity.

As you will learn in later chapters, theories of short-run variations in economic activity do indicate that interest-rate variations can lead to changes in prices and output. In the basic classical framework, however, interest rates do not perform such a "causal" role. Instead, they adjust to equate quantities demanded and supplied in markets for credit.

Not everyone spends all the income that he or she earns. Many people save a portion of their earnings. This means that somewhere along the multiple chains of expenditures that take place in the economy, there is a *leakage* from the total flow of expenditures when people save. To achieve equilibrium in the market for real output, however, all goods and services produced ultimately must be purchased. Hence, all saving ultimately must find its way back into the aggregate flow of spending on goods and services. In the classical model, the role of interest rates is to ensure that this occurs in equilibrium.

Real versus Nominal Interest Rates

Before we discuss how interest rates matter, it is important to understand the distinction between *nominal interest rates* and *real interest rates.* Nominal interest rates are easy to understand. These are the interest rates that appear in the daily and weekly financial periodicals. They also are the loan and deposit interest rates that your bank, savings institution, or credit union posts on its walls. A nominal interest rate is simply the current market rate of interest expressed as the nominal value of a flow of interest relative to a nominal base, or principal amount of funds. For example, a quoted annual auto loan rate of 9 percent means that for every $100 borrowed to finance an auto purchase, the borrower must pay $9 per year in interest to the lender.

Suppose, though, that when the auto loan was negotiated, both the lender and the borrower anticipated an annual inflation rate of 3 percent during the term of the loan. In this case, the real value of the principal amount of the loan would decline by $3 each year. As a result, the *real* interest payment that the borrower anticipates making and the lender anticipates receiving would be reduced by this $3 amount each year. Consequently, the real interest paid each year on the initial $100 principal would be $9 − $3,

REAL INTEREST RATE: The nominal interest rate minus the expected rate of inflation.

LOANABLE FUNDS: The term used by classical economists to refer to the amount of real income that households save, representing claims on real output.

or $6 per year. The *real interest rate,* therefore, would be 6 percent, or the nominal interest rate of 9 percent minus the expected inflation rate of 3 percent. Thus, we can define the **real interest rate** as the difference between the nominal interest rate and the expected rate of inflation. If we denote the nominal interest rate as r, the expected inflation rate as π^e (the Greek letter pi denotes the inflation rate, and the e superscript indicates an expectation of that rate), then the real interest rate, r_r, is equal to

$$r_r = r - \pi^e.$$

Saving and the Supply of Loanable Funds

In the classical theory, the main determinant of real saving per unit of time is the real interest rate, r_r. People care about the real interest rate because this is the correct measure of their real return on saving. The key hypothesis is that there is a direct relationship between the real interest rate and the amount that households save out of a given level of real income, holding all other factors unchanged. If the real interest rate rises, the real return on saving rises, and households will save more of a given level of income and thereby choose to consume a smaller portion of that income. If the real interest rate falls, households will save less and consume more of a given level of income. Figure 4–1 illustrates this direct relationship between real saving, s, and the real interest rate, r_r.

The saving of households represents claims on real goods and services, so the original classical economists called these financial claims **loanable funds.** Therefore, the saving schedule s in Figure 4–1 is a supply schedule in the market for these loanable funds, and the real interest rate is the price of loanable funds. (In recent years official measures of the saving of U.S. households have been drawn into question; see *Policy Notebook: Has the U.S. Saving Rate Really Declined So Dramatically?*)

Figure 4–1   The Classical Market for Loanable Funds

For a given level of real income, individuals save more and consume less as the real interest rate rises. Therefore, the saving schedule, which is the supply of loanable funds, slopes upward. In contrast, desired real investment spending by firms declines as the real interest rate increases. As a result, the investment schedule slopes downward. In the absence of a government budget deficit, or surplus, the equilibrium real interest rate equilibrates investment and saving.

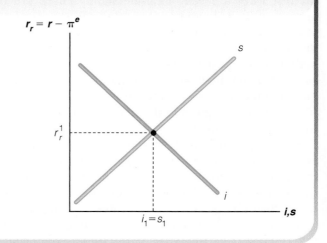

Has the U.S. Saving Rate Really Declined So Dramatically?

At various times during the past few years, the U.S. government's official measure of the rate at which individuals save from their income has generally hovered around 3 percent. As panel (a) of Figure 4–2 indicates, when measured on a quarterly basis, it fell dramatically during the 1990s.

Why has the official saving rate declined? The reason is that when the Bureau of Economic Analysis constructs the National Income and Product Accounts (NIPA), it has a relatively easy time determining domestic consumption spending, taxes, and import spending. To calculate saving, it subtracts these items from total income. It then divides this measure of saving by income to determine the saving rate. Thus, in the NIPA, saving is a *residual,* or leftover, item. Domestic consumption and import spending soared after 1992. As a consequence, the official saving rate fell, as shown in the figure.

In reality, saving is not a residual. It is an addition to household wealth that takes place over time. Part of household wealth includes stocks and bonds, held either directly or indirectly through pension and employee thrift plans. As the market values of stocks and bonds change, so does the market valuation of household wealth. In principle, this means that when households allocate more wealth to bonds and stocks or experience capital gains when the prices of these assets increase, their saving rises as well. Panel (b) of Figure 4–2 displays annual measures of both the official, NIPA saving rate and an adjusted saving rate that takes account of changing market valuations of household wealth within sav-

Figure 4–2   **Official and Adjusted Saving Rates**

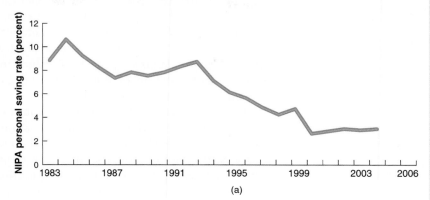

(a)

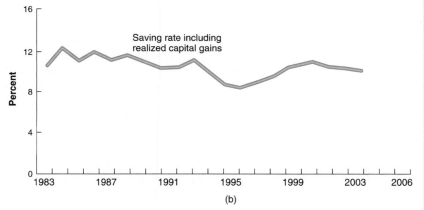

(b)

Panel (a) displays quarterly values of the government's official (NIPA) saving rate, which has fallen below zero at times. Panel (b) shows annual measures of both the official saving rate and an adjusted saving rate that counts market valuations of household wealth as part of saving.

SOURCES: Richard Peach and Charles Steindel, "A Nation of Spendthrifts? An Analysis of Trends in Personal and Gross Saving," Federal Reserve Bank of New York *Current Issues in Economics and Finance* 6 (September 2000); *Economic Report of the President,* various issues; authors' estimates.

ing. This adjusted saving rate has been much more stable over time, and it has remained well above zero.

For Critical Analysis
According to the classical model, why should policymakers care how much individuals wish to save?

Investment and the Demand for Loanable Funds

Not everyone saves. At any given time many people desire to spend more than their incomes would otherwise permit them to spend. This is especially true for owners of businesses. To be able to produce goods and services, owners of business firms often need to purchase or build expensive capital goods such as machines and factories. The required capital expenditures commonly exceed the real incomes of the individuals who own these firms. For this reason, firm owners often desire to borrow funds from those who save; that is, those who *invest* in new capital equipment *demand loanable funds.* Then they use these funds to purchase capital goods. In this way, a large portion of the saving leakage from the economy's flow of spending is *reinjected* into that flow.

In the classical framework, the amount of desired investment spending depends negatively upon the real interest rate. As the real interest rate rises, the price of loanable funds for firm investment increases, and business owners respond by reducing the quantity of loanable funds demanded. As the real interest rate declines, the quantity of loanable funds demanded by firms rises. This inverse relationship between desired investment spending and the interest rate is shown as the *investment schedule,* labeled i in Figure 4–1.

The saving schedule and investment schedule cross at the real interest rate r_r. At this real rate of interest, the quantity of loanable funds supplied by household savers, s_1, is equal to the quantity of loanable funds demanded by business owners to fund private investment, i_1.

If businesses are the only source of demand for loanable funds in the economy, then r_r is the *equilibrium* real rate of interest. It also is the real interest rate at which the market for real output is in equilibrium. This is so because at this real interest rate the equality of desired saving and desired investment implies that all leakages from the flow of real expenditures in the form of savings are reinjected into that flow as investment expenditures.

FUNDAMENTAL ISSUE #1

How is the real interest rate determined in the classical theory?   Within the classical model, the supply of loanable funds is real saving by households. Because real saving is directly related to the real interest rate, the supply schedule of loanable funds is upward sloping. The key source of the demand for loanable funds is real investment spending by firms. The amount of real investment that firms desire to undertake depends negatively on the real interest rate, so the demand schedule for loanable funds slopes downward. The real interest rate adjusts to equalize the quantity of loanable funds supplied, or aggregate private saving, with the quantity of loanable funds demanded, or real investment spending; this occurs at the intersection of the loanable funds demand and supply schedules.

Government budgetary policies can also influence the equilibrium real interest rate in the classical model. Governments adjust their budgets by increasing or reducing taxes imposed on households and by raising or lowering their expenditures. Typically, government budgets are established over an annual interval called a *fiscal year,* so economists commonly refer to variations in taxes or government spending as **fiscal policies.** In the classical theory, governmental fiscal policy actions exert their effects in the market for loanable funds.

Government Deficits and the Real Interest Rate

Governments borrow loanable funds when they spend more on goods and services than they receive in tax revenues. We denote the quantity of real government spending on goods and services as g and the amount of real government tax revenues less transfer payments as t. Then, if government spending exceeds taxes, it needs to fund a deficit equal to $g - t$. This is known as the *primary deficit,* which is the most basic measure of the government's deficit. It ignores other potentially important government expenditures, such as interest payments on outstanding government debt issued in earlier periods.

GOVERNMENT DEFICITS AND THE DEMAND FOR LOANABLE FUNDS   Panel (a) in Figure 4–3 on page 84 shows the effect of including a government's budget deficit as a component of the total demand for loanable funds. If we assume that the government simply desires to fund a lump-sum deficit of amount $g - t$ at any given real interest rate, then we can add this quantity of loanable funds demanded by the government horizontally to the private loanable funds demanded by business firms. We do this by adding the amount $g - t$ to the amount of desired investment by business firms at each possible interest rate. This produces the total demand schedule for loanable funds in panel (a).

At the intersection of the saving, or loanable funds supply, schedule with the schedule for combined demand for loanable funds by both businesses and the government, the equilibrium real interest rate is r_r^2. At this real interest rate, households save the amount s_2, which is the equilibrium quantity of loanable funds supplied. This amount is equal to the equilibrium quantity of loanable funds demanded, which is the sum of the amount of desired investment by firms at the equilibrium real interest rate, r_r^2, plus the amount of the government's deficit, $g - t$.

GOVERNMENT BUDGET DEFICITS IN THE CLASSICAL MODEL   Panel (a) of Figure 4–3 illustrates the classical view of the effects of expansionary fiscal policy. The effect of increasing the government's deficit from a value of zero to the amount $g - t$ results in a rightward shift in the demand schedule for loanable funds that is equal to $g - t$. This causes the equilibrium real interest

On the Web

What are the current outlays and revenues of the U.S. government, and is the government currently operating with a deficit or a surplus? View the historical tables of the U.S. government's budget at http://www.access.gpo.gov/usbudget, where you can click on the budget for the latest fiscal year.

FISCAL POLICY: Actions by the government to vary its spending or taxes.

Figure 4–3   Government Deficits and Surpluses in the Classical Market for Loanable Funds

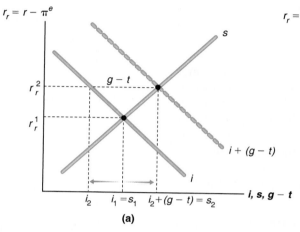

(a)

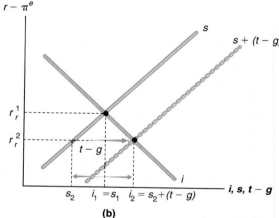

(b)

Panel (a) shows that in the presence of a government deficit, investment and the government budget deficit together constitute the downward-sloping demand for loanable funds. The result is a rise in the equilibrium real interest rate that induces greater saving and lower consumption. The increase in the real interest rate also causes investment to decline. The total decline in private consumption and investment is equal to the rise in the government budget deficit; thus, deficit spending "crowds out" an equal amount of private spending in the classical model. By way of contrast, panel (b) depicts the effects of a government surplus, which adds to the supply of loanable funds. This pushes down the equilibrium real interest rate, thereby inducing lower private saving (hence, higher private consumption) and higher investment. The total increase in private consumption and investment is equal to the rise in the government budget surplus.

rate to rise from r_r^1, to r_r^2. This increase in the real interest rate induces households to raise the amount of saving from s_1 to s_2. Because real income in the classical model is determined by the position of the aggregate supply schedule, which is fixed in the short run, a rise in household saving corresponds to a decline in household consumption spending on real goods and services. Therefore, one effect of an increase in government spending or reduction in taxes that widens the deficit is a *fall in private consumption.*

There is also another effect, however: the rise in the real interest rate from r_r^1, to r_r^2 raises the price of loanable funds for business firms. This causes firm owners to reduce their desired investment expenditures from

i_1 to i_2. Consequently, another outcome induced by a rise in government spending or a tax cut that increases the government's deficit is a *fall in private investment*.

Consequently, the classical theory of the loanable funds market indicates that a fiscal policy action that increases the government's deficit causes an increase in the real rate of interest that induces reductions in private consumption and investment. The total decline in private spending—the sum of the amount by which private saving rises and private investment falls—exactly equals the amount by which the deficit rose, which is the distance $g - t$ in panel (a) of Figure 4–3.

This reduction in private spending caused by an increase in the government deficit is known as the **crowding-out effect.** Panel (a) shows that expansions of government deficits through fiscal policies that raise government spending and/or reduce government tax revenues "crowd out" an equal amount of private spending. In the classical model, therefore:

> **If the government consumes a larger share of the total output of goods and services via deficit finance, an equally smaller amount of output is available for private use.**

Government Surpluses and the Real Interest Rate

In recent years, the U.S. government has been able to reduce its deficit significantly. Indeed, a key political issue today is whether the government should aim to achieve future *budget surpluses,* which arise when the government's tax revenues, t, exceed its expenditures, g. In this situation, the government *saves* its surplus, which is the amount $t - g$. That is, the government supplies loanable funds—it effectively saves on behalf of the citizens it taxes.

Panel (b) of Figure 4–3 depicts the effects of a government surplus on the market for loanable funds under the assumption that the government saves a lump-sum surplus equal to $t - g$ at any given real interest rate. We add this amount to the amount of private saving at each real interest rate. This effectively shifts the supply schedule for loanable funds rightward, from s to $s + (t - g)$. At the intersection of the investment schedule, the demand for loanable funds, and the combined private and government supply of loanable funds, the equilibrium real interest rate is r_r^2, which is less than the initial equilibrium real interest rate r_r^1. This interest-rate reduction induces a reduction in private saving, from s_1 to s_2, and an increase in investment, from i_1 to i_2.

Recall that real income in the classical model is determined by the position of the aggregate supply schedule and thus is fixed in the short run. Thus, the reduction in private saving corresponds to an increase in private consumption. The sum of the amount by which private saving falls and investment rises in response to the increase in the budget surplus, therefore, is exactly equal to the increase in the surplus. By running a budget surplus, the government brings about an increase in private spending on goods and services—the "inverse" of the crowding-out effect caused by a government deficit.

macro**xtra!**
Economic Applications

What should the U.S. government do in years when it operates with a surplus? To review alternative perspectives on this debate and make your own judgment, go to EconDebate Online.
http://macroxtra.swcollege.com

CROWDING-OUT EFFECT: The situation when private spending is reduced due to a rise in the real interest rate induced by an increase in the government's deficit.

FUNDAMENTAL ISSUE #2

How do government spending and taxation policies influence the real interest rate in the classical model?   Higher government deficits induce a rise in the demand for loanable funds. This increases the equilibrium real interest rate and thereby induces a fall in private investment and a rise in private saving, which corresponds to a fall in private consumption. Hence, higher government deficits crowd out private expenditures on goods and services. In contrast, higher government surpluses increase the supply of loanable funds, which pushes down the equilibrium real interest rate and stimulates private spending.

The Classical Theory of Nominal Interest-Rate Determination

We intentionally started by considering the equilibrium real interest rate in the classical model because that is the natural starting point for considering how the nominal interest rate is determined within the classical approach to macroeconomics.

The Equilibrium Nominal Interest Rate

Recall that the real interest rate equals the nominal interest rate minus the expected rate of inflation, or $r_r = r - \pi^e$. As discussed above, in the classical model the real interest rate adjusts to equate the quantities of loanable funds supplied and demanded. Thus, the equilibrium real interest rate is determined in the market for loanable funds. For instance, the equilibrium real interest rate might equal r_r^1 in Figure 4–1 on page 80. As a result, the equilibrium *nominal* interest rate equals the equilibrium real interest rate plus the expected inflation rate, or $r = r_r^1 + \pi^e$.

This means that factors that influence the equilibrium real interest rate also affect the equilibrium nominal interest rate. Changes in the position of the real saving schedule or the real investment schedule, for example, will induce movements in the equilibrium real interest rate that then, given the expected inflation rate, will cause the nominal interest rate to move in the same direction.

Likewise, fiscal policy actions that influence the demand for or supply of loanable funds will bring about changes in the equilibrium nominal interest rate. For example, because an increase in a government budget deficit increases the demand for loanable funds and pushes up the equilibrium real interest rate, given the current expected inflation rate the equilibrium nominal interest rate must also increase in response to the higher deficit. A higher government surplus, by way of contrast, raises the supply of loanable funds and causes a decline in the real interest rate that translates into a lower nominal interest rate, given the anticipated inflation rate.

Money and Interest Rates

CLOSED ECONOMY: An economy that operates in isolation from the rest of the world.

OPEN ECONOMY: An economy that is linked by trade with other economies of the world.

87

CHAPTER 4 Classical Macroeconomic Theory: Interest Rates and Exchange Rates

It is important to recognize that in the classical theory, monetary policy plays no role in determining the real interest rate. Changes in the quantity of money in circulation can only influence the nominal rate of interest.

To see how monetary policy can affect the nominal interest rate, recall that in the classical theory changes in the quantity of money cause the price level to rise, holding all other factors unchanged. Thus, in the classical model, an increase of 3 percent in the rate of money growth will cause the price level to rise by 3 percent, assuming real GDP and velocity are unchanged. Lenders and borrowers expect a sustained 3 percent inflation rate, so the nominal rate of interest that they negotiate in bond or loan contracts accounts for this anticipated rate of inflation. Therefore, given the equilibrium real interest rate determined in the loanable funds market, the growth rate of the quantity of money determines the nominal interest rate. Higher money growth raises expected inflation and causes an increase in the nominal interest rate. Lower money growth reduces expected inflation and causes a decrease in the nominal interest rate. (Some support for this prediction of the classical theory is provided by U.S. interest rates and inflation rates; see on the following page *Policy Notebook: Interest Rates and Inflation Rates Really Do Tend to Move Together.*)

FUNDAMENTAL ISSUE #3

How is the nominal interest rate determined in the classical theory? The nominal interest rate equals the real interest rate plus the expected rate of inflation. The equilibrium interest rate is determined in the market for loanable funds, so one way that the equilibrium nominal interest rate can change is if there is a change in the real interest rate, induced by a variation in a factor that influences the demand for or supply of loanable funds, such as saving, investment, or a government deficit or surplus. Alternatively, the equilibrium nominal interest rate can change if there is a change in the expected inflation rate, which in the classical model occurs when there is a change in the rate of growth of the quantity of money in circulation.

International Dimensions of Classical Theory

To this point, we have considered the classical theory of a **closed economy.** This is an economy that functions in isolation from the rest of the world. In a closed economy, either no international trade occurs, or the government prohibits such trade.

Few economies are truly closed. Like most other nations of the world, the United States is increasingly becoming an **open economy,** in which international trade accounts for a significant portion of a nation's total income. In 2003, exports and imports accounted for about 11 and 13

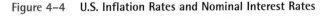

Interest Rates and Inflation Rates Really Do Tend to Move Together

According to the classical theory, the nominal interest rate should equal the real interest rate, which is determined in the market for loanable funds, plus the expected rate of inflation. This means that if inflation expectations come reasonably close to matching the actual inflation rate, there should be a positive relationship between nominal interest rates and the *actual* inflation rate.

Figure 4–4 shows that this generally has been true for the United States. The nominal interest rate (measured as the interest rate on three-month Treasury bills) has usually declined at roughly the same time that the inflation rate has fallen. The nominal interest rate also has typically increased when the inflation rate has risen.

For Critical Analysis
What factors might cause movements in the nominal interest rate and the inflation rate to diverge from time to time?

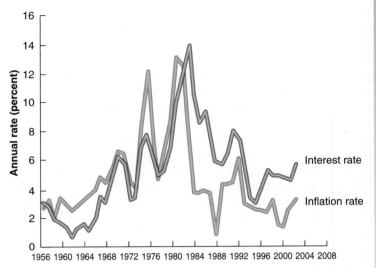

Figure 4–4   U.S. Inflation Rates and Nominal Interest Rates

Nominal interest rates in the United States have tended to move in the same direction as the inflation rate.

SOURCES: *Economic Report of the President* and *Economic Indicators*, various issues.

percent, respectively, of U.S. GDP, as compared with 1960 figures of 5 and 4 percent.

Greater openness engenders greater interest in determinants of the exchange value of a nation's currency relative to other world currencies. As Figure 4–5 indicates, the U.S. dollar's relative value has varied considerably since the 1970s. How would a classical theorist explain these movements in the dollar's value? Before answering this question, let's consider some important facts about the exchange rate.

The Exchange Rate, Depreciation, and Appreciation

First, recall from Chapter 1 that the *exchange rate* is the value of one nation's currency in terms of the currency of another nation. In the case of the U.S. dollar ($) and the European Monetary Union's euro (€), for instance, the dollar-euro exchange rate may be calculated as the price of the euro, measured in dollars per euro. Table 4–1 on page 90 shows exchange-rate data provided by the Federal Reserve Bank of New York on September 6, 2002. The table indicates that on this date, a U.S. resident would have to pay $0.9843 to obtain one euro, and so the exchange rate

Figure 4–5   The Value of the Dollar

This figure displays annual values of an index of the dollar's value relative to currencies of U.S. trading partners.

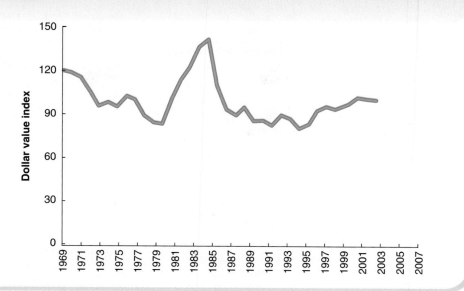

SOURCES: *Economic Report of the President,* 2002; *Federal Reserve Bulletin* (various issues).

could be expressed as $E = \$0.9843/€$, or 0.9843 dollars per euro. Another way to express the same rate of exchange, however, is to calculate the exchange rate as the price of the euro measured in dollars. This is the reciprocal of the dollar price of the euro, or $1/E = 1/(\$0.9843/€1) = €1.0160/\$1$, or 1.0160 euros per dollar. This can be seen by reading down the "Currency per U.S. Dollar" column to "Euro" in Table 4–1.

Suppose that the dollar-euro exchange rate were to *rise* to $E' = \$0.9950/€1$, or 99.5 cents per euro. Now an individual would have to pay more dollars to obtain one euro. Consequently, the dollar would lose some of its value relative to the euro. A currency that loses value relative to the currency of another country has experienced a **depreciation.** Hence, a *rise* in the value of E implies a *depreciation* of the value of the dollar relative to the euro. At the same time that the dollar depreciates relative to the euro, the euro experiences an **appreciation** relative to the dollar. Looking at the reciprocal, $1/E' = 1/(\$0.995/€1) = €1.0050/\$1$, we can see that now fewer euros are needed to obtain a dollar. The euro's dollar value increases with a rise in the exchange rate E.

Exchange-Rate Determination in the Classical System

What might cause such a dollar depreciation? According to the classical theory, the key to the answer is found in a concept known as **purchasing power parity.** Under purchasing power parity, the price of a good in one nation should be the same as the price of the same good in another nation, adjusted for the exchange rate. For instance, suppose that an economics textbook sells for a euro price of $P^* = €50$ in a country in the Eurpoean Monetary Union, such as Germany, where P^* is the price in the

DEPRECIATION: A decline in the relative value of a nation's currency.

APPRECIATION: A rise in the relative value of a nation's currency.

PURCHASING POWER PARITY: A condition that states that if international arbitrage is possible, then the price of a good in one nation should be the same as the price of the same good in another nation, adjusted for the exchange rate.

Table 4–1   **Exchange Rates**

Country	Monetary Unit	U.S. Dollar Equivalent	Currency per U.S. Dollar
European Monetary Union	Euro	0.9843	1.0160
Australia	Dollar	0.5467	1.8292
Brazil	Real	0.3150	3.1750
Canada	Dollar	0.6395	1.5637
China, P.R.	Yuan	0.1208	8.2770
Denmark	Krone	0.1325	7.5450
Hong Kong	Dollar	0.1282	7.7800
India	Rupee	0.0206	48.5700
Japan	Yen	0.0844	118.4800
Malaysia	Ringgit	0.2632	3.8000
Mexico	Peso	0.1003	9.9685
New Zealand	Dollar	0.4702	2.0371
Norway	Krone	0.1336	7.4860
Singapore	Dollar	0.5718	1.7490
South Africa	Rand	0.0953	10.4950
South Korea	Won	0.0008	1196.6000
Sri Lanka	Rupee	0.0104	96.1000
Sweden	Krona	0.1067	9.3696
Switzerland	Franc	0.6745	1.4825
Taiwan	N.T. dollar	0.0293	34.1200
Thailand	Baht	0.0236	42.3000
United Kingdom	Pound	1.5597	0.6411
Venezuela	Bolivar	0.0007	1444.0000

SOURCE: Federal Reserve Bank of New York, Daily Noon Buying Rates, September 6, 2002.

foreign currency. If the rate of exchange of euros for dollars is equal to E = \$0.9843/€1, then according to purchasing power parity the price of the same book in the United States should be $P = P^* \times E$ = (€50) × (\$0.9843/€1) = \$49.22.

According to the purchasing power parity idea, the only factor causing the prices of the textbooks in the two nations to differ is that they are measured in different currency units. If not for the fact that the textbook is priced in different currencies, its price would be the same in both countries. If E were equal to one, so that dollars and euros could be traded one for one, the U.S. price would be $P = P^* \times E$ = (€50) × (\$1/€1) = \$50. In other words, the only reason that the currency price of the same textbook differs in the two countries is that the currencies *cannot* be exchanged on a one-for-one basis. Otherwise, the textbook would have the same price in both nations.

THE RATIONALE FOR PURCHASING POWER PARITY   The main motivation for purchasing power parity is the classical hypothesis of pure competition. If the

INTERNATIONAL ARBITRAGE: The act of buying a good in one nation and selling it in another.

91

CHAPTER 4   Classical Macroeconomic Theory: Interest Rates and Exchange Rates

exchange rate is $E = \$0.9843/\text{€}1$ and the €50 textbook were to sell for, say, $25 in the United States, then a smart college student could buy, say, 1,000 copies of the textbook at $25 each, box them up, and ship them to Germany for a shipping cost of $1,000. Thus, the student's total expenditures would be $26,000. In Germany the textbooks could be sold at €50 each to yield revenues of €50,000. Converted to dollars at the exchange rate of $0.9843/€1, these revenues would amount to ($0.9843/€1) × €50,000 = $49,215. Thus the profit from this enterprise would be $49,215 − $26,000 = $23,215. This might pay the student's tuition for the next year or two.

In our example, the college student engaged in **international arbitrage,** which is the act of buying a good in one nation and selling it in another nation. The student profited from a *deviation* from purchasing power parity. What would happen if enough students (and others) engaged in international arbitrage? Eventually, enough textbooks would make their way from the United States to Germany that the German textbook price would begin to fall toward the U.S. textbook price. This process would continue until the textbook price was approximately the same in both countries, adjusting for the exchange rate, or until $P = P^* \times E$.

PURCHASING POWER PARITY AND THE EXCHANGE RATE   Not all goods and services can be bought and sold internationally. As an extreme example, it is impossible for a Canadian mother to hire an Italian baby-sitter for an evening, so international arbitrage in short-run baby-sitting services is not feasible. This is true of many services, although some types of services, such as those that banks provide in financial markets, can be provided by computer connections that extend beyond national borders.

The original classical economists recognized that there are limits on international arbitrage for some goods and services, but they regarded purchasing power parity as a *benchmark* for understanding how a nation's exchange rate is determined. Figure 4–6 on the next page shows how purchasing power parity can be combined with the theory of price-level determination to provide an explanation of why a nation's currency might depreciate over time. The diagram in panel (a) displays an initial equilibrium price level, denoted P_1, at the intersection of the classical aggregate demand and aggregate supply schedules. Panel (b) is a diagram of the purchasing power parity condition, $P = P^* \times E$. Recall that the intercept-slope equation for a straight line says that a variable measured along the y-axis of a diagram is equal to an intercept plus the slope times a variable measured on the x-axis. Hence, the condition $P = P^* \times E$ is just the equation of a straight line in which the domestic price level, P, is measured along the y-axis in panel (b), and the exchange rate, E, is measured along the x-axis. The intercept of this equation is equal to zero, and the foreign price level, P^*, is the *slope* of the line. At the current price level in our home nation, P_1, the purchasing power parity condition yields an equilibrium exchange rate equal to E_1.

As we discussed earlier, the classical model indicates that a likely reason for persistent inflation is consistently high growth in the quantity of money that shifts the aggregate demand schedule to the right over time. Panel (a) in Figure 4–6 shows such a rightward shift in aggregate demand that causes

Figure 4–6   Exchange-Rate Determination in the Classical Model

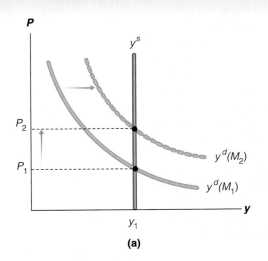

(a)

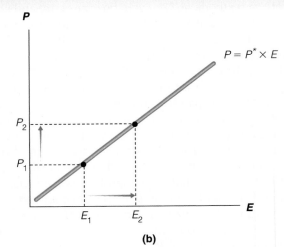

(b)

In the classical model, a nation's price level is determined in the market for real output, as in panel (a). A rise in aggregate demand caused by an increase in the nation's money stock causes an increase in the price level. According to the purchasing power parity relationship, the price level can be expressed as $P = P^* \times E$, where P^* is the foreign price level and E is the exchange rate in units of home currency per unit of foreign currency. The graph of this relationship is a straight line, as shown in panel (b). There you can see that a rise in the price level results in an increase in the exchange rate, so more units of the home currency must be given up in exchange for units of the foreign currency. Consequently, the home currency depreciates relative to the foreign currency.

the home price level to rise to P_2. According to the purchasing power parity condition, if foreign prices remain unchanged at P^*, our nation's exchange rate must rise to E_2. If the "home nation" is the United States, then the exchange rate E would be measured in dollars per unit of foreign currency (for instance, euros). Hence, when the exchange rate rises from E_1 to E_2, more dollars will be needed to purchase foreign currency. The value of the dollar will have *depreciated*. In other words, the classical model predicts that persistent growth in the quantity of money in the United States will cause a fall in the value of the dollar as well as persistent U.S. inflation.

FUNDAMENTAL ISSUE #4

According to the classical model, how is the value of a nation's currency determined?   The value of a country's currency is its exchange rate. In the classical model, a key benchmark for understanding how the exchange rate is determined is the purchasing power parity condition, which states that the home price level is equal to the foreign price level times the exchange rate. Given the foreign price level and the determination of the home price level in the market for real output, the exchange rate adjusts to maintain purchasing power parity.

Biting into Purchasing Power Parity at McDonald's

Among business travelers, the most popular version of purchasing power parity (PPP) is the Big Mac Index. *The Economist* magazine first published the Big Mac Index in 1986 as a satirical approach to predicting exchange-rate movements, based on the idea that a Big Mac sandwich is made up of the same ingredients (two all-beef patties, special sauce, etc.) around the globe and information about its price is readily available. The 2002 version of the Big Mac Index appears in Table 4–2 (p. 94).

Table 4–2 shows that the price of a Big Mac in the United States is $2.49, whereas the price of a Big Mac in Japan is ¥262. We can rearrange our equation for PPP, $P = P^* \times E$ (P^* in $ per U.S. Big Mac) to solve for E, $E = P/P^*$. Using this equation, the implied exchange rate is 105¥/$, which is shown in the "Implied PPP" column of the table. The next column gives the actual value of the yen-dollar exchange rate at the time, 130¥/$. The true, market-determined value of the yen relative to the dollar is lower than the value implied by PPP. The Big Mac Index, therefore, indicates that the yen is undervalued relative to the dollar. We can express this under-valuation as the percentage difference between the implied value of the yen according

to the Big Mac PPP measure and the market value. This works out to be 19 percent for the yen. Hence, according to the Big Mac measure of PPP, the yen should appreciate relative to the dollar.

How does the Big Mac perform as a guide to exchange-rate movements? In the short run, the index certainly is not an accurate predictor of exchange rates. The index performs better in the long run, but most of the adjustment to PPP occurs through price changes.

Research Project

Studies have found that the Big Mac Index is closely related to several other more elaborate measures of purchasing power parities. These indicators provide more evidence favoring PPP in the long run than in the short run. What does this imply about the likely usefulness of PPP within the classical theory of exchange-rate determination?

Web Resource

Where can calculations of purchasing power parity exchange rates for major economies be found? Go to the home page of the Organization for Economic Cooperation and Development (http://www.oecd.org) and click on "Statistics" along the top margin of the page. Next click on "PPPs and derived indices for all OECD countries."

macroxtra!
Online
Perspective

For a discussion of the Big Mac Index as a PPP measure, go to the Chapter 4 reading from the Federal Reserve Bank of St. Louis, entitled "For Here or to Go? Purchasing Power Parity and the Big Mac," by Michael Pakko and Patricia Pollard.
http://macroxtra.swcollege.com

Continued on next page

Link to The Global Economy, continued

Table 4–2   The "Big Mac Index" of Currencies' Purchasing Power

	Big Mac Prices		Implied PPP* the Dollar	Actual Dollar Exchange Rate 4/23/02	Under(−)/Over(+) Valuation against the Dollar, %
	In Local Currency	In Dollars			
United States[†]	$2.49	2.49	—	—	—
Argentina	Peso2.50	0.78	1.00	3.13	−68
Australia	A$3.00	1.62	1.20	1.86	−35
Brazil	Real3.60	1.55	1.45	2.34	−38
Britain	£1.99	2.88	1.25[‡]	1.45[‡]	+16
Canada	C$3.33	2.12	1.34	1.57	−15
Chile	Peso1,400	2.16	562	655	−14
China	Yuan10.50	1.27	4.22	8.28	−49
Czech Rep.	Koruna56.28	1.66	22.6	34.0	−33
Denmark	DKr24.75	2.96	9.94	8.38	+19
Euro area	€ 2.67	2.37	0.93§	0.89§	−5
Hong Kong	HK$11.20	1.40	4.50	7.80	−42
Hungary	Forint459	1.69	184	272	−32
Indonesia	Rupiah16,000	1.71	6,426	9,430	−32
Israel	Shekel12.00	2.51	4.82	4.79	+1
Japan	¥262	2.01	105	130	−19
Malaysia	M$5.04	1.33	2.02	3.80	−47
Mexico	Peso21.90	2.37	8.80	9.28	−5
New Zealand	NZ$3.95	1.77	1.59	2.24	−29
Peru	NewSol8.50	2.48	3.41	3.43	−1
Philippines	Peso65.00	1.28	26.1	51.0	−49
Poland	Zloty5.90	1.46	2.37	4.04	−41
Russia	Rouble39.00	1.25	15.7	31.2	−50
Singapore	S$3.30	1.81	1.33	1.82	−27
South Africa	Rand9.70	0.87	3.90	10.9	−64
South Korea	Won3,100	2.36	1,245	1,304	−5
Sweden	SKr26.00	2.52	10.4	10.3	+1
Switzerland	SFr6.30	3.81	2.53	1.66	+53
Taiwan	NT$70.00	2.01	28.1	34.8	−19
Thailand	Baht55.00	1.27	22.1	43.3	−49
Turkey	Lira4,000,000	3.06	1,606,426	1,324,500	+21
Venezuela	Bolivar2,500	2.92	1,004	857	+17

*Purchasing power parity; local price divided by price in the United States.
†Average of New York, Chicago, San Francisco, and Atlanta   ‡Dollars per pound   § Dollars per euro
SOURCES: McDonald's; *The Economist.*

1. **How the Real Interest Rate Is Determined in the Classical Theory:** In the classical model, the equilibrium real interest rate is determined in the market for loanable funds, in which the key source of the supply of loanable funds is real saving by households, which is positively related to the real interest rate. The key source of the demand for loanable funds is real investment spending by firms, which is negatively related to the real interest rate, so the demand schedule for loanable funds slopes downward. The real interest rate adjusts to equate the quantities of loanable funds demanded and supplied, so in the absence of a government deficit or surplus, saving equals investment at the equilibrium real interest rate.

2. **How Government Spending and Taxation Policies Influence the Real Interest Rate in the Classical Model:** A government's budget is in deficit when its spending exceeds its tax receipts; there is a surplus whenever the reverse is true. A rise in the government's deficit increases the demand for loanable funds, thereby causing a crowding-out effect as the resulting rise in the real interest rate induces a decrease in private spending. In contrast, a rise in the government's budget surplus increases the supply of loanable funds, which causes a reduction in the real interest rate and an increase in private spending.

3. **How the Nominal Interest Rate Is Determined in the Classical Theory:** The nominal interest rate equals the real interest rate, which is determined in the market for loanable funds, plus the expected rate of inflation, which depends on the rate of growth in the quantity of money in circulation. Thus, one factor that can cause the equilibrium nominal interest rate to change is any variation in the equilibrium real interest rate induced by a rise or fall in the demand for or supply of loanable funds resulting from a change in saving, investment, or a government deficit or surplus. Another factor that can bring about a change in the equilibrium nominal interest rate is a change in the expected inflation rate caused by a rise or fall in the rate of growth of the quantity of money in circulation.

4. **The Value of a Nation's Currency:** The exchange rate is the value, or price, of one nation's currency in terms of that of another nation. The classical theory's benchmark for understanding how exchange rates are determined is purchasing power parity, which states that if international arbitrage can occur, then the price level in one nation should equal the foreign price level times the exchange rate. Once a home nation's price level is determined in its market for real output, and given the foreign price level, the home nation's exchange rate adjusts to maintain purchasing power parity. Persistent inflation in the home nation caused by excessive money growth will thereby be accompanied by persistent depreciation in, or decline in the value of, the home nation's currency.

Self-Test Questions

1. A nation's government initially has a balanced budget, but then it decides to push up real government spending without changing the level of real taxes. The government finances the resulting deficit by selling bonds to private individuals. Explain the effects that this policy action will have on equilibrium real and nominal interest rates in the classical model, all other things being equal.

2. Suppose that the government discussed in question 1 decides to sell the bonds that it issues to finance the deficit only to the nation's central bank, which purchases the bonds by creating new money that it offers in exchange for the bonds. Would this affect the classical model's predictions for effects on real and nominal interest rates? Explain your reasoning.

3. Explain how, according to the classical theory, a nation's nominal interest rate could decline without a change in the real rate of interest. Would it be possible for the real interest rate to rise even as the nominal rate of interest declined? Explain your reasoning.

(Answers to odd-numbered questions may be found on the Web at **http://macro. swcollege.com** under "Student Resources.")

4. Suppose that the central bank of a small European nation keeps the quantity of money in circulation stable. Its government's budget is balanced. In addition, its income velocity of money is stable, as are conditions in its labor market. Its technology and other factors of production also have not changed. Nevertheless, the value of the nation's currency is persistently depreciating relative to that of its major trading partner. Given the conditions the small country faces, what *single* factor would the classical model indicate must account for this steady depreciation of its currency?

5. During recent decades, several governments in South America have experienced significant deficits that they funded in large measure by purchasing government bonds with new money printed by central banks. Apply the classical model to explain the effects that such government actions would likely have on prices, real GDP, the real interest rate, the nominal interest rate, *and* the exchange rate of a nation that finds itself in this situation.

Problems

(Answers to odd-numbered problems may be found on the Web at **http://macro. swcollege.com** under "Student Resources.")

1. A nation's demand for loanable funds (denoted l) is given by $r = 20 - (0.5)l$, where r is the nominal interest rate. The supply of loanable funds is given by $r = 2 + l$.

    a. What is the equilibrium nominal interest rate?

    b. If the real interest rate is equal to 3 percent, then what is the expected rate of inflation in this nation?

2. Currently, the rate of exchange between the U.S. dollar and the British pound is $1.60 per pound.

    a. Suppose that the equilibrium British price level has a value of 2.0. If purchasing power parity holds, then what is the equilibrium price level in the United States?

    b. In the United States, equilibrium real output is $10 trillion, and the current-dollar value of the quantity of money is $4 trillion. What is the income velocity of money?

Before the Test

Test your understanding of the material covered in this chapter by taking the Chapter 4 interactive quiz at **http://macro.swcollege.com**.

Online Application

Internet URLs: **http://www.oecd.org/EN/statistics/** and **http://federalreserve. gov/releases/H10/hist**

Titles: *Purchasing Power Parities—Organization for Economic Cooperation* and *Development and Exchange Rates—Board of Governors of the Federal Reserve System*

Navigation: To obtain data on exchange rates consistent with purchasing power parity, first go to the home page of the OECD (**http://www.oecd.org**). Then click on *Statistics* and then *Purchasing Power Parities for all OECD*

Countries. Print this document. Next, go to the Federal Reserve Board's home page (http://federalreserve.gov), and click on *Economic Research and Data.* Then click on *Statistics: Releases and Historical Data,* and under the H.10 "Weekly Releases," click on *Historical Bilateral Rates.*

Application: Use the reports at each Web site to apply the purchasing power parity doctrine to real-world data.

1. The first set of columns in the OECD table gives the currency-per-U.S.-dollar exchange rates that would be consistent with purchasing power parity (PPP) for various OECD countries. The Federal Reserve Board provides data on actual exchange rates for a number of countries. Select a nation in the OECD table, and compare the exchange rates predicted by PPP for a selected year in the table with the nation's *actual* exchange rates in the Federal Reserve's H.10 release. During the year you selected, did PPP indicate that this nation's currency was over- or undervalued?

2. Look over the nation's exchange rates in the Federal Reserve's H.10 release for all five years in the OECD table. In your view, were the actual exchange rates for the country you have selected even "roughly" consistent with PPP over this five-year period?

For Group Study and Analysis: Assign questions 1 and 2 to several groups, each of which will examine the data for a different country. Have each group report its conclusions. Discuss possible reasons that PPP may have been a better approach to understanding exchange-rate determination for some countries than for others.

Selected References and Further Reading

Fisher, Irving. *The Theory of Interest.* New York: Macmillan, 1930.

Humpage, Owen. "Foreign Economic Growth and the Dollar." Federal Reserve Bank of Cleveland *Economic Commentary,* September 1, 2000.

Pakko, Michael, and Patricia Pollard. "For Here or to Go? Purchasing Power Parity and the Big Mac." Federal Reserve Bank of St. Louis *Review,* January/February 1996, pp. 3–21.

Wicksell, J. G. K. *Interest and Prices,* trans. R. F. Kahn. London: Macmillan, 1936.

macro**xtra!**

Log on to the MacroXtra Web site at http://macroxtra.swcollege.com for additional learning resources such as practice quizzes, Interactive Key Graphs, readings, and additional economic applications.

Utopia Just Beyond the Horizon or
Future Shock?—

The Theory of
Economic Growth

FUNDAMENTAL ISSUES

1. **How do economists measure economic growth?**

2. **What key factors determine the rate of economic growth?**

3. **How does labor-force participation affect economic growth? Do population growth and immigration increase or reduce economic growth?**

4. **How do changes in labor productivity influence economic growth?**

5. **Why are saving and capital investment important for economic growth?**

6. **What role does human knowledge play in economic growth? Is growth self-perpetuating?**

During the spring of 2000, average prices on the New York Stock Exchange rose by nearly 5 percent. Between June of 2000 and March of 2001, stock prices proceeded to fall by more than 7 percent. Within another three months, however, average share price had jumped 5 percent once again. Then share prices fell off again in 2002.

To most observers, these are just typical examples of unpredictable gyrations in stock prices. Nonetheless, some economists think that important information can be gleaned from such changes in market valuations of companies' shares of stock. The amounts that investors are willing to pay for stocks, these economists argue, reflect investors' forecasts of how productive firms are likely to be in the future. Consequently, stock price movements may be useful in predicting overall business productivity—how much output companies can produce using given volumes of inputs—which is a key determinant of both firms' profitability and aggregate economic growth.

The potentially important effects of the pace of productivity enhancements and the speed of economic growth are not limited to financial market activity. Productivity growth and the growth of overall economic activity also influence the rate of joblessness and the level of prices of goods and services. In this chapter you will learn how economists gauge economic growth. In addition, you will learn why business productivity is an important factor influencing the long-term growth of a nation's economy.

ECONOMIC GROWTH: The annual rate of change in per capita real GDP.

99

CHAPTER 5 Utopia Just Beyond the Horizon or Future Shock?—The Theory of Economic Growth

Measuring Economic Growth

Most people have a general idea of what economic growth means. When the economy of a nation grows, its residents must be better off in terms of their material well-being. Nevertheless, we do not measure the well-being of any nation solely in terms of its total output of real goods and services, or real GDP, without making some adjustments. After all, GDP in India typically is roughly triple the size of GDP in Switzerland, yet the Indian population is about 125 times larger than the Swiss population. Clearly, measuring a country's growth in terms of annual increases in real GDP requires adjusting for population growth. This leads to the following measure of a nation's overall **economic growth:**

A nation's economy grows when it experiences increases in per capita real GDP. We measure economic growth as *the rate of change in per capita real GDP (income) per year.*

Table 5–1 displays average annual rates of growth of per capita real GDP for several nations since 1965. Notice that during this period the economic growth rate of the United States was comparable to the growth rates of these other nations. This illustrates an important point: Current wealth and productive capacity are not necessarily indicators of current or future economic growth. A nation with considerable wealth at a point in time, such as the United States at the beginning of the twenty-first century, may not necessarily enjoy higher rates of growth in the future.

Some Problems with the Per Capita GDP Growth Measure

Defining growth as the rate of change in per capita income should, in principle, make economic growth relatively straightforward to measure. Nevertheless, this growth measure suffers from some problems.

Table 5–1	Average Per Capita Growth Rates in Selected Countries, 1965–Present (%)			
Country			**Country**	
Colombia	2.1		Russia	1.7
Canada	2.0		United States	1.5
Congo	1.9		Mexico	1.5
Turkey	1.7		Nepal	1.3

SOURCE: World Bank.

DATA PROBLEMS   Per capita income growth can be computed easily provided that economists can obtain dependable data about a nation's real GDP and its population. In many developing nations, however, governments do not have the resources to collect accurate real income data. Furthermore, a number of nations do not conduct careful censuses of their populations. Even the United States, which devotes considerable resources to census taking, conducts a complete census only once each decade. All media reports of world population depend on population *estimates* of varying quality for a large fraction of the countries of the world. Likewise, annual figures on per capita GDP growth necessarily are economists' best estimates.

GROWTH FOR WHOM?   In addition to data problems, some conceptual problems can arise when using per capita income as a measure of economic growth. One is that this measure tells us nothing about how output is *distributed* among the residents of a nation. During a period when a country's measured per capita output grew very rapidly, its poorest residents might have become even poorer. Therefore, when using the rate of increase in GDP per capita as a growth measure, we must recognize that it tells us nothing about relative incomes of various groups within a country.

GROWTH IN LIVING STANDARDS?   Furthermore, the rate of increase in real GDP per capita is at best an indicator of improvements in the average living standard of a nation's residents. Real standards of living can advance without per capita income growth. This can happen if people, on average, enjoy more leisure time while producing as much as they did before. For example, if a country's per capita real income remained unchanged for ten years while the average hours of work per week declined, we could not automatically conclude that its residents were, on average, no better off. In fact, their average standard of living would definitely be higher at the end of the ten-year period, because they would be working fewer hours per week to produce and consume the same real output. In the United States, for instance, average hours worked per week fell steadily until the 1960s before leveling off. Hence, before the 1970s, measured U.S. economic growth, in terms of increased real income per capita, tended to understate the true growth in living standards that had taken place.

THE QUALITY PROBLEM   Finally, measured per capita GDP growth does not fully account for *quality* changes that take place over time. In the 1960s, for instance, athletic shoes were known as tennis shoes or, in some locales, "sneakers." Though there was some variety in athletic shoes, typically they were relatively flat-soled and shaded a single-toned white. Now there are athletic shoes specifically designed for walking, jogging, running, or heavy-duty jumping on basketball courts. Athletic shoes also come in every imaginable color. Yet official measures of output lump athletic shoes together into the same basic category of the "sneakers" of old. The official statistics on athletic shoe production tabulate the large growth in the number of athletic shoes produced between the 1960s and the 2000s without accounting for the simultaneous improvement in the quality and variety of the shoes.

macroxtra!
Economic Applications

Do technological advances result in higher unemployment? To review alternative perspectives on this debate and make your own judgment, go to EconDebate Online. http://macroxtra.swcollege.com

COMPOUNDED GROWTH:
Accumulated growth in per
capita real GDP over a given
interval.

COMPOUND GROWTH RATE: The
annual rate at which per capita
real GDP accumulates over a
given interval.

101

Why Economic Growth Matters

Table 5–1 indicates that the growth rates in real per capita income for most countries typically differ by just a few percentage points or even by just tenths of percentage points. Nevertheless, a small difference in growth rates between any two nations can translate into considerable differences in future per capita output levels.

COMPOUND GROWTH   The reason for these differences is that growth has a cumulative, or *compound,* effect over the years. Suppose, for example, that Country A's per capita real GDP was $10,000 at the end of 2002. Then suppose that this economy grew at a sizable rate of 20 percent per year in 2003 and 2004. At the end of 2003, Country A's per capita GDP would equal the sum of the initial $10,000 and an additional GDP growth during the year of $10,000 × 0.2 = $2,000, for a total of $12,000. During 2004, the economy would grow by another 20 percent. By the end of 2004, then, its real income per capita would equal the initial 2002 per capita GDP of $10,000 plus the $2,000 in growth that occurred in 2003, *plus* 20 percent of the initial 2002 per capita GDP of $10,000 *plus* 20 percent of the $2,000 growth in per capita GDP that took place in 2003. Thus, Country A's per capita real GDP for 2004 would be $10,000 + ($10,000 × 0.2) + ($12,000 × 0.2) = $14,400. Note that this 2004 per capita GDP figure would reflect accumulated growth that occurred during both 2003 and 2004. Such accumulated growth in per capita income is called an economy's **compounded growth.** The 20 percent annual rate of growth that accumulates across years is the economy's **compound growth rate.**

To see why an economy's compound growth rate makes such a difference over time, consider Table 5–2 on the following page. It shows how a dollar in per capita real GDP compounds across years with different growth rates. For instance, in our example of Country A, each dollar of 2002 per capita income grew at 20 percent for two years. Referring to Table 5–2, we see that this rate would yield $1.44 in accumulated income after two years of growth. Applying this figure to Country A's $10,000 in per capita income in 2002 again yields the $14,400 we computed for 2004.

We can use Table 5–2 to determine how much difference a nation's compound growth rate can make. Consider Country B, where the per capita 2002 income was $20,000, or double that of Country A. If Country B's compound growth rate is 3 percent for the next ten years, then Table 5–2 indicates that its real income per capita in 2012 would be $20,000 × 1.34 = $26,800. Suppose, though, that Country A—which was much poorer in 2002 with a per capita income of only $10,000—could maintain its 20 percent compound growth rate for ten years. By the year 2012, its per capita income would have grown to $10,000 × 6.19 = $61,900. Thus, by 2012 the nation that was much poorer initially would have well over twice the per capita income of the nation with the higher 2002 income.

CATCHING UP TAKES TIME   Few nations ever achieve a compound growth rate as high as 20 percent, however. Even countries that are able to achieve such growth rates typically cannot maintain them. Although differences in compound growth rates explain why nations' relative per capita incomes have

Table 5–2   One Dollar in Real Income Per Capita Compounded Annually at Different Growth Rates

This table displays the value of a dollar in income at the end of a given period during which it has compounded annually at a specified growth rate. For instance, suppose $1 in income today grows at 6 percent per year. At the end of one year, it will have grown to $1.06. At the end of 10 years, $1.79, and at the end of 50 years, it will be $18.40.

Number of Years	Growth Rate						
	3%	4%	5%	6%	8%	10%	20%
1	1.03	1.04	1.05	1.06	1.08	1.10	1.20
2	1.06	1.08	1.10	1.12	1.17	1.21	1.44
3	1.09	1.12	1.16	1.19	1.26	1.33	1.73
4	1.13	1.17	1.22	1.26	1.36	1.46	2.07
5	1.16	1.22	1.28	1.34	1.47	1.61	2.49
6	1.19	1.27	1.34	1.41	1.59	1.77	2.99
7	1.23	1.32	1.41	1.50	1.71	1.94	3.58
8	1.27	1.37	1.48	1.59	1.85	2.14	4.30
9	1.30	1.42	1.55	1.68	2.00	2.35	5.16
10	1.34	1.48	1.63	1.79	2.16	2.59	6.19
20	1.81	2.19	2.65	3.20	4.66	6.72	38.30
30	2.43	3.24	4.32	5.74	10.00	17.40	237.00
40	3.26	4.80	7.04	10.30	21.70	45.30	1,470.00
50	4.38	7.11	11.50	18.40	46.90	117.00	9,100.00

changed so much over the course of history, these changes typically occur over a number of years. The reason is that nations' growth rates typically differ only by small amounts over long spans of time.

As an example, consider the United Kingdom and Sweden. In 1870, the United Kingdom's GDP per capita was nearly twice that of Sweden, meaning that the typical British resident had a real income two times the income of a Swede. During the next 120 years, the United Kingdom's average annual rate of per capita income growth was 1.4 percent, whereas Sweden's rate was slightly higher at 2.1 percent. By 1920, British per capita income was still about one and a half times that of Sweden. By 1950, however, per capita real GDP was only 6 percent higher in the United Kingdom than in Sweden. By the 1990s, Sweden's slightly higher compound growth rate had allowed it to pass the United Kingdom in per capita income. The typical resident of Sweden then earned about 10 percent more than a resident of the United Kingdom.

How quickly a nation's relative position in per capita income changes clearly depends on how fast it can grow. Before examining the factors that determine the speed of a nation's economic growth, though, let's first consider whether economic growth is always *desirable*.

Is High Economic Growth Always a Good Thing?

A number of modern commentators maintain that defining economic growth in terms of real GDP per capita ignores potential ill effects of income growth. Some even contend that per capita growth can make people worse off in some respects. Economic growth, they argue, also creates new "needs" that can make human beings feel worse off as they grow richer. Psychologists, for instance, sometimes find that people's expectations for "success" increase as their real incomes rise. As a result, individuals may be disappointed with their economic achievements even though their real incomes have grown considerably.

INTERGENERATIONAL EXTERNALITIES: Spillover effects of economic growth that take years to influence human welfare and therefore have different effects across generations.

NEGATIVE SPILLOVERS FROM GROWTH Critics of "too much" economic growth also point to the potential for other negative spillover effects arising from growth. Economists call such a spillover effect an *externality*. Economic growth can create **intergenerational externalities,** or spillover effects that span decades and thereby affect the well-being of people born in different periods. For instance, when oil drilling led to significant economic growth in Pennsylvania during the 1890s, gasoline was regarded as a useless by-product of the oil refining process. (Remember that gasoline-driven automobiles did not appear on the scene until a couple of decades later.) Refiners dumped gasoline into rivers and streams, creating an ecological mess that was not fully cleaned up for more than a decade. Discarding the gasoline not only saddled future residents of Pennsylvania with polluted streams but also deprived them of higher incomes that they could have earned when future uses of gasoline were developed.

COSTS AND BENEFITS OF GROWTH Any economic activity has costs and benefits. Economic growth is widely credited with significantly improving health care and extending life expectancies. It permits greater expenditures on education, which has led to higher literacy rates. Economic growth also can contribute to political stability, particularly if it is shared to some extent by all residents of a nation. At the same time, economic growth can lead to intergenerational externalities such as the pollution caused by the dumping of gasoline in Pennsylvania in the 1890s. Critics of economic growth also cite urban congestion and the psychological problems it can create as significant externality effects. Some commentators also blame economic growth for perceived deteriorations in traditional social structures, such as the widely documented breakdown of family units for many people. Others blame economic growth for the increase in crime rates in the late twentieth century.

Economists and other social scientists continue to try to understand all the costs and benefits that stem from economic growth. Placing value judgments on these costs and benefits, however, is up to each individual. Our goal for the rest of this chapter is to try to explain recent patterns in economic growth around the world, how economic growth occurs, and what factors contribute to or detract from economic growth.

> **FUNDAMENTAL ISSUE #1**
>
> **How do economists measure economic growth?**   The key measure of a nation's overall economic growth is the annual rate of growth in per capita real GDP. This measure tells how much the real income of an average resident of a country grows from year to year. Economists recognize that this is an imperfect measure, because it does not tell us how total income is distributed within a country, does not account for changes in product quality, and fails to consider possible intergenerational externalities. Nevertheless, per capita real GDP is the best available measure of the growth of a nation's economy.

The Great Growth Slowdown

Today, economists are asking a very fundamental question: Has economic growth all but ended for a number of nations? Although several nations, such as China and Azerbaijan, have experienced rapid growth since the early 1990s, the same has not been true for much of Europe and Japan.

Documenting the Slowdown

Table 5–3 shows average annual growth rates in per capita incomes for selected industrialized countries over three intervals: 1974–1983, 1984–1993, and 1994–2003. As you can see, growth rates in most of these nations had peaked by the 1980s. Since then all but the United Kingdom have experienced generally lower rates of economic growth.

Note that the figures in Tables 5–1 and 5–3 show growth rates for *intervals* of years. When assessing trends in economic growth, it is important not to get caught up in *annual* growth rates. To see why, consider Figure 5–1. Panel (a) shows actual per capita real GDP for the United States since 1959. As you can see, aside from a few dips U.S. per capita income has experienced steady growth. Panel (b) shows the year-to-year growth rates that correspond to the data displayed in panel (a). As panel (b) makes clear, year-to-year growth rates in per capita real GDP can be extremely volatile.

Table 5–3	Economic Growth Rates in Selected Industrialized Nations (%)		
	1974–1983	**1984–1993**	**1994–2003**
Canada	2.1	1.5	1.9
France	2.4	1.5	2.0
Germany	2.0	2.3	1.7
Italy	2.3	2.2	1.8
Japan	3.5	3.3	0.8
United Kingdom	1.4	1.8	2.2

NOTE: Figures are average annual percentage changes in per capita real GDP.
SOURCE: International Monetary Fund, *World Economic Outlook*, various issues.

Figure 5–1   Real GDP Per Capita and Year-to-Year Changes in Real GDP Per Capita in the United States

As panel (a) indicates, U.S. real GDP per capita has trended upward in recent decades. Nevertheless, panel (b) shows that annual rates of change in per capita real GDP have been highly variable from year to year.

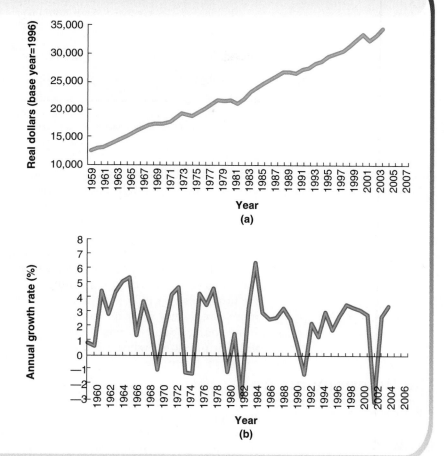

(a)

(b)

SOURCES: *Economic Report of the President,* 2002; *Economic Indicators* (various issues).

Looking at ranges of years smooths out such annual variations and helps us identify longer-term trends in economic growth rates. Table 5–4 on the next page shows two ways that we can do this. One is to look at averages of year-to-year rates of growth in per capita income for ranges of years. Another is to look at compound rates of growth for such ranges. Either way, however, it is clear that the experience of the United States has tended to parallel that of the other developed nations of the world, as summarized in Table 5–3. U.S. economic growth has been steady for a long period, but average growth since the early 1990s remains lower than before the 1970s.

Is Slowed Growth a Cause for Concern?

Recall that growth rates are compounded over time. For any nation, relatively low economic growth this year ultimately means relatively lower real GDP per capita in all future years. For the United States and other developed nations, reduced growth rates during the past two decades

Table 5-4   Slowed Economic Growth Rates in the United States

	Average Growth Rate (%)	Compound Growth Rate (%)
1961–1970	2.9	2.9
1971–1980	2.2	2.1
1981–1990	2.3	2.2
1991–2003	2.0	2.1

NOTE: Figures are percentage changes in per capita real GDP.
SOURCES: *Economic Report of the President,* 2002; *Economic Indicators* (various issues).

ultimately will lead to significantly smaller per capita incomes than these nations otherwise might have attained.

As discussed earlier, lower economic growth is not necessarily bad. Indeed, critics of the negative intergenerational spillovers that growth can cause would regard reduced growth as a good thing. Nevertheless, the United States and other low-growth nations have reasons to be concerned. One is that to the extent that economic growth *does* reflect living standards, the consistently lower growth rates of recent years indicate a poor outlook for improvement in overall living standards. Another is that some government programs, such as social security programs that transfer incomes from young people to members of older generations, can come under significant pressures when economic growth fades.

The Determinants of Economic Growth

Why do economic growth rates differ so much across nations? Why do growth rates for any given nation differ over time? Finally, why has average worldwide economic growth slowed in recent decades?

These are tough questions. Although economists still argue about which answers are "right," they generally agree about how to try to find those answers. This, you will see, is because the per capita real GDP measure of economic growth implies that there are three important factors that determine growth.

The Key Factors That Determine Economic Growth

Recall from our analysis of the classical macroeconomic model in Chapter 3 that the *short-run* aggregate production function is $y = F(N)$, where y is real GDP and N is the amount of labor employed. We called this the *short-run* production function because we considered only a period short enough that labor was the only factor of production whose quantity firms could vary. But the economy has another crucial factor of production. This is **capital,** or goods such as tools, machinery, and factories that may be used to produce other goods and services in the future. Although there are other factors of production, such as land and entrepreneurship, let's focus our attention on labor and capital, because these are the most important productive factors.

CAPITAL: Goods that people can use to produce other goods and services in the future.

THE LONG-RUN AGGREGATE PRODUCTION FUNCTION   In the long run, real output of goods and services depends on the nature of the production function that applies to a period lengthy enough that firms can adjust the amount of capital that they employ. Consequently, any consideration of economic growth must include capital in the production function. In addition, over a number of years the technology that firms can use also can change. The long-run production function must therefore account for technological change as well. These considerations indicate that a long-run aggregate production function for the economy is

$$y = F(N, K) \times A,$$

where capital, K, is a factor of production along with labor and where A is a measure of the degree to which technical progress permits firms to increase the amount of goods and services that they produce using labor and capital. This factor A is commonly referred to as a measure of *long-run overall productivity of capital and labor*. As we shall explain shortly, this factor captures the potential for economic growth through technological change rather than through growth in labor and capital.

In the short-run classical model in Chapter 3, we assumed that technology was fixed, which allowed us to abstract from long-run productivity changes. In addition, we assumed that capital was fixed in the short run, which allowed us to ignore it. When thinking about the long run, however, both must be considered.

THE COMPONENTS OF GDP GROWTH   Our measure of economic growth is the rate at which real GDP per capita increases each year. In terms of our notation, a proportionate increase in real GDP, which is how we measure real GDP growth, is $\Delta y / y$. We can see from the expression for the aggregate production function that a proportionate increase in y could arise for any one of three reasons. One possibility is a proportionate rise in productivity, which is a change in productivity relative to total productivity, or $\Delta A / A$. If the amounts of labor and capital are unchanged, but both become more productive, then more output can be produced.

Another reason that output might grow is a proportionate rise in output caused by growth in labor employment. Suppose that β_N is the proportionate increase in output induced by a proportionate increase in employment. Then the contribution of employment growth to output growth would be $\beta_N \times \Delta N / N$, where $\Delta N / N$ is the proportionate growth in the labor input.

Finally, output could grow because of a proportionate increase in output induced by growth in the amount of capital. If β_K is the proportionate increase in output induced by a proportionate increase in capital, then the contribution of capital growth to output growth would be $\beta_K \times \Delta K / K$, where $\Delta K / K$ is the proportionate growth in capital. (During the late 1980s and 1990s, businesses made big investments in capital relating to information technologies, and in the late 1990s, those investments began to boost overall U.S. productivity; see on the following page *Management Notebook: The Contribution of Information Technology to Productivity Gains in the U.S. Economy*.)

On the Web

What are recent trends in labor productivity in the U.S. economy? You can get these data for various sectors from the Bureau of Labor Statistics at **http://stats.bls.gov**. Under the heading, "Productivity," click on "Multifactor Productivity." Then click on "Most Requested Statistics," and select data to consider.

The Contribution of Information Technology to Productivity Gains in the U.S. Economy

etween 1973 and 1995, overall U.S. productivity grew at a rate of only about 1.4 percent per year. Since 1995, productivity growth has been closer to 2.4 to 2.6 percent per year. Economists call an increase in the productivity growth rate an *acceleration* of productivity growth.

Numerous economists have tried to determine what factors have accounted for the acceleration of U.S. productivity growth since 1995. Businesspeople have long argued that the huge information technology investments they undertook beginning in the late 1980s were largely responsible for the surge in productivity growth, but several prominent economists had trouble crediting the adoption of new information technologies with generating even as much as one-fourth of the productivity-growth acceleration that occurred after the mid-1990s.

More recent studies have developed more accurate ways to measure the effect of the adoption of new information technologies on overall U.S. productivity. One such study, by Federal Reserve economists Stephen Oliner and Daniel Sichel, finds that as much as *70 percent* of the acceleration of U.S. productivity growth after 1995 stemmed from the use of new information technologies. Thus, the businesspeople may have been right all along.

For Critical Analysis
In what ways might the adoption of new information technologies have contributed to the increase in overall U.S. productivity?

Consequently, we can write a nation's overall output growth over a year's time as the sum of these three components, or

$$\Delta y / y = (\beta_N \times \Delta N / N) + (\beta_K \times \Delta K / K) + (\Delta A / A).$$

We could then divide by the nation's population (which typically would be larger than N, because not all people are in the labor force or employed) to calculate per capita output growth. The above expression tells us that economic growth is equal to the contribution of employment growth to output growth plus the contribution of capital growth to output growth plus the rate of growth in the productivity of capital and labor. Hence, an understanding of the determinants of economic growth must focus on these three factors.

FUNDAMENTAL ISSUE #2

What key factors determine the rate of economic growth?   The growth of real GDP has three components. One is the growth in labor's contribution to real GDP, and another is the growth in capital's contribution to real GDP. The third is the growth in productivity of labor and capital. Any attempt to understand why cross-country differences in economic growth exist or why countries grow at different rates over time must focus on these three factors.

Economists have estimated that the proportionate response of output to a proportionate rise in labor employment, β_N, is approximately equal to 0.7. This means that a 10 percent increase in employment would, holding other determinants of growth unchanged, cause output to grow by about 7 percent. Consequently, we might expect that employment growth would have a lot to do with output growth.

LABOR–FORCE PARTICIPATION   To understand how employment growth affects output growth, let's return to the classical model that we developed in Chapters 3 and 4. There you learned that a key determinant of the amount of labor services that people supply to firms is the real wage.

Nevertheless, the real wage is not the only factor that influences a person's decision to enter the labor force and work for a wage. A number of other factors also play important roles in this decision. For instance, consider the choices that a married couple may make during their years together. Early on, they may both choose to enter the labor force to earn the highest possible combined income so that they can make major investments in education, housing, and so on that will have long-term benefits for their household. Then, if the couple has a child, one of the parents may leave the workforce for a time until the child is old enough for day care or school. To pay for the child's college education, one or both parents may take on extra work, such as moonlighting or consulting. All of these decisions naturally depend in part on the real wages that both parents can earn in the labor market. Clearly, though, the decisions are also influenced by other factors, including actions and policies of local, state, and federal governments.

For instance, the extent of labor-force participation depends in part on the taxes that governments impose on wage income. Suppose that the federal government significantly reduces taxes on wage income. The couple in our example may decide that after-tax earnings from work are now high enough that they can afford to hire outside child care. Consequently, such a tax cut could induce the parent who stayed home to reenter the labor force. Likewise, reductions in government benefits, such as unemployment insurance or other governmentally supported supplemental income benefits, could induce more individuals to enter the labor force.

AN INCREASE IN THE LABOR FORCE, EMPLOYMENT, AND AGGREGATE SUPPLY   Figure 5–2 on the next page illustrates the effects of a rise in overall labor-force participation, caused perhaps by a cut in taxes on wage income. At any given real wage [panel (a)] or money wage [panel (b)], people supply more labor services, so the labor supply schedule shifts rightward. As a result, the equilibrium money wage declines, and equilibrium employment rises. This causes a rightward movement along the aggregate production function [panel (c)] and an increase in real output. Consequently, the aggregate supply schedule shifts rightward [panel (d)]. The result is short-run growth in real output. Whether this growth will be sustained over a long horizon will depend upon the duration of the tax cut. (As you learned in Chapter 3, a rightward shift in aggregate supply will, if aggregate demand is stationary,

Figure 5–2   The Effects of a Rise in Labor-Force Participation on the Equilibrium Money Wage, Employment, Aggregate Supply, and Real Output

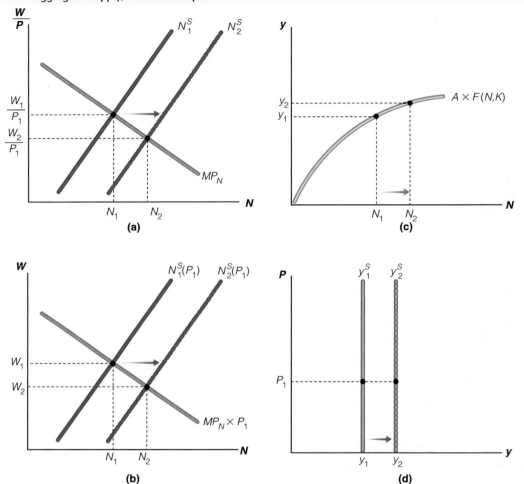

As panels (a) and (b) show, increased labor-force participation results in a rightward shift in the labor supply schedule. The equilibrium money wage declines, and equilibrium employment rises. As a result, as panel (c) indicates, aggregate output increases. Thus, as panel (d) shows, the economy's aggregate supply schedule shifts to the right. At a given price level, real output rises. If population is unchanged, the result is an increase in per capita real output.

SUPPLY-SIDE ECONOMICS: A school of economic thought that promotes government policies intended to influence real GDP by affecting the position of the economy's aggregate supply schedule.

lead to a decline in the price level. Of course, in most countries aggregate demand is not really unchanging over time, which complicates the assessment of how inflation and economic growth may be related; see *Global Notebook: Inflation and GDP Growth—Is There a Relationship?*)

Figure 5–2 illustrates a key argument proposed by adherents of the school of thought known as **supply-side economics.** According to this view, the primary way for governmental policy actions to have real effects

Inflation and GDP Growth—Is There a Relationship?

According to the basic classical model, a rightward shift in the aggregate supply curve generates a rightward movement along the aggregate demand curve, which causes a reduction in the price level. During much of the nineteenth century, and especially at the height of the Industrial Revolution between the 1860s and 1890s, the result was deflation in many nations.

During the second half of the twentieth century and the early years of the twenty-first century, however, nearly all nations with positive economic growth also experienced positive inflation rates. The simultaneous observation of GDP growth and inflation can still be consistent with the classical theory if aggregate demand grows at a faster rate than aggregate supply.

Nevertheless, the classical theory would predict that over a large number of countries, we should expect to see less inflation in countries with higher GDP growth. The reason is that relatively large rightward shifts of a vertical aggregate supply curve would do much to counter the inflationary effects of increased aggregate demand.

Figure 5-3 plots the relationship between GDP growth and a measure of inflation for 140 nations over the four decades following 1960. As you can see, higher-growth nations do, as the theory predicts, tend to experience lower inflation than countries with lower rates of GDP growth.

Figure 5–3   **GDP Growth and Inflation for 140 Countries**

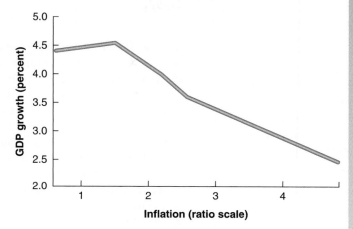

The classical theory predicts that countries that experience greater economic growth will, given the growth of aggregate demand, experience lower rates of inflation. There is some support for this prediction in the experience of 140 of the world's nations.

SOURCE: Mohain Khan and Abdelhak Senhadji, "Threshold Effects in the Relationship between Inflation and Growth," *IMF Staff Papers* 48 (January 2001): 1–21.

For Critical Analysis
Are there any circumstances under which higher inflation might actually contribute to lower economic growth?

is by influencing the position of the aggregate supply schedule. Policies that encourage labor-force participation, such as low tax rates on wage income, are central supply-side policy prescriptions.

POPULATION GROWTH AND ECONOMIC GROWTH   The world's population has passed 6 billion people, and it will continue to grow by about 100 million people per year. Population growth does not occur evenly over the earth's surface, however. Women in the relatively wealthy nations of Europe bear an average of 1.6 children during their life spans. In the United States, a typical woman has slightly more than 2 children. Meanwhile, in the generally poorer nations of Africa, women bear an average of 6 children.

Does a large population contribute to or detract from economic growth? On the one hand, population growth naturally tends to induce a rise in a nation's labor-force participation. As we have discussed, this expands equilibrium

On the Web

How does GDP growth currently vary across nations and regions of the world? To find out, go to the International Monetary Fund's home page at http://www.imf.org, and click on "Publications." Under "Search by," type in "World Economic Outlook." Download the latest issue of this report, which contains detailed statistical information contrasting national and regional growth rates.

employment and spurs economic growth. On the other hand, a larger population directly reduces growth in *per capita* real GDP.

Which of these effects dominates? The answer seems to depend on which nation one considers. In some nations with high population densities, such as Japan, Singapore, and Hong Kong, population growth historically has been positively related to economic growth. In nations such as Bangladesh, Kenya, and Nigeria, however, so far there has been a negative relationship between population growth and per capita real GDP growth.

IMMIGRATION AND ECONOMIC GROWTH In centuries past, people in nations with relatively low economic growth often could escape their predicament by emigrating to other lands. Today, however, believing that continued immigration will harm their interests, the citizens of many democratic nations have erected significant barriers to immigrants. Indeed, many social commentators argue that immigration slows economic growth. This view has recently gained broader currency in the United States, which previously was one of the most open nations to immigration. Indeed, with the exception of Native Americans, every citizen of the United States is descended from immigrants.

From one perspective, immigration is just a form of population growth. According to this perspective, the answer to whether immigration spurs or inhibits economic growth is the same as the answer to the question of whether population growth speeds or slows economic growth. In both cases, a crucial factor appears to be the extent of economic freedom—the right to own private property and to exchange goods, services, and financial assets with minimal government interference—available to the residents of a nation. In nations with significant economic freedom, immigration should stimulate growth, but in nations lacking economic freedom, immigration likely will stunt the economy's growth. Consequently, a nation such as the United States should gain from immigration over the long term. This has been the rationale for relative openness to immigration in the United States, and it paid off handsomely during the first two centuries of the nation's existence.

FUNDAMENTAL ISSUE #3

How does labor-force participation affect economic growth? Do population growth and immigration increase or reduce economic growth? A rise in labor-force participation causes an increase in labor supply, which spurs employment and causes a rise in real GDP. Hence, if more members of the current population enter the labor force, per capita income definitely rises. A larger population has two effects on per capita income. One is the positive effect from a rise in the labor force, but another is the negative effect of reducing the average share of GDP available to each person in a nation. Whether population growth leads to economic growth seems to be related to the extent of the nation's economic freedom. Immigration is a form of population growth, so its effects on economic growth also depend on how the positive and negative effects net out.

As we have seen, labor-force participation affects growth. So does the productivity of labor that firms employ. We can also use the classical model of Chapters 3 and 4 to understand why labor productivity can be an important determinant of a nation's growth.

LABOR PRODUCTIVITY, EMPLOYMENT, AND AGGREGATE SUPPLY   Business and financial publications such as the *Wall Street Journal* often feature articles on recent developments in labor productivity. Improvements in labor productivity are treated as "good news" for businesses because of the cost savings—and potentially higher short-run profits—that productivity improvements yield.

Nevertheless, a key effect of a productivity improvement arises in the labor market, and a general rise in labor productivity can have important economy-wide effects. We can see this in Figure 5–4 (p. 114). A rise in labor productivity means that each unit of labor is capable of producing a larger amount of output. Another way of saying this is that the marginal product of labor increases at any given quantity of labor, so the MP_N schedule shifts upward, as shown in panel (a). Because the value of marginal product is equal to the marginal product of labor times the price of output, the VMP_N schedule also shifts rightward, as shown in panel (b). Consequently, a rise in labor productivity results in an increase in the demand for labor, which induces a rise in the money wage and an increase in employment.

This is not the only effect of the rise in productivity, however. Recall that the marginal product of labor is the slope of the aggregate production function. Hence, a rise in labor's marginal product means that the slope of the production function increases at any given quantity of labor. As panel (c) shows, the result is an *upward rotation* in the production function. A rise in labor productivity thereby leads to a rise in equilibrium real output that has two causes. First, with any given quantity of labor, firms can produce more output. As shown in panel (c), even if employment were to remain at N_1, real output would increase to y'. Second, the rise in equilibrium employment, from N_1 to N_2, that is induced by the increase in labor's marginal product leads to a further increase in the production of output. Panel (d) shows that as a result of these combined increases in production of output, the aggregate supply schedule shifts rightward. A rise in labor productivity, like an increase in labor-force participation, leads to growth in real output.

LABOR PRODUCTIVITY GROWTH AND EMPLOYMENT GROWTH MOVE TOGETHER   Note that employment and productivity very naturally often move in the same direction. Figure 5–5 on page 115 verifies this essential relationship between employment growth and output growth, which can make it difficult for economists to separate the effects of productivity improvements from those arising solely from employment growth.

This relationship also tends to confuse journalists who write about economic growth. Sometimes their writings seem to suggest that improvements in labor productivity necessarily lead to fewer people being employed by firms. As you can see, however, economic theory indicates that this is not necessarily true. If people generally become more productive, perhaps by

macroxtra!
Economic
Applications

How much has labor productivity recently been rising? Take a look at movements in U.S. productivity via EconData Online.
http://macroxtra.swcollege.com

macro**xtra!**
Interactive Key Graph

The following graph shows how a rise in labor productivity affects employment and output. What happens if there is technological change? What occurs if there is a change in labor-force participation? You can discover the answers to these questions by interacting with this graph on the Web.
Go to http://macroxtra.swcollege.com

Figure 5–4   The Effects of a Rise in the Marginal Product of Labor on Employment and Real Output

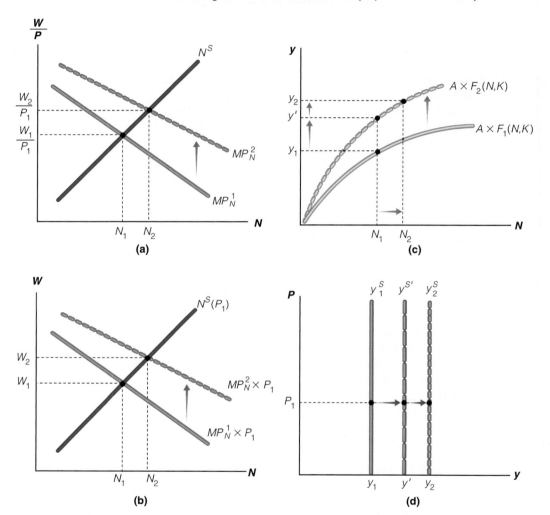

A rise in the marginal product of labor leads to an increase in the demand for labor, as shown in panels (a) and (b). As a result, the equilibrium money wage and employment level increase. Thus, if the economy's productive capabilities were to remain the same, real output would increase as a result of the rise in employment, and the aggregate supply schedule would shift rightward as in panel (d). Nevertheless, the marginal-product-of-labor schedule shows the slope of the production function at each level of employment. Hence, an increase in the marginal product of labor rotates the production function upward, as in panel (c). For this reason, an additional increase in real output occurs as a result of the greater productive capabilities owing to the rise in labor's marginal product, and the aggregate supply schedule shifts farther to the right in panel (d).

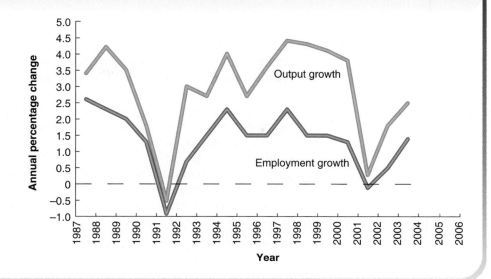

Figure 5–5   Employment Growth and Output Growth in the United States

Annual U.S. employment growth rates and output growth rates are positively related.

SOURCE: International Monetary Fund, *World Economic Outlook*, April 2002.

making personal investments in education and training that improve their ability to produce goods and services, then the result is increased per capita incomes. The big issue, as we shall discuss shortly, is the extent to which people can make themselves sufficiently productive to avoid being replaced by machines.

FUNDAMENTAL ISSUE #4

How do changes in labor productivity influence economic growth?   A rise in the marginal product of labor enables firms to produce more output with any given amount of employment. A rise in labor's marginal product also leads to an increase in the demand for labor by firms, which stimulates employment. These two effects together yield growth in real GDP per capita.

Capital Investment, Saving, and Growth

As you learned in Chapter 2, when economists use the term *investment,* they have in mind the accumulation of capital goods. **Gross investment** is the term for total spending on capital goods during a year. Such expenditures typically include spending to repair existing capital. For instance, a part on a machine in a factory may wear out, or *depreciate,* during the year and need to be replaced. Spending to repair or replace existing capital goods is called the *depreciation allowance* or, more simply, **depreciation.**

The difference between gross investment and depreciation is **net investment.** This is the amount of spending during the year that adds to the existing stock of capital goods. Hence, by engaging in net investment

GROSS INVESTMENT: Total spending on capital goods during a year, including depreciation expenditures.

DEPRECIATION: Spending to repair or replace existing capital goods.

NET INVESTMENT: Gross investment minus depreciation; the result is equal to total expenditures on new capital goods.

expenditures during a year, a society creates new capital that can help fuel future economic growth.

CAPITAL AND ECONOMIC GROWTH   To see why capital accumulation via net investment induces economic growth, recall first that the long-run aggregate production function indicates that the amount of real output produced depends on capital as well as labor. To this point, we have graphed the production function with output (y) and employment (N) on the axes, but we can also draw a diagram of the production function in which we relate output to the amount of capital (K), as in Figure 5–6. Holding employment of labor unchanged, an increase in the amount of capital causes real output to increase.

It follows that greater capital accumulation leads to higher economic growth. Capital accumulation, in turn, requires people and businesses to undertake net investment. Therefore, to understand the factors that can influence capital formation and its contribution to economic growth, we must consider the determinants of net investment.

INVESTMENT AND THE MARGINAL PRODUCT OF CAPITAL   Recall from Chapter 4 that desired investment is a component of the demand for loanable funds. According to the classical theory, the desired investment schedule is downward sloping in a diagram in which the real interest rate appears on the vertical axis. *Equilibrium* investment then is determined by the interplay between saving by households, investment spending that is done mainly by firms, and the demand for loanable funds by the government to finance its deficit.

How do we come up with the desired investment schedule used in the diagram of the loanable funds market? Let's begin by assuming that depreciation is a small enough component of gross investment that the difference between gross and net investment is negligible. (In fact, depreciation typically is just a fraction of gross investment.) Now consider Figure 5–7.

Figure 5–6   Capital Accumulation and Growth in Real Output

Holding other factors unchanged, an increase in the capital stock will induce a movement along the production function and an increase in real output.

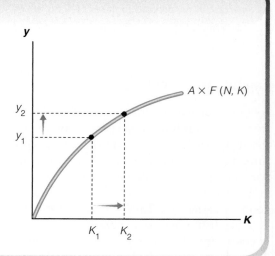

Panel (a) shows the diagram of the aggregate production function from Figure 5–6. As in Figure 5–6, panel (a) of Figure 5–7 shows that a rise in the amount of capital, from K_1 to K_2, causes real output to increase from y_1 to y_2. In addition, however, panel (a) shows that the slope of lines tangent to the production function declines as the amount of capital increases. The slope of each of these tangent lines is the rise divided by the run, or a change in output divided by a change in the capital stock. In words, the slope of each line tangent to the production function is the additional output resulting from an additional unit of capital, which is the **marginal product of capital,** denoted MP_K.

Panel (b) of Figure 5–7 displays a marginal-product-of-capital schedule, or MP_K schedule, corresponding to the production function. Because the production function is concave, the law of diminishing marginal returns holds, and the MP_K schedule slopes downward. The rise in the amount of capital displayed in panel (a) causes a movement downward and rightward along the MP_K schedule.

Why would a firm choose to increase its capital stock? Recall from Chapter 4 that the real interest rate is the real rate of return from an investment in capital. The real interest rate, r_r, is the additional output that a firm receives from making an investment expenditure on new capital. These are the same units of measurement used to calculate the marginal product of capital. Consequently, there must be a relationship between the marginal product of capital, the real interest rate, and investment.

(MP_K): The additional output that can be produced following the addition of another unit of capital.

Figure 5–7   The Marginal-Product-of-Capital (MP_K) Schedule

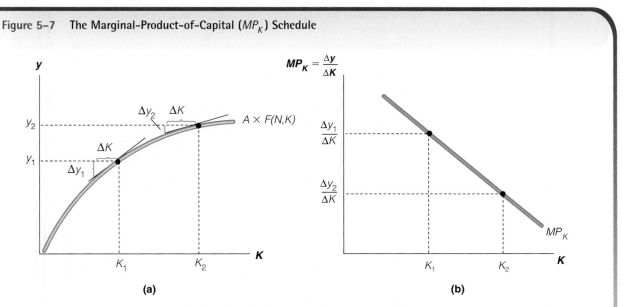

(a)   (b)

As shown in panel (a), we can graph the aggregate production function with the amount of capital measured along the horizontal axis. The slope of the production function at any given quantity of capital is the marginal product of cap-ital, which declines as the amount of capital increases. Hence, the marginal-product-of-capital schedule slopes downward, as in panel (b).

Figure 5–8   The Real Interest Rate and the Investment Schedule

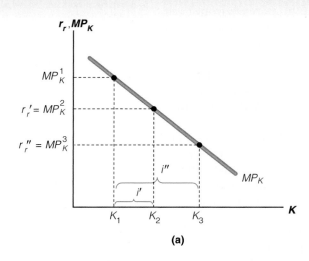

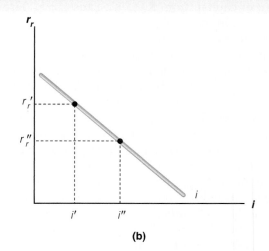

(a)   (b)

Firms install new capital equipment to the point at which the marginal product of capital is equal to the real interest rate. Hence, a decline in the real interest rate induces firms to increase the amount of capital employed in production, as shown in panel (a). Investment is an increase in the capi-tal stock, so the rise in capital accumulation indicated in panel (a) corresponds to an increase in investment. Therefore, the investment schedule is downward sloping, as shown in panel (b).

The diagrams in Figure 5–8 explain this relationship. Suppose that the current amount of capital is equal to K_1, so that the marginal product of capital is equal to MP_K^1, as shown in panel (a). The real interest rate, however, is equal to r_r'. Because the real interest rate is the market return on saving, it is the price of new capital to owners of the firm. By using the amount of capital K_1, the firm would be using too little capital relative to the amount consistent with the price of capital, r_r'. The firm would earn fewer profits than it otherwise could by increasing its capital to K_2, thereby reducing the marginal product of capital to MP_K^2, which is equal to the real interest rate r_r'. This capital increase would be the firm's investment, $i' = K_2 - K_1$. Hence, as panel (b) shows, at the real interest rate r_r', the firm's desired investment would equal i'.

Now consider how a firm currently using the amount of capital K_1 would respond to a fall in the current real interest rate to r_r''. As panel (a) indicates, the firm would increase its use of capital goods further, to K_3. Consequently, it would undertake a larger amount of capital investment of $i'' = K_3 - K_1$. A reduction in the real interest rate would stimulate more capital investment by the firm. As a result, the firm's desired investment schedule would slope downward, as shown in panel (b).

What happens if capital becomes more productive? For example, suppose part of a firm's capital consists of computer equipment, and a software breakthrough improves the computers' functioning, so the firm can produce more output with the same amount of computers. How does this improvement in productivity influence the firm's investment decision?

Figure 5–9   Desired Investment and a Rise in the Marginal Product of Capital

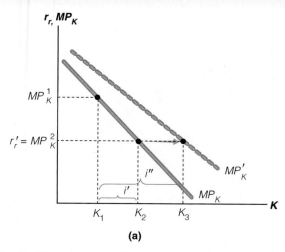

(a)

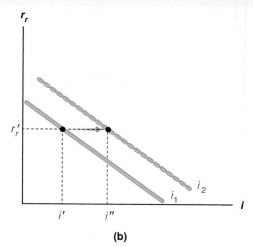

(b)

At a given real interest rate, an increase in the marginal product induces firms to employ additional capital in production, as shown in panel (a). The result, displayed in panel (b), is an increase in investment spending. Thus, a rise in the marginal product of capital shifts the investment schedule rightward.

Figure 5–9 provides the answer to this question. If capital becomes more productive, then its marginal product increases at any given amount of capital. As panel (a) shows, the marginal-product-of-capital schedule would shift upward and to the right. Consequently, at any given market real interest rate, the firm would desire to make a greater capital investment. This means that the investment schedule would shift to the right, following a rise in the marginal product of capital, as shown in panel (b).

A rise in investment, or increased capital formation, leads to an increase in the capital stock. A rise in the capital stock, in turn, yields an increase in real output. Therefore:

> **An increase in the productivity of capital leads to a rise in output growth. Thus, nations that are successful in developing ways to make their capital more productive generally grow faster than other nations.**

INVESTMENT, SAVING, AND ECONOMIC GROWTH   The productivity of capital is only one factor influencing capital formation and economic growth. Any factor that affects the equilibrium amount of investment by all firms affects how much the capital stock and output will expand.

Figure 5–10 on the next page illustrates one factor that affects equilibrium aggregate investment. This factor is total desired saving. The figure shows the market for loanable funds, where for the moment we ignore the possible existence of a government deficit. As we discussed in Chapter 4, the supply of loanable funds is the saving schedule, and in the absence of a government deficit, the demand for loanable funds is the investment

Figure 5–10   The Effect on Equilibrium Investment of a Rise in Saving

A rise in saving at any given real interest rate implies a rightward shift in the saving schedule. As a result, equilibrium saving and investment rise.

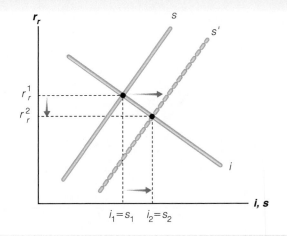

schedule. At the equilibrium real interest rate r_r^1, the amount of loanable funds supplied, saving, is equal to the amount of loanable funds demanded, investment, or $s_1 = i_1$.

If household saving were to increase at any given real interest rate, the saving schedule would shift to the right. This would cause the equilibrium real interest rate to decline to r_r^2, which would induce firms to increase their investment. Capital formation would increase, as would economic growth, at least in the near term.

What might cause saving to rise? The answer is that saving would increase if households had incentives to save a larger portion of their earnings. For this reason, supply-side proponents often argue that income tax rates applied to households' returns from saving should be reduced or even eliminated. Such an action would cause the saving schedule to shift rightward, as in Figure 5–10, and induce greater capital investment.

Another factor that plays a role in determining equilibrium investment is a government deficit. As you learned in Chapter 4, an increase in a government deficit *crowds out* private investment. To the extent that government spending financed by the deficit is purely consumption spending instead of investment in capital goods such as roads or bridges, the result is a decline in capital formation. For this reason supply-side enthusiasts also argue for reductions in government deficits as a way to stimulate greater capital formation and economic growth.

DOES CAPITAL CROWD OUT LABOR?   Classic science fiction stories of the 1940s and 1950s envisioned a future world where machines based on robotics technology could perform many of the mental and physical tasks previously performed only by human labor. In some of the darker stories, many human workers were unemployed as a result of the new technology, and only a few human beings reaped the rewards from the use of robots—a then futuristic type of capital good.

Although today's robots have not quite achieved the level of sophistication of the old science fiction stories, robot machines are commonplace in many of today's factories. Many factories also employ fewer workers than they did in the past. Does this mean that the science fiction stories were correct? Are capital and labor **substitutes in production**—meaning that greater use of capital leads to less use of labor in the production of goods and services? Or were the stories operating under a false premise? Could capital and labor be **complements in production,** so that greater use of capital goods actually stimulates employment of labor?

At the level of an individual firm or a specific industry, it turns out that some capital goods are substitutes for labor, while others are complements. In most cases, for instance, robot machines *do* substitute for human workers. Personal computers also can substitute for human beings. Accountants and actuaries who once needed human clerks to operate calculators by hand for hours on end now can program their personal computers to do the calculations for them in seconds.

At the same time, however, capital and labor can be complements in other environments. To the extent that there are **economies of scale** in a production process, meaning that savings in average production costs can be realized by increasing the size of a firm's operations by expanding the use of capital and other resources, it can pay for a business to grow larger. This can lead to a simultaneous increase in both capital and labor.

The development of new types of capital, such as robots or personal computers, can also create a need for human workers who can operate and repair the new capital equipment. For instance, even as the ranks of human clerks at accounting and actuarial firms have declined, the firms' staffs of human computer consultants have expanded.

The implication of these offsetting effects across firms and industries is that human beings will not be replaced by new and improved capital as long as they are willing and able to adapt to the new capital goods. Humans who cannot adapt, or who choose not to do so, may find themselves substitute inputs in firms' production processes. Such humans may join the ranks of the unemployed. Those who do adapt, however, can find that the rewards are very high.

SUBSTITUTES IN PRODUCTION: The term for the situation in which increased use of capital leads to reduced use of labor in the production of real output.

COMPLEMENTS IN PRODUCTION: The term for the situation in which an increased use of capital goods leads to greater use of labor in the production of goods and services.

ECONOMIES OF SCALE: The realization of reduced average production costs via an increase in the size of a firm's operations through acquisition of new capital.

FUNDAMENTAL ISSUE #5

Why are saving and capital investment important for economic growth?   A firm maximizes its profit when the marginal product of capital is equal to the real interest rate. A rise in the marginal product of capital or a decline in the real interest rate induces a firm to increase its investment in additional capital. Equilibrium total investment depends on the flow of saving. A rise in saving leads to greater investment, as does a decline in the government's deficit. Greater investment lays a foundation for higher economic growth.

Humans adapt to new types of capital and ways of doing things by *learning*. That is, they acquire *knowledge* about new forms of capital and new ways to produce goods and services.

Knowledge, Innovation, and Growth

INNOVATION: The process by which a new invention is integrated into the economy, where it reduces production costs or provides people with new types of goods and services.

HUMAN CAPITAL: The knowledge and skills possessed by people in a nation's labor force.

macroxtra!
Economic
Applications

Is there a new economy? To review alternative perspectives on this debate and make your own judgment, go to EconData Online.
http://macroxtra.swcollege.com

Innovation and Knowledge

Typically, we think of technological progress as, say, the invention of the electric motor, motion pictures and television, or the microchip. By themselves, however, inventions do not translate into greater economic growth. For instance, nearly a quarter of a century passed before the electric motor transformed the workplace and induced rapid growth in productive capabilities in the United States. The fact that a swift succession of moving images can trick the eye into perceiving motion was first understood in the 1830s, but more than fifty years passed before the first motion pictures were shown in theaters. The radio technology necessary for television was in wide use by the 1920s, but televisions did not become widespread in U.S. homes until the 1950s. Personal computers have been around since the 1970s, but only since the 1990s have they begun to change the way that the average U.S. employee works. Despite the significant growth in computer technology, computers amount to only 2 percent of the net investment by businesses and an even smaller percentage of all the machinery, equipment, and buildings owned by firms.

These examples illustrate that more than invention is needed to change the way that people produce goods and services. **Innovation,** or the transformation of something new, such as an invention, into something that benefits the economy either by lowering production costs or by providing new types of goods and services, is required.

A natural question is how the process of innovation works. For instance, have innovations in the United States been fueled by rising demand for new products in a rapidly expanding nation? Or does innovation itself spur a demand for goods and services that a new invention like the personal computer can make possible? Economists do not yet know the answer to this chicken-or-the-egg puzzle. What they do know, however, is the following:

Innovation cannot occur without the capacity for human beings to *create*. People must have knowledge of their world and must have the ability to *apply* that knowledge if innovation is to occur.

Human Capital

The knowledge and skills that people in the labor force possess constitute their **human capital.** People develop human capital through education, on-the-job training, and self-teaching. Just as physical capital cannot be accumulated without investment in capital goods, human capital accumulation requires investment in activities and experiences that add to people's knowledge and train their minds to apply that knowledge in new tasks.

Productivity, innovation, and human capital are all related. A poorly trained workforce cannot be highly innovative and productive. As we have discussed, productivity is a key component of growth. Yet total productivity in the United States has not grown much during the past three decades. As Figure 5–11 shows, overall productivity grew slowly and steadily from 1870 until 1930. After the Great Depression of the 1930s, productivity grew at a rapid pace until the 1970s. Since then, however, aside from upticks in the mid-1970s, mid-1980s, and the past few years, productivity appears to

Figure 5–11 Overall Productivity in the United States, 1870–Present

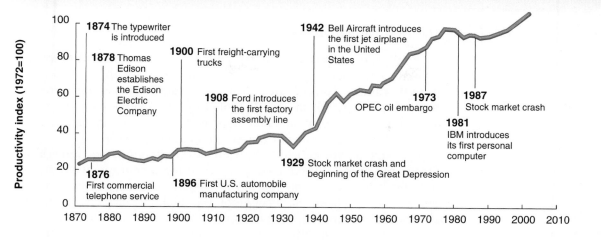

Relative to preceding years, overall U.S. productivity grew significantly between the 1930s and the 1970s and then leveled off for nearly twenty years. Since the mid-1990s productivity growth has showed signs of returning to its previous upward trend.

SOURCES: Louis Uchitell, "Not Making It: We're Leaner, Meaner, and Getting Nowhere Fast," *New York Times,* May 12, 1996, p. 1; *Economic Report of the President,* 2002.

have slowed somewhat, although its overall performance since the 1980s has bettered the 1870s, a period that predated mass electric power generation and distribution plus other innovations, such as the adoption and use of automotive and air travel, radio and television, and computers.

Some economists argue that one explanation for the leveling off of U.S. productivity from the 1970s through the mid-1990s was a relative decline in human capital investment in the United States. This is one of the reasons why concerned citizens and political leaders have been rethinking the structure of the nation's education system. As Figure 5–11 indicates, the highest productivity growth occurred between the mid-1930s and the 1970s, which was also a period of rapid development of the nation's secondary schools and colleges and universities. These schools and colleges became the centers of human capital development. Most provided firm grounding in science and mathematics—precisely the areas that are required for developing better technology.

On the Web

In what ways did the U.S. government improve its measures of service-sector productivity in 2002? To find out, go to the Bureau of Economic Analysis, **http://www.bea.doc.gov**, and next to "National," click on "Articles," and then click on "Comprehensive NIPA Revision—Improved Estimates of the NIPA's for 1929–1999: Results of the Comprehensive Revision."

New Growth Theory: Does Growth Feed on Itself?

Economists' interest in the determinants of productivity growth is a relatively recent phenomenon. Although economists have always recognized that growth in productivity is important to economic growth, traditionally they tended to focus their attention on the contributions that stemmed from the relatively more easily measured and understood growth of labor

NEW GROWTH THEORY: A theory of economic growth that focuses on productivity growth as a key determinant of technological progress and the rate of growth of an economy.

and capital. Typically, economists regarded productivity growth as an external factor and did not try very hard to explain it.

The New Growth Theory

In contrast, economists called *new growth theorists* now focus on productivity and technology as driving forces of economic growth. According to **new growth theory,** technological growth is crucial to economic growth, and technological growth in turn is fueled by improvements in productivity. This means that to understand what makes an economy grow, we must understand what factors determine productivity growth.

Two factors have helped to spur the development of new growth theory. One is the apparent relationship between the recent twenty-year drop-off in economic growth and the slight slowing of productivity growth. The other factor has been the recognition that technological change can play a significant role in explaining even the slow growth rates of recent years.

Consider some startling statistics about the growth in computer technology. Microprocessor speeds may increase to previously unimaginable speeds by 2010. By that same year, the size of the thinnest circuit line in a transistor likely will decrease by over 100 percent. The typical memory capacity of computers may increase by a factor of one thousand. Even before these changes have occurred, microchip manufacturers should be able to produce a thousand transistors a week for every person on earth.

As noted earlier, investment in computer hardware accounts for only a small fraction of total capital investment. To new growth theorists, however, this is not the main contribution of computers. The key issue for growth, they contend, is the extent to which people can raise their productivity and the productivity of the other capital they use to produce goods and services by adapting technological improvements in computers. In other words, the relative importance of computers in the overall capital stock may be less important than how much the use of computers contributes to production and manufacturing knowledge and innovation.

macroxtra!
Online
Perspective

For a more detailed evaluation of the implications of new growth theory, go to the Chapter 5 reading, entitled "What Drives Productivity Growth," by Kevin Stiroh of the Federal Reserve Bank of New York.

http://macroxtra.swcollege.com

Knowledge and Self-Perpetuating Growth

To new growth theorists, production and manufacturing knowledge is at least as important to determining economic growth as other factors. These adherents of new growth theory argue that as an aspect of human capital accumulation, knowledge is a factor of production that people accumulate by forgoing current consumption. Nations must therefore invest in knowledge just as they invest in machines.

New growth theorists view recent advances in computer technology as an example of how economic growth can be *self-perpetuating*. An investment in capital such as computer equipment can make it more profitable to acquire more knowledge. This newly acquired knowledge then creates a need for new and better computer equipment. As a result, an initial investment in computer technology can increase knowledge, but then the new knowledge can stimulate greater investment.

According to the traditional theory of economic growth, a onetime increase in the rates of saving and investment leads to a higher plateau for a nation's standard of living, but the standard of living does not continue to rise as a result. If knowledge itself stimulates economic growth, however, as suggested by new growth theory, then a onetime increase in a country's rate of investment may permanently raise that country's growth rate. This means that economic growth can continue as long as people keep coming up with new ideas and developing greater knowledge.

New growth theory, therefore, places greater emphasis on human capital and education. The process of acquiring and applying knowledge may be the key to continuous economic growth. For this process to work, however, people must be able to apply their minds effectively.

FUNDAMENTAL ISSUE #6

What role does human knowledge play in economic growth? Is growth self-perpetuating? According to new growth theory, the acquisition and use of knowledge that people gain from investment can contribute to further investment. As a result, economic growth can be self-perpetuating, provided that people make human capital investments that enable them to engage in the process of acquiring and using knowledge.

Does the Stock Market Forecast Business Productivity?

Stock prices should depend positively on anticipated annual future earnings of companies that issue stocks, because companies will pay annual dividends to shareholders from those earnings. Companies' earnings, in turn, are positively related to business productivity, or the ability of businesses to produce a given amount of output from a fixed quantity of inputs. When business productivity increases, firms are able to produce a given volume of output at lower cost, thereby boosting both their demand for labor and their output of final goods and services.

The Relationship between Productivity and Stock Prices

Because companies' current and future earnings are related to productivity, investors have good reason to keep close tabs on productivity trends when deciding how much they are willing to pay for shares of stock. Other things being equal, when investors are convinced that productivity is on an upswing, stock prices should increase. If investors have good reason to anticipate a drop-off in business productivity, then if other factors are unchanged, they will tend to bid lower amounts for shares of stock, and market share prices should fall.

Because investors have strong incentives to forecast business productivity and act on their forecasts in ways that influence stock prices, some economists have suggested that movements in stock price indexes can provide good signals of future business productivity. Certainly, we often observe a positive relationship between stock prices and business productivity. During quarters when stock prices have risen, business

productivity has also tended to increase, and vice versa. On the surface, this relationship does seem to suggest that movements in stock prices may help firms gauge current trends in overall productivity.

Using Stock Prices to Forecast Business Productivity

But are the observed co-movements of stock prices and productivity positively related because investors do a particularly good job of anticipating future productivity or because investors are simply adept at reacting quickly to previously unexpected productivity increases or declines? If stock prices rise or fall because of speedy investor reactions to recent productivity movements, then stock prices are not likely to provide much information about *future* productivity trends. Instead, stock price movements would simply reflect changes in business productivity already observed in the marketplace.

To evaluate whether it is possible to use stock price measures to forecast future productivity growth, Evan Koenig, an economist at the Federal Reserve Bank of Dallas, used ratios of stock prices to firms' earnings and dividends to try to predict business productivity growth in following quarters between 1982 and 2000. His forecasting method controlled for movements in interest rates, inflation expectations, and trends in employment. As you can see in Figure 5-12, movements in ratios of stock prices to earnings and dividends yielded relatively accurate predictions of productivity growth during this period. Hence, there is some evidence that variations in stock prices really can assist in forecasting future changes in business productivity.

Research Project

Why might a firm be interested in trying to forecast future movements in productivity for the economy as a whole? Provide a list of potential reasons, and evaluate the ways that successfully anticipating aggregate productivity could help an individual company improve its own current and future profitability.

Web Resources

1. What are the broader economic implications of the relationship between the stock market and productivity? Find out by going to the home page of the Federal Reserve Bank of Dallas, http://www.dallasfed.org, where you can click on "Economic Research," then "Southwest Economy." At this page, scan down to "January/February 2000," click on text, and download that issue to read Evan Koenig's paper entitled, "Productivity, the Stock Market, and Monetary Policy in the New Economy."

2. What are the recent trends in U.S. business productivity? Find out by going to the home page of the Bureau of Labor Statistics (http://www.bls.gov) and, under "Productivity," clicking on "Productivity and Costs."

Figure 5–12   Actual and Predicted Productivity Growth

Predictions of productivity growth using stock prices closely match actual growth in business productivity.

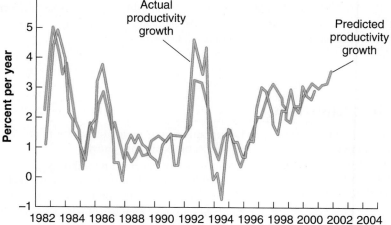

SOURCE: Evan Koenig, "Productivity, the Stock Market, and Monetary Policy in the New Economy," Federal Reserve Bank of Dallas *Southwest Economy,* January/February 2000, pp. 6–12.

1. Measuring Economic Growth: The annual rate of change in per capita real GDP is the measure of economic growth. This measure is imperfect, because it fails to account for changes in the quality of goods and services, does not always reflect improvements in living standards, and does not tell us how many residents of a nation actually benefit from growth. This measure also cannot capture negative intergenerational externalities that growth may create. Nevertheless, it is the best available measure of how much the real income of a nation's average resident grows over time.

2. The Key Factors Determining the Rate of Economic Growth: Three crucial factors influence the growth of per capita GDP. One is the growth of labor's contribution to GDP resulting from a rise in the number of workers. A second factor is the growth in the contribution of capital to GDP as a nation accumulates a larger amount of capital. Finally, higher productivity of existing labor and capital can add to economic growth.

3. The Growth Effects of Increased Labor-Force Participation, Larger Populations, and Immigration: Holding a nation's population unchanged, greater labor-force participation leads to higher employment of labor and increased real GDP, which raises the rate of economic growth. Population growth tends to increase the number of workers, which adds to real GDP, but it also increases the number of people among whom real GDP is divided. As a result, the effect of population growth on economic growth is not obvious. Current evidence favors the view that population growth enhances economic growth in nations with a greater degree of economic freedom but depresses growth in nations with restraints on economic freedom. Traditionally, immigration has spurred economic growth, although the growth effects of immigration are hotly debated today.

4. Labor Productivity and Economic Growth: Greater productivity of labor enhances economic growth. Until a recent uptick, however, labor productivity in the United States and other developed countries had stagnated, as had economic growth.

5. How Saving and Capital Investment Matter for Economic Growth: Nations accumulate new capital by forgoing consumption and saving resources. This permits capital investment to occur. Firms add to their use of capital by investing to the point at which the marginal product of capital is equal to the real interest rate. Consequently, increased national saving, a fall in the real interest rate, or a rise in the productivity of capital leads to a rise in capital accumulation and greater long-run economic growth.

6. Human Knowledge and the Idea of Self-Perpetuating Growth: The new growth theory emphasizes the importance of productivity growth as a determinant of economic growth. According to this view, investments in human capital, or the ability of people to use their minds to acquire and use knowledge, and in knowledge-enhancing technologies are crucial for raising rates of long-term economic growth. Such investments lead to growth in knowledge, which then spurs further investment, which can make economic growth a self-perpetuating process.

Self-Test Questions

(Answers to odd-numbered questions may be found on the Web at **http://macro.swcollege.com** under "Student Resources.")

1. Explain in your own words why population growth has theoretically uncertain effects on economic growth.

2. Immigration has become a thorny political issue in the United States in the early twenty-first century, just as it was in the early twentieth century. In light of what you have learned in this chapter, discuss why this is not surprising.

3. Explain in your own words why nations with more productive capital grow faster.

4. A lower real rate of interest tends to spur investment spending, thereby stimulating expansion of the nation's capital stock. Based on this relationship, some observers argue that the Federal Reserve should "keep interest rates low" to encourage greater economic growth. Based on what you learned about real and nominal interest-rate determination in Chapter 4, does it appear that the Federal Reserve could actually play a central role in regulating a nation's real GDP growth? Explain your reasoning.

5. Explain in your own words why the new growth theory regards education as central to a nation's long-term growth prospects.

6. Theories of economic growth developed during the 1960s assumed that aggregate production exhibits "constant returns to scale," which means that a proportionate change in all factors of production leads to an equal proportionate increase in output produced. Is the new growth theory consistent with this assumption? Explain your reasoning.

Problems

1. The following table presents growth rate data for four countries (A, B, C, and D) between 2001 and 2011:

	Annual Growth Rate (%)			
	A	B	C	D
Nominal GDP	30	22	15	8
Price level	18	10	5	2
Population	10	8	2	1

(Answers to odd-numbered problems may be found on the Web at **http://macro. swcollege.com** under "Student Resources.")

   a. Which country has the largest rate of output growth per capita?

   b. Which country has the smallest rate of output growth per capita?

2. Use Table 5–2 to answer the following questions:

   a. Country X has a growth rate of 3 percent, and Country Y has a growth rate of 4 percent. Assume that they both start off with equal incomes. How much richer will Country Y be after twenty years? After fifty years?

   b. Assume that Country H has twice the income per capita of Country K. Country H is growing at 3 percent, and Country K is growing at 4 percent. Will Country K ever catch up? If so, when?

3. During a given interval, a nation's overall productivity grows at a compounded rate of 2 percent. Its population growth rate and degree of labor-force participation do not change over this time span. The nation accumulates new capital at a compounded rate of growth of 1 percent, and the coefficient governing the proportionate increase in real GDP production in response to a proportionate rise in the amount of capital is equal to 0.3. What is the compound growth rate of real GDP during this interval?

4. A nation's rate of economic growth in 2003 was 5 percent. It accumulated capital at a rate of 5 percent and added to its employment of labor at a rate of 5 percent. The proportionate increase in real GDP in response to a proportionate increase in capital was 0.2, and the proportionate rise in real GDP following a proportionate increase in labor was 0.8. What was the growth in the overall productivity of labor and capital during 2003?

Before the Test

Test your understanding of the material covered in this chapter by taking the Chapter 5 interactive quiz at **http://macro.swcollege.com**.

Online Application

As discussed in this chapter, growth in productivity is a key factor determining a nation's overall economic growth. This application helps you to perform your own evaluation of the factors contributing to U.S. growth.

macroXtra!

Log on to the MacroXtra Web site now http://macroxtra.swcollege.com for additional learning resources such as practice quizzes, Interactive Key Graphs, readings, and additional economic applications.

Internet URL: http://stats.bls.gov/news.release/prod3.toc.htm

Title: *Bureau of Labor Statistics: Multifactor Productivity*

Navigation: Begin at the home page of the Bureau of Labor Statistics (http://stats.bls.gov). Under the heading, "Economic News Releases," click on "Multifactor Productivity Trends." Then click on "Summary of Methods" for the most recent available year.

Application: Read the report and answer the following questions:

1. What does multifactor productivity measure? Based on your reading of this chapter, how does multifactor productivity relate to the determination of economic growth?

2. Click on *Manufacturing industries: Multifactor productivity trends.* According to these data, which industries have exhibited the greatest productivity growth in recent years? Which industries have shown the least productivity growth?

For Group Study and Analysis: Divide the class into three groups to examine multifactor productivity data for the private business sector, the private nonfarm business sector, and the manufacturing sector. (Be sure to tell each group to read the "Sources and footnotes" discussion following the multifactor productivity tables so that they will know how the sectors are defined.) Have each group identify periods when multifactor productivity growth was particularly fast or slow. Then compare notes. Does the sector one looks at make a big difference when evaluating periods of largest and smallest growth in multifactor productivity?

Selected References and Further Reading

Aaronson, Daniel, and Kenneth Housinger. "The Impact of Technology on Displacement and Reemployment." Federal Reserve Bank of Chicago *Economic Perspectives* 23 (Second Quarter 1999): 14–30.

Federal Reserve Bank of Kansas City. *Policies for Long-Run Economic Growth.* 1992.

Filardo, Andrew. "Has the Productivity Trend Steepened in the 1990s?" Federal Reserve Bank of Kansas City *Economic Review,* Fourth Quarter 1995, pp. 41–59.

Gould, David, and Roy Ruffin. "What Determines Economic Growth?" Federal Reserve Bank of Dallas *Economic Review,* Second Quarter 1993, pp. 25–40.

Greenwood, Jeremy, "The Third Industrial Revolution: Technology, Productivity, and Income Equality." Federal Reserve Bank of Cleveland *Economic Review* 35 (Second Quarter 1999): 2–12.

Ireland, Peter. "Two Perspectives on Growth and Taxes." Federal Reserve Bank of Richmond *Economic Review,* Winter 1994, pp. 1–18.

Kozicki, Sharon. "The Productivity Growth Slowdown: Diverging Trends in the Manufacturing and Service Sectors." Federal Reserve Bank of Kansas City *Economic Review* 81 (First Quarter 1997): 31–46.

Romer, Paul. "Increasing Returns and Economic Growth." *Journal of Political Economy* 95 (October 1986): 1002–1037.

Solow, Robert. "A Contribution to the Theory of Economic Growth." *Quarterly Journal of Economics* 70 (February 1956): 65–94.

Stiroh, Kevin. "What Drives Productivity Growth?" Federal Reserve Bank of New York *Economic Policy Review,* March 2001, pp. 37–59.

Stiroh. Kevin. "Investment in Information Technology: Productivity Payoffs for U.S. Industries." Federal Reserve Bank of New York *Current Issues in Economics and Finance,* 7 (June 2001).

Webb, Roy. "National Productivity Statistics." Federal Reserve Bank of Richmond *Economic Quarterly* 84 (Winter 1998): 45–64.

Unit III

Keynesian and Monetarist Macroeconomic Perspectives

The Keynesian Revolution and a New Tradition

The Great Depression of the 1930s did much to make classical economics appear less useful, if not invalidated. Worldwide levels of prices and wages fell significantly during the Depression, and so did output and labor employment. In the United States, real national income fell by about 25 percent between 1929 and 1933, and the unemployment rate rose to nearly 17 percent of the labor force in the depths of the Depression years.

Led by the British economist John Maynard Keynes, economists of the post-Depression years sought to establish a new tradition of thought about how the economy functions and about what role monetary and fiscal policies play in influencing aggregate output, employment, expenditures, and prices. According to this new tradition, capitalistic economies were not self-regulating. Instead, they were plagued by problems of insufficiently flexible wages and prices and incomplete information.

Addressing these problems, Keynes and his followers contended, required active governmental stabilization policies to assure attainment of full employment. Indeed, in its most extreme form, this new "Keynesian" tradition of thought turned the classical dictum, "Supply creates its own demand," upside down to "Demand creates its own supply."

It is not an overstatement to regard much economic policymaking during the post–World War II period, especially from the late 1950s through the late 1970s, as a social experiment in *demand management,* a term Keynesian economists used to describe the use of fiscal and monetary policies to "fine-tune" the economy's total level of expenditures. Whether this experiment was successful is a topic of continued debate. A central issue of this debate is the *Phillips curve,* a negative relationship between the inflation rate and the unemployment rate predicted by Keynesian theory.

One group that raised serious doubts about the policy implications of the Keynesian perspective was the *monetarists.* These economists accepted the short-run implications of a few specific aspects of the Keynesian theory. In contrast to the Keynesian focus on the alleged benefits of fiscal-policy-centered demand management, however, the monetarists emphasized a role for monetary policy actions as the main determinants of real output and employment in the short run and of the price level in the long run. A key monetarist prediction, which has appeared to receive some support from actual experience, is that an inverse relationship between inflation and unemployment should at best be a short-run phenomenon. According to the monetarist view, in the long run the unemployment rate is determined independently of the inflation rate.

Business Cycles and Short-Run Macroeconomics—

Essentials of the Keynesian System

6

FUNDAMENTAL ISSUES

1. What are business cycles, and what are their key features?

2. What are the key relationships implied by the circular flow of income and expenditures?

3. What are the components of aggregate desired expenditures in the basic Keynesian model?

4. How is equilibrium real income determined in the basic Keynesian model, and how does this theory explain short-run business cycles?

5. How is the equilibrium trade balance determined?

During the summer of 2000, the market interest rate for three-month U.S. Treasury bills fell below the interest rate for ten-year Treasury bonds for the first time since 1989. This relatively uncommon event set off alarm bells among economists. In years past, when interest rates on short-maturity financial instruments fell below interest rates on longer-maturity instruments, business downturns often occurred sometime within the next six to eighteen months.

More alarm bells sounded in late 2000 when businesses that specialize in supplying raw materials and components reported slowing deliveries, which was also consistent with drops in new orders by manufacturers. In addition, average prices in the stock market began to fall. Soon economic forecasters began raising the probability that an economic downturn was in the offing. Sure enough, by the spring of 2001 a broad U.S. economic slowdown had begun.

Economists often regard movements in the difference between long- and short-term interest rates, supplier deliveries, manufacturers' orders, and stock prices as *leading indicators* of future swings in output and employment. In this chapter you will learn how economists classify cyclical patterns of economic activity, and you will also consider a traditional macroeconomic theory of why we observe these patterns.

From the Long Run to the Short Run: Business Cycles

A nation's rate of economic growth determines the future standard of living of its citizens. Typically, however, a nation's citizens care more about their living standards *today* than about their well-being down the road. To at least some extent, people typically *discount* the future, meaning that they place less weight on possible future outcomes relative to events that affect them in the present. As a result, although people recognize that economic choices they make today will affect their lives in future years, they tend to care more about how those choices influence their lives right now.

A single parent of two young children, for instance, certainly would be pleased if her real income prospects would grow at a compounded rate of 6 percent over the next twenty years instead of at the current U.S. average real per capita income growth rate of 2.7 percent. If business conditions this month have been so poor, however, that her employer has cut back on production and placed her on a long-term layoff from her full-time job, differences in long-term growth rates become purely academic issues. The issue in her mind this month is not her income prospects twenty years from now, but her ability to earn sufficient income to feed, clothe, and provide supervision for her children during the coming weeks and months.

Business Cycles

This natural human concern about current economic prospects is why people typically worry about fluctuations in their real incomes. Fluctuations in aggregate real income relative to its long-run growth path are **business cycles.** Figure 6–1 illustrates some key concepts associated with a single complete business cycle. The dashed line in the figure shows a hypothetical growth path for **natural GDP,** or the level of real GDP along the long-run growth path that the economy would tend to follow in the absence of cyclical fluctuations. The solid curve is a hypothetical growth path for *actual* GDP, which fluctuates over time.

RECESSIONS AND BUSINESS CYCLE TROUGHS   When actual real GDP declines, the economy is said to be in a phase in the business cycle known as a **recession.** The National Bureau of Economic Research defines a recession as a period of at least two consecutive quarters in which real GDP falls.

At the low point of a recession, actual real GDP is at its lowest point relative to its natural path, meaning that the downward vertical distance between the natural GDP growth path and the actual growth path reaches its maximum size for the cycle. This point is called the **trough** of the business cycle. At the trough, actual real GDP may be well below the economy's

BUSINESS CYCLE: Fluctuations in aggregate real income above or below its long-run growth path.

NATURAL GDP: The level of real GDP that is consistent with the economy's natural rate of growth.

RECESSION: A decline in real GDP lasting at least two consecutive quarters, which can cause real GDP to fall below its long-run, natural level.

TROUGH: The point along a business cycle at which real GDP is at its lowest level relative to the long-run natural GDP level.

Figure 6–1   A Hypothetical Business Cycle

At a business cycle trough, actual real GDP is at its lowest point relative to the long-run growth path of real GDP, so the downward vertical distance between long-run and actual real GDP levels reaches its largest size over the cycle. The period in which real GDP declines toward this trough is a recession. Beyond the trough, actual real GDP rises back toward and beyond its long-run growth path until it reaches its peak for the cycle. This period is called a business cycle expansion. At the peak of the expansion, the upward vertical distance between the long-run real GDP growth path and the actual growth path reaches its maximum size.

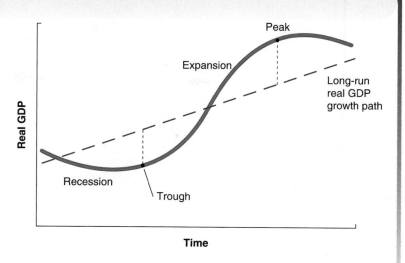

natural level. If such a significant recession and trough are particularly long lasting, then economists say that the economy experiences a severe recession, or a **depression.** Although economists often disagree about when recessions are sufficiently severe for this term to apply, all agree that a depression occurred in the United States during the 1930s.

EXPANSIONS AND BUSINESS CYCLE PEAKS   When actual real GDP begins to rise again, the economy enters the **expansion** phase of the business cycle. At the point where actual real GDP rises to its highest level relative to natural GDP, the business cycle is at its **peak.** Then the cycle begins anew.

Actual business cycles are not as simple as the one illustrated in Figure 6–1. The actual path of real GDP typically is much less smooth than the hypothetical path shown in the figure, and the durations of expansions and recessions are rarely of equal length. Table 6–1 on the following page tabulates the durations between troughs and peaks of the twenty-two business cycles that the United States has experienced since 1899. As the table indicates, the lengths of expansion and recession phases of business cycles have varied considerably.

Unemployment and the Business Cycle

Business cycles entail movements in aggregate GDP that have implications for all of us. When business cycle recessions cause more people to lose their jobs, as in our earlier example, the effects can hit especially hard. In contrast, expansions can pave the way to brighter futures for many families as they bring about an overall reduction in unemployment.

DEPRESSION: An especially severe recession.

EXPANSION: The period during a business cycle when actual GDP begins to rise, perhaps even above its natural, long-run level.

PEAK: The point along a business cycle at which real GDP is at its highest level relative to its long-run, natural level.

On the Web

Where can you find out when the National Bureau of Economic Research has determined that a recession is under way? The answer is to visit the NBER's home page at http://www.nber.org, where you can click on "Business Cycle Dates" under the heading "Data."

Table 6–1   Business Cycle Expansions and Recessions in the United States

Peak	Trough	Peak	Duration in Months* Recession	Expansion	Cycle
June 1899	December 1900	September 1902	18	21	39
September 1902	August 1904	May 1907	23	33	56
May 1907	June 1908	January 1910	13	19	32
January 1910	January 1912	January 1913	24	12	36
January 1913	December 1914	August 1918	23	44	67
August 1918	March 1919	January 1920	7	10	17
January 1920	July 1921	May 1923	18	22	40
May 1923	July 1924	October 1926	14	27	41
October 1926	November 1927	August 1929	13	21	34
August 1929	March 1933	May 1937	43	50	93
May 1937	June 1938	February 1945	13	80	93
February 1945	October 1945	November 1948	8	37	45
November 1948	October 1949	July 1953	11	45	56
July 1953	May 1954	August 1957	10	39	49
August 1957	April 1958	April 1960	8	24	32
April 1960	February 1961	December 1969	10	106	116
December 1969	November 1970	November 1973	11	36	47
November 1973	March 1975	January 1980	16	58	74
January 1980	July 1980	July 1981	6	12	18
July 1981	November 1982	July 1990	16	92	108
July 1990	March 1991	March 2001	8	120	128
March 2001	May 2002				

*Cycles are measured from peak to peak.
SOURCES: National Bureau of Economic Research; *Survey of Current Business*; authors' estimates.

macro**xtra!**
Economic
Applications

Has the U.S. unemployment rate recently been rising or falling? Take a look at movements in U.S. unemployment via EconData Online. http://macroxtra.swcollege.com

UNEMPLOYMENT RATE: The percentage of the civilian labor force that is unemployed.

THE UNEMPLOYMENT RATE   To track the extent of aggregate unemployment in the U.S. economy, the government tabulates the **unemployment rate,** which is simply the percentage of the civilian labor force that is unemployed. Terminology is important here: The civilian labor force consists of all individuals sixteen to sixty-five years of age who are not in the military, confined to an institution such as a hospital, or enrolled in school full-time and who either have a job or are actively seeking a job. The number of people in the civilian labor force who are unemployed includes all who are not working, yet are available for and actively seeking a job. People who are not employed but who also are not actively looking for work are not included in either the civilian labor force or the ranks of the unemployed. Such *discouraged workers* are not counted in calculations of the unemployment rate.

It is important to understand that the official unemployment rate is an *estimate.* The government does not calculate the entire labor force. On behalf of the Bureau of Labor Statistics, the Bureau of the Census conducts a monthly *Current Population Survey* covering 60,000 households in about 2,000 counties and cities across the fifty states and the District of Columbia.

The Bureau of Labor Statistics uses the information from this monthly survey to calculate its estimates of the size of the labor force and of the number of people in the labor force who are unemployed. It then uses these estimates to calculate the unemployment rate.

BUSINESS CYCLES AND THE UNEMPLOYMENT RATE   The unemployment rate varies systematically across business cycles, as Figure 6–2 shows. Recessions, which are the shaded periods in the figure, always are accompanied by higher unemployment rates. During expansion phases of business cycles, in contrast, unemployment rates tend to decline.

Economists identify three components of the unemployed portion of the civilian labor force. One is **frictional unemployment,** which refers to the portion of the labor force consisting of people who are qualified for gainful employment but are temporarily out of work. They may be in this situation because they recently quit a job to accept another job that will begin in a few weeks.

Another component of unemployment is **structural unemployment.** This refers to the portion of the civilian labor force made up of people who would like to be gainfully employed but lack skills and other attributes necessary to obtain a job. The duration of unemployment for these individuals can stretch into months or perhaps even years.

As we shall discuss in more detail in Chapter 11, most economists consider the ratio of those who are frictionally and structurally unemployed to the civilian labor force to be the **natural rate of unemployment,** or the unemployment rate that would exist if the economy could stay on its long-run

FRICTIONAL UNEMPLOYMENT: The portion of total unemployment arising from the fact that a number of workers are between jobs at any given time.

STRUCTURAL UNEMPLOYMENT: The portion of total unemployment resulting from a poor match of workers' abilities and skills with current needs of employers.

NATURAL RATE OF UNEMPLOYMENT: The portion of the unemployment rate that is accounted for by frictional and structural unemployment.

137

CHAPTER 6   Business Cycles and Short-Run Macroeconomics—Essentials of the Keynesian System

Figure 6–2   Unemployment Rates and Phases of the Business Cycle

The cyclical component of the unemployment rate increases during business cycle downturns. As a result, the overall unemployment rate typically rises during recessions (the shaded intervals).

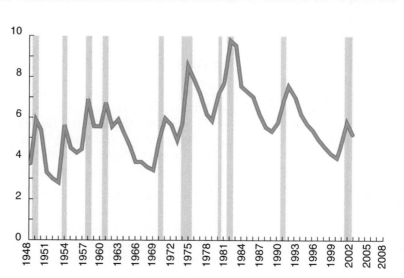

SOURCES: *Economic Report of the President,* 2002; National Bureau of Economic Research; *Economic Indicators* (various issues).

CYCLICAL UNEMPLOYMENT: The portion of total unemployment resulting from business cycle fluctuations.

growth path. The variations in the overall unemployment rate shown in Figure 6–2 arise from changes in the third category of unemployment, called **cyclical unemployment.** This is the portion of the civilian labor force composed of those who lose their jobs because of business cycle fluctuations.

FUNDAMENTAL ISSUE #1

What are business cycles, and what are their key features? Business cycles are fluctuations in real income above or below the level that is consistent with the economy's long-run growth. Recessions occur when real income falls below its long-run level, and expansions take place when real income rises back to or even above its long-run level. Although the existence of frictional and structural unemployment implies that there is a natural unemployment rate, the overall unemployment rate has a cyclical component that rises during recessions and falls during expansions.

Keynes's Critique of the Classical Theory

In a 1930 radio broadcast, the British economist John Maynard Keynes surveyed the severe recession the United Kingdom was experiencing and concluded, "If we just sit tight there will be still more than a million men unemployed six months or a year hence. That is why I feel that a radical policy of some kind is worth trying, even if there are risks about it." The "radical policy" that Keynes advocated entailed a departure from the policy prescriptions of the classical macroeconomic model that we presented in Chapters 3 and 4. Rather than keep government deficits low and maintain steady money growth, Keynes advocated active governmental policies to reduce the high cyclical unemployment rates of the 1930s. Indeed, Keynes proposed a broad abandonment of many aspects of classical theory and in its place offered a different way of looking at macroeconomics. This approach became known as "Keynesian macroeconomics."

The Potential Shortsightedness of Long-Run Analysis

As a student, Keynes had learned all the elements of the classical theory. He did not advocate tossing aside all its features. The problem, he argued, was that the classical theory did not do a good job of explaining short-run movements in real GDP away from its long-run growth path. To Keynes, classical theory did not satisfactorily explain the business cycles that affected so many lives in the near term.

SHORT-RUN LABOR MARKET RIGIDITIES Keynes felt that the classical theory of the labor market was especially defective. According to that theory, as you learned in Chapter 3, the labor supply schedule is upward sloping. Workers supply more labor services as the real wage rises and fewer labor services as the real wage falls. In either circumstance, the adjustment of the quantity of labor supplied to changes in real wages would bring about a new labor market equilibrium in which both workers and firms were satisfied with the prevailing real wage.

According to Keynes, actual observations did not support this prediction of the classical labor market model. Real wages in Britain, the United States, and elsewhere declined during the 1930s, yet millions of prospective workers could not find jobs. Furthermore, in Keynes's view the real wage did not fall as quickly or as much as classical theory predicted. Both of these observations of short-run labor market adjustments induced Keynes to reject the classical theory of labor supply in favor of an alternative theory.

MONEY AND FINANCIAL MARKETS   Keynes also questioned key aspects of the classical theory of money and financial markets. Recall from Chapter 3 that a change in the quantity of money by a government or central bank should, according to the quantity theory, have a direct effect on the aggregate demand for goods and services. Keynes argued that the quantity theory overstated the extent to which monetary policy actions influence aggregate demand.

The problem, Keynes contended, was that classical theory ignored the fact that money is an asset that is part of a person's financial wealth along with bonds and stocks. Whenever people revise their bond or stock holdings based on speculations about interest-rate movements, the resulting reshuffling of financial assets entails short-run changes in desired money holdings. Consequently, a person's demand for money ought to depend on the interest rate. Classical theory did not give sufficient consideration to this relationship between desired money holdings and the interest rate, according to Keynes. This led him to develop a new theory of money demand.

CONSUMPTION, SAVING, AND INVESTMENT   Finally, Keynes questioned the classical model's view of the roles of consumption, saving, and investment. As you learned in Chapters 3 and 4, in the classical theory output is determined on the supply side, and then its division among households, firms, and the government is a distributional issue. The real interest rate adjusts in the loanable funds market to equate saving with the sum of investment and the government's deficit. The amount that households do not save (or pay in taxes) then is available for current consumption of goods and services.

To Keynes, this view reversed the proper order for understanding short-run fluctuations in real GDP. Key sources of such fluctuations, it seemed to him, were year-to-year variations in household consumption expenditures and investment spending by firms. For this reason, Keynes formulated a new theory of aggregate demand with consumption and investment as the centerpieces.

The Short-Run Focus: The Circular Flow of Income and Expenditures

As you will see in later chapters, many economists today disagree with Keynes's notion that the classical model was seriously flawed. Nevertheless, Keynes's reformulation of macroeconomic theory has had dramatic effects on the way that economists think about macroeconomics today. For this reason, it is important to understand how Keynes's approach to macroeconomic analysis differed from the classical theory.

REAL NET TAXES: The amount of real taxes paid to the government by households, net of transfer payments.

TRANSFER PAYMENTS: Governmentally managed income redistributions.

REAL CONSUMPTION: The real amount of spending by households on domestically produced goods and services.

REAL IMPORTS: The real flow of spending by households on goods and services produced by firms in other countries.

REAL SAVING: The amount of income that households save through financial markets.

INCOME IDENTITY: An identity that states that real national income equals the sum of real household consumption, real household saving, real net taxes, and real imports.

REAL REALIZED INVESTMENT SPENDING: Actual real expenditures by firms in the product markets.

We will start where Keynes began—with the circular flow of income and expenditures, which we discussed in Chapter 2. The flow chart in Figure 6–3 provides a more detailed version of the circular flow diagram you saw there. This figure shows financial flows as well as flows of taxes and expenditures by the government. Despite the greater detail, one key point is the same:

The value of the flow of income to households must equal the value of the output produced by firms.

Conceptually, if we abstract from depreciation and indirect business taxes and transfers that distinguish their definitions in the national income accounts, real income and real output are the same.

THE INCOME IDENTITY   As Figure 6–3 indicates, households use their earnings of real income, denoted y, for four purposes. First, they use part of their real income to pay taxes to the government. **Real net taxes,** denoted t, are the total taxes that households pay net of any **transfer payments,** which are income redistributions that the government manages through programs such as Social Security, unemployment compensation, and so on. Hence, real net taxes are the funds that the government actually has available from total tax proceeds to purchase goods and services for its own use.

Second, households may spend some of their real income on goods and services produced in *domestic* markets, or markets for goods and services produced in their home country. Such domestic consumption spending is called **real consumption,** denoted c. Of course, households may also purchase goods and services produced in other nations. This is real import consumption or, more simply, **real imports,** denoted im.

Finally, households may allocate any untaxed or unspent portion of their real income earnings to **real saving,** denoted s. Households save by purchasing financial claims issued in the economy's financial markets.

Because households use their total real income in these four ways, real income must, by definition, equal the sum of real consumption, real saving, real net taxes, and real imports:

$$y \equiv c + s + t + im.$$

We use the three-bar equality symbol to indicate that this relation is a truism, or identity. Because it is a truism for how real income must be allocated in the circular flow, economists call it the **income identity.**

THE PRODUCT IDENTITY   As the classical model emphasized, owners of business firms borrow a portion of real household saving by issuing financial claims, such as stocks and bonds, in the financial markets. The firms use these funds saved by households to finance purchases of capital goods, as well as other goods and services, from other firms. Firms may also use these funds to finance the maintenance of inventories of produced goods that they have not yet sold. Such actual real expenditures by firms constitute **real realized investment spending,** denoted i_r.

Any household saving that is not borrowed by firms is borrowed by the government, which issues bonds and other financial claims to households

Figure 6–3 Circular Flow of Income and Expenditures

Firms' earnings from goods and services produced and supplied through product markets ultimately flow to households, which own the firms and the factors of production. Households consume domestic goods and services, import foreign goods and services, save, and pay net taxes. The goods and services produced by firms are purchased by households, firms, the government, and foreign residents.

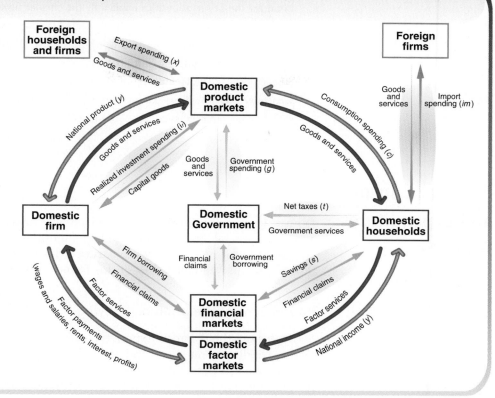

in exchange for the use of their saving. The government uses these funds to cover any deficit, which would be the difference between real government spending, g, and real net taxes, t.

Note that there are three sources of spending on goods sold in domestic product markets: household consumption, realized investment by firms, and government spending. In addition, foreign residents may purchase goods and services produced by domestic firms. These purchases from abroad are exports by domestic firms, so they constitute the nation's **real exports,** denoted x. Adding this final type of spending on the output produced by domestic firms yields the **product identity** for the domestic economy:

$$y \equiv c + i_r + g + x.$$

Because this relationship is a truism, we again use the three-bar equality symbol.

Keynes was not the first to recognize the identities that the circular flow implies—the classical economists were well aware of them. Keynes, however, used the identities extensively in his effort to understand the nature of the short-run variations in real income that business cycles generate.

REAL EXPORTS: The real value of goods and services produced by domestic firms and exported to other countries.

PRODUCT IDENTITY: An identity that states that real national product is the sum of real household consumption, real realized investment, real government spending, and real export spending.

FUNDAMENTAL ISSUE #2

What are the key relationships implied by the circular flow of income and expenditures?   We can infer two fundamental identities from the circular flow diagram. One is the income identity, which states that all real income is allocated to domestic consumption, saving, taxes, and import spending. The other is the product identity. This identity says that the real value of output of goods and services is equal to real expenditures on that output in the form of household consumption, business investment, government spending, and export spending by foreigners.

Aggregate Income and Expenditures from the Ground Up

Keynes viewed the flows among households, firms, and the government, and the national income and product identities that they imply, as the building blocks necessary to construct a foundation for macroeconomic theory. He analyzed each part of this foundation as a separate component.

Household Consumption and Saving

Because household consumption typically represents about two-thirds of total expenditures on goods and services, Keynesian theory emphasized its importance. The basic proposition of the Keynesian theory of household consumption is that the amount of such consumption depends positively upon **real disposable income,** or real income after taxes, denoted $y_d \equiv y - t$.

Note that we can rearrange the income identity, $y \equiv c + s + t + im$, by subtracting real net taxes, t, from both sides of the identity, which gives us $y - t \equiv c + s + im$. Thus, disposable income can be defined as $y_d \equiv c + s + im$. That is, households can allocate their after-tax income to consumption of domestic goods and services, saving, or purchases of imported goods and services.

DISPOSABLE INCOME IDENTITIES   Because disposable income by definition is equal to $y_d \equiv c + s + im$, it follows that a *change in* disposable income must equal

$$\Delta y_d \equiv \Delta c + \Delta s + \Delta im.$$

Thus, households use any additional disposable income for additional consumption, additional saving, and additional spending on imports. If we divide both sides of this identity by Δy_d, we obtain the following relationship:

$$\frac{\Delta y_d}{\Delta y_d} = 1 \equiv \frac{\Delta c}{\Delta y_d} + \frac{\Delta s}{\Delta y_d} + \frac{\Delta im}{\Delta y_d}.$$

This disposable income identity says that the sum of a change in consumption resulting from a change in disposable income ($\Delta c/\Delta y_d$), a change in saving resulting from a change in disposable income ($\Delta s/\Delta y_d$), and a

macroxtra!
Economic
Applications

What is the current level of U.S. real disposable income per capita? Take a look at EconData Online.
http://macroxtra.swcollege.com

Real Disposable Income: A household's real after-tax income.

change in real imports resulting from a change in disposable income $(\Delta im/\Delta y_d)$ must be equal to 1.

Keynes called the first ratio on the right side of this identity, $\Delta c/\Delta y_d$, the **marginal propensity to consume (MPC),** or the change in real consumption that is induced by a change in real disposable income. For instance, a value of 0.85 for $\Delta c/\Delta y_d$ means that a one-dollar increase in real disposable income will induce households to increase their real consumption of domestically produced goods and services by 85 cents.

Keynes referred to the second ratio, $\Delta s/\Delta y_d$, as the **marginal propensity to save (MPS),** which is the change in real saving caused by a change in real disposable income. A value of 0.10 for $\Delta s/\Delta y_d$ means that a one-dollar rise in real disposable income will induce households to increase their real saving by 10 cents.

Finally, $\Delta im/\Delta y_d$ is the **marginal propensity to import (MPIM),** or the additional spending on imported goods and services by households. If $\Delta im/\Delta y_d$ is equal to 0.05, then each additional dollar of real disposable income to households will induce them to spend 5 cents on additional imported goods and services.

The identity says that all three marginal propensities must sum to 1, or $MPC + MPS + MPIM \equiv 1$. Consequently, the 85 cents of each additional dollar of real disposable income used for domestic real consumption, the 10 cents of each additional dollar of real disposable income allocated to saving, and the 5 cents of each new dollar of real disposable income spent on imports must sum to the total 1 dollar of additional real disposable income.

Because real disposable income is identically equal to $y_d \equiv c + s + im$, we can divide both sides by y_d to get another disposable income identity:

$$\frac{y_d}{y_d} = 1 \equiv \frac{c}{y_d} + \frac{s}{y_d} + \frac{im}{y_d}.$$

Keynes called the first ratio on the right side of this identity, c/y_d, or the ratio of real consumption to real disposable income, the **average propensity to consume (APC).** He termed the second ratio, s/y_d, or the ratio of real saving to real disposable income, the **average propensity to save (APS).** The third ratio, im/y_d, or imports divided by disposable income, is the **average propensity to import (APIM).** Again, because households may only spend disposable income on domestic goods, allocate it to saving, or spend it on imports, these average propensities also must sum to 1, or $APC + APS + APIM \equiv 1$.

THE SAVING FUNCTION In the Keynesian theory of household saving, a key determinant of households' annual saving flow is their disposable income. The basic idea is that as disposable income rises, households can increase their saving. This notion is captured by the function

$$s = -s_0 + (MPS \times y_d).$$

As panel (a) of Figure 6–4 on page 144 shows, this is a straight-line function in its intercept-slope form, where $-s_0$ is the intercept and MPS is the slope. This *saving function* says that aggregate household saving is equal to a constant amount, $-s_0$, plus an amount that depends on disposable income, $MPS \times y_d$. Recall that $MPS \equiv \Delta s/\Delta y_d$, which is the slope of the saving

MARGINAL PROPENSITY TO CONSUME (MPC): The additional consumption caused by an increase in disposable income; the change in consumption spending divided by the corresponding change in disposable income; the slope of the consumption function.

MARGINAL PROPENSITY TO SAVE (MPS): The additional saving caused by an increase in disposable income; the change in saving divided by the corresponding change in disposable income; the slope of the saving function.

MARGINAL PROPENSITY TO IMPORT (MPIM): The additional import expenditures stimulated by an increase in disposable income; the change in import spending divided by the corresponding change in disposable income; the slope of the import function.

AVERAGE PROPENSITY TO CONSUME (APC): Real household consumption of domestically produced goods and services divided by real disposable income; the portion of disposable income allocated to consumption spending.

AVERAGE PROPENSITY TO SAVE (APS): Real household saving divided by real disposable income; the portion of disposable income allocated to saving.

AVERAGE PROPENSITY TO IMPORT (APIM): Real household spending on imports divided by real disposable income; the portion of disposable income allocated to spending on imported goods and services.

Figure 6–4 The Saving, Import, and Consumption Functions

Panel (a) displays the saving function, in which the intercept $-s_0$ represents autonomous dissaving. The slope of the saving function, $MPS = \Delta s/\Delta y_d$, is the marginal propensity to save. Panel (b) shows the import function. The intercept of this function, im_0, is the amount of autonomous imports, and the slope, $MPIM = \Delta im/\Delta y_d$, is the marginal propensity to import. Finally, panel (c) shows the consumption function. Because real consumption of domestic goods and services, c, is equal to disposable income less saving and import expenditures, the intercept of the consumption function is $s_0 - im_0$, which is autonomous consumption. The consumption function's slope, MPS, is equal to $1 - MPS - MPIM$, or one minus the marginal propensity to save and the marginal propensity to import.

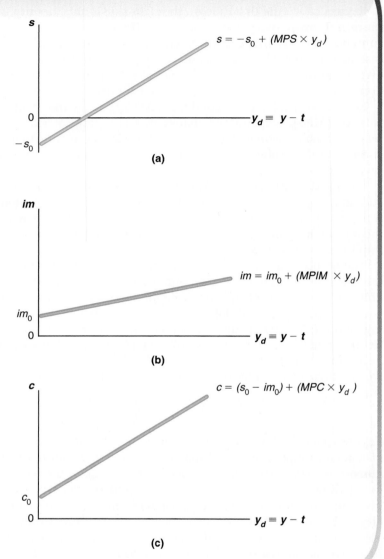

function. Thus, the slope of the saving function tells us how much real saving rises with additional real disposable income, y_d. Note that the constant intercept of the saving function, $-s_0$, is a negative number. The reason is that if disposable income were equal to zero, then households would need to draw down existing wealth to buy domestic and foreign goods. For instance, suppose that you had to make it through a semester of college with no disposable income and without any outside assistance from family members. Undoubtedly, you would have to withdraw funds from bank accounts and other accumulated wealth to buy books, food, and housing.

Hence, the basic Keynesian theory of household saving says that real domestic saving has two components. One is *induced saving, MPS* $\times y_d$, which is the saving brought about by the receipt of disposable income. The other component is *autonomous dissaving,* $-s_0$, or the amount by which households wish to draw from their wealth to make purchases of domestic goods and services and foreign imports.

THE IMPORT FUNCTION   Import expenditures also consist of autonomous and induced components. This is captured by using the straight-line *import function:*

$$im = im_0 + (MPIM \times y_d).$$

Here im_0 denotes *autonomous import spending,* which is the amount of spending on imports by households irrespective of their total disposable income. As panel (b) of Figure 6–4 shows, im_0 is the constant intercept of the import function. The amount $MPIM \times y_d$ is *induced import spending.* This is the level of households' spending on imports that is related directly to their earnings of disposable income where the marginal propensity to import, $MPIM \equiv \Delta im/\Delta y_d$, is the slope of the import function.

The import function slopes upward. This means that growth in disposable income in the households' home country will induce a rise in imports. Recall from Chapter 2 that a nation's trade balance is exports minus imports. Consequently, if exports are unchanged, a rise in a nation's real disposable income causes its trade balance to decline. We shall return to this issue later in the chapter.

Note that in this chapter we shall abstract from another important determinant of desired import spending, which is the price of foreign goods relative to the price of domestic goods. A key factor influencing this relative price is the rate of exchange between foreign and domestic currency. To keep our basic Keynesian model as simple as possible for now, however, we shall postpone consideration of this issue until Chapter 9.

THE CONSUMPTION FUNCTION   Finally, we shall consider the consumption function, $c = c_0 + (MPC \times y_d)$, where the slope of the consumption function is equal to $MPC \equiv \Delta c/\Delta y_d$. The intercept, as shown in panel (c) of Figure 6–4, is c_0.

By definition, $y_d \equiv c + s + im$, so household disposable income is split among consumption expenditures on domestically produced output, saving, and import spending. This means that the saving and import functions automatically imply a domestic consumption function. To see this, let's substitute the saving function, $s = -s_0 + (MPS \times y_d)$, and the import function, $im = im_0 + (MPIM \times y_d)$, into the disposable income identity to get

$$y_d = c + s + im,$$

or

$$y_d = c - s_0 + (MPS \times y_d) + im_0 + (MPIM \times y_d).$$

Note that we now use an equals sign instead of a three-bar identity symbol because our saving and import functions are hypotheses that may or may not be true. If we rearrange the last equation and solve for c, we obtain

$$c = (s_0 - im_0) + [(1 - MPS - MPIM) \times y_d].$$

Thus, it must be true that **autonomous consumption,** the amount of households' domestic consumption expenditures that would take place irrespective of their disposable income, is $c_0 \equiv s_0 - im_0$, or autonomous dissaving allocated to domestic consumption less autonomous import spending. Furthermore, the marginal propensity to consume is $MPC \equiv 1 - MPS - MPIM$. Note that adding $MPS + MPIM$ to both sides of this relationship implies that $MPC + MPS + MPIM = 1$. And so, as discussed earlier, the three marginal propensities sum to 1.

Investment Spending by Firms

The Keynesian theory of investment expenditures is based on the classical approach. As in the classical loanable funds theory, desired investment, which we shall assume takes place only domestically, depends negatively on the real interest rate, as shown in panel (a) of Figure 6–5. A decline in the real interest rate from r_r^0 to r_r^1 causes desired real investment spending to rise from i_0 to i_1. As you learned in Chapter 4, the real interest rate is equal to the nominal interest rate minus the expected inflation rate, so a fall in the real interest rate could take place because of a decline in the nominal interest rate or a rise in the expected inflation rate.

It is important to recognize the distinction between *desired* investment, *i,* and *realized* investment, i_r. The two can—and for short periods often do—deviate from one another. This occurs whenever firms experience unintended depletions or accumulations of inventories of finished goods, which are included in realized investment but were not desired by the firms. As we shall discuss shortly, such unplanned changes in inventories induce firms to vary their production and perform a key role in achieving an equilibrium flow of real income.

Panel (b) of Figure 6–5 shows another way that investment could rise from i_0 to i_1. Holding the real interest rate unchanged, the desired investment schedule itself could shift to the right, causing the same rise in desired investment. Keynes argued that such shifts in the desired investment schedule were commonplace and that they resulted from changes in firms' expectations of future profits. The rightward shift of the investment schedule in panel (b), for instance, could result from firms' general anticipation of higher profits in the future. This would induce the firms to increase both their total investment in capital goods, so as to expand future production, and their inventories of produced goods, which they would expect to sell in the near future.

Panel (c) of Figure 6–5 shows that, whether induced by a fall in the real interest rate or expectations of higher future profits, an increase in desired investment would cause investment to rise at any given level of aggregate income, y. Although some amount of investment is income induced, we shall assume for the sake of simplicity that investment is autonomous, or unrelated to income. Consequently, with investment measured along the vertical axis and real income measured along the horizontal axis, a rise in desired investment implies an upward shift in a horizontal desired invest-

Figure 6–5   Factors Causing Changes in Desired Investment

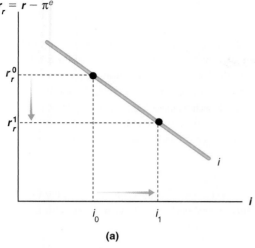

(a)

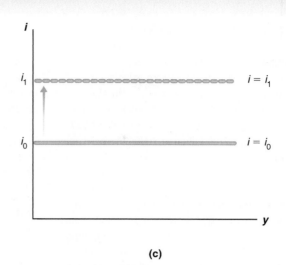

(c)

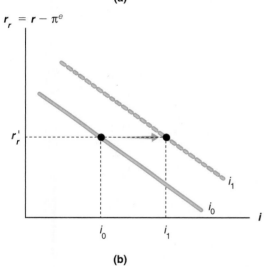

(b)

Panels (a) and (b) show two key factors that might induce an increase in desired real investment expenditures. In panel (a), a decline in the real interest rate, owing to a fall in the nominal rate of interest or a rise in anticipated inflation, causes a movement along the investment schedule graphed against the real interest rate. In panel (b), a shift occurs in the investment schedule itself, so a rise in desired investment will take place at any given real interest rate. Such a shift could arise from an increase in firms' expectations of future profitability from new investment. As panel (c) indicates, either cause of an increase in desired investment spending would result in an upward shift in the investment schedule graphed against real income.

ment schedule, from $i = i_0$ to $i = i_1$. (Since the 1990s, a big part of business investment has involved purchases of computing equipment; see on the next page *Management Notebook: Investing in Computing Power.*)

Government Spending and Taxation

A number of factors can influence the levels of government spending and taxation. How much a government spends may reflect its concern about national defense and law enforcement; its wish to maintain national parks, monuments, and buildings; or even purely political factors such as the desire to satisfy certain constituencies. We shall simplify considerably by

Investing in Computing Power

Business spending on computers is a component of equipment and software investment, which, in turn, is a large part of total fixed investment in the U.S. National Income and Product Accounts. As Figure 6–6 shows, business spending on computers increased from about $37 billion in 1987 to nearly $120 billion in 2000 before declining somewhat in the early 2000s. Business purchases of computers typically account for about 75 percent of all computer purchases. Households buy only about 17 percent of all computers, and the government buys the remaining 8 percent. Undoubtedly, a key factor motivating businesses, households, and the government to boost their purchases of computing equipment has been the 95 percent decline in the real price of computers—the average nominal price of computers relative to the overall price level—also shown in the figure.

All told, business purchases of computers now account for almost 9 percent of total nonresidential business fixed investment in the United States. Counting investment in computer software and communications technologies that link computers as well as investment in computing equipment, total investment in information technology now accounts for between 35 and 40 percent of aggregate business investment each year.

For Critical Analysis
What factors other than computer prices are likely to influence businesses' decisions about how much to invest in computers that they will use for a number of years?

Figure 6–6   U.S. Final Sales of Computers and the Real Price of Computers

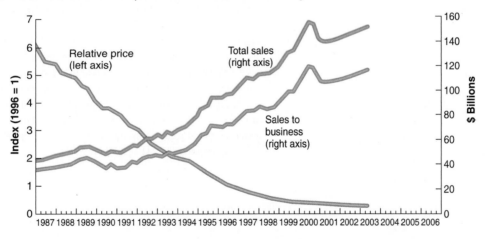

As the real price of computers has declined, sales of computers have increased. A large portion of these sales has been to companies and recorded as business investment.

SOURCES: Michael Pakko, "Accounting for Computers," Federal Reserve Bank of St. Louis *National Economic Trends,* May 2001; authors' estimates.

treating all these factors as beyond the scope of our theory and assuming that real government spending on domestic output is just equal to an autonomous amount, $g = g_0$. As panel (a) of Figure 6–7 shows, this means that the *government spending schedule* is horizontal. Suppose the government increases its spending on national defense or decides to build a new dam in West Virginia or an office building in Washington, D.C. Then the

Figure 6–7   The Government Spending and Net Tax Schedules

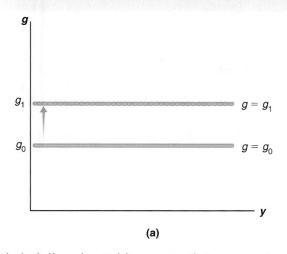

(a)

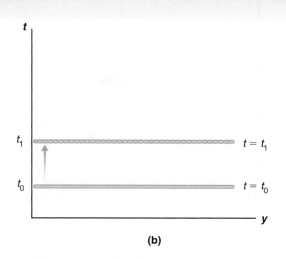

(b)

In the basic Keynesian model, we assume that government spending is autonomous, meaning that the amount of government spending does not vary with changes in the level of real income. Hence, the government spending schedule is horizontal, as shown in panel (a). An increase in government spending therefore causes an upward shift in this schedule. Likewise, in our basic model we assume that net taxes are autonomous, so the net tax schedule in panel (b) is also horizontal. An increase in net taxes results in an upward shift in this schedule.

government spending schedule will shift upward by the rise in spending, to $g = g_1$, where g_1 is the new, higher level of government expenditures.

Governments have a number of possible sources of net taxes, including income taxes, sales taxes, excise taxes, and the like. Because a government's income tax revenues depend on the level of income, net taxes realistically depend on aggregate real income. Nevertheless, we again shall keep things simple by assuming that net taxes are equal to a lump-sum, autonomous amount. (We shall consider how income taxes change the nature of the basic Keynesian model in Chapter 7.) Under this simplification, the net tax schedule also is horizontal, as shown in panel (b) of Figure 6–7. If the government increases net taxes from an amount $t = t_0$ to a larger amount $t = t_1$, then the net tax schedule will shift upward by the amount of the tax increase, as shown in Figure 6–7.

Spending on Exports

The final component of total spending in a nation's economy is the level of expenditures by foreign residents on the exports produced and sold by domestic firms. As we shall discuss briefly later in this chapter and in greater detail in Chapter 9, two key factors affect spending on a nation's exports. One is the real incomes of the nations whose residents purchase domestically produced goods. As other nations' incomes rise, their residents desire to purchase more domestic output. The other key factor influencing

On the Web

How much does the U.S. Congress expect that it will tax and spend during the next few years? To obtain the latest printout of the Joint Committee on Taxation's "Estimates of Tax Expenditures," go to http://www.house.gov/jct, and click where it says "Click Here to Continue." Then click on "JCT Publications" for the most recent year, and select "Estimates of Federal Tax Expenditures."

spending on a nation's exports is the rate of exchange between its domestic currency and the currencies of its trading partners. For instance, if the domestic currency *depreciates,* so that fewer units of foreign currency are required to obtain the domestic currency, then domestic exports become less expensive to foreigners, and they are likely to increase their spending on domestic exports.

Domestic income, y, has no effect on real exports, however. Consequently, the *export schedule* is horizontal, as shown in Figure 6–8. A rise in foreign nations' incomes or a depreciation of the domestic currency will cause exports to increase from an amount $x = x_0$ to a larger amount $x = x_1$. Thus, either type of change will cause the export schedule to shift upward, as shown in the figure.

Putting the Pieces Together: Aggregate Desired Expenditures

Total spending on domestically produced goods and services is the sum of household consumption spending, desired investment spending, government expenditures, and spending on domestic exports by residents of foreign nations. In terms of our notation, therefore, total expenditures on domestic output are equal to $c + i + g + x$.

Figure 6–9 shows how to add up these components of aggregate desired expenditures. Panel (a) sums up the purely autonomous components, which are desired investment spending, $i = i_0$, government spending, $g = g_0$, and spending on exports, $x = x_0$. This yields the horizontal schedule $i_0 + g_0 + x_0$ in panel (a).

Total spending on domestically produced goods and services also includes domestic consumption spending by households. In panel (b) of Figure 6–9, we again display the upward-sloping household consumption function, $c = c_0 + (MPC \times y_d)$. Note however, that we now recognize that disposable income, y_d, is equal to total real income, y, minus real net taxes, t.

Figure 6–8   The Export Schedule

Because foreign residents purchase domestic export goods, domestic income has no direct effect on export expenditures. Consequently, the export schedule is horizontal. If foreign incomes rise or the domestic currency's value depreciates, however, export spending will rise, causing an upward shift in the export schedule.

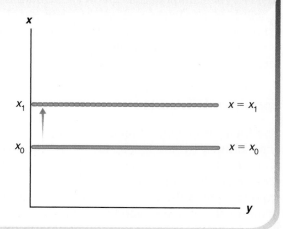

Figure 6–9   Deriving the Aggregate Expenditures Schedule

Adding together the autonomous levels of desired investment spending, government spending, and export expenditures yields the schedule $i_0 + g_0 + x_0$ in panel (a). Summing this amount with the level of consumption at each income level, given by the consumption function, yields the aggregate expenditures schedule $c + i + g + x$, displayed in panel (b).

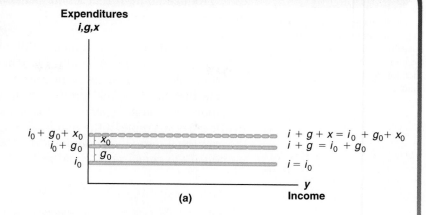

(a)

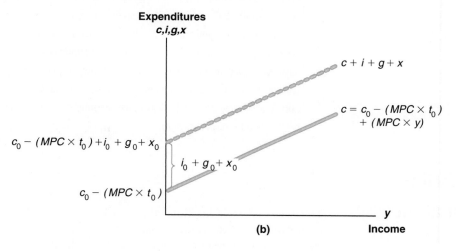

(b)

Hence, if t_0 is the current lump-sum amount of net taxes, we can substitute $y - t_0$ for y_d to get $c = c_0 + [MPC \times (y - t_0)]$. This implies that the consumption function is

$$c = c_0 - (MPC \times t_0) + (MPC \times y).$$

With total real income measured on the horizontal axis, the consumption function's intercept, $c_0 - (MPC \times t_0)$, takes into account the consumption-reducing effect of taxes. Its slope remains equal to the marginal propensity to consume.

At each level of income, we then add the vertical distance $i_0 + g_0 + x_0$ to the amount of consumption. This gives us the **aggregate expenditures schedule,** $c + i + g + x$. This schedule tells us how much households, firms, the government, and foreign residents combined will desire to spend on domestically produced output at any given level of domestic real income,

AGGREGATE EXPENDITURES SCHEDULE: A schedule that represents total desired expenditures by all the relevant sectors of the economy at any given level of real national income.

AGGREGATE NET AUTONOMOUS EXPENDITURES: The sum of autonomous consumption, autonomous investment, autonomous government spending, and autonomous export spending, all of which are independent of the level of national income in the basic Keynesian model.

y. Its intercept is **aggregate net autonomous expenditures,** or $c_0 - (MPC \times t_0) + i_0 + g_0 + x_0$. This is the total net amount of spending on domestically produced output that is independent of the current level of total real income.

Because we have constructed the aggregate expenditures schedule by adding a fixed vertical distance all along the consumption function, the slope of the aggregate expenditures schedule is equal to the consumption function's slope. This slope is the marginal propensity to consume. We shall assume that the marginal propensity to save and the marginal propensity to import are relatively small fractions, so that the MPC is a relatively large fraction. For example, if the marginal propensity to save is equal to 0.10 and the marginal propensity to import is equal to 0.08, then the marginal propensity to consume is equal to $1 - 0.10 - 0.08 = 0.82$.

FUNDAMENTAL ISSUE #3

What are the components of aggregate desired expenditures in the basic Keynesian model?   Aggregate desired expenditures are composed of household consumption on domestically produced goods and services, investment spending desired by firms, government spending, and export spending by foreigners. In the basic Keynesian model, we assume that desired investment, government spending and net taxes, and export spending are autonomous. Consumption spending, however, is positively related to disposable income. As a result, the aggregate expenditures schedule slopes upward.

Equilibrium
National Income

The detailed circular flow diagram in Figure 6–3 on page 141 depicts the relationships that must exist among the various components of total income and aggregate expenditures. While it tells us the direction of the overall flow of income and spending, the circular flow diagram does not tell us anything about the total *magnitude* of the flow. The flow of water along a riverbed, for instance, might run from east to west, but it could be either a trickle or a torrent. Likewise, the size of the flow of income to households that ultimately flows to firms in the form of expenditures on goods and services could be meager, implying a weak economy, or it could be large, implying a robust economy.

The *equilibrium* flow of real income is the level at which households, firms, the government, and foreign residents desire to purchase all real output that is produced and sold by domestic firms. In other words, in equilibrium, households, firms, the government, and foreign residents are satisfied with the actual flow of income and expenditures through the domestic economy. If the actual flow were to differ from the desired level, then households, firms, the government, and foreign residents would have an incentive to change their expenditures, which in turn would affect the total flow of spending and income. Therefore, in equilibrium there is no tendency for the flow of real income and expenditures to change from its current level.

Determining the Equilibrium Flow of Income and Expenditures

In light of this definition of equilibrium, we can define a nation's **equilibrium real income** as the real income level at which aggregate desired expenditures are equal to the real value of domestically produced output. The circular flow diagram tells us that the real value of output is equal to real income. Consequently, in equilibrium real income is equal to aggregate desired expenditures, or $y = c + i + g + x$.

THE INCOME-EXPENDITURE EQUILIBRIUM   Figure 6–10 depicts a schedule of all the possible combinations of real income and aggregate desired expenditures that can satisfy our definition of equilibrium. This schedule is a **45-degree line,** because it cuts in half the 90-degree angle formed by the coordinate axes on the diagram. At any point along this 45-degree line, the level of real income along the horizontal axis is equal to the level of aggregate desired expenditures along the vertical axis. This means that every point on the 45-degree line could, in principle, satisfy our definition of equilibrium.

Panel (a) of Figure 6–11 on the following page shows the determination of a single income-expenditure equilibrium. This figure combines Figures 6–9 and 6–10. The aggregate expenditures schedule, $c + i + g + x$, is taken from Figure 6–9. It displays all combinations of real income and desired expenditures by households, firms, the government, and foreign residents. As just discussed, the 45-degree line (Figure 6–10) displays all combinations of real income levels that could be equal to aggregate desired expenditures. Hence, the point at which the two schedules intersect is the single point that satisfies the equilibrium condition $y = c + i + g + x$. The equilibrium level of real income at this point is denoted y_e.

EQUILIBRIUM REAL INCOME: The real income level at which aggregate desired expenditures are equal to the real value of domestic output.

45-DEGREE LINE: A line that cuts in half the 90-degree angle of the coordinate axes on a diagram relating real income to aggregate desired expenditures; every point on the 45-degree line could, in principle, be a point of equilibrium at which real income equals aggregate desired expenditures.

Figure 6–10   The 45-Degree Line

The economy is in equilibrium when aggregate desired expenditures equal aggregate real income. This will be true along the 45-degree line. If aggregate desired expenditures equal the amount y_1, then by reading over to the 45-degree line and downward to the horizontal axis, we find that this level of total spending is equal to the aggregate income level y_1. The same is true for the higher level of expenditures y_2. Consequently, any point along the 45-degree line is a potential equilibrium point.

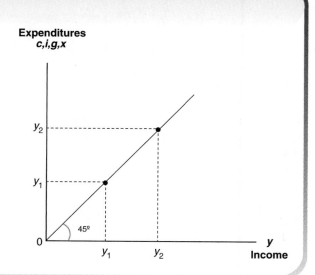

Figure 6–11   Two Approaches to Determining Equilibrium Real Income

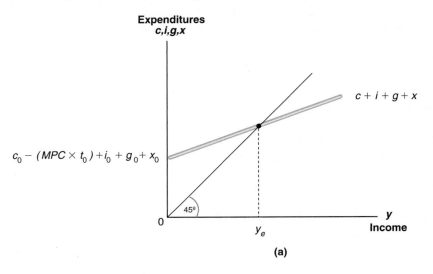

(a)

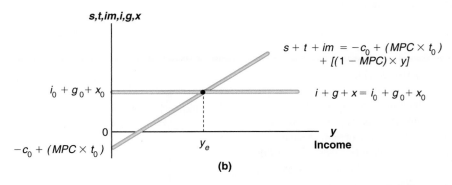

(b)

Equilibrium real income arises at the point at which aggregate desired real expenditures, $c + i + g + x$, equal aggregate real income. This is true at the single real income level, y_e, where the aggregate expenditures schedule crosses the 45-degree line in panel (a).

Alternatively, as shown in panel (b), equilibrium income also arises at the point at which leakages from the flow of spending on domestic output, given by $s + t + im$, equal total injections back into the spending flow, $i + g + x$.

THE LEAKAGES-INJECTIONS APPROACH TO DETERMINING EQUILIBRIUM REAL INCOME

We can also think about equilibrium in another way. Substituting the real income identity, $y \equiv c + s + t + im$, for y in the equilibrium condition $y = c + i + g + x$ gives us

$$c + s + t + im = c + i + g + x.$$

If we subtract c from both sides of this equation, we get another expression for the equilibrium condition:

$$s + t + im = i + g + x.$$

If you look back at the circular flow diagram in Figure 6–3 on page 141, you will see that the left side of this new condition is the sum of all *leakages* from the flow of spending on domestic output that take place because households save, pay taxes, and purchase imports from foreign firms. The right side consists of *injections* back into the flow of spending on domestically produced goods and services that take place when firms, the government, and foreign residents purchase domestically produced output. Hence, this equation says that in equilibrium, all leakages from the flow of spending ultimately are *reinjected* back into that flow.

Panel (b) of Figure 6–11 shows this alternative leakages-injections approach to determining equilibrium real income. The right side of the leakages-injections equilibrium condition is described by the horizontal schedule $i_0 + g_0 + x_0$ from panel (a) of Figure 6–9. Using our saving and import functions discussed earlier, the left side of the equation, $s + t + im$, is equal to $-s_0 + (MPS \times y_d) + t_0 + im_0 + (MPIM \times y_d)$. Remembering that $y_d \equiv y - t$, where $t = t_0$ is the current lump-sum level of taxes, we can rearrange this expression as

$$s + t + im = -(s_0 - im_0) + t_0 + [(MPS + MPIM) \times (y - t_0)].$$

Finally, by factoring out the terms relating to t_0 and recalling that $c_0 = s_0 - im_0$, we can rearrange a little more to obtain

$$s + t + im = -c_0 + (MPC \times t_0) + [(1 - MPC) \times y],$$

which is the equation of the upward-sloping "$s + t + im$" schedule displayed in panel (b) of Figure 6–11. The intersection of these two schedules then determines equilibrium real income, y_e. This is the same as the equilibrium real income level determined via the income-expenditures approach to equilibrium in panel (a) of Figure 6–11.

THE COMPLETE DEPICTION OF EQUILIBRIUM REAL INCOME   Figure 6–12 on the next page summarizes the graphical depiction of the determination of a nation's equilibrium real income flow. Households, firms, the government, and foreign residents purchase all the output produced domestically ($y = c + i + g + x$), and leakages from the spending flow ultimately are reinjected into that flow ($s + t + im = i + g + x$). From either perspective, equilibrium real income is equal to the same level, y_e.

Figure 6-12 The Determination of Equilibrium Real Income

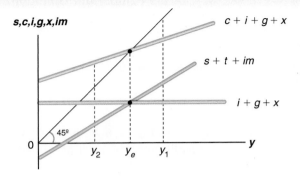

Equilibrium real income is attained both when aggregate desired expenditures, $c + i + g + x$, equal real income and when spending-flow leakages, $s + t + im$, equal spending-flow injections, $i + g + x$. At an income level above the equilibrium level of real income, y_e, such as y_1, desired expenditures would be less than the value of real output, so firms would begin to accumulate inventories of unfinished goods. As a result, realized investment, i_r, would exceed desired investment at the income level y_1. Firms would cut back on production, and real income would fall back toward the equilibrium level y_e. In contrast, at an income level below the equilibrium income level, such as y_2, desired expenditures would be greater than the value of real output, so firms would begin to experience unplanned inventory depletions. Realized investment, i_r, would be less than desired investment at the income level y_2. Firms would increase production, and real income would rise toward the equilibrium level y_e.

Finally, remember that the national product identity is $y \equiv c + i_r + g + x$, where i_r is the amount of realized, or actual, investment spending by firms. In equilibrium, $y = c + i + g + x$. If we substitute the national product identity for y in this equilibrium condition, we obtain $c + i_r + g + x = c + i + g + x$ in equilibrium. After subtracting $c + g + x$ from both sides of this equation, we find a third and final way to express equilibrium:

$$i_r = i.$$

This equation says that in equilibrium firms undertake the amount of investment spending that they *desire* to undertake. Thus, in equilibrium firms do not hold more inventories of finished goods than they desire to hold. Nor do firms hold fewer inventories of finished goods than they desire when the economy is in equilibrium.

In Figure 6-12, if real income somehow increased to y_1, above the equilibrium income level y_e, the increase could be only temporary. The reason is that at this higher income level y_1, real income—the real value of output—exceeds the level of desired spending on output, or $y > c + i + g + x$. Consequently, realized real investment would be greater than desired investment, or $i_r > i$. Firms would observe that their inventories of unsold goods had risen above desired levels and would cut their inventories. As a result, production of new output would decline, causing the value of real output, or real income, to decline toward the equilibrium level y_e.

In contrast, if real income declined to y_2, below the equilibrium income level y_e in Figure 6–12, real income would be less than the level of desired spending on output, or $y < c + i + g + x$. Realized real investment would therefore be lower than desired investment, or $i_r < i$. Firms would see their inventories of unsold goods fall below desired levels and would add to their inventories. As a result, production of new output would increase, causing the value of real output, or real income, to rise toward the equilibrium level y_e.

The Multiplier Effect and Short-Run Business Cycles

What factors could cause equilibrium real income to change, thereby generating cyclical changes in real income that we observe over business cycles? What factors account for the magnitudes of such cyclical income variations? To answer these questions, we need to understand one of the key implications of the basic Keynesian model of real income determination: the **multiplier effect.** This effect refers to the fact that a given 1-unit change in aggregate net autonomous expenditures—a 1-unit movement in the intercept of the aggregate desired expenditures schedule $c + i + g + x$ in panel (a) of Figure 6–11 and in Figure 6–12—causes a greater-than-1-unit change in equilibrium real income in the same direction.

THE AUTONOMOUS EXPENDITURES MULTIPLIER   To see how the multiplier effect occurs, let's begin with a little algebra. The income-expenditure equilibrium condition is $y = c + i + g + x$. If we substitute from our consumption function, $c = c_0 - (MPC \times t_0) + (MPC \times y)$, and assume that net taxes and desired investment, government spending, and export spending are all autonomous, we can rewrite this condition as

$$y = c_0 - (MPC \times t_0) + (MPC \times y) + i_0 + g_0 + x_0.$$

Now, if we subtract $(MPC \times y)$ from both sides of this equation, we obtain

$$y - (MPC \times y) = c_0 - (MPC \times t_0) + i_0 + g_0 + x_0.$$

Finally, if we divide both sides of the preceding equation by $(1 - MPC)$, we get

$$y = \frac{1}{(1 - MPC)} [c_0 - (MPC \times t_0) + i_0 + g_0 + x_0].$$

This final expression is an equation for equilibrium real income. It tells us that equilibrium real income is equal to the ratio $1/(1 - MPC)$ times aggregate net autonomous expenditures, $c_0 - (MPC \times t_0) + i_0 + g_0 + x_0$. The ratio $1/(1 - MPC)$ is the Keynesian **autonomous expenditures multiplier,** which we shall simply call the "multiplier." This is a measure of the size of the multiplier effect on equilibrium real income caused by a change in the level of aggregate net autonomous expenditures. The MPC is between 0 and 1, so the multiplier is greater than 1. For example, if the marginal propensity to save is equal to 0.08 and the marginal propensity to import is equal to 0.12, the marginal propensity to consume is $MPC = 0.8$. Then the multiplier is equal to $1/(1 - MPC) = 1/(1 - 0.8) = 1/0.2 = 5$.

MULTIPLIER EFFECT: The ratio of a change in equilibrium real income to an increase in autonomous net aggregate expenditures. When the aggregate expenditures schedule shifts vertically, the equilibrium level of national income changes by a multiple of the amount of the shift.

AUTONOMOUS EXPENDITURES MULTIPLIER: A measure of the size of the multiplier effect on equilibrium real income caused by a change in aggregate net autonomous expenditures; in the simple Keynesian model, the multiplier is equal to $1/(MPS + MPIM) = 1/(1 - MPC)$.

Thus, a $1 billion reduction in aggregate net autonomous expenditures per year would cause a $5 billion decline in equilibrium real income per year.

The multiplier effect is illustrated in Figure 6–13, where the initial equilibrium is point A, at the level of real income y_1. Now suppose that autonomous investment spending declines, perhaps because owners of business firms anticipate lower future profits. A decline in autonomous investment equal to Δi_0 causes the aggregate desired expenditures schedule to shift downward by that amount. As a result, equilibrium real income falls by a larger amount, from y_1 to y_2, or Δy, at point B. In fact, our final equation for equilibrium real income tells us that the exact amount of the decline in real income is equal to $\Delta y = [1/(1 - MPC)] \times \Delta i_0$. Real income would decline by the fall in autonomous investment times the autonomous spending multiplier, $1/(1 - MPC)$.

WHAT LIES BEHIND THE MULTIPLIER?   What accounts for the multiplier effect? Consider the following example in which $MPC = 0.80$. This means that each dollar reduction in household disposable income induces a reduction in disposable income of 80 cents. If autonomous investment declines by an amount $\Delta i_0 = \$1$ million, then firms now spend $1 million less than before on capital goods and inventories of finished goods. This spending reduction immediately reduces real income by $1 million. The result is a $1 million decline in disposable income, which in turn reduces household consumption spending by 80 percent of $1 million, or $800,000. This in turn leads to an $800,000 reduction in the real income of the firms from which households would have purchased domestically produced goods and services. To this point, therefore, the $1 million decline in autonomous investment has reduced total real income by $1.8 million.

The process of spending reduction is not yet complete, however. The owners and workers at the firms that have lost $800,000 in sales and income earnings will reduce their consumption spending by 80 percent of this amount or $0.8 \times \$800,000 = \$640,000$. Furthermore, this spending

---

Figure 6–13   The Multiplier Effect on Real Income Caused by a Decline in Real Investment

A decline in real autonomous investment expenditures equal to Δi_0 causes the aggregate expenditures schedule to shift downward by that amount and induces a movement from equilibrium point A to equilibrium point B. As a result, equilibrium real income declines by a larger amount than the fall in autonomous investment, given by $\Delta y = y_2 - y_1$. The amount of the fall in equilibrium real income is equal to $\Delta y = [1/(1 - MPC)] \times \Delta i_0$.

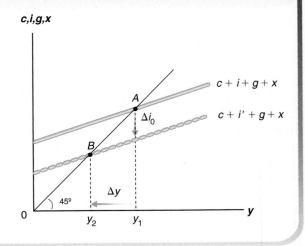

reduction will generate a fall in real income of $640,000 for owners and workers at other firms, who then will reduce their consumption spending by 0.8 × $640,000 = $512,000.

Ultimately, the total reduction in real income will be the sum of all these declines ($1 million + $800,000 + $640,000 + $512,000 + · · ·) in spending. As we determined earlier, if the *MPC* is equal to 0.8, the total decline in real income caused by a $1 million fall in autonomous investment will be equal to $1 million times $1/(1 - 0.8)$, or $1 million times 5 or a real income reduction of $5 million. (Most economists agree that the latest recession resulted from a fall in autonomous investment; see on the following page *Policy Notebook: An Investment Recession.*)

A BASIC KEYNESIAN THEORY OF BUSINESS CYCLES   Note that a multiple decline in real income caused by a fall in autonomous investment would, if all other factors were unchanged, lead to a recession. Real income would fall relative to its long-run growth path, and equilibrium real income would not rise again until autonomous investment or some other component of aggregate net autonomous investment increased. The result would be a downturn in the business cycle.

Our final equation for equilibrium real income indicates that a number of factors could cause such a downturn. Any change causing a reduction in aggregate net autonomous expenditures, $c_0 - (MPC \times t_0) + i_0 + g_0 + x_0$, could induce a recession. For instance, a fall in the value of c_0 equal to Δc_0 would cause real income to decline by $\Delta c_0 \times 1/(1 - MPC)$. Recall that autonomous consumption is equal to $s_0 - im_0$, and this would imply a decline in autonomous consumption of domestically produced goods and services, either because people decide to save more than they did before or because they choose to purchase more imports from abroad. The result would be a fall in equilibrium real income and a recession.

In addition, a significant fall in real export spending by foreign residents could induce an economic downturn. A decline in spending on real exports equal to Δx_0 would cause real income to decline by $\Delta x_0 \times 1/(1 - MPC)$.

Finally, changes in autonomous net taxes or government spending can also influence equilibrium real income. A rise in net taxes would reduce real income, as would a fall in government spending. The fact that the government can induce equilibrium real income to change via alterations in these *fiscal policy* variables led Keynes and his followers to propose a stabilization role for government, as we discuss in Chapter 7.

FUNDAMENTAL ISSUE #4

How is equilibrium real income determined in the basic Keynesian model, and how does this theory explain short-run business cycles?   In equilibrium, a nation's real income is equal to the aggregate desired expenditures on domestically produced goods and services by households, firms, the government, and foreign residents. Equilibrium real income changes are a multiple of any changes in aggregate net autonomous expenditures. Consequently, variations in autonomous spending can cause equilibrium real income to vary from a level consistent with the economy's long-run growth path.

An Investment Recession

Most people link the recession that began in early 2001 to the terrorist attacks on New York and Washington, D.C., that took place in September of that year. The climate of uncertainty created by those attacks undoubtedly contributed to the economic downturn. Nevertheless, economists at the National Bureau of Economic Research (NBER) formally dated the onset of the recession to March 2001, six months before the attacks.

Accounting for the Decline in Aggregate Expenditures

Panel (a) of Figure 6–14 displays real consumption, government spending, investment, and export expenditures since 1993. As you can see, government spending and consumption continued to grow as the recession commenced in early 2001, although the rate of increase in consumption began to decline at the recession's onset as the decline in real income generated a drop-off in induced consumption.

Both investment spending and export expenditures, which are both part of autonomous spending in the basic Keynesian model, fell just as the recession began. Hence, both of these factors contributed to bringing about the decline in U.S. real income that took place beginning in spring of 2001.

The Main Culprit: Reduced Investment in Information Technology

A close look at panel (a) indicates that export spending by foreign residents began to fall *after* the decline in U.S. investment. Although economists are still studying the role of exports in the 2001 recession, some believe that foreign exports began to fall partly *in response* to the onset of the U.S. downturn. As U.S. national income began to fall, so did import spending by U.S. residents, which dropped by 7 percent between the end of 2000 and the fall of 2001. The resulting decline in U.S. purchases of other nations' goods and services tended to depress incomes in those countries, whose residents then reduced their purchases of U.S. goods and services.

This leaves the drop in investment spending at the beginning of 2001 as the main factor that brought about the U.S. recession. This decline followed a major upswing in investment, which by 1998 had passed government spending to become the second-largest component of aggregate expenditures on U.S. goods and services. The main factors accounting for the investment boom that ended in 2001 were purchases of equipment and software relating to information technologies, biotechnologies, and communications technologies. Panel (b) of Figure 6–14 displays the considerable growth in investment in equipment and software from the beginning of 1993 until 2000. In the latter part of 2000, however, business purchases of equipment and software began to fall slightly, and this decline accelerated in the early part of 2001 and accounted for the bulk of the overall drop in investment spending that most economists agree ultimately was most responsible for bringing about the recession.

For Critical Analysis

Based on the information in Figure 6–14, what was the main factor that contributed to the long economic expansion of the 1990s?

National Income and the Balance of Trade

As we discussed in Chapter 2, the United States has run significant trade and current account deficits in recent years. What factors might explain these deficits? What policies might be enacted to address them? We can apply the Keynesian model that we have just developed to find some initial answers to these questions.

Figure 6–14   Real Consumption, Government Spending, Exports, and Investment since 1993

Panel (a) shows that total business investment expenditures leveled off in late 2000 and then dropped in early 2001, and export spending declined shortly thereafter. Panel (b) indicates that a key factor affecting total business investment was that investment spending on equipment and software rose steadily until 2000 and then leveled off and abruptly declined at the end of 2000 and into 2001.

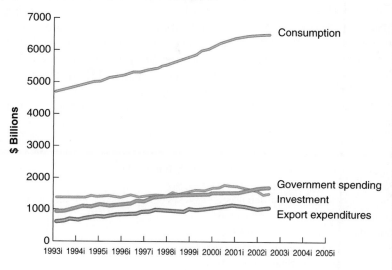

(a)

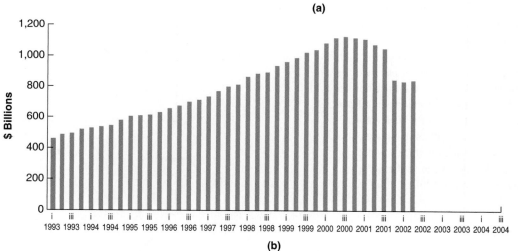

SOURCES: Bureau of Economic Analysis; *Economic Indicators,* various issues.

(b)

Exports, Imports, and National Income

Recall that the balance of trade is equal to exports minus imports. Using the model developed in this chapter, we can explore factors that influence the trade balance by looking at the quantity $x - im$. Our assumptions are that export spending is autonomous, so $x = x_0$, and that the import function is $im = im_0 + (MPIM \times y_d)$. It follows that our measure of the trade balance is

On the Web

What countries and regions contribute most to U.S exports and imports? To find out, visit the Web site of the Bureau of Economic Analysis, http://www.bea.doc.gov. Under "International," click on "Balance of payments and related data." Then click on "Printable versions of tables 1 through 10" from the latest issue of the *Survey of Current Business.*

$$x - im = x_0 - im_0 - (MPIM \times y_d)$$
$$= x_0 - im_0 + (MPIM \times t_0) - (MPIM \times y).$$

As panel (b) in Figure 6–15 shows, this expression for the trade balance is a downward-sloping, straight-line function. We shall call this the *trade balance schedule*. The reason the trade balance schedule slopes downward is that a rise in aggregate real income raises household disposable income and stimulates higher import spending, which reduces the nation's balance of trade.

Note that a rise in autonomous exports or a fall in autonomous imports naturally would increase the trade balance at any given level of real income. Consequently, a rise in x_0 or a fall in im_0 would raise the intercept of the trade balance schedule, thereby *shifting* the trade balance schedule upward. In addition, a tax increase would reduce household disposable income even if total real income is unchanged, thereby improving the trade balance.

Figure 6–15   Determining the Equilibrium Trade Balance

The trade balance is the difference between export spending and import expenditures, or $x - im$. Import expenditures rise as real income increases, so the trade balance declines with a rise in real income. Hence, the trade balance schedule slopes downward, as shown in panel (b). At a current equilibrium real income level, such as y_e in panel (a), the equilibrium trade balance can be determined by reading off the trade balance schedule. Here, there initially is a trade deficit. To eliminate the trade deficit, policymakers might contemplate policies that would shift the trade balance schedule upward and to the right, as illustrated in panel (b).

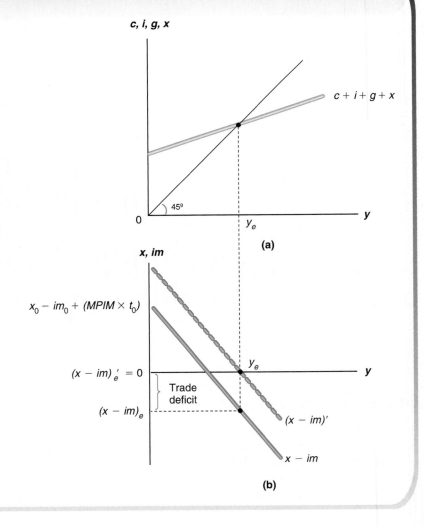

Therefore, a rise in autonomous net taxes, t_0, also raises the value of the intercept of the trade balance schedule and shifts the schedule upward.

The Equilibrium Balance of Trade

Figure 6–15 illustrates the determination of the equilibrium trade balance. Panel (a) shows the income-expenditure approach to the determination of the equilibrium level of real income, y_e. We can then read off the trade balance schedule $x - im$ in panel (b) to determine the equilibrium trade balance $(x - im)_e$. As drawn, these figures show a situation in which there is a trade deficit, so $(x - im)_e < 0$.

This theory of the equilibrium balance of trade can help to explain factors that cause a country to experience a trade deficit. Clearly, holding all other things constant, one factor that can induce a trade deficit is a high level of real income, which induces greater import spending, which, in turn, worsens the trade balance. Notice that any nation faces a potential trade-off: Holding other factors constant, higher growth of real output tends to improve the likelihood of running a trade deficit.

One way a trade deficit might be reduced is by inducing an upward shift of the trade balance schedule. For instance, if the trade balance schedule is shifted to the position shown by the dashed schedule $(x - im)'$ in panel (b) of Figure 6–15 while holding equilibrium real income constant, then exports would equal imports, and the nation's trade would be balanced at $(x - im)'_e = 0$. Such a shift might be accomplished by enacting policies intended to increase autonomous exports and reduce autonomous imports. One possibility is an exchange-rate depreciation, which would make foreign goods more expensive to domestic households and domestically produced goods less expensive to foreigners. Another approach is to provide subsidies to domestic industries to promote exports and to impose **tariffs,** or taxes on imports, to discourage their consumption. Finally, higher net taxes at home would reduce household disposable income and thereby reduce import spending. Many nations have adopted such policies in the past in an effort to improve their trade balance.

It is important to recognize, however, that all the policies mentioned here would also affect panel (a) in Figure 6–15. For instance, a currency depreciation or subsidy policy that stimulated export spending would cause the aggregate desired expenditures schedule to shift upward, which would cause equilibrium real income to rise. This would tend to offset somewhat the trade balance improvement otherwise induced by the policy change. In addition, a tax increase would cause the aggregate desired expenditures schedule to shift downward, which would cause equilibrium real income to decline. This would reinforce the improvement in the trade balance induced by the tax increase, but at the cost of reduced real income for home residents.

macroxtra!
Online Perspective

To think about factors that have contributed to relatively large trade deficits in the United States, go to the Chapter 6 reading, entitled "Is the Large U.S. Current Account Deficit Sustainable?" by Jill Holman of the Federal Reserve Bank of Kansas City.
http://macroxtra.swcollege.com

macroxtra!
Economic Applications

Does the U.S. economy benefit from foreign trade? To review alternative perspectives on this debate and make your own judgment, go to EconData Online.
http://macroxtra.swcollege.com

FUNDAMENTAL ISSUE #5

How is the equilibrium trade balance determined?   Because import spending is positively related to disposable income, a nation's trade balance will, holding other factors unchanged, decline as its real income increases. Consequently, the equilibrium size of the trade balance varies with the equilibrium level of real income.

TARIFFS: Taxes imposed on the values of goods and services that are traded internationally.

Using Leading Indicators to Predict Recessions

If a recession catches the managers of a business off guard, it can damage the firm's long-term fortunes even if the company has a highly regarded product and a solid business plan. Thus, businesses commonly search for information from so-called leading indicators of recessions. The most popular of these is the Leading Economic Indicators Index (LEI Index), which is a weighted average of the most commonly used leading indicators.

The Leading Economic Indicators Index

Table 6–2 lists the current components of the LEI Index, which the Conference Board compiles based on their ability to predict past recessions. Most of these indicators are relatively straightforward. It makes sense that changes in hourly employment and unemployment claims, new manufacturing orders and vendor deliveries, and building permits might provide information about the economy's direction. In addition,

changes in the level of money holdings, stock prices, and consumer expectations also might provide relevant information about whether economic activity is likely to rise or fall in the future.

The idea behind including the spread between the ten-year Treasury bond rate and the federal funds rate (the rate on U.S. interbank loans) relates to a concept known as the expectations theory of the term structure of interest rates—the relationship between yields on otherwise identical bonds with differing terms to maturity. This theory predicts that longer-term bond rates should be nearly equal to the average of current and expected future shorter-term bond rates. Thus, if the spread between the ten-year Treasury bond rate and the current federal funds rate narrows, that could indicate that investors expect that *future* federal funds rates will be lower. Interest rates tend to fall when the demand for credit falls due

---

Table 6–2   Components of the Index of Leading Economic Indicators

1. Average weekly hours, manufacturing
2. Average weekly initial claims for unemployment insurance
3. Manufacturers' new orders, consumer goods and materials (in 1996 dollars)
4. Vendor performance, slower deliveries diffusion index
5. Manufacturers' new orders, nondefense capital goods (in 1996 dollars)
6. Building permits, new private housing units
7. Stock prices, 500 common stocks
8. Money supply, M2 (in 1996 dollars)
9. Interest rate spread, ten-year Treasury bonds less federal funds
10. Index of consumer expectations

SOURCE: Conference Board.

to declining economic activity, so a drop in this interest rate spread might help predict a coming recession.

In-Sample versus Out-of-Sample Forecasting

Figure 6–16 displays values of the LEI Index since 1970. In addition, shading in the figure indicates recession periods. As you can see, the LEI Index typically drops in advance of officially declared recessions. Many economists use a rule of thumb that three consecutive drops in the LEI Index should be regarded as a clear signal that a recession is on the horizon.

There is a problem with the LEI Index, however. The Conference Board selects the components of the index based on their *in-sample* performance—that is, their ability to predict recessions within the sample of available historical economic data. Yet the point of using the LEI Index is to try to predict *future* recessions, or to engage in *out-of-sample* forecasting. Typically,

after each recession the Conference Board revises the components of the LEI Index when it discovers that one or two of them turned out not to be such good predictors after all.

Research Project
Explain why it is important to evaluate the out-of-sample performance of a leading indicator. Discuss how you might go about doing this if you were in charge of putting together the LEI Index for the United States.

Web Resource
1. What is the latest direction of the U.S. LEI Index? Find out by going to the home page of the Conference Board (http://www.conference-board.org/) and clicking on "U.S. Leading Indicator Index."

2. What are the components of the leading economic indicator indexes for other countries, and how do they differ from those used in the U.S. LEI Index? To find out, elect other nations' leading economic indicator indexes at the above Web site.

Figure 6–16   The Leading Economic Indicators Index since 1970

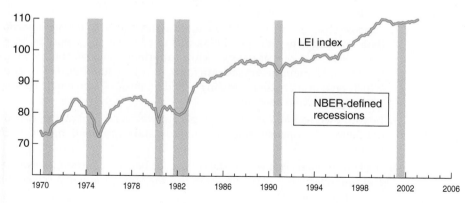

Drops in the value of the LEI Index are often followed by recessions.

SOURCES: Marco Del Negro, "Turn, Turn, Turn: Predicting Turning Points in Economic Activity," Federal Reserve Bank of Atlanta *Economic Review,* Second Quarter 2001, pp. 1–12; Conference Board; National Bureau of Economic Research.

1. Business Cycles and Their Characteristics: Business cycles are variations in real income around its long-run growth path. Recessions are periods of a decline in real income below its long-run level, and expansions are increases in real income to levels that for a time can exceed its long-run level. Frictional and structural unemployment exist even without business cycles, but the overall unemployment rate has a cyclical component that tends to rise during recessions and decline during expansions.

2. The Key Relationships Implied by the Circular Flow of Income and Expenditures: One fundamental identity that can be inferred from the circular flow is the income identity. This identity says that all real income is allocated to domestic consumption, saving, taxes, and import spending. The other identity is the product identity, which states that the real value of output of goods and services is equal to real expenditures on that output in the form of household consumption, business investment, government spending, and export spending by foreigners.

3. The Components of Aggregate Desired Expenditures in the Basic Keynesian Model: Aggregate desired expenditures are equal to the sum of household consumption of domestically produced goods and services, investment spending desired by firms, government expenditures, and export spending by foreigners. In the most basic Keynesian theory, desired investment, government spending and net taxes, and export spending are autonomous, but consumption spending is positively related to disposable income. Therefore, the aggregate expenditures schedule is upward sloping.

4. The Determination of Equilibrium Real Income and the Keynesian Explanation for Short-Run Business Cycles: The fundamental equilibrium condition of the Keynesian model is that a nation's real income is equal to the aggregate desired expenditures on domestically produced goods and services by households, firms, the government, and foreign residents. Because equilibrium real income changes are a multiple of a change in aggregate net autonomous expenditures, such changes in autonomous spending can cause equilibrium real income to vary from its long-run level.

5. The Determination of the Equilibrium Trade Balance: Import spending is positively related to disposable income. Therefore, holding other factors unchanged, a nation's trade balance will tend to fall as its real income rises.

Self-Test Questions

(Answers to odd-numbered questions may be found on the Web at **http://macro. swcollege.com** under "Student Resources.")

1. In light of the definitions of business cycle peaks and troughs, explain why the trough of the idealized business cycle in Figure 6–1 does not correspond to the lowest level of real GDP over the cycle depicted and why the peak is not at the highest level of real GDP.

2. Suppose that the citizens of the United States decide to devote a portion of their tax dollars to reducing the natural rate of unemployment by increasing expenditures on one of the following: (a) primary and secondary education, (b) unemployment insurance programs, or (c) income transfer programs. Which type of increased spending would be most effective in achieving the goal? Explain your reasoning.

3. In your own words, without relying on any algebraic equations, explain why the marginal propensities to save, import, and consume domestic goods must sum to 1.

4. Explain, in your own words, the difference between desired investment and realized investment. Why are these two magnitudes equal at the equilibrium level of real income?

Problems

(Answers to odd-numbered problems may be found on the Web at **http://macro. swcollege.com** under "Student Resources.")

1. In the simple Keynesian model, suppose that $MPS = 0.04$ and $MPC = 0.90$. What is the marginal propensity to import ($MPIM$)? Suppose disposable income increases from $900 billion to $1,000 billion. By how much would consumption rise? By how much would saving rise? By how much would imports rise? Is the sum of your answers equal to the change in income?

2. If the consumption function (in billions of dollars) for a closed economy is $c = \$20 + (0.8)y_d$, determine the level of consumption and the level of saving for $y_d = \$50$ billion, 150 billion, and 250 billion. Compute the associated values of the average propensity to consume (APC).

3. Suppose that the value of the autonomous spending multiplier is equal to 4, the marginal propensity to save is equal to 0.10, and the economy is open to international trade. What is the value of the marginal propensity to import? Show your work.

4. Suppose that the level of government spending is equal to $200 billion (in base-year dollars) and that the level of real net taxes is equal to $100 billion. This economy is closed to international trade. In equilibrium, will saving be equal to real desired investment? Why or why not?

5. Suppose that equilibrium real income is $y = \$500$ billion (in base-year dollars). The consumption function is $c = \$50 + (0.75)y_d$. Real net taxes are equal to $100 billion, and real government spending is equal to $125 billion.

  a. What is the equilibrium level of consumption?

  b. If real desired investment is equal to $10 billion, what is the amount of autonomous real exports?

Before the Test

Test your understanding of the material covered in this chapter by taking the Chapter 6 interactive quiz at **http://macro.swcollege.com**.

Online Application

Internet URL: http://research.stlouisfed.org/fred/data.gdp.html

Title: *Gross Domestic Product and Components*

Navigation: Begin at the home page of the Federal Reserve Bank of St. Louis (**http://www.stls.frb.org**). Click on "FRED." Then click on *Economic Research,* and then click on *Economic Data–Gross Domestic Product and Components.*

Application:

1. Under "Personal Income and Its Disposition (Quarterly)," click on *Real Personal Consumption Expenditures.* Write down consumption expenditures for the past eight quarters. Now back up to *Gross Domestic Product and Components,* click on *Gross Domestic Product,* and write down GDP for the past eight quarters. Use these data to calculate implied values for the marginal propensity to consume, assuming that taxes do not vary with income. Is there any problem with this assumption?

2. Back up to *Gross Domestic Product and Components.* Under "3 Decimal," click on *Real Gross Domestic Product in Chained (1996) Dollars.* Scan through the data since the mid-1960s. In which years did the largest variations in GDP take place? What component(s) of GDP appear to have accounted for these large movements?

For Group Study and Analysis: Assign groups to use the FRED database to try to determine the best measure of aggregate U.S. disposable income for the past eight quarters. Reconvene the class, and discuss each group's approach to this issue.

and Further Reading

Dillard, Dudley. *The Economics of John Maynard Keynes.* Englewood Cliffs, N.J.: Prentice Hall, 1948.

Haimowitz, Joseph. "The Longevity of Expansions." Federal Reserve Bank of Kansas City *Economic Review* 83 (Fourth Quarter 1998): 13–34.

Hansen, Alvin. *A Guide to Keynes.* New York: Macmillan, 1953.

Holman, Jill. "Is the Large U.S. Current Account Deficit Sustainable?" Federal Reserve Bank of Kansas City *Economic Review,* First Quarter 2001, pp. 5–23.

Keynes, John Maynard. *The General Theory of Employment, Interest, and Money.* New York: Harcourt Brace Jovanovich, 1964.

Klein, Lawrence. *The Keynesian Revolution.* 2d ed. New York: Macmillan, 1966.

LeKachman, Robert. *The Age of Keynes.* New York: Random House, 1966.

LeKachman, Robert, ed. *Keynes and the Classics.* Boston: Heath, 1965.

Valletta, Robert. "Changes in the Structure and Duration of U.S. Unemployment." Federal Reserve Bank of San Francisco *Economic Review,* Third Quarter 1998, pp. 29–40.

macroxtra!

Fiscal Policy—What Can Government Spending and Taxation Policies Accomplish?

FUNDAMENTAL ISSUES

1. Why does the basic Keynesian model indicate that there may be a potential stabilizing role for fiscal policy?

2. How can the basic Keynesian model be adapted to account for income taxes?

3. Do cuts in income tax rates necessarily reduce the government's tax revenues?

4. What is the Ricardian equivalence proposition?

In the United States, the story has become a familiar one. A municipality that has recently lost a number of businesses and is experiencing slow growth decides to try to steal firms away from other cities and states. Sometimes the municipality offers individual businesses specially tailored inducements. If the municipality really wants to reverse its overall fortunes, however, it resorts to blanket reductions in taxes on corporate assets and financing. That is, it cuts the tax rates it assesses on capital.

Today this form of tax competition in search of capital investment is also taking place well beyond U.S. borders. Ireland, for instance, attracted significant business investment during the 1990s after it cut its marginal tax rate on capital—the additional amount of tax required on the next unit of capital—to just over 9 percent, almost half the average marginal tax rate for the European Union as a whole.

The upsurge in tax competition is bad news for locales that maintain high marginal tax rates on capital. Just as U.S. municipalities that keep their marginal tax rates high in the face of competition from other cities and states have lost out on business and economic growth, so have Germany, with its 25 percent marginal tax rate on capital, and France, which assesses a marginal tax rate in excess of 30 percent on capital investment.

How can economists assess the broad economic effects of tax policies? When is a tax rate "too high" or "too low"? This chapter addresses the macroeconomic roles of both taxation and government spending.

Fiscal Policy and Income Stabilization

The basic Keynesian model provides a theory of the determination of equilibrium real income and of how changes in aggregate net autonomous expenditures can, through the multiplier effect, cause short-run cyclical variations in real income. Keynes argued that such variations in equilibrium real income from the economy's natural growth path were inefficient and, for the many people who lose their jobs during business downturns, even harmful. Because the government can affect the volume of aggregate net autonomous expenditures, Keynes felt that it was the government's obligation to offset business cycles.

Recessionary and Inflationary Gaps

To understand the essence of Keynes's argument, consider Figure 7–1, which displays three possible levels of equilibrium real income resulting from three different positions of the aggregate desired expenditures schedule. The middle equilibrium point, A, is assumed to be an equilibrium real income level, y_{LR}, consistent with the economy's long-run growth path.

A fall in autonomous consumption, investment, or exports, however, would cause a decline in aggregate net autonomous expenditures and thereby shift the aggregate desired expenditures schedule downward by the

Figure 7–1   Recessionary and Inflationary Gaps

If the income-expenditure equilibrium is at point A, which is consistent with the economy's long-run path for real GDP at the amount y_{LR}, then there is no tendency for the economy to experience either a recession or a period of inflation. If the equilibrium point were at point B, however, then the income level y_1 would be below the economy's long-run growth path, and there would be a recession. The distance $A–C$ would be the recessionary gap in aggregate expenditures, or the amount by which aggregate expenditures would need to increase to raise real income back to its long-run equilibrium level. In contrast, if the equilibrium point were at point D, then the income level y_2 would be above the economy's long-run growth path, and inflation would result. The distance $E–A$ would be the inflationary gap in aggregate expenditures, or the amount by which aggregate expenditures would need to decline to reduce real income to its long-run equilibrium level.

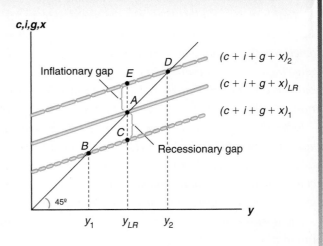

distance A–C. The new short-run equilibrium point would be at B, which would yield a short-run equilibrium income level of y_1. The economy's real income would be lower than its long-run potential income level, y_{LR}. The result would be a recession and, as we discussed in Chapter 6, a higher unemployment rate. For this reason, economists call the distance A–C a **recessionary gap** in spending, or the amount by which aggregate desired expenditures would need to increase to move equilibrium real income back to its *natural level,* or the natural GDP level along its long-run growth path.

Recall that total *nominal* income is $Y \equiv y \times P$, where P is the GDP price deflator. In a recessionary gap situation at point B, real income is lower than its long-run level, which would imply lower nominal income as well. For this reason, there may be downward pressure on prices when the economy is in a recessionary gap. Indeed, during the Great Depression of the 1930s when Keynes was formulating his theory, there was significant deflation.

Now consider the situation that arises if the economy is at point D in Figure 7–1. At this point, aggregate desired expenditures are at a sufficiently high level that real income is equal to y_2, which is above the long-run potential income level, y_{LR}. Because the economy is operating above its long-run potential production level, there likely would be upward pressure on prices in this situation. Consequently, the amount by which the aggregate desired expenditures schedule lies above the long-run equilibrium point A, or the distance E–A, is called an **inflationary gap.** This is an excess amount of real aggregate desired expenditures relative to the amount necessary to keep the economy at its natural GDP.

Countercyclical Fiscal Policy

Because autonomous consumption, investment, or exports could vary over time, Keynes and his followers viewed recessionary and inflationary gaps as events that were likely to make short-run business cycles commonplace occurrences. Furthermore, unexpectedly large variations in aggregate net autonomous expenditures could induce large gaps, causing equilibrium real income to diverge considerably from its natural level. In other words, severe recessions could not be ruled out.

USING GOVERNMENT SPENDING TO CLOSE A RECESSIONARY GAP   In Keynes's view, however, the severity of the downturns could be reduced significantly by government action. For instance, suppose that the long-run real income level given by y_{LR} in Figure 7–1 is equal to $12,000 billion ($12,000,000,000,000), but the economy is in a recessionary gap with equilibrium real income y_1 equal to $11,500 billion. Thus, to reattain its long-run level of real income, the economy would need to witness a rise in real income equal to $\Delta y = \$12,000$ billion $- \$11,500$ billion $= \$500$ billion.

Let's also continue to suppose that the marginal propensity to save is equal to 0.08 and the marginal propensity to import is equal to 0.12, so that the marginal propensity to consume is $MPC = 1 - MPS - MPIM = 1 - 0.08 - 0.12 = 0.8$. Then, as we calculated in Chapter 6, the autonomous spending multiplier is equal to $1/(MPS + MPIM) = 1/(1 - MPC) = 1/(1 - 0.8) = 1/0.2 = 5$. Then we can calculate the amount of the recessionary gap, A–C, by dividing $\Delta y = \$500$ billion by the autonomous spending multiplier, $1/(1 - MPC) = 5$,

RECESSIONARY GAP: The amount by which aggregate desired expenditures lie below the level that would cause equilibrium real income to equal its long-run, natural level.

INFLATIONARY GAP: The amount by which aggregate desired expenditures exceed the level that would cause equilibrium real income to equal its long-run, natural level.

which yields \$100 billion. Aggregate desired expenditures need to rise by this amount to reattain the economy's long-run level of real GDP.

Recall that our final expression for equilibrium real income is

$$y = \frac{1}{(1 - MPC)} [c_0 - (MPC \times t_0) + i_0 + g_0 + x_0],$$

where in our example $1/(1 - MPC)$ is equal to 5. This tells us that one way to induce a rise in equilibrium real income of $\Delta y = \$500$ billion is to raise real government spending by \$100 billion. In other words, the government could increase its autonomous spending level g_0 by exactly the amount of the recessionary gap $A-C$ in Figure 7–1, which in this example is equal to \$100 billion. This action would shift the aggregate desired expenditures schedule upward from $(c + i + g + x)_1$ to $(c + i + g + x)_{LR}$ and eliminate the recessionary gap. Equilibrium real income then would be at its long-run level, $y_{LR} = \$12{,}000$ billion.

CLOSING A RECESSIONARY GAP WITH A TAX CUT   The equation for equilibrium real income also indicates that a tax change could achieve the same outcome. A change in autonomous net taxes, Δt_0, would be multiplied by $-MPC$ times $1/(1 - MPC)$ to yield a change in equilibrium real income. This factor, $-MPC/(1 - MPC)$, is called the *autonomous tax multiplier,* because it indicates that a tax increase has a negative multiplier effect on real income. In our example, the value of this multiplier is equal to $-0.8/(1 - 0.8) = -0.8/0.2 = -4$, and the needed increase in real income is $\Delta y = \$500$ billion. Consequently, to achieve the long-run equilibrium level of income, the government could enact a *tax cut,* $\Delta t_0 = -\$125$ billion. Multiplying $-\$125$ billion times the autonomous tax multiplier of -4 yields the desired increase in real income of \$500 billion.

Our example illustrates why Keynes concluded that a recessionary gap could be eliminated by government deficit spending. He likewise argued that inflationary gaps could be eliminated through government surpluses. The surpluses would be achieved either by reductions in government spending that were not balanced by tax cuts or by tax increases that were not balanced by hikes in government spending. Because short-run business cycles are relatively commonplace events, Keynes advocated **countercyclical fiscal policy,** in which the government runs deficits during times of recessions and surpluses during inflationary times. Such policies, he argued, would offset business cycle fluctuations.

COUNTERCYCLICAL FISCAL POLICY: A process for managing government spending and taxation so as to smooth out business cycles; the government runs deficits during times of recessions and surpluses during inflationary periods.

FUNDAMENTAL ISSUE #1

Why does the basic Keynesian model indicate that there may be a potential stabilizing role for fiscal policy? In the basic Keynesian theory, changes in government spending and taxation policies can influence aggregate net autonomous expenditures and the equilibrium level of real income. Because the theory indicates that short-run business cycle fluctuations result from variations in autonomous expenditures, fiscal policy potentially can play a role in smoothing out these variations, thereby stabilizing real income near its long-run, natural level.

The Income Tax System in the Keynesian Framework

173

CHAPTER 7 Fiscal Policy—What Can Government Spending and Taxation Policies Accomplish?

In the basic Keynesian model, the government assesses taxes as a lump-sum amount. We doubt that many of you have ever paid lump-sum taxes to the government, however. In the United States, the federal and state governments typically assess *excise taxes, sales taxes, tariffs,* and *income taxes.* Excise taxes typically are assessed on consumer expenditures on specific goods and services. Sales taxes, which are imposed in many states, are a form of excise taxes that apply to consumer expenditures on *all,* or nearly all, goods and services in general. Tariffs, which are imposed by the federal government, are taxes on imported goods and services. Finally, income taxes are assessed on earnings of wages, interest, rents, and profits.

Trying to account for all of these various types of taxes in a single macroeconomic model would be complicated. Modifying the traditional Keynesian model to account for income taxes is a straightforward procedure, however. The income tax is the key source of tax revenues for the U.S. government, so we shall focus our attention on this form of taxation. (In nations of the European Union, taxes both on wage income *and* on consumption are key sources of governmental tax revenues; see on page 175 *Global Notebook: High Tax Rates on Labor and Consumption in Europe.*)

The Income Tax System

Figure 7–2 on the next page shows the relative sizes of the various sources of tax revenues received by the U.S. government. The three basic types of income taxes—personal income taxes, corporate income taxes, and social insurance payroll taxes—together account for about 90 percent of the federal government's total tax revenues. The personal income tax is a tax on all household income, and the corporate income tax is a tax on the accounting profits of corporations. Social insurance payroll taxes apply only to the wages and salaries of individuals.

PROGRESSIVE VERSUS REGRESSIVE INCOME TAX SYSTEMS Any tax system is a **progressive tax system** if the amount of the tax assessed on an individual rises as a percentage of the individual's income as his income increases. In a **regressive tax system,** in contrast, the total tax paid by a person rises as a percentage of the person's income as her income declines.

Finally, in a **proportional tax system,** the total tax that a person pays remains a constant percentage of the individual's income as the individual's income rises. A proportional tax system is neither progressive nor regressive.

MARGINAL VERSUS AVERAGE TAX RATES In the United States, the income tax system is designed to be progressive. **Marginal tax rates,** or the rates at which taxes change as a person's income increases (the change in taxes divided by the corresponding change in income, $\Delta t/\Delta y$), rise as an individual's income increases. Some of the progressivity of the system is reduced by the ability to *deduct* various types of expenditures from taxable income, but on net the U.S. system is relatively progressive.

PROGRESSIVE TAX SYSTEM: A system of taxation in which the amount of a tax that a person must pay increases as a percentage of the individual's income as that income rises.

REGRESSIVE TAX SYSTEM: A system of taxation in which the amount of a tax that a person must pay declines as a percentage of the individual's income as that income rises.

PROPORTIONAL TAX SYSTEM: A system of taxation in which the amount of a tax that a person must pay remains a constant percentage of the individual's income as that income rises.

MARGINAL TAX RATE: The rate at which tax payments rise when an individual's income increases; the change in taxes divided by the corresponding change in income, $\Delta t/\Delta y$.

Figure 7–2   The Sources of the U.S. Government's Tax Receipts

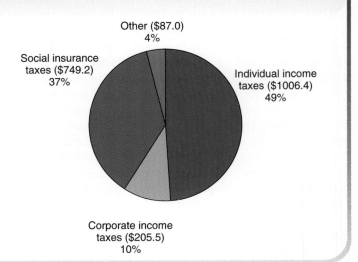

Together, individual and corporate income taxes and social insurance payroll taxes account for more than 90 percent of total federal tax revenues.

Other ($87.0)
4%

Social insurance
taxes ($749.2)
37%

Individual income
taxes ($1006.4)
49%

Corporate income
taxes ($205.5)
10%

NOTE: Amounts are in billions of dollars.
SOURCES: *Economic Report of the President,* 2002; *Economic Indicators* (various issues).

In contrast to the marginal tax rate, the **average tax rate** is simply the ratio of total tax payments to total income, or t/y. The marginal and average *income* tax rates that a person faces are identical in a proportional income tax system, because the individual always pays the same percentage of income taxes at any income level. In progressive or regressive income tax systems, however, the marginal and average income tax rates differ at various income levels. Suppose that a progressive system imposes a 10 percent income tax rate on the first $10,000 in income and a 20 percent tax rate on all income earnings above $10,000. In this system, an individual who earns $15,000 would pay $1,000 in income taxes on the first $10,000 in income and $1,000 on the additional $5,000 in income earnings. His total bill would be $2,000, and his average tax rate would be $2,000/$15,000, or 13⅓ percent. The 15,000th dollar earned would be taxed at a rate of 20 percent, however, so that would be the marginal tax rate faced at a level of income equal to $15,000.

AVERAGE TAX RATE: The ratio of total net taxes to total income.

Adapting the Keynesian Model to the Income Tax

A macroeconomic model with a progressive income system is very difficult to construct and analyze without using some sophisticated math. Nevertheless, we can illustrate all the essential ways that income taxes alter the Keynesian framework by examining a proportional income tax system. You should not confuse a proportional income tax with proposals for a *flat income tax system,* in which there is a constant marginal tax rate for all levels of taxable income. A flat tax system can be progressive if

On the Web

What distinguishes proposals for a so-called flat tax from a proportional income tax system? To learn more about various flat tax schemes, go to the flat tax Web site of the National Center for Policy Analysis, **http://www.ncpa.org/ pi/taxes/tax7.html**, and click on "Flat Tax Proposals."

Global NOTEBOOK

175

CHAPTER 7 Fiscal Policy—What Can Government Spending and Taxation Policies Accomplish?

High Tax Rates on Labor and Consumption in Europe

Like the U.S. government, national governments in the European Union (EU) depend considerably on taxes on the income of workers. As Panel (a) of Figure 7–3 shows, however, EU tax rates on labor income typically are much higher than the average U.S. tax rate of just over 20 percent. The EU labor tax rates range from nearly 23 percent in Ireland to as high as 51 percent in Sweden. As far back as 1970, the labor tax rate in most EU nations was well above 20 percent. Tax rates throughout the EU tended to increase between 1970 and 1980 before leveling off or even falling somewhat since then.

Forty-five U.S. states impose taxes on consumption through sales taxes, but state sales tax rates rarely exceed 10 percent. By way of contrast, as panel (b) of the figure indicates, national governments of EU nations impose much higher tax rates on consumption—mostly in the form of value-added taxes. Currently, the lowest tax rate on consumption in the EU is the approximately 18 percent set in Germany and Spain. Denmark currently has the highest tax rate on consumption, at about 30 percent.

Figure 7–3 Tax Rates on Labor and Consumption in Nations of the European Union

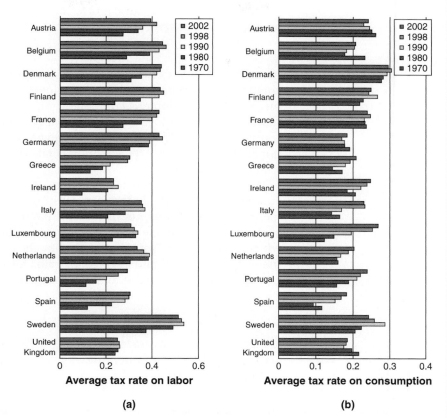

(a)

(b)

Panel (a) shows that several nations in the EU assess average tax rates on labor in excess of 40 percent. Panel (b) shows that average tax rates on consumption in the EU are typically in the range of 20 to 30 percent.

SOURCES: Carlos Martinez-Mongay, "ECFIN's Effective Tax Rates: Properties and Comparisons with Other Tax Indicators," Directorate for Economic and Financial Affairs, European Commission, October 2000; and authors' estimates.

For Critical Analysis

What are some possible consequences of differential tax rates on labor and consumption among nations that are as interconnected as those in the EU? (Hint: What incentives do the lower tax rates in some EU nations impart to people who currently reside in countries with higher tax rates?)

income earnings ranging from zero to some cutoff level are exempted from taxation. Under a proportional income tax, *all* income is taxed at the same marginal tax rate. Consequently, the marginal and average income tax rates faced by an individual are always equal under a proportional income tax, but these tax rates can differ under a flat tax that exempts low income levels from taxation.

THE TAX FUNCTION   We can capture the workings of a proportional income tax system in a macroeconomic model by using the following tax function:

$$t = t_0 + \tau y.$$

According to this tax function, the government's total real tax revenues are equal to an autonomous component plus a component that depends on real income. The autonomous component, t_0, includes tax revenues from other sources than the income tax, net of any transfer payments. The second component represents income tax revenues, which are directly proportional to real income. The marginal tax rate is τ (the Greek letter tau), which is a fraction.

Figure 7–4 shows the tax function on a diagram. The amount of net autonomous taxes, t_0, is the vertical intercept of the function, or governmental tax collections net of transfer payments if real income is equal to zero. The slope of the function, $\Delta t / \Delta y$, is the *overall* marginal tax rate, which is equal to τ. Note that even though the income tax is proportional, the overall marginal and average tax rates for the entire tax system are not equal, because the ratio of total net taxes to real income is equal to

$$t/y = (t_0 + \tau y)/y$$
$$= t_0/y + \tau.$$

Hence, the overall average tax rate, $t_0/y + \tau$, equals the marginal income tax rate, τ, only if net autonomous taxes are equal to zero. This typically will not be the case.

Figure 7–4   The Tax Function with a Proportional Income Tax System

In the tax function, $t = t_0 + \tau y$, t_0 denotes net tax revenues from sources other than the income tax and constitutes the vertical intercept of the tax function. The slope of the tax function is the income tax rate, τ.

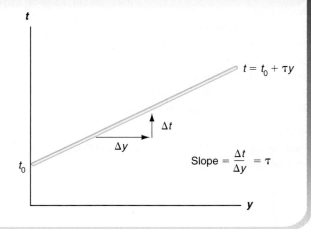

CONSUMPTION AND THE INCOME TAX RATE To determine how accounting for an income tax system affects equilibrium real income in the traditional Keynesian model, we need to retrace the solution for an income-expenditure equilibrium using our new tax function. The first step in this process is to think about how an income tax affects household consumption. Recall from Chapter 6 that the consumption function is

$$c = c_0 + (MPC \times y_d),$$

where c_0 denotes autonomous consumption, MPC is the marginal propensity to consume, and $y_d \equiv y - t$ is real disposable income.

If we substitute our new tax function into the consumption function, we get

$$
\begin{aligned}
c &= c_0 + (MPC \times y_d) \\
&= c_0 + [MPC \times (y - t)] \\
&= c_0 + [MPC \times (y - t_0 - \tau y)] \\
&= c_0 - (MPC \times t_0) + [(1 - \tau) \times MPC \times y].
\end{aligned}
$$

The slope of the consumption function, $\Delta c / \Delta y$, therefore is equal to $(1 - \tau) \times MPC$, or 1 minus the marginal tax rate times the marginal propensity to consume. This indicates that when a person receives an additional dollar of real income, the first thing that happens to that dollar is that it is taxed at the rate τ. Then only the portion $(1 - \tau)$ is available to allocate to additional consumption.

Figure 7–5 displays the consumption function. Autonomous consumption is equal to $c_0 - (MPC \times t_0)$, so this is the vertical intercept of the consumption function. The slope of the consumption function is equal to $(1 - \tau) \times MPC$, or 1 minus the marginal tax rate times the marginal propensity to consume. This means that an increase in the tax rate, from a rate equal to τ to a higher rate equal to τ', will reduce the slope of the consumption function. Thus, an increase in the tax rate will *rotate* the consumption function downward, as shown in Figure 7–5.

Figure 7–5   The Consumption Function with a Proportional Income Tax System

If the government raises taxes by imposing a proportional tax rate τ on aggregate real income, then the slope of the consumption function is equal to $(1 - \tau)$ times the marginal propensity to consume, or $(1 - \tau) \times MPC$. Consequently, an increase in the income tax rate from an initial rate τ to a higher rate given by τ' will reduce the slope of the consumption function, causing it to rotate downward.

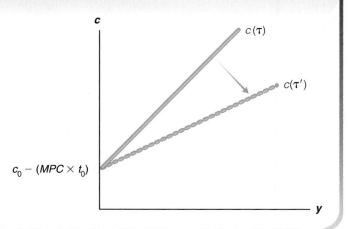

177

CHAPTER 7   Fiscal Policy—What Can Government Spending and Taxation Policies Accomplish?

THE INCOME TAX RATE AND EQUILIBRIUM REAL INCOME   To determine equilibrium real income, we now follow the same steps that we used in Chapter 6. First, we impose the income-expenditure equality condition, $y = c + i + g + x$. For now, let's assume that desired investment spending is completely autonomous and equal to an amount i_0. If government spending and exports also are autonomous, then we can substitute our consumption function into our equilibrium expression to get

$$y = c + i + g + x$$
$$= c_0 - (MPC \times t_0) + [(1 - \tau) \times MPC \times y] + i_0 + g_0 + x_0.$$

Now, we can solve for y by subtracting $[(1 - \tau) \times MPC \times y]$ from both sides to get

$$y - [(1 - \tau) \times MPC \times y] = c_0 - (MPC \times t_0) + i_0 + g_0 + x_0$$

or

$$\{1 - [(1 - \tau) \times MPC]\} \times y = c_0 - (MPC \times t_0) + i_0 + g_0 + x_0.$$

Now, if we divide both sides by $\{1 - [(1 - \tau) \times MPC]\}$, we get our final solution for equilibrium real income with an income tax system:

$$y = \frac{1}{1 - [(1 - \tau) \times MPC]} \times [c_0 - (MPC \times t_0) + i_0 + g_0 + x_0].$$

As in Chapter 6, the equilibrium level of real income is equal to an autonomous expenditures multiplier times net autonomous expenditures.

With an income tax system, however, the size of the autonomous expenditures multiplier depends on the income tax rate τ. A reduction in the income tax rate reduces the denominator of the multiplier and therefore increases the size of the multiplier. Thus, a cut in the income tax rate increases the size of the autonomous expenditures multiplier.

Figure 7–6 explains why this is so. Panel (a) shows the effect of a decline in net autonomous expenditures, perhaps resulting from a fall in autonomous investment, when the tax rate is relatively low, so that the slope of the consumption function is relatively steep. Panel (b) displays the effect of an identical decline in net autonomous expenditures when the tax rate is relatively high, so that the consumption function's slope is relatively shallow.

As you can see, the multiplier effect is larger when the tax rate is lower. This phenomenon can be readily explained. A fall in, say, autonomous investment spending causes real income to decline. This causes a fall in consumption spending, which causes an additional fall in real income, and so on. At each step in this multiplier process, the fall in consumption spending is larger with a lower tax rate because the effect on disposable income is greater when the tax rate is lower. Consequently, the total size of the multiplier effect is larger with a lower income tax rate.

AUTOMATIC FISCAL STABILIZER: A mechanism of government policy that automatically reduces volatility in real income caused by changes in autonomous expenditures.

The Income Tax System as an Automatic Stabilizer

The comparison in Figure 7–6 illustrates the claim of many economists: an important by-product of a government's use of an income tax system is that the system functions as an **automatic fiscal stabilizer,** or a governmental

Figure 7-6 The Multiplier Effect with Different Income Tax Rates

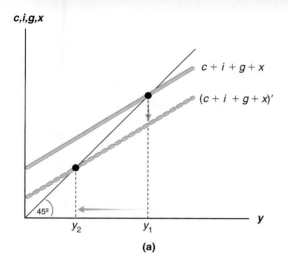

(a)

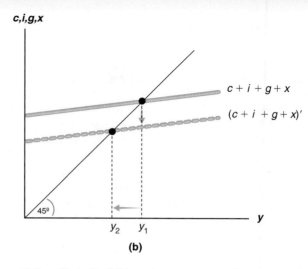

(b)

Both panels of this figure illustrate the effects of a decline in autonomous expenditures. The income tax rate in panel (a), however, is lower than the tax rate in panel (b). Consequently, the autonomous expenditures schedule is more steeply sloped in panel (a), and the result is a larger fall in equilibrium real income. This illustrates that the mul-tiplier effect of a fall in autonomous expenditures on equilibrium real income is larger for lower income tax rates. Thus, an increase in the income tax rate tends to make equilibrium real income more stable in the face of variations in aggregate expenditures, as shown in panel (b).

policy mechanism that automatically mutes variations in real income arising from changes in autonomous expenditures.

To see this, imagine the result if the income tax rate were set equal to zero, which would imply elimination of the income tax. The consumption function would be as steep as possible, thereby steepening the aggregate desired expenditures schedule, $c + i + g + x$, as much as possible. Consequently, in the absence of the income tax system, equilibrium real income would respond as fully as possible to variations in autonomous aggregate expenditures, such as a fall in desired investment spending.

The income tax system is not the only type of automatic stabilizer constructed by governments. In the United States and many other nations, the government has linked transfer programs, such as unemployment benefits, Social Security, and welfare programs, to the incomes of recipients. Thus, when aggregate real income declines, more individuals' incomes fall below thresholds that qualify them for government benefits. Therefore total transfer payments increase as real income declines. In our model, we have assumed that transfer payments are a lump sum. If we were to link them to income, we would find that income-conditioned transfer payments also function as an automatic fiscal stabilizer. (Recent estimates indicate that the U.S. income tax system has possessed very consistent stabilizing properties since the 1960s; see on the following page *Policy Notebook: Quantifying the Stabilization Gains from the Income Tax.*)

Unit III Keynesian and Monetarist Macroeconomic Perspectives

 **Policy** NOTEBOOK

Quantifying the Stabilization Gains from the Income Tax

Since the 1960s, numerous changes in the U.S. tax laws have tinkered considerably with the tax rates for people in different income groups. The net effect on the average income tax rate, nonetheless, has been relatively small.

Alan Auerbach of the University of California at Berkeley and Daniel Feenberg of the National Bureau of Economic Research have estimated that the U.S. tax structure automatically offsets as much as 8 percent of any unexpected change in aggregate expenditures. Thus, a decline in autonomous investment equal to $10 billion results in an increase in consumption expenditures of about $800 million owing to the reduced taxation of income.

Auerbach and Feenberg have concluded that aside from a short interval during the late 1970s and the early 1980s, this stabilizing effect has been nearly constant for more than four decades. All the various changes in the U.S. income tax structure during that period have tended to have offsetting effects on the automatic-stabilizer properties of the U.S. tax system.

For Critical Analysis
How could the government adjust the tax rate to push the tax system's stabilizing effect above 8 percent?

FUNDAMENTAL ISSUE #2

How can the basic Keynesian model be adapted to account for income taxes? This can be done by recognizing that the government's real net tax revenues must equal an autonomous component plus a component that is equal to the average income tax rate times the level of real income. As a result, the slope of the consumption function and the aggregate desired expenditures schedule depend on the income tax rate. A reduction in the tax rate steepens these schedules, which raises equilibrium real income while making equilibrium real income more sensitive to the effects of changes in autonomous aggregate expenditures.

Taxes, the Federal Budget, and Real Income

The comparison in Figure 7–6 tells us that the stabilization benefit of the income tax system increases with higher income tax rates. Most of us, of course, do not like high income tax rates, because they leave us with lower disposable income to allocate to saving, import spending, and domestic consumption. Governments interested in the performances of their economies must recognize this as well. As you will see, when the government determines the income tax rate, it faces a trade-off between real income stability and the absolute size of income. A higher tax rate makes income more stable but also depresses real income. A lower tax rate stimulates real income but also makes income less stable in the face of a change in autonomous aggregate expenditures.

With an income tax system, the tax revenues of the government depend on both the tax rate and real income. Together with government expendi-

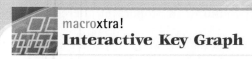

macroxtra!
Interactive Key Graph

The graph below shows how equilibrium real income responds to a cut in the income tax rate. How do different values of the tax rate affect the aggregate expenditures schedule and real income? You can discover the answer to this question by interacting with this graph on the Web.

Go to http://macroxtra.swcollege.com

Figure 7–7   The Effect of a Cut in the Income Tax Rate on Equilibrium Real Income

Because a cut in the income tax rate steepens the consumption function, the rate cut must also steepen the aggregate expenditures schedule. The result is an increase in equilibrium real income that arises from the stimulus to consumption spending owing to the cut in the tax rate.

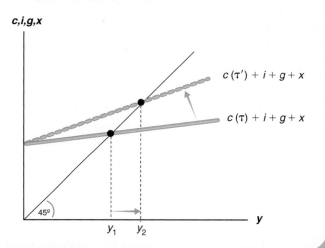

tures, governmental tax collections also determine the size of the government's budget surplus or deficit. Hence, income tax rates, real income, and the state of the government's budget all must be related, as you will see shortly.

Tax Rate Changes and Equilibrium Real Income

Changes in the tax rate alter the slope of the consumption function by changing the portion of real income available for household consumption. Hence, tax rate changes must affect aggregate desired expenditures and, therefore, equilibrium real income.

Figure 7–7 shows the effect of a tax rate reduction on equilibrium real income. A cut in the income tax rate steepens the consumption function and thereby steepens the aggregate desired expenditures schedule. This schedule rotates upward along the 45-degree line. Equilibrium real national income increases.

A cut in the income tax rate increases the portion of each dollar of real income that may be allocated to saving, import expenditures, and consumption spending. Every individual thereby responds to a tax cut by allocating a greater share of total income earnings to consumption spending.

On the Web

What fractions of GDP were government spending and taxes in the most recent period? To find out, go to the Federal Reserve Bank of St. Louis's Federal Reserve Economic Data (FRED) Web site at http://research.stlouisfed.org/fred, and use the most recent data to calculate these ratios.

This raises aggregate desired expenditures in proportion, thereby pushing up equilibrium real income.

Thus, a cut in the tax rate stimulates an increase in real income. As shown earlier, however, a tax rate reduction also tends to make equilibrium real income more susceptible to changes in autonomous expenditures. Any government faces this fundamental trade-off in determining the "best" overall income tax rate.

Do Cuts in Income Tax Rates Necessarily Reduce Tax Revenues?

Figure 7–8 shows the federal government's expenditures and tax revenues as a percentage of GDP since 1959. The figure also displays the difference between government outlays and tax collections as a percentage of GDP for the same years. This net amount was almost always positive through 1997, indicating that the government experienced a budget deficit. The net of outlays over tax revenues as a percentage of GDP dropped below zero in 1998. Hence, the federal government officially operated at a surplus for a time, until the war on terrorism began in 2001.

GOVERNMENT SPENDING, TAXES, DEFICITS, AND SURPLUSES   As you learned in Chapter 4, the *primary deficit* is simply the difference between the government's expenditures and its tax revenues. Total government outlays include interest payments on outstanding debt that the government issued to finance deficits in past years. The government cannot do much about the interest portion of each year's outlays after the fact, however. Indeed, if the government wants to contain deficits or increase its budget surpluses, all it can do is either reduce its spending or increase its tax revenues.

Figure 7–8   The Net of Federal Government Outlays over Taxes as a Percentage of U.S. GDP

This figure displays government outlays, tax revenues, and the net outlays (government spending minus tax revenues) as percentages of GDP. Although there is year-to-year variability in both government spending and tax receipts, tax revenues as a fraction of GDP have risen in recent years. Government spending generally has trended downward until the early 2000s.

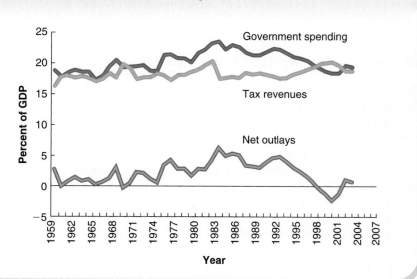

SOURCES: *Economic Report of the President,* 2002; *Economic Indicators* (various issues).

Nearly all political leaders say that the government should spend efficiently. In light of evidence of inefficiencies in various governmental programs, therefore, many candidates for political office are safe in saying that they favor less government spending.

Figure 7–8 indicates that, as a percentage of GDP, government expenditures increased considerably between 1959 and 1983, but declined after 1984 before leveling off since the late 1990s. The federal deficit as a percentage of GDP began to decline after 1993 and officially disappeared between 1998 and 2001. The government was running a surplus, taking into account a surplus in the Social Security system. Although the surplus arose in part because of a slight decline in government spending, the key reason was that U.S. government tax revenues increased relative to GDP, as Figure 7–8 indicates. Recall that the average tax rate is the ratio of total tax payments to total real income. Consequently, the plot of government tax receipts relative to GDP in Figure 7–8 is really a graph of the overall average tax rate in the United States since 1959. As you can see, the average federal tax rate is about four percentage points higher today than it was in 1959.

macroxtra!
Online
Perspective

To learn about how the state of the government's budget quickly changed when the war on terrorism began, go to the Chapter 7 reading, entitled "The Federal Budget: What a Difference a Year Makes," by Alan Viard of the Federal Reserve Bank of Dallas. http://macroxtra.swcollege.com

THE STATIC VIEW OF THE TAX RATE AND TAX REVENUES Because income taxes account for the bulk of the U.S. government's tax revenues, an issue of considerable concern is how income tax rates, real income, and the government's budget are related. There are two perspectives on this issue: the static view and the dynamic view. The purely *static view* is based on the tax function we discussed earlier, which is given by

$$t = t_0 + \tau y.$$

Under this static view, we can visualize the relationship between the tax rate τ and tax revenues t by considering the diagram of the tax function in Figure 7–9. This is just a graph of the tax function, in which tax revenues are measured along the vertical axis and the tax rate is measured along the

183

CHAPTER 7 Fiscal Policy—What Can Government Spending and Taxation Policies Accomplish?

Figure 7–9   The Static View of the Relationship between the Income Tax Rate and Total Tax Revenues

If we graph the tax function with real tax revenues measured against the income tax rate, then the slope of the function is real income, y. Given the level of real income, a cut in the tax rate reduces government tax receipts.

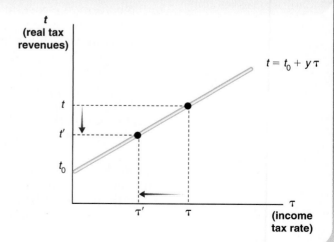

horizontal axis. In this diagram, therefore, t_0 is the horizontal intercept of the straight-line tax function, and real income, y, is the slope. This function tells us that as the tax rate declines, say, from a value τ to a smaller value τ', the government's tax revenues fall, from t to t'. Thus, according to this perspective, if Congress wishes to cut deficits or build surpluses, but prefers not to do so only by reducing government spending, it will need to increase the income tax rate. Certainly, the static view implies that Congress would not reduce tax rates if it wants to maintain or increase the government's tax revenues.

THE DYNAMIC VIEW OF THE TAX RATE AND TAX REVENUES   Careful consideration of Figure 7–9, however, indicates that there is a problem with the static view. An upper bound on the income tax rate is 100 percent, or $\tau = 1$. At this maximum possible tax rate, do you think it is likely that the government would collect any income tax revenues? After all, if the government is going to take all of people's income, they are likely to respond either by halting all work effort or, more likely, by finding ways to hide most or all of their income from the government. Indeed, nations with very high tax rates commonly also have the largest *underground economies,* or portions of their economies in which people conduct unrecorded transactions for the purpose of avoiding taxes (and, potentially, arrest for engaging in these and other illegal transactions).

Although the diagram in Figure 7–9 is mathematically correct, it really indicates that a reduction in the tax rate, τ, necessarily causes a fall in income tax revenues and hence total government tax receipts, *only if all other things, including* real income, *are equal.* The problem is that a change in the tax rate will alter real income, as we showed in Figure 7–6 on page 179. This change, in turn, will affect the slope of the tax schedule in Figure 7–9. The purely static view of the relationship between the tax rate and tax revenues ignores the fact that equilibrium real income changes when the tax rate is altered.

THE LAFFER CURVE   Figure 7–10 shows what happens when we take into account that tax rate cuts cause real income to rise. As we noted, at a tax rate of 100 percent, the government receives no income tax revenues. Hence, at point A the government's net tax receipts are autonomous taxes, t_0.

The figure also shows the tax function from Figure 7–9. Again, at a relatively high tax rate τ, real tax revenues would be equal to t at point B. A cut in the tax rate to τ' would cause equilibrium real income to rise, from y to a larger amount y', so the tax function would steepen. Indeed, real income could rise sufficiently that even though the tax rate applied to income would be lower, the net income tax revenues of the government would be equal to the higher level t' at point C. Under this dynamic view, therefore, *an income tax rate cut could actually cause tax revenues to rise.*

Nonetheless, at some point further cuts in the tax rate would reduce the government's tax revenues on net. For instance, reducing the tax rate once more, from τ' to τ'', would cause real income to rise from y' to a larger amount y'', which again would steepen the tax function. Yet tax revenues

Figure 7–10   The Dynamic View of the Relationship between the Income Tax Rate and Total Tax Revenues

With a tax rate equal to 1 (100 percent) at point A, individuals would have no incentive to earn income, so the government would collect no income tax revenues, and its only net tax receipts, t_0, would come from other sources. At point B, the tax rate is less than 100 percent, so the government collects some income tax revenues. A cut in the income tax rate reduces the portion of income that must be paid to the government as taxes, which tends to reduce the government's tax revenues but also raises equilibrium real income, causing the tax function to steepen. Consequently, a tax rate reduction could result in a movement from point B to point C, implying that a cut in the income tax rate could actually raise the government's total tax receipts. Of course, at a zero tax rate, at point E, the government could collect no income tax revenues. Therefore, continual tax rate cuts would ultimately reduce tax revenues, as indicated by a movement from point C to point D. The *Laffer curve* traced out by points A through E shows that at sufficiently high tax rates,

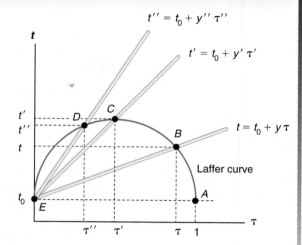

cuts in income tax rates can yield increases in government tax receipts.

on net would decline as a result of this second tax rate reduction, from t' to t'' at point D.

Finally, if the tax rate were equal to zero, the government again would collect no income taxes, and its net tax receipts would equal only the autonomous amount of taxes, t_0, at point E.

Points A, B, C, D, and E trace out a hill-shaped schedule known as the **Laffer curve,** after Arthur Laffer, the economist who popularized the dynamic view in the late 1970s and early 1980s. The Laffer curve indicates that if the income tax rate is sufficiently high, cutting the tax rate will raise income tax revenues. Only at lower rates will tax rate reductions necessarily reduce tax revenues.

The difficult problem, naturally, is determining the location of the top point of the Laffer curve. The evidence on this issue is mixed. Shortly after significant reductions in average tax rates were enacted in the early 1980s, tax revenues declined, and the deficit increased sharply. At first glance, these events seem to support the static view. The difficulty with this off-the-cuff judgment, however, is that the U.S. economy went into a sharp recession in the early 1980s even as tax rates were cut, because autonomous investment and consumption declined sharply. Even though government spending also increased in the early 1980s (see Figure 7–8 on page 182), these declines in private spending led to a net reduction in equilibrium real income. Consequently, the true result of the 1980s experiment with the Laffer curve is difficult to judge.

LAFFER CURVE: A relationship between income tax rates and income tax revenues, which shows that at sufficiently high tax rates, tax rate reductions can increase tax revenues, whereas at lower tax rates, tax rate reductions necessarily reduce tax revenues.

FUNDAMENTAL ISSUE #3

Do cuts in income tax rates necessarily reduce the government's tax revenues?   A tax rate cut reduces the government's tax receipts if government expenditures and real income do not change. A tax rate cut also causes a rise in equilibrium real income, which raises the government's revenues from the income tax system. Consequently, if the tax rate is sufficiently high, a cut in the tax rate can actually induce a rise in the government's total tax revenues.

Ricardian Equivalence: Can Tax Policy Matter?

During almost every electoral cycle in the United States, candidates for Congress or for president seem to debate the merits of a cut in income tax rates or "tax rebates" or some other type of short-term, autonomous tax reductions. To this point, our discussion indicates that these debates ought to center on the implications of such proposals for the volume and variability of economic activity and the size of the government's deficit or surplus.

In recent years, however, debates about tax changes have also focused on their implications for the *distribution* of income. Typically, one politician will propose a tax cut plan, and then another will respond that the plan would benefit high-income people disproportionately as compared with low-income people. The potential macroeconomic effects of tax cuts sometimes get lost in the rhetoric of these discussions.

Some macroeconomists believe that the income distribution issue is an appropriate topic for debate. They contend that tax cuts cannot actually affect aggregate economic activity. In addition, they argue, tax changes cannot influence the variability of real income in response to changes in autonomous aggregate expenditures. All that changes in tax rates or autonomous taxes can do is affect the size of the government's deficit or surplus and, as many politicians emphasize, the distribution of income. In other words, according to this view, on the question of the effects of tax changes, the politicians have it right, and most economists have got it wrong.

Ricardian Equivalence

The basis for this argument is the *Ricardian equivalence proposition.* The elements of this proposition were outlined by a classical economist of eighteenth- and nineteenth-century Britain named David Ricardo (1772–1823). Ricardo advanced the idea that a cut in lump-sum taxes theoretically might have no effect on aggregate consumption. His reasoning was as follows. If a government maintains its current level of spending, then it must finance a tax cut today by issuing more bonds. In the future, the government must pay interest on these bonds. To pay this interest, which will be a flow of future expenditures by the government, taxes eventually will have to be increased. Foresighted taxpayers understand this and realize that a current tax cut implies a future tax increase. Consequently, rational, self-interested individuals will respond to a current tax cut by saving the increase in their disposable, after-tax income until the future time when the government increases taxes to pay interest on the debts arising from the current tax cut. Thus, a current tax cut cannot raise current consumption and, therefore, cannot stimulate real income.

In a nutshell, therefore, the **Ricardian equivalence proposition** is a simple idea. It states that a current tax cut implies a future tax increase to make interest payments on debt issued to finance the tax cut. Consequently, people allocate the current increase in their disposable income to saving, from which they can draw to pay the higher future taxes. That is, a tax cut today essentially is *equivalent* to a tax increase in the future. As a result, consumption and equilibrium real income are unaffected by a tax cut.

Note that the argument hinges on the maintenance of a constant level of government spending. An increase in government spending, according to the Ricardian equivalence proposition, increases the flow of taxes that ultimately will be necessary to finance those government expenditures today and into the future. Hence, increases in government spending *do* affect equilibrium real income, because these actions permanently increase lifetime flows of tax transfers to the government and thereby induce people to reduce their private saving and consumption.

The Ricardian equivalence reasoning also works in the opposite direction for the case of a tax increase. If the government raises taxes today while keeping its spending level constant, then it will be able to pay off any existing debt more quickly and will be able to reduce taxes in the future. Consequently, people respond to a current tax increase by drawing from their stock of accumulated savings. They realize they will be able to replenish their savings when their future tax burden declines. As a result, they maintain their current level of consumption, and so equilibrium real income does not change.

Intergenerational Ricardian Equivalence

Until the early 1980s, modern economists had largely ignored or dismissed the Ricardian equivalence proposition. They argued, as we have throughout this text up to this point, that a current tax cut would increase present after-tax income and cause a rise in present consumption. Ricardo's reasoning, they suggested, relied on too much foresight by taxpayers. In addition, even if people realize that a tax cut today will require a future tax increase, such an increase might be so far in the future that today's generation will be dead and gone before the tax increase takes place. As a result, current autonomous changes in lump-sum taxes or changes in income tax rates should affect equilibrium real income for the current generation's economy.

Nevertheless, several modern economists, including Robert Barro of Harvard University, have contended that Ricardo may have had it right two centuries ago. Barro and others contend that self-interested individuals will indeed realize that a current tax cut is equivalent to a future tax increase. They also argue that individuals who care about the welfare of future generations, which will include their children, grandchildren, and other relatives, will also care about the tax burdens that those generations

RICARDIAN EQUIVALENCE PROPOSITION: The proposition that if government spending will be unchanged in the future, people regard a current tax cut as equivalent to a future tax increase and therefore save the proceeds of a tax cut rather than increasing their consumption.

BEQUEST: A sum payable to one's offspring at the time of death.

INTERGENERATIONAL TRANSFERS: Transfers of disposable income, in the form of gifts or bequests, from one generation to another generation.

will face. Thus, Barro and others propose that Ricardian equivalence applies not only to members of a current generation but to people *across* generations. Ricardian equivalence, they believe, is an *intergenerational* concept.

BEQUESTS AND INTERGENERATIONAL TRANSFERS   Consider the following example. Suppose that a political party adopts a platform proposing significant tax cuts without changes in prevailing levels of government expenditures. If a sufficient number of the party's candidates are elected and enact this plan, current taxes will decline, and the government will run a deficit. Suppose also that this party becomes entrenched in power for a number of years and holds to its platform. Then taxes will be lower than before for a long interval, and the government will continue to run deficits.

Members of the current generation who are in their highest-income years (roughly ages forty-five to sixty-five) will be the primary beneficiaries of this long-lasting cut in taxes. Their disposable income will be larger than before and will remain at a higher level for several years. Nevertheless, these individuals will realize that the government is constantly running deficits because of these tax cuts. They also will recognize that their children and grandchildren will ultimately face higher taxes to pay off the debt that will accumulate after a number of years of the low-tax policy. Because these members of the current, older generation care about their offspring, they will allocate the increase in their disposable income attributable to tax cuts to saving.

As members of the older generation age, their children and grandchildren will become taxpayers and will face higher tax burdens. These younger men and women will have a hard time paying their taxes while maintaining a standard of living as good as the older generation enjoyed. Out of concern for the welfare of their offspring, members of the older generation will pass along their accumulated savings to the younger generation, either in the form of gifts or in the form of **bequests,** or sums payable to their offspring after their deaths. In essence, then, *the older generation will effectively pay the taxes that have fallen on the young generation.* In this way, the tax decrease that *apparently* benefited the older generation nevertheless ultimately will be paid for by that generation.

Note that Ricardian equivalence still holds in this example because of **intergenerational transfers,** or transfers of disposable income via gifts or bequests from members of one generation to those of another. Ultimately, instead of changing their consumption levels, the members of the older generation in our example save the proceeds of the tax cuts that they received and pass them on to their offspring. On net, then, the long-lasting tax cut for the older generation does not influence their consumption spending. In addition, the tax cut does not influence economic activity for *either* generation. The older generation saves the proceeds to give to the younger generation, who then pay higher taxes later from the proceeds of the gifts and bequests. Members of the younger generation are able to spend the same amounts as before even though they, on paper at least, face a higher tax burden than the older generation faced.

IS THE LOGIC OF THE RICARDIAN EQUIVALENCE PROPOSITION INESCAPABLE?   By the late 1980s, the group of macroeconomists supporting the Ricardian equivalence proposition and its implications for tax policy had grown to include many more than just Robert Barro and a few others. Indeed, among macroeconomists the notion of Ricardian equivalence transformed the topic of debate from how large the effects of tax cuts might be to whether tax cuts could have any effects at all.

One irony about the timing of this transformation of the economic debate was that it took place during the 1980s. As Figure 7–11 indicates, when U.S. government deficits were historically high relative to GDP, national saving rates were at historically low levels. This appears to contradict the Ricardian equivalence proposition, which indicates that saving rates should have *risen* as the federal deficit increased, as people saved to pay anticipated higher future taxes.

In the view of a number of economists, a number of factors stand in the way of Ricardian equivalence:

- *Shortsightedness.* A number of economists contend that proponents of Ricardian equivalence give people too much credit for looking ahead. In fact, they argue, people are not nearly so sophisticated. Members of any given generation often struggle just to make their own ends meet, goes this counterargument, and cannot concern themselves with the tax burdens of their offspring until it is truly too late. As a result of this shortsightedness, members of a current generation *do* raise their consumption in response to a tax cut.

- *Liquidity constraints.* Even some economists who believe that people are rational and farsighted argue that the Ricardian equivalence

189

CHAPTER 7 Fiscal Policy—What Can Government Spending and Taxation Policies Accomplish?

Figure 7–11   U.S. Government Deficits and Saving as Percentages of GDP

The Ricardian equivalence proposition indicates that individuals should respond to increased government budget deficits by saving more funds to pay the implied higher future taxes that they will face to repay those deficits. In reality, however, private saving trended downward even as U.S. government deficits trended upward.

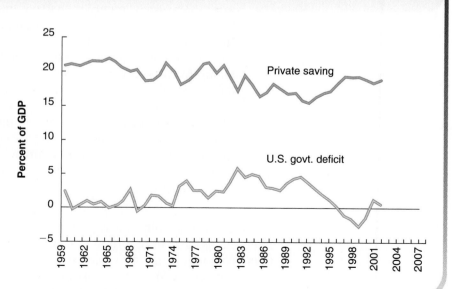

SOURCE: *Economic Report of the President,* 2002.

logic is still flawed, in that it fails to take into account **liquidity constraints** that people face during their lives. These are constraints that people face on the availability of cash and credit to meet their spending needs at various points in their life spans. For instance, a couple in their thirties with several children may use the proceeds of a tax cut to purchase a larger house, simply because they are low on cash and cannot find lenders willing to extend them sufficient credit. Instead of saving the proceeds of the tax cut to pass on to their children, the couple facing a liquidity constraint will allocate the tax cut to higher consumption.

- *Tax rate changes.* The logic of Ricardian equivalence applies most directly to lump-sum tax changes. Changes in marginal tax rates, however, affect decisions about how much to work and thereby influence production of real goods and services. As a result, real incomes and consumption and saving choices could be affected by changes in marginal tax rates. Consequently, many opponents of Ricardian equivalence argue that the hypothesis fails to apply to changes in *tax rates,* though it might be relevant for tax rebates and other lump-sum tax changes.

- *Gift and bequest motives.* Other economists point out that people give gifts and bequests to their offspring for many reasons. One reason might be to help the offspring maintain their own living standards in the face of altered tax burdens. Another, however, might be to induce behavior that the parents desire from their offspring, such as caring for the parents when they reach old age. Such additional motives could explain many of the gifts and bequests parents give to their children, but the Ricardian equivalence reasoning ignores such factors.

- *Income uncertainty.* Martin Feldstein, who like Barro is an economist at Harvard University, has pointed out a potentially critical flaw in the fundamental Ricardian equivalence logic: Intergenerational Ricardian equivalence does not necessarily hold true when members of the older generation face *income uncertainty.* Even if they care about their offspring, at the time of a tax cut members of the older generation do not know what their future flows of income will turn out to be in later years—the situation that all of us arguably face. Therefore, to protect themselves against the risk that their incomes and consumption levels may turn out to be lower than they might otherwise wish, members of the older generation take advantage of a tax cut by increasing their consumption.

The debate about the Ricardian equivalence proposition is still in progress. At this point, most economists agree that Ricardian equivalence likely holds to at least a limited extent, thereby muting the effects of tax cuts on economic activity. David Ricardo developed many other theories, especially concerning labor market behavior and wages, but only his theory of tax policy continues, after two centuries, to be a significant source of controversy in macroeconomics. It appears that the Ricardian equivalence proposition was Ricardo's own bequest to the current generation of macroeconomists.

> FUNDAMENTAL ISSUE #4
>
> **What is the Ricardian equivalence proposition?** This proposition states that tax reductions will not affect total consumption or aggregate desired expenditures. The reasoning behind this proposition is that people recognize that a current tax reduction entails a rise in the government's debt that they will have to repay in the future. Therefore, they respond by saving the proceeds of a tax cut so that they or their offspring will be able to pay higher future taxes. Many economists concur with this proposition, although others point out that its relevance hinges on the degree to which people are shortsighted, the extent to which people face liquidity constraints, the applicability of the proposition to changes in tax rates, the motivations that people have for providing gifts and bequests to their offspring, and the degree of uncertainty that people have about their future incomes.

191

Chapter 7 Fiscal Policy—What Can Government Spending and Taxation Policies Accomplish?

Tax Competition Sweeps the Globe

The Laffer curve analysis indicates that nations with relatively low tax rates tend to have relatively higher tax bases. This is one reason why nations' governments sometimes engage in *tax competition,* reducing their tax rates below those prevailing in other countries in an effort to induce individuals and businesses to engage in taxable activities within their borders instead. By reducing their tax rates, nations actually might be able to broaden their tax bases sufficiently to generate net *increases* in their tax revenues.

Fighting Over Capital

When entrepreneurs are considering starting a new business or when existing businesses are assessing where to construct a new facility, what they care about are *marginal* tax rates, or the tax rates that they will face on earnings generated by the *next additional* unit of capital. Joeri Gorter and Ashok Parikh of the Netherlands Bureau for Economic Policy Analysis have estimated marginal tax rates on capital in EU nations, and their estimates are reported in Figure 7–12.

These estimates indicate that if managers are equally inclined to consider capital investments in any given EU country, taking into account marginal tax rates on their investment will push them toward such relatively low-tax locales as Greece and Ireland. Managers are less likely to consider France and Germany, which have the highest marginal tax rates on capital.

This has important implications for flows of foreign direct investment within Europe. Gorter and Parikh find that for each percentage-point reduction in the marginal tax rate on capital relative to the EU average tax rate, any given EU nation's flow of foreign direct investment tends to increase by about 4 percent.

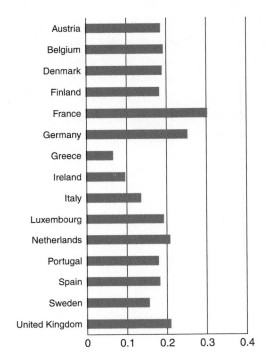

Figure 7–12   Marginal Tax Rates on Capital in the European Union

Marginal tax rates on capital are much higher in France and Germany than in Greece and Ireland.

SOURCE: Joeri Gorter and Ashok Parikh, "How Mobile Is Capital within the European Union?" Research Memorandum, CPB Netherlands Bureau for Economic Policy Analysis, The Hague, November 2000.

Trying to Reduce Tax Competition: International Coordination among Taxing Authorities

There are two basic perspectives on the increased tax competition that has accompanied the recent globalization trend. One perspective is that tax competition constrains taxation and thereby makes governments operate more efficiently. According to another view, however, national governments realize that if they maintain relatively high tax rates, the tax base will shrink because some residents will attempt to become free riders by reducing their contributions to the tax base. To avoid inducing declines in national tax bases, governments will set tax rates lower than they otherwise would. But with these low rates, the governments will be unable to earn enough revenues to maintain socially desirable spending programs.

Those who view tax competition as harmful typically favor international coordination of tax policies. A number of governments in industrialized nations with well-developed tax bases promote tax coordination. Some nations have even coordinated efforts to try to force other countries to join their tax-coordination schemes. In 2001, the thirty member nations of the Organization for Economic Cooperation and Development (OECD), which includes the United States, Japan, Canada, and major European nations, signed a "Memorandum of Understanding" requiring OECD nations to "blacklist" nations with "harmful tax regimes." Specifically, countries that the OECD determined had set tax rates sufficiently low to "unfairly erode the tax bases of other countries and distort the location of capital and services"

would be targeted for various sanctions, such as imposing withholding taxes on payments to residents of harmful tax regimes, denying foreign tax credits for taxes paid to their governments, and perhaps even adopting overt trade sanctions. Interestingly, the tax systems of four OECD members—Luxembourg, Switzerland, the United Kingdom, and the United States—all qualified as harmful tax regimes under the OECD's definition, but the OECD nations aimed their coordinated tax sanctions only against nonmembers.

Research Project

Based on the estimates of Gorter and Parikh and assuming all other factors are equal, which EU nations would you predict are most likely to experience the largest capital inflows? Given what you learned in Chapter 5 about economic growth, which countries are most likely and least likely to experience greater future growth in per capita incomes? Explain your reasoning.

Web Resources

1. What are arguments favoring reducing international tax competition? For one perspective, visit http://www.imf.org/external/np/fad/itd/2002/031302.htm.

2. How have global flows of capital changed in recent years? For a good review of developments into the early 2000s, go to the home page of the International Monetary Fund (http://www.imf.org), and click on "Publications." Under "Search by," type in the title, "International Capital Markets." Then select "International Capital Markets, August 2001."

1. The Potential Stabilizing Role of Fiscal Policy in the Basic Keynesian Model: According to Keynesian theory, changes in government spending and taxation policies can affect the equilibrium level of real income by changing aggregate net autonomous expenditures. Consequently, fiscal policy potentially can play a role in smoothing out variations in autonomous expenditures, thereby stabilizing real income and smoothing business cycles.

2. How the Basic Keynesian Model Can Be Adapted to Account for Income Taxes: This can be accomplished by recognizing that the government's net tax receipts consist of autonomous net taxes plus income taxes, which equal the average income tax rate times income. Consequently, the slope of the consumption function and the aggregate desired expenditures schedule vary with changes in the income tax rate. A reduction in the tax rate steepens these schedules, thereby causing a rise in equilibrium real income. At the same time, however, a tax rate cut makes equilibrium real income more sensitive to the effects of changes in autonomous aggregate expenditures.

3. How Cuts in Income Tax Rates Affect the Government's Tax Revenues: Holding government spending and real income unchanged, a reduction in the average income tax rate reduces the government's tax revenues. Nevertheless, a cut in the income tax rate also causes equilibrium real income to increase. This, in turn, raises the government's income tax receipts. Therefore, at a sufficiently high tax rate, a reduction in the tax rate can actually cause the government's total tax revenues to increase.

4. The Ricardian Equivalence Proposition: According to this proposition, tax cuts cannot affect total consumption or aggregate desired expenditures. The logic leading to this proposition is that a current tax reduction causes the government's debt to increase, so people will realize that this higher debt implies higher future taxes. Consequently, they save the proceeds of a tax cut so that they or their offspring will be able to pay these higher future taxes. Although a number of economists are swayed by the logic of this position, others contend that it is weakened by shortsightedness, liquidity constraints, the fact that tax changes typically are made via changes in tax rates, other factors that motivate gifts and bequests, and income uncertainty.

Self-Test Questions

(Answers to odd-numbered questions may be found on the Web at **http://macro.swcollege.com** under "Student Resources.")

1. Explain in your own words the distinction between the marginal income tax rate and the average income tax rate.

2. Explain in your own words how the income tax system performs the role of "automatic stabilizer."

3. Why does a lump-sum tax cut *shift* the aggregate expenditures schedule, whereas a cut in the income tax rate *rotates* the aggregate expenditures schedule? Explain your answer.

4. Assuming that the Ricardian equivalence proposition is correct, would the structure of an income tax system be completely irrelevant? Take a stand, and support your answer.

5. Why do some economists view the fact that saving and government deficits were generally inversely related during the high-deficit period of the late 1980s and early 1990s as evidence against the applicability of Ricardian equivalence? Explain your reasoning.

Problems

(Answers to odd-numbered problems may be found on the Web at **http://macro.swcollege.com** under "Student Resources.")

1. Suppose that the marginal propensity to save is equal to 0.20, the marginal propensity to import is equal to 0.05, and the income tax rate is equal to zero. How much would equilibrium real income rise following a $1 billion increase in government spending? Explain briefly.

195

CHAPTER 7 Fiscal Policy—What Can Government Spending and Taxation Policies Accomplish?

2. Suppose that the marginal propensity to save is equal to 0.20 and the marginal propensity to import is equal to 0.05. Calculate the autonomous expenditures multiplier for each of the following values of the income tax rate, assuming that the income tax system is proportional (round to the nearest hundredth): (a) $\tau = 0.10$; (b) $\tau = 0.20$; (c) $\tau = 0.50$. For which tax rate would equilibrium real income be most stable in the face of a change in autonomous aggregate expenditures? Explain your answer.

3. Suppose that the peak of the Laffer curve is at an income tax rate of 18 percent and that the current income tax rate is 22 percent. If the government maintains its current spending level, then would a cut in the income tax rate to 19 percent increase or reduce the government's deficit? Explain.

Before the Test

Test your understanding of the material covered in this chapter by taking the Chapter 7 interactive quiz at http://macro.swcollege.com.

Online Application

Internet URL: http://www.access.gpo.gov/usbudget

Title: *Historical Tables: Budget of the United States Government*

Navigation: Begin at the home page of the U.S. Government Printing Office (http://www.access.gpo.gov). Under "Executive Office of the President," select *Office of Management and Budget*. Then click on the latest fiscal year budget, and click on *Historical Tables*.

Application: After the document downloads, perform the indicated operations, and answer the questions:

1. Go to section 2, entitled "Composition of Federal Government Receipts." Take a look at Table 2.2—Percentage Composition of Receipts by Source. Before World War II, what was the federal government's key source of revenues? What has been the key revenue source since World War II?

2. Now scan down the document to Table 2.3—Receipts by Source as Percentages of GDP. Have any of the government's revenue sources declined as a percentage of GDP? Which ones have noticeably risen in recent years?

For Group Study and Analysis: Split the class into four groups, and have each group examine Section 3: Federal Government Outlays by Function, and in particular Table 3.1—Outlays by Superfunction and Function. Assign one group to each of the following functions: National Defense, Health, Income Security, and Social Security. Have each group prepare a brief report concerning long-term and recent trends in government spending on its function. Which functions have captured growing shares of government spending in recent years? Which are receiving declining shares of total spending?

Selected References and Further Reading

Blejer, Mario, and Adrienne Cheasty. "The Measurement of Fiscal Deficits: Analytical and Methodological Issues." *Journal of Economic Literature* 39 (December 4, 1991): 1644–1678.

Eichenbaum, Martin, and Jonas Fisher. "How Does an Increase in Government Purchases Affect the Economy?" Federal Reserve Bank of Chicago *Economic Perspectives* 22 (Third Quarter 1998): 29–43.

Federal Reserve Bank of Kansas City. *Budget Deficits and Debt: Issues and Options.* 1995.

Hakkio, Craig. "The Effects of Budget Deficit Reduction on the Exchange Rate." Federal Reserve Bank of Kansas City *Economic Review,* Third Quarter 1996, pp. 21–38.

Mann, Catherine. *Is the U.S. Trade Deficit Sustainable?* Washington, D.C.: Institute for International Economics, 1999.

Schultze, Charles. "Is There a Bias toward Excess in U.S. Government Budgets or Deficits?" *Journal of Economic Perspectives* 6 (Spring 1992): 25–43.

Sill, D. Keith. "Managing the Public Debt." Federal Reserve Bank of Philadelphia *Business Review,* July/August 1994, pp. 3–13.

Viard, Alan. "The Federal Budget: What a Difference a Year Makes." Federal Reserve Bank of Dallas *Southwest Economy,* January/February 2002, pp. 1–10.

macro**xtra!**

Log on to the MacroXtra Web site at http://macroxtra.swcollege.com for additional learning resources such as practice quizzes, Interactive Key Graphs, readings, and additional economic applications.

Do Central Banks Matter?—

Money in the Traditional Keynesian System

FUNDAMENTAL ISSUES

1. What are the key motives for holding money, and what variables do they indicate should influence the demand for money?

2. How is the nominal interest rate determined in the traditional Keynesian model?

3. What is the *LM* schedule, and what factors determine its elasticity and position?

4. What is the *IS* schedule, and what factors determine its elasticity and position?

5. What is an *IS–LM* equilibrium, and what are the implications of the *IS–LM* framework for the transmission mechanism of monetary policy?

6. How does government spending influence real income in the traditional Keynesian model?

Since the early 1990s, the performance of the Japanese economy can per-haps be best described as rocky. Any hint of a recovery seems to have been swiftly followed by an economic reversal. Although the unemploy-ment rate has remained below 6 percent, since the early 2000s many Japanese high school graduates have had trouble finding jobs outside of fast-food and other low-level service occupations. A number of Japanese youths have begun to despair of ever moving up in the world.

Critics of the Bank of Japan contend that it bears much of the blame for the nation's economic weakness. What Japan has needed for the past several years, they contend, is higher growth in the quantity of yen in circulation, which would push up aggregate desired spending and boost output and employment.

Some economists, however, worry that there may be little the Bank of Japan can do. Japanese money growth rates have averaged about 7 percent for the past several years, and interest rates in Japan have hovered close to zero. Expansionary monetary policy actions exert their effects on spending by pushing down interest rates, these economists argue, and interest rates cannot go much lower. The Bank of Japan, these economists suggest, may be trapped by the extremely low interest rates its own policies have produced.

In this chapter you will learn how money and the interest rate fit into the traditional Keynesian framework. As you will see, within this framework interest-rate adjustments are crucial to determining the effects of both monetary policy and fiscal policy.

The Demand for Money

The traditional Keynesian income-expenditure theory forms the heart of a simple theory of short-run business cycles and of the balance of trade. Missing from the basic framework discussed in Chapter 6, however, were any meaningful roles for money and other financial assets, interest rates, and monetary policy. You will learn in this chapter that the traditional Keynesian macroeconomic theory actually indicates that central banks potentially can assist in smoothing out business cycles via their ability to determine national monetary policies.

The reason for this conclusion is that the Keynesian theory proposes interactions among the interest rate, money, prices, and real income that are absent from the classical macroeconomic model that we discussed in Chapters 3 and 4. Part of the rationale for these interactions is provided by Keynes's theory of the demand for money, which emphasized the role of interest rates.

Recall that classical theorists emphasized the use of money as a medium of exchange. This led them to propose the Cambridge equation, $M^d = k \times Y$, where M^d denotes total desired money holdings, Y denotes total nominal income, and k represents the fraction of income that people wish to hold as money to use in planned exchanges for goods and services. As you will see later in the chapter, Keynes agreed that total income is an important determinant of desired money holdings. Nevertheless, he also argued that interest rates influence the prices of financial assets that people hold alongside the cash in their portfolios of financial wealth. This fact, Keynes contended, creates an important link between money demand and interest rates and, furthermore, implies mechanisms for interest-rate determination and monetary policy that operate very differently from those originally proposed by the classical economists.

The Transactions and Precautionary Motives for Holding Money

Keynes's theory of money demand starts by considering the specific motives that people have to hold money. It might seem obvious that people want to hold money, but consider that currency pays no interest and that checking deposits typically pay interest rates well below the rates that people can earn by holding other financial assets. Indeed, a key type of checking account, called a *demand deposit,* pays no interest at all. What Keynes tried to do was to identify the reasons why people hold coins, pieces of paper, and bank accounts that offer them little or no financial return.

TRANSACTIONS MOTIVE: The motive to hold money for use in planned exchanges.

PRECAUTIONARY MOTIVE: The motive to hold money for use in unplanned exchanges.

THE TRANSACTIONS MOTIVE   To Keynes, the classical theory of money demand, as summarized by the Cambridge equation, relied on two basic motives for holding money. One of these he called the **transactions motive.** This was the incentive to hold non-interest-bearing currency and non- (or low-) interest-bearing checking deposits for use as media of exchange in planned transactions. For instance, you need some cash on hand if you have a snack while you study between classes every afternoon. Money is also useful for buying groceries each week and for paying your rent and utility bills each month.

In turn, how lavishly you can afford to eat and live depends on your income. If you are a student with a relatively low income, your daily meals and apartment will likely be less elaborate than those of a student from a wealthy family who receives a monthly stipend from a trust fund. Consequently, Keynes agreed with the classical economists' argument that total income is a key determinant of total desired money holdings. As income rises, Keynes concluded, so does the total quantity of money demanded to satisfy the transactions motive for holding money.

THE PRECAUTIONARY MOTIVE   Another related reason to hold money was what Keynes called the **precautionary motive,** or the desire to hold money in the event of a need to make unplanned transactions. For instance, your car might break down and require repair, or you might run across a great sale on an item that you had not previously planned to purchase. Most of us typically try to budget some extra cash to cover such unexpected transactions.

How much extra cash we include in our budgets as a precaution is likely to depend on our respective real incomes. Returning to our college student example, a low-income student with an eight-year-old automobile would probably experience lower repair bills in the event of a breakdown than would a high-income student with a late-model sports car with a high-performance engine. Likewise, the low-income student is likely to find an unexpectedly good buy while shopping at a discount store, while the high-income student is more likely to come across a sale at an upscale department store. Consequently, Keynes hypothesized that the amount of money held to satisfy the precautionary motive should also depend positively on total income.

The Portfolio Motive for Holding Money

Both the transactions and the precautionary motive justify the classical theorists' emphasis on the importance of income as a key determinant of aggregate desired money holdings. What distinguishes Keynes's theory of the demand for money from the classical approach is the idea that interest

PORTFOLIO MOTIVE: The modern term for Keynes's basic idea of a speculative motive for holding money, in which people hold both money and bonds and adjust their holdings of both types of financial assets based on their speculations about interest-rate movements.

rates affect desired money holdings. According to Keynes, there is also a *speculative motive* for holding money that arises from the interplay between interest rates and the prices of financial assets such as bonds. The modern term for this rationale for holding money is the **portfolio motive.** The idea behind the portfolio motive is that speculations about interest-rate changes and movements in bond prices induce people to adjust their desired holdings of bonds and money. As a result, interest-rate variations influence the quantity of money demanded.

MONEY, BONDS, AND FINANCIAL WEALTH   People can hold accumulated wealth in a number of ways. One possibility is to hold nonfinancial assets, such as land, residential housing, or durable goods such as automobiles. Another is to hold financial assets, such as bonds, stocks, and savings accounts. Keynes also viewed money as a key part of a person's financial wealth.

To keep things simple, let's assume that an individual's financial wealth may be allocated only between money holdings, M, and another financial asset called "bonds," B. Money differs from bonds in that the nominal price of money is always equal to 1 unit of money (for instance, $1, 1 euro, 1 yen, and the like). In contrast, the nominal price of a bond can change over time. As a result, an individual who holds a bond earns a *capital gain* if the nominal price of the bond increases over a given interval of time or a *capital loss* if the nominal price of the bond falls during some other period. A $1 bill of U.S. currency or a $1 portion of a checking account at a bank has the same $1 *nominal* value over any given interval. Consequently, people cannot earn nominal capital gains or incur nominal capital losses if they hold all their financial wealth as currency or deposit forms of money.

To see how a person might decide to allocate financial wealth between money and bonds, let's suppose that at some given point in time, the person's nominal financial wealth is equal to some amount F. The individual can split this wealth between money holdings, M, which we shall assume are non-interest-bearing cash, and bond holdings, B, that earn a nominal interest rate of return r. Thus, at the point in time under consideration, the individual's financial wealth must be equal to holdings of money plus holdings of bonds:

$$F = M + B.$$

Because wealth is constant at a point in time, it must be true that the sum of changes in money and bond holdings must equal zero, or $\Delta M + \Delta B = 0$. That is, any change in bond holdings, ΔB, must be offset by an equal change in money holdings in the opposite direction, $-\Delta M$. For example, suppose that a person has $10,000 in financial wealth, with $5,000 in money and $5,000 in bonds. Suppose further that she wishes to increase her bond holdings by $2,000. Then, to maintain the same total financial wealth of $10,000, she must reduce her money holdings by $2,000, leaving her with $3,000 in cash and $7,000 in bonds.

This constraint that an individual faces in allocating a fixed amount of financial wealth provides the foundation for a relationship between the demand for money and the interest rate. Because bonds earn a nominal interest return, changes in the interest rate affect the market prices of

On the Web

How can a person keep track of U.S. interest rates from day to day? One way is to view statistics made available by the Federal Reserve Bank of New York at http://www.ny.frb. org/pihome/statistics.

bonds and an individual's desired bond holdings. Changing bond holdings, however, requires changes in money holdings. Consequently, interest-rate variations typically will induce changes in desired holdings of money.

BOND PRICES AND INTEREST RATES   How do interest-rate changes affect bond prices? To answer this question, let's consider the simplest kind of bonds, which are **perpetuities.** These are nonmaturing bonds, or bonds that have no final date of maturity. Over the years the governments of the United Kingdom and several nations of the British Commonwealth have issued such bonds, called *consols*. Perpetuities typically pay a fixed annual amount, or coupon return C, per year forever. If the nominal interest rate is r, then one important issue for anyone contemplating buying a perpetuity is how much to pay for this infinite-life bond.

To determine this, we must first think about the concept of **discounted present value,** or the value from today's perspective of funds to be received at a future date. If the annual interest rate is r, then the discounted present value of C dollars a year from now is equal to $C/(1 + r)$ dollars. This is true because if we had $C/(1 + r)$ dollars today, we could earn interest on this amount during the coming year, thereby obtaining $[C/(1 + r)] \times (1 + r) = C$ dollars a year from now. Likewise, the discounted present value of C dollars two years from now is equal to $C/(1 + r)^2$ dollars. If we had that sum today and saved it until next year, we would have $[C/(1 + r)^2] \times (1 + r) = C/(1 + r)$ dollars next year. Then, if we save that sum into the second year, we again would have $[C/(1 + r)] \times (1 + r) = C$ dollars. In general, therefore, we can reach an important conclusion:

The discounted present value of any amount C when the market interest rate is r is equal to $C/(1 + r)^n$, where n denotes the number of years into the future that we are considering.

A perpetuity that we purchase today will pay C dollars next year, the year after that, and every other year into the future. That means that the discounted present value of this bond is the sum of the discounted present values of C dollars for all those years, or the infinite sum $C/(1 + r) + C/(1 + r)^2 + C/(1 + r)^3 + C/(1 + r)^4 + \cdots$. In the absence of risk and exchange costs, this is the amount that we would be willing to pay for this bond, because it is today's value of the coupon returns the bond will yield. Consequently, the price of the perpetual bond, P_B, will equal

$$P_B = C/(1 + r) + C/(1 + r)^2 + C/(1 + r)^3 + C/(1 + r)^4 + \cdots.$$

When confronted with an infinite sum, it is tempting to throw up one's hands. Notice, though, that if we multiply both sides of the preceding equation by $(1 + r)$, we get

$$(1 + r) \times P_B = C + C/(1 + r) + C/(1 + r)^2 + C/(1 + r)^3 + C/(1 + r)^4 + \cdots$$

From algebra, we know that we can always subtract one equation from another. So let's subtract the first equation from the second to get

$$[(1 + r) \times P_B] - P_B = $$
$$[C + C/(1 + r) + C/(1 + r)^2 + C/(1 + r)^3 + C/(1 + r)^4 + \cdots]$$
$$- [C/(1 + r) + C/(1 + r)^2 + C/(1 + r)^3 + C/(1 + r)^4 + \cdots].$$

PERPETUITY: A nonmaturing bond that pays an infinite stream of coupon returns.

DISCOUNTED PRESENT VALUE: The value from today's perspective of funds to be received at a future date.

Notice that $[(1 + r) \times P_B] - P_B$ is equal to $P_B + (r \times P_B) - P_B = r \times P_B$. In addition, we can see that all the terms on the right side of the last equation cancel out except for C. Consequently, this very messy equation involving differences between infinite sums reduces to

$$r \times P_B = C.$$

If we now divide both sides of this much simpler equation by r, we get a final expression for the price of a perpetuity, which is

$$P_B = C/r.$$

The price of a perpetual, nonmaturing bond is its annual coupon return divided by the market interest rate. Therefore, if the perpetuity pays $C = \$100$ per year forever and the market interest rate is 7 percent, then the price of the bond is equal to $P_B = C/r = \$100/(0.07) = \$1,428.57$.

Suppose that the market interest rate r increases. Then the ratio C/r would fall, and the price of the bond would decline. In our numerical example, if the market interest rate rises to 8 percent, then the price of the perpetuity with a \$100 annual coupon return would be equal to $P_B = C/r = \$100/(0.08) = \$1,250.00$.

We can conclude that:

Holding the coupon return and all other factors unchanged, there is an inverse relationship between the price of existing bonds and the current nominal interest rate.

If the market nominal interest rate rises, then bond prices will fall, and people who hold bonds will incur a nominal capital loss. If the market nominal interest rate declines, then bond prices will rise, and people who hold bonds will earn a nominal capital gain.

THE PORTFOLIO MOTIVE   Now let's consider how a person might adjust her money and bond holdings as part of a speculative strategy involving expected changes in interest rates. This individual recognizes that her future capital gains or losses from bond holdings depend directly upon whether nominal market interest rates rise or fall in the future. Consequently, she will adjust the composition of her portfolio of money and bonds in light of her *anticipation* of future interest-rate movements.

Suppose that the market interest rate rises, in the present, to a level that our individual believes is rather high. As a result, she anticipates that the interest rate will decline in the future, causing bond prices to rise and providing her with a future capital gain on bonds that she holds as part of her financial wealth. To further increase her anticipated capital gains from bond holdings, she will allocate more of her financial wealth to bonds in the present. Her financial wealth is fixed in the present, however, so to do this, she will have to reduce her holdings of money. Consequently, for this individual a current rise in the market interest rate causes a present reduction in her desired money holdings. Her demand for money depends negatively on the market interest rate.

Suppose instead that the market interest rate falls, at present, to levels that our individual perceives to be rather low. Therefore, she anticipates

that the market interest rate will rise in the future, causing bond prices to fall and causing her to incur capital losses on her existing bond holdings. To avoid some of these anticipated future losses, she will sell bonds in the present, thereby allocating more of her fixed current financial wealth to holdings of money. Hence, a current fall in the market interest rate induces her to increase the amount of money demanded. Again, the individual's demand for money is inversely related to the market interest rate.

Keynes concluded from this line of reasoning that the portfolio motive for holding money implies that a person's real income is not the only determinant of desired money holdings. The demand for money should also depend on the nominal interest rate. Furthermore, *there should be a negative relationship between the quantity of money demanded and the nominal interest rate.*

The Demand for Money

Our examination of the three motives for holding money indicates that two key variables should influence desired money holdings. One is real income. A rise in real income intensifies the transactions and precautionary motives for holding money, which we predict should lead to a rise in total desired money balances. Additionally, the quantity of money demanded depends on the nominal interest rate. The logic of the portfolio motive for holding money indicates that there should be an inverse relationship between the quantity of money demanded and the nominal interest rate, holding other factors unchanged.

THE MONEY DEMAND SCHEDULE   We can capture these relationships with a simple diagram of a *money demand schedule,* or a graphical depiction of the relationship between the quantity of money demanded and the nominal interest rate. A typical money demand schedule is shown in panel (a) of Figure 8–1 on the following page. The downward slope of this schedule reflects the inverse relationship between the quantity of money demanded and the nominal interest rate that the portfolio motive indicates should exist. In addition, we label the money demand schedule $M^d(Y_1)$ to indicate that its *position* depends on the current level of nominal income, such as a nominal income level Y_1.

Panel (b) of Figure 8–1 illustrates the effect of an increase in nominal income, from Y_1 to a larger amount Y_2. Such a rise in income will increase the volume of planned transactions by all individuals in the economy. In addition, it will raise people's precautionary money holdings. Consequently, at any given nominal interest rate, people will demand more money. This means that the money demand schedule will shift rightward, from $M^d(Y_1)$ to $M^d(Y_2)$, as a result of the rise in total nominal income, as shown in panel (b).

THE DEMAND FOR REAL MONEY BALANCES   To simplify our notation, we have emphasized the demand for nominal, or current-dollar, money balances. When people decide how much cash to carry, however, what really matters is the purchasing power of the money that they hold. Suppose, for instance, that you decide one morning to carry $15 in cash to cover your intended

macroxtra!
Online
Perspective

Consider how the growing use of online payments may affect the demand for monetary aggregates by going to the Chapter 8 reading, entitled "Personal On-Line Payments," by Kenneth Kuttner and James McAndrews of the Federal Reserve Bank of Cleveland.
http://macroxtra.sw.college.com

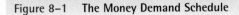

Figure 8-1   The Money Demand Schedule

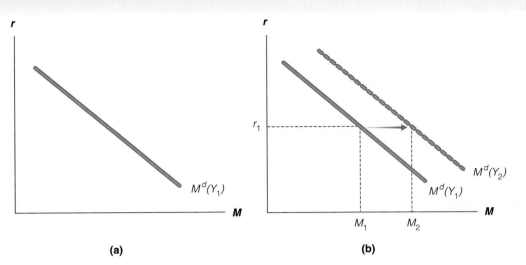

(a)

(b)

As shown in panel (a), the inverse relationship between the nominal interest rate and holdings of money resulting from the portfolio motive implies that the money demand schedule slopes downward. The money demand schedule's position depends on the level of nominal national income. If nominal national income increases, then, as panel (b) indicates, people hold more money balances at any given interest rate, and the money demand schedule shifts rightward.

purchases, say, lunch for $10 and an afternoon snack for $5. Imagine, however, that after you leave home the price level doubles. As a result, the price of lunch increases to $20, and the price of an afternoon snack rises to $10. Now your $15 will not even cover the cost of the lunch that you had planned to eat, and you will have to forgo your afternoon snack altogether. The problem is that the purchasing power of your $15 is now half its previous value. To purchase the same lunch and snack, you would have to double your nominal money balances to $30. A doubling of prices requires a doubling of nominal money balances to maintain the required purchasing power for the day's expenses.

The upshot of this example is that the real purchasing power of a person's nominal cash balances is the price-adjusted value of the money holdings, or $m = M/P$, where m denotes **real money balances.** These are equal to nominal money holdings, M, divided by the price level, which we measure using the GDP deflator, P. Panel (a) of Figure 8–2 depicts a demand schedule for real money balances, $m^d = M^d/P$. The portfolio motive for holding money continues to apply to holdings of real money balances, so the demand schedule for real money balances also slopes downward. (The real purchasing power of $1 is a lot less than it used to be; see on page 206 *Policy Notebook: A Dollar Really Doesn't Buy Much Anymore.*)

The total real purchasing power that an individual desires to maintain will depend on the person's *real* income. As a person's real income rises,

REAL MONEY BALANCES: The value of the nominal quantity of money adjusted for the price level; defined as the nominal money stock divided by the price level.

Figure 8-2   The Demand for Real Money Balances

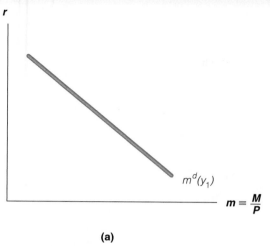

(a)

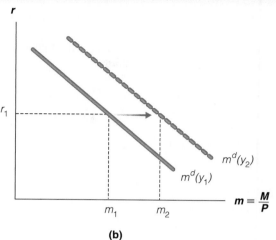

(b)

The demand for real money balances, $m = M/P$, is the total demand for real purchasing power. As shown in panel (a), the demand for real money balances slopes downward as a result of the portfolio motive for holding real money bal-

ances. The demand for real money balances shifts rightward when real income rises, as shown in panel (b), because of the transactions and precautionary motives for holding real money balances.

the real value of planned and unplanned transactions will increase, spurring the transactions and precautionary motives for holding real money balances. Therefore, a rise in real income, from an initial level y_1 to a larger amount y_2, causes an individual to increase desired holdings of real money balances at each possible interest rate. This means that a rise in real income shifts the position of the demand schedule for real money balances to the right, $m^d(y_1)$ to $m^d(y_2)$, as shown in panel (b) of Figure 8–2.

FUNDAMENTAL ISSUE #1

What are the key motives for holding money, and what variables do they indicate should influence the demand for money? There are three key motives for holding money. The transactions and precautionary motives refer to the desire to hold money for use in planned and unplanned exchanges, respectively; both indicate that the demand for real money balances should depend positively on the level of real income. The portfolio motive refers to the allocation of a portion of financial wealth to money holdings as part of speculative strategies involving expectations about future interest-rate movements. This motive indicates that the quantity demanded for real money balances should depend negatively on the nominal interest rate.

Policy NOTEBOOK

A Dollar Really Doesn't Buy Much Anymore

You have probably heard your parents or grandparents talk about the days when a dollar could buy much more than it does today. They are not making it up. Inflation dramatically eroded the purchasing power of $1 during the past century.

Figure 8–3 illustrates just how much erosion has taken place by starting with a $1 value of goods and services in 1900 and showing the market value of goods and services that a dollar bill would have been able to purchase in the years following. By 1918 a dollar was only able to buy what 40 cents could have purchased in 1900. During the Great Depression, a decline in the overall price level caused the value of a dollar to recover somewhat, so through much of the 1930s a dollar could purchase an amount of goods and services that about 60 cents could have obtained in 1900.

Gradual inflation since the late 1930s has resulted in a steady decline in the dollar's purchasing power. Today a one-dollar bill will allow you to buy an amount of goods and services that a nickel would have purchased in 1900.

Figure 8–3   The Falling Purchasing Power of a Dollar

A dollar bill issued today buys less than what a nickel would have purchased in 1900.

SOURCE: Bureau of Labor Statistics.

For Critical Analysis
One way to make a dollar worth approximately what it was back in 1900 might be for the government to print new U.S. currency, announce that five units of old currency must be traded for each unit of new currency on a particular date, and require all prices to be reduced by a factor of five as of that date. Would society necessarily come out ahead if the government were to do this?

The Money Supply and the Equilibrium Nominal Interest Rate

The nominal quantity of money, or the *money stock,* is the total amount of circulating exchange media. As already noted, in our modern world these media of exchange include coins and currency and checking deposits. Each week, the Federal Reserve sums the amounts of these components of the total quantity of money to get a basic overall measure of the money stock, which it calls M1. The Federal Reserve also tabulates broader measures of money, such as M2 and M3, which add other types of bank deposits to M1. Most other central banks around the world have adopted analogous measures of the money stocks of their respective nations.

The Supply of Money

Because central banks' measures of the money stock include various bank deposits, the nominal quantity of money in any nation responds in part to events that affect the nation's banking system. To influence a nation's nominal money stock, a central bank such as the Federal Reserve must institute policies that affect decisions made by the nation's banks and thereby alter the total amounts of deposits that they issue.

THE MONEY SUPPLY SCHEDULE   Realistically, any central bank's ability to bring about desired changes in bank deposits is likely to be imperfect, and a central bank such as the Federal Reserve typically cannot precisely control the total amount of nominal money balances in circulation. Because banks likely will respond to interest-rate changes by altering the amount of deposits that they issue, the nominal quantity of money supplied in the economy usually will depend in part on interest rates.

Nevertheless, we shall simplify by assuming that a typical central bank can supply any desired quantity of nominal money balances in the form of non-interest-bearing cash and deposits. This assumption means that the quantity of money supplied will not, in our analysis, depend on the nominal interest rate. As a result, as shown in Figure 8–4, the nominal money supply function is *vertical,* and its position is determined by policies of the central bank. If the central bank institutes policies that increase the amount of currency in circulation or induce banks to issue more checkable deposits, then the money supply function will shift to the right, as shown in the figure.

THE SUPPLY OF REAL MONEY BALANCES   As we discussed earlier, the real purchasing power of money (M/P) is what really matters to all individuals in an economy. From the viewpoint of any central bank, therefore, it would be desirable to be able to control the quantity of real money balances directly. This is not possible, however. Central banks do not *set* prices,

On the Web

What are the latest trends in measures of the U.S. money supply? To find out, go to the Federal Reserve's H.6 Statistical Release at **http://federalreserve.gov/releases/**.

Figure 8–4   The Nominal Money Supply Schedule

We assume that a nation's central bank can completely control the quantity of nominal money balances in the economy and that the quantity of money the central bank supplies is independent from the nominal interest rate. Under these assumptions, the nominal money supply schedule is vertical. It shifts rightward if the central bank increases the stock of money in circulation.

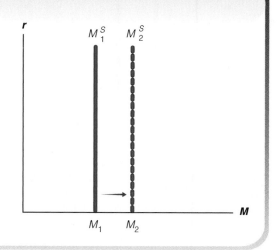

which are determined in markets for goods and services. As you will learn, all that a central bank can do is to conduct policies that influence the *equilibrium* price level. This means that the actual quantity of real money balances will depend on what the equilibrium price level turns out to be.

Figure 8–5 depicts diagrams of the supply of real money balances, denoted M^s/P. Panel (a) shows the effect on real money balances of a reduction in the nominal money stock, from M_1 to M_2, when the price level remains unchanged at P_1. The result is a decline in real money balances, from M_1/P_1 to M_2/P_1.

Panel (a) shows that if the price level were to remain constant, a central bank could, in principle, determine the quantity of real money balances. Realistically, however, the price level can change without a central bank implementing any policy actions. As panel (b) of the figure shows, a rise in the price level, from P_1 to P_2, shifts the real money supply schedule leftward even if the central bank leaves the nominal money stock unchanged, at an amount M_1. As a result, real money balances decline, from M_1/P_1 to M_1/P_2, without any action by the central bank.

We can conclude that the position of the supply schedule for real money balances depends on *both* the nominal money stock *and* the price level. A fall in the nominal money stock shifts this supply schedule leftward, while

Figure 8–5   The Supply of Real Money Balances

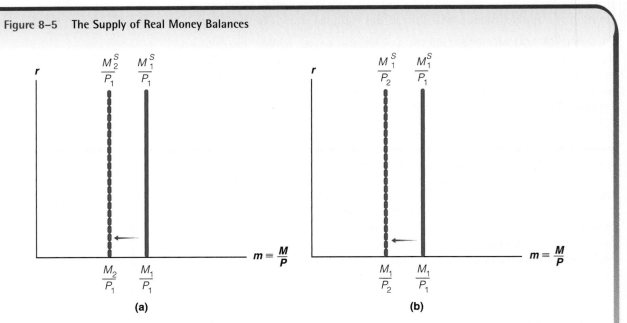

(a)   **(b)**

The supply of real money balances is the purchasing power of the nominal quantity of money supplied by the central bank. As illustrated in this figure, two factors can cause a reduction in the supply of real money balances. One, illustrated in panel (a), is a reduction by the central bank in the nominal quantity of money in circulation at a given price level. The other, shown in panel (b), is a rise in the price level while the nominal money stock remains unchanged. In either instance, the supply of real money balances shifts leftward.

a rise in the nominal money stock shifts the schedule to the right. A rise in the price level shifts the supply schedule leftward, whereas a fall in the price level shifts the schedule to the right.

The Equilibrium Nominal Interest Rate

Both the supply and demand schedules for real money balances appear in Figure 8–6. The crossing point of the two schedules describes a situation in which all individuals in the economy are satisfied holding the nominal money stock supplied by the central bank, M_1, deflated by the current price level, P_1. Consequently, at this single point the quantity of real money balances demanded by the public is equal to the quantity of real money balances supplied by the central bank.

ATTAINING EQUILIBRIUM IN THE MARKET FOR REAL MONEY BALANCES　The nominal interest rate adjusts to achieve this equilibrium point. Therefore, the nominal interest rate, r_1, is the *equilibrium* rate. To understand the adjustment process by which the equilibrium interest rate is determined, consider the situation in which the nominal interest rate is equal to r_2 in Figure 8–6. At this higher interest rate, there is an excess quantity of real money balances supplied. Individuals wish to hold fewer real money balances than the central bank has supplied. At the nominal interest rate r_2, people wish to hold more bonds than currently are available. Hence, there is an excess quantity of bonds demanded, which will cause bond prices to rise. Because there is an inverse relationship between the price of bonds and the nominal interest rate, the interest rate must fall toward the equilibrium level, r_1. At this equilibrium interest rate, both the bond market and the market for real money balances are in equilibrium.

Figure 8–6　Attaining Equilibrium in the Market for Real Money Balances

At the equilibrium rate r_1, the quantity of real money balances demanded is equal to the quantity of real money balances supplied. If instead the nominal interest rate is equal to r_2, then there will be an excess quantity of real money balances supplied. This implies that at the interest rate r_2, people desire to hold more bonds than currently are available in financial markets. As a result of this excess quantity of bonds demanded, equilibrium bond prices will begin to rise, so the nominal interest rate will decline toward its equilibrium level of r_1.

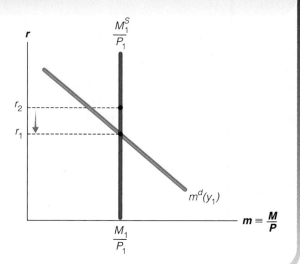

LIQUIDITY EFFECT: A fall in the equilibrium nominal interest rate resulting from a rise in the nominal quantity of money, holding the price level unchanged.

THE LIQUIDITY EFFECT OF MONETARY POLICY   Figure 8–7 shows the effect of an increase in the nominal quantity of money supplied by the central bank, from M_1 to M_2, assuming that the price level is fixed at an amount P_1. The rise in the nominal money supply causes the real money supply schedule to shift to the right. This results in an excess quantity of money supplied at the initial equilibrium interest rate, r_1. As in Figure 8–6, there now will be an excess quantity of bonds demanded, and bond prices will increase. This implies that the nominal interest rate must fall to a new equilibrium level, r_2.

This fall in the interest rate caused by an increase in the nominal quantity of money without a change in the price level is the **liquidity effect** of monetary policy. It is called a liquidity effect because such an increase in the nominal quantity of money raises the overall liquidity in the economy. People will be satisfied with this higher liquidity level only if the equilibrium nominal interest rate declines. The resulting rise in bond prices discourages individuals from buying additional bonds, because of their concern that future bond price declines will yield capital losses. Thus, as long as the interest rate declines and bond prices increase, people will be willing to hold the larger quantity of money in circulation.

THE REAL BALANCE EFFECT   Figure 8–8 shows what will happen if the price level rises, from P_1 to P_2, while the nominal money stock is unchanged. The increase in the price level reduces the supply of real money balances. This means that the real purchasing power of the nominal money balances supplied by the central bank will decline. As a result, there will be an excess quantity of real money balances demanded at the initial equilibrium interest rate, r_1. At this initial equilibrium interest rate, people now desire more real purchasing power. To achieve this, they reduce their holdings of

Figure 8–7   The Liquidity Effect of Monetary Policy

Given an unchanged price level, an increase in the nominal quantity of money in circulation will cause the supply of real money balances to rise. At an initial equilibrium nominal interest rate r_1, there then will be an excess quantity of money supplied, which corresponds to an excess quantity of bonds demanded. As a result, bond prices will increase, and the nominal interest rate will fall to a new equilibrium level, r_2. This fall in the equilibrium nominal interest rate caused by a rise in the nominal money stock without a change in the price level is called the *liquidity effect*.

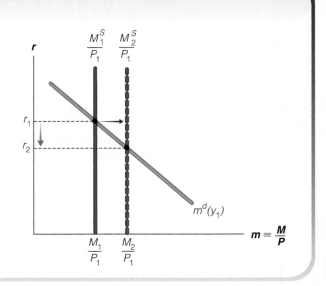

Figure 8–8 The Real Balance Effect

If the nominal quantity of money in circulation is unchanged, a rise in the price level will reduce the supply of real money balances. At an initial equilibrium interest rate r_1, therefore, there will be an excess quantity of money demanded, which corresponds to an excess quantity of bonds supplied. As a result, bond prices will decline, and the nominal interest rate will increase toward a new equilibrium value of r_2. This rise in the nominal interest rate caused by an increase in the price level is the *real balance effect*.

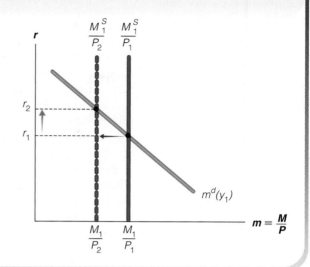

bonds at the interest rate r_1, and the result is an excess quantity of bonds supplied at that interest rate. Bond prices therefore begin to fall, and the nominal interest rate rises to a new equilibrium level, r_2.

This rise in the nominal interest rate caused by an increase in the price level with a constant nominal money stock is called the **real balance effect,** because it results from a change in the real purchasing power of the nominal money stock caused by a change in the price level.

REAL BALANCE EFFECT: An increase in the nominal rate of interest that results from an increase in the price level, holding the nominal quantity of money unchanged.

FUNDAMENTAL ISSUE #2

How is the nominal interest rate determined in the traditional Keynesian model? The equilibrium nominal interest rate is the nominal rate of interest at which people are satisfied holding the quantity of real money balances supplied through policies of the central bank. A rise in the supply of real money balances caused solely by an increase in the nominal money stock results in a liquidity effect, which causes a reduction in the equilibrium nominal interest rate. A reduction in the supply of real money balances caused solely by an increase in the price level results in a real balance effect, which causes an increase in the equilibrium nominal interest rate.

The *LM* Schedule

The liquidity effect and the real balance effect on the equilibrium nominal interest rate both stem from changes in the supply of real money balances. The equilibrium nominal interest rate can also be affected by changes in the demand for real money balances. As we discussed earlier in this chapter, a key factor affecting the position of the money demand schedule is the level of real income. Consequently, there must be a relationship between real income and the equilibrium nominal interest rate. As you will learn shortly, this relationship is summed up graphically by a schedule known as the *LM schedule.*

At the same time, as we showed in Chapter 6, a change in the real interest rate induces a change in desired real investment spending, which, in turn, causes a change in aggregate desired expenditures and in equilibrium real income. The real interest rate, in turn, is equal to the nominal interest rate minus the expected inflation rate. Therefore, there also is a relationship between equilibrium real income and the nominal interest rate, which can be captured on a diagram as a schedule called the *IS schedule.*

Because the equilibrium nominal interest rate depends on real income while, at the same time, equilibrium real income depends on the nominal interest rate, the equilibrium nominal interest rate and the equilibrium level of real income must be determined simultaneously. Our objective in the remainder of this chapter is to explain this process. Once we have done that, we shall be able to explore the traditional Keynesian theory of monetary policy.

Deriving the *LM* Schedule

The **LM schedule** is a set of all combinations of real income levels and nominal interest rates that maintain equilibrium in the market for real money balances. Figure 8–9 traces the derivation of the *LM* schedule. If real income rises from y_1 at point A to y_2 at point B, then due to the transactions and precautionary motives for holding money, the demand for real money balances will also increase. As a result, the demand schedule for real money balances shifts to the right, from $m^d(y_1)$ to $m^d(y_2)$, as shown in panel (a).

MAINTAINING MONEY MARKET EQUILIBRIUM   Following the rise in real income, there will be an excess quantity of real money balances demanded at the initial equilibrium interest rate, r_1. Because people will desire to hold fewer bonds as they seek to increase their real money balances, the result will be an excess quantity of bonds supplied. Bond prices will decline, and the equilibrium nominal interest rate will rise, to r_2. As a result, the economy will move from a real income–nominal interest rate combination, y_1 and r_1 at point A, at which the market for real money balances initially was in equilibrium, to a new combination, y_2 and r_2 at point B, that continues to maintain money market equilibrium. These real income–nominal interest rate combinations are two representative points of money market equilibrium along the *LM* schedule displayed in panel (b).

The *LM* schedule's name stems from the notation used by an economist named John Hicks in 1937. He referred to the demand for money as desired liquidity, *L*. Money market equilibrium required setting desired liquidity equal to the quantity of money balances supplied by the Federal Reserve, *M*. Hence, in Hicks's original terminology, $L = M$ always held along the schedule for money market equilibrium.

Figure 8–9   The Derivation of the *LM* Schedule

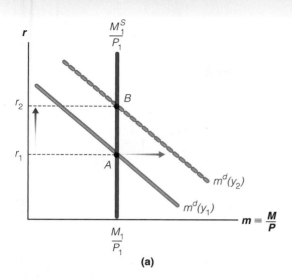

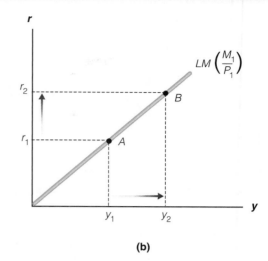

(a)

(b)

If real income rises from an initial amount to a higher level, y_2, then the demand for real money balances will increase, causing the equilibrium nominal interest rate to rise from r_1 at point *A* in panel (a) to r_2 at point *B*. Hence, as shown in panel (b), the real income–interest rate combinations y_1 and

r_1 at point *A* and y_2 and r_2 at point *B* will both maintain equilibrium in the market for real money balances given the current supply of real money balances. Hence, both points lie on the *LM* schedule.

A CONSTANT REAL MONEY SUPPLY   It is important to recognize that our derivation of the *LM* schedule in Figure 8–9 depended on an unchanging supply of real money balances equal to M_1/P_1. To emphasize this fact, we have labeled the *LM* schedule in panel (b) as $LM(M_1/P_1)$.

This notation makes clear that we have derived this set of real income–nominal interest rate combinations *given* the nominal money stock M_1 and the price level P_1. If the supply schedule for real money balances had been in a different position, then we would have come up with a different set of combinations of real income and the nominal interest rate consistent with money market equilibrium. We would have derived a different *LM* schedule.

Determining the Elasticity of the *LM* Schedule

What determines the elasticity of the *LM* schedule? Answering this question will help us to understand the factors that determine the overall effectiveness of monetary policy in the traditional Keynesian framework.

THE INTEREST ELASTICITY OF THE DEMAND FOR REAL MONEY BALANCES   Figure 8–10 on the next page displays two demand schedules for real money balances. In both panels, we show how a rise in the nominal interest rate affects desired holdings of real money balances. We do this beginning with point *A*, which

Figure 8–10   The Interest Elasticity of Money Demand

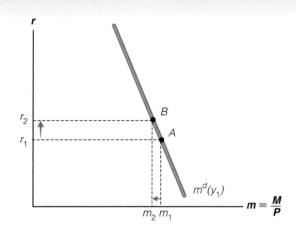

(a)

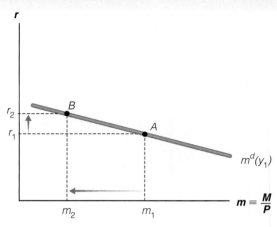

(b)

In panel (a), a given proportionate rise in the nominal interest rate from point A to point B causes a relatively small proportionate reduction in the quantity of real money balances demanded, so the demand for real money balances is relatively interest-inelastic. In contrast, in panel (b), the

same proportionate interest-rate increase induces a relatively larger proportionate decline in the quantity of real money balances demanded. Thus, money demand is relatively more interest-elastic in panel (b) than in panel (a).

INTEREST-INELASTIC MONEY DEMAND: Demand for money that is relatively insensitive to interest-rate variations.

INTEREST-ELASTIC MONEY DEMAND: Demand for money that is relatively sensitive to interest-rate variations.

the two schedules share in common. At this point, the interest rate is r_1 and the quantity of real money balances demanded is m_1 in each panel. Any proportionate change in the interest rate, such as the proportionate interest-rate change entailed in a movement from point A to point B in each panel, will always yield a smaller proportionate rise in desired real money holdings for the demand schedule shown in panel (a), as compared with panel (b). Consequently, around point A the money demand schedule in panel (a) is *less elastic* as compared with the money demand schedule in panel (b).

The money demand schedule in panel (a) of Figure 8–10, therefore, illustrates a situation of relatively more **interest-inelastic money demand** around point A, as compared with the money demand schedule in panel (b). This means that the interest sensitivity, or interest elasticity, of the demand for real money balances is lower in panel (a) than in panel (b) around point A. Alternatively, we can say that the money demand schedule in panel (b) shows a situation of relatively more **interest-elastic money demand** around point A, as compared with the money demand schedule in panel (a). This means that the interest sensitivity, or interest elasticity, of the demand for real money balances is higher in panel (b) than in panel (a) around point A.

INTEREST ELASTICITY OF MONEY DEMAND AND THE ELASTICITY OF THE *LM* SCHEDULE

Figure 8–11 shows how the interest elasticity of money demand affects the

Figure 8–11   The Interest Elasticity of Money Demand and the Elasticity of the *LM* Schedule

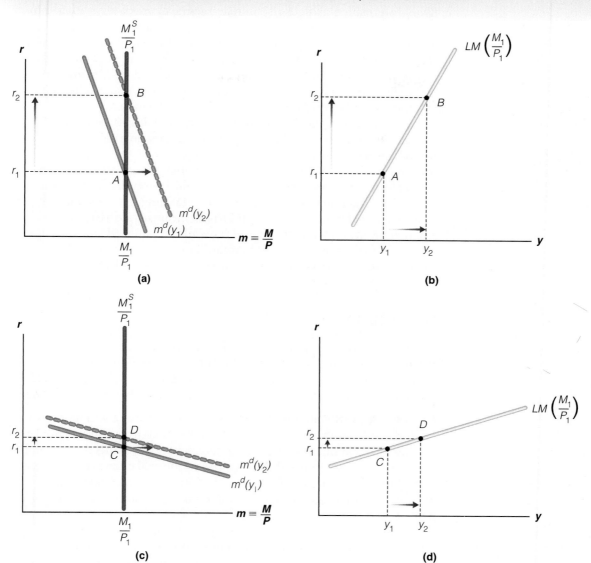

(a)

(b)

(c)

(d)

Panels (a) and (b) display the derivation of an *LM* schedule when the demand for money balances is relatively interest-inelastic. A rise in money demand induced by a rise in real income causes a movement from point *A* to point *B* in the market for real money balances in panel (a). These points correspond to points *A* and *B* along the relatively inelastic *LM* schedule in panel (b). By way of contrast, panels (c) and

(d) show the derivation of an *LM* schedule when money demand is relatively interest-elastic. In panel (c), an increase in the demand for real money balances induced by a rise in real income produces a movement from point *C* to point *D*. These points correspond to points *C* and *D* along the relatively elastic *LM* schedule that results, as shown in panel (d).

elasticity of the *LM* schedule. In panels (a) and (b), we again derive an *LM* schedule, but we assume that the demand for real money balances is relatively interest-inelastic. A rise in real income causes a rightward shift in the interest-inelastic money demand schedule in panel (a). Because individuals' money holdings are not very responsive to changes in the interest rate, they are satisfied holding the same quantity of real money balances at a significantly higher equilibrium nominal interest rate. As shown in panel (b), this means that the *LM* schedule, like the money demand schedule in panel (a), must be relatively inelastic in the relevant range.

In contrast, panels (c) and (d) of Figure 8–11 illustrate the derivation of the *LM* schedule when the demand for real money balances is relatively more interest-elastic and, therefore, comparatively more elastic (less inelastic) than in panel (a). Because people are much more sensitive to interest-rate changes when money demand is very interest-elastic, following a rise in real income they are satisfied holding the same quantity of real money balances only if the equilibrium interest rate rises by a relatively small amount. As a result, the *LM* schedule in panel (d) for the case of relatively interest-elastic money demand is more elastic than the *LM* schedule in panel (b) for the case of relatively interest-inelastic money demand in the relevant range.

Factors That Shift the *LM* Schedule

As we emphasized when we first derived the *LM* schedule in Figure 8–9, the position of the *LM* schedule depends upon the quantity of real money balances. This is so because we derive the *LM* schedule by increasing real income while keeping the quantity of real money balances unchanged.

A CHANGE IN THE NOMINAL MONEY STOCK   Now imagine a situation in which a central bank, such as the Federal Reserve, increases the nominal money stock while real income and the price level are unchanged. As panel (a) of Figure 8–12 shows, this will cause a rise in the real quantity of money, from M_1/P_1 to M_2/P_1. Although real income will be unchanged at y_1, the equilibrium nominal interest rate will decline because of the liquidity effect, from r_1 to r_2.

Following the increase in the nominal money stock, there will now be a new real income–interest rate combination, y_1 and r_2 at point *B*, that will maintain equilibrium in the market for real money balances. Consequently, as shown in panel (b) of Figure 8–12, this combination will be on a new *LM* schedule, $LM(M_2/P_1)$, that lies below and to the right of the initial *LM* schedule, $LM(M_1/P_1)$. With the price level unchanged, therefore, a rise in the nominal money stock will increase the supply of real money balances and shift the *LM* schedule downward and to the right. In contrast, a decline in the money stock with an unchanged price level will shift the *LM* schedule upward and to the left.

A CHANGE IN THE PRICE LEVEL   Panels (c) and (d) of Figure 8–12 illustrate the effects of a rise in the price level with the nominal quantity of money and

Figure 8–12   Changes in the Real Money Supply and in the Position of the *LM* Schedule

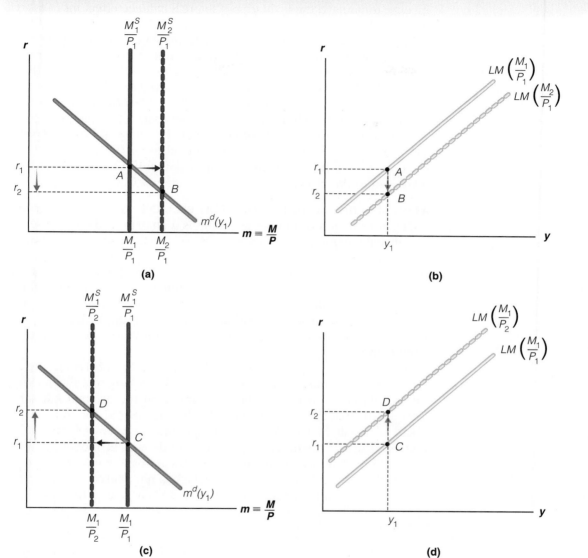

(a)

(b)

(c)

(d)

Panels (a) and (b) show the effects of an increase in the nominal money stock if the price level is unchanged. As shown in panel (a), the result is a rise in the supply of real money balances and a resulting movement from equilibrium point *A* to equilibrium point *B*. The new real income–interest rate combination y_1 and r_2 at point *B* in panel (b) lies directly below the original combination y_1 and r_1 at point *A*. Hence, the *LM* schedule will shift downward and to the

right. Panels (c) and (d), in contrast, show that a rise in the price level with the nominal money stock unchanged results in a movement from equilibrium point *C* to equilibrium point *D*, as shown in panel (c). The new real income–interest rate combination y_1 and r_2 at point *D* in panel (d) lies directly above the original combination y_1 and r_1 at point *C*. Therefore, the *LM* schedule shifts upward and to the left.

real income unchanged. In panel (c), an increase in the price level, from P_1 to P_2, will cause a fall in real money balances, from M_1/P_1 to M_1/P_2. Real income remains at the level y_1, but the real balance effect induces a rise in the equilibrium nominal interest rate, from r_1 to r_2.

After the rise in the price level, there will be a new real income–interest rate combination, y_1 and r_2 at point D, that will maintain equilibrium in the market for real money balances. Hence, as indicated in panel (d), this combination will be on a new LM schedule, $LM(M_1/P_2)$, above point C on the original LM schedule, $LM(M_1/P_1)$. With the nominal money stock unchanged, therefore, an increase in the price level will reduce the supply of real money balances and shift the LM schedule upward and to the left. In contrast, a decline in the price level with an unchanged nominal quantity of money will shift the LM schedule downward and to the right.

A CHANGE IN THE DEMAND FOR REAL MONEY BALANCES   The final factor that can affect the position of the LM schedule is a change in the demand for real money balances not caused by a variation in real income. For instance, suppose that there is a significant increase in the use of credit cards to make retail payments. As a result, people reduce their demand for real money balances at any given nominal interest rate. As panel (a) of Figure 8–13 shows, the demand for real money balances will decline, from $m_1^d(y_1)$ to $m_2^d(y_1)$, with the quantity of real money balances supplied, M_1/P_1, and real income, y_1, unchanged. This causes the equilibrium interest rate to fall from r_1 to r_2.

As a result, as panel (b) of Figure 8–13 shows, equilibrium in the market for real money balances will be maintained at a new real income–interest rate combination at point B below point A on the original LM schedule. This means that the LM schedule will shift downward and to the right as a result of a fall in the demand for real money balances caused by the increased use of credit cards. Indeed, any decline in money demand not induced by a fall in real income would cause this to happen. In contrast, a rise in the demand for real money balances not caused by an increase in real income would shift the LM schedule upward and to the left.

FUNDAMENTAL ISSUE #3

What is the *LM* schedule, and what factors determine its elasticity and position?   The *LM* schedule is an upward-sloping set of all combinations of real income and the nominal interest rate that maintain equilibrium in the market for real money balances. The *LM* schedule is more inelastic if money demand is relatively interest-inelastic, and it is more elastic if money demand is relatively interest-elastic. The *LM* schedule shifts downward and to the right if there is an increase in the nominal money stock, a fall in the price level, or a decline in money demand not caused by a change in real income. A decrease in the money stock, a rise in the price level, or a rise in money demand causes the *LM* schedule to shift upward and to the left.

Figure 8–13   The Effect of a Fall in the Demand for Real Money Balances on the Position of the *LM* Schedule

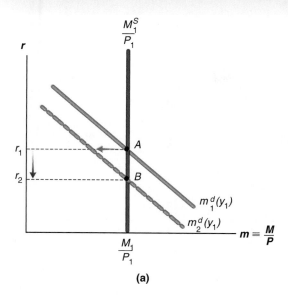

(a)

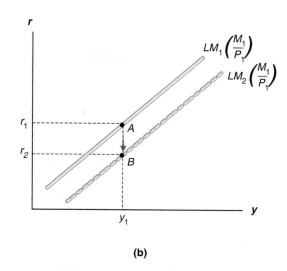

(b)

A fall in the demand for money caused by any factor other than a decline in real income will cause a decline in the equilibrium nominal interest rate, from r_1 at point A to r_2 at point B in panel (a). Because real income remains unchanged at y_1, the new real income–interest rate combination that will maintain money market equilibrium, given by point B in panel (b), will lie below the initial real income–interest rate combination given by point A. Thus, a decline in the demand for real money balances not stemming from a fall in real income implies a downward and rightward shift in the *LM* schedule.

The *IS* Schedule

As you learned in Chapter 6, *equilibrium* real income must satisfy the condition that real income is equal to the sum of consumption spending, desired business investment spending, government expenditures, and export spending. You also know that desired investment spending is negatively related to the interest rate. This means that the interest rate must affect equilibrium real income. It follows that there must be combinations of real income and the nominal interest rate that maintain *equilibrium* real income. This set of real income–nominal interest rate combinations is the *IS schedule*.

Deriving the *IS* Schedule

Figure 8–14 on the following page shows the derivation of the *IS* schedule. Panel (a) shows the desired investment schedule. Recall from Chapter 6 that desired real investment spending is negatively related to the real interest rate, which is equal to the nominal interest rate less the expected inflation rate. If inflation expectations are unchanged, therefore, investment is

Figure 8–14   The Derivation of the *IS* Schedule

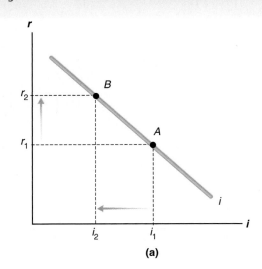

(a)

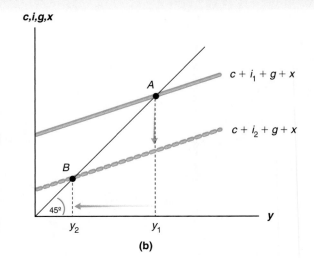

(b)

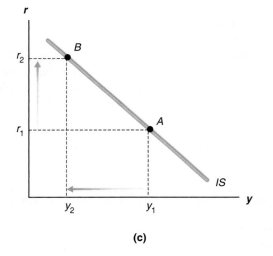

(c)

As shown in panel (a), an increase in the nominal interest rate will cause a movement from point *A* to point *B* along the investment schedule and result in a decline in desired investment expenditures. As panel (b) shows, this will reduce aggregate desired expenditures, causing a reduction in equilibrium real income, from y_1 at point *A* to y_2 at point *B*. As a result, the new combination of real income and the nominal interest rate, y_2 and r_2 at point *B* in panel (c), that is consistent with equilibrium real income and expenditures will lie above and to the left of the original combination y_1 and r_1 at point *A*. Hence, the *IS* schedule, which shows all combinations of real income and the nominal interest rate consistent with equilibrium real income and expenditures, slopes downward.

inversely related to the *nominal* interest rate, as shown in the figure. As a result, a rise in the nominal interest rate, from r_1 to r_2, will cause desired real investment spending to fall from i_1 at point *A* to i_2 at point *B*.

As panel (b) indicates, this decline in desired investment spending caused by a rise in the nominal interest rate will cause the aggregate desired expenditures schedule to shift downward. As a result, equilibrium real income will decline, from y_1 to y_2. Hence, as shown in panel (c), the economy will move from the initial real income–nominal interest rate combination, y_1 and r_1 at point *A*, that is consistent with equilibrium real income to a new combination, y_2 and r_2 at point *B*.

These real income–nominal interest rate combinations A and B lie on an **IS schedule,** which is a set of combinations of levels of real income and nominal interest rates that maintain equilibrium real income. The *IS* schedule also was named in 1937 by John Hicks, who first derived the schedule by assuming a simple economy with no government sector or international trade and who used the leakages-injections approach to determining equilibrium real income. Because income is equal to desired expenditures all along the *IS* schedule, it is also true that, with no government or international trade, saving "leakages" from the income-expenditure flow will equal investment "reinjections." Thus, investment (i) will equal saving (s); hence, Hicks's term "*IS*."

Determining the Elasticity of the *IS* Schedule

Just as the elasticity of the *LM* schedule depends on the interest elasticity of real money balances, the elasticity of the *IS* schedule depends on the interest elasticity of desired investment. Figure 8–15 on the next page illustrates this by considering a situation of relatively **interest-elastic desired investment** in panel (a), so that the investment schedule is very elastic in the relevant range. As a result, a relatively small increase in the nominal interest rate induces a relatively large decline in desired investment. This causes a relatively large downward shift in the aggregate expenditures schedule, resulting in a comparatively large reduction in equilibrium real income due to the multiplier effect. Thus, as shown in panel (c), when desired investment spending is relatively interest-elastic, the derived *IS* schedule is relatively elastic.

In contrast, in a situation of relatively **interest-inelastic desired investment** in the relevant range, relatively large changes in the interest rate cause comparatively small changes in desired investment, aggregate desired expenditures, and equilibrium real income. As a result, with relatively *interest-inelastic* desired investment the *IS* schedule is also relatively *inelastic.*

Factors That Shift the *IS* Schedule

To derive the *IS* schedule in Figures 8–14 and 8–15, we considered only the effects of a rise in the nominal interest rate on desired investment spending, with all other factors that would affect autonomous desired expenditures unchanged. These factors include autonomous saving, autonomous imports, government expenditures, autonomous net taxes, and autonomous export spending. Reductions in autonomous saving, imports, or net taxes all will stimulate consumption spending and, at any given interest rate, induce a rise in aggregate desired expenditures, as shown in panel (b) of Figure 8–16 on page 223. Likewise, an increase in government expenditures or autonomous export spending also induces an upward shift in the aggregated desired expenditures schedule. The result is a rise in equilibrium real income, from y_1 at point A to y_2 at point B, even though desired investment spending has not changed in panel (a).

IS SCHEDULE: A set of possible combinations of real income and the nominal interest rate that are necessary to maintain an income-expenditure equilibrium, $y = c + i + g + x$.

INTEREST-ELASTIC DESIRED INVESTMENT: Desired investment spending that is relatively sensitive to interest-rate variations.

INTEREST-INELASTIC DESIRED INVESTMENT: Desired investment that is relatively insensitive to interest-rate variations.

Figure 8–15   The Interest Elasticity of Desired Investment and the Elasticity of the *IS* Schedule

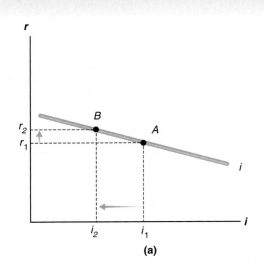

(a)

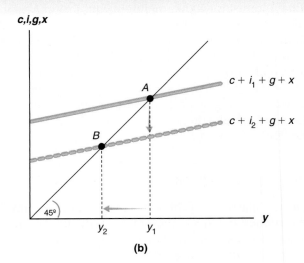

(b)

If desired investment is relatively interest-elastic, so that a relatively small proportionate rise in the interest rate causes a relatively large proportionate reduction in desired investment, as in the movement from point *A* to point *B* in panel (a), then the result is a relatively large reduction in aggregate desired expenditures, as shown in panel (b). Thus, equilibrium real income falls by a relatively large proportionate amount, from y_1 at point *A* in panel (b) to y_2 at point *B*. Panel (c) shows that the result is a relatively elastic *IS* schedule containing corresponding real income–interest rate combinations at points *A* and *B*.

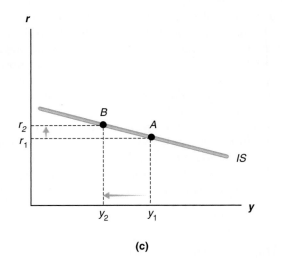

(c)

Any one of these possible sources of an increase in autonomous expenditures would induce a rise in equilibrium real income equal to the increase in aggregate autonomous expenditures times the autonomous spending multiplier. As panel (c) of Figure 8–16 indicates, the result would be a new real income–nominal interest rate combination, y_2 and r_1 at point *B*, that lies to the right of the original combination, y_1 and r_1 at point *A*. Therefore, any factor that causes an increase in aggregate desired expenditures, other than a rise in investment stemming from a fall in the nominal interest rate, shifts the *IS* schedule rightward by the amount of the result-

Figure 8–16   A Change in Autonomous Expenditures and the Position of the *IS* Schedule

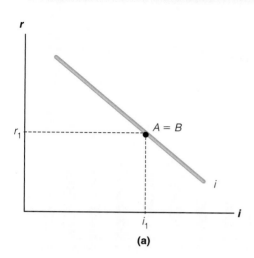

(a)

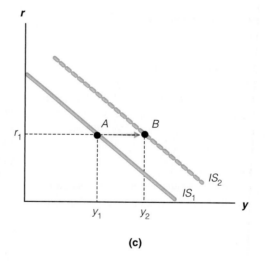

(b)

An increase in aggregate desired expenditures, perhaps because of a reduction in autonomous saving, autonomous import expenditures, or net taxes, or because of an increase in autonomous government spending or autonomous export expenditures, causes the aggregate expenditures schedule to shift upward, as shown in panel (b). Thus, at a given interest rate and level of investment spending, displayed in panel (a), equilibrium real income will increase following the movement from point *A* to point *B* in panel (b). This implies that a new real income–interest rate combination maintaining equilibrium real income and expenditures, y_2 and r_1 at point *B* in panel (c), will lie on a new *IS* schedule to the right of the original combination y_1 and r_1 at point *A* on the initial *IS* schedule. Hence, a rise in autonomous expenditures shifts the *IS* schedule to the right.

(c)

ing multiplier effect on equilibrium real income. In contrast, any factor that causes a *reduction* in aggregate desired expenditures, other than a fall in investment resulting from a rise in the nominal interest rate, shifts the *IS* schedule *leftward* by the amount of the resulting multiplier effect on equilibrium real income. (There is some evidence that falling stock prices can induce a leftward shift in the *IS* schedule by reducing autonomous consumption; see on the following page *Policy Notebook: Gauging the Stock Market's Effect on Consumption.*)

Gauging the Stock Market's Effect on Consumption

Figure 8–17 shows that the portion of households owning shares of corporate stock held steady for a number of years before rising steadily after the mid-1980s. Stocks are part of total household wealth, and changes in their market values that affect total wealth potentially influence the amount of consumption spending by households.

John Duca of the Federal Reserve Bank of Dallas has studied the effect of changes in stock wealth valuations on aggregate consumption spending. He found that the near doubling of the market value of all U.S. stocks during the late 1990s tended to push up household consumption by nearly 3.5 percentage points. The drop in stock prices during 2000 and early 2001, however, reduced the overall increase in stock prices to about 150 percent. Hence, after taking into account the falloff in stock wealth valuation in the early 2000s, Duca found that the overall boost in consumption generated by stock prices between 1994 and 2001 was just over 2.5 percentage points.

For Critical Analysis
Stock prices, like prices of bonds, are inversely related to interest rates, and they also depend on investors' percep-

tions of firms' future earnings. Does it make any difference, in terms of evaluating whether stock price changes relate to movements along versus shifts of the *IS* schedule, whether changes in stock prices result mainly from interest-rate movements or from altered perceptions of future corporate earnings?

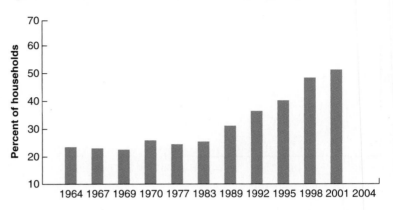

Figure 8-17   The Portion of U.S. Households Owning Corporate Stock

The fraction of households owning shares of stock was stable until the late 1980s but has been gradually increasing since.

SOURCES: John Duca, "How Does the Stock Market Affect the Economy?" *Federal Reserve Bank of Dallas Southwest Economy* 5 (September/October 2001): 1–12; Federal Reserve *Survey of Consumer Finances.*

FUNDAMENTAL ISSUE #4

What is the *IS* schedule, and what factors determine its elasticity and position?   The *IS* schedule is a downward-sloping set of all combinations of real income and the nominal interest rate for which aggregate desired expenditures equal real income. The *IS* schedule is more inelastic if desired investment is relatively interest-inelastic, and it is more elastic if desired investment is relatively interest-elastic. The *IS* schedule shifts to the right if there is an increase in autonomous desired expenditures stemming from a fall in autonomous saving, import spending, or taxes or from a rise in autonomous government spending, investment, or export spending. In contrast, a rise in autonomous saving, import spending, or taxes or a fall in autonomous government spending, investment, or export spending shifts the *IS* schedule to the left.

The *IS* schedule is a set of real income–nominal interest rate combinations that maintain equilibrium real income, and the *LM* schedule consists of real income–nominal interest rate combinations that maintain equilibrium in the market for real money balances. Thus, combining the two schedules on one diagram will permit us to find a single combination of real income and the nominal interest rate that achieves equilibrium real income while simultaneously achieving equilibrium in the market for real money balances.

Combining *IS* and *LM*

Figure 8–18 on the next page combines the *IS* and *LM* schedules. At point *E* in panel (a), the two schedules cross. Real income is equal to aggregate desired expenditures at the real income level y_1, because point *E* is on the *IS* schedule. At the same time, point *E* is also the *LM* schedule. Thus, the market for real money balances is in equilibrium at the interest rate r_1.

We call point *E* a point of **IS-LM equilibrium.** At any point such as *E*, the following is true:

> **A point of *IS-LM equilibrium* is a point that is common to both the *IS* schedule and the *LM* schedule, so that equilibrium real income is attained simultaneously with the nominal interest rate that attains equilibrium in the market for real money balances.**

IS-LM Equilibrium and Disequilibrium

The reason that point *E* is an *equilibrium* point is explained in panel (b) of Figure 8–18. For instance, at point *A*, above the *LM* schedule at the interest rate r_2 and income level y_2, the nominal interest rate is too high to achieve equilibrium in the market for real money balances. As a result, there will be an excess quantity of money supplied at this interest rate. Consequently, the nominal interest rate will tend to fall toward r_1, and equilibrium real income will tend to rise along the *IS* schedule toward point *E* and the real income level y_1.

Now consider point *B*, below the *LM* schedule at the nominal interest rate r_3 and real income level y_3. At point *B*, the nominal interest rate is too low to maintain equilibrium in the market for real money balances. The result is an excess quantity of real money balances demanded, which causes the interest rate to rise toward r_1, inducing a movement up along the *IS* schedule toward point *E* and real income y_1.

Now think about point *C* in panel (b), which is to the right of the *IS* schedule at the nominal interest rate r_2 and real income level y_3. At point *C*, the level of real income is above its equilibrium level, which means that real income is greater than aggregate desired expenditures at the interest rate r_2. As we discussed in Chapter 6, in such a situation realized investment will be greater than desired investment, and firms will find themselves making undesired investment expenditures on inventories. Firms therefore reduce their real investment, which causes real income to fall toward its equilibrium level, y_1. As real income falls, the demand for real

IS-LM EQUILIBRIUM: The point at which the *IS* and *LM* schedules cross, so that the economy simultaneously attains both an income-expenditure equilibrium and equilibrium in the market for real money balances.

The graph below shows how real income and the nominal interest rate are determined in the Keynesian model. What happens if the money stock changes? What occurs if there is a change in government spending? You can discover the answers to these questions by interacting with this graph on the Web. **Go to** http://macroxtra.swcollege.com

Figure 8–18   *IS-LM* Equilibrium and Disequilibrium

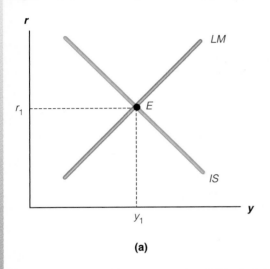

(a)

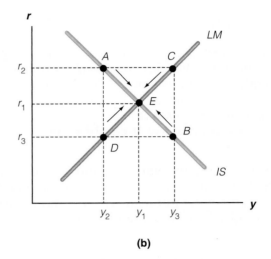

(b)

At point *E* in panel (a), where the *IS* and *LM* schedules cross, the market for real money balances is in equilibrium at the same time that real income equals aggregate desired expenditures. Points *A* and *B* in panel (b) are on the *IS* schedule but not the *LM* schedule, so at these points the market for real money balances is not in equi-

librium. The interest rate must move back toward r_1 to reattain money market equilibrium. Points *C* and *D* are on the *LM* schedule but not the *IS* schedule, so at these points real income is not equal to aggregate desired expenditures. Real income must move back toward y_1 to reattain real income–expenditure equilibrium.

money balances will decline, causing a fall in the interest rate and a movement along the *LM* schedule from point *C* toward the equilibrium point *E*.

Finally, at point *D*, to the left of the *IS* schedule at the nominal interest rate r_3 and real income level y_2, the opposite situation would arise. At point *D*, the level of real income is below its equilibrium level, which means that real income is less than aggregate desired expenditures at the interest rate r_3. As a result, realized investment is less than desired investment. Firms will wish to increase their real investment spending, which will cause real income to rise toward its equilibrium level, y_1. As real income rises, the demand for real money balances will increase, inducing a rise in the interest rate and a movement along the *LM* schedule from point *D* toward the equilibrium point *E*.

The Effects of Monetary Policy Actions in the *IS-LM* Model

Monetary policy actions change the nominal money stock, thereby changing the real money supply (as long as the price level is unchanged) and altering the position of the *LM* schedule. Such actions must also change the location of an *IS-LM* equilibrium, thereby affecting *both* the equilibrium nominal interest rate *and* the equilibrium level of real income. This is why Keynes concluded that a linkage may exist among monetary policy, the nominal interest rate, and real economic activity.

To understand the nature of the monetary policy linkage that Keynes proposed, let's use the *IS-LM* framework to explore the effects of an increase in the nominal money stock by a central bank such as the Federal Reserve. To keep things simple, for the time being let's assume that the price level remains unchanged. (We shall allow the price level to vary in response to monetary policy actions in Chapter 10.)

Figure 8–19 illustrates the effects of this central bank policy action. The first effect of an increase in the nominal money stock, shown in panel (a),

Figure 8–19 The Effect of an Increase in the Nominal Money Stock

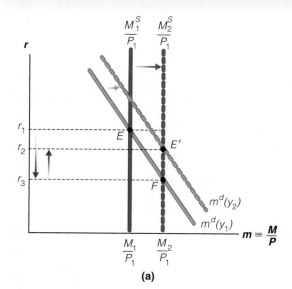
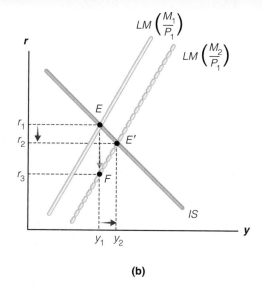

(a)   (b)

The result of an increase in the nominal money stock is a decline in the equilibrium interest rate in the market for real money balances from r_1 at point E to r_3 at point F in panel (a). This results in a downward shift in the *LM* schedule by the distance E–F in panel (b). The decline in the interest rate, however, induces a rise in desired investment and a consequent movement down along the *IS* schedule to a new *IS*-*LM* equilibrium at point E' at the higher real income level

y_2. As real income increases, the demand for real money balances rises in panel (a), causing the equilibrium interest rate to rise to r_2, which corresponds to an upward movement along the new *LM* schedule in panel (b), from point F to point E'. On net, therefore, the rise in the nominal money stock causes a reduction in the equilibrium nominal interest rate and an increase in equilibrium real income.

is a shift in the LM schedule downward and to the right, from $LM(M_1/P_1)$ to $LM(M_2/P_1)$ displayed in panel (b). This shift reflects the liquidity effect: Holding real income and the price level unchanged, an increase in the nominal quantity of money supplied by the central bank reduces the equilibrium interest rate in the market for real money balances. Now, however, we can take into account the response of real income.

As the nominal interest rate declines, from r_1 at point E in the direction of r_3 at point F, desired investment spending begins to increase. This causes a rise in aggregate desired expenditures, thereby inducing a movement down along the IS schedule from point E toward point E' in panel (b). Furthermore, as real income rises, so does the demand for real money balances in panel (a), which places upward pressure on the nominal interest rate. This keeps the nominal interest rate from declining all the way to r_3. Instead, the final equilibrium interest rate is r_2 at point E'. Likewise, the final equilibrium income level, y_2, is also at point E', where the IS schedule and the new LM schedule intersect in panel (b).

We may conclude that the effects of an increase in the nominal money stock, holding the price level unchanged, are a decline in the equilibrium nominal interest rate and an increase in equilibrium real income. If instead the nominal money stock were reduced while the price level remained unchanged, the opposite results would follow: the equilibrium nominal interest rate would rise, and equilibrium real income would decline.

The Keynesian Monetary Policy Transmission Mechanism

The discussion in the preceding section illustrates the **Keynesian monetary policy transmission mechanism,** which is the fundamental Keynesian explanation for how a change in the nominal money stock is transmitted to real income. Our discussion indicates that there are two linkages by which this transmission takes place. First, an increase in the nominal money stock causes a liquidity effect that reduces the equilibrium nominal interest rate. Second, a fall in the interest rate causes desired investment and desired expenditures to rise. In the end, therefore, as summarized in Figure 8–20, an increase in the nominal money stock causes a rise in equilibrium real income.

THE FIRST LINK: THE LIQUIDITY EFFECT   According to this proposed mechanism for monetary policy effects, the magnitude of the effect of a monetary policy action on real income depends on two factors. One is the size of the liquidity effect on the interest rate. If the liquidity effect is large, then the ultimate effect of a monetary policy action on real income is more likely to be sizable. If the liquidity effect is small, then the ultimate effect on real income is more likely to be negligible.

The size of the liquidity effect is determined by the elasticity of the LM schedule, which in turn depends on the interest elasticity of the demand for real money balances. If the demand schedule for real money balances is relatively interest-elastic, then the LM schedule is relatively elastic, and a change in the nominal money stock causes a relatively small change in

Figure 8–20   The Keynesian Transmission Mechanism of Monetary Policy

According to the Keynesian model, an increase in the nominal quantity of money in circulation causes a change in the equilibrium nominal interest rate. This, in turn, induces a change in desired investment spending, which brings about a change in equilibrium real income.

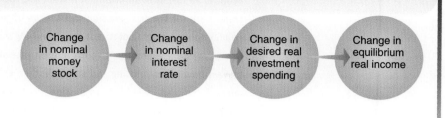

the nominal interest rate. In contrast, if the demand schedule for real money balances is relatively interest-inelastic, then the *LM* schedule is relatively inelastic, and a change in the nominal money stock causes a relatively large change in the nominal interest rate. Consequently, the lower the interest elasticity of the demand for real money balances—that is, the more inelastic the *LM* schedule is—the larger the liquidity effect resulting from a change in the quantity of money.

THE SECOND LINK: THE INVESTMENT RESPONSE   The other linkage, relating a given interest-rate change to the responsiveness of desired investment spending, depends on the interest elasticity of desired investment and the elasticity of the *IS* schedule. If desired investment is relatively interest-inelastic, then the *IS* schedule also is relatively inelastic, and a given change in the interest rate will have a comparatively small effect on desired investment, aggregate desired expenditures, and real income. If desired investment is relatively interest-elastic, then the *IS* schedule is relatively elastic, and a given change in the interest rate will have a comparatively larger effect on desired investment, aggregate desired expenditures, and real income. Therefore, the more interest-elastic desired investment spending is—that is, the more elastic the *IS* schedule is—the stronger the second linkage in the monetary policy transmission mechanism will be.

We can conclude that, according to the Keynesian monetary policy transmission mechanism, a constant-price increase in the nominal money supply will cause the equilibrium nominal interest rate to fall and the equilibrium level of real income to rise. A constant-price decrease in the nominal money supply will cause the equilibrium nominal interest rate to rise and the equilibrium level of real income to fall. The size of the effect on real income will be larger when the demand for real money balances is relatively more interest-inelastic, so that the *LM* schedule is more inelastic. When desired investment spending is relatively more interest-elastic, the *IS* schedule is more elastic, and the real income effect of monetary policy is enhanced.

FUNDAMENTAL ISSUE #5

What is an _IS-LM_ equilibrium, and what are the implications of the _IS-LM_ framework for the transmission mechanism of monetary policy?   An _IS-LM_ equilibrium is a single point that the _IS_ and _LM_ schedules have in common. At this point, real income and the nominal interest rate are both consistent with an equilibrium flow of real income and an equilibrium in the market for real money balances. The monetary policy transmission mechanism is the set of linkages by which the Keynesian framework indicates that monetary policy actions should influence equilibrium real income. According to this proposed mechanism, an increase in the nominal money stock reduces the equilibrium nominal interest rate, thereby stimulating desired investment spending. This, in turn, raises aggregate desired expenditures, thereby increasing equilibrium real income.

Government Spending and Crowding Out

As we discussed in Chapters 6 and 7, fiscal policy actions, such as changes in government spending or taxes, have multiplier effects on equilibrium real national income in the traditional Keynesian model. The _IS-LM_ model emphasizes that real income and the nominal interest rate _both_ must adjust simultaneously to achieve an equilibrium flow of aggregate desired expenditures and equilibrium in the market for real money balances. Because total spending affects real income and, as a result, the demand for money, fiscal policy actions should influence the nominal interest rate. Changes in the interest rate should, in turn, feed back to affect total spending and, therefore, the degree to which fiscal policy can influence equilibrium real income.

Fiscal Policy in the Basic _IS-LM_ Model

To understand how fiscal policy influences interest rates and how the resulting interest-rate changes affect real income, let's evaluate the effects of changes in government expenditures. Consider the effect of a rise in real government spending, from an amount equal to g_1 to a larger amount equal to g_2, holding everything else, including taxes, constant. In this situation, the government would have to finance the increase in its spending either by reducing an existing budget surplus or, more likely, by adding to an existing budget deficit.

Figure 8–21 depicts the effects of this fiscal policy action in the _IS-LM_ framework. The rise in government expenditures causes the _IS_ schedule to shift rightward by the amount of the spending increase times the autonomous expenditures multiplier, $1/(1 - MPC)$. Consequently, at the initial equilibrium interest rate, r_1, real income will rise from y_1 to y_3, which is equal to the distance between the initial equilibrium at point E and point F. This rise in real income, however, will act through the transactions and precautionary motives to increase the demand for real money balances. This will cause an increase in the equilibrium nominal interest rate, from r_1 to r_2, that is shown by an upward movement along the _LM_ schedule from point E

Figure 8–21   The Effects of an Increase in Government Spending in the *IS-LM* Model

An increase in government spending shifts the *IS* schedule rightward. This causes equilibrium real income to rise, thereby inducing an increase in the demand for real money balances. As a result, the equilibrium nominal interest rate will increase, as shown by the movement upward along the *LM* schedule from point *E* to point *E'*. Holding inflation expectations unchanged, the real interest rate will increase, thereby causing a decline in desired investment expenditures and a movement back along the *IS* schedule from point *F* to point *E'*. Nevertheless, on net the increase in government spending generally will cause a rise in the equilibrium nominal interest rate and an increase in equilibrium real income.

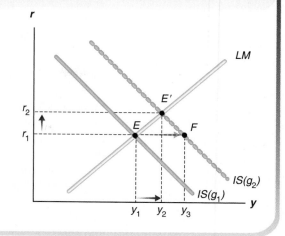

to point E'. If inflation expectations are unchanged, the rise in the nominal interest rate will correspond to an increase in the real rate of interest.

Recall, however, that desired investment spending is inversely related to the real interest rate. Hence, the rise in the real interest rate owing to the upward movement in the nominal rate with unchanged inflation expectations will reduce investment expenditures and thus cause aggregate desired expenditures to decline once again. This causes real income to decline somewhat, to y_2. This decline in real income is shown by a movement back along the new *IS* schedule from point *F* to point *E'*. The amount of the fall in real income from y_3 back toward y_2 will equal the decline in investment spending times the autonomous expenditures multiplier, $1/(1 - MPC)$.

In the end, even though the rise in government spending initially causes real income to rise by a multiple amount, the induced rise in the interest rate will also cause investment expenditures to decline by a multiple amount. The *net* effect of the increase in real government expenditures on equilibrium real income typically is positive, as shown in Figure 8–21. Clearly, however, the fundamental nature of the Keynesian multiplier effect changes when we account for a change in the nominal interest rate that is induced by a rise in government spending. Equilibrium real income no longer rises by the full amount predicted by the basic multiplier framework developed in Chapter 6. In fact, the increase in equilibrium real income induced by fiscal policy could be much less than that model would indicate. How much less, it turns out, depends on the size of the *crowding-out effect*.

The Crowding-Out Effect

We encountered the crowding-out effect in Chapter 4. There we found that in the classical model there is *complete* crowding out: A deficit-financed increase in government expenditures crowds out an equal amount of private spending. In the classical model, complete crowding out also takes place because a rise in government spending causes private spending to decline by inducing an increase in the real interest rate, which could result from a rise in the nominal interest rate with unchanged inflation expectations.

Real income is predetermined in the classical model, however, by the position of the vertical aggregate supply schedule. In contrast, in the traditional Keynesian model, real income can vary in response to an alteration in government expenditures. Thus, complete crowding out generally does not occur.

THE AMOUNT OF CROWDING OUT   What determines the relative size of the crowding-out effect? Suppose that we had drawn Figure 8–21 with a very inelastic *IS* schedule in the relevant range (so that investment was very interest-inelastic) and a very elastic *LM* schedule in the relevant range (so that the demand for money was very interest-elastic). With these elasticities, the amount of the final increase in real income would have been very nearly the same as the amount of the rightward *IS* shift. The crowding-out effect would have been very small.

In contrast, if we had drawn Figure 8–21 with a very elastic *IS* schedule in the relevant range (so that desired investment was relatively interest-elastic) and a very inelastic *LM* schedule in the relevant range (so that the demand for real money balances was relatively interest-inelastic), then the final increase in equilibrium real income would have been very nearly equal to zero. Crowding out would have been very nearly complete. We may conclude that:

> **The crowding-out effect becomes larger as the interest elasticity of desired investment increases. The crowding-out effect also increases as the interest elasticity of the demand for real money balances declines.**

COMPLETE CROWDING OUT   The extreme case of complete crowding out occurs with a perfectly elastic *IS* schedule (completely interest-elastic investment) and a perfectly inelastic *LM* schedule (completely interest-inelastic money demand). In this case, a rise in government expenditures shifts the *IS* schedule along itself, and no change takes place in the equilibrium real income level as a result. This outcome can occur only when desired investment spending falls by exactly the same amount as government expenditures rise. This special case is the *IS-LM* analogue to the classical model, in which there is complete crowding out. This is a sensible conclusion, because the classical model emphasizes the interest sensitivity of desired investment but assumes that money demand is completely interest insensitive.

FUNDAMENTAL ISSUE #6

How does government spending influence real income in the traditional Keynesian model?   The initial effect of a rise in government expenditures is an increase in real income equal to the increase in government spending times the autonomous expenditures multiplier. The rise in real income, however, causes an increase in the demand for money that pushes up the equilibrium nominal interest rate. Given current inflation expectations, this leads to a rise in the real interest rate and a reduction in desired real investment. As a result, some private spending is crowded out by the rise in government expenditures, so equilibrium real income rises by less than predicted by the basic multiplier analysis.

Is Japan Stuck in a "Liquidity Trap"?

Since the early 1990s, Japan has faced rising unemployment, price deflation, and sluggish growth in real incomes. The nation's central bank, the Bank of Japan, has responded by reducing interest rates in an effort to stimulate real expenditures. As Figure 8-22 indicates, by early 1999 short-term interest rates in Japan were virtually zero.

The Theory of the Liquidity Trap

Keynes suggested that very low interest rates could create a *liquidity trap*. In this situation, he argued, interest rates are so low that very few people are willing to hold bonds instead of the most liquid asset, money.

In a liquidity trap environment, therefore, the portfolio motive for holding money predominates, and the demand for money is highly interest-elastic. The economy's *LM* schedule, therefore, is very elastic, and rightward shifts in the *LM* schedule can do little to induce increases in aggregate spending and equilibrium real income. Thus, a central bank's effort to stimulate aggregate expenditures by boosting the quantity of money is rendered impotent by the willingness of domestic residents to hold money rather than spending it.

Evaluating the Evidence

Two pieces of evidence point to the possible existence of a liquidity trap in Japan. One is the fact that interest rates in Japan have been so very low—the lowest for any major industrialized nation since the Great Depression of the 1930s.

Another piece of evidence is that even though the Bank of Japan has steadily increased

Figure 8-22   **Short-Term Interest Rates in Japan since 1990**

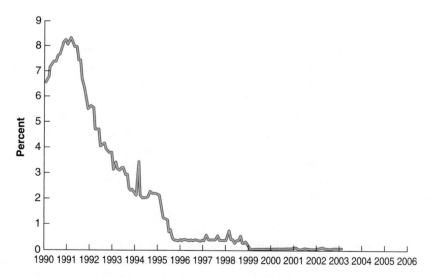

Interest rates have hovered near zero in Japan since 1999.

SOURCES: Michael Hutchison, "Japan's Recession: Is the Liquidity Trap Back?" Federal Reserve Bank of San Francisco *Economic Letter*, No. 2000-19, June 16, 2000; Bank of Japan.

Continued on next page

Link to The Global Economy, continued

bank reserves, the monetary base, and monetary aggregates, there has been little noticeable effect on economic activity. When the Bank of Japan has induced increases in reserves in the banking system, Japanese banks have seemed content to hold them alongside other assets that offer zero rates of return, and the Japanese public likewise has been willing to hold more cash in the form of currency and checking account balances. Thus, increases in bank reserves have not been bringing about increased spending on goods and services. Every month since the beginning of 2000, Japan's M1 has grown at annual rates of 4 to 9 percent, and M2 has increased at annual rates of 2 to 4 percent, but the nation has continued to experience a series of recessions interrupted by short-lived, meager recoveries.

Research Project

Use an *IS-LM* diagram to verify that monetary policy action has little effect on equilibrium real income if the *LM* schedule is highly elastic at very low rates of interest. If a liquidity trap prevents monetary policy actions from helping to boost national income, is there any potential role for additional forms of government policy actions? Explain how the actions you have proposed might provide a stimulus to economic activity even in a liquidity trap situation.

Web Resources

1. What recent monetary policy actions has the Bank of Japan undertaken? Find out at its English-language home page, http://www.boj.or.jp/en/index.htm.

2. What recent policies regarding public expenditures and taxation has Japan undertaken? To learn more, visit the English-language home page of Japan's Ministry of Finance at http://www.mof.go.jp/english/.

Chapter Summary

1. The Key Motives for Holding Money and the Variables That They Indicate Should Influence the Demand for Money: Two key motives for holding money are the transactions and precautionary motives, which have to do with the need to hold money for use in planned and unplanned exchanges, respectively. Both motives indicate that the demand for real money balances should depend positively on the level of real income. The third key motive is the portfolio motive. This refers to the allocation of a portion of financial wealth to money holdings as part of speculative strategies based on anticipated future changes in interest rates and bond prices. The portfolio motive indicates that desired holdings of money should depend negatively on the nominal interest rate.

2. The Determination of Nominal Interest Rates in the Traditional Keynesian Model: At the equilibrium nominal interest rate, people are satisfied holding the quantity of real money balances supplied by the central bank. A liquidity effect on the nominal interest rate occurs when an increase in the nominal money stock alone causes a rise in the supply

of real money balances that reduces the equilibrium nominal interest rate. A real balance effect on the nominal interest rate occurs when an increase in the price level causes a reduction in the supply of real money balances that raises the equilibrium nominal interest rate.

3. The *LM* Schedule and the Factors That Determine Its Elasticity and Position: The *LM* schedule is the set of all combinations of real income and the nominal interest rate that maintain equilibrium in the market for real money balances. It is more inelastic if money demand is relatively interest-inelastic, and it is more elastic if money demand is relatively interest-elastic. An increase in the nominal money stock, a fall in the price level, or a decline in money demand not caused by a change in real income shifts the *LM* schedule downward and to the right. A decrease in the money stock, a rise in the price level, or a rise in money demand shifts the *LM* schedule upward and to the left.

4. The *IS* Schedule and the Factors That Determine Its Elasticity and Position: The *IS* schedule is the set of all combinations of real income and the nominal interest rate for which aggregate desired expenditures equal real income. The *IS* schedule is more inelastic if desired investment is relatively interest-inelastic, and it is more elastic if desired investment is relatively interest-elastic. An increase in autonomous desired expenditures stemming from a fall in autonomous saving, import spending, or taxes or from a rise in autonomous government spending, investment, or export spending shifts the *IS* schedule upward and to the right. A rise in autonomous saving, import spending, or taxes or a fall in autonomous government spending, investment, or export spending shifts the *IS* schedule downward and to the left.

5. *IS-LM* Equilibrium and the Traditional Keynesian Transmission Mechanism for Monetary Policy: At the single point where the *IS* and *LM* schedules cross, real income and the nominal interest rate simultaneously achieve an equilibrium flow of real income and an equilibrium in the market for real money balances. According to the Keynesian

IS-LM framework, a rise in the nominal money stock reduces the equilibrium nominal interest rate. This causes a rise in desired investment spending that increases aggregate desired expenditures and induces an increase in equilibrium real income.

6. How Government Spending Affects Real Income in the Traditional Keynesian Model: The direct effect of an increase in government spending is a rise in real income equal to the increase in government spending times the autonomous expenditures multiplier. When real income increases, the demand for real money balances rises, which causes an increase in the equilibrium nominal interest rate. Given current expected inflation, this implies a rise in the real rate of interest. The result is a crowding-out effect, as desired real investment declines. Consequently, equilibrium real income rises by less than predicted by the simplest Keynesian multiplier model.

Self-Test Questions

1. Explain in your own words why the *LM* schedule generally slopes upward. Would a change in real income cause a shift in the *LM* schedule or a movement along the schedule? Explain your reasoning.

2. Explain in your own words why the *IS* schedule generally slopes downward. Would a change in real income cause a shift in the *IS* schedule or a movement along the schedule? Explain your reasoning.

3. Explain in your own words what occurs at a point of *IS-LM* equilibrium.

4. If graphed on a diagram where the nominal interest rate is measured on the vertical axis and the quantity of real money balances is measured on the horizontal axis, what would the *classical* money demand schedule look like? Based on your answer, would you argue that the classical theory of the demand for money is more or less general than the Keynesian theory? Explain your reasoning.

(Answers to odd-numbered questions may be found on the Web at **http://macro. swcollege.com** under "Student Resources.")

Problems

1. Suppose that the GDP deflator is equal to 1 and that the nominal money stock is equal to $1.5 trillion. If the demand schedule for real money balances is given by the straight-line function (measured in trillions of dollars), $m^d = (0.9 \times y) - (80 \times r)$, what is the equation for the economy's *LM* schedule? Show your work, and solve for r on the left side of the equation that you derive.

2. Using the information from problem 1, if y is equal to $7 trillion, what is the equilibrium nominal interest rate?

3. Suppose that desired investment spending is determined by the equation (measured in trillions of dollars), $i = 5.8 - (80 \times r)$. If government spending is equal to $2 trillion, real consumption spending is equal to a *fixed* value of $3 trillion, and export spending is equal to $1 trillion, what is the straight-line equation for the *IS* schedule? (Hint: Set y equal to $c + i + g + x$ and solve the resulting expression with r on the left side of your solution.)

4. Using the information in problem 3, if the nominal interest rate is 5 percent (that is, 0.05), what is the equilibrium level of real income?

(Answers to odd-numbered problems may be found on the Web at **http://macro. swcollege.com** under "Student Resources.")

5. Use your answers to problems 1 and 3 to calculate the single real income–nominal interest rate combination for an *IS-LM* equilibrium.

Before the Test

Test your understanding of the material covered in this chapter by taking the Chapter 8 interactive quiz at http://macro.swcollege.com.

Online Application

As we discussed in this chapter, the Federal Reserve can influence market interest rates by changing the quantity of money in circulation. This application explores the Federal Reserve's role in determining interest rates.

Internet URL: http://research.stlouisfed.org/fred/

Title: *Federal Reserve Economic Data (FRED)*

Navigation: Go to the above Web page

Application: Follow the instructions below, and answer the questions:

1. Click on "Monetary Aggregates," and then click on "M2 Money Stock—1959:01." Print the M2 data so that you can have the information by your side as you continue. Now go back to the opening page of FRED, and click on "Interest Rates," followed by "6-Month Treasury Constant Maturity Rate—1982.01." According to the Keynesian theory of the demand for money, the quantity of money demanded varies inversely with market interest rates. Reviewing the M2 and 6-month Treasury security rates since 1982, does this relationship appear in the data? Based on the discussion in this chapter, can you offer some reasons for why the relationship might not be apparent in the data?

2. Go back to "Monetary Aggregates" and click on "M2 Own Rate—1979.01." Explain what these data measure. How would you expect this factor to influence the relationship between other market interest rates and the quantity of money (M2) demanded?

For Group Study and Analysis: FRED contains a number of financial data series. Break the class up into three groups, and assign one of the monetary aggregates—M1, M2, and M3—to each group. Have the groups take a look at the rest of the FRED database and determine what data might be helpful in trying to estimate the demand for their assigned monetary aggregate.

macro**xtra!**

Log on to the MacroXtra Web site at http://macroxtra.swcollege.com for additional learning resources such as practice quizzes, Interactive Key Graphs, readings, and additional economic applications.

Selected References
and Further Reading

Branson, William. *Macroeconomic Theory and Policy*. New York: Macmillan, 1978.

Hansen, Alvin. *A Guide to Keynes*. New York: Macmillan, 1953.

Harris, Laurence. *Monetary Theory*. New York: McGraw-Hill, 1981.

Hicks, John. "Mr. Keynes and the Classics: A Suggested Interpretation." *Econometrica* 5 (April 2, 1937): 147–159.

Keynes, John Maynard. *The General Theory of Employment, Interest, and Money*. New York: Harcourt Brace Jovanovich, 1964.

The Open Economy—

Exchange Rates and the Balance of Payments

Fundamental Issues

1. **How is the private payments balance determined in the *IS-LM* model?**

2. **How do government budget policies affect the private payments balance in the traditional Keynesian theory?**

3. **How do monetary and fiscal policy actions affect a nation's real income under fixed exchange rates?**

4. **How do monetary and fiscal policy actions affect a nation's real income under floating exchange rates?**

N *ations within the European Monetary Union (EMU) established their currency, the euro, in January 1999. At the time of its introduction, the euro's value in foreign exchange markets was just over 0.88 euros per dollar. Hence, every euro was worth more than a U.S. dollar. During the months that followed, the euro steadily lost value relative to the dollar. By the summer of 2000, Europeans who wished to obtain dollars had to provide 1.23 euros per dollar, or about 39 percent more euros than three years earlier. Consequently, the euro had lost more than one-third of its value during the first year and a half of its existence as a major world currency.*

The European Central Bank (ECB) did little to try to halt the euro's slide until September 2000, when the ECB conducted its first significant interventions in foreign exchange markets. It sold large amounts of dollars for euros in an effort to push up the euro's relative value in foreign exchange markets. Continued dollar sales by the ECB did little to slow the fall in the euro's market value, however.

Some observers criticized the ECB for failing to intervene more dramatically to stabilize the euro's value in foreign exchange markets. A number of economists, however, concluded that the ECB's intervention policy prevented its actions from having any long-term effects on the euro's value. Whenever the ECB sold dollars for euros, which otherwise would have reduced the total quantity of euros in circulation, the ECB always countered by issuing more euros within the EMU nations. By issuing sufficient euros domestically to more than offset the reduction in euros held abroad, the ECB allowed the total quantity of euros in circulation to increase on net. According to a traditional theory of how monetary policy affects a nation's exchange rate, called the monetary approach to the balance of payments, *only central bank interventions that cause the quantity of domestic money to decline relative to the amounts of money in circulation elsewhere can reduce a currency's value in foreign exchange markets. According to these economists, the reason for the euro's continuing decline in value despite the ECB's interventions was the excess growth in the overall quantity of euros in circulation.*

In this chapter you will apply what you have learned in previous chapters to examine how changes in the quantity of money can influence the rate of exchange of a nation's currency, the market interest rate, and the equilibrium quantity of real income. In addition, you will learn about the transmission of monetary and fiscal policy actions to the economy when the exchange rate is fixed. As you will see, the monetary approach to the balance of payments has important implications for the ultimate effects of policy actions under a fixed exchange rate.

The Balance of Payments and the *IS-LM* Model

In the Keynesian *IS-LM* model, both fiscal and monetary policy actions can affect domestic income and interest rates. Accordingly, fiscal and monetary policymakers may decide to try to push the level of real income toward the long-run level discussed in Chapter 5. By doing so, they would be trying to help the nation's economy achieve **internal balance,** or the attainment of the level of real income consistent with the economy's long-run growth path.

Policymakers may also care about how their actions influence the nation's international payment flows. That is, they may also want to achieve **external balance,** which would entail the attainment of some objective for private international flows of goods, services, income, and assets.

Maintaining Private Payments Balance

Achieving "external balance" is likely to mean different things to policymakers in different nations. In some nations, for instance, it may mean a goal of consistently running a trade surplus. In others, it might mean maintaining a surplus on the current account.

INTERNAL BALANCE: The attainment of the level of real income consistent with the domestic economy's long-run growth path.

EXTERNAL BALANCE: The attainment of an objective for the composition of a nation's balance of payments.

Recall from Chapter 2 that the balance of payments is the sum of the current account balance, the private capital account balance, and the official settlements balance. Let's suppose that policymakers would like the *private payments balance*—the sum of the balances on the current account and the capital account—to be equal to zero. That is, the policymakers desire neither a surplus nor a deficit in the sum of the current account and the capital account. To aim for this objective, the policymakers need to understand how their policies will influence the size of the private payments balance.

REAL INCOME AND THE PRIVATE PAYMENTS BALANCE   To understand the factors that determine the private payments balance in the balance of payments, let's first remember that the current account balance is equal to the balance of merchandise trade plus net service flows and net flows of cross-border income and transfers. The predominant component of the current account balance is the balance of merchandise trade. In addition, recall from Chapter 6 that the main determinant of the trade balance is domestic real income. A rise in domestic real income induces an increase in import spending, which pushes down the trade balance, while a fall in domestic real income depresses import spending, thereby improving the trade balance.

To see how this ultimately relates to fiscal and monetary policies, consider Figure 9–1 on the following page. Suppose that the private payments balance is equal to zero at point A, at a nominal interest rate equal to r_1 and a real income level equal to y_1. Now suppose that real income rises, to level y_2 at point C. In line with our reasoning above, at point C higher real income will stimulate a rise in import spending, which will reduce the trade balance, thereby pushing down the current account balance. Although higher real income at point C indicates that activity in the domestic economy has increased as compared with point A, it also implies higher imports and a worsened private payments balance. Consequently, under our assumption that the private payments balance is equal to zero at point A, it follows that at point C there is a *private payments deficit.*

THE NOMINAL INTEREST RATE AND THE PRIVATE PAYMENTS BALANCE   If real income were to remain at y_2, then would the economy necessarily be "stuck" with a private payments deficit in its balance of payments? The answer is no. To see this, suppose that income remains equal to y_2 but that the nominal interest rate rises. This would produce a point such as point B in Figure 9–1, at a nominal interest rate of r_2.

An increase in the domestic nominal interest rate will make domestic financial assets, such as domestic bonds, more attractive to residents of other nations by increasing the returns they can earn on such assets. Consequently, foreign residents will increase their holdings of domestic financial assets. As you learned in Chapter 2, such an increase in foreign holdings of domestic assets will increase the private capital account balance. This, in turn, will improve the private payments balance.

Let's assume that the interest-rate increase from r_1 to r_2 is sufficient to return the private payments balance to zero. If so, point B, like point A, represents a situation in which the nation's private payments balance is equal to zero. Indeed, points A and B both lie on a set of real income–nominal interest rate combinations that will maintain a zero private payments

Figure 9–1   The *BP* Schedule

If real income rises from y_1 at point *A*, at which the private payments balance is equal to zero, to y_2 at point *C*, then the nation's import expenditures will increase, and its trade balance will decline. The result is a private payments deficit at point *C*. Reattaining a private payments balance will require an increase in the nominal interest rate, which will induce foreign residents to hold more of the nation's financial assets, thereby improving its capital account balance. Hence, a point such as point *B*, which is above and to the right of point *A*, could represent another real income–interest rate combination consistent with a private payments balance. The set of all such combinations is the *BP* schedule.

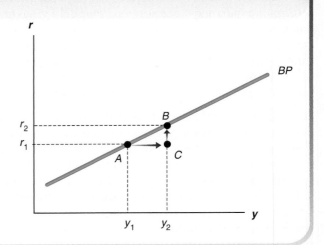

balance. This set of combinations slopes upward, because at higher real income levels the resulting increases in imports that will drive down the private payments balance will need to be offset by higher nominal interest rates to stimulate the purchases of domestic assets that will push the private payments balance back up to zero.

Traditionally, the set of real income–nominal interest rate combinations that maintains the private payments balance in the balance of payments accounts is referred to as the **BP schedule,** so we use this label in Figure 9–1. As we noted in Chapter 2, a common, albeit somewhat misleading, term for a private payments balance is "balance of payments equilibrium"; hence, the traditional notation "*BP*." In actuality, along the *BP* schedule, the sum of the current account balance and the capital account balance remains equal to zero at any given point.

Balance of Payments Deficits and Surpluses in the *IS-LM* Framework

The implication of the *BP* schedule is that at a given time there is a limited set of combinations of real income and the nominal interest rate along which a nation can achieve a private payments balance of zero. As you learned in Chapter 8, *equilibrium* values for real income and the nominal interest rate are determined by the intersection of the *IS* and *LM* schedules. This means that a private payments balance of zero can be achieved only if the *IS* and *LM* schedules happen to cross *on* the economy's *BP* schedule.

ACHIEVING EXTERNAL BALANCE   Panel (a) of Figure 9–2 shows a situation in which a nation has achieved external balance as we have defined this concept: The nation's *IS-LM* equilibrium occurs at a point on the country's *BP*

BP SCHEDULE: A set of real income–nominal interest rate combinations that maintains a zero balance for private payments—sometimes called a "balance of payments equilibrium"—in the balance of payments accounts.

Figure 9–2   *IS–LM* Equilibrium and the *BP* Schedule

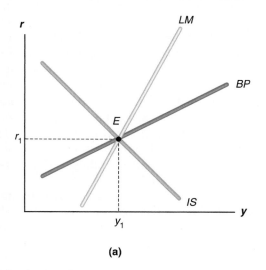

(a)

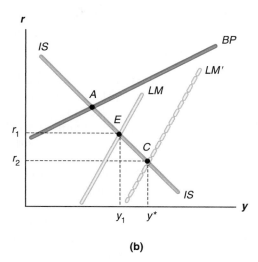

(b)

Panel (a) displays a situation in which an *IS–LM* equilibrium occurs at a point, denoted point *E*, on the *BP* schedule. At point *E*, therefore, the nation's economy attains a private payments balance. In contrast, the *IS–LM* equilibrium point *E* in panel (b) is below and to the right of the *BP* schedule, so there is a private payments deficit at that point. At the same time, equilibrium real income at point

E in panel (b) is below a policy target income level. Attaining *internal balance* via monetary policy would require increasing the quantity of money and thereby inducing the *LM* schedule to shift to the right, but this action would move the economy farther away from point *A*, at which *external balance* could be attained via achievement of a private payments balance.

schedule, at point *E*. This implies that the equilibrium nominal interest rate and the equilibrium real income level are consistent with a private payments balance of zero.

As you might imagine, a nation's fiscal and monetary policymakers will face a challenge in determining the nominal interest rate and real income level consistent with its external balance objective. In fact, for a typical nation, achieving just the right real income–nominal interest rate combination to achieve external balance could be a difficult undertaking. Furthermore, achieving external balance *and* internal balance objectives *simultaneously* is likely to be a truly daunting task.

THE POTENTIAL TRADE-OFF BETWEEN EXTERNAL AND INTERNAL BALANCE Panel (b) of Figure 9–2 illustrates the nature of the difficulties that a monetary policy-maker—a central bank—can face in trying to achieve both external and internal balance. Again, external balance is achieved at any point along the *BP* schedule. In addition, however, let's suppose that attaining internal balance requires reaching the real income level y^* at an *IS-LM* equilibrium such as the one at point *C*. At present, however, there is a private payments deficit at the *actual IS-LM* equilibrium point, at point *E*.

Keep in mind that a central bank can influence real income and the nominal interest rate solely by varying the nominal money stock to influence the position of the *LM* schedule. This means that the situation in panel (b) will be a "no-win scenario" for a central bank. The central bank could reduce the nominal money stock to attain point *A* along the *BP* schedule, thereby achieving its external balance goal, but this action would yield a real income level below the level consistent with the bank's internal balance objective. Suppose, instead, that the central bank increases the nominal money stock and shifts the *LM* schedule to the position *LM'*, thereby attaining an *IS-LM* equilibrium at point *C* at the income level y^* that is consistent with internal balance. At point *C*, however, real income is too high for external balance, because import spending will increase and depress the nation's trade balance even further.

Hence, we usually would not expect that a central bank acting alone could achieve both internal and external balance objectives. Typically, the central bank would need some assistance from fiscal policymakers, who can influence the position of the *IS* schedule. In addition, governments may use exchange-rate changes to influence the position of the *BP* schedule. Let's now consider how fiscal and exchange-rate policies affect the private payments balance.

FUNDAMENTAL ISSUE #1

How is the private payments balance determined in the *IS-LM* model? A particular objective for the private payments balance may be achieved only along a set of real income–nominal interest rate combinations called the *BP* schedule. The *BP* schedule is a set of real income–nominal interest rate combinations for which the sum of the current account balance is equal to zero. Hence, if an *IS-LM* equilibrium occurs at a point on the *BP* schedule, then private payments balance is attained. An *IS-LM* equilibrium above or below the *BP* schedule, however, results in a private payments surplus or deficit, respectively.

Fiscal Policy, the Balance of Payments, and the Exchange Rate

As you learned in Chapter 2, the U.S. merchandise trade balance and current account balance have consistently been negative since the early 1980s. Thus, in most recent years the United States has experienced a private payments deficit. As an initial application of the *IS-LM-BP* framework, let's consider whether fiscal policies might do anything about this.

Fiscal Policy and the Private Payments Deficit

A number of factors influence the size of a nation's private payments deficit (or surplus). For instance, by definition the sum of the private payments deficit and the official reserves transactions account must equal zero. If governments of other countries alter their holdings of a nation's currency, then the nation's private payments deficit will necessarily be affected by those official reserve transactions.

Nevertheless, government budgetary policies and private payments deficits in the balance of payments clearly appear to be related. Economists disagree, however, as to the appropriate mix of policies for reducing private payments deficits. To explore the nature of this disagreement, we will use the framework that we just developed, in which the *BP* schedule is added to the *IS-LM* model so as to consider the international dimensions of policy actions.

CAPITAL MOBILITY AND THE PRIVATE PAYMENTS DEFICIT   One of the sources of disagreement over how fiscal authorities might respond to private payments deficits arises from the issue of **capital mobility.** This term refers to the degree to which financial assets and funds are free to flow across a nation's borders. A nation with high capital mobility permits such flows. A country with low capital mobility often has legal impediments, known as **capital controls,** which typically include restrictions on the ability of the country's residents to hold and exchange assets denominated in the currencies of other nations. Capital controls thereby inhibit flows of funds and assets across the borders of a country. Capital mobility is often low in less-developed nations that do not have advanced banking systems or financial markets. (Economists remain divided about whether countries can benefit from imposing capital controls; see on the following page *Global Notebook: Were Capital Controls Malaysia's Salvation?*)

THE CASE OF LOW CAPITAL MOBILITY   Recall that eliminating a private payments deficit entails attaining *external balance* by achieving an *IS-LM* equilibrium along the *BP* schedule, or the set of real income–nominal interest rate combinations consistent with a private payments balance of zero. Capital mobility plays an important role in the process of attaining external balance, because it affects the slope of the *BP* schedule. If capital mobility is very low because of capital controls and other impediments to flows of funds and assets, then the *BP* schedule is relatively steep. To understand why this is so, suppose that real income rises, thereby causing imports to rise and causing a current account deficit to occur. A capital inflow will then be needed to improve the nation's capital account balance sufficiently to maintain private payments balance. If capital mobility is low, however, foreigners will be reluctant to undertake the expense of overcoming capital controls and other barriers so as to hold financial assets issued in the country. Only a very large interest-rate increase that will provide a high interest return will induce foreigners to hold the country's financial assets.

Panel (a) of Figure 9–3 on page 245 illustrates the situation that the government faces if it seeks both to balance its own budget and to attain private payments balance when capital mobility is low. Suppose that the

CAPITAL MOBILITY: The extent to which funds and financial assets may flow freely across a country's borders.

243

CHAPTER 9   The Open Economy—Exchange Rates and the Balance of Payments

CAPITAL CONTROLS: Legal restrictions on the holdings of foreign currencies or assets by the residents of a nation.

UNIT III Keynesian and Monetarist Macroeconomic Perspectives

Were Capital Controls Malaysia's Salvation?

In the fall of 1997, the international section of a major news outlet contained a story under the headline "Malaysia Learns Curbs on Currency Don't Work." The story told how the Malaysian government had decided within a week's time to remove restrictions imposed on the ability of international investors to short-sell shares of stock. The purpose of the restrictions had been to prop up Malaysian stock prices and support the value of the Malaysian currency, the ringgit, but during the week after the controls were imposed, stock prices and the ringgit's exchange value had each fallen by more than 10 percent. During the following months, the value of the ringgit continued to plummet, and by the fall of 1998, the ringgit had lost nearly half its value relative to the dollar. In September 1998, a new headline announced, "Malaysia Imposes Sweeping Capital Controls."

The Controls

The government began by ordering the Kuala Lumpur Stock Exchange to halt trading of Malaysian shares outside the country, especially in neighboring Singapore. It then declared an immediate ban on Malaysian trading of the ringgit in foreign exchange markets located in other countries, which left banks and their customers stuck with suddenly illegal agreements to exchange dollars for ringgits at previously agreed-on exchange rates at dates months and years into the future.

Under the government's edict, all ringgit held outside Malaysia were to be repatriated within a month's time or be declared worthless. In addition, foreign residents who sold Malaysian stocks or bonds were barred from exporting the proceeds for a year. The government also placed limits on how much money Malaysians could carry abroad and required all Malaysian export and import transactions to be settled with foreign currencies.

What Did the Controls Accomplish?

By February 1999, the Malaysian government had replaced its complete ban on cross-border currency movements with less draconian rules. In the meantime, the Malaysian economy had stabilized, and the value of the ringgit had recovered somewhat in foreign exchange markets. A few months later, the directors of the International Monetary Fund (IMF) formally commended Malaysian authorities for making good use of the breathing space that IMF economists had concluded the controls had provided Malaysia's policymakers.

Other economists, however, questioned whether the controls really deserved much credit for Malaysia's improved economic performance. Even though the controls were sweeping, they were imposed weeks after most foreign investors had sold off large amounts of Malaysian assets. Furthermore, other Southeast Asian nations that did not resort to controls experienced large inflows of investment that helped their economies experience recoveries during the early 2000s that eclipsed the more modest boost in Malaysian economic activity.

For Critical Analysis

In what ways might capital controls give policymakers "breathing space" to address national economic problems?

current *IS-LM* equilibrium is at point *A*. This point is below and to the right of the *BP* schedule. Consequently, real income is high enough to stimulate imports that induce a trade deficit, and the interest rate is low enough that it will not attract sufficient capital into the country to improve the capital account balance and offset this trade deficit. In the absence of any monetary policy actions, attaining private payments balance will require a leftward shift of the *IS* schedule to point *B*. The government can accomplish this by increasing taxes, reducing government expenditures, or using a combination of both types of fiscal policy actions. Such policy actions will attack both deficits at the same time. The cost, of course, is the reduction in real income entailed by the movement from point *A* to point *B*.

THE CASE OF HIGH CAPITAL MOBILITY   Many economists do not believe that panel (a) of Figure 9–3 is a good representation of the situation faced by the United States, which has relatively high capital mobility as compared with most other nations. They argue that panel (b) provides a better indication of the U.S. situation since the 1980s. Here, the *BP* schedule is very shallow. In this case, if an increase in real income causes imports to rise, thereby causing a trade deficit, then a small increase in the interest rate will attract enough flows of funds and assets from other nations to improve the capital account balance sufficiently to reattain a private payments balance along the *BP* schedule.

With high capital mobility, a private payments deficit again will arise if there is an *IS-LM* equilibrium below and to the right of the *BP* schedule, as at point *A* in panel (b). In this case, as shown in the diagram, reattaining external balance by eliminating the private payments deficit will require a *rightward* shift of the *IS* schedule, to the dashed schedule labeled *IS"*. To eliminate the private payments deficit that exists at point *A*, the government will need to *reduce* taxes or *increase* its spending or adopt some combination of these policies. This government action will raise the nominal interest rate. With high capital mobility, this interest-rate increase will

Figure 9–3   Policy Actions to Eliminate Private Payments Deficits

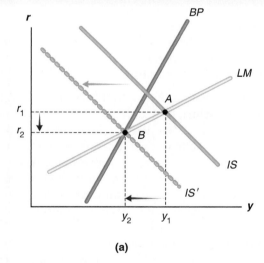

(a)

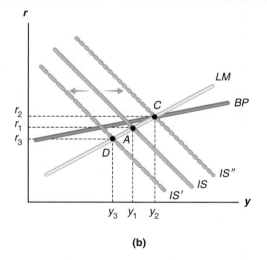

(b)

At point *A* to the right of the steeply sloped *BP* schedule in panel (a), there is a private payments deficit. If there is also a government budget deficit at point *A*, then a reduction in government spending will cause a movement to a new equilibrium point *B*, thereby reducing the budget deficit and reattaining private payments balance. Panel (b), in contrast, illustrates a situation of relatively high capital mobility. The *BP* schedule is much more shallowly sloped than in panel (a), although point *A* still lies below and to the right of the *BP*

schedule, indicating a private payments deficit. Even though the resulting movement from point *A* to point *D* will reduce the budget deficit, it will lead to a higher private payments deficit. Eliminating the private payments deficit would actually require an increase in government spending via a movement to point *C*. This action would raise the equilibrium interest rate and stimulate greater capital inflows from abroad.

attract sufficient volumes of funds and financial assets from foreigners to raise the nation's capital account balance by a large amount, thereby attaining private payments balance at point C.

Reducing taxes or increasing spending, however, will also worsen the government's budget deficit. Consequently, when an economy is at point A in panel (b), reducing the budget deficit will cause the IS schedule to shift in the *wrong direction*, to a position such as IS'. As a result, the interest rate will decline, and foreigners will remove their funds and assets, causing the nation's private payments deficit to worsen at point D. If the government is intent upon reducing its deficit, the only way out of this quandary is for the central bank to assist by conducting a contractionary monetary policy and shifting the LM schedule leftward. This could raise the nominal interest rate sufficiently to induce a net rise in the nation's capital account balance.

EXCHANGE RATES AND PRIVATE PAYMENTS DEFICITS   As we noted earlier, panel (a) of Figure 9–3 is not very applicable to the U.S. situation of the 1990s and 2000s because U.S. capital mobility is very high. Panel (b) does not fit the U.S. experience very well either, because it indicates that reducing the nation's private payments deficit will require actions that push the government's budget into deficit or that increase an existing budget deficit. Clearly, some important real-world factor must be missing from the examples in Figure 9–3.

The missing factor is the exchange rate. Since the early 1970s, both the Federal Reserve and the U.S. Treasury generally have permitted the exchange value of the dollar to move relatively freely in foreign exchange markets. Although both the Fed and the Treasury have tried to influence the exchange rate from time to time since then, for the most part the dollar's value has adjusted to prevailing conditions.

THE EFFECT OF CHANGES IN THE EXCHANGE RATE ON THE IS AND BP SCHEDULES
Figure 9–4 shows how a **depreciation,** or decline, in the value of a nation's currency affects the IS and BP schedules. Panel (a) shows the effect of a currency depreciation on the IS schedule. A decline in the value of a nation's currency, which also corresponds to an **appreciation,** or rise, in the value of the foreign currency, makes imports more expensive, so the nation's residents cut back on their import expenditures. At the same time, the nation's goods become less expensive for residents of other nations to purchase, so export expenditures rise. Both of these effects will lead to a rise in the nation's aggregate autonomous expenditures at any given interest rate, such as r_1 in panel (a). Hence, the level of real income consistent with an income-expenditure equilibrium will increase from y_1 at point A to y_2 at point B. Thus, following a currency depreciation, the IS schedule will shift rightward, from IS_1 to IS_2, as shown in panel (a).

A currency depreciation will also affect the position of the BP schedule. Recall that the BP schedule is the set of real income–interest rate combinations that maintains a private payments balance equal to zero, holding all other factors unchanged. As we just noted, however, a currency depreciation will cause a nation's exports to rise and its imports to fall at any given level of real income and at any given interest rate. Consequently, as shown in panel (b) of Figure 9–4, at a given real income–interest rate com-

DEPRECIATION: A decline in the value of one nation's currency in terms of the currency of another nation.

APPRECIATION: A rise in the value of one nation's currency in terms of the currency of another nation.

Figure 9–4   The Effects of a Domestic Currency Depreciation on the *IS* and *BP* Schedules

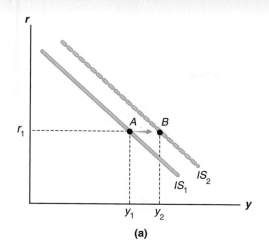

(a)

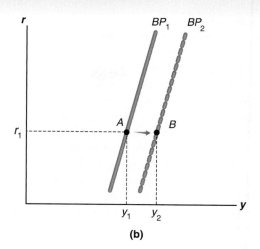

(b)

Depreciation of a nation's currency effectively makes the nation's goods less expensive for foreign residents and makes foreign goods more expensive for the nation's residents. Hence, export expenditures rise and import spending declines. The result is a rightward shift in the *IS* schedule from point *A* to point *B* in panel (a). At the same time, if point *A* in panel (a) corresponds to a situation in which the nation has a private payments balance equal to zero, then

point *A* will lie on the *BP* schedule, as shown in panel (b). The improvement in the merchandise trade balance and current account owing to the currency depreciation will then tend to induce a private payments surplus, so real income will have to increase to induce a rise in import spending. Hence, a currency depreciation will cause the *BP* schedule to shift rightward, as illustrated in panel (b).

bination, such as y_1 and r_1 at point *A* on the *BP* schedule labeled BP_1, a currency depreciation will cause a trade balance improvement that will result in a private payments surplus at point *A*. To keep the private payments balance equal to zero, real income will have to increase to y_2, thereby stimulating increased import spending that will return the trade balance and, therefore, the private payments balance to zero. Thus, point *B* will be a point on a new *BP* schedule, denoted BP_2, that will result from a currency depreciation. A currency depreciation, we may conclude, will shift the *BP* schedule rightward, as shown in panel (b).

CURRENCY APPRECIATIONS, DEPRECIATIONS, AND THE GOVERNMENT BUDGET   Figure 9–5 on the next page shows how exchange-rate movements might apply in the situation of the United States. Consistent with the high capital mobility of the United States, it shows a very shallow *BP* schedule. The initial *IS-LM* equilibrium is at point *A*, at which there is a private payments deficit. Let's also assume the government experiences a budget deficit at this point.

If the exchange rate adjusts freely to the situation illustrated by point *A* in Figure 9–5, then the following sequence of events must take place. First, at point *A* the existence of a U.S. private payments deficit means, by definition, that U.S. residents pay more dollars to foreign residents than foreign residents pay to U.S. residents. To make the payments to foreign residents,

Figure 9-5   Fiscal Policy and Exchange-Rate Adjustments That Would Eliminate Budget and Private Payments Deficits

At point *A*, which is below and to the right of the initial *BP* schedule, there is a private payments deficit. Suppose that there is also a government budget deficit at point *A*. With a floating exchange rate, the private payments deficit will tend to decline naturally, as the value of the nation's currency depreciates, causing a reduction in import spending and a rise in export expenditures that improve the nation's trade balance, thereby inducing the *BP* schedule to shift downward to the position denoted *BP'*. To reduce its budget deficit, however, the government needs to reduce its spending, which will cause the *IS* schedule to shift to the left, resulting in the new equilibrium point *B*. This point lies below and to the right of *BP'*, so again there is a private payments deficit. Further currency depreciation will ultimately eliminate this deficit by causing the *BP* schedule to shift once more, to *BP''*.

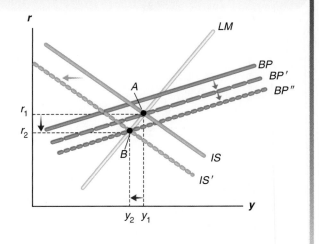

U.S. residents must exchange their dollars for foreign currencies. This raises the demand for such currencies, so their values increase in terms of the dollar. In other words, foreign currencies appreciate, and the dollar depreciates. Second, when the dollar loses value relative to other nations' currencies, the prices of goods imported to the United States from those countries become more expensive in terms of foreign currencies. This induces U.S. residents to reduce their imports at any given level of real income and interest rate. The result is a *shift* of the *BP* schedule, such as that shown in Figure 9–5 by the movement to the new position *BP'*. In principle, therefore, such an exchange-rate depreciation will automatically eliminate the U.S. private payments deficit without the need for any fiscal (or monetary) policy actions whatsoever.

If the government also wishes to reduce its budget deficit, however, it still will need to increase taxes or reduce its expenditures. This action causes the *IS* schedule to shift leftward, to *IS'*, thereby producing a new *IS-LM* equilibrium at point *B*, where once again there is a private payments deficit. With a flexible exchange rate, however, the exchange rate will depreciate further, and the *BP* schedule will again shift downward, toward the schedule labeled *BP''*. Ultimately, the government can balance its own budget as the exchange rate adjusts to reattain private payments balance at point *B*.

THE PRIVATE PAYMENTS BALANCE AND THE VALUE OF THE DOLLAR   Does the story told by Figure 9–5 appear to match reality? Figure 9–6 provides some evidence on this issue. The figure shows the exchange value of the U.S. dollar in terms of the currencies of the United States' major trading partners since 1976. Notice how the value of the dollar changed following the large runup in the federal budget deficit and the trade deficit that occurred after 1982. Clearly, the value of the dollar gradually declined after 1985, just as theory would have predicted.

Figure 9–6   The Value of the Dollar, the Federal Budget Deficit, and the Private Payments Deficit

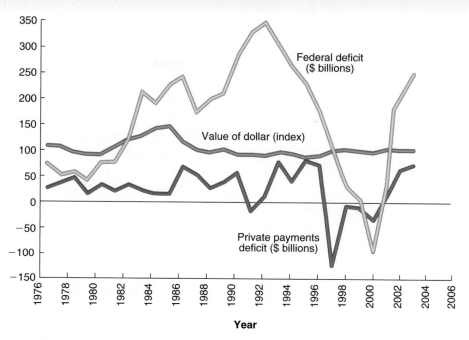

In accordance with the theory of adjustments under floating exchange rates, the downward trend in the U.S. private payments deficit after 1996 was accompanied by a general upward trend in the value of the U.S. dollar in world currency markets. Thus, in the early 2000s the United States was very near an overall *IS-LM-BP* equilibrium.

SOURCES: *Economic Report of the President,* 2002; *Economic Indicators.*

Figure 9–6 indicates that the U.S. private payments deficit initially continued to rise in the early 1990s. This happened even as the federal budget deficit rapidly declined and ultimately turned negative (that is, the government began to operate with a budget surplus) in 1998. In normal circumstances, theory would have predicted a gradual downturn in the size of the private payments deficit. Figure 9–6, however, shows that a sudden decline took place in 1997. This immediate drop in the private payments deficit to a sizable negative value—that is, a relatively large private payments *surplus*—was caused mainly by a significant flow of funds into the United States that occurred during the currency crises that swept through Southeast Asia and Russia during that year. Thus, the drop in the private payments deficit in 1997 was consistent with theory but received an additional boost from external world events. Nevertheless, both the U.S. government budget and private payments approached simultaneous balance in 1999 and 2000 when the fallout from the Asian crisis dissipated. Between 1998 and 2000, therefore, the United States was very close to an overall *IS-LM-BP* equilibrium with a slight government budget surplus.

Consistent with theory, the overall value of the dollar increased slightly in response to the improvement in the U.S. private payments balance.

Nonetheless, the dollar's value fluctuated relatively little through the entire 1990s and into the 2000s.

> **FUNDAMENTAL ISSUE #2**
>
> **How do government budget policies affect the private payments balance in the traditional Keynesian theory?**   If capital mobility is relatively low, so that the *BP* schedule is relatively steeply sloped, then a contractionary fiscal policy action will enable the government to reduce a budget deficit and a private payments deficit simultaneously. If capital mobility is relatively high, however, so that the *BP* schedule is relatively shallow, then reducing spending or raising taxes to reduce a budget deficit will contribute to a rising private payments deficit. In an environment in which the exchange rate floats freely in foreign exchange markets, however, the traditional Keynesian model predicts that a private payments deficit should induce a currency depreciation that automatically tends to reduce the private payments deficit.

Macroeconomic Policy with Fixed Exchange Rates

About 40 percent of the world's nations—mostly developing countries—currently attempt to fix their exchange rates or at least to prevent their exchange rates from floating freely in foreign exchange markets. How does the adoption of a fixed exchange rate influence the transmission of macroeconomic policies? What complications do policymakers face when they peg their exchange rate? Let's try to answer these questions using the analytical framework that we have now developed.

Monetary Policy under Fixed Exchange Rates

Let's suppose that a country has established a fixed-exchange-rate commitment. Given this assumption, we can examine how monetary policy actions would affect interest rates and real income.

INITIAL EFFECTS OF AN EXPANSIONARY MONETARY POLICY   Figure 9–7 shows the immediate effects of a central bank action to increase the nominal money stock under a fixed exchange rate. In both panels, a monetary expansion, from M_1 to M_2, causes the *LM* schedule to shift rightward from an initial point *A,* at which the country's private payments balance is equal to zero along the *BP* schedule. This results in a new *IS-LM* equilibrium point, point *B,* below and to the right of the *BP* schedule. Hence, a monetary expansion will result in a private payments deficit at point *B* in each panel.

In panel (a), capital mobility is low, so the *BP* schedule is relatively inelastic in the relevant range. Here, the main reason that a private payments deficit will occur is that the monetary expansion causes a rise in real income. This induces an increase in imports and a consequent trade deficit. Although the equilibrium interest rate will decline, the low capital mobility implies that little capital will flow out of the country. Thus, the

macroxtra!
Online
Perspective

To consider the potential advantages and disadvantages of fixed exchange rates for developing nations, go to the Chapter 9 reading, entitled "Pegging and Stabilization Policy in Developing Countries," by Ramon Moreno of the Federal Reserve Bank of San Francisco.

http://macroxtra.swcollege.com

Figure 9-7   The Initial Effects of Monetary Policy with Fixed Exchange Rates

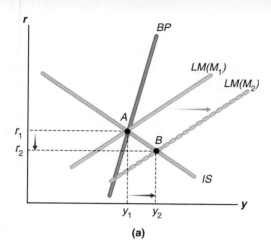

(a)

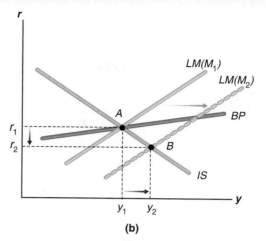

(b)

Both panels show how a monetary expansion initially affects the nominal interest rate and real income under a fixed exchange rate. In panel (a), the *BP* schedule is relatively inelastic, indicating a situation of low capital mobility. The decline in the equilibrium interest rate that occurs following a movement from point *A* to point *B* induces little capital outflow, but the rise in equilibrium real income stimulates greater import spending. The result is a private payments deficit at point *B*. In panel (b), the *BP* schedule is much more elastic, implying a situation of high capital mobility. In this case, the decline in the equilibrium interest rate spurs a significant capital outflow that makes a key contribution to the resulting private payments deficit at point *B*.

main reason for the private payments deficit that arises at point *B* is the trade deficit caused by greater import expenditures at the higher income level y_2.

In contrast, in panel (b) capital mobility is high, so the *BP* schedule is relatively more elastic in the relevant range. In this case, a decline in the nation's equilibrium interest rate to r_2 will cause a significant outflow of capital, so at point *B* the nation runs a sizable capital account deficit, which is a key contributor to the private payments deficit it will experience at this new equilibrium point.

STERILIZED MONETARY POLICIES   Following a period of monetary expansion that reduces the equilibrium interest rate and raises equilibrium real income, can a nation run private payments deficits indefinitely while maintaining a commitment to a fixed exchange rate? In principle, the answer is yes. A nation's ability to do this, however, depends on the amount of foreign exchange reserves held by its central bank and government. In addition, the ultimate effects of a monetary expansion depend on whether or not the nation's central bank conducts a policy of *sterilization*.

Sterilization is a central bank action to prevent changes in its foreign exchange reserves from affecting its nation's money stock. The money that any central bank issues is a liability of the central bank that must be backed

STERILIZATION: A central bank action to prevent variations in its foreign exchange reserves from affecting the total amount of money in circulation.

by its assets. In the United States, for instance, more than 90 percent of the liabilities of the Federal Reserve System are currency in circulation and dollar reserves held by U.S. banks with the Federal Reserve. The Federal Reserve backs these money liabilities with holdings of U.S. government bonds and other assets, *including* assets denominated in foreign currencies, or the Federal Reserve's foreign exchange reserves. Only a small fraction of the U.S. money stock is backed by foreign exchange reserves of the Federal Reserve. In many other nations, foreign exchange reserves account for a much greater portion of central bank assets.

At point *B* in either panel of Figure 9–7, the fact that a nation runs a private payments deficit means that there will be market pressures for the nation's exchange rate to change. With low capital mobility, as in panel (a), the rise in real income at point *B* will induce the nation's residents to seek to acquire other nations' currencies so that they can purchase more imports, thereby raising their demand for foreign exchange and placing downward pressure on the value of their own nation's currency. At point *B* in panel (b), in contrast, a decline in the equilibrium interest rate will cause residents to wish to acquire more foreign capital. This also will entail purchasing more foreign currencies with their own nation's currency, which will tend to depress the value of their nation's currency in the foreign exchange markets.

To prevent the exchange value of its currency from declining at point *B* in either panel of Figure 9–7, the nation's central bank will have to sell some of its assets that are denominated in foreign currencies. This action will offset the rise in the demand for foreign currencies by its own citizens by increasing the supply of foreign currencies in the foreign exchange markets. Thus, this policy response will be required at point *B* if the central bank wishes to maintain the nation's fixed exchange rate. If the central bank sells some of its foreign currency reserves, however, its total assets will decline. This would require a decline in the bank's liabilities, including some of its money liabilities in circulation. To keep this situation from occurring, the central bank will have to add sufficient *domestic* assets, such as domestic government bonds, to prevent its total assets from falling. This is the process of sterilization.

THE MONETARY APPROACH TO THE BALANCE OF PAYMENTS   What will happen if the central bank chooses not to sterilize after a monetary expansion that induces a private payments deficit and a decline in its foreign exchange reserves? Figure 9–8 illustrates the implications of such a decision. As in Figure 9–7, panels (a) and (b) of Figure 9–8 show the immediate effects of a monetary expansion with low capital mobility and high capital mobility, respectively. In both cases, at a new equilibrium point *B*, the nation experiences a private payments deficit. This tends to depress the value of the nation's currency in foreign exchange markets, so the nation's central bank must sell some of its foreign exchange reserves to keep the exchange rate fixed.

If the central bank does not sterilize these outflows of foreign exchange reserves, its assets will decline, necessitating a decrease in the money liabilities that it issues. The nation's nominal money stock will start to fall. As

Figure 9–8   The Final Effects of a Monetary Policy Expansion without Sterilization

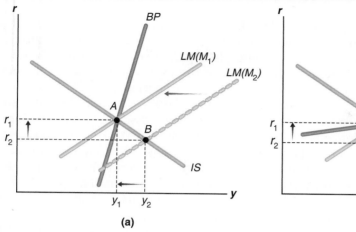

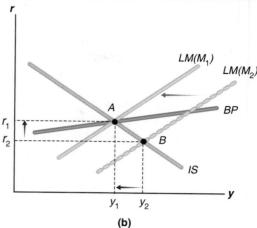

(a)   (b)

Panels (a) and (b) illustrate the final effects of an increase in the nominal quantity of money that first causes a movement from point *A* to point *B* and results in a private payments deficit, as shown in Figure 9–7. In panel (a), capital mobility is relatively low, so the resulting private payments deficit stems mainly from higher import expenditures. In panel (b), there is significant capital mobility, so the private payments deficit at point *B* results mainly from capital outflows. In either case, the private payments deficit implies an increased demand for foreign currencies by the nation's residents. To keep the exchange rate from changing, the nation's central bank will have to sell foreign exchange reserves. If the central bank does not sterilize this action, it will cause a reduction in the quantity of money in circulation and an ultimate movement back to point *A*.

shown in both panels of Figure 9–8, failure to sterilize ultimately will cause the nation's quantity of money to decline from M_2, the level to which the central bank originally had expanded the nation's money stock, back to M_1, the original quantity of money before the monetary expansion. The central bank's efforts to keep the exchange rate fixed by selling foreign exchange reserves ultimately will cause the nation's money stock to contract once more. As a result, the *LM* schedule will shift back to its original location, and the initial *IS-LM* equilibrium point *A* will be reattained.

A *nonsterilized* monetary expansion with a fixed exchange rate ultimately leads to a contraction of the money stock and a return to the economy's initial equilibrium real income level and interest rate.

As a result of the fall in real income, in panel (a) imports decline and the trade deficit falls. In panel (b), a rise in the nominal interest rate leads to the return of capital and a decrease in the nation's capital account deficit. In both panels, the private payments balance ultimately returns to zero at point *A*.

Figure 9–8 illustrates the **monetary approach to the balance of payments.** Under this view, a commitment to a fixed exchange rate

MONETARY APPROACH TO THE BALANCE OF PAYMENTS: A theory of unsterilized monetary policy under fixed exchange rates; changes in foreign exchange reserves required to maintain a fixed exchange rate cause a nation's money stock to adjust automatically in a direction that leads to attainment of a private payments balance of zero.

causes a nation's money stock to vary with changes in foreign exchange reserves that are necessary to keep the exchange rate fixed. Without central bank sterilization, the result is an automatic adjustment toward a private payments balance.

Note that if a central bank tries to sterilize indefinitely, so as to keep real income at y_2 at point B, it must attempt to maintain a continuing private payments deficit that would place perpetual downward pressures on the nation's currency value. To keep the exchange rate fixed, therefore, the nation's central bank would have to continually sell foreign exchange reserves in the foreign exchange markets. No central bank has sufficient reserves of foreign-currency-denominated assets to mount such an effort for very long. Indeed, even sporadic efforts by the Federal Reserve and U.S. Treasury to maintain the dollar's value have led to significant losses of foreign currency reserves since the early 1980s. Since the United States began running significant private payments deficits in the early 1980s, these efforts have resulted in a cumulative loss of more than half of the foreign exchange reserves held by these two policymaking institutions. Smaller countries such as Mexico and Bolivia rarely have sufficient foreign exchange reserves available to fix exchange rates for a lengthy period via sterilized monetary expansions. Ultimately, nations such as these that attempt to expand real income via expansionary monetary policies must either permit their money stocks to contract or devalue their currencies by altering their exchange-rate targets.

Fiscal Policy under Fixed Exchange Rates

As you learned earlier, the degree of capital mobility influences the macroeconomic effects of fiscal policy actions. Let's contemplate how maintaining a fixed exchange rate automatically produces an interaction between fiscal and monetary policy decisions that depends crucially on the relative mobility of capital across a nation's borders.

FISCAL POLICY EFFECTS WITH DIFFERENT DEGREES OF CAPITAL MOBILITY   Both panels in Figure 9–9 depict the effects of a bond-financed rise in government spending. In panel (a), capital mobility is low, so the BP schedule is relatively inelastic in the relevant range. In panel (b), capital is highly mobile, so the BP schedule is more elastic in the relevant range. In each panel we consider an initial point A at which there is an IS-LM equilibrium along the BP schedule, which implies that the private payments balance initially is equal to zero. In addition, a rise in government spending causes a rightward shift in the IS schedule, from $IS(g_1)$ to $IS(g_2)$, that yields a new equilibrium point B in each panel, with a higher nominal interest rate r_2 and a higher level of real income y_2.

In panel (a), the increase in real income causes a rise in imports that leads to a trade deficit. Although the rise in the equilibrium interest rate induces some capital to flow into the nation, with low capital mobility this effect will be small. Consequently, on net there will be a private payments deficit, indicated by point B's position below and to the right of the BP schedule. In panel (b), capital is much more mobile, so a significant capi-

Figure 9–9   The Initial Effects of a Rise in Government Spending with a Fixed Exchange Rate

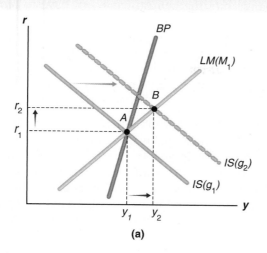

(a)

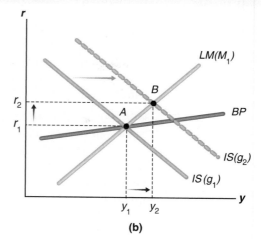

(b)

Both panels show how an increase in real government expenditures initially induces an increase in the equilibrium nominal interest rate and a rise in equilibrium real income. In panel (a), the BP schedule is relatively inelastic, which implies a situation of low capital mobility. The increase in the equilibrium interest rate that occurs following a movement from point A to point B induces little capital inflow, but the rise in equilibrium real income stimulates greater import spending.

The net result is a private payments deficit at point B. In panel (b), the BP schedule is much more elastic, which indicates a situation of high capital mobility. In this case, the rise in the equilibrium interest rate spurs a significant capital inflow that more than offsets the higher imports owing to the increase in equilibrium real income. This results in a private payments surplus at point B in panel (b).

tal inflow will occur as a result of the higher equilibrium interest rate. The resulting capital account surplus will more than counterbalance the trade deficit resulting from higher income and imports. Thus, panel (b) shows that with very high capital mobility, an increase in government spending results in a private payments surplus, because point B is above and to the left of the BP schedule.

A FIXED EXCHANGE RATE AS A SOURCE OF FISCAL PRESSURE ON MONETARY POLICY   At point B in both panels of Figure 9–9, a nation will experience a private payments imbalance that will place market pressures on the exchange rate, thereby forcing the central bank to trade foreign exchange reserves to support the fixed exchange rate. When the central bank sterilizes by trading domestic bonds to keep the money stock from changing, the nation can remain at equilibrium point B in panel (a) only as long as the central bank's foreign exchange reserves hold out. Running a continuous private payments deficit will place downward pressure on the nation's currency value, however, so the central bank will have to keep selling its foreign-currency-denominated assets. Eventually, it may run out of these assets and have to let the nation's currency value fall, but in the meantime the economy will remain at point B.

In panel (b), where there is a private payments surplus at point B, there will be *upward* pressure on the value of the nation's currency. As a result, to maintain a fixed exchange rate the central bank will have to *purchase* foreign-currency-denominated assets. Thus, the central bank will begin to accumulate more foreign exchange reserves. Sterilizing the effect that this accumulation otherwise would have on the money stock will require the central bank to sell domestic bonds. Then the economy can remain at point B in panel (b) as long as the central bank's holdings of domestic bonds remain undepleted.

MONETARY ADJUSTMENTS WITH NONSTERILIZED OPERATIONS   Figure 9–10 shows what will happen if the central bank is unable or unwilling to conduct sterilization operations following a rise in government spending. Again both panels show movements from an initial point A with a private payments balance of zero to point B where there is a private payments imbalance. In the case of low capital mobility depicted in panel (a), a failure to sterilize will result in a decline in the nation's quantity of money in circulation as

---

Figure 9–10   The Final Effects of an Increase in Government Spending without Sterilization

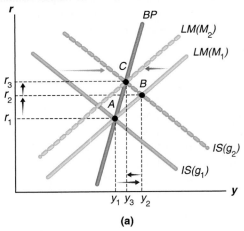
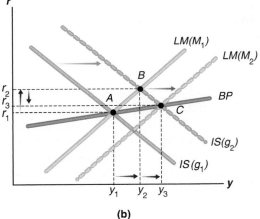

(a)

(b)

The panels of this figure illustrate the final effects of an increase in real government expenditures that initially causes a rightward shift in the *IS* schedule and a movement from point A to point B, as shown in Figure 9–9. In panel (a), capital mobility is relatively low, so a private payments deficit results from higher import expenditures that more than off-set meager capital inflows. Hence, the nation's residents increase their demand for foreign currencies. To keep the exchange rate from changing, the nation's central bank will have to sell foreign exchange reserves, which without sterili-

zation will cause a movement to point C. In contrast, in panel (b) there is significant capital mobility, so significant capital outflows more than offset increased imports, result-ing in a private payments surplus at point B. As the nation's residents reduce their desired holdings of foreign currencies, the value of the nation's currency in foreign exchange markets will tend to rise. To keep the exchange rate from chang-ing, the nation's central bank will purchase foreign exchange reserves, inducing a movement to point C.

the central bank sells foreign exchange reserves to maintain the nation's fixed exchange rate in the face of a private payments deficit at point B. This will cause the LM schedule to shift leftward as the nation's money stock declines from M_1 to M_2, as predicted by the monetary approach to the balance of payments. This ultimately will lead to a new IS-LM equilibrium at point C, with a higher equilibrium interest rate r_3 and a somewhat lower equilibrium real income level y_3. The fall in real income will cause import spending to decline, thereby reducing the trade deficit and helping to produce a private payments balance equal to zero at point C. In this situation, the central bank no longer feels pressure to sell foreign exchange reserves to defend the fixed exchange rate.

RETURNING TO PRIVATE PAYMENTS BALANCE   In panel (b) of Figure 9–10, there is a private payments surplus at point B following a rise in government spending, because capital mobility is so high that the nation experiences a significant capital account surplus when its interest rate increases. As noted earlier, the central bank then will begin to accumulate foreign exchange reserves as it buys foreign-currency-denominated assets to maintain the fixed exchange rate. If the central bank does not sterilize, the nation's money stock will grow as the central bank's foreign exchange reserves increase. Thus, the LM schedule will shift to the right as the quantity of money in circulation increases from M_1 to M_2. As a result, the equilibrium interest rate will decline to r_3, causing a capital outflow that will return the private payments balance to zero at point C along the BP schedule.

Figures 9–9 and 9–10 illustrate an important implication of the monetary approach to the balance of payments under a fixed exchange rate: with a fixed exchange rate, fiscal policy actions place pressures on a nation's central bank. The central bank must respond to private payments imbalances induced by fiscal policy changes by depleting or accumulating foreign exchange reserves. In addition, it must decide whether or not to conduct sterilization operations by buying or selling domestic bonds to keep the nation's money stock from changing. As Figures 9–9 and 9–10 indicate, the effects of fiscal policy actions on a nation's real income depend on the choice that the central bank makes.

FUNDAMENTAL ISSUE #3

How do monetary and fiscal policy actions affect a nation's real income under fixed exchange rates?   The effects of monetary policy actions with a fixed exchange rate depend in large measure upon the extent to which a nation's central bank sterilizes by preventing variations in its foreign exchange reserves from affecting the nation's nominal money stock. Under the monetary approach to the balance of payments, the immediate effects of unsterilized monetary policy actions on real income ultimately are reversed by offsetting changes in the quantity of money. Likewise, fiscal policy effects on a nation's real income also depend on a central bank's decision about sterilization. In general, however, an expansionary fiscal policy causes an unambiguous rise in real income, at least in the short run, when the exchange rate is fixed.

Policy with Floating Exchange Rates

As we have seen, with fixed exchange rates a nation's central bank must buy and sell foreign-currency-denominated assets to keep the exchange rate unchanged, and it must decide whether or not to conduct sterilization operations as its foreign exchange reserves change. With floating exchange rates, a central bank is relieved of these responsibilities. As you will now learn, this tends to make the immediate real income and aggregate demand effects of monetary policy more potent, particularly in a world where capital is highly mobile. In contrast, under floating exchange rates fiscal policy may lose at least some of its ability to bring about initial real income and aggregate demand effects. (Under a floating exchange rate, business managers benefit from being able to make speedy currency trades in foreign exchange markets, and the Internet is helping in this regard; see *Management Notebook: Currency Trading Moves Online.*)

Monetary Policy under Floating Exchange Rates

We examine the effect of an expansionary monetary policy action under floating exchange rates in panels (a) and (b) of Figure 9–11, where we begin with an initial *IS-LM* equilibrium point *A* on an initial *BP* schedule labeled

Management NOTEBOOK

Currency Trading Moves Online

An alliance of fifteen worldwide foreign exchange dealers, including Bank of America, operate FXall.com, a Web-based currency-trading site linking multinational corporations, institutional investors, and investment funds that wish to trade currencies in spot and forward markets. The FXall.com exchange permits traders to enter offers to buy or sell currencies online. The Web exchange then executes the orders automatically. A competing online currency exchange, Currenex.com, links traders to the foreign exchange operations of twenty-five major banks, such as ABN Amro.

Foreign exchange dealers affiliated with these Web sites do not use the systems to trade with each other. Instead, the sites are virtual locations where banks' clients gain immediate access to the banks' quotes in a competitive auction environment and obtain speedier settlement of transactions. An estimated 15 percent of foreign exchange trading is now taking place online, and some forecasts indicate that this percentage could double within the next five years.

Increasingly, online trading is also catching on with those who buy and sell currency futures and options. For instance, Deutsche Boursche and the London International Futures and Options Exchange, the two key European futures and options exchanges that compete with the Chicago Mercantile Exchange and the Chicago Board of Trade, have begun merging their operations. The two European exchanges have considered maintaining their separate trading centers and linking them via the Internet. Indeed, some industry experts anticipate that within a few years most trading in derivative securities will take place on the Internet.

For Critical Analysis
What might foreign exchange traders gain from arranging and completing transactions online instead of through traditional channels?

Figure 9–11   The Effects of an Increase in the Money Stock with Floating Exchange Rates

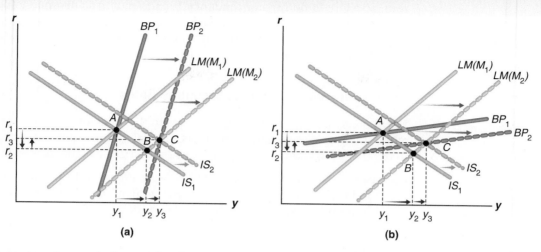

(a)   **(b)**

In both panels, an increase in the quantity of money in circulation causes a rightward shift in the *LM* schedule, thereby
inducing a movement from point *A* to point *B*. In addition,
in both panels the result is a private payments deficit at

point *B*. This will induce a currency depreciation that will
shift both the *IS* and the *BP* schedules rightward, leading to
a final equilibrium with a zero private payments balance at
point *C*.

BP_1. Thus, initially the nation's private payments balance is equal to zero
in both panels. In panel (a), the *BP* schedule is relatively inelastic in the relevant range, which indicates low capital mobility. In panel (b), capital
mobility is much greater, so the *BP* schedule is relatively more elastic in the
relevant range.

As usual, an increase in the money stock from M_1 to M_2 will cause the *LM*
schedule to shift rightward. In both panels of Figure 9–11, therefore, there
will be an initial movement from point *A* to point *B*, which lies below and to
the right of the BP_1 schedule. Consequently, there is a private payments
deficit at point *B*. With low capital mobility, in panel (a), the main reason for
the private payments deficit is the rise in import spending spurred by an
increase in real income from y_1 to y_2. With high capital mobility in panel (b),
the key factor spurring the private payments deficit is the outflow of capital
stemming from the decline in the interest rate from r_1 to r_2.

As a result of the private payments deficit that arises at point *B* in both
panels of Figure 9–11, there will be a depreciation of the nation's currency
in the foreign exchange markets, as the nation's residents increase their
import spending and acquisition of foreign capital and as foreign citizens
reduce their export spending and acquisition of the nation's capital. A currency depreciation, however, will make foreign goods more expensive to
domestic residents and the nation's goods cheaper for foreign residents.
Thus, the depreciation will cause export spending to rise and import
spending to fall, and so the *IS* schedule will shift rightward, from IS_1 to IS_2.
In addition, as we discussed earlier, the depreciation will cause the *BP*

schedule to shift to the right, from BP_1 to BP_2. The eventual equilibrium point will be point C, at which the private payments balance will equal zero, so there is no further tendency for the nation's currency to depreciate. As Figure 9–11 shows, with both low and high capital mobility, a monetary expansion will cause a rise in real income, holding the price level and other factors unchanged.

Fiscal Policy under Floating Exchange Rates

Fiscal policy actions also induce changes in the value of a nation's currency when the nation's exchange rate floats. Capital mobility performs a key role in determining whether the currency's value rises or falls, however.

THE CASE OF LOW CAPITAL MOBILITY   Panel (a) of Figure 9–12 shows the effects of a bond-financed increase in government spending when a nation's capital mobility is low. With the exchange rate initially unchanged, a rise in gov-

Figure 9–12   The Effects of an Increase in Government Spending with a Floating Exchange Rate

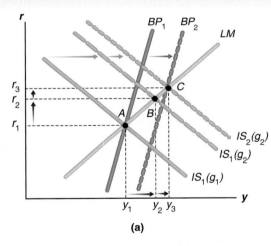

(a)

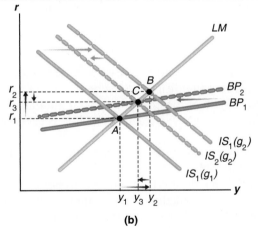

(b)

In both panels, an increase in government expenditures causes an initial rightward shift in the *IS* schedule, thereby inducing a movement from point *A* to point *B*, which leads to an increase in the equilibrium nominal interest rate and an increase in equilibrium real income. In panel (a), where the relatively low elasticity of the *BP* schedule implies low capital mobility, greater import spending will more than offset a small capital inflow and cause a private payments deficit to arise at point *B*. This will induce a currency depreciation that will shift both the *IS* and the *BP* schedules to

the right, leading to a final equilibrium with a zero private payments balance at point *C*. In panel (b), where the relatively high elasticity of the *BP* schedule implies high capital mobility, significant capital inflows will more than offset greater import expenditures and cause a private payments surplus to occur at point *B*. This will induce a currency appreciation that will shift both the *IS* and the *BP* schedules leftward, leading to a final equilibrium with a zero private payments balance at point *C*.

ernment spending causes the IS schedule to shift rightward, from $IS_1(g_1)$ to $IS_1(g_2)$, resulting in a movement from point A to point B. Point B lies to the right of the BP_1 schedule, so the immediate effect of the rise in government spending will be a private payments deficit resulting from an increase in import spending stemming from a rise in real income. As a result of the private payments deficit, the nation's currency will depreciate, and net export spending will increase, thereby causing the IS schedule to shift rightward once more, to $IS_2(g_2)$. In addition, the depreciation will cause the BP schedule to shift to the right, from BP_1 to BP_2. The final equilibrium point, with other factors such as the price level unchanged, will be point C, at which there once again is a zero private payments balance and, thus, no tendency for the nation's currency to depreciate further.

THE CASE OF HIGH CAPITAL MOBILITY   When capital is very mobile, as in panel (b) of Figure 9–12, the effects are different from those shown in panel (a). A bond-financed increase in government expenditures initially has an identical effect, as shown by the immediate movement from point A to point B in panel (b). With high capital mobility, however, the rise in the interest rate from r_1 to r_2 will cause significant capital inflows that will lead, on net, to a private payments *surplus* at point B, which lies above the BP_1 schedule. Consequently, foreign residents will seek to acquire more of the nation's currency to purchase domestic capital, so the value of the nation's currency will *appreciate.* This will make foreign goods cheaper to the nation's own residents but will make the nation's goods more expensive for foreign residents, spurring import spending and slowing export expenditures. As a result, the nation will experience a fall in autonomous expenditures, and the IS schedule will shift *leftward*, from $IS_1(g_2)$ to $IS_2(g_2)$. The currency appreciation will also cause the BP schedule to shift leftward, from BP_1 to BP_2. At the final equilibrium point C, real income on net will be higher, at y_3, than it was at the beginning level of y_1. Nevertheless, high capital mobility clearly alters the economy's adjustment to a bond-financed rise in government spending by muting the effects of the government spending increase on equilibrium real income.

FUNDAMENTAL ISSUE #4

How do monetary and fiscal policy actions affect a nation's real income under floating exchange rates?   An expansionary monetary policy action results in a private payments deficit that leads to a depreciation of a nation's currency, thereby stimulating export expenditures while inhibiting import spending. Consequently, expansionary monetary policy actions cause a nation's real income to rise in the short run. The effects of fiscal policy actions on a nation's private payments balance and the value of its currency depend on the degree of capital mobility. Under most circumstances, an expansionary fiscal policy action causes at least a slight short-term increase in a nation's real income level. The extent of the rise in real income declines as the degree of capital mobility increases, however.

Can Nonsterilized Central Bank Interventions Influence Exchange Rates?

According to the monetary approach to exchange rates, nonsterilized central bank interventions in foreign exchange markets bring about adjustments in the quantity of money in circulation that can either detract from or enhance intended effects of monetary and fiscal policies. About two-thirds of the world's central banks fail to sterilize their interventions by preventing changes in the quantity of money. A question that arises, however, is whether fully sterilized interventions by other central banks really accomplish anything. This is not an unimportant question, because major central banks such as the Federal Reserve, the European Central Bank, and the Bank of Japan regularly sterilize their foreign exchange market interventions.

The Effects of Interventions—in Theory

Most economists believe that sterilized foreign exchange interventions can, at least in theory, have two possible effects on exchange rates. One of these is a *portfolio balance effect:* If the exchange rate is viewed as the relative price of imperfectly substitutable assets such as bonds, then changes in government or central bank holdings of bonds and other assets denominated in various currencies can influence exchange rates by affecting the equilibrium prices at which traders are willing to hold these assets. For example, if an intervention reduces the supply of domestic assets relative to foreign assets held by individuals and firms, then the expected return on domestic assets must fall to induce individuals and firms to readjust their portfolios. A reduction in the anticipated rate of return on domestic assets, in turn, requires an appreciation of the domestic currency. Hence, a finance ministry or central bank purchase of domestic currency can, through the portfolio balance effect, cause the value of the domestic currency to rise.

The other possible effect is an intervention *announcement effect,* in which foreign exchange interventions may provide traders with previously unknown information that alters their willingness to demand or supply currencies in the foreign exchange markets. The announcement effect can exist, therefore, only if a government or central bank intervention clearly reveals some kind of "inside information" that traders did not have prior to the intervention. For instance, a central bank that plans to conduct a future anti-inflation policy by contracting its money stock may reveal this intention by leaning against the wind in the face of a recent downward trend in the value of its nation's currency. If currency traders believe this message provided by the central bank's intervention, then they will expect a future appreciation and will increase their holdings of the currency. This concerted action by currency traders then causes an actual currency appreciation. Thus, the announcement effect of the intervention, like the portfolio balance effect, induces a rise in the value of the domestic currency.

Gauging the Actual Effects of Interventions

Assessing whether the theoretical effects of sterilized interventions amount to anything in reality turns out to be a challenging endeavor. One reason is that central banks typically intervene infrequently, and when they do intervene, they usually engage in foreign exchange transactions only for relatively short periods ranging from a single day to a couple of weeks. For instance, consider the dollar intervention activity by the Swiss National Bank since 1986 displayed in Figure 9–13, which is typical of the pattern of interventions conducted by most central banks. Even though many of the Swiss interventions amounted to more than $100 million, they occurred infrequently and lasted for relatively short intervals.

To assess whether sterilized interventions can affect exchange rates, economists often conduct *event studies* that focus on exchange-rate movements immediately following interventions. Several such studies have found evidence that both portfolio balance and announcement effects of sterilized interventions can cause market exchange rates to change, at least in the short run.

Nevertheless, a number of economists contend that the longer-term effects of sterilized interventions are likely to be meager. The portfolio balance effect, they argue, ultimately leads to changes in asset returns that induce flows of funds that reverse the initial exchange-rate effects of the interventions. In addition, announcement effects tend to be short-lived at best, so such effects are unlikely to bring about long-lasting changes in exchange rates.

Research Project

The examples considered in this chapter assumed that all central bank foreign exchange interventions to maintain a fixed exchange rate were nonsterilized. Reevaluate the effects of expansionary monetary and fiscal policy actions under fixed exchange rates if central banks are able to influence exchange rates using sterilized interventions.

Web Resources

1. How has the Federal Reserve intervened in foreign exchange markets in recent years? For a helpful summary provided by the Federal Reserve Bank of New York, go to http://www.ny.frb.org/pihome/fedpoint/fed44.html.

2. What are the activities of the Federal Reserve's Foreign Exchange Committee? Find out at http://www.ny.frb.org/fxc/.

Figure 9–13   Swiss National Bank Foreign Exchange Market Interventions since 1986

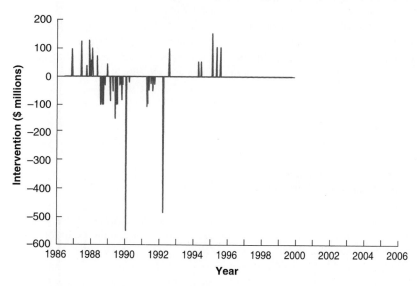

As is typical of the pattern of foreign exchange market interventions by the world's central banks, interventions by the Swiss National Bank have been both infrequent and short-lived.

SOURCE: Richard Payne and Paolo Vitale, "A Transaction Level Study of the Effects of Central Bank Interventions on Exchange Rates," Centre for Economic Policy Research Discussion Paper No. 3085, November 2001.

1. **Determination of the Private Payments Balance in the IS-LM Model:**   In the *IS-LM* framework, the private payments balance is implied by the location of the *IS-LM* equilibrium relative to a set of real income–nominal interest rate combinations called the *BP* schedule. The *BP* schedule consists of real income–nominal interest rate combinations for which the sum of the current account balance and the capital account balance is equal to zero. At any *IS-LM* equilibrium along the *BP* schedule, the private payments balance equals zero. An *IS-LM* equilibrium above or below the *BP* schedule, however, generates a private payments surplus or deficit, respectively.

2. **How Government Budget Policies Affect the Private Payments Balance in Traditional Keynesian Theory:**   In an environment with relatively low capital mobility and a relatively steep *BP* schedule, a reduction in government spending or a tax increase will reduce both a government budget deficit and a private payments deficit. By way of contrast, if capital mobility is relatively high and the *BP* schedule is relatively shallow, then a contractionary fiscal policy action aimed at reducing a government budget deficit will contribute to a rising private payments deficit. If the exchange rate floats freely in foreign exchange markets, however, then the traditional Keynesian model indicates that a private payments deficit ultimately should induce a currency depreciation. This decline in the value of the domestic currency then should automatically tend to induce an offsetting decline in the size of the private payments deficit.

3. **How Monetary and Fiscal Policy Actions Affect a Nation's Real Income under Fixed Exchange Rates:**   If a nation's central bank sterilizes by preventing variations in its foreign exchange reserves from affecting the nation's nominal money stock, then a rise in the money stock can induce at least a short-term increase in real income as long as the central bank has sufficient reserves to keep the exchange rate fixed in the face of private payments deficits. The effects of unsterilized monetary policy actions on real income, however, eventually dissipate as changes in foreign exchange reserves cause the quantity of money to return to its initial level. The effects of fiscal policy actions also are influenced by a central bank's decision about sterilization, but with a fixed exchange rate, an expansionary fiscal policy action typically causes real income to increase in the short run.

4. **How Monetary and Fiscal Policy Actions Affect a Nation's Real Income under Floating Exchange Rates:**   A central bank action that increases the quantity of money in circulation causes a private payments deficit, which induces a currency depreciation that spurs export spending and reduces import spending. Thus, expansionary monetary policy actions cause short-run increases in a nation's real income level. Expansionary fiscal policy actions can result in private payments deficits or surpluses and currency depreciations or appreciations, depending on the degree of capital mobility. The size of the effect of a fiscal policy action on real income declines as capital mobility increases.

Self-Test Questions

(Answers to odd-numbered questions may be found on the Web at **http://macro. swcollege.com** under "Student Resources.")

1. Suppose that the home currency appreciates in value relative to other nations' currencies. What are the effects on the positions of the nation's *IS* and *BP* schedules?

2. Explain in your own words why capital mobility and exchange-rate flexibility matter for evaluating the response of the private payments balance to a reduction in government spending.

3. If a central bank maintains a fixed exchange rate but conducts unsterilized monetary policies, how would a contractionary monetary policy action ultimately affect the nation's private payments balance and its real income level, assuming that the price level is unchanged? Support your answer.

4. If a nation's central bank maintains a fixed exchange rate and conducts unsterilized monetary policies, how could a contractionary fiscal policy induce a change in the quantity of money in circulation? If capital mobility is low, would the nation's money stock expand or contract as a result? Explain.

5. Explain in your own words how a contractionary monetary policy action would affect a nation's private payments balance and the value of its currency under a floating exchange rate.

6. Explain in your own words how a contractionary fiscal policy action would, if capital mobility is low, affect a nation's private payments balance and the value of its currency under a floating exchange rate.

Problems

1. Use the following equations to work out an equation for the *BP* schedule, where *e, f, g,* and *h* are positive numbers and r^w is the market interest rate in the rest of the world outside this nation:

    Current account balance: $CA = e - (f \times y)$.

    Capital account balance: $KA = g + [h \times (r - r^w)]$.

2. Draw a rough graph of the *BP* schedule from problem 1. What is its slope? What happens as the value of *h* increases? What happens as the value of *h* decreases? Why does this make sense?

(Answers to odd-numbered problems may be found on the Web at **http://macro. swcollege.com** under "Student Resources.")

Before the Test

Test your understanding of the material covered in this chapter by taking the Chapter 9 interactive quiz at **http://macro.swcollege.com**.

Online Application

Internet URL: http://www.bankofengland.co.uk

Title: *Bank of England*

Navigation: The above address connects you with the home page for the Bank of England.

Application: Click *Enter.* Then click on *Statistics* at the top of the page, and then click on the *Monetary and Financial Statistics* main page; then click on *Latest Statistical Releases and Publications.* Answer the following questions.

1. In the right-hand margin, click on *Growth rates of M4 and M4 lending* to download this table. Examine the recent three- and six-month growth rates in M4, Britain's main measure of the quantity of money.

2. Go back to *Monetary and Financial Statistics,* and in the left-hand margin, click on *Exchange rates* to download these data. Use the data for the U.S. dollar exchange rate of the British currency, the pound sterling, to calculate rates of British currency depreciation (or appreciation) during recent months. Does there appear to be a relationship between the M4 money growth rate and the rate of depreciation of the pound sterling? Does this square with theory?

For Group Study and Analysis: The Bank of England reports rates of exchange for the pound relative to a dozen other world currencies. Divide the class into three groups, and have each group repeat exercise 2 above for four of the exchange rates. Are there any differences in the relationships between money growth and exchange-rate depreciation (or appreciation) depending on which exchange rate is considered?

UNIT III Keynesian and Monetarist Macroeconomic Perspectives

and Further Reading

Calvo, Guillermo, and Carmen Reinhart. "Fear of Floating." *Quarterly Journal of Economics* 117 (May 2002): 379–408.

Daniels, Joseph, and David VanHoose. *International Monetary and Financial Economics,* 2d ed. Cincinnati: Thomson/Southwestern, 2002.

Frankel, Jeffrey, Sergio Schmukler, and Luis Servén. "Global Transmission of Interest Rates: Monetary Independence and Currency Regime." National Bureau of Economic Research Working Paper No. 8828, March 2002.

Humpage, Owen, and William Osterberg. "Why Intervention Rarely Works." Federal Reserve Bank of Cleveland *Economic Commentary,* February 1, 2000.

Humpage, Owen, and James Thomson. "The Exchange Stabilization Fund: How It Works." Federal Reserve Bank of Cleveland *Economic Commentary,* December 1999.

International Monetary Fund. *World Economic Outlook.* Washington, D.C., various issues.

Moreno, Ramon. "Pegging and Stabilization Policy in Developing Countries." Federal Reserve Bank of San Francisco *Economic Review,* 2001, pp. 17–29.

macro**xtra**!

Is There a Trade-off between
Unemployment and Inflation?—

The Keynesian and Monetarist Views on Price and Output Determination

10

FUNDAMENTAL ISSUES

1. What factors determine aggregate demand in the traditional Keynesian model?

2. What factors determine the shape and position of the Keynesian aggregate supply schedule?

3. According to traditional Keynesian theory, what are the price and output effects of expansionary fiscal and monetary policies?

4. What is the Phillips curve?

5. How does monetarism differ from the traditional Keynesian theory?

6. How has the relationship between the inflation rate and the unemployment rate changed in the 1990s and 2000s?

I t is called the Phillips curve—a postulated inverse relationship between a nation's unemployment rate and the rate of growth of its price level. The existence of a Phillips curve relationship between the unemployment rate and the inflation rate is a key prediction of the traditional Keynesian theory. This relationship held up so well during the 1960s that by the start of the 1970s Keynesian theory predominated in all discussions of macroeconomic theory and policy.

At the end of the 1960s, however, Nobel Prize–winning economist Milton Friedman predicted the demise of the inverse inflation-unemployment

267

relationship. Unlike many economic predictions, this one turned out to be exactly right. During the years that followed, it was hard to find anything more than a short-lived hint of an inverse relationship between the rate of U.S. unemployment and the rate of growth of the U.S. price level. Today, many economists completely dismiss the notion of a stable Phillips curve relationship.

Something Friedman also proposed back in the late 1960s, however, was that the short-run adjustment of wages to changes in the price level should lead to a different sort of relationship. According to Friedman, the inverse relationship that ought to emerge over a period of years is between the rate of unemployment and the rate of increase *in the inflation rate. Thus, according to this* accelerationist approach *to the Phillips curve, what economists really ought to observe is a long-term inverse relationship between a nation's unemployment rate and the acceleration or deceleration of its price level.*

In this chapter, you will learn why the traditional Keynesian theory predicts a Phillips curve relationship between unemployment and inflation. In addition, you will learn why Friedman and others—known as *monetarists* who both built upon and departed from the Keynesian approach—argued that an inverse relationship between unemployment and inflation at best will be fleeting. First, however, you must understand how nominal wages, prices, employment, and output are determined in the traditional Keynesian theory.

Chapters 6–9 have developed the key features of this approach to short-run business cycles and the potential roles that monetary and fiscal policy may play in helping to smooth these cycles. Absent from our discussion to this point, however, has been a consideration of the determination of the price level and inflation in the Keynesian framework. This chapter considers this issue, which most sharply divides traditional Keynesian theory from the classical framework of Chapters 3 and 4 and from the modern renditions of the classical perspective that we shall take up in Chapters 11 and 13. The basic Keynesian theory of price and inflation determination also provides a foundation for more modern Keynesian approaches to explaining business cycles, which we shall discuss in Chapters 12 and 13.

As you will learn in this chapter, the fundamental differences between Keynesian macroeconomics and the classical model or other alternative theories concern whether there is a short- or long-run relationship between output and inflation. According to the classical theory, output is determined independently from inflation. In contrast, the Keynesian theory indicates that increased output can be achieved by incurring higher inflation, which also implies that lower unemployment will be associated with higher inflation rates. The reason for this conclusion, it turns out, is that the traditional Keynesian theory of price and inflation determination is significantly different from the one proposed by proponents of the classical framework. Eventually, monetarists such as Milton Friedman would help to reconcile—or at least illuminate—the differences between the approaches.

Aggregate 269
Demand in
the Keynesian
Framework

CHAPTER 10   Is There a Trade-off between Unemployment and Inflation?—The Keynesian and Monetarist Views on Price and Output Determination

According to the classical theory discussed in Chapters 3 and 4, aggregate demand depends primarily on the quantity of money supplied by a central bank such as the Federal Reserve. Consequently, the quantity of money is the main determinant of the position of the aggregate demand schedule, which in the classical model is the set of real output–price level combinations at which people are satisfied holding the quantity of money supplied.

The traditional Keynesian model also implies a theory of aggregate demand. This theory is richer than the classical theory, however. Although this does not mean that the Keynesian model is necessarily the correct approach to understanding aggregate demand, it does mean, as you will see, that the Keynesian approach to aggregate demand is more "general." The classical aggregate demand schedule, it turns out, is a "special case" of the Keynesian aggregate demand schedule.

The Keynesian Aggregate Demand Schedule

As you learned in Chapter 8, in the Keynesian *IS-LM* diagram, the point at which the *IS* schedule and the *LM* schedule cross represents a combination of the nominal interest rate and real income for which aggregate desired expenditures equal income at the same time that the market for real money balances is in equilibrium. In addition, however, the Keynesian framework also includes a *real balance effect* on the nominal interest rate stemming from changes in the price level. A rise in the price level reduces the supply of real money balances, thereby causing the nominal interest rate to rise at any given level of real income. This causes the *LM* schedule to shift upward and to the left.

Panel (a) of Figure 10–1 on the next page shows the real balance effect in a full *IS-LM* equilibrium. The initial equilibrium point in panel (a) is point *A*. An increase in the price level, from P_1 to P_2, causes a real balance effect on the nominal interest rate. This shifts the *LM* schedule upward, from $LM(M_1/P_1)$ to $LM(M_1/P_2)$. As the interest rate rises, however, desired investment spending declines. As a result, aggregate desired expenditures decline, inducing a fall in equilibrium real income. This decline in equilibrium real income from y_1 to y_2 causes a leftward movement along the *IS* schedule to point *B*. The fall in real income reduces the demand for real money balances, which places a somewhat offsetting downward pressure on the nominal interest rate, which on net thereby increases from r_1 to r_2.

Panel (b) of the figure illustrates that the fall in real income resulting from the real balance effect means that both real income–price level combinations, y_1 and P_1 at point *A* and y_2 and P_2 at point *B*, are consistent with *IS-LM* equilibrium. Consequently, both of these real income–price level combinations maintain equilibrium real income and equilibrium in the market for real money balances. They are two possible combinations of real income and the price level that lie on a set of points that will maintain *IS-LM* equilibrium as the price level changes. This set of real income–price

Figure 10–1   Deriving the Keynesian Aggregate Demand Schedule

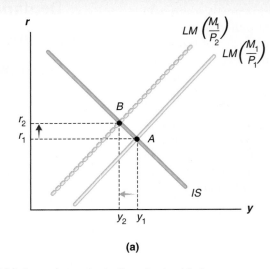

(a)

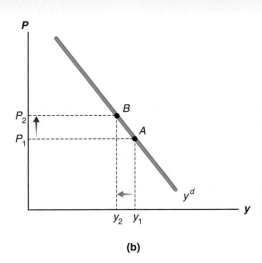

(b)

Panel (a) shows that a rise in the price level induces an increase in the equilibrium nominal interest rate through the real balance effect, as the *LM* schedule shifts back along the *IS* schedule from point *A* to point *B*. Because equilibrium real

income falls as the price level increases, the aggregate demand schedule containing the real income–price level combinations *A* and *B* slopes downward in panel (b).

level combinations consistent with *IS-LM* equilibrium is the Keynesian aggregate demand schedule, denoted y^d. Thus:

> **The Keynesian theory of aggregate demand stems directly from the *IS-LM* model. At all price levels and real income levels along the Keynesian aggregate demand schedule, *IS-LM* equilibrium is attained.**

Monetary Policy and Aggregate Demand

In Figure 10–1, we derived the aggregate demand schedule by considering only the real balance effect arising from an increase in the price level. All other factors, including the nominal money stock, M_1, were unchanged. Hence, a change in other factors affecting the positions of the *IS* or *LM* schedules will alter the position of the aggregate demand schedule.

HOW A CHANGE IN THE QUANTITY OF MONEY AFFECTS AGGREGATE DEMAND   For instance, suppose that actions of the central bank increase the nominal quantity of money supplied from M_1 to a larger amount, M_2. Panel (a) of Figure 10–2 shows that at an initial real income–price level combination y_1 and P_1 at point *A*, the rise in the nominal money stock will induce a downward and rightward shift of the *LM* schedule. There is a new *IS-LM* equilibrium at point *B*. The liquidity effect arising from the increase in the nominal money stock will reduce the nominal interest rate from r_1 to r_2, and equilibrium real income will rise, from y_1 to y_2.

Figure 10-2 The Effect of an Increase in the Money Stock on Aggregate Demand

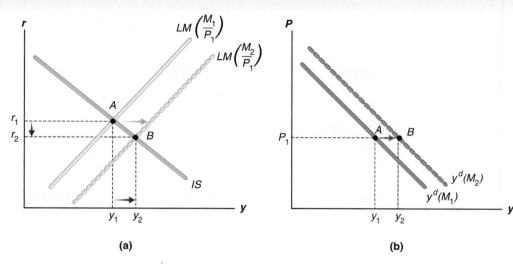

(a) **(b)**

With an unchanged price level, an increase in the nominal quantity of money in circulation causes an increase in the amount of real money balances and shifts the *LM* schedule downward and to the right along the *IS* schedule from point *A* to point *B* in panel (a). Because the resulting real income level at point *B* in panel (b) corresponds to the same price level, this new equilibrium real income–price level combination lies on a new aggregate demand schedule to the right of the real income–price level combination at point *A* on the original aggregate demand schedule. Thus, an increase in the nominal money stock will cause an increase in aggregate demand to $y^d(M_2)$.

The real income–price level combination y_2 and P_1 lies to the right of the original aggregate demand schedule, denoted $y^d(M_1)$ in panel (b). Nevertheless, this new point *B* in panel (b) is consistent with the *IS-LM* equilibrium at point *B* in panel (a). Because the Keynesian aggregate demand schedule is a set of real income–price level combinations that maintain *IS-LM* equilibrium, point *B* in panel (b) is on a *new* aggregate demand schedule. Consequently, a rise in the nominal quantity of money will shift the aggregate demand schedule to the right. That is, a rise in the nominal money stock will *increase aggregate demand.*

In contrast, a reduction in the nominal money stock will shift the *LM* schedule to the left, causing equilibrium real income to fall at any given price level. The aggregate demand schedule will shift leftward as a result of the fall in the nominal quantity of money supplied. Thus, a decline in the nominal money stock will reduce aggregate demand.

THE ELASTICITY OF THE *LM* SCHEDULE MATTERS It is important to recognize that the amount aggregate demand shifts as a result of a change in the money stock depends on the size of the liquidity effect that the change in the money stock exerts. The size of the liquidity effect, in turn, depends on the relative elasticities of *IS* and *LM*. As discussed in Chapter 8, these relative elasticities depend on the interest elasticity of desired investment to spending and on the interest elasticity of money demand, respectively. In other words, the size of the effect of a change in the money stock on aggregate demand depends on the linkages of the Keynesian monetary policy transmission mechanism. As you learned in Chapter 8, the linkages in this mechanism strengthen as the *LM* schedule becomes more inelastic (as the demand for real money balances becomes more interest-inelastic) and as the *IS* schedule becomes more elastic (as desired investment spending becomes more interest-elastic).

It follows that the effects of monetary policy actions on aggregate demand become larger as the *LM* schedule becomes more inelastic. If the *LM* schedule is perfectly inelastic, so that money demand is completely interest-inelastic, monetary policy actions have the largest possible effects on aggregate demand. This case corresponds to the classical model of Chapters 3 and 4. Changes in the nominal interest rate had no effect on desired money holdings, which were determined by the Cambridge equation of money demand, so the classical version of the *LM* schedule is perfectly inelastic. In this sense, therefore, the classical model's aggregate demand schedule is a "special case" of the Keynesian aggregate demand schedule.

Fiscal Policy and Aggregate Demand

In Chapter 4, we showed that in the classical model, deficit-financed government spending completely crowds out an equal-sized amount of private spending. Fiscal policy actions have no effect on aggregate demand, but simply redistribute existing goods and services between the government and the private sector. As discussed in Chapter 8, however, the Keynesian framework proposes that the fiscal crowding-out effect is incomplete. As a result, fiscal policy should be able to influence aggregate demand in traditional Keynesian theory.

Figure 10–3 demonstrates that this reasoning is correct. Panel (a) displays the *IS-LM* effects of a rise in real government expenditures, from g_1 to g_2, with the price level unchanged at P_1. The immediate result is a rightward shift in the *IS* schedule by the amount of the increase in government spending times the autonomous spending multiplier, $1/(1 - MPC)$. The rise in real income causes the demand for real money balances to rise, which, in turn, leads to a rise in the equilibrium nominal interest rate that causes investment spending to decline. Crowding out is not complete, however, so equilibrium real income will rise, from y_1 at point *A* to y_2 at point *B*.

Point *B* in panel (a) is a new *IS-LM* equilibrium, so the real income–price level combination y_2 and P_1 must lie on a new aggregate demand schedule at point *B* in panel (b). That is, the rise in government spending shifts the aggregate demand schedule outward and to the right, which means that the rise in real government expenditures will raise aggregate demand.

It is important to recognize that changes in private spending have an analogous effect on aggregate demand. For instance, an autonomous increase in consumption spending or net export spending also will shift the *IS* schedule rightward, thereby causing an increase in aggregate demand.

Note that a tax cut will have the same basic effects as a rise in government spending. In the case of a lump-sum tax reduction, the only differ-

Figure 10–3 The Effect of an Increase in Government Spending on Aggregate Demand

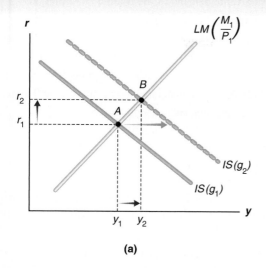
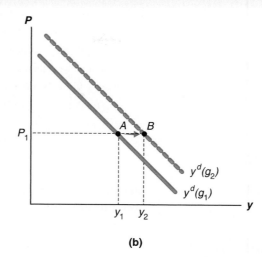

(a) **(b)**

With an unchanged price level, an increase in government spending will shift the *IS* schedule rightward along the *LM* schedule from point *A* to point *B* in panel (a). The resulting real income level at point *B* in panel (b) corresponds to the same price level. This new equilibrium real income–price

level combination will be located on a new aggregate demand schedule to the right of the real income–price level combination at point *A* on the original aggregate demand schedule. Consequently, an increase in government spending will cause an increase in aggregate demand to $y^d(g_2)$.

ence is that the *IS* schedule will shift rightward by the amount of the tax cut times the tax multiplier, $-MPC/(1 - MPC)$. In the more realistic case of a cut in the income tax rate, the *IS* schedule will shift by a different amount, but again aggregate demand will rise.

The extent to which fiscal policy actions can influence aggregate demand depends on how much crowding out occurs. As you learned in Chapter 8, the extent of the crowding-out effect increases as the *LM* schedule becomes more inelastic (as the demand for real money balances becomes more interest-inelastic) and as the *IS* schedule becomes more elastic (as desired investment spending becomes more interest-elastic). In the extreme case when the *LM* schedule is perfectly inelastic and the *IS* schedule is perfectly elastic, crowding out is complete, and fiscal policy has no influence on aggregate demand in the economy. Hence, if money demand is completely interest-inelastic and desired investment is completely interest-elastic, the traditional Keynesian model mimics the classical theory's prediction that fiscal policy cannot affect aggregate demand. More generally, however, the Keynesian model proposes a potential role for fiscal policy in influencing aggregate demand, prices, and real output. To understand how both fiscal and monetary policy may exert short-run effects on prices and real output, however, we must develop the Keynesian theory of how these macroeconomic variables are determined.

FUNDAMENTAL ISSUE #1

What factors determine aggregate demand in the traditional Keynesian model? Two key factors influence the position of the Keynesian aggregate demand schedule. One is the set of elements that together compose autonomous aggregate expenditures, such as government spending and taxation and autonomous consumption, investment, and net exports. The other is the nominal money stock. As a result, both fiscal and monetary policy actions can influence the position of the Keynesian aggregate demand schedule.

Keynesian Aggregate Supply: Sticky Nominal Wages

Recall from Chapter 3 that the classical economists made three important assumptions when they examined the market for labor and derived the classical aggregate supply schedule:

1. Workers, consumers, and entrepreneurs are motivated by rational self-interest.

2. People do not experience money illusion.

3. Pure competition prevails in the markets for goods and services and for factors of production.

Proponents of the Keynesian approach to aggregate supply typically have no trouble accepting the first classical proposition. They doubt the generality of the latter two assumptions, however. The Keynesians argue that because information is imperfect, in the short run people have no choice but to exhibit money illusion, even if they are rationally motivated by self-interest. In addition, they contend that self-interest can induce workers and firms to set up institutional arrangements that inhibit pure competition, thereby making wages and prices less than fully flexible. We begin our discussion of the Keynesian approach to aggregate supply by considering the effects of wage stickiness (we postpone the slightly more complicated issue of potential price inflexibilities until Chapter 13). Then we discuss the implications of imperfect information for the theory of aggregate supply.

Explaining Wage Inflexibility

Why might nominal wages be inflexible, or "sticky"? One possible explanation is the existence of minimum-wage laws that place artificial floors on wages that firms can pay. Other factors that could artificially boost workers' effective nominal compensation, such as legal impediments to nominal wage cuts, also might make nominal wages sticky, at least in a downward direction.

Another potential reason for wage inflexibility might be widespread unionization of a nation's workforce. Organized groups of workers may seek to keep their nominal wages at levels that they feel are appropriate relative to other occupations. In a highly unionized economy, **explicit contracts**— legally binding contracts laying out the terms for workers' compensation,

EXPLICIT CONTRACTS: Contractual arrangements in which the terms of relationships between workers and firms, especially about wages, are in writing and legally binding upon both parties.

benefits, and so on—establish wages for specified periods, such as one, two, or three years. Union contracts typically allow wages to rise above specified levels but do not permit wages to fall below those levels, even though some workers are laid off as a result. Consequently, widespread unionization could also account for downward inflexibility of the nominal wage.

IMPLICIT CONTRACTS: Unwritten agreements between workers and firms, concerning terms of employment such as wages; the agreements may or may not be legally binding.

Of course, wage contracts are not limited to unionized industries. Many white-collar workers, for instance, have explicit contracts with their employers. In addition, a number of labor economists contend that workers and firms adopt **implicit contracts.** These are tacit agreements that firms will not reduce workers' wages when economic activity ebbs in exchange for the right not to raise wages as much as the market wage would indicate when business conditions improve. In effect, such a contract is an insurance scheme: Workers pay an insurance premium in the form of lower-than-market wages in good times in exchange for insurance coverage in the form of higher-than-market wages in bad times. Widespread use of implicit contracts could result in relatively rigid nominal wages across upturns and downturns of business cycles.

Proponents of the view that nominal wages are inflexible typically offer one or more of these rationales for their position. We shall discuss the real-world evidence on the importance of contracts in the U.S. economy in greater detail in Chapter 12. For now, let's try to evaluate how widespread nominal wage inflexibility will affect the theory of aggregate supply.

Wage Stickiness and the Aggregate Supply Schedule

Recall from Chapter 3 that the aggregate supply schedule for an economy is the set of real output–price level combinations that maintain labor market equilibrium. To see how nominal wage inflexibility affects the nature of the aggregate supply schedule, consider Figure 10–4 on the following page. Panel (a) is a diagram of the labor market with the nominal wage measured on the vertical axis. Panel (b) shows the aggregate production function. Panel (c) is a diagram of real output–price level combinations.

THE RELATIONSHIP BETWEEN THE PRICE LEVEL AND REAL OUTPUT   In the classical model, the labor supply schedule slopes upward, as shown by the dashed schedule $N^s(P_1)$ in panel (a). If the general level of nominal wages is determined by legal requirements and explicit and implicit contracts, however, the aggregate wage rate in the economy may be regarded as fixed in the short run, at $W = \overline{W}$. This means that workers supply whatever amount of labor that firms demand at this nominal wage. Recall from Chapter 3 that if the price level is P_1, then the value-of-marginal-product schedule, $MP_N \times P_1$, represents the labor demand schedule. At the fixed nominal wage $W = \overline{W}$, the amount of labor demanded is equal to N_1 at point A in panel (a). Referring to the aggregate production function in panel (b), this yields the level of real output y_1. Consequently, at the price level P_1, the real output level consistent with equilibrium employment with a fixed nominal wage $\overline{W}$ is y_1. This is one point, labeled point A in panel (c), on the economy's aggregate supply schedule.

Now consider the effect of a rise in the price level, from P_1 to P_2. This causes the value of labor's marginal product to rise to $MP_N \times P_2$. Hence, the

Figure 10–4   The Keynesian Aggregate Supply Schedule with Wage Inflexibility

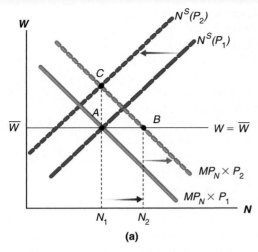

(a)

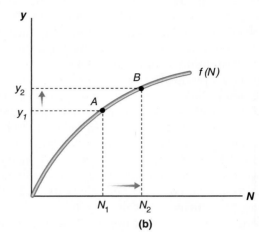

(b)

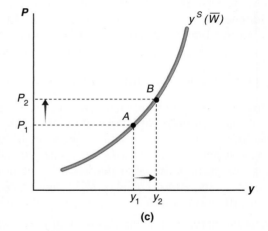

(c)

A rise in the price level causes an increase in the value of labor's marginal product, $MP_N \times P$. As a result, the demand for labor by firms will increase. If the money wage is flexible, as in the classical model, then the labor supply will shift back to the left as well, as workers perceive a decline in their real wage due to higher prices and respond by supplying fewer labor services at any money wage. Thus, in the classical model, equilibrium employment will remain unchanged, at N_1 at point C in panel (a). With an inflexible money wage, however, the rise in labor demand will induce an increase in employment via a movement from point A to point B in panel (a), causing production of output to increase [panel (b)]. A rise in the price level will induce an increase in real output and a movement from point A to point B in panel (c), so the aggregate supply schedule will slope upward.

demand for labor in panel (a) will increase. In the classical model, the labor supply will then decline, from $N^s(P_1)$ to $N^s(P_2)$, as workers recognize that the rise in the price level reduces the real wage that they earn. Thus, in the classical theory, the resulting labor market equilibrium is at point C, with no change in employment. If nominal wages are fixed through laws and contracts, however, then the classical labor supply schedule no longer plays any role, and point C is not attained. Instead, the rise in labor demand leads to an increase in employment to N_2, at point B in panel (a). As a result, real output rises to y_2 in panel (b). The result is a new real output–price level combination y_2 and P_2 at point B in panel (c).

AGGREGATE SUPPLY Points A and B are both consistent with fixed-wage equilibrium outcomes in the labor market. Therefore, both of these points lie on an upward-sloping *Keynesian aggregate supply schedule.* Because we have derived this aggregate supply schedule under the assumption that the nominal wage is fixed at $W = \overline{W}$, we label it $y^s(\overline{W})$. Note also that the aggregate supply schedule is convex, or bowed upward. It has this shape because the production function is concave, or bowed downward (due to the law of diminishing marginal returns). Therefore, successive increases in the price level stimulate increases in labor demand and employment that induce successively smaller gains in real output production.

Finally, because we derive the aggregate supply schedule for a *given* fixed wage, a change in the fixed nominal wage rate will require us to derive a new aggregate supply schedule. At a higher nominal wage, employment levels and, hence, corresponding output levels will always be lower. As a result, if the fixed nominal wage increases, the amounts of real output corresponding to various price levels will be lower, and the aggregate supply schedule will lie to the left of its original position. A rise in the nominal wage, perhaps as a result of union demands for wage increases or from an increase in the legal minimum wage, will shift the aggregate supply schedule upward and to the left. The higher value for the fixed nominal wage will reduce aggregate supply.

Keynesian Aggregate Supply: Imperfect Information

As we noted earlier, proponents of the Keynesian approach also disagree with the classical assumption that people never exhibit money illusion. Economists typically believe that well-informed people always care about their real wages. Therefore, if people did possess complete information, the classical and Keynesian theorists would not disagree on this issue. If people live in a world of uncertainty, however, then information about the actual price level may not always be available. Furthermore, people are never fully informed about *future* events. These observations form the basis for an alternative Keynesian theory of aggregate supply.

The Sources of Uncertainty

Let's consider a worker's decision to supply labor services today. He may have a reasonably good idea about some specific prices of goods and services today, because he has made recent trips to retail stores. Nevertheless, he will not have up-to-date information about prices at all stores. Nor will he have full information about how prices may have changed at stores that he recently visited. Certainly, he can consult newspaper ads, and he could even subscribe to government and Federal Reserve publications that report recent price indexes. Nevertheless, ads constitute small samples, and reliable price index numbers are available only on a monthly basis, after the fact. The worker's information about the overall price level will always be somewhat uncertain.

This means that when our worker tries to decide how much labor to supply, he must base his decision on his *perception* of what the current real wage is and on his *anticipation* of what it will be during the period when he agrees to work at that wage. In other words, he must form an *expectation* of the value of the real wage that he will earn if he works at any given nominal wage that a firm offers him. To do this, he must form an expectation of the price level, which we shall denote P^e.

Imperfect Information and Aggregate Supply

To see how imperfect information motivates a Keynesian theory of aggregate supply, consider Figure 10–5. Here, we assume that nominal wages are flexible (we shall consider wage contracts in the presence of imperfect information in Chapter 12). Consequently, as in the classical model, the equilibrium nominal wage is determined by the intersection of the labor demand and labor supply schedules in panel (a). As in the classical theory,

Figure 10–5   The Keynesian Aggregate Supply Schedule with Imperfect Information

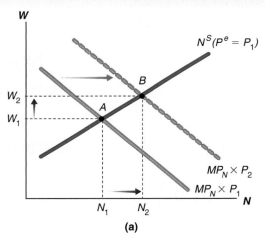

(a)

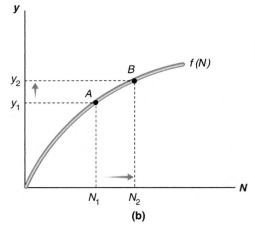

(b)

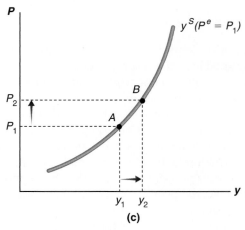

(c)

If workers have imperfect information about price changes that they receive with a lag, then the workers' price expectations may fail to reflect actual price movements. As a result, the position of the labor supply schedule does not adjust immediately to a change in the price level. An increase in the price level raises the value of labor's marginal product, $MP_N \times P$, thereby raising the demand for labor by firms and inducing a movement along the labor supply schedule from point A to point B in panel (a). As shown in panel (b), this causes an increase in the production of output. Hence, a rise in the price level will cause an increase in real output and a movement from point A to point B in panel (c). The aggregate supply schedule will slope upward.

we assume that if the current price level is equal to P_1, then the labor demand schedule is the value of labor's marginal product, $MP_N \times P_1$. If workers base their labor supply decisions on their anticipation of the overall price level, however, the position of the labor supply schedule depends on their price expectation. Let's suppose that the specific value of this price expectation is $P^e = P_1$, so that workers anticipate that the price level during their period of employment will be equal to P_1, and the position of the labor supply schedule is given by $N^s(P^e = P_1)$. Consequently, at point A in each panel of Figure 10–5, workers correctly anticipate the *actual* price level. Given this correct expectation, the equilibrium nominal wage in panel (a) is equal to W_1, and equilibrium employment is equal to N_1. The amount of real output produced is equal to y_1 in panel (b), and the resulting real output–price level combination is y_1 and P_1 in panel (c).

TRACING OUT AGGREGATE SUPPLY   Suppose however, that the price level rises to P_2, above the value P_1 that workers expected. Because information about this change is not readily available, workers do not immediately recognize that this price change has taken place. Thus, they maintain their price expectation at $P^e = P_1$, and the position of the labor supply schedule in panel (a) does not change. Firms, however, observe the rise in the prices of the goods and services that they sell and the resulting increase in the value of labor's marginal product, to $MP_N \times P_2$. As a result, labor demand rises, and the equilibrium nominal wage increases to W_2 at point B in panel (a).

Because workers do not have sufficient information to realize that the nominal wage has risen because of an increase in the price level, they perceive the increase in the nominal wage as an increase in the real wage. Workers therefore supply more labor services, as shown by the movement upward along the labor supply schedule to the new equilibrium employment level N_2 at point B. As panel (b) shows, this rise in employment then induces an increase in real output, from y_1 to y_2. As a result, there is a new real output–price level combination, y_2 and P_2 at point B in panel (c), that lies above and to the right of the original combination at point A. The schedule containing both point A and point B is the aggregate supply schedule. We label this schedule $y^s(P^e = P_1)$, because we have derived it given this specific value for workers' expected price level.

SHIFTING AGGREGATE SUPPLY   Now consider what would happen if workers were to raise their price expectation. This would shift the labor supply schedule back to the left somewhat. Then we could derive another aggregate supply schedule like the one in Figure 10–5, except that for any given price level we would plot lower employment and output levels. Consequently, the aggregate supply schedule that we would derive would lie to the left of the one in Figure 10–5. We can conclude that a rise in the expected price level will shift the aggregate supply schedule leftward. In other words, higher price expectations will reduce aggregate supply.

This Keynesian aggregate supply schedule, like the one we derived for the case of inflexible nominal wages, slopes upward and has a convex, or bowed, shape. In this case, however, the rationale for the slope and shape of the aggregate supply schedule is imperfect information. As you can see, removing *either* the classical assumption of pure, unhindered determination of market wages *or* the classical presumption that no basis exists for worker money illusion is sufficient to produce an upward-sloping aggregate supply schedule. We may conclude that in the Keynesian model there is a positive relationship between the price level and the amount of real output produced by firms.

> ### FUNDAMENTAL ISSUE #2
>
> **What factors determine the shape and position of the Keynesian aggregate supply schedule?**   There are two Keynesian theories of aggregate supply, and both imply that the aggregate supply schedule slopes upward and is convex. One proposes that nominal wages are inflexible. According to this theory, a rise in nominal wages following union demands for higher wages or increases in a legal wage minimum will shift the aggregate supply schedule upward and to the left. The other theory follows from the assumption that workers have imperfect information about the price level. This theory indicates that a rise in the expected price level will shift the aggregate supply schedule upward and to the left.

The Keynesian Market for Real Output

Let's summarize the traditional Keynesian theories of aggregate demand and aggregate supply. The Keynesian aggregate demand schedule is the set of all combinations of real income (output) that maintain *IS-LM* equilibrium or, in other words, in which aggregate desired expenditures equal real income and the quantity of real money balances demanded equals the quantity of real money balances supplied. The aggregate demand schedule slopes downward, and its position depends on the nominal money stock and on factors that influence aggregate autonomous expenditures, including fiscal policy instruments such as government spending and taxation.

The Keynesian aggregate supply schedule slopes upward, either because nominal wages are inflexible or because workers have imperfect information concerning the price level. For the remainder of this chapter, we shall simply draw the aggregate supply schedule as upward sloping (and convex) and offer a specific rationale for the upward slope only when doing so is required for the purposes of the specific issue under consideration.

Combining Aggregate Demand and Aggregate Supply

Figure 10–6 combines the two schedules on a single diagram of the market for real output. They intersect at point *E*, where the equilibrium price level, labeled P_1, is determined. Several conditions hold simultaneously at point *E*:

1. Because point *E* is on the aggregate demand schedule, the economy is operating on its *IS* schedule, and aggregate desired expenditures are equal to the level of real income y_1.

2. Because point *E* is on the aggregate demand schedule, the economy is operating on its *LM* schedule, and the quantity of real money bal-

Interactive Key Graph

The graph below shows how real output and the price level are determined in the Keynesian model. What happens if the money stock changes? What occurs if there is a change in the nominal wage rate? You can discover the answers to these questions by interacting with this graph on the Web.
Go to http://macroxtra.swcollege.com

Figure 10–6   Equilibrium in the Keynesian Market for Real Output

In the Keynesian model, the equilibrium price level and the equilibrium level of real output arise at the intersection of the aggregate demand and aggregate supply schedules. This point, denoted E, is on the aggregate demand schedule and corresponds to a point of *IS-LM* equilibrium. Therefore, the market for real money balances is in equilibrium, and real income is equal to aggregate desired expenditures. At the same time, this point is on the aggregate supply schedule, so at the price level P_1 corresponding to point E, workers and firms are willing and able to produce the equilibrium real output level.

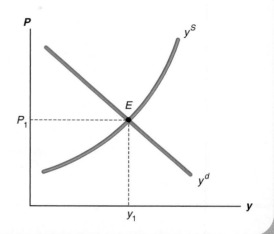

ances demanded at this real income level y_1 is equal to the real value of the quantity of money balances supplied, evaluated at the price level P_1.

3. Because point E is on the aggregate supply schedule, workers and firms are willing and able to produce the level of real output y_1 at the price level P_1.

Point E satisfies all of these conditions *given* the factors that determine the positions of the aggregate demand and aggregate supply schedules. Changes in aggregate desired expenditures or in the nominal money stock, which may be induced by fiscal and monetary policy actions, can change the positions of the schedules and thereby alter the location of point E.

Fiscal Policy, Prices, and Real Output

Recall that in the classical model of Chapters 3 and 4, fiscal policy actions leave both real output and the price level unaffected. The reason is that changes in government spending or taxes only cause redistributions of existing output. Hence, they are unable to affect the position of the classical aggregate demand schedule.

In contrast, fiscal policy actions typically influence equilibrium real output and prices in the traditional Keynesian model. To see why, consider Figure 10–7. In panel (b), the economy begins at point E at an equilibrium price level equal to P_1 and an equilibrium real output level y_1. Because point E in panel (b) is on the aggregate demand schedule, there is a corresponding IS-LM equilibrium at point E in panel (a). Suppose that government expenditures increase from an initial amount g_1 to g_2. This fiscal policy action will shift the IS schedule rightward from $IS(g_1)$ to $IS(g_2)$ in panel (a), causing real income to rise toward y_3 at point F. The aggregate demand schedule will shift rightward by the amount of this increase in real income on the IS-LM diagram, or the distance from point E to point F, in panel (b).

Following the rise in aggregate demand from $y^d(g_1)$ to $y^d(g_2)$, however, workers and firms will not produce all the output demanded by households, firms, and the government at the price level P_1. Workers and firms will be willing to increase production of real output only if the price level rises toward a new equilibrium value equal to P_2. Hence, there will be a movement upward along the aggregate supply schedule in panel (b), from point F to point E'. The rise in the price level will cause real money balances to decline, which will result in a leftward shift of the LM schedule in panel (a). This shift implies a movement upward along the new aggregate

Figure 10–7 The Price and Output Effects of a Rise in Government Expenditures

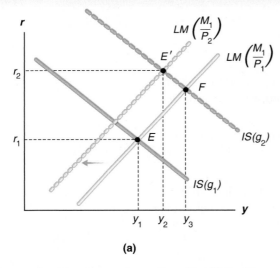

(a)

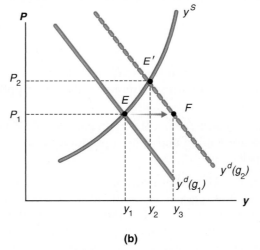

(b)

An increase in real government spending will shift the IS schedule rightward along the LM schedule, causing a movement from point E to point F in panel (a) and inducing a rightward shift of the aggregate demand schedule by the distance E–F in panel (b). Workers and firms will be willing to produce more real output, however, only if the price level increases as shown by the upward movement from point E to point E' along the aggregate supply schedule in panel (b). This increase in the price level will reduce the quantity of real money balances, thereby shifting the LM schedule leftward in panel (a). On net, the increase in real government expenditures leads to a rise in the equilibrium price level and an increase in the equilibrium level of real output.

demand schedule in panel (b), from point F to point E', to the final equilibrium real output level, y_2.

283

CHAPTER 10   Is There a Trade-off between Unemployment and Inflation?—The Keynesian and Monetarist Views on Price and Output Determination

The net effect, therefore, of an increase in real government expenditures is a rise in both the equilibrium real output and the equilibrium price level. (Recently, some economists have argued that ultimately the government's fiscal policy stance is the main determinant of the price level; see *Policy Notebook: The Fiscal Theory of the Price Level—A Deep Idea or a Crazy Notion?*) Note that a tax reduction will induce analogous effects. Indeed, any rise in net autonomous aggregate expenditures, such as a rise in autonomous investment, consumption, or exports, will induce a rise in equilibrium output and prices.

 **Policy** NOTEBOOK

The Fiscal Theory of the Price Level—A Deep Idea or a Crazy Notion?

The traditional Keynesian theory's implication that it is possible for fiscal policy actions to affect a nation's price level conflicts with the classical model's conclusion that monetary policy actions are the primary means by which government authorities can alter the price level. In recent years, however, some economists have proposed going a step further. In their view, fiscal policy, not monetary policy, is the predominant link between government policymaking and the price level.

A Central Bank Captive to the Whims of the Government

There are two versions of this perspective, which is known as the *fiscal theory of the price level.* One holds that even though changes in the quantity of money ultimately are the main factors affecting the price level, monetary policy is essentially a "slave" to fiscal policy. This argument is based on the current *government budget constraint,* which states that all government spending not funded by taxes must be funded either by issuing bonds or by creating money.

If the government refuses to alter its spending, taxation, and bond issuance policies, proponents of this perspective contend, a central bank has no choice but to create sufficient new quantities of money to support the government's fiscal policies, with associated inflationary consequences. In this way, the government's fiscal policy stance is responsible for the price level, albeit indirectly.

The Case of an Irrelevant Central Bank

Another version of the fiscal theory of the price level goes even further in claiming predominance for fiscal policy in determining the price level. This stronger version of the theory focuses on the government's long-term budget constraint, which indicates that eventually the government must be able to pay off all its debts if it wishes people to hold its bonds today.

Proponents of this theory argue that the current price level must adjust until the real value of the government's current debt is consistent with the public's anticipations of current and future flows of government spending and taxes, *given* the quantity of money in circulation. Thus, according to this theory, a multiplicity of possible price levels may exist given the current money stock. Fiscal policies that establish the total volume of government debt outstanding, not monetary policies that affect the quantity of money, ultimately determine the price level.

Most economists see the potential for merit in the first version of the fiscal theory of the price level, which appears to describe the experiences of many nations that have subjugated their central banks to the whims of government fiscal authorities. So far, however, only a few are convinced that the stronger form of the theory has any real-world relevance. Most economists remain convinced that the quantity of money in circulation plays a key role in determining any nation's price level.

For Critical Analysis
In the quantity equation, $M \times V \equiv P \times y$, what variable must adjust to cause the price level to change if the stronger form of the fiscal theory of the price level is correct?

In the classical model discussed in Chapters 3 and 4, monetary policy actions are able to influence aggregate demand, but because the aggregate supply schedule is vertical, money stock changes have no effect on equilibrium real output. As a result, in the classical macroeconomic model, money is said to be neutral.

Money is nonneutral in the traditional Keynesian macroeconomic framework. To understand why this is so, consider Figure 10–8. At an initial output-market equilibrium at point E in panel (b), with the nominal stock M_1, the aggregate demand schedule is given by $y^d(M_1)$, and the equilibrium price level and quantity of real output are equal to P_1 and y_1, respectively. This output-market equilibrium point must correspond to point E on the IS-LM diagram in panel (a). Suppose now that the central bank raises the nominal money stock from M_1 to M_2. This action will cause the LM schedule to shift to the right in panel (a), from $LM(M_1/P_1)$ to $LM(M_2/P_1)$, resulting in a new IS-LM equilibrium at point F, at the higher

Figure 10–8   The Price and Output Effects of a Rise in the Money Stock

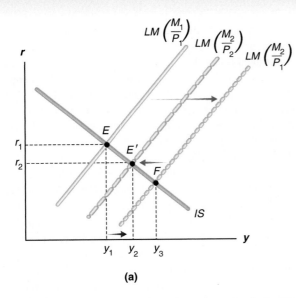

(a)

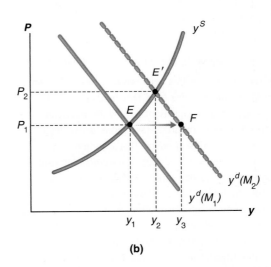

(b)

An increase in the nominal quantity of money in circulation will shift the LM schedule downward and to the right, thereby causing a movement from point E to point F in panel (a) and inducing a rightward shift of the aggregate demand schedule by the distance E–F in panel (b). Nevertheless, workers and firms will be willing to produce more real output only if the price level increases, as shown by the upward movement from point E to point E' along the aggregate supply schedule in panel (b). This increase in the price level will reduce the quantity of real money balances, thereby shifting the LM schedule back up and to the left in panel (a). On net, the increase in the money stock leads to a rise in the equilibrium price level and an increase in the equilibrium level of real output.

real income level y_3. The aggregate demand schedule in panel (b) will shift rightward by the same amount, the distance from point E to point F.

After the rightward shift in aggregate demand from $y^d(M_1)$ to $y^d(M_2)$, workers and firms continue to produce only the real output level y_1 at the price level P_1 in panel (b). Firms will increase their production only if the price level increases to the new equilibrium level, P_2. This increase will induce a movement upward along the aggregate supply schedule in panel (b), from point F to point E'. The rise in the price level will cause a decline in the amount of real money balances, so the LM schedule will shift back to the left, from $LM(M_2/P_1)$ to $LM(M_2/P_2)$ in panel (a). This will cause a movement back along the new aggregate demand schedule in panel (b), from point F to point E', and a fall in the quantity of real output demanded, to y_2.

On net, therefore, a central bank expansion of the nominal money stock increases both the equilibrium price level *and* equilibrium real output. Because monetary policy is nonneutral in the traditional Keynesian model, proponents of this model typically prescribe expansionary or contractionary monetary policy actions to stabilize real economic activity. The notion that the Federal Reserve and other central banks can stabilize real output—and, by implication, employment—contrasts sharply with the classical position, which contends that price-level stabilization is all that monetary policy can accomplish. (In recent years, critics of the Bank of Japan have argued that it has not done enough to try to boost the Japanese economy by stimulating aggregate demand; see on the following page *Global Notebook: The Effects of Monetary Policy on Aggregate Demand—Trying to Have It Both Ways at the Bank of Japan.*)

FUNDAMENTAL ISSUE #3

According to traditional Keynesian theory, what are the price and output effects of expansionary fiscal and monetary policies?   In the Keynesian aggregate demand–aggregate supply model, a rise in government expenditures, a tax cut, or an increase in the nominal money stock will cause an increase in aggregate demand. The result will be a rise in the equilibrium price level and an increase in equilibrium real output.

The Phillips Curve

Speculation about Federal Reserve actions to "spur employment" or "slow the pace of economic growth" appears every week or two in such financial news publications as the *Wall Street Journal*. Many media commentators also discuss the pros and cons of using monetary and fiscal policy actions to reduce the unemployment rate. Periodically, politicians debate the merits of policy proposals aimed at such goals.

The prevalence of these discussions indicates how widely the Keynesian model has influenced thinking about macroeconomic policy. These discussions are consistent with traditional Keynesian theory, which predicts an

The Effects of Monetary Policy on Aggregate Demand— Trying to Have It Both Ways at the Bank of Japan

Since the mid-1990s, the Japanese economy has experienced simultaneous declines in the price level and real output, which the traditional Keynesian theory indicates are associated with a fall in aggregate demand. Recently, the *Diet,* Japan's parliament, decided that it was time for the Bank of Japan to make serious efforts to halt deflation. To try to force the hand of the central bank's policymakers, leaders of the ruling political party in the Diet proposed a law requiring the Bank of Japan to aim for a target of positive inflation.

Officials at the Bank of Japan offered two criticisms of the proposed restriction on its activities. First, they pointed out that the central bank had already pushed up money growth to annual rates as high as 10 percent, yet prices of goods and services in Japan continued to fall. This experience, they argued, revealed that the Bank of Japan faced significant impediments to its ability to raise aggregate demand by boosting the monetary base and thereby bringing about increases in the price level and national output.

In addition, however, the officials contended that any faster growth of the monetary base would be "dangerous."

What was the alleged danger? Speeding the growth of the monetary base could, they warned, pose serious inflation risks for the Japanese economy.

Members of the Japanese Diet, as well as economists around the world, were left scratching their heads. The essence of the central bank officials' argument, after all, was that they had only a meager ability to generate increases in aggregate demand, yet felt that if they were to make the attempt, aggregate demand could rise so rapidly and so dramatically that dangerously high inflation might result. Officials at the Bank of Japan could not really have it both ways, but this did not stop them from making an inconsistent argument that a U.S. economist was quick to point out would have earned them zero credit in a macroeconomics course.

For Critical Analysis
If boosting the growth of the monetary base caused aggregate demand to expand sufficiently to raise the price level beyond some desired level, what could a central bank such as the Bank of Japan do to push inflation back down again?

---

inverse relationship between the inflation rate, which Federal Reserve policies can influence, and the unemployment rate. This proposed inverse relationship is widely known as the *Phillips curve,* and it has been a controversial topic in modern macroeconomics.

The Origins of the Phillips Curve

The Phillips curve is named for its discoverer, A. W. Phillips, who conducted a study of British data. He found strong evidence for an inverse relationship between nominal wages and unemployment rates. Other economists then noticed that nominal wages typically moved in the same direction as the inflation rate. This led to the idea of plotting the inflation rate and the unemployment rate on the same diagram. The result was the modern **Phillips curve,** which is a plot of the relationship between unemployment and inflation rates for a given period.

Figure 10–9 displays unemployment rate–inflation rate combinations for the United States from 1961 to 1969. As you can see, during that interval there was a strikingly smooth, inverse relationship between the two

PHILLIPS CURVE: A curve that shows an inverse relationship between inflation and unemployment rates.

Figure 10–9   Inflation and Unemployment Rates in the United States, 1961–1969

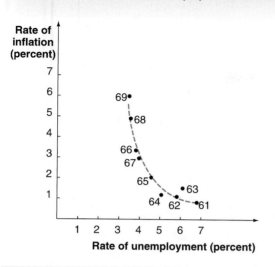

During the 1960s, there was a smooth, downward-sloping Phillips curve relating the rate of inflation inversely to the rate of unemployment.

SOURCE: *Economic Report of the President*, 2002.

macroeconomic variables. Higher inflation rates were associated with lower rates of unemployment.

The Keynesian Model and the Phillips Curve

The discovery of the Phillips curve appeared to support the Keynesian theory of aggregate supply. To see why this is so, consider Figure 10–10 on the next page. Panel (a) displays a Keynesian aggregate supply schedule together with four possible positions of the aggregate demand schedule and, hence, four possible points of aggregate output–market equilibrium. Panel (b) shows the aggregate production function. Panel (c) depicts a diagram in which the inflation rate, π, is measured on the vertical axis and the unemployment rate, u, is measured on the horizontal axis.

DERIVING THE PHILLIPS CURVE   Now consider two extreme cases: a sharp, aggregate demand–induced recession versus a significant aggregate demand–induced economic expansion. Let's contemplate the recession first. This situation results from relatively low levels of aggregate demand, as illustrated by the positions y_1^d and y_2^d on the aggregate demand schedule in panel (a), which lead to relatively low equilibrium output levels y_1 and y_2, respectively, at points A and A'. Note that a movement from point A to point A' causes a relatively small increase in the price level, from P_1 to P_2. Because the rate of inflation is the proportionate change in the level of prices per unit of time, or $\pi = (\Delta P/P)/(\Delta \text{time})$, such a rise in aggregate demand yields a relatively low inflation rate, denoted π_A in panel (c). In addition, in panel (b) output levels at points A and A' are low relative to the scale on the horizontal axis. As panel (b) indicates, at these low levels of output, employment is also low. This, in turn, implies that the average

Figure 10-10   The Theoretical Basis for the Phillips Curve

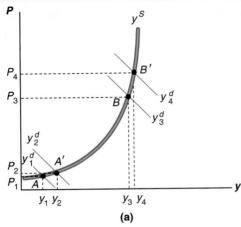

(a)

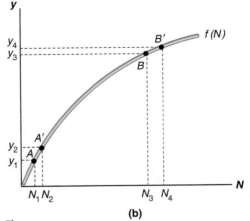

(b)

Comparing the movement from point B to point B' in panel (a) and the movement from point A to point A' shows that a given shift in the aggregate demand schedule causes a larger proportionate increase in the price level for high levels of real output as compared with low levels of output. Therefore, the inflation rate is greater at higher output levels. At the same time, as panel (b) indicates, employment is lower at smaller output levels, implying higher measured unemployment rates at lower levels of real output. As a result, the Keynesian theory of aggregate supply yields an inverse relationship between the inflation rate and the unemployment rate, or a Phillips curve, as shown in panel (c).

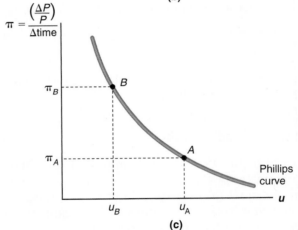

(c)

of the unemployment rates at points A and A', denoted u_A, is high. The result of this comparison of points A and A' in panels (a) and (b), therefore, is the unemployment rate–inflation rate combination u_A and π_A at point A in panel (c).

Now let's consider the second situation in which real output is in an expansion phase of the business cycle. Then positions such as y_3^d and y_4^d on the aggregate demand schedule are applicable, and equilibrium real output levels at points B and B' are high relative to the scale on the horizontal axis in panel (a). An increase in aggregate demand illustrated by these two aggregate demand schedules leads to a larger proportionate increase in the price level as a result of the absolute rise in the price level, from P_3 to P_4. Hence, there is a relatively high inflation rate, denoted π_B, entailed in the movement from point B to point B'. The reason is that at high levels of aggregate demand, equilibrium occurs along the steepest portion of the aggregate supply schedule, where the law of diminishing returns yields the smallest effects on the quantity of real output following a rise in the price level. As shown in panel (b), at points B and B', workers and firms are producing output along the shallower portion of the aggregate production function. Along this portion of the production function, employment is high. Therefore, the average of the unemployment rates at points B and B', denoted u_B, is low. This new unemployment rate–inflation rate combination that we have deduced is point B in panel (c).

Points A and B in panel (c) of Figure 10–10 are two points along a Phillips curve. This Phillips curve is convex, or bowed inward, because of the law of diminishing marginal returns. Theoretically, a given increase in the inflation rate tends to push unemployment down by a larger amount when unemployment is high than when unemployment is low. In addition, our derivation of the Phillips curve has intentionally been simplified, in that we have looked only at one-time changes in the price level instead of more realistically considering continuous variations. Nevertheless, the important point that stems from Figure 10–10 is that the Phillips curve slopes downward. The Keynesian theory of aggregate supply yields the trade-off between the inflation rate and the unemployment rate that U.S. data from the 1960s fit so well. Even though we have varied the positions of the aggregate demand schedule to trace out the Phillips curve in Figure 10–10, the key point is that it is the upward-sloping, convex aggregate supply schedule that implies the Phillips curve relationship. Thus, we may conclude that:

> **An essential implication of the Keynesian theory of aggregate supply is the existence of a trade-off between the inflation rate and the unemployment rate. The Keynesian model predicts that a rise in the rate of inflation should lead to a decline in the rate of unemployment.**

THE PHILLIPS CURVE AND THE BENEFITS AND COSTS OF INFLATION   As we noted earlier, the Phillips curve has been a controversial idea in macroeconomics. It has engendered debate for two reasons. One reason, as we will see in the next section, is that many economists have doubts about the validity of the concept. The other reason involves the effects that would follow from the application of the concept, assuming that it is valid. Assuming for this discussion that the Phillips curve concept is correct, then we could reduce unemployment by creating inflation and being willing to live with any costs due to the inflation. Indeed, people who particularly abhor unemployment regard the Phillips curve trade-off as beneficial: Sufficiently high inflation could, in principle, nearly eradicate unemployment.

Those who strongly dislike unemployment would be more willing to accept inflation-related costs than those who would bear them most heavily, however. Table 10–1 (p. 290) summarizes the costs of inflation and inflation variability. As it indicates, all members of society bear these costs to some extent, but some are hurt more than others. Those who are hurt most include owners of businesses that lose out on profit opportunities and must incur costs of changing prices, savers and financial institutions that are creditors, and those who pay taxes that are not indexed to inflation. U.S. income tax brackets have been indexed to inflation since the 1980s, but in many countries

On the Web

Have you ever wanted to try your hand at being a macroeconomic policymaker? If so, visit the Biz/ed/Institute for Fiscal Studies at http://www.bized.ac.uk, where you can try your hand at policymaking in a "virtual economy" model of the United Kingdom (http://www.bized.ac.uk/virtual/economy/policy). To contemplate implications of your policy decisions within the context of the Phillips curve, click on "Outcomes," and then "Unemployment."

Table 10-1   The Costs of Inflation and Inflation Variability

Type of Cost	Cause
Resources expended to economize on money holdings (more trips to banks, etc.)	Rising prices associated with inflation
Costs of changing price lists and printing menus and catalogues	Individual product/service price increases associated with inflation
Redistribution of real incomes from individuals to the government	Inflation that pushes people into higher, nonindexed nominal tax brackets
Reductions in investment, capital accumulation, and economic growth	Inflation variability that complicates business planning
Slowed pace of introduction of new and better products	Volatile price changes that reduce the efficiency of private markets
Redistribution of resources from creditors to debtors	Unexpected inflation that reduces the real values of debts

individuals can be subject to higher tax rates simply because inflation has pushed their nominal incomes into income ranges subject to higher rates.

Consequently, if the Phillips curve idea is "true," then it creates scope for sharp divisions in society. Some groups will be more likely to prefer inflationary policies, while others will be more likely to oppose such policies. Indeed, as we shall discuss shortly, the Phillips curve provides a potential basis for a political theory of business cycles.

> ### FUNDAMENTAL ISSUE #4
>
> **What is the Phillips curve?**   The Phillips curve is an inverse relationship between the unemployment rate and the inflation rate predicted by the Keynesian theory of aggregate supply. The existence of such a trade-off between unemployment and inflation would imply that society must make a choice between low inflation and low unemployment.

The Long-Run Phillips Curve and Political Business Cycles

As we noted, the other reason that the Phillips curve has proved to be so controversial is that a number of economists believe that it is, at best, a very tenuous relationship. While not discounting its existence during the 1960s, they have pointed to evidence of its breakdown in years afterward, and they have questioned its usefulness over any long-run period. This challenge to the long-term relevance of the Phillips curve has been led by a group of economists known as *monetarists*.

MONETARISTS: Economists who believe that the main factor influencing aggregate demand is the nominal money stock and that there is not a long-run trade-off between inflation and unemployment.

The Monetarist Challenge to the Unemployment-Inflation Trade-off

The **monetarists** are so named because their original contribution to macroeconomics was their focus on the role of money as the primary determinant of aggregate demand. This group of economists, which was led by

Milton Friedman, the late Karl Brunner, and Allan Meltzer, reemphasized the classical view that monetary stability was the key to price stability.

The monetarists' overarching contribution, however, has been on the subject of the Phillips curve. Beginning in the late 1960s, they challenged the then-prevailing view that the Phillips curve was a stable relationship that policymakers could exploit to reduce unemployment at the cost of higher inflation. In the long run, the monetarists contended, such policies would succeed only in raising inflation, while having little measurable impact on the unemployment rate.

During the 1960s, few economists were receptive to this argument. After all, as Figure 10–9 on page 287 indicates, Keynesian theory seemed to explain the data very well. Beginning in the 1970s, however, more economists began to pay attention to the monetarists. In 1969, Milton Friedman predicted that the smooth unemployment-inflation trade-off summarized in Figure 10–9 could not last very long. As Figure 10–11 shows, the experience of the following decades verified this prediction: There was no smooth Phillips curve from the 1970s through the early 1990s.

THE LONG RUN AND THE NATURAL RATE OF UNEMPLOYMENT What reasoning led the monetarists to forecast that the Phillips curve trade-off would break down? Their argument has its roots in the Keynesian imperfect-information theory of the upward-sloping aggregate supply schedule. According to the monetarists, this theory applies only to the **short run,** or a period short enough that information is imperfect and expectations of inflation do not necessarily match actual inflation. In the long run, they contend, the aggregate supply schedule is vertical, as in the classical model.

The key to the monetarists' argument is their definition of the *long run.* Monetarists define the **long run** as a period sufficiently lengthy that workers can compile enough information about developments in the economy that their inflation expectations correctly match true inflation rates. In the long run, therefore, workers are fully informed, as the classical model assumes. Unlike the classical theorists, however, the monetarists do not contend that the economy is always in this long-run position. Instead, they

To read an evaluation of the monetarist position that the quantity of money in circulation is the main determinant of the price level, go to the Chapter 10 reading, entitled "What Remains of Monetarism?" by R. W. Hafer, published by, the Federal Reserve Bank of Atlanta.
http://macroxtra.swcollege.com

SHORT RUN: According to the monetarists, an interval short enough that workers do not have complete information about aggregate prices and inflation; therefore, expected prices and inflation may differ from actual prices and inflation.

LONG RUN: According to the monetarists, an interval long enough that workers can compile full information about aggregate prices and inflation; therefore, expected prices and inflation are equal to actual prices and inflation.

291

CHAPTER 10 Is There a Trade-off between Unemployment and Inflation?—The Keynesian and Monetarist Views on Price and Output Determination

Figure 10–11   Inflation and Unemployment Rates in the United States, 1971–1991

From the 1970s through the early 1980s, there was no apparent Phillips curve relationship. The basic Keynesian model was unable to explain this breakdown in the predicted inverse relationship between the inflation rate and the unemployment rate.

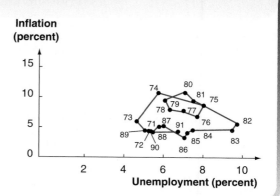

SOURCE: *Economic Report of the President,* 2002.

argue that it naturally tends toward that state over the passage of several years.

This reasoning leads to the logical conclusion that in the long run, when full information is available, expected inflation equals actual inflation, and the classical presumption of a vertical aggregate supply schedule will actually hold. Price-level changes then will not affect real output, because they will not influence equilibrium employment. As a result, changes in the inflation rate will not affect the unemployment rate. Therefore, as discussed in Chapter 6, in the long run the economy will tend toward a *natural rate of unemployment,* or the rate of unemployment that arises under full information when the economy is on its long-run growth path (see Chapter 5's discussion of economic growth). The natural unemployment rate stems from structural and frictional unemployment, as discussed in Chapter 6.

GETTING FROM THE SHORT RUN TO THE LONG RUN   This is not to say that the monetarists entirely rule out the existence of a trade-off between unemployment and inflation. Monetarists agree with Keynesian theorists that cyclical variations in the unemployment rate do occur. They also do not argue with the evidence that during some short-run periods these cyclical components of unemployment may be inversely related to the inflation rate.

Indeed, the monetarists have no quarrel with the traditional Keynesian theory's assumption that workers can have incomplete information about prices and inflation. Their point is that incomplete information is a short-run phenomenon. In the long run, people are more nearly fully informed, and so the Keynesian theory of aggregate supply is not as useful over the long term.

Figure 10–12 summarizes the monetarist perspective. Panel (a) is an aggregate demand–aggregate supply diagram relating the price level and real output, while panel (b) is a Phillips curve diagram relating the inflation rate and the unemployment rate. Panel (a) depicts two aggregate supply schedules. One, which corresponds to the Keynesian aggregate supply schedule, is the *short-run aggregate supply schedule* implied by the monetarists' reasoning. Along this short-run aggregate supply schedule, workers have imperfect information, so they form an expectation of the price level, such as $P^e = P_1$, that varies in the face of actual price changes that are unknown to the workers in the short run. As a result, if the actual price level rises from P_1 to P_2 in the short run, real output will increase from y_1 toward y_2 at point B. Alternatively, if the actual price level declines from P_1 to P_3 in the short run, real output will fall from y_1 toward y_3 at point D.

In the long run, however, workers become fully informed, so their expectation of the price level is always equal to the actual price level, and the *long-run aggregate supply schedule* is the vertical schedule of the classical model. In the long run, therefore, changes in the price level leave real output unaffected. A rise in the price level ultimately will cause a movement from point A to point C in the long run. A fall in the price level eventually will cause a movement from point A to point E in the long run.

SHORT-RUN AND LONG-RUN PHILLIPS CURVES   Likewise, panel (b) displays two Phillips curves. One, the downward-sloping Phillips curve, is derived from

Figure 10–12 Aggregate Supply and the Phillips Curve in the Short Run and the Long Run

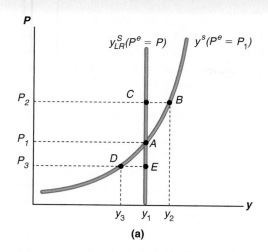

(a)

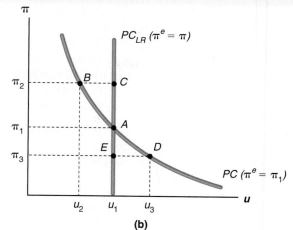

(b)

In the short run, which is a period sufficiently short that price and inflation expectations do not adjust in the face of actual inflation, the level of real output can vary as the actual price level changes, as shown by movements along the aggregate supply schedule between points B and D in panel (a). Likewise, variations in the actual inflation rate can result in changes in the unemployment rate, as shown by movements between points B and D in panel (b). In the long run, however, price and inflation expectations can fully adjust, so as the price level varies between points C and E in panel (a) there are no changes in real output, and the long-run aggregate supply schedule is vertical, and the long-run Phillips curve in panel (b) also is vertical.

the upward-sloping short-run aggregate supply curve (see Figure 10–10 on page 288). A price-level increase will raise the inflation rate, causing a short-run decline in the unemployment rate along the downward-sloping *short-run Phillips curve (PC),* from point A to point B. Because workers' price expectations cannot adjust in the short run, they have a temporarily fixed *inflation expectation,* denoted $\pi^e = \pi_1$. As a result, in the short run a rise in the inflation rate, from π_1 to π_2 in panel (b), can induce workers to supply more labor to firms, and the unemployment rate will fall. In contrast, a decline in the inflation rate from π_1 to π_3 can cause workers to reduce the quantity of labor services that they supply, and the unemployment rate can rise in response, as shown by the movement from point A to point D.

The *long-run Phillips curve (PC$_{LR}$),* however, is vertical, because the long-run aggregate supply schedule is vertical. In the long run, workers are fully informed, so their inflation expectation π^e is equal to actual inflation. Hence, a rise in the inflation rate ultimately leaves the unemployment rate unaffected, as shown by the movement along the long-run Phillips curve from point A to point C. Furthermore, a fall in the inflation rate ultimately has no long-term impact on the unemployment rate, as shown by the movement from point A to point E. The unemployment rate u_1 therefore will be the economy's natural rate of unemployment.

Political Business Cycles and Alternative Theories of Stagflation

The monetarists essentially proposed a link between the traditional Keynesian theory's short-run emphasis and the classical model's long-run aspects. The link is based on price and inflation expectations, which are ill-informed in the short run but based on full information in the long run. This combination of the two theoretical approaches to macroeconomics provides the foundation for what is known as the theory of *political business cycles*. It also forms the basis for alternative theories of *stagflation,* or the simultaneous occurrence of high inflation and unemployment rates.

THE POLITICAL BUSINESS CYCLE   How might political factors influence the business cycle? It is a short step from Figure 10–12 to an answer to this question. To see why, consider Figure 10–13. Suppose that, as shown in panel (a), the natural rate of unemployment is equal to u_N, which gives the position for the vertical, long-run Phillips curve. In addition, suppose that the current inflation rate is equal to π_1. Finally, suppose that this is also the inflation rate that people anticipate, so that the short-run Phillips curve crosses point A, which illustrates the current unemployment rate–inflation rate combination.

Figure 10–13   Political Business Cycles

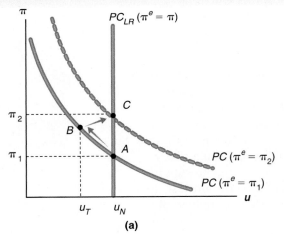

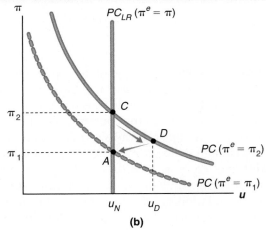

Suppose that a policymaker tries to reduce the unemployment rate toward a target level, u_T, in an effort to pursue short-term political gains by taking advantage of a short-run trade-off between inflation and unemployment. Panel (a) shows that increasing the inflation rate toward point B along the short-run Phillips curve might reduce the unemployment rate somewhat in the short run, but in the long run a rightward shift in the Phillips curve caused by

increased inflation expectations would lead to an increase in the unemployment rate back toward the natural rate at point C. Then, as panel (b) indicates, reducing the inflation rate would require a short-run rise in the unemployment rate at point D, until a decline in inflation expectations would induce a leftward shift of the Phillips curve and a fall in the unemployment rate toward point A.

Attempting to Push Down the Unemployment Rate   Imagine now that a political party campaigns on the platform of reducing unemployment to a target unemployment rate, u_T, that is below the natural rate of unemployment. After winning sufficient offices, the party embarks on monetary and fiscal policies that expand aggregate demand and push up the price level. The result is a rise in the inflation rate. In the short run, this can achieve the unemployment rate target u_T by moving the economy back along the short-run Phillips curve *toward* point B. The decline in the unemployment rate occurs because workers temporarily fail to recognize the rise in inflation that erodes the real value of their wages. As a result, they supply more labor services to firms, and unemployment declines.

According to the monetarist theory, however, workers will eventually begin to recognize that the inflation rate has increased. As their inflation expectations rise, the short-run Phillips curve *shifts* upward and to the right. After sufficient time has passed for workers to become fully informed, the short-run and long-run Phillips curves cross at a new point, at point C. As the short-run Phillips curve shifts, the unemployment rate begins to rise once again. Ultimately, the economy reaches point C at the natural rate of unemployment u_N, but at a higher inflation rate π_2 that is fully anticipated by workers.

Attempting to Reduce the Inflation Rate   At this point, another political party argues that inflation is the economy's number-one problem and promises that, if elected, it will enact a program to cut the inflation rate. After winning the next election, this new party in power embarks on its program. The effects that the political business cycle theory predicts are illustrated in panel (b) of Figure 10–13. Now that the economy is at the unemployment rate–inflation rate combination at point C, the new party in power must engage in monetary and fiscal policies that reduce aggregate demand and depress price increases. These policies reduce the inflation rate from π_2 to, say, π_1 once again. In the near term, however, this will require a movement downward and to the right along the short-run Phillips curve, to point D. As a result, the unemployment rate will rise above the natural rate of unemployment, *toward* u_D. The unemployment rate will fall back toward the natural rate only after sufficient time has passed for workers to recognize the lower inflation in the economy. As their inflation expectations decline from $\pi^e = \pi_2$ to $\pi^e = \pi_1$, the short-run Phillips curve will shift back down and to the left, and the unemployment rate once again will return to its natural level, at point A.

A prediction of the political business cycle theory, therefore, is that a democratic society can easily fall into a cyclical pattern of seeking lower unemployment in the short run, only to find that the cost is higher inflation. Efforts to reduce inflation will follow, but at the short-run cost of higher unemployment rates. The inflation and unemployment experience of the United States between 1971 and 1991 in Figure 10–11 on page 291 appears to fit the theory's prediction. After two decades of higher inflation accompanied by short-run declines, increases, and then declines in the unemployment rate, the United States in 1991 was not too far from the point from which it might have embarked on a quest for lower unemployment in 1971.

macro**xtra!**
Economic
Applications

How much has the U.S. consumer price index increased lately? Find out via EconData Online.
http://macroxtra.swcollege.com

STAGFLATION: The simultaneous observation of rising inflation rates and declining real output and rising unemployment rates.

SUPPLY SHOCKS: Changes in the position of the aggregate supply schedule caused by significant changes in the costs of factors of production or in technological capabilities.

EXPLAINING STAGFLATION   Embedded in the political business cycle theory is one possible explanation for **stagflation,** a rather awkward but nevertheless descriptive term for the occurrence of high inflation at the same time that real output is declining and the unemployment rate is rising. As panel (a) of Figure 10–13 shows, the theory indicates that stagflation typically will occur as inflation expectations increase following a politically motivated attempt by policymakers to reduce the unemployment rate below its natural rate.

Stagflation can also occur for another reason that does not rely so much on cynical views about the motives of politicians. If you look at the unemployment rate–inflation rate combinations that occurred in the 1970s and 1980s in Figure 10–11 on page 291, you will notice that one can trace out three distinct periods: the first three years of the 1970s, the period 1974–1978, and the period 1979–1983. In each interval the short-run Phillips curve apparently shifted to the right. If the monetarist-based political business cycle theory were the only explanation available to us, we would have to conclude that inflation expectations appear to have increased three times in succession after the 1960s to yield these three separate short-run Phillips curves.

In fact, however, other events transpired during the 1970s. These were **supply shocks,** which are changes in the position of the aggregate supply schedule caused by significant changes in the costs of factors of production or in technological capabilities. The supply shocks of the 1970s largely stemmed from large increases in oil prices brought about first by an Arab oil embargo and then by the coordinated actions of the broader group of OPEC nations in the later 1970s. Both of these supply shocks undoubtedly account for the multiple shifts of the Phillips curve that took place in the 1970s. To the extent that the political business cycle theory may account for the U.S. experience in the 1970s and 1980s, therefore, higher inflation expectations and supply shocks *together* will have accounted for the periods of stagflation that took place during these years.

FUNDAMENTAL ISSUE #5

How does monetarism differ from the traditional Keynesian theory?   The monetarists have argued that the nominal money stock is the main determinant of aggregate demand. Furthermore, they have proposed a blend of the Keynesian and classical theories of aggregate supply, in which the short-run imperfection of information makes the aggregate supply schedule slope upward in the short run but the availability of full information in the long run produces a vertical aggregate supply schedule. According to the monetarist view, the Phillips curve slopes downward in the short run. In the long run, however, it is vertical at the natural rate of unemployment. This provides a basis for the political business cycle model of how political pressures to reduce unemployment can lead to higher inflation and inflation expectations, thereby leading to lower unemployment initially but higher unemployment later on. It also explains how higher inflation expectations and supply shocks together can cause the short-run Phillips curve to shift upward, so that both higher inflation and higher unemployment—stagflation—can result.

Panel (a) of Figure 10–14 plots inflation and unemployment rate combinations since 1985. A quick look at the panel shows a "cluster" of points that appear to indicate a return to a generally downward-sloping relationship between inflation rates and unemployment rates. This might be taken as evidence that reductions in unemployment can be achieved at the cost of slight increases in inflation. Indeed, one can still find major political figures arguing that the U.S. government should embark on new policies to take advantage of the trade-off.

A closer look at panel (a) of Figure 10–14, however, makes clear that the cluster of points derives its apparent downward slope from inflation-unemployment combinations from the 1980s. As you can see in panel (b), if we consider only the period since 1991, the relationship between inflation and unemployment rates has been, if anything, a shallow, *upward-sloping* relationship. From the 1990s up to the recession in 2001, lower inflation accompanied gradual reductions in the U.S. unemployment rate.

GOOD NEWS AND BAD NEWS   This sudden change in the behavior of inflation and unemployment sparked considerable optimism. Many commentators argued that the Internet and other information technologies had transformed the economic landscape. These and other newfound sources of

Figure 10–14   U.S. Inflation and Unemployment Rates since 1985

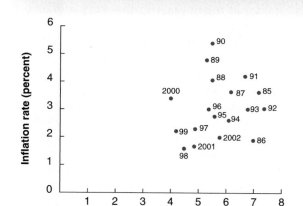

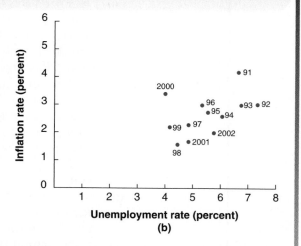

(a)

(b)

Panel (a) shows that a plot of U.S. inflation and unemployment rates since the mid-1980s appears to reveal a generally downward-sloping relationship between the inflation rate and the unemployment rate. As panel (b) indicates, however, when only the 1990s and the early 2000s are considered, in an apparent contradiction to the standard theory of the short-run Phillips curve, there was an *upward-sloping relationship* between inflation and unemployment rates in the United States.

SOURCES: *Economic Report of the President*, 2002; *Economic Indicators* (various issues).

economic growth, they claimed, had become self-perpetuating. The United States had crossed into the territory of a "new economy," and eventually inflation would become a distant memory.

For the Federal Reserve, however, the inverted slope of the Phillips curve posed problems. Fed economists' forecasts of future inflation traditionally have been based on Phillips curve models of the inflation process. Starting in the 1990s, the Fed's inflation-forecasting equations indicated that inflation was "too low" relative to actual unemployment rates. Or, from an alternative perspective, unemployment was "too low" relative to observed rates of inflation. The Fed's forecasting models consistently indicated that the natural rate of unemployment was at least 6 percent, but, as panel (b) of Figure 10–14 indicates, until the economic downturn in 2001, the unemployment rate was consistently 1 to 2 percentage points below this level. Throughout the 1990s and early 2000s, then, the Federal Reserve was in the uncomfortable position of working with models that yielded estimates of the natural rate of unemployment that the nation would actually reach only in periods of recession.

EXPLAINING THE RECENT BEHAVIOR OF INFLATION AND UNEMPLOYMENT Economists have struggled to explain the shifting inflation-unemployment relationship. Here, we consider two possible explanations, neither of which by itself can fully explain the changed relationship. One emphasizes changes in the competitive landscape of the U.S. economy. The other focuses on changes in the age distribution of the U.S. population.

Increased Competition Beginning in the late 1970s, the U.S. government launched a major effort to deregulate many major industries that previously had been subject to a number of restrictions on the entry and exit of firms and to regulation on prices or quantities. As deregulation continued into the 1980s and 1990s, many barriers to international trade also fell by the wayside. Furthermore, Internet commerce grew dramatically in the 1990s and 2000s. Together, these changes led to a significant increase in the overall extent of competition in U.S. industries.

This opened up the range of product choice for U.S. consumers. As a result, firms in most industries found that the demand for their products was more price-sensitive than it had been before. This left firms with less scope for price changes, which automatically tended to restrain price increases in the face of rising demand. At any given unemployment rate, therefore, increased competition across the economy tends to restrain inflation even as the unemployment rate falls. Thus, greater economy-wide competition should make the short-run Phillips curve *more shallow*.

In addition, greater competition for goods and services theoretically can reduce the natural rate of unemployment. To the extent that any markets for goods and services previously were less than fully competitive, firms in such markets would have used their monopoly power to restrain their output. Hence, they hired fewer workers than they would have otherwise. As competition increases, therefore, basic economic theory implies that employment should tend to rise. Consequently, the natural unemployment rate should decline.

Panel (a) of Figure 10–15 displays estimates of an index measure of the overall degree of competition in the United States. As these estimates indi-

Figure 10–15 Increased U.S. Product Market Competition and Implications for Short- and Long-Run Phillips Curves

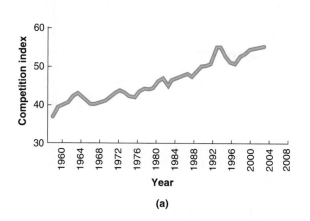

(a)

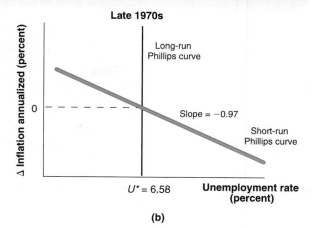

(b)

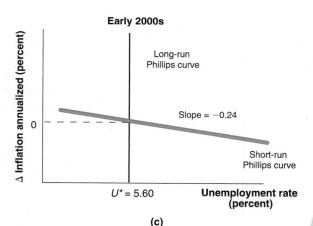

(c)

Panel (a) shows that an index of aggregate competition in U.S. markets for goods and services has increased since the early 1970s. Panels (b) and (c) provide estimates of the position of the short- and long-run Phillips curves in the late 1970s and early 2000s. They indicate that the short-run Phillips curve became more shallow and the long-run Phillips curve shifted leftward. One possible factor accounting for these changes was greater competition in U.S. markets for goods and services.

SOURCES: John Duca and David VanHoose, "Has Greater Competition Restrained U.S. Inflation?" *Southern Economic Journal* 67 (2000); authors' estimates.

cate, competition in U.S. product markets has been steadily increasing as a result of both greater competition among U.S. firms and increased competition from foreign sources. Panels (b) and (c) show estimated Phillips curve relationships for the late 1970s and early 2000s that take into account the changing degree of economy-wide competition. As you can see, there is evidence that rising competition since the late 1970s has had two effects. It has tended to make the short-run Phillips curve more shallow, and it has shifted the long-run Phillips curve to the left.

These estimates indicate that the natural rate of unemployment declined from about $6\frac{1}{2}$ percent in the late 1970s to nearly $5\frac{1}{2}$ percent by the early 2000s. The study from which these estimates are taken, coauthored by John Duca of the Federal Reserve Bank of Dallas and one of the text authors, indicates that about half the estimated 1 percentage point drop in the natural unemployment rate has resulted from greater competition in U.S. product markets. In this sense, part of the drop in unemployment may result from heightened competition in a "new economy."

Shifting Population Distributions   As panel (b) of Figure 10–14 on page 297 clearly indicates, after the mid-1990s the actual unemployment rate remained well below $5\frac{1}{2}$ percent until the economic downturn in 2001. Thus, there must be more to the story of the altered Phillips curve relationship than changes in the competitive structure of U.S. markets.

One possible explanation focuses on the age distribution of the U.S. population. A large fraction of the current population consists of the so-called baby boom generation born between the late 1940s and the late 1950s. This large generation of people reached working age during their teens in the 1960s and 1970s. In contrast, fewer people were born between the early 1970s and early 1980s. These people reached their teen working years in the late 1980s and 1990s.

Unemployment rates for teenagers are always higher than for other groups in the labor force. Hence, from the mid-1960s to the late 1970s, there were a lot of teenage baby boomers who were unemployed. This factor pushed up the unemployment rate during those years. Then population growth declined. By the 1990s, far fewer teens were in the labor force, so the unemployment rate fell.

A study by Robert Shimer of Princeton University has estimated that between $\frac{1}{2}$ and 1 percentage points of the observed reduction in the U.S. unemployment rate may result from the "age effect." This effect on unemployment and the $\frac{1}{2}$ percentage point estimated reduction in the unemployment rate stemming from increased competition could account for why the U.S. unemployment rate fell below $4\frac{1}{2}$ percent in the 1990s and 2000.

FUNDAMENTAL ISSUE #6

How has the relationship between the inflation rate and the unemployment rate changed in the 1990s and 2000s?   The relationship between inflation and unemployment rates in the 1990s and early 2000s has sloped upward. One factor that may account for this is increased overall competition in U.S. markets for goods and services, which has tended to make the short-run Phillips curve more shallow while shifting the long-run Phillips curve inward. Another is the changing U.S. population distribution. In the late 1960s and 1970s, a large number of relatively unemployable teenagers of the baby boom generation created a bulge in U.S. unemployment rates. As members of this generation became better trained, the natural rate of unemployment tended to decline after the 1980s. In addition, a chance combination of lower employee costs, reduced energy prices, and lower import prices contributed to lower inflation after the early 1990s.

A Different Sort of Phillips Curve—A Long-Run Trade-off between the Unemployment Rate and the Rate of Price-Level *Acceleration?*

The starting point for the Phillips curve was A. W. Phillips's study of the relationship between the rate of change in nominal wages and the unemployment rate. Economists who developed the alternative traditional perspectives on Keynesian aggregate supply then realized that these approaches implied that there should also be a relationship between price inflation and the unemployment rate. This led to the modern idea of the Phillips curve, but since the 1960s an inverse relationship between the inflation rate and the unemployment rate does not seem to have held up in the long run. Such a relationship between the inflation rate and the unemployment rate has appeared to last a few years at most, and often it has been even more fleeting

Friedman's Accelerationist Hypothesis

As you have learned, one way to generate an upward-sloping aggregate supply curve—and, by implication, a downward-sloping relationship between the inflation rate and the unemployment rate—is to assume that there are nominal wage contracts between workers and firms that make nominal wages inflexible. Nevertheless, when Milton Friedman predicted in the 1960s that the inflation-unemployment relationship could not hold up in the long run, he also suggested an alternative approach to understanding how inflation and unemployment rates might relate. This is known as the *accelerationist* approach to the Phillips curve. According to this approach, which combines elements of both the fixed-wage and the imperfect-information approaches to the aggregate supply schedule, workers and firms actually bargain over *real* wages. Because of imperfect information about the current price level, however, workers and

firms perceive the current real wage to equal the currently observable nominal wage divided by the price level from the previous period. As nominal wages change over time and more information about changes in the price level becomes available, firms raise or reduce their employment of labor.

What Friedman's hypothesis implies is that the unemployment rate should actually be inversely related to the difference between nominal wage inflation and price inflation that took place one period earlier. Instead of A. W. Phillips's inverse relationship between the rate of change in nominal wages and the unemployment rate, Friedman suggested that the actual Phillips curve should entail an inverse relationship between the unemployment rate and the differential between nominal wage inflation in a current period and price inflation one period earlier.

As turns out, this also means that there is not necessarily a negative relationship between the unemployment rate and the rate of price inflation. Instead, Friedman's hypothesis predicts a negative relationship between the unemployment rate and the rate of change in price inflation. Inflation is the rate of change in the price level over time, so the rate of change in price inflation is a rate of change of a rate of change, or an *acceleration.* That is, there should be a downward-sloping relationship between the unemployment rate and the rate at which the price level *accelerates* upward over time.

Wage and Price Acceleration and a Different Sort of "Phillips Curve"

Figure 10–16 on the next page provides some evidence favoring Friedman's reinterpretation of

Continued on next page

Link to Policy, continued

the Phillips curve idea. Panel (a) displays unemployment rates and associated differences between current wage inflation and price inflation a year earlier for the United States since 1955. Just as Friedman suggested, there appears to have been an inverse relationship over this period spanning more than four decades.

Panel (b) displays annual unemployment rates and associated annual changes in the rate of inflation, or annual acceleration or deceleration rates of inflation, since 1955. This diagram also provides some support for Friedman's accelerationist hypothesis.

It is important to recognize that Figure 10–16 does not necessarily *prove* that Friedman's specific theory is correct. It does, however, indicate that a different sort of Phillips curve relationship than the standard unemployment-inflation trade-off highlighted by the traditional Keynesian theory may be relevant. Furthermore, this reformulated relationship may be more stable over the long run.

Research Project

Evaluate the promises and pitfalls of using the accelerationist approach to the Phillips curve as a guide to policy. Would the existence of a long-run relationship between the unemployment rate and the change in the inflation rate necessarily imply that policymakers could bring about a permanent reduction in the unemployment rate via successive bursts of inflation?

Web Resource

Do data from other countries provide any evidence of an inverse relationship between the unemployment rate and the differential between wage inflation and lagged price inflation and of an inverse relationship between the unemployment rate and the change in price inflation? You can find data on employment costs, consumer price indexes, and unemployment rates in several nations at the Bureau of Labor Statistics International–Foreign Labor Statistics site, http://www.bls.gov/fls.

Figure 10-16   U.S. Unemployment Rates and Associated Wage Inflation-Lagged Price Inflation Differentials and Changes in Price Inflation since 1955

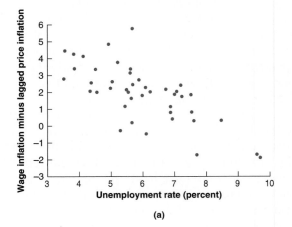

(a)

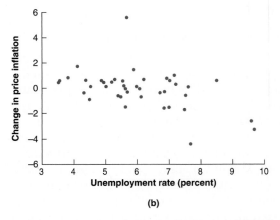

(b)

Panel (a) shows that as predicted by the wage-adjustment process of the accelerationist hypothesis proposed by Milton Friedman, there tends to be a negative relationship between the difference between wage inflation and lagged price inflation and the unemployment rate in the United States. Panel (b) indicates that there also tends to be an inverse relationship between the change in the U.S. Inflation rate and the U.S. unemployment rate.

SOURCES: Karl Whalen, "Real Wage Dynamics and the Phillips Curve," Division of Research and Statistics, Board of Governors of the Federal Reserve System, December 1999; and *Economic Report of the President* and *Economic Indicators*, various issues.

1. The Factors That Determine Aggregate Demand in the Traditional Keynesian Model: Two key factors affect the position of the Keynesian aggregate demand schedule. One is the set of elements that comprise autonomous aggregate expenditures. These include government spending and taxation and autonomous consumption, investment, and net exports. The other key factor is the nominal quantity of money. Consequently, both fiscal and monetary policy actions can affect the position of the Keynesian aggregate demand schedule.

2. The Factors That Determine the Shape and Position of the Keynesian Aggregate Supply Schedule: According to the sticky-wage and imperfect-information theories of aggregate supply, the aggregate supply schedule is upward sloping and has a convex shape. Under the sticky-wage theory, a rise in nominal wages, perhaps as a result of union demands for higher wages or an increase in a legal wage minimum, will shift the aggregate supply schedule upward and to the left. Under the imperfect-information theory, a rise in the expected price level will also shift the aggregate supply schedule upward and to the left.

3. The Price and Output Effects of Expansionary Fiscal and Monetary Policies in the Traditional Keynesian Model: According to this theory, an increase in government expenditures, a tax cut, or a rise in the nominal quantity of money will raise aggregate demand. This will cause an increase in both the equilibrium price level and equilibrium real output.

4. The Phillips Curve: This is a downward-sloping schedule that traces a proposed inverse relationship between the unemployment rate and the inflation rate. Such a relationship, which is an implication of the Keynesian theory of aggregate supply, will indicate that society must trade off higher inflation for lower unemployment, and vice versa.

5. How Monetarism Differs from the Traditional Keynesian Theory: The monetarists have argued that the nominal quantity of money is the primary factor influencing aggre-

gate demand. In addition, the monetarists have developed a theory in which imperfect information makes the short-run aggregate supply schedule slope upward and the short-run Phillips curve slope downward. The availability of full information in the long run, however, makes both the aggregate supply schedule and the Phillips curve vertical. Using the monetarist theory as a foundation, the political business cycle theory provides a potential explanation for how politically motivated efforts to reduce unemployment can lead to higher inflation and inflation expectations, resulting at first in lower unemployment but eventually causing higher unemployment. It also provides a possible reason for why efforts to reduce inflation can push unemployment up initially but lead to lower unemployment later on. Increased inflation expectations and supply shocks together can shift the short-run Phillips curve upward, thereby causing stagflation, or simultaneous high inflation and unemployment rates.

6. The Relationship between the Inflation Rate and the Unemployment Rate in the 1990s and 2000s: In apparent contrast to the predictions of Keynesian and monetarist theory, the relationship between inflation and unemployment rates in the 1990s and early 2000s has sloped upward. It is likely that several factors account for the simultaneously low inflation and low unemployment from the early 1990s up to the 2001 slowdown. One of these is increased overall competition in U.S. markets for goods and services, which has tended to make the short-run Phillips curve more shallow while shifting the long-run Phillips curve inward. Another is the changing U.S. population distribution. In the late 1960s and 1970s, a large number of relatively unemployable teenagers of the baby boom generation created a bulge in U.S. unemployment rates. As members of this generation became better trained, the natural rate of unemployment tended to decline after the 1980s. In addition, a chance combination of lower employee costs, reduced energy prices, and lower import prices undoubtedly contributed to lower inflation after the early 1990s.

Self-Test Questions

1. In the classical model, fiscal policy actions cannot influence aggregate demand, but in the Keynesian theory, they can. Why is this so?

2. In Chapter 9, you learned that the ability of monetary policy actions to affect equilibrium real income varies depending on whether the exchange rate floats or is fixed. Use the *IS-LM-BP* diagram from Chapter 9 to evaluate

(Answers to odd-numbered questions may be found on the Web at **http://macro. swcollege.com** under "Student Resources.")

whether expansionary monetary policy can boost aggregate demand with both floating and fixed exchange rates.

3. In Chapter 9, you also learned that the ability of fiscal policy actions to affect equilibrium real income varies depending on whether the exchange rate floats or is fixed, as well as on the degree of capital mobility.

   a. Suppose that a nation has low capital mobility and a fixed exchange rate. Use the *IS-LM-BP* diagram from Chapter 9 to determine the extent to which an increase in government spending can induce an increase in aggregate demand.

   b. Repeat part (a) for the case of a nation with high capital mobility and a floating exchange rate.

4. List the various factors that can cause inflation in the classical model. Then construct a similar list for the Keynesian theory. Which list is longer? Explain why this is so.

5. Explain verbally, and with diagrams to the extent that they assist, why a sudden decline in price expectations shifts the short-run aggregate supply schedule downward and to the right.

6. Explain in your own words why money is nonneutral in the traditional Keynesian model.

7. In 1996, a few senators delayed for several months the full Senate's approval of Alan Greenspan's nomination to a third term as chair of the Federal Reserve Board. One of this group was quoted as saying in the floor debate, "Every time growth starts to go up, they [the Federal Reserve] push on the brakes [reduce money growth], robbing working families and businesses of the benefits of faster growth." (Interpretations are in brackets.) Were this senator's views more likely swayed by classical, Keynesian, or monetarist theory?

8. Explain verbally, and with diagrams to the extent that they assist, why a sudden decline in price-level and inflation expectations shifts the short-run Phillips curve downward and to the left. (Hint: You should find that your answer to question 5 will be helpful in answering this question.)

9. Explain why the long-run Phillips curve is vertical.

10. Economists have not reached agreement on how lengthy the time horizon for the "long run" is in the context of the long-run Phillips curve. Would you anticipate that this period is likely to have been shortened or extended by the advent of more sophisticated computer and communications technology? Explain your reasoning.

11. Evaluate the ability of the political business cycle theory alone to explain the behavior of inflation and unemployment rates since the 1960s. Explain your reasoning.

Problems

(Answers to odd-numbered problems may be found on the Web at **http://macro.swcollege.com** under "Student Resources.")

1. Consider the following equations for a fictitious economy, which has no government:

   LM schedule: $r = 160 - [2 \times (M/P)] + (8 \times y)$

   IS schedule: $r = 160 - (8 \times y)$

   a. Suppose that the nominal money stock is equal to 160 and the price level is equal to 2. What is the equilibrium level of real income?

   b. Suppose that the nominal money stock remains equal to 160 but the price level falls to 1. What is the new equilibrium real income level? What does this imply about the slope of the aggregate demand schedule?

2. Consider the following straight-line equation expressing a Phillips curve relationship (at least, as a rough approximation, since theory indicates that the Phillips curve probably is not a straight line): $u = u_N - b \times (\pi - \pi^e)$ where u and π are the actual unemployment rate and inflation rate, π^e is the expected inflation rate, u_N is the natural rate of unemployment, and b is a constant. All rates are measured as percentages in this equation. Suppose that u_N is estimated at 5.5 percent and b is equal to 0.5. The current unemployment rate is 5 percent, and the current inflation rate is 2 percent. According to the equation, what is the expected inflation rate?

3. Imagine that you are an economic adviser to a policymaker, and you decide to use the Phillips curve equation and the values for u_N, b, and π^e in problem 2 to forecast *future* inflation.

   a. Prove that the equation can be rearranged into the expression, $\pi = \pi^e + (1/b) \times (u_N - u)$.

   b. Suppose that expected inflation does not change, but the unemployment rate unexpectedly drops to 4 percent at the end of the year. Using the Phillips curve equation, what is your forecast of the inflation rate at year-end?

Before the Test

Test your understanding of the material covered in this chapter by taking the Chapter 10 online quiz at http://macro.swcollege.com.

Online Application

Internet URL: http://stats.bls.gov/data/top20.html

Title: *Bureau of Labor Statistics: Most Requested Series*

Navigation: Begin at the home page of the Bureau of Labor Statistics (http://stats.bls.gov). Then click on *Get Detailed Statistics,* followed by *Overall Most Requested BLS Series.*

Application: Perform the indicated operations, and answer the following questions:

1. Click checkmarks in the boxes for "Civilian Labor Force," "Civilian Employment," and "Civilian Unemployment." (Note that all data are seasonally adjusted.) At the bottom of the screen click on "retrieve data." Change the year to the earliest at change output options. Click on "go," or at the top click on "More Formatting Options." Select table format, select "All Years," and click on "Retrieve Data." Can you identify periods of sharp cyclical swings? Do they show up most readily in data for the labor force, employment, or unemployment?

2. Do cyclical factors appear to have been important during the past couple of years?

For Group Study and Analysis: This site also has data series for consumer and producer price indexes. Divide the class into groups, and assign a price index to each group. Ask each group to take a look at the index for "All Years" and to identify periods during which their index accelerated or decelerated (or even fell). Reconvene the class, and discuss periods in which the indexes provided similar indications about inflation and disinflation (or deflation). Do the indexes ever provide opposing implications about inflation and disinflation (or deflation)? Are there periods in which an inverse relationship between unemployment and inflation is apparent? What about from the early 1990s into the 2000s?

UNIT III   Keynesian and Monetarist Macroeconomic Perspectives

and Further Reading

Alesina, Alberto, and Howard Rosenthal. *Partisan Politics, Divided Government, and the Economy.* Cambridge: Cambridge University Press, 1995.

Atkeson, Andrew, and Lee Ohanian. "Are Phillips Curves Useful for Forecasting Inflation?" Federal Reserve Bank of Minneapolis *Quarterly Review* 25 (Winter 2001): pp. 2–11.

Brinner, Roger. "Is Inflation Dead?" Federal Reserve Bank of Boston *New England Economic Review,* January/February 1999, pp. 37–49.

Cross, Rod. *The Natural Rate of Unemployment: Reflections on 25 Years of the Hypothesis.* Cambridge: Cambridge University Press, 1995.

Duca, John, and David VanHoose. "Has Greater Competition Reduced Inflation?" *Southern Economic Journal* 67 (January 2000): 729–741.

Fuhrer, Jeffrey. "The Phillips Curve Is Alive and Well." Federal Reserve Bank of Boston *New England Economic Review,* March/April 1995, pp. 41–56.

Laidler, David. "The Legacy of the Monetarist Controversy." Federal Reserve Bank of St. Louis *Review,* March/April 1990, pp. 49–64.

Mayer, Thomas, ed. *The Political Economy of American Monetary Policy.* Cambridge: Cambridge University Press, 1990.

Roberts, John. "New Keynesian Economics and the Phillips Curve." *Journal of Money, Credit, and Banking* 27 (November 1995): 975–984.

Shimer, Robert. "Why Is the U.S. Unemployment Rate So Much Lower?" *NBER Macroeconomics Annual* (Cambridge, Mass.: MIT Press, 1998), pp. 11–61.

Tootell, Geoffrey. "Restructuring, the NAIRU, and the Phillips Curve." Federal Reserve Bank of Boston *New England Economic Review,* September/October 1994, pp. 31–44.

Whalen, Karl. "Real Wage Dynamics and the Phillips Curve." Division of Research and Statistics, Board of Governors of the Federal Reserve System, December 1999.

macro**xtra!**

Unit IV

Rational Expectations and Modern Macroeconomic Theory

Recent Macroeconomic Theories: Mixing Something(s) Old with Something(s) New

Events that occurred beginning in the mid-1970s caused a growing number of economists to question the postclassical tradition established by Keynes and his followers. Particularly bothersome was the problem of *stagflation,* or the simultaneous existence of relatively high levels of inflation and unemployment. The Keynesian tradition had not predicted this problem and, indeed, appeared ill-suited for offering a solution. The stagflation of the 1970s may have been as damaging to the Keynesian theory as the Great Depression was to the classical school of thought.

The 1970s and 1980s ushered in an ongoing period of sharp disagreement among many economists about the best model of the aggregate economy and the "best"—that is, most successful at predicting actual outcomes—theory of the proper roles of monetary and fiscal policies. Although various economists have promoted several specific theories, the views of most economists during the past two decades fall into two basic groupings. One set of economists seeks to rejuvenate the essential elements of the classical model while incorporating some features of the twentieth-century Keynesian tradition that they regard as useful. Central among this group are the *new classical* economists, who follow in the footsteps of the original classical theorists by arguing that the assumption of flexible prices and wages is the foundation for a successful model of the economy.

The new classical economists accept the traditional view that informational constraints sometimes interfere with the economy's self-adjustment process. Yet they do not see such constraints as a significant impediment to the attainment of full-employment output. Nor do they accept the view that systematic, predictable policy actions necessarily influence real economic activity. Thus, within the new classical theory as in the original classical tradition, individuals rationally act in their own best interest,

albeit in an environment in which they are incompletely informed, and ultimately find their own way to full employment without the need for government intervention. Ultimately, this new classical perspective evolved into what economists today call *real-business-cycle theory,* in which "Supply creates its own demand," just as in the original classical model.

Another group of economists has sought to preserve the essential elements of the Keynesian tradition. These economists believe that informational imperfections together with various potential sources of rigidities in prices and wages are central to understanding and predicting economic performance. They argue that theories incorporating these elements are necessary for the successful application of monetary and fiscal policies. These modern Keynesian economists, however, recognize flaws inherent in the original Keynesian tradition and have sought to develop new approaches using certain aspects of the classical, new classical, and even real-business-cycle theories that they believe to be relevant. Consequently, these modern Keynesian theorists work with theories in which price and wage rigidities result from rational decision making by self-interested individuals. Some of these modern theories have also led to the development of a so-called *new Keynesian economics* that promotes the view that "Demand creates its own supply."

The prevailing lack of consensus about the workings of the economy and the proper roles of monetary and fiscal policies can make the study of modern macroeconomics both challenging and potentially frustrating for students and instructors alike. Yet the unsettled state of affairs also makes today's macroeconomics both intellectually stimulating and exciting. The issues discussed in this unit will continue to dominate the time and effort of economists and policymakers in the coming decades.

The Pursuit of Self-Interest—

Rational Expectations, New Classical Macroeconomics, and Efficient Markets

FUNDAMENTAL ISSUES

1. What is the distinction between adaptive and rational expectations?

2. What are the key assumptions underlying new classical macro-economics?

3. How do policy anticipations determine the actual effects of policy actions in the new classical model, and what is the new classical policy ineffectiveness proposition?

4. What is the efficient markets theory, and what is its main implication?

5. How are exchange rates determined, and what is foreign exchange market efficiency?

From the perspective of many Europeans, it was not supposed to turn out this way. In their view, after its formal establishment in 1999 the European Central Bank (ECB) was supposed to emerge as an independent world policymaker. As one of the world's most independent central banks— in some respects, the most independent—the ECB was free to challenge the Federal Reserve for preeminence among global central banking institutions.

To the dismay of its European critics, so far the ECB appears to have remained well within the shadow of the Fed. Whenever the Fed has conducted *a monetary expansion that has pushed down U.S. interest rates, the ECB has tended to respond in kind by pushing down European rates. Likewise, the ECB has generally matched Fed policies that boosted U.S. interest rates, often point for point. Instead of conducting a truly independent,* European *monetary policy, to these critics, the ECB seems to be behaving more like a Fed subsidiary on the other side of the Atlantic. One disparaging European commentator has even suggested that the ECB's policymaking officials should be replaced with a single individual who simply does whatever the Federal Reserve does—because that is what current officials seem to do anyway.*

If the ECB really does adjust its monetary policies to mimic Federal Reserve policy actions, does this necessarily mean that the ECB is subservient to the Fed? Or could there be other reasons that the central banks tend to conduct policies that move interest rates in similar directions? When you have completed this chapter, you will understand why relationships might exist among interest rates in different nations. You will also be able to evaluate possible reasons for the apparent codependence of U.S. and European monetary policies.

The Rational Expectations Hypothesis

The monetarists blended aspects of the classical and traditional Keynesian approaches in their effort to explain how macroeconomic policies affect real output, employment, and the rate of inflation in the short run and in the long run. In the short run, the monetarist approach looks much like the traditional Keynesian theory, whereas in the long run the monetarist model essentially duplicates the classical theory.

Binding together the classical and Keynesian approaches was no mean feat for the monetarists. As you have seen, the hybrid model that the monetarists and others have pieced together provides the basis for the idea of political business cycles and for simple theories of stagflation. The monetarist model also identifies the important role that inflation expectations can perform in determining the pace of economic activity, the unemployment rate, and the rate of inflation.

Missing from the basic monetarist theoretical framework, however, was a clear explanation for how people form inflation expectations. As macroeconomists sought to apply the monetarist ideas to develop a more complete understanding of factors that might influence business cycles, they began to recognize that how people forecast inflation is a key determinant of business cycle peaks, troughs, and durations. Hence, economists needed to carefully consider the assumptions about expectation formation in their theories.

Expectations and Macroeconomics

In Chapter 10 you learned that the monetarist model indicates that adjustment to the long-run, classical equilibrium takes place when workers have information about true changes in the rate of inflation. In the long run, therefore, workers experience no money illusion, and the unemployment rate is equal to the natural rate of unemployment.

FROM THE SHORT RUN TO THE LONG RUN   Before this long-run, classical equilibrium is reached, however, the monetarist framework implies that workers essentially are handicapped by a lack of full information. Because of information imperfections in the short run, workers must forecast the price level and the inflation rate so that they can decide how much labor to supply at prevailing nominal wages. If the actual price level and inflation rate differ from the expectations, workers' perceptions of their real wage earnings will turn out to be incorrect. The short-run results are a deviation in the unemployment rate from the natural rate of unemployment, variations in real output from the long-run, classical level of output, and fluctuations in the price level and inflation rate. In other words, business cycles occur.

At what point does the short-run period of the traditional Keynesian theory end? In other words, how does the economy make the transition to the long-run state described by the classical theory? The basic monetarist model tells us only that the long run is an interval whose length is determined by the availability of information. As long as expectations are based on imperfect information, the short-run Keynesian theory is applicable, and real output and the unemployment rate can vary with changes in the price level and the inflation rate.

Exactly what information is really available to people in the short run? How do they use this information to forecast the price level and the inflation rate? Clearly, the choices that people make depend on such factors, yet the macroeconomic theories that we have considered to this point are silent on these issues.

THE ROLE OF EXPECTATIONS   One element that separates *modern* macroeconomics—the study of the aggregate economy during the late twentieth and early twenty-first centuries—from the macroeconomics of the past is a greater effort to clarify the role that the *expectations formation process* plays in macroeconomic models. Modern macroeconomists have developed clear-cut hypotheses for how people forecast the price level and inflation rate, and they incorporate these hypotheses into their theories of the determination of real output, employment, the price level, and the inflation rate.

Macroeconomists have adopted two basic types of hypotheses about how people form expectations. One is the hypothesis of *adaptive expectations.* The other is the *rational expectations hypothesis,* which has dominated modern macroeconomic thinking. Our first task in this chapter is to explain why this is so.

Adaptive Expectations

Many of the choices that we make each day depend on our anticipations of future events. Should you register for a course this term when the instructor is a professor with an average-quality reputation, or should you wait until next term when the course will be taught by a better instructor, but the tuition rate may be higher? Should you buy a sweater at a department store today, or do you expect that it will be on sale in a couple of

311

CHAPTER 11   The Pursuit of Self-Interest—Rational Expectations, New Classical Macroeconomics, and Efficient Markets weeks? Should you take a job at the salary you have been offered for the coming year, or would you be better off searching for a position at a higher salary, given that you expect the price level to rise during the coming year?

Clearly, to make any decisions that have future consequences, you must act on forecasts that you make based on whatever information you currently possess. This information includes the prices of goods and services that you buy each day in your own town or city, prices of items that you see advertised in local and national media, and information that you can glean from reports on regional or national television news programs.

How do you use such information to infer the current aggregate inflation rate for the United States? How do you forecast future inflation? Most likely, you would have trouble providing a detailed, scientific answer to either of these questions. Certainly, it is unlikely that you engage in any formal statistical analysis or use a computer to make your forecast. You probably just make your "best guess" based on the information available to you.

What is a person's best guess of inflation? Simply saying that people do the best they can with limited information is not a very specific statement. As you have learned, macroeconomists need to make more specific assumptions when they construct theories of output and price-level determination. For this reason, in recent years they have developed precise conceptions about alternative processes by which people form expectations.

ADAPTIVE EXPECTATIONS PROCESSES   One way to make an inference of the aggregate price level or to forecast the future inflation rate is to do so "adaptively." Let's consider an example. Imagine that someone asks you for your forecast of the U.S. inflation rate for next year. How would you come up with an answer?

One approach might be to collect data on inflation rates for the past twenty or twenty-five years. You then could plot this information on a chart and make a rough drawing of the "trend line" along the points and beyond. The next point on your trend line would be your forecast of next year's inflation rate.

If you have taken a statistics course, you might use a more sophisticated method. You could use statistical techniques to determine the specific equation for the trend line that best fits the inflation data that you have collected. With this equation, you could give a predicted value, or forecast, of the inflation rate for a given year, including next year.

Either method would require you to sacrifice time and effort to collect and analyze years of inflation data. If you do not wish to incur this opportunity cost to make a sophisticated forecast, you could choose a simpler method. For instance, you might just guess that next year's inflation rate will turn out to be an average of the inflation rates over the past three years. Even simpler, you might guess that next year's inflation rate will turn out to be similar to the inflation rate during the past year.

Each of the above forecasting methods is an example of an **adaptive expectations** process, because each method uses only past information. Whether you draw a rough trend line, use statistical techniques to calculate an exact trend line, compute a three-year average, or just extrapolate from

ADAPTIVE EXPECTATIONS:
Expectations that are based only on information from the past up to the present.

the current inflation rate, you are basing your inflation forecast solely on past data.

IMPLICATIONS OF ADAPTIVE EXPECTATIONS   As you learned in Chapter 10, one way to derive an upward-sloping Keynesian aggregate supply schedule and a downward-sloping Phillips curve is to assume that workers make choices based on imperfectly informed forecasts of the price level and inflation rate. If the workers' forecasts turn out to be incorrect, then the results are movements along the aggregate supply schedule and the Phillips curve. Misperceptions caused by imperfect information lead to changes in real output and the unemployment rate.

The production of real output by more or fewer workers requires the passage of time, however. Consequently, short-run output and employment adjustments cannot occur until an interval passes and workers realize that their forecasts of the price level and inflation rate were wrong. During this interval, which corresponds to the monetarists' notion of the short run, workers can fail to realize that a rise in the nominal wage may stem solely from an increase in the price level. As a result, when the nominal wage rises, for a time workers can misperceive this rise in the nominal wage as a rise in their real wage, leading them to supply more labor services. This permits firms to produce more real output.

The hypothesis that workers use adaptive expectations processes is consistent with this traditional Keynesian theory of aggregate supply and the Phillips curve. If workers make their price-level and inflation forecasts adaptively, then they must always wait until new information about the price level and inflation rate appears before changing their expectations. Consequently, over some intervals workers will not be able to avoid experiencing money illusion concerning their wages, and policy actions that raise the price level will always cause workers to misperceive their true real wages, at least for a short time. Thus, such policies can have short-run effects on real output and the unemployment rate.

DRAWBACKS OF ADAPTIVE EXPECTATIONS   Just because an expectations hypothesis happens to fit a theory does not mean that it is a reasonable hypothesis. Indeed, many economists reject the idea of adaptive expectations. For one thing, if people really were to use adaptive expectations processes, they would often make forecasts that they realize in advance should turn out to be wrong. Suppose, for instance, that your adaptive method for forecasting next year's inflation rate is to calculate an average of the inflation rates for the past three years. If this average is equal to 3 percent, then that will be your forecast of the inflation rate for next year. Now suppose that you read in the newspaper that a new majority on the Federal Reserve have decided to increase money growth significantly, as compared with previous years. Sticking with your three-year-averaging procedure for calculating the average inflation rate means that you must consciously ignore this new information, even though any reasonable person would recognize that higher money growth may push up next year's inflation rate. As a result, a macroeconomic model based on the hypothesis of adaptive expectations will yield forecasts of the rate of inflation that are consistently less than the actual inflation rate. Thus, any macroeconomic theory based on adaptive expectations will be internally inconsistent, because the people whose behavior the model attempts to mimic behave in a way inconsistent with new information.

Another troublesome aspect of the hypothesis is that there is no way to say, in advance, which adaptive expectations process is "best." For example, one individual might draw a chart of twenty-five years of past annual inflation rate data to plot a rough trend line to guide her forecasts, another person might use the same technique using data from the previous forty years, and yet another might use fifty years of data. Someone else might calculate a weighted average of inflation over the past five years. Indeed, the number of possible adaptive expectations schemes is infinite. Which one should we include in a macroeconomic model? There is no good way to answer this question.

Rational Expectations

In the 1970s, macroeconomists began to confront the quandary that adaptive expectations posed for evaluating the traditional Keynesian and monetarist efforts to allow for imperfect information in their theories. Motivating an upward-sloping aggregate supply function and a downward-sloping Phillips curve seemed to require adaptive expectations, yet incorporating specific schemes for adaptively formed price-level and inflation rate expectations in macroeconomic models seemed both arbitrary and inconsistent.

In 1969, an Indiana University economist named John Muth proposed an alternative way to think about how people form expectations. Then Robert Lucas of the University of Chicago and others, including Thomas Sargent of Stanford University, Neil Wallace of Pennsylvania State University, and Robert Barro of Harvard University, followed up on Muth's idea to derive a possibly better way to think about how price-level and inflation rate expectations are formed.

The approach to expectations that Muth, Lucas, and others developed is called the **rational expectations hypothesis.** According to this hypothesis, an individual makes the best possible forecast of a macroeconomic variable such as the price level or inflation rate using all available past *and current* information *and* drawing on an understanding of what factors affect the macroeconomic variable. In contrast to an adaptive forecast, which only looks backward because it is based on past information, a rational forecast looks forward while taking past information into account as well.

Consider, for instance, our earlier example of someone who initially made an inflation forecast using an average of the past three years' inflation rates but then learned that the Fed intended to increase the money growth rate substantially. If your goal is to make the best prediction of inflation so as to make the best possible choices for the coming year, then sticking with your original, adaptive forecast clearly would not be in your own best interest. The *rational* way to respond to the new information is to use your own understanding of how a higher money growth rate will influence the price level and the inflation rate. Then you update your inflation rate forecast accordingly.

RATIONAL EXPECTATIONS HYPOTHESIS: The idea that individuals form expectations based on all available past and current information and on a basic understanding of how the economy works.

Hence, the difference between adaptive and rational expectations can be summarized in the following manner:

An *adaptive* expectation is based only on past information. In contrast, a *rational* expectation takes into account both past and current information, plus an understanding of how the economy functions.

ADVANTAGES OF THE RATIONAL EXPECTATIONS HYPOTHESIS   Because the rational expectations hypothesis does not impose artificial constraints on how people use information, it is a more general theory of expectations formation than the hypothesis of adaptive expectations. Whereas the adaptive expectations process is restricted to past information, the rational expectations hypothesis states that if an individual can improve upon an adaptive forecast, then that individual will do so.

Under some circumstances, a person's rationally formed expectation may look like an adaptive expectation. If a person has only past information and no special insight into how the economy functions, then an adaptive forecast may be the best that person can do. In this case, an adaptive expectation will be the individual's rational expectation.

Usually, however, people will use all available current information plus all their knowledge about the economy's workings when they try to infer the price level and forecast the inflation rate. Consequently, under most circumstances, a rationally formed expectation will differ from a purely adaptive expectation.

We must emphasize that even though rational expectations generally are better than adaptive expectations, forecasts based on all current information and an understanding of how the economy works still will not always be correct. For instance, the widespread adoption of Doppler radar by the National Weather Service has improved the ability of weather forecasters to predict where tornadoes may form. As a result, tornado forecasts are better than before, but they still are not always on the mark. Likewise, rationally formed forecasts are better, on average, than adaptive forecasts. Nevertheless, the actual price level and inflation rate can still turn out to be different than people rationally predicted.

ARE THERE LIMITS ON RATIONALITY?   The rational expectations hypothesis presents a couple of conceptual problems of its own. One problem is that the hypothesis is very broad, so broad that incorporating it fully into a macroeconomic model can prove challenging. For instance, each individual in an economy has her or his own perspective on how the economy works. In addition, at any given instant each person is informed to a somewhat different extent about current economic developments. Should economists therefore try to model every individual's expectations formation procedure?

A related difficulty is that each individual in the economy should act on his or her rationally formed expectation of the price level and the inflation rate. This means that the actual price level and inflation rate will depend on how all form their expectations. If each person realizes that others' expectations affect the actual price level and inflation rate, does this mean that each person should attempt to forecast others' forecasts?

To get around these problems, macroeconomists often use two simplifying assumptions when they construct theories that include rational expectations.

On the Web

Take a look at the latest survey of professional economic forecasts at http://www.phil.frb. org/econ/liv/.

Representative Agent Assumption: The assumption that all people in an economy have access to the same information and have the same understanding of how the economy works.

Under the **representative agent assumption,** a macroeconomic model presumes that each person in the economy has access to the same information and has the same conception of how the economy works. This gets around the issue of different expectations across individuals in the economy. Furthermore, by assuming that all people make the same forecast, the representative agent assumption also avoids the problem of individuals worrying about others' forecasts.

The second common assumption used in macroeconomic models with rational expectations is that people in the economy understand how the economy functions. That is, a macroeconomist using the rational expectations hypothesis typically assumes that the people whose aggregate behavior the models try to describe behave *as if* they understand that the economy works according to the macroeconomist's own theory. This assumption boils down to presuming that the people in a macroeconomic model *know the model*.

As you will learn in Chapter 13, a number of macroeconomists today question the wisdom of assuming that people are all the same and understand exactly how the price level and inflation are determined. Nevertheless, both the representative agent assumption and the assumption that people act as though they understand the workings of the economy greatly simplify the inclusion of the rational expectations hypothesis in any macroeconomic model. For this reason, we shall also adopt these assumptions in this chapter and in Chapter 12.

> **FUNDAMENTAL ISSUE #1**
>
> **What is the distinction between adaptive and rational expectations?**   An adaptive expectation is formed using only past information. In contrast, a rationally formed expectation is based on past and current information and on an understanding of how macroeconomic variables are determined.

New Classical Hypotheses

The first macroeconomists to incorporate the rational expectations hypothesis in their theories are known as *new classical economists*. Beginning in the 1970s, this group argued that expectations are so important that they should play a key role in any macroeconomic theory. The theory that the new classical economists promoted returned to themes of the classical theory that we surveyed in Chapters 3 and 4.

Because the new classical economists were the first to include the rational expectations hypothesis in their macroeconomic models, at one time many economists used the terms "new classical theory" and "rational expectations theory" interchangeably. As we shall discuss in Chapters 12 and 13, however, most other macroeconomists—including some whose theories are very nonclassical—now use the rational expectations hypothesis in their models as well. Thus, it is important to recognize that the rational expectations hypothesis does not necessarily lead to new classical conclusions. Instead, the rational expectations hypothesis is just a part of a broader theory now known as *new classical macroeconomics*.

The Basis of New Classical Theory: Wage and Price Flexibility

The key assumption of the new classical theory is that pure competition, with completely flexible wages and prices, prevails in the economy. This, you will recall from Chapter 3, is also a primary presumption of classical theory.

Adopting this assumption means ruling out stickiness of nominal wages that might result from explicit or implicit wage contracts or from minimum-wage laws. While not denying that such contracts exist in the real world, many new classical theorists conclude that the contracts play such a minor role in the larger scheme of things that they cannot keep wages from moving to levels consistent with equating the quantity of labor demanded with the quantity of labor supplied in the labor market. This, of course, is exactly what the original classical economists proposed. This assumption, of course, conflicts with traditional Keynesian theory. As you will learn in Chapter 12, it also conflicts with Keynesian approaches that incorporate the rational expectations hypothesis.

In addition, the pure competition assumption rules out the possibility that prices of goods and services may adjust slowly to changes in economic conditions. As we shall discuss in Chapter 13, some modern Keynesian theorists argue that pure competition is so rare that prices of goods and services typically are not determined in purely competitive markets. The new classical economists, in contrast, contend that competitive markets are the rule, rather than the exception.

Self-Interest and Rational Forecasts

The new classical theory is based on two additional assumptions. The first is that people are motivated by rational self-interest. Most economists would say this assumption should underlie any economic model. Macroeconomic models typically assume that people pursue their own self-interest.

The other key assumption of new classical theory is that no one has complete information, but all individuals nevertheless form rational expectations. To do so, they use all available past and current information and their understanding of how the economy functions.

As you will now see, these assumptions lead to some striking implications about the effects—and the lack of effects—of macroeconomic policies intended to stabilize the economy. These implications have engendered considerable debate among macroeconomists. This ongoing debate is the subject of most of the remainder of this book.

> **FUNDAMENTAL ISSUE #2**
>
> **What are the key assumptions underlying new classical macroeconomics?** As in other macroeconomic theories, the new classical model assumes that people pursue their self-interest. Like the classical model, the new classical framework is based on the assumption that purely competitive behavior leads to the determination of flexibly adjusting wages and prices. Finally, like the Keynesian and monetarist theories of aggregate supply, the new classical model assumes that information is imperfect in the short run. People form price-level and inflation rate expectations rationally, however, in the new classical model.

The Essential Features of the New Classical Model

You learned in Chapter 10 that the traditional Keynesian theory of aggregate supply relies on the assumption that workers decide how much labor to supply based on fixed expectations of the price level and the inflation rate. Consequently, a higher price level and inflation rate induced by increased aggregate demand cause workers to misperceive resulting nominal wage increases as higher real wages. Thus, workers supply more labor services, equilibrium employment rises, and firms produce more real output. Because the monetarist theory of short-run price-level and output determination shares this feature, it yields these same short-term implications.

The new classical theory challenges the idea of fixed expectations, because rigid expectations typically arise under the hypothesis of adaptive expectations. Under the rational expectations hypothesis, the traditional Keynesian predictions about workers' behavior indicate that they behave irrationally, unless one is willing to argue that workers cannot observe factors that will raise aggregate demand or fail to understand that rises in aggregate demand will increase the price level and the inflation rate. Typically, the new classical economists argue, workers are smarter than the traditional Keynesian and monetarist theories give them credit for being. They pay attention to factors that affect aggregate demand, and they update their forecasts based on a recognition that such factors ultimately will affect the price level and the inflation rate.

Making Rational Forecasts by Anticipating Policy Actions

Among the factors that affect aggregate demand are monetary policy actions and, at least according to traditional Keynesian theory, fiscal policy actions. According to the new classical theory, people understand this and therefore pay close attention to current and anticipated future policy actions by central bank or governmental officials. They follow current policy actions by keeping up with media reports, and from such reports they make inferences about likely future policy actions.

POLICY ANTICIPATIONS AND RATIONAL FORECASTS To capture the idea that people track current policies and try to forecast future policies, the new classical economists propose that workers' expectation of the price level, P^e, depends in part on their expectation of the money stock, M^e. In addition, to the extent that people believe that fiscal policies affect aggregate demand and the price level, P^e also depends on their expectation of government expenditures, g^e, and their expectation about the level of taxes, t^e.

It is important to recognize that M^e, g^e, and t^e all denote the settings of monetary and fiscal policy variables that people *anticipate*. The central bank, of course, determines the actual quantity of money, M. Likewise, the government determines its actual expenditures, g, and actual taxes, t. Actual policy choices by the central bank and the government may or may not correspond to what people anticipate. How closely actual events correspond to expectations depends on how well people are able to predict central bank and government policy choices.

FED WATCHING   A real-world example of the sort of forecasting behavior that the new classical model proposes is known as **Fed watching.** A number of economists make a living by observing each nuance of Federal Reserve policymaking and selling forecasts of likely Fed policy actions during the coming weeks or months. Many of these professional "Fed watchers" work as independent consultants, but some are employed by banks, investment firms, and other financial services corporations.

In terms of the new classical model, Fed watchers help people keep their forecasts of monetary policy, M^e, as up-to-date as possible. You might wonder why people are willing to pay for Fed watchers' services instead of just watching the Fed themselves. The reason is that the Fed is a quasi-independent agency of the federal government that has been able to keep many aspects of its decision-making process secret. Consequently, forecasting the Fed's next move is more of a challenge than, say, anticipating how politicians, who typically make their views on spending or tax policies very public, are likely to vote on fiscal policy actions. People with some inside knowledge of the Fed, such as former Fed economists, often become Fed watchers. Although former Fed employees are "out of the loop" once they leave their Fed jobs, they still may have more insight into how the Fed is likely to act than people with no Fed experience. People lacking any Fed background then may be willing to pay for the expertise of the Fed watchers.

FED WATCHING: An occupation that involves developing and selling forecasts of Federal Reserve monetary policy actions based on careful examination of the process by which the Fed appears to make its policy decisions.

The Effects of Macroeconomic Policy Actions in the New Classical Model

Now let's consider the new classical theory of short-run output and price-level determination. The foundation of the new classical theory is the monetarist short-run model, which in turn corresponds to the traditional Keynesian theory. As shown in Figure 11–1 on the next page, the aggregate demand schedule slopes downward, and its position depends on the actual values of the money stock, government expenditures, and taxes, denoted M_1, g_1, and t_1, respectively. As in the Keynesian imperfect-information theory of aggregate supply, the aggregate supply schedule slopes upward. Its position depends on people's expectation of the price level, P^e.

Figure 11–1   Real Output and Price-Level Determination in the New Classical Model

According to the new classical theory, individuals form their current expectation of the price level P_1^e, which influences the position of the aggregate supply function, based on their rational forecast of monetary and fiscal policy choices, M_1^e, g_1^e, and t_1^e. A nation's central bank determines the actual money stock, M_1, while its government sets the actual level of government spending, g_1, and net real taxes, t_1. These policy changes affect the position of the aggregate demand schedule. Together, aggregate demand and aggregate supply determine the equilibrium price level and the equilibrium amount of real output.

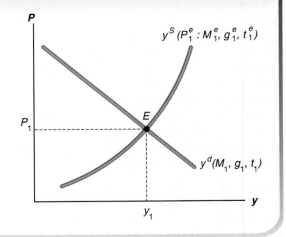

As discussed above, however, key determinants of the price-level expectation that people form are their specific anticipations of monetary and fiscal policy choices, denoted M_1^e, g_1^e, and t_1^e. Hence, we label the aggregate supply schedule as $y^s(P^e: M_1^e, g_1^e, t_1^e)$ to indicate that its position depends on the expectation of the price level, which in turn depends on anticipated values of policy variables.

Policy anticipations may not always be correct. Nevertheless, we shall assume that initially these anticipations *are* correct, so that $M_1^e = M_1$, $g_1^e = g_1$, and $t_1^e = t_1$. Consequently, $P^e = P_1$ at point E in Figure 11–1, so initially people expect the equilibrium current price level. The question now is what effects policy *changes* will have on the equilibrium price level and real output, depending on whether or not people correctly anticipate them.

THE EFFECTS OF ANTICIPATED POLICY ACTIONS   Figure 11–2 illustrates the effects of policy actions that are *correctly* anticipated. These actions are an increase in the money stock, from M_1 to M_2, a rise in government spending from g_1 to g_2, and a tax reduction from t_1 to t_2. These policy actions together shift the aggregate demand schedule rightward, as shown in the figure.

Suppose that people correctly anticipate these policy actions, meaning that they alter their expectations of the monetary and fiscal policy variables to $M_2^e = M_2$, $g_2^e = g_2$, and $t_2^e = t_2$. As a result, people anticipate the rise in the price level brought about by the policy-induced increase in aggregate demand. This rise in their price expectation implies an expectation that the real wage will fall. Workers cut back on their supply of labor to firms, and firms supply less real output at any given price level. As a result, the aggregate supply schedule, y^s, will shift leftward, as shown. At the new short-run equilibrium point, E', the equilibrium price level is higher, at P_2, but real output remains unchanged, at y_1. Correct anticipations of the monetary and fiscal policy actions effectively neutralize their effects on actual real output. Correctly anticipated monetary and fiscal policy actions thereby will have no real output effects, *even in the short run*. They will result only in a higher price level.

Figure 11–2   The Effects of Correctly Anticipated Policy Actions

Expansionary monetary and fiscal policy actions, such as an increase in the money stock, an increase in real government expenditures, or a reduction in real net taxes, will cause a rightward shift in the aggregate demand schedule. In the new classical theory, if people correctly forecast these policy actions, then they will fully anticipate the increase in the price level that the actions will induce. Accordingly, individuals will raise their price expectation, causing a leftward shift in the aggregate supply schedule. On net, the equilibrium price level will rise, but the equilibrium amount of real output will remain unchanged.

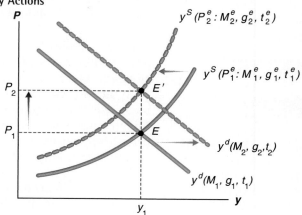

To understand why these effects occur, recall from Chapter 3 that the classical aggregate supply schedule is vertical, because in the classical model people have full information. As a result, any increase in the price level resulting from a rise in aggregate demand will be fully anticipated, so real output will not change. The example in Figure 11–2 differs from the classical model of Chapters 3 and 4 only in that information is not complete. Nevertheless, by correctly anticipating policy actions that will raise aggregate demand and the price level, the people in our example act as though they had complete information. Consequently, the outcome looks very "classical": Real output is not affected by a policy-induced rise in aggregate demand.

THE EFFECTS OF UNANTICIPATED POLICY ACTIONS   Of course, people cannot always correctly predict macroeconomic policies. A majority of Congress might enact a spending increase, but the president might unexpectedly veto the spending bill. The Federal Reserve might announce that it plans a particular growth rate for the money stock but may not successfully induce that money growth rate. The Fed might even intentionally deviate from the planned money growth rate it previously announced because of changes in economic activity that it believes require a policy response. If the Fed fails to communicate its change in policy, people will not correctly anticipate its action.

POLICY INEFFECTIVENESS PROPOSITION: The new classical conclusion that if policy actions are anticipated, they have no real effects in the short run; nor do policy actions have real effects in the long run even if the policy actions are unanticipated.

macroxtra!
Online
Perspective

To learn why the new classical theory's implications cause some economists to question whether the Phillips curve could be a useful forecasting tool, go to the Chapter 11 reading, entitled "Are Phillips Curves Useful for Forecasting Inflation?" by Andrew Atkeson and Lee Ohanian, published by the Federal Reserve Bank of Minneapolis.

http://macroxtra.swcollege.com

Figure 11–3 displays the effects of monetary and fiscal policy actions that people completely fail to anticipate. Again, the policy actions are an increase in the money stock, from M_1 to M_2, a rise in government spending from g_1 to g_2, and a tax reduction from t_1 to t_2, which together shift the aggregate demand schedule rightward.

Because workers anticipated that the money stock, government spending, and taxes would remain equal to M_1, g_1, and t_1, respectively, in the short run they misperceive any rise in the nominal wage as indicating an increase in their real wage. The nominal wage increase occurs because a rise in the price level caused by the unanticipated increase in aggregate demand raises the demand for labor. Workers increase the quantity of labor services that they supply, and firms produce more real output. In the short run, therefore, the equilibrium price level will rise, from P_1 to P_2, and equilibrium real output will increase, from y_1 to y_2, as the aggregate demand schedule shifts along the aggregate supply schedule from point E to point E'.

In the long run, according to the new classical model, people ultimately recognize that these monetary and fiscal policy actions have taken place. They eventually adjust their policy anticipations appropriately, and their price-level expectations increase. In the long run, therefore, the aggregate supply schedule will shift leftward as in Figure 11–2. As in the monetarist framework, an unanticipated policy-induced increase in aggregate demand will exert no effects on longer-run equilibrium real output. In the short run, however, real output will rise.

The Policy Ineffectiveness Proposition

The concepts illustrated in Figures 11–2 and 11–3 form the basis for a key implication of the new classical theory—the **policy ineffectiveness proposition.** This proposition states that *systematic,* or predictable, macro-

Figure 11–3   The Effects of Completely Unanticipated Policy Actions

If the central bank increases the nominal quantity of money in circulation and if the government raises real government spending or reduces real net taxes, then the aggregate demand schedule will shift rightward. If these policy actions are completely unanticipated, then individuals will not have forecast the actions, and their price expectations will remain unchanged. Consequently, the aggregate supply schedule's position does not change, and the rise in aggregate demand induces an increase in both the equilibrium price level and the equilibrium level of real output.

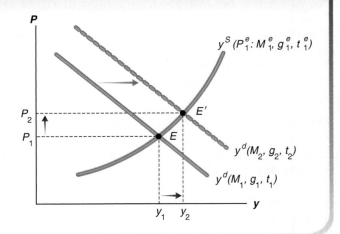

economic policy actions should have no short-run effects on real variables, such as employment, the unemployment rate, or real GDP. Systematic policy actions that people can anticipate lead only to changes in the price level and the inflation rate.

The policy ineffectiveness proposition applies only to the effects of systematic policy actions that people can anticipate. *Unsystematic policies,* which people cannot always anticipate fully, can still have short-run real effects. Although these effects disappear in the long run, as in the monetarist model, in principle they could be sizable in the short run.

Hence, the new classical theory has the following key implications for macroeconomic policymaking:

According to new classical theory, macroeconomic policy actions that individuals and firms fully anticipate have no effects on real variables such as output and employment. Only unanticipated policy actions that people cannot predict in advance can influence real GDP and employment.

macroxtra!
Economic Applications

Should the Fed pursue a fixed policy rule? To review alternative perspectives on this debate and make your own judgment, go to EconDebate Online.
http://macroxtra.swcollege.com

FUNDAMENTAL ISSUE #3

How do policy anticipations determine the actual effects of policy actions in the new classical model, and what is the new classical policy ineffectiveness proposition? On the one hand, if people are able to anticipate monetary or fiscal policy actions correctly, then they will adjust their price and inflation expectations accordingly. As a result, correctly anticipated policy actions have no real effects. On the other hand, policy actions that people are not able to anticipate have short-run effects on real output, employment, and the unemployment rate that mirror those predicted by Keynesian and monetarist theory. These implications of the new classical theory provide the foundation for the policy ineffectiveness proposition, which states that systematic, or predictable, monetary and fiscal policies can have no short-run or long-run effects on real output, employment, or unemployment. This means that if policymakers wish to induce changes in such real variables, they must undertake policy actions that are unsystematic, or unpredictable.

Rational Expectations and Efficient Markets

The new classical economists have applied the rational expectations hypothesis to the theory of the determination of the price level and real output. Another important application of the rational expectations hypothesis, however, is in the area of financial markets.

Efficient Markets Theory

You learned in Chapter 8 that bond prices are inversely related to interest rates. To demonstrate this inverse relationship, we considered perpetual bonds that pay an infinite stream of coupon returns. To calculate the price that someone would be willing to pay for such a bond, we summed up the discounted present value of the stream of coupon returns. To compute the discounted present value of each year's coupon return, we used the current market interest rate. What if the market interest rate might vary from year to year? Then the price of the bond would actually equal the *expected* discounted present value of the stream of coupon returns, based on people's *expectations* of future market interest rates.

RATIONAL EXPECTATIONS AND FINANCIAL ASSET RETURNS Let's think about how we might apply the rational expectations hypothesis to this more realistic view of how bond prices are determined. Under the rational expectations hypothesis, an optimal forecast reflects all available past *and* current information as well as an understanding of how the relevant variable is determined. In the case of an interest return, therefore, the rational expectations hypothesis would indicate that the expected future market interest rates used in bond-price calculations would be the rational forecast of future interest returns by those who purchase and hold financial assets.

As a result, the price of a perpetual bond is equal to the rationally anticipated discounted present value of the sum of future coupon returns. The market price thereby incorporates rationally formed expectations.

EFFICIENT MARKETS THEORY This reasoning forms the basis for the **efficient markets theory.** This theory states that prices of financial assets should reflect all available information, including bond traders' understanding of how financial markets determine asset prices. As applied to the perpetual bond we studied in Chapter 8, the theory of efficient markets indicates that the current price of a bond should be equal to the rational forecast of the discounted value of the sum of coupon returns yielded by the bond.

More generally, the efficient markets theory says that the price of *any* financial asset should reflect the rational forecast of the asset's returns. Consequently, any bond price should reflect a recognition of all available information by those who trade the bonds. If the market bond price failed to reflect all such information, then the implication would be that the market functions inefficiently, because traders could earn higher returns on bonds by considering the unused information.

Can People "Beat the Market"?

Recognition that failure to use all available information will lead to lower returns than bond traders otherwise could earn leads to the key implication of the efficient markets theory: In an efficient financial market, there should be no unexploited opportunities for traders to earn higher returns. If such opportunities existed, some traders would buy or sell more bonds. This would cause the market price of the bonds to change.

What direction would the bonds' price move? The answer is that it would adjust to its efficient-market price that would reflect the rational forecasts of traders. Rational expectations in the bond market would lead to trading that would yield this efficient-market price.

Does this mean that no trader can ever earn profits from trading bonds? The answer clearly must be no, otherwise people would not earn their livelihoods by speculating in bond markets. Nevertheless, the efficient markets theory does indicate that bond speculators should not be able to earn profits from taking advantage of unused information for very long. Any unexploited information will quickly be recognized by a sufficient number of bond traders that bond prices will adjust quickly. Profits from such trades may be significant, but they will also be fleeting. (Sometimes traders can earn profits when government policymakers accidentally create the potential for only a few people to have inside information; see on the following page *Policy Notebook: The Demise of the 30-Year Treasury Bond— Insider Trading or a Bureaucratic Comedy?*)

FUNDAMENTAL ISSUE #4

What is the efficient markets theory, and what is its main implication? The efficient markets theory states that the market price of a financial asset should take into account all available information in that market. This theory, which follows from the application of the rational expectations hypothesis to financial markets, indicates that unexploited opportunities to earn higher returns in a financial market should not exist at the equilibrium price of the financial asset traded in that market.

Interest Parity and Foreign Exchange Market Efficiency

The concept of market efficiency does not apply only to financial asset prices and interest rates that are determined in a nation's domestic financial markets. It may also be extended to markets for financial assets that are traded internationally, such as bonds and national currencies. Ultimately, then, currency exchange rates, national interest rates, and expectations all must be related.

Exchange-Rate Determination

How is the exchange rate, or the dollar's exchange value in terms of other currencies, determined? We touched on this issue in Chapter 4, but let's consider it in more detail now that you understand the importance of information and expectations.

The exchange rate is a price that is determined in markets for foreign exchange. Therefore, the value of the exchange rate is determined by the interactions between the forces of demand and supply in **foreign exchange markets,** which are the markets in which individuals, businesses, governments, and central banks exchange currencies of various nations.

FOREIGN EXCHANGE MARKETS: Markets in which currencies of different nations are exchanged.

The Demise of the 30-Year Treasury Bond— Insider Trading or a Bureaucratic Comedy?

On Wednesday, October 31, 2001, the U.S. Treasury Department accidentally created a Halloween monster. It made two big mistakes, and as a consequence, it lost considerable credibility with private securities firms on Wall Street.

Both of the Treasury's mistakes occurred as it prepared to formally announce that it was immediately discontinuing the issuance of 30-year government bonds. For years, the 30-year Treasury bond had been a key vehicle for U.S. government borrowing. Beginning in the late 1990s, the Treasury had made it clear that it planned to phase out the bonds. Financial markets did not know exactly when that would happen, but the Treasury had settled on October 31 as the day for the formal announcement.

At 9 A.M. on that day, Treasury officials conducted a news briefing intended solely for media representatives. Officials told the reporters that news of the bond's demise would be made public as of 10 A.M., but that they were being informed in advance so that they could write stories for release at that time. Officials failed to check the credentials of everyone who attended the meeting, however, and one of those present was a financial consultant who did not understand that this early news of the bond's end was "embargoed" until 10 A.M.. After the briefing ended just before 9:30 A.M., the consultant called some of his clients and relayed the news.

Shortly before the formal public release of the information at 10 A.M., bond prices jumped as many traders began betting that bond investors who could no longer hold 30-year bonds would begin shifting some of their funds to stocks, thereby causing bond rates to decline. If not for a second mistake, the Treasury could easily have argued that the consultant had helped his clients profit from inside information. The difficulty was that the Treasury had accidentally posted the public announcement of the bond's demise on its Web site at 9:49 A.M.. Almost immediately, several news wire services noticed the announcement on the Web site and began to file reports. Hence, although some traders may have earned profits on insider information gleaned from the consultant's release, it is also possible that some traders earned profits simply because they were paying close attention to the Treasury's own Web site.

For Critical Analysis
Why might it be in the Treasury's interest to give advance notice to the media before announcing major policy actions such as the elimination of a type of bond?

EXCHANGE RATES Before we discuss foreign exchange markets, you need to understand how exchange rates are measured. Consider Table 11–1, which displays exchange rates for selected nations' currrencies as they appear each day on the Web site of the Federal Reserve Bank of New York.

For purposes of discussion, we shall confine our attention to the value of the dollar in terms of the European Monetary Union's euro ($\in$). Table 11–1 indicates that as of September 26, 2002, \$1 could have purchased about $\in$1.0266. This meant that the exchange rate at that time was $\in$1.0266 per dollar, which we can write as 1.0266 $\in$/\$. But it also meant that $\in$1.0266 could have purchased \$1, or that 1 euro could have purchased $1/(1.0266)$ = \$0.9741. Hence, the 2002 dollar–euro rate of exchange could also have been expressed as 0.9741 dollars per euro, or 0.9741 \$/$\in$.

As you can see, because the exchange rate measures the value of one nation's currency in terms of the currency of another nation, it can always be expressed in two ways. Consequently, we must specify which measure we are using when we discuss changes in exchange rates. Just

Table 11-1   Exchange Rates

Country	Monetary Unit	U.S. Dollar Equivalent	Currency per U.S. Dollar
European Monetary Union	Euro	0.9741	1.0266
3-month forward		0.9704	1.0305
6-month forward		0.9671	1.0342
Canada	Dollar	0.6340	1.5772
Denmark	Krone	0.1314	7.6086
Japan	Yen	0.0081	122.71
3-month foward		0.0082	122.17
6-month forward		0.0082	121.67
Norway	Krone	0.1333	7.5006
Sweden	Krona	0.1069	9.3532
Switzerland	Franc	0.6656	1.5025
United Kingdom	Pound	1.5568	0.6423

SOURCE: Federal Reserve Bank of New York, Daily 10 A.M. Midpoint Foreign Exchange Rates from the New York Interbank Market, September 26, 2002.

saying that the exchange rate "rose" or "fell" means little unless we know which of the two measures we have in mind. Throughout our discussion, we shall look at the dollar–euro exchange rate from a U.S. perspective: We shall express the exchange rate in terms of dollars that must be given up in exchange for euros, such as the 0.9741 $/€ exchange rate that applied in September 2002. This is the dollar value of the euro. An increase in this exchange rate indicates an appreciation of the value of the euro relative to the dollar and, equivalently, a depreciation of the value of the dollar relative to the euro.

IMPORTS AND THE DEMAND FOR FOREIGN CURRENCY   The primary reason that U.S. residents might desire to obtain the currency of another country is that they wish to buy goods and services produced in that nation. To help envision the factors that influence the quantity of a foreign currency, such as the euro, that U.S. residents might wish to obtain, consider an example. Suppose that a U.S. consumer purchased a German-manufactured coffeemaker in September 2001. The German manufacturer sent the coffeemaker to the United States to be sold that year at a price of €30. Thus, at the 2001 exchange rate of 0.9395 $/€, the dollar price of the coffeemaker was equal to €30 × 0.9395 $/€, or $28.19.

Now imagine that the same consumer considered buying the same coffeemaker model in September 2002. Suppose further that the euro price of the coffeemaker remained unchanged, at €30, between 2001 and 2002. Nevertheless, the euro strengthened relative to the dollar, so the exchange rate increased to about 0.9741 $/€. As a result, the dollar price of the coffeemaker rose to €30 × 0.9741 $/€ = $29.22. Hence, in dollar terms the price of the coffeemaker increased by $1.03, which amounted to about a 3.7 percent price increase.

On the Web

Where on the Internet can one find daily updates concerning euro and yen forward exchange rates relative to the U.S. dollar? One place to check for these forward exchange rates is the Federal Reserve Bank of New York's daily 10 A.M. foreign exchange statistical release located at http://www.ny.frb.org/pihome/statistics/forex10.shtml.

When faced with such an increase in the dollar price of the German-manufactured coffeemaker, the U.S. consumer may have decided not to buy a coffeemaker made in Germany. Likewise, other U.S. residents likely tended to reduce their purchases of goods manufactured in Germany, which experienced similar dollar price increases. Consequently, U.S. importers decreased their orders for German-made products. So importers cut back purchases from German firms using euros acquired in the foreign exchange market. Hence, the amount of euros demanded in the foreign exchange market declined as a result of the rise in the dollar–euro exchange rate from 0.9395 \$/€ to 0.9741 \$/€. It follows that the *demand schedule* for euros slopes downward, as shown in Figure 11–4.

EXPORTS AND THE SUPPLY OF FOREIGN CURRENCY   We must also think about the effect of a rise in the dollar–euro exchange rate from the perspective of German residents. Suppose that a German importer buys U.S.-manufactured computer microchips for resale in Germany. For the sake of argument, suppose also that a typical lot of microchips has a dollar price of \$500 and that this base price did not change between 2001 and 2002. At the 2001 exchange rate of 0.9395 \$/€, the euro price of the lot of microchips during that year would have been \$500/(0.9395 \$/€), or €532.20. In 2002, however, at the exchange rate of 0.9741 \$/€, the same computer sold at a euro price of \$500/(0.9741 \$/€), or about €513.29. Therefore, from the perspective of a German consumer, the U.S. price of the lot of microchips fell by 18.91 euros, or by about 3.6 percent.

This decrease in the euro price of the U.S.-manufactured microchips tended to induce an increase in German purchases of U.S. microchips. In like manner, reductions in prices of other U.S. export goods caused German

Figure 11–4   The Market for European Monetary Union Euros

Holding other factors constant, as the dollar price of the euro rises, U.S. residents are inclined to purchase fewer goods made in Germany and elsewhere in the European Monetary Union. Therefore they convert fewer dollars into euros, thereby decreasing the quantity of euros demanded in the foreign exchange market. Hence, the demand schedule for euros slopes downward. At the same time, a rise in the dollar price of the euro induces German residents to increase their purchases of U.S.-made goods, thereby increasing the quantity of euros supplied in the foreign exchange market. Consequently, the euro supply schedule slopes upward. At the equilibrium exchange rate, or dollar price of the euro, the quantity of euros supplied is equal to the quantity of euros demanded.

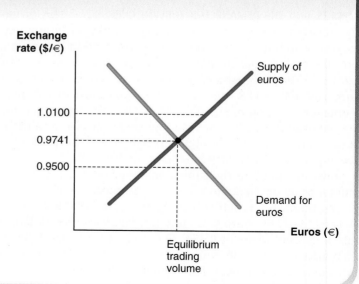

purchases of U.S. goods to rise. German importers increased their orders for U.S. export goods, which they bought with dollars that they obtained in the foreign exchange market. These German importers supplied more euros in exchange for dollars. Consequently, the rise in the dollar–euro exchange rate from 0.9395 $/€ to 0.9741 $/€ increased the quantity of euros supplied in the foreign exchange market. As Figure 11–4 shows, the *supply schedule* for euros generally was upward sloping.

THE EQUILIBRIUM FOREIGN EXCHANGE RATE   Figure 11–4 also depicts the determination of an *equilibrium exchange rate* between the euro and the dollar. This is the rate of exchange of dollars for euros at which the amount of euros demanded is equal to the amount of euros supplied in the foreign exchange market.

In Figure 11–4, we assume that the equilibrium exchange rate is 0.9741$/€. If the exchange rate happened to be above this level, perhaps at the rate of 1.0100 $/€, then there would be fewer euros demanded than supplied. Some German residents who wished to supply euros for dollars would be unable to sell their euros at this exchange rate, so they would be obliged to offer the euros at a lower exchange rate. Consequently, the exchange rate would fall toward the equilibrium rate of 0.9741 $/€. In contrast, if the exchange rate fell below the equilibrium rate, say, to 0.9500 $/€, then there would be more euros demanded than supplied, and so the exchange rate would tend to rise back toward the equilibrium rate of 0.9741 $/€.

Covered and Uncovered Interest Parity

Although we have explained demand and supply in the foreign exchange market solely by referring to exports and imports of goods, U.S. residents also hold financial assets issued in Germany, and German residents hold financial assets issued in the United States. U.S. financial assets are denominated in dollars and pay dollar-denominated interest returns, while German financial assets are denominated in euros and pay euro-denominated interest returns. Because the exchange rate measures the relative values of the two currencies, the exchange rate must play a role in relating interest rates in the two countries.

COVERED INTEREST PARITY   Table 11–1 on page 327 reports several **spot exchange rates,** which are the rates of exchange for currencies to be traded immediately, or "on the spot." Each day, the interactions among financial institutions, nonfinancial firms, and individual foreign exchange market traders also determine **forward exchange rates.** These are the market exchange rates on **forward currency contracts,** which call for delivery of a unit of a nation's currency in exchange for another at a predetermined price on a specified date. Table 11–1 also lists forward exchange rates for 3-month and 6-month forward euro and yen contracts.

The existence of forward currency contracts plays a central role in relating national interest rates. To see why, suppose that a U.S. resident has two alternatives. One is to purchase a one-period, dollar-denominated bond that has a market interest yield of r_{US}. After one year, the U.S. resident will have accumulated $1 + r_{US}$ dollars for each dollar saved.

SPOT EXCHANGE RATE: The rate of exchange for currencies to be traded immediately.

FORWARD EXCHANGE RATE: The rate of exchange for currencies specified in forward currency contracts.

FORWARD CURRENCY CONTRACTS: Agreements to deliver a unit of a nation's currency in exchange for another at a specified price on a given date.

The other option is to use each dollar to buy euros at the spot exchange rate of S dollars per euro, thereby obtaining $1/S$ euros with each dollar. The U.S. resident could use the $1/S$ euros to buy a one-year German bond that pays the rate r_E. After a year, he will have accumulated $(1/S)(1 + r_E)$ *euros.* When the U.S. resident buys the German bond, however, at the same time he sells this quantity of euros in the forward market at the forward exchange rate of F dollars per euro. This "covers" him against risk of exchange-rate changes by ensuring that the effective return on the German bond will be $(F/S)(1 + r_E)$.

The returns on the two bonds will be the same if $1 + r_{US} = (F/S)(1 + r_E)$. As you will demonstrate in a problem at the end of the chapter, this means that the U.S. resident will be willing to hold bonds only if r_{US} is approximately equal to r_E plus the quantity $(F - S)/S$:

$$r_{US} = r_E + (F - S)/S.$$

This is called the **covered interest parity** condition. If positive, the quantity $(F - S)/S$ is called the *forward premium,* so covered interest parity says that the interest rate on a U.S. bond should approximately equal the interest rate on the foreign (German) bond plus the forward premium. If $(F - S)/S$ is negative, there is a *forward discount.*

In Table 11–1, for a 6-month forward contract, F is equal to 0.9671 dollars per euro. In addition, S is equal to 0.9741 dollars per euro, so $(F - S)/S$ is equal to $(0.9671 - 0.9741)/0.9741 = -0.0072$, a negative number. This means that the dollar would have a higher value in terms of euros—it would take fewer dollars to buy euros—in the forward exchange market than in the spot exchange market. Consequently, covered interest parity tells us that the interest rate on the U.S. dollar–denominated bond should be lower than the interest rate on the German euro-denominated bond.

In contrast, if F were equal to 0.9862 dollars per euro and S remained at 0.9741 dollars per euro $(F - S)/S$ would be equal to $(0.9862 - 0.9741)/0.9741 = 0.0124$, a positive number. Then covered interest parity tells us that, as a consequence, the interest rate on the U.S. dollar–denominated bond should be higher than the interest rate on the German euro-denominated bond.

UNCOVERED INTEREST PARITY   The covered interest parity condition is very useful for evaluating why nations' interest rates may differ. It does not tell us, however, why a forward premium exists. This is where expectations come into the story.

Suppose that a U.S.-based mutual fund is considering holding either U.S. Treasury bonds or euro-denominated bonds issued by the German government. The bonds have the same maturity, and the mutual fund perceives that they are equally risky. Hence, the mutual fund views the bonds as perfect substitutes. Suppose that the current spot dollar–euro exchange rate is $S = 0.9741$ $/€. Note that if S were to rise during an interval, say, to 0.1.0100 $/€, more dollars would be required to obtain one euro. The dollar would *depreciate* relative to the euro.

Suppose that the dollar depreciates relative to the euro at a rate s over time. A positive value of s indicates a positive *rate of depreciation* of the dollar versus the euro. This implies that the value of the dollar falls relative to the euro. In fact, between September 2001 and September 2002, the dollar depreciated relative to the euro almost 4 percent. Thus, s had a *positive* value during this interval.

Now consider the situation faced by the mutual fund. If it holds the dollar-denominated U.S. Treasury bond, then its total return is simply the interest return r_{US}. If it holds the German government bond, then it earns interest at the rate r_E. In addition, however, the mutual fund anticipates that the dollar value of the euro-denominated bond will fall at an expected rate of s^e. Consequently, the mutual fund anticipates future *appreciation* of the dollar, so s^e is negative.

This mutual fund—as well as others making a similar choice—will be willing to hold either U.S. or German government bonds only if the expected returns on the two bonds are the same. This will be the case when

$$r_{US} = r_E + s^e.$$

For the mutual fund to be willing to hold *both* the U.S. and German government bonds, the U.S. Treasury bond rate must equal the German government bond rate minus the rate at which the dollar is expected to appreciate relative to the euro.

This condition makes a lot of sense. Because the dollar is expected to appreciate in the future, so that s^e is negative, it says that a dollar-denominated U.S. Treasury bond will yield a return comparable to the return on a German bond only if the U.S. bond's yield is lower to compensate for any expected appreciation in the dollar relative to the euro. Hence, the amount by which the U.S. Treasury bond yield will be less than the German government bond yield is equal to the rate at which the dollar is expected to appreciate relative to the euro, or s^e, which is negative.

The last equation is the **uncovered interest parity** condition. It applies to interest yields on bonds with identical risks and terms to maturity that are denominated in different national currencies. According to uncovered interest parity, the yield on a bond denominated in a currency that is expected to depreciate must exceed another nation's bond yield by the rate at which the currency is expected to depreciate. Or it must be less by the expected rate of appreciation.

We have simplified by assuming that the U.S. and German bonds are equally risky. Even though both U.S. and German bonds should be relatively free of the risk of default by the respective governments, people may still regard one government's bond as slightly more risky than the other government's bond. For instance, in the event of a financial crisis in the Western Hemisphere, such as the Mexican peso crisis of 1995, the devaluations of the Brazilian *real* in 1999 and 2002, or the devaluation of the Argentine peso in 2002, people might worry that the U.S. government's finances might become entangled, affecting returns on U.S. government bonds. If the U.S. bond is relatively more risky than another, then the uncovered interest parity condition becomes

$$r_{US} = r_E + s^e + RP,$$

where RP denotes a risk premium, or an extra amount that must be built into the U.S. bond's interest rate to induce people to hold both U.S. and

UNCOVERED INTEREST PARITY: A prediction that the interest rate on a bond denominated in a currency that is expected to depreciate must exceed another nation's bond rate by the rate at which the currency is expected to depreciate plus a risk premium.

German bonds of equal maturities. (If bonds have the same risk characteristics and uncovered interest parity still fails to hold, then traders can earn *excess returns* by engaging in international bond trading; see *Management Notebook: Excess Returns and Uncovered Interest Parity.*)

Foreign Exchange Market Efficiency

Note that the two interest parity conditions just discussed provide two reasons why the interest rate on a U.S. bond might be different from the interest rate on an otherwise identical German bond. One reason, provided by the *covered* interest parity condition, is that there may be a forward premium (or discount) in the foreign exchange market. In that case, the differential between the U.S. bond's rate and the German bond's rate would equal

$$r_{US} - r_E = (F - S)/S.$$

The other reason is implied by the *uncovered* interest parity condition, which says that the U.S. bond's interest rate should exceed the German bond's interest rate by an amount equal to the expected rate of depreciation of the dollar plus any risk premium:

$$r_{US} - r_E = s^e + RP.$$

The only way that both of these interest parity conditions are satisfied is if the right-hand terms in both are equal, or if

$$(F - S)/S = s^e + RP,$$

which states that the forward premium for the dollar relative to the euro is equal to the rate at which the dollar is expected to depreciate relative to the euro plus any risk premium. This last condition is known as the condition for **foreign exchange market efficiency.** It states that in an efficient foreign exchange market, spot and forward exchange rates should adjust to the point at which the forward premium reflects the expected rate of currency depreciation and any risk premium. Under the rational expectations hypothesis, the expected rate of currency depreciation should be the rational forecast of the depreciation rate, or the forecast of depreciation based on all available information and an understanding of how exchange rates are determined.

Another way of thinking about the foreign exchange market efficiency condition is to relate it to the efficient markets theory. This theory broadly states that the price of a financial asset should reflect all available information. The foreign exchange market efficiency condition is analogous. It states that the spot and forward exchange rates, which are the spot and forward prices of a nation's currency, should take into account rational forecasts of the extent to which the nation's currency will depreciate. As a result, the forward premium relating the spot and forward exchange rates should reflect all available information.

Considerable evidence indicates that covered interest parity holds in foreign exchange markets. The evidence on uncovered interest parity and, consequently, of foreign exchange market efficiency is more mixed. If the rational expectations hypothesis is correct, then the expected rate

Excess Returns and Uncovered Interest Parity

As you have learned, if the uncovered interest parity condition is satisfied, the interest rate on a U.S. bond, r, should equal the interest rate on a foreign bond, r^*, plus the rate at which the domestic currency is anticipated to depreciate during the period that the two bonds mature, s^e. What happens if the uncovered interest parity condition fails to hold even if bonds are equally risky? In this situation, the expected rate of domestic currency depreciation is greater than the differential between the U.S. and foreign bonds, so s^e exceeds the difference between r and r^*.

This means that instead of simply holding the U.S. bond and earning the rate r, a U.S. resident can anticipate earning more by converting dollars to the foreign currency, holding foreign bonds and earning the rate r^*, and then obtaining more dollars per unit of foreign currency after the foreign bond matures and the domestic currency depreciates. In this way, the U.S. resident could earn an "excess return" equal to $s^e - (r - r^*)$. For instance, if the expected rate of depreciation of the dollar relative to the euro is 2 percent, the annual return on a U.S. bond is 6 percent, and the annual

Figure 11–5   Estimates of Excess Returns on International Bond Trading

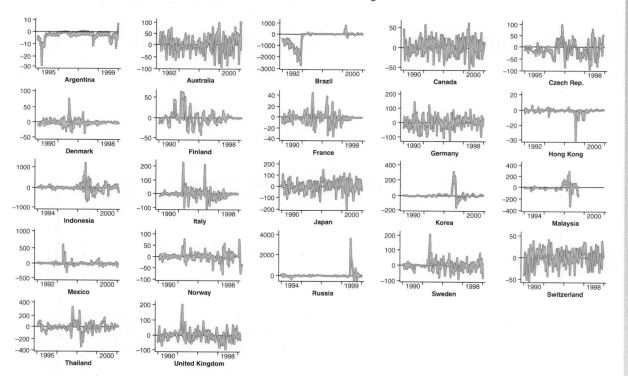

These charts display annualized excess returns (in basis points, or hundredths of a percentage point) for various nations.

These excess returns are estimated expected percentage changes in the exchange rate minus interest-rate differentials.

SOURCE: Robert Flood and Andrew Rose, "Uncovered Interest Parity in Crisis: The Interest Rate Defense of the 1990s," Center for Economic Policy Research Discussion Paper No. 2943, September 2001.

Continued on next page

Management Notebook, continued

return on a German bond is 5 percent, then the excess return equals 2 percent − (6 percent − 5 percent) = 1 percent.

Traditionally, economists have argued that U.S. residents should have less opportunity to earn excess returns from bonds of nations that have the most developed and open financial markets. For this reason, we might expect that measured excess returns should be relatively smaller in more developed nations than in less-developed, emerging nations.

Figure 11–5 on the previous page displays estimates of excess returns during the 1990s from a study by Robert Flood of the International Monetary Fund and Andrew Rose of the University of California at Berkeley. As you can see, it is not readily apparent that larger excess returns are available to U.S. residents who have held bonds issued in nations with emerging economies. For instance, the excess returns available from holding Indonesian bonds have tended to be no greater than those available from holding Italian bonds. Likewise, excess returns from holding bonds issued in the

Czech Republic are comparable to those available from holding bonds issued in the United Kingdom.

Even though U.S. residents can sometimes earn significant excess returns by holding bonds of other nations, Flood and Rose determined that *average* excess returns in many countries are not very large. Although Figure 11–5 indicates that the uncovered interest parity condition is rarely satisfied at any given point in time, over longer-run periods excess returns tend to disappear. Interestingly, this appears to be as true for emerging nations as it is for highly developed countries. Foreign exchange markets are not fully efficient in less-developed countries, but apparently these markets are not significantly less efficient than those in more developed countries.

For Critical Analysis
If excess returns average out to zero over the long term, then how can firms that specialize as broker-dealers in international bond trading stay in business?

of depreciation should reflect a rational forecast. Consequently, studies of foreign exchange market efficiency also entail trying to determine if exchange-rate expectations are formed rationally. Trying to determine statistically whether foreign exchange market efficiency and rational expectations both hold at the same time is a difficult proposition, and economists continue to investigate the efficiency of foreign exchange markets.

FUNDAMENTAL ISSUE #5

How are exchange rates determined, and what is foreign exchange market efficiency?   Exchange rates are determined by the forces of demand and supply in foreign exchange markets. The spot exchange rate is the exchange rate for currency to be exchanged immediately, and the forward exchange rate is the rate of exchange on currency to be delivered at a later date. Foreign exchange market efficiency requires that the forward premium, or the difference between the forward and spot exchange rates divided by the spot exchange rate, equal the expected rate of currency depreciation plus a risk premium. This efficiency condition holds if both the covered and the uncovered interest parity conditions are satisfied.

Explaining International Interest–Rate Linkages

In a world of floating exchange rates, interest rates of different countries should not necessarily move together, because movements in actual and expected exchange rates can be consistent with declining interest rates in one nation and rising interest rates in another. Nevertheless, in recent years, interest rates in several major industrialized nations have tended to move in conjunction. As you can see in Figure 11–6 on the following page, the main explanation for this is that central banks have aimed to move interest rates nearly in lockstep.

Common Rationales for Similar Interest-Rate Adjustments

Economists can offer at least three rationales for why central banks might desire for interest rates to move in similar directions over time:

1. **Reacting to common events** One reason that central banks might, say, engage in policies that push down interest rates simultaneously is that the economies of their nations have experienced a temporary, worldwide oil price shock. Because a temporary increase in global energy prices tends to push down aggregate supply within countries throughout the world, central banks may respond with similar monetary expansions that reduce interest rates and increase aggregate demand so as to stabilize real output levels.

2. **Reacting to international spillovers** In some situations, economic fluctuations in one nation may spill over to affect economic activity in other countries. A recession in the United States, for example, could cause U.S. imports from Canada, the United Kingdom, and the nations of the European Monetary Union to decline, thereby reducing the aggregate demand for goods and services in those countries. Thus, as the Federal Reserve engages in a monetary expansion that pushes down interest rates and stimulates aggregate demand in the United States, the Bank of Canada, the Bank of England, and the European Central Bank might engage in expansionary monetary policies at roughly the same time in an effort to address spillover effects of the U.S. recession on their economies.

3. **Smoothing exchange rates** Central banks might wish to minimize swings in the exchange values of their currencies by adjusting their monetary policies in tandem. Basic international interest parity conditions imply that if interest rates of different countries move together, actual and expected exchange rates will not change very much. If international interest rates move in equal measure, exchange rates will remain unchanged.

The Federal Reserve as "Policy Leader"

Take another look at Figure 11–6, and you will see that central banks rarely engage in policies that bring about equal adjustments of interest rates. Thus, even though central banks may have exchange-rate smoothing in mind, their actions do not appear to be intended to fix exchange rates. Furthermore, although interest-rate changes tend to happen at about the same time, they do not always occur simultaneously.

During the period charted in Figure 11–6, the United States experienced a major expansion followed by a relatively sharp recession. During this interval, the Bank of Canada, the Bank of England, and the European Central Bank often tended to follow Federal Reserve policy changes by bringing about similar adjustments in their market interest rates. This could be evidence of reactions by those nations to spillover effects from cyclical movements in U.S. output and prices.

Continued on next page

Link to the Global Economy, continued

In addition, however, the tendency for other nations' interest-rate adjustments to lag behind those in the United States is also consistent with the notion that the Fed sometimes acts as the lead central bank of the world. According to this interpretation, the Federal Reserve pays attention mostly to factors that affect the U.S. economy and tends to be less concerned with external world economic events. Then other central banks follow the Fed's lead by adjusting their own policies.

Research Project

Some economists argue that because the formation of the European Monetary Union (EMU) is effectively creating an economy that rivals the United States in size, in the future the European Central Bank will be less concerned with external factors when determining its own monetary policies. Are there reasons to agree with this perspective? To disagree? If this prediction turns out to be accurate, how are the rela-

tionship between U.S. and EMU interest rates and the behavior of the dollar–euro exchange rate likely to be affected in future years?

Web Resources

What are the current interest-rate targets of major central banks? U.S. data are available by clicking on "Monetary Policy" and the "Federal Funds Rate" at http://federalreserve.gov, and information on the European Central Bank's current interest-rate targets is available at http://www.ecb.int. You can find current Canadian overnight interest-rate targets at http://www.bankofcanada.ca, and information about targets for interest rates in the United Kingdom is available at http://www.bankofengland.co.uk, where you can click on "Latest MPC Minutes." To search for information about targets of other central banks, go to the home page of the Bank for International Settlements (http://www.bis.org), scroll down to "Links to Central Banks," and click on the pop-up "Central Bank Web Sites."

Figure 11–6 Interest-Rate Targets of Major Central Banks since 1993

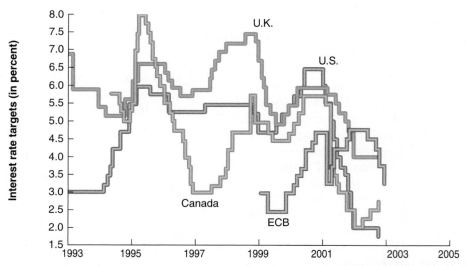

In conjunction with, or shortly after, the Federal Reserve engages in policies that generate movements in U.S. interest rates, other major central banks engage in monetary policy actions that cause short-term interest rates to move in similar ways.

SOURCES: Christopher Neely, "International Interest Rate Linkages," Federal Reserve Bank of St. Louis *International Economic Trends,* August 2001; Bank of Canada, Bank of England, European Central Bank, and Board of Governors of the Federal Reserve System.

Chapter Summary

1. The Distinction between Adaptive and Rational Expectations: An expectation that is formed adaptively is based only on past information. A rational expectation is formed using all available past and current information and relying on an understanding of how the economy works.

2. The Key Assumptions Underlying New Classical Macroeconomics: The new classical model assumes that people pursue their self-interest, and it also follows the classical model by assuming that flexible wages and prices are determined in purely competitive markets. In contrast to the classical theory, the new classical model is based on the assumption of imperfect information in the short run. In contrast to the traditional Keynesian and monetarist theories, however, in the new classical model people form rational price-level and inflation rate expectations.

3. The Actual Effects of Correctly and Incorrectly Anticipated Policy Actions in the New Classical Model and the Policy Ineffectiveness Proposition: If people can fully anticipate monetary or fiscal policy actions, then they will adjust their price-level and inflation rate expectations, and the policy actions will have no real effects. Policy actions that are not fully anticipated, however, have short-run effects on real output, employment, and the unemployment rate that are the same as those predicted by traditional Keynesian and monetarist theory. The new classical policy ineffectiveness proposition states that systematic, pre-dictable macroeconomic policy actions cannot exert either short-run or long-run effects on real output, employment, or unemployment. Hence, if monetary or fiscal policymakers wish to change real output, employment, and unemployment, they must find ways to enact policies that are unsystematic, or unpredictable.

4. The Efficient Markets Theory and Its Main Implication: According to the efficient markets theory, which stems from applying the rational expectations hypothesis to the determination of bond prices, the market price of any financial asset should reflect information available in that market. As a result, opportunities to earn interest returns higher than the equilibrium market return should not exist.

5. Exchange-Rate Determination and Foreign Exchange Market Efficiency: Demand and supply in foreign exchange markets interact to determine the equilibrium exchange rate. The spot exchange rate applies to currencies traded immediately, and the forward exchange rate applies to currency delivered at a later date. The foreign exchange market efficiency condition states that the forward premium, which is the difference between the forward and spot exchange rates divided by the spot exchange rate, should be equal to the expected rate of currency depreciation plus a risk premium. This efficiency condition is met if both the covered and the uncovered interest parity conditions hold.

Self-Test Questions

(Answers to odd-numbered questions may be found on the Web at **http://macro. swcollege.com** under "Student Resources.")

1. In your own words, explain the distinction between an adaptive expectation and a rational expectation. Could the two ever be the same? Explain.

2. In your view, what are the two strongest arguments in favor of the rational expectations hypothesis? What are the two strongest arguments against the hypothesis? Support your answers.

3. Suppose that people are partly, but not fully, successful in anticipating a reduction in the money stock. Assuming that all other factors are the same, would real output decline in the short run, according to the new classical model? If so, would real output decline by as much as the traditional Keynesian and monetarist theories would predict? Explain your reasoning.

4. Evaluate the following statement: "In an important sense, the term *policy ineffectiveness proposition* is misleading." Justify your position.

5. Some new classical economists have argued that secrecy is necessary if monetary policy is to influence real GDP, but that the presence of monetary policy secrecy destabilizes GDP. Can you rationalize this perspective? Explain.

6. Which is more "general," in that it could still be correct even if the other were not—the rational expectations hypothesis or the efficient markets theory? Justify your position.

7. Explain, in your own words, the distinction between covered interest parity and uncovered interest parity.

8. Could the covered interest parity condition be met if the uncovered interest parity condition is not also satisfied? Why or why not?

Problems

(Answers to odd-numbered problems may be found on the Web at **http://macro. swcollege.com** under "Student Resources.")

1. Suppose that three years ago, a country experienced an inflation rate of 4 percent. The year before last, its inflation rate rose to 5 percent, and last year the country's inflation rate was 6 percent. Propose two different ways to form an adaptive expectation of the inflation rate for the current year.

2. Consider the data from question 1. Now suppose that you have two additional pieces of information: (a) the country's inflation rate in all previous years that data have been tabulated has been the same as the rate of growth of the quantity of money in circulation, and (b) the current year's money growth rate is 10 percent. In your view, what is a rational expectation of the current year's inflation rate? Is there any guarantee that this expectation will turn out to match the *actual* inflation rate this year, however?

3. Suppose that the equation for the aggregate demand schedule is $y^d = (b \times M) - (c \times P)$, where b and c are positive numbers. The equation for the aggregate supply schedule is $y^s = y^* + [a \times (P - P^e)]$, where y^* and a are positive numbers.

    a. Work out an expression for the equilibrium price level, which will involve the expected price level, P^e. Now consider a situation in which people have full information. What is the equilibrium price level in this situation? (Hint: What is the expected price level when people are fully informed?) Does a monetary policy action—a change in M—influence the price level when people have full information?

    b. What is the output level in the long run when people have full information? Does a monetary policy action affect real output under full information?

4. As discussed in this chapter, a U.S. resident who can cover risks of exchange-rate movements with a forward currency contract will be willing to hold both U.S. and German bonds if the return on each dollar held in the U.S. bond, $1 + r_{US}$, is equal to the return on the German bond, $(F/S)(1 + r_E)$. Note that F/S can be written as $[S + (F - S)]/S = 1 + (F - S)/S$, and use this fact to derive the covered interest parity condition. [Hint: Note that if $(F - S)/S$ is a small fraction and if r_{US} is a small fraction, then the product of r_E and $(F - S)/S$ is very close to zero.]

Before the Test

Test your understanding of the material covered in this chapter by taking the Chapter 11 online quiz at **http://macro.swcollege.com**.

Online Application

You can track exchange rates each day by clicking onto the Federal Reserve Bank of New York's home page (see "Navigation" below).

Title: *The Federal Reserve Bank of New York — Foreign Exchange 12 Noon Rates*

Navigation: Start at the Federal Reserve Bank of New York's home page (http://www.ny.frb.org). Select *Statistics* (http://www.ny.frb.org/pihome/mktrates). Click on *Foreign Exchange 12 Noon Rates.*

Application:

1. For each currency listed, how many dollars does it take to purchase a unit of the currency in the spot foreign exchange market?

2. For each day during a given week (or month), choose a currency from those listed and keep track of its value relative to the dollar. Based on your tabulations, try to predict the value of the currency at the end of the week *following* your data collections. Use any information you may have, or just do your best without any additional information. How far off was your prediction?

For Group Study and Analysis: Each day, you can also click on a report entitled *Foreign Exchange 10 a.m. Rates,* which shows exchange rates for a subset of countries listed in the 12 noon report. Assign each country in the 10 a.m. report to a group. Ask the group to determine whether the currency's value appreciated or depreciated relative to the dollar between 10 a.m. and 12 noon. In addition, ask each group to discuss what kinds of demand or supply shifts could have caused the change that occurred within this interval.

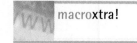

Log on to the MacroXtra Web site at http://macroxtra.swcollege.com for additional learning resources such as practice quizzes, Interactive Key Graphs, readings, and additional economic applications.

Selected References and Further Reading

Daniels, Joseph, and David VanHoose. *International Monetary and Financial Economics.* Cincinnati: ITP/Southwestern, 1998.

Flood, Robert, and Andrew Rose. "Uncovered Interest Parity in Crisis: The Interest Rate Defense of the 1990s." Center for Economic Policy Research Discussion Paper No. 2943, September 2001.

Lucas, Robert. *Studies in Business-Cycle Theory.* Cambridge, Mass.: MIT Press, 1981.

McCallum, Bennett. *Monetary Economics: Theory and Policy.* New York: Macmillan, 1989.

Minford, Patrick, and David Peel. *Rational Expectations and the New Macroeconomics.* Oxford: Martin Robertson, 1983.

Neely, Christopher. "International Interest Rate Linkages." Federal Reserve Bank of St. Louis *International Economic Trends,* August 2001.

Sargent, Thomas, and Neil Wallace. "Rational Expectations and the Theory of Economic Policy." *Journal of Monetary Economics* 2 (April 1976): 169–183.

Stein, Jerome. *Monetarist, Keynesian, and New Classical Economics.* New York: New York University Press, 1982.

Taylor, Mark. "The Economics of Exchange Rates." *Journal of Economic Literature* 43 (March 1995).

Rational Wage Stickiness—

Modern Keynesian Theory with Rational Expectations

FUNDAMENTAL ISSUES

1. What are the essential elements of the modern Keynesian theory of wage stickiness?

2. In what respect is the modern Keynesian theory observationally equivalent to the new classical model?

3. How does the degree of wage indexation affect the elasticity of the aggregate supply schedule, and what role does this elasticity play in determining the optimal degree of indexation?

4. What factors determine the duration of wage contracts, and what are the macroeconomic implications of overlapping contract intervals?

5. Are the wage contracting models proposed by the modern Keynesian theorists relevant in today's world?

E
mployee stock ownership plans, stock options, bonus plans, pension profit-sharing schemes—all are examples of profit-linked compensation that companies can offer their workers in addition to standard hourly wages or annual salaries. A little over two decades ago, only a small portion of U.S. employers offered these and other forms of profit-sharing arrangements. Firms paid salespeople commissions based on the revenues they generated, of course, and a number of companies paid managers annual bonuses based on the firms' profitability performances.

The world of work has changed dramatically since the early 1980s. Today, nearly half of all companies offer stock options as part of their compensation package. All told, about nineteen out of every twenty private firms now offer some type of profit-sharing arrangement.

Profit-sharing arrangements are often part of contractual agreements between firms and their employees. In Chapter 10 you learned that if such contracts make nominal wages rigid, then the economy's aggregate supply schedule slopes upward. Profit sharing, however, causes workers' wages to vary automatically as firms' profits change. This is just one example of an *indexed* wage contract, in which a worker's compensation is linked to some other economic variable. Another example is a contract that adjusts wages to inflation.

One subject of this chapter is the macroeconomic effects of indexed contracts. More broadly, however, this chapter examines how modern Keynesian theorists have attempted to integrate rational expectations into an approach to aggregate supply that includes a role for nominal wage contracts.

The Rationale for Wage Contracts

The new classical theory discussed in Chapter 11 brought about a revolution in macroeconomics. Its proponents were the first economists to include the rational expectations hypothesis in their models of the economy. The theory's predictions—that systematic (and, therefore, anticipated) macroeconomic policies should have no real effects and that only unanticipated policy actions should affect short-run real output and employment—changed the terms of the debate among macroeconomists. Before new classical theory, arguments had centered on whether monetary or fiscal policy had the greater effects and whether the effects of policy actions were long-lasting or short-lived. Following the new classical revolution, the main topic of discussion was under what circumstances macroeconomic demand management policies could matter at all.

Among proponents of traditional Keynesian and monetarist macroeconomics, there have been two reactions to this state of affairs. The initial response was a denial of the relevance of the rational expectations hypothesis. This, however, did not turn out to be a very fruitful course, given the greater generality of rational expectations as compared with adaptive expectations. The other reaction was to admit that prior theory had suffered from a poor treatment of expectations and to consider the implications of rational expectations for the traditional Keynesian and monetarist approaches.

Those who have followed the second course have sought to develop theories that include a role for rational expectations but, at the same time, accept that nominal wages may be sticky in the short run. As you learned in Chapter 10, nominal wage rigidity leads to an upward-sloping short-run aggregate supply schedule. Hence, even if people have rational expectations, wage stickiness might allow for gradual price adjustment to policy actions and for short-term employment and real output responses.

Long-Term Contracts

The reason that wages and prices might be inflexible, according to these modern Keynesians, is that workers and firms in the real world often agree to contracts that set the terms, such as wages and benefits, over a given time period. The existence of such long-term contracts, argue modern Keynesians, can make the instantaneous adjustments of expectations to monetary policy actions moot even if such adjustments are possible. If workers agree to wage contracts with firms, for instance, they cannot adjust their behavior to changed expectations even if they might like to do so. As a result, as you will see, modern Keynesian theories conclude that monetary policy has real effects even with the incorporation of the rational expectations hypothesis into macroeconomic theory.

This approach, which was spearheaded by Stanley Fischer of the International Monetary Fund, Jo Anna Gray of the University of Oregon, and John Taylor of Stanford University, led to the development of what we shall call the *modern Keynesian model*. As you will learn in this chapter, the modern Keynesian model follows the new classical theory by relying on the rational expectations hypothesis. Its implications for macroeconomic policy turn out to be very different, however.

The assumption that workers and firms set wages using contracts has been a central feature of the modern Keynesian model. Let's begin by considering the features of wage contracts and possible explanations for their existence.

Explicit and Implicit Contracts

Recall that *explicit contracts* are formal, written agreements between workers and firms. Explicit one- to three-year contracts are common in unionized industries, but formal contracts are also used frequently in industries without unionized workers. For instance, firms hiring workers with undergraduate degrees typically extend formal position offers that state initial salaries and policies concerning the timing of future salary reviews.

Implicit contracts are unwritten, tacit agreements between firms and workers. Some modern Keynesian theorists argue that implicit contracts are more common than explicit contracts, but these claims are difficult to document because the contracts are not written. Nevertheless, the idea of implicit contracts is that workers and firms both try to follow certain unstated patterns of behavior in establishing standards for worker performance and remuneration.

Why Contract?

Economists in general recognize that labor contracts have been an important feature of many labor markets. What is less apparent to many economists is why workers and firms have been willing to bind themselves to contracts that set nominal wages over fixed intervals. On the one hand, firms surely would prefer to pay lower, market-determined nominal wages if consumers demand fewer of the goods and services that they produce. On the other hand, workers arguably would prefer to earn higher, market-determined nominal wages if the demand for their skills rises. Why, then, would either firms or workers be willing to enter into agreements that establish a nominal wage that may turn out to be inconsistent with demand and supply conditions in the market for labor?

There are three possible rationales for nominal wage contracts:

1. *Avoiding auction-market transaction costs.* One rationale for nominal wage contracts is that using the contracts saves firms and workers the trouble of "auctioning" workers' skills when labor demand and supply conditions go through temporary fluctuations. In the labor market theory of the classical model that we discussed in Chapter 3, wages and employment adjust very quickly to changes in labor demand and supply conditions. This adjustment can occur, however, only if workers auction their skills continuously to firms making the highest bids for their talents. In many labor markets, it is difficult to visualize such instantaneous and continuous adjustments taking place.

   For example, consider the situation faced by an engineer whose specialty is nuclear power. If the market for nuclear engineers continuously auctioned their skills, then nuclear engineers would have to be willing to move themselves and their families to a different nuclear power plant at any time. These continual relocations would impose sizable costs upon the engineers. A continuous auction would also force the firms that operate nuclear power plants to conduct constant searches for replacement engineers, making it difficult for the firms to maintain a stable production process. Economists call such costs of maintaining an auction market for labor skills *labor market transaction costs.* One explanation for the existence of wage contracts is that labor market transaction costs could be large enough to induce nuclear engineers and other workers to negotiate contracts with their employers.

2. *Risk aversion.* Another possible reason for the existence of contracts is *risk aversion.* If market wages rise unexpectedly, workers will be better off while firms will not. If market wages fall unexpectedly, firms will be better off while workers will not. Consequently, to protect themselves from the risks that can arise when wages are market determined, workers and firms may agree to fix the wage in advance.

3. *Asymmetric information.* A final, related rationale for nominal wage contracts is **asymmetric information,** or information possessed by one party to an economic transaction but not by the other party. Individual workers may not always be privy to information about their employer's revenues, costs, and profits, so they may perceive benefits from contractual agreements that bind the employer to providing guaranteed wage payments. From an employer's perspective, information about the productivity of various workers also is imperfect. By providing a guaranteed wage payment for a specified amount of work effort, the employer may give each worker an incentive to produce a minimum desirable amount of work effort. Consequently, both workers and firms might see a wage contract as a way to offset problems arising from asymmetric information.

ASYMMETRIC INFORMATION:
Information that is possessed by one party to an economic transaction but is unavailable to the other party.

# of Rational Contracting

The modern Keynesian theory combines both wage stickiness and imperfect information from the traditional Keynesian model. In addition, it follows the new classical theory by adopting the rational expectations hypothesis. Consequently, the modern Keynesian model adopts the new classical assumption that people make rational forecasts of the price level and the inflation rate in the face of imperfect information, but it forgoes the new classical assumption that purely competitive markets determine flexible nominal wages.

The traditional Keynesian theory of wage stickiness that we discussed in Chapter 10 assumes that workers and firms fix nominal wages via contracts, but it provides no explanation of how workers and firms determine a particular contract wage. The modern Keynesian theory, in contrast, seeks to explain what nominal wage workers and firms will set via a contractual agreement. The theory proposes that both parties to a wage contract choose a contract wage based on their rational expectations of the conditions that will prevail in the labor market during the period in which the wage contract is in force. Consequently, the modern Keynesian model of wage contracts follows the new classical theory by imposing the requirement that workers and firms act on the basis of rational forecasts.

Expected Labor Market Equilibrium

To develop their theory of rational wage contracts, the modern Keynesian economists begin by thinking about how labor markets would work if there were no wage contracts at all and if workers and firms had complete information. In these circumstances, the nominal wage would adjust to ensure that the quantity of labor supplied would equal the quantity of labor demanded. At this equilibrium nominal wage, denoted W^* in Figure 12–1, the equilibrium quantity of labor services supplied by workers and demanded by firms is equal to N^*. The equilibrium values of the nominal wage and employment in Figure 12–1 are the *full-information* values of the wage and employment, because they would arise if workers and firms have complete information about the price level, so that $P^e = P$.

ATTAINING CLASSICAL LABOR MARKET EQUILIBRIUM   Recall from Chapter 3 that Figure 12–1 displays the classical labor market equilibrium. The desirable property of the classical equilibrium is that at the full-information nominal wage W^*, firms wish to purchase the same quantity of labor services that workers wish to supply. Thus, the desires of both producers and workers are satisfied at this nominal wage rate, and there is neither a shortage of labor nor a surplus (or unemployment) at this nominal wage.

As discussed above, however, there also are potential drawbacks associated with allowing market forces to determine the nominal wage. As noted above, these could include transaction costs that workers and firms must incur to continually auction labor services, the risk of significant wage volatility arising from shifts in labor demand and supply, and problems in dealing with asymmetric information. In light of these difficulties, workers

Figure 12–1   Full-Information Labor Market Equilibrium

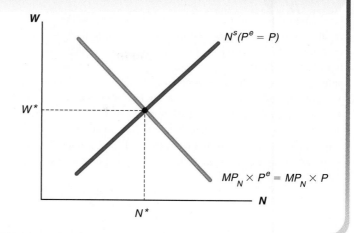

If workers and firms both possessed full information, then they would correctly anticipate the actual price level that would prevail. Hence, the expected price level, P^e, would equal the actual price level, P, and W^* and N^* would be the full-information values of the money wage and employment, respectively.

and firms may choose to fix the nominal wage over a period of time. The lengths of contracts vary in the real world, and terms of contracts typically overlap. For the sake of simplicity, however, we shall assume that all contracts are for one year and that they all begin and end at the same time.

THE WAGE OBJECTIVE   Nevertheless, we assume that workers and firms in an otherwise competitive labor market would like to preserve the desirable properties, such as the absence of unemployment, that a classical labor market equilibrium could attain. Consequently, the shared goal of workers and firms when they negotiate a contract wage for a coming year is to try to achieve the same equilibrium wage and employment level that they *anticipate* would arise in the classical labor market equilibrium.

The problem is that when workers and firms conduct their contract negotiations, they do not know the precise conditions that will prevail during the forthcoming contract year. What they *can* do, however, is to do the best that they can to set the same nominal wage that would hold, on average, in the absence of contracts. In other words, at the time that workers and firms negotiate a wage contract, they can try to achieve the full-information nominal wage rate that they *expect* the classical labor auction market otherwise would yield during the contract period. If this effort is successful, they will exactly replicate the classical labor market equilibrium without having to incur transaction costs, face risks of wage volatility, or experience the full scope of problems arising from asymmetric information.

The Wage Contract

Figure 12–2 on the next page illustrates how rational wage contracting would work according to the modern Keynesian theory. At the beginning of a contract interval, workers and firms agree to set the contract wage at the level that they expect the classical, full-information nominal wage will

Figure 12–2 Determining the Contract Wage

According to the modern Keynesian contract theory, workers and firms determine the contract wage based on their expectation of the price level that will prevail during the term of the contract. This price expectation implies anticipated positions for the labor demand and supply schedules and, consequently, an expectation of the full-information money wage and employment level, denoted W^{*e} and N^{*e}, respectively. In an effort to achieve the full-information employment level, workers and firms then set the contract wage, W^c, equal to the expected full-information wage.

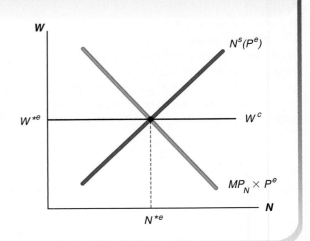

turn out to be, denoted W^{*e}. This is the nominal wage at which workers and firms expect the quantity of labor demanded will equal the quantity of labor supplied during the year in which the contract will be binding.

Of course, at the beginning of the contract year, workers and firms do not know what the actual price level will be during that year. Hence, they have to make a rational forecast of the price level, labeled P^e. Figure 12–2 indicates that, in light of their rational expectation of the price level, both workers and firms anticipate that during the coming year the labor supply schedule of workers will, on average, be in the position $N^s(P^e)$. In addition, they anticipate that the average position of the labor demand schedule will be the expected value of labor's marginal product, $MP_N \times P^e$. The expected wage consistent with classical labor market equilibrium, W^{*e}, conceptually is determined by the intersection of these two schedules. To assure that they will achieve the expected equilibrium employment level, N^{*e}, at least on average, workers and firms set the contract wage, denoted W^c, equal to the anticipated market-clearing nominal wage, W^{*e}.

The Aggregate Supply Schedule

This rationally constructed nominal wage contract only assures that workers and firms will *anticipate* achieving the classical labor market equilibrium. Once the contract wage is contractually set, however, the price level may or may not turn out to be equal to the price level that workers and firms anticipated when they conducted their contract negotiations.

Suppose that the actual price level, P_1, turns out to be the level workers and firms expected when they set the contract wage, P^e. Panel (a) of Figure 12–3 shows that, in this situation workers and firms correctly anticipate the value of labor's marginal product during the contract period, so that $MP_N \times P^e = MP_N \times P_1$. This determines the location of the labor demand sched-

Figure 12-3   Deriving the Aggregate Supply Schedule with Rational Wage Contracts

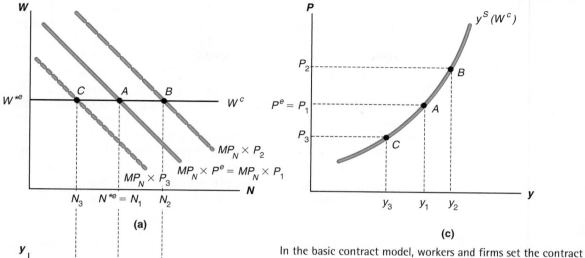

In the basic contract model, workers and firms set the contract wage, W^c, equal to the anticipated wage that would have prevailed in the absence of contracting, given by W^{*e} in panel (a). If workers and firms correctly anticipate the price level consistent with this outcome, so that $P^e = P_1$, then employment will equal N_1 at point A in panel (a), so that real output is y_1 at point A in panel (b). This yields the price level–real output combination P_1 and y_1 at point A in panel (c). If the price level is higher than workers and firms expected, however, then the result is a rise in employment at the contract wage, shown by the movement to point B in panel (a). Thus, real output will rise to point B in panel (b), yielding the price level–real output combination at point B in panel (c). Likewise, if the price level is lower than workers and firms expected, then employment will fall to point C in panel (a), causing a decline in real output to point C in panel (b). The result will be the price level–real output combination at point C in panel (c). Points A, B, and C thereby will lie on an upward-sloping aggregate supply schedule. The position of this schedule will depend on the contract wage, W^c.

ule, and the equilibrium employment level, N_1, will be the quantity of labor demanded at the contract wage, $W^c = W^{*e}$, at point A. At this employment level, firms produce the real output level y_1, at point A in panel (b). Hence, at the price level P_1, the corresponding real output level is y_1, and this price level–real output combination is point A in panel (c).

Now consider the outcomes that result if the actual price level rises above $P^e = P_1$, to P_2. This price level is higher than workers and firms anticipated when they negotiated their contracts, so the value of labor's marginal product is also higher, at $MP_N \times P_2$. Consequently, firms demand more labor than they anticipated, and workers provide more labor services at the contract wage than they expected. Equilibrium employment is equal to N_2 at point B in panel (a). Given this quantity of labor, panel (b) indicates that firms will produce the real output level y_2, thereby yielding the price level–real output combination P_2 and y_2 at point B in panel (c).

In contrast, if the actual price level is below the value that workers and firms anticipated, at P_3, then the value of labor's marginal product during the contract period will be below its anticipated level, at $MP_N \times P_3$, and employment and real output will equal N_3 and y_3, respectively, at points C in panels (a) and (b). This will yield the price level–real output combination P_3 and y_3 given by point C in panel (c).

The schedule containing points A, B, and C in panel (c) is the economy's aggregate supply schedule under rational wage contracting. Because we have derived this aggregate supply schedule given the specific contract wage W^c, we label it $y^s(W^c)$. As in the traditional Keynesian theory, the aggregate supply schedule slopes upward. (One way to gauge overall wage costs faced by all firms in the economy is the Employment Cost Index; see *Management Notebook: Tracking Business Labor Costs in the United States.*)

On the Web

What do the most recent changes in ECIs reveal about current trends in wages and salaries and in benefits? Find out by going to the home page of the Bureau of Labor Statistics at http://www.bls.gov, clicking on "Employment Costs" under the heading "Wages, Earnings, & Benefits," and then clicking on "Get Detailed Statistics," where you can go to "Employment Cost Index" and select an ECI.

FUNDAMENTAL ISSUE #1

What are the essential elements of the modern Keynesian theory of wage stickiness?   According to the modern Keynesian theory, workers and firms may wish to establish wage contracts to save on transaction costs, reduce the risk of wage variability, or address informational asymmetries that they face. To establish contract wages, workers and firms must rationally forecast the price level for the interval that the contract will be in force. Once the contract wage has been established, however, unexpected variations in the price level can cause employment and real output to change. As a result, the aggregate supply schedule slopes upward.

Observational
Equivalence

Like the new classical theory, the modern Keynesian contract-based theory is based on the rational expectations hypothesis. In contrast to the new classical theory, however, which assumes that pure competition ensures flexibility of all wages and prices, the modern Keynesian theory assumes that contracts cause stickiness in the nominal wage.

Another feature shared by both theories is the concept of a full-information employment level toward which the economy gravitates in the long run. This aspect of the monetarist elaboration of the traditional Keynesian model has become a common element of both modern approaches. We shall touch on this issue again when we consider the theory of macroeconomic policy in Chapters 14 and 15.

In what respects are the theories different? To answer this question, we begin by thinking about how policy actions can influence real output and

Tracking Business Labor Costs in the United States

nvestors and economists both pay close attention to the Employment Cost Indexes (ECIs) computed by the Bureau of Labor Statistics (BLS). Investors track changes in ECIs to assist in forecasting the future direction of overall business profits. Economists use them to help gauge how aggregate wage pressures may affect aggregate supply and, consequently, output and prices.

To calculate the ECIs, the BLS surveys about 7,400 private companies and 800 state and local governments. The survey questions cover hourly pay and annual salaries and benefits ranging from overtime, health insurance, and paid vacations to Social Security taxes and workers' compensation insurance.

Figure 12–4 displays annual changes in the ECIs for civilian wages and salaries and benefits. These are the data that investors and economists watch most closely, because increases in these ECIs relative to inflation indicate that firms' real wage costs are increasing. This is likely to reduce the growth of aggregate supply over time, thereby restraining output growth and placing upward pressure on the price level.

For Critical Analysis
Why do increases in aggregate wages and salaries cause a reduction in aggregate supply in the traditional Keynesian model?

Figure 12–4   Annual Changes in Employment Cost Indexes for Wages and Salaries and for Benefits

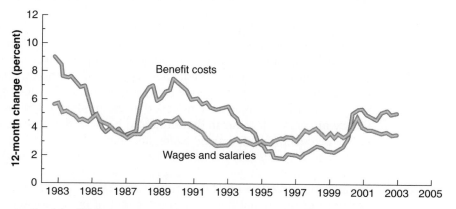

The year-to-year growth of the ECI for wages and salaries has been more stable than the annual changes in the ECI for employee benefits.

SOURCE: Bureau of Labor Statistics.

prices in the modern Keynesian model. As you will see, in the basic version of this theory, the new classical and modern Keynesian approaches are not easy to distinguish individually.

Policy Effects in the Basic Modern Keynesian Framework

Figure 12–5 on the following page shows that in the one-period contracting framework that we have discussed, policy actions typically have short-run effects on real output and employment. The nominal wage is rigid during the

Figure 12–5   The Effects of Unanticipated Policy Actions

If workers and firms fail to anticipate a rise in aggregate demand during the term of wage contracts, an unexpected rise in the price level will result. The result will be a movement from point E to point E' and an increase in equilibrium real output. Hence, unanticipated policy actions that cause aggregate demand to change will induce variations in real output.

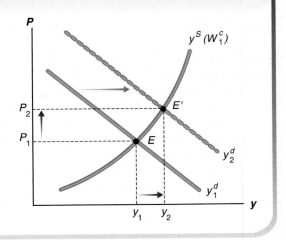

contract interval, so an expansionary monetary or fiscal policy action will lead to a rise in aggregate demand that will induce increases in both the price level and real output, as shown by the movement from point E to point E'. To produce the higher output level, firms will hire more labor services, thereby raising employment and reducing the unemployment rate.

This does not mean, however, that macroeconomic policies will always have short-run effects on real GDP. Suppose that the central bank and the government follow systematic, predictable policies. If so, then workers and firms will be able to predict the policy actions that will occur during the contract period. Figure 12–6 shows the effects that the modern Keynesian contracting theory predicts will occur in this situation. If workers and firms do not expect policy actions that will expand aggregate demand, they will agree to the contract wage W_1^c, which is the nominal wage that they expect during the period of the contract. This yields the aggregate supply schedule $y^s(W_1^c)$, and the equilibrium price level and real output are P_1 and y_1 at point E in the figure.

Consider now what happens in the event of expansionary monetary and fiscal policies that workers and firms anticipate before reaching a contractual agreement. As the figure shows, these policies shift the aggregate demand schedule outward and to the right, to y_2^d, causing the price level to rise. Workers and firms anticipate this rise in the price level, however, so they also anticipate a rise in the market nominal wage during the contract interval. As a result, they agree to a higher contract wage, W_2^c, which shifts the aggregate supply schedule leftward. As a result, during the contract period there will be a higher price level at point E', but no change in equilibrium real output. The expansionary monetary and fiscal policies have no real effects.

Observationally Equivalent Theories

The examples illustrated in Figures 12–5 and 12–6 are very similar to those that we examined in our discussion of the new classical theory in Chapter 11. They imply that policies that workers and firms cannot correctly antic-

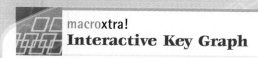

macroxtra!

Interactive Key Graph

The graph below shows how real output and the price level adjust to a rise in aggregate demand when it is fully anticipated by workers. What happens if workers partly anticipate an increase in aggregate demand? What occurs if they fail to anticipate this change? You can discover the answers to these questions by interacting with this graph on the Web.

Go to http://macroxtra.swcollege.com

Figure 12–6   The Effects of Policy Actions That Workers and Firms Anticipate

If workers and firms fully anticipate a rise in aggregate demand during the term of wage contracts, then they will expect a higher price level and will raise the contract wage. As a result, the aggregate supply schedule will shift leftward. The actual price level will rise from the initial equilibrium level P_1 at point E to a higher level P_2 at point E', but equilibrium real output will remain unchanged. Consequently, fully anticipated policy actions that induce changes in aggregate demand will have no real output effects.

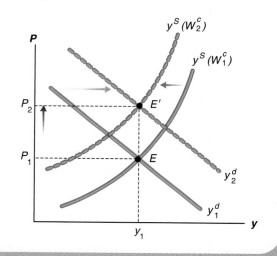

ipate before reaching contractual agreements will affect real output and employment during the term that the agreements are binding. In contrast, fully anticipated policy actions will induce workers and firms to adjust the contract wage accordingly, so the policy actions will have no influence on equilibrium real output or employment.

This similarity between the policy predictions of the basic new classical and modern Keynesian theories is known as **observational equivalence.** It poses something of a problem for macroeconomists because it complicates efforts to determine whether the new classical approach or the modern Keynesian theory better "fits" real-world data. Even though the two theories are based on very different assumptions—pure competition with completely flexible wages in the new classical theory versus contractual wage setting with fixed wages in the modern Keynesian model—in their most basic forms they offer very similar policy predictions. Both theories predict that real employment and output variations should occur only in the event of unanticipated changes in the price level, which macroeconomists often call price-level "misperceptions" or "surprises." As you learned in Chapter 11, in the new classical model price-level misperceptions can occur, for instance, when a central bank or government makes mistakes, is misunderstood, or is insincere in its policy announcements. In the modern

OBSERVATIONAL EQUIVALENCE: The fact that the basic version of the modern Keynesian theory, which assumes sticky wages, makes some of the same fundamental policy predictions as the new classical model, which is based on pure competition with completely flexible wages.

Keynesian model, surprise changes in the price level can take place whenever the price level differs from the level that workers and firms anticipated when they negotiated their wage contracts. This price-level misperception can occur for the same reasons proposed in the new classical theory.

Hence, both theories provide the same fundamental message:

In both the new classical and the modern Keynesian models, actual real output should differ from full-information output whenever price-level misperceptions take place.

Consequently, both theories are observationally equivalent in their predictions, making testing one theory against the other a tricky proposition. Although the modern Keynesian theory indicates that real output and employment responses to price-level surprises might be longer lived than under the new classical theory, especially if long-term contracts are widespread in the economy, such subtle differences are hard to capture in real-world data.

For this reason, economists interested in determining which, if either, theory has greater relevance have pursued two lines of research. One has been to determine if real output and employment really do respond only to price-level misperceptions, as *both* theories predict. If not, this would indicate that *neither* theory fits the facts very well. In contrast, if the evidence indicates that real output and employment do vary directly with surprise movements in the price level, then at least one of the theories may fit the facts. The initial research on this issue, which was conducted in the 1980s, found little evidence that price-level surprises had real output effects. In the 1990s, however, Jo Anna Gray of the University of Oregon and David Spencer of Brigham Young University along with Magda Kandil of the University of Wisconsin—Milwaukee used more advanced measures of full-information output and employment and found more evidence supporting both theories.

The second line of research has been to identify aspects of the modern Keynesian theory of wage contracting that separate it more clearly from the new classical approach. The idea here is that wage contracting may have other features that will lead to further predictions that will distinguish the contracting theory. We turn next to some of these potential features of wage contracts that could have macroeconomic implications.

FUNDAMENTAL ISSUE #2

In what respect is the modern Keynesian theory observationally equivalent to the new classical model?   Basic versions of both the modern Keynesian theory and the new classical approach make the same fundamental prediction: Unanticipated policy actions are more likely to have effects on employment and real output, whereas fully anticipated policy actions should have no real effects. Hence, the theories are observationally equivalent in that they have similar basic implications even though they stem from very different perspectives on how the labor market functions.

The basic one-period contracting model that we have discussed ignores some important issues with considerable real-world relevance. One is the possibility that contracts could contain clauses calling for a **cost-of-living adjustment (COLA),** which automatically adjusts nominal wages to changes in the price level. Another is the issue of contract length. As noted above, longer contracts extend the interval during which unexpected policy actions can affect real output and employment. Finally, in the real world contracts do not begin or end at the same time. Instead, they overlap. Let's consider how proponents of the modern Keynesian theory have sought to extend the basic contracting framework to incorporate each of these issues.

Nominal Wage Indexation

In the past (and to a lesser degree in the present, as discussed later in the chapter), workers and firms have frequently negotiated wage agreements that provide for the automatic adjustment of wages during the interval in which the contract is binding. Usually, these COLA contracts set a *base wage* that creates a floor on workers' earnings and then specify additional wage payments in the event of inflation. Under a standard COLA contract, if the price level rises, the wage paid to workers automatically increases, typically at set intervals of time, such as every quarter or every six months. The presence of COLA clauses in wage contracts is an explicit example of what economists call **wage indexation.** In this situation, contracted wages are "indexed," or adjusted automatically to changes in the price level.

Another common way to index wages is to relate them to a firm's performance through payments of commissions, bonus plans, or other types of profit-sharing arrangements. Thus, when the firm's sales increase as a result of price increases, workers share in the higher revenues, and their wage effectively adjusts automatically.

Considering all types of wage indexation can be a difficult task. To keep things as simple as possible, let's consider a situation in which all wages in the economy are determined via contracts with COLA clauses requiring fully proportionate adjustment of the wage to changes in the price level. In other words, the contracts specify that every time the price level rises by one unit, the nominal wage must increase by one unit. Furthermore, let's suppose that the contracts call for continuous adjustment of the wage during the contract interval (though continuous adjustment is rare in practice). Finally, let's assume that the contracts permit full upward *or* downward movement of the nominal wage as the price level rises or falls, even though clauses calling for both types of adjustments also are rare.

COMPLETELY INDEXED WAGES Under these assumptions, Figure 12–7 on the next page shows what would happen during the contract term if the price level turned out to be higher than workers and firms anticipated when they set the base contract wage, W^c. As in the basic contracting model that we discussed earlier, W^c is set equal to the nominal wage that workers and

COST-OF-LIVING ADJUSTMENT (COLA): A clause in a wage contract that calls for the nominal wage to be adjusted in response to changes in the price level.

WAGE INDEXATION: The automatic adjustment of contract wages to changes in the price level.

Figure 12–7   The Aggregate Supply Schedule with Fully Indexed Nominal Wages

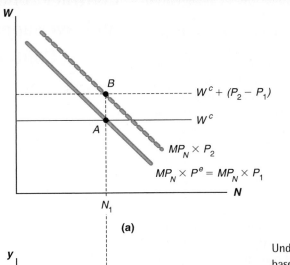

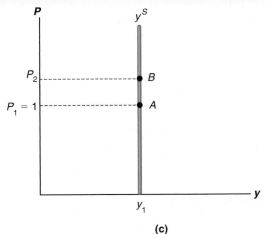

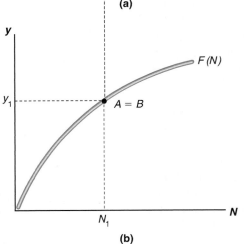

Under a fully indexed wage contract, workers and firms set the base wage of the contract based on their expectation of the price level, which in panel (a) is equal to $P^e = P_1$. If the actual price level is equal to this value, then employment will equal N_1 at point A in panel (a), real output will equal y_1 at point A in panel (b), and the resulting price level–real output combination will be P_1 and y_1 at point A in panel (c). If the price level rises unexpectedly to P_2, the value of labor's marginal product will rise as a result, as shown in panel (a). With a fully indexed wage contract, however, the contract wage automatically will rise as well, by an amount equal to the increase in the price level. As a result, the equilibrium employment level will be unchanged at point B in panel (a), and equilibrium real output will be unchanged in panel (b). This will yield the price level–real output combination P_2 and y_1 at point B in panel (c), which lies directly above point A. Therefore, with fully indexed wage contracts, the aggregate supply schedule will be vertical.

firms anticipate will arise in the absence of the contract. In the absence of any price-level changes, the points labeled A in panels (a), (b), and (c) show the determination of equilibrium employment and output at this base wage, where we have assumed that initially workers and firms correctly anticipate the actual price level, so that $P^e = P_1$. We simplify further by assuming that the initial value of the price level is equal to one, so that a variation in the price level is equivalent to a proportionate price-level change.

Fully indexed contracts require that the nominal wage rise in proportion to any price-level increase. Thus, if the price level rises from P_1 to P_2, then the actual wage received by workers will equal W^c plus an amount equal to the rise in the price level, or $W^c + (P_2 - P_1)$. The rise in the price level causes labor demand to increase as the value of labor's marginal product rises. At the same time, however, firms also have to pay a proportionately higher nominal wage. As shown in panel (a), this means that employment does not change. As a result, as panel (b) indicates, real output also is unaffected. Therefore, the new real output–price level combination y_1 and P_2, shown by point B in panel (c), lies directly above point A. The aggregate supply schedule with completely indexed wages is completely inelastic.

The shape of this aggregate supply schedule is, of course, the same as in the classical model of Chapter 3. Wages under a completely indexed wage contract adjust equiproportionately to changes in the price level. This mirrors the one-for-one adjustment of nominal wages to price changes that arises in the classical framework with full information and flexible wages and prices. Hence, the aggregate supply schedule under complete indexation also is vertical.

PARTIAL INDEXATION AND THE SLOPE OF THE AGGREGATE SUPPLY SCHEDULE Many U.S. industries use wage contracts without COLA clauses. Indeed, as shown in Figure 12–8, the portion of U.S. employment contracts containing indexation clauses has fallen from 61 percent in the mid-1970s to about 20 percent in the 2000s (later on we shall consider some possible reasons for this sharp decline). Furthermore, in industries that use contracts with COLA clauses, indexation has rarely been as full or as flexible as we assumed in our example in Figure 12–7. Hence, most modern Keynesian theorists would argue that, in the aggregate, nominal wages have been only *partially* indexed to the inflation rate in the United States. Thus, according to the modern Keynesian contracting theory, the aggregate supply schedule has

Figure 12–8   The Share of U.S. Labor Contracts Containing Indexation Clauses, 1956–Present

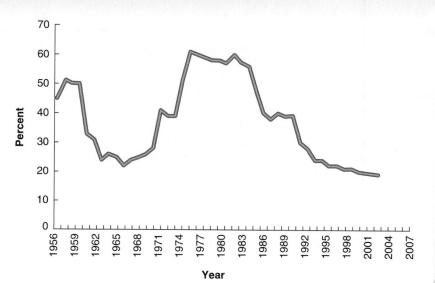

The portion of contracts with COLA clauses peaked at 61 percent in 1976 and has declined considerably since then.

SOURCES: John Duca and David VanHoose, "The Rise of Goods-Market Competition and the Decline in Wage Indexation," *Journal of Macroeconomics* 20 (Summer 1998); authors' estimates.

not been completely inelastic, but neither has it been as elastic as a fixed-wage theory would imply.

Note that the example in Figure 12–7 indicates that under complete wage indexation and a completely inelastic aggregate supply schedule, changes in the price level induced by variations in aggregate demand will have no effects on real output and employment. Consequently, full indexation of all wages in the economy would be optimal if the only sources of economic fluctuations were factors causing greater variability in aggregate demand, such as volatility in autonomous consumption, investment, or imports. In that case, by completely indexing wages to price changes workers and firms could ensure that they would always maintain the desired, full-information levels of employment and real output.

In light of this implication, why aren't all contracted wages completely indexed? One likely reason is that volatility of relative prices of key resources such as oil or sudden technological changes can cause the aggregate supply schedule to shift. Figure 12–9 shows that if both relatively elastic and completely inelastic aggregate supply schedules (around point E) shift leftward by the same amount, then, for a given position for the aggregate demand schedule, the effect on real output (and, hence, employment) is larger when the aggregate supply schedule is completely inelastic. As we noted earlier, complete indexation of nominal wages makes the aggregate supply schedule vertical, so full wage indexation is not always best for workers and firms.

This reasoning indicates that aggregate wage indexation should decline if variability in aggregate demand declines relative to variability in aggregate supply. To the extent that this may have occurred in the United States since the mid-1970s, it could represent one possible explanation for the decrease in the share of contracts with indexed contracts shown in Figure 12–8.

Figure 12–9   The Effects of a Decline in Aggregate Supply with Nonindexed and Completely Indexed Contract Wages

If aggregate supply schedules that arise under nonindexed and fully indexed wage contracts shift leftward by the same amount, then the effect on equilibrium real output is greater in the case of the fully indexed wage contracts. Higher variability of output under full wage indexation implies that employment will also be more variable. Consequently, full wage indexation is less desirable for workers and firms when aggregate supply is highly variable.

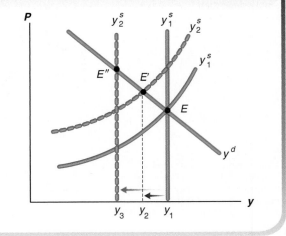

FUNDAMENTAL ISSUE #3

How does the degree of wage indexation affect the elasticity of the aggregate supply schedule, and what role does this elasticity play in determining the optimal degree of indexation?   If contract wages are completely indexed to changes in the price level, then wages adjust equiproportionately with price-level variations as in the classical model, which yields a completely inelastic aggregate supply schedule. In contrast, with nonindexed wage contracts, the aggregate supply schedule is relatively elastic around a particular price level, because the nominal wage does not adjust at all in response to changes in the price level. Complete wage indexation insulates real output and employment from the effects of variability in aggregate demand, but magnifies the output and employment responses to variability in aggregate supply. Consequently, in the presence of both sources of macroeconomic fluctuations, neither completely indexed nor nonindexed wage contracts are best for limiting variability of employment and real output.

Optimal Contract Length

So far we have assumed that the length of a wage contract is a year. Some wage contracts have terms two to three times that long. Others have shorter durations. What factors determine the length of a contract that sets nominal wages?

NEGOTIATION COSTS   As we noted earlier, one of the primary reasons that people might agree to fix wages via contracts is to avoid having to haggle over wages from week to week and month to month. Negotiating new contracts can be very time-consuming. Consequently, a key component of the total *negotiation cost* for a contract is the opportunity cost that is entailed. Both workers and firm owners and managers could do other things with the time that they spend nailing down the terms of a contract.

In addition, contract negotiations entail potentially sizable direct costs. A union, for instance, may pay professional negotiators or consultants to help make a strong case for why the workers deserve higher base wages. A business may incur similar expenses to explain why it cannot raise base wages as much as workers desire.

The total negotiation cost of contracting is the sum of these opportunity costs and direct costs. Naturally, we would predict that as the cost of contract negotiation increases, the duration of a typical contract should also rise. By lengthening the term of a contract, workers and firms can postpone incurring contract negotiation costs.

THE OPTIMAL CONTRACT DURATION   In light of these potentially high negotiation costs, why don't contracts last for several years? The answer is that as the term of a nonindexed contract lengthens, so does the period over which workers and firms must try to anticipate factors that could cause the price level to vary, thereby inducing variability in the full-information wage and employment level.

For example, suppose that a union is contemplating adopting either a one-year or a two-year contract. With the one-year contract, the union must try to rationally forecast the labor demand and supply conditions for the coming year. With the two-year contract, the union's horizon for trying to anticipate these conditions stretches out another year.

If factors that can affect labor demand over a two-year period, such as the price level, are expected to be relatively stable, then the union may feel comfortable going with the two-year contract and saving on the negotiation costs that two successive one-year contracts would entail. If the union anticipates a highly variable price level, however, resulting from significant variability in aggregate demand and aggregate supply, then it would tend to prefer one-year agreements. In that case, the union could negotiate a more appropriate base wage after a year has passed and uncertainty about labor market conditions has been resolved.

As this reasoning indicates, the determination of the optimal length of a wage contract involves a trade-off between contract negotiation cost and the variability of aggregate demand and aggregate supply. As the cost of negotiating a contract increases, the optimal contract length tends to rise. As variability of aggregate demand or aggregate supply rises, the optimal contract length tends to decline.

Overlapping Contracts and Persistence

Because the duration of wage contracts in an industry or at an individual firm depends on the nature of the trade-off between industry- and firm-specific negotiation costs and volatility in the price level induced by aggregate demand and supply variability, we would expect to see contract lengths differ across industries and firms. In addition, because workers and firms make their own decisions about the timing of contract negotiations, we would anticipate that the dates when contracts begin and end would be *staggered.* In other words, all one-year contracts would be unlikely to begin on January 1 of each year. Some might begin on that day, but many others might begin on any other day of a year.

As a result of different durations and contract staggering, contracts across the economy *overlap.* Figure 12–10 shows how contracts might overlap in an economy. Some firms, denoted group *A*, have one-year contracts that begin and end on January 1 of each year, while the firms in group *B* have one-year contracts beginning and ending on June 30. At the same time, workers in some unionized industries (groups *C* and *D*, respectively) have two- and three-year contracts that overlap with the one-year contracts.

POLICY IMPLICATIONS OF OVERLAPPING CONTRACTS   Does the overlapping nature of contracts make any difference for the effects of macroeconomic policies? Consider Figure 12–10. The groups of workers whose new contracts begin on January 1, 2005 (groups *A* and *D*) will negotiate contract wages with their employers based on the information they possess at that date. Workers whose contracts begin on June 30, 2005 (groups *B* and *C*) will set base wages using any additional information that became available between January 1, 2005, and June 30, 2005. Note that if the four groups,

Figure 12–10   Overlapping Wage Contracts

This figure illustrates how wage contracts can overlap. For some firms, denoted group *A*, contracts begin and end on January 1 of each year. For other firms, denoted group *B*, contracts begin and end at the midpoint of each calendar year. At the same time, firms in group *C* have two-year contracts, while firms in group *D* have three-year contracts.

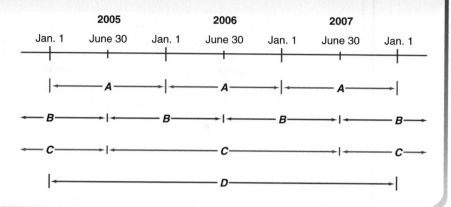

A through *D*, include all workers in the economy, then the aggregate wage for any period, such as the six-month interval between June 30, 2005, and January 1, 2006, will be just the weighted average of the contract wages established by the four groups of workers and firms.

Workers and firms in groups *B* and *C* will be able to take into account any policy changes that take place between January 1, 2005, and June 30, 2005, when they make rational forecasts of the price level for their contract intervals. Consequently, the aggregate wage during the June 30, 2005–January 1, 2006 interval will *partially* take into account any changes in macroeconomic policy. Firms and workers in groups *A* and *D*, however, cannot consider these policy changes when they negotiate wages. Thus, even some systematic changes in monetary policy will *not* be fully taken into account by these groups of workers and firms, who will be constrained by the contract decisions that they made earlier. Even if workers and firms in groups *A* and *D* made rational choices on January 1, 2005, they cannot respond to systematic policy changes until their next contract renewal dates.

The implication of this example is that in an economy with overlapping contracts, the modern Keynesian theory indicates that systematic macroeconomic policy actions potentially can have longer-lasting real effects. This can happen simply because a portion of all workers and firms set their wages via long-term contracts, which limit their ability to respond quickly to systematic policy changes. As a result, the modern Keynesian theory with overlapping contracts indicates that the effects of both anticipated and unanticipated policy actions on employment and real output should be much longer lasting than predicted by the new classical model. Hence:

> **A key prediction of modern Keynesian theory is greater persistence in policy-induced business cycle recessions or expansions.**

SHOULD WAGE CONTRACTS BE SYNCHRONIZED?   The potential for more persistent recessions that is implied by staggered and overlapping contracts has led some macroeconomists to propose that employment and real output would be more stable if all wage contracts had the same term. Contracts that begin and end at the same times would be *synchronized,* or identically timed. Contract synchronization, these macroeconomists argue, would ensure that all workers and firms have the same information when they anticipate conditions during the coming contract period. A possible drawback of synchronization is that it would induce greater aggregate wage response to past and expected future policy actions each period when contracts are renegotiated, as compared with a world of overlapping contracts. An advantage is that persistence in business cycles in a contract-dominated economy would be limited to the common interval of all the synchronized contracts.

Many other macroeconomists, however, believe that staggered contracting has significant advantages that help to offset the persistence of the output change that it induces. As we noted earlier, one advantage is that staggered, overlapping contracts help to mute responses of the aggregate wage to changes in aggregate demand conditions, thereby limiting the size of wage changes and the effects that they ultimately may have on the price level. Consequently, even though staggered, overlapping contracts theoretically may lead to more persistent business cycles, such contracts also tend to limit the size of business cycle downturns.

FUNDAMENTAL ISSUE #4

What factors determine the duration of wage contracts, and what are the macroeconomic implications of overlapping contract intervals?   The optimal length of a wage contract declines as the cost of negotiating a contract decreases and as the variability in the price level caused by aggregate demand and supply fluctuations increases. Because negotiation costs typically vary across firms and industries, contracts typically have different durations and consequently are staggered. The modern Keynesian theory indicates that overlapping contracts lead to persistent long-term effects of aggregate demand fluctuations on employment and real output.

Can Wage Contracting Theories Explain Business Cycles?

The contract-based modern Keynesian theory represents the main response of Keynesian proponents to the new classical revolution. In key respects the theory's predictions mirror those of the new classical approach. Nevertheless, the modern Keynesian theory indicates that wages are unlikely to be nearly as flexible as the new classical theory presumes, unless wages are fully indexed to changes in the price level. In the presence of variability in aggregate supply, however, the theory predicts that complete wage indexation should be rare.

The modern Keynesian theory also implies that there is greater scope for aggregate demand fluctuations to have more persistent effects on real economic activity. Consequently, proponents of contract-based macroeconomic theories have argued that such theories can help to explain short-run business cycles. They also contend that the theories can be used to develop policies that stabilize aggregate demand and thereby limit the magnitude of business cycles.

As you will learn in Chapter 13, a number of macroeconomists disagree completely with this view. They doubt the ability of the modern Keynesian approach to explain key macroeconomic regularities, and they question the usefulness of the approach as a guide for macroeconomic policy.

Key Predictions and Evidence on Wage Contracting Theories

The first line of attack on modern Keynesian theory focuses on some basic predictions that stem from contract-based theories. Critics of these theories contend that they simply do not do a good job of predicting the economy's performance.

REAL WAGES: COUNTER- OR PRO-CYCLICAL? According to the modern Keynesian theory, nominal wages typically will be nonindexed or at most partially indexed. Consequently, a rise in the price level should not lead to an equiproportionate rise in the nominal wage. This has an important implication: If the contract-based theories are correct, then rises in the price level induced by increases in aggregate demand should cause real wages to decline. In other words, real wages should move *countercyclically*. During expansions caused by rising aggregate demand, average real wages should decline. During recessions induced by declining aggregate demand, average real wages should rise.

In fact, however, many studies of the overall behavior of real wages in the United States have found that real wages tend to rise during business cycle expansions and fall during business cycle contractions. This apparent *procyclical* behavior of the average U.S. real wage, argue critics, casts serious doubt on the applicability of the modern Keynesian theory, at least to the U.S. economy.

Proponents of contract-based theories have responded that studies of the cyclical behavior of the aggregate real wage are very sensitive to how wages are averaged and to the frequency of the data that one analyzes (that is, whether the researcher looks at monthly, quarterly, or annual wage and price-level data). In addition, David Card of Princeton University has pointed out that contract wages theoretically are countercyclical only if all other things are held constant. In the real world, however, other factors that influence contract wages do change over time. As a result, looking at the behavior of the aggregate real wage over time without taking into account other factors that affect wage negotiations could lead to misleading conclusions. After controlling for various factors that might affect negotiated wages, such as issues specific to individual firms and industries, Card has concluded that observed patterns in real wages are consistent with the predictions of modern Keynesian contract theory.

WAGE INDEXATION: DO THE FACTS FIT THE THEORY? The modern Keynesian theory also indicates that significant variability in aggregate demand relative to variability in aggregate supply should induce workers and firms to increase the extent of wage indexation. In contrast, reduced relative aggregate demand volatility should lead to decreased use of COLA contracts.

Nevertheless, average U.S. wages have shown a fairly low level of indexation to price-level changes during periods of high aggregate demand variability. Indeed, indexation has been used so infrequently that Robert

Gordon of Northwestern University has called the low overall degree of wage indexation the "indexation puzzle." Studies conducted during the late 1980s found that even among industries with explicit contracts, the use of COLA clauses did not always appear to increase during periods of highly volatile aggregate demand or of low variability in aggregate supply, as the basic theory of indexation would predict. To critics, this apparent failure of the modern Keynesian theory's key prediction provided further evidence of its inapplicability to the U.S. economy.

Proponents of the contract-based approach have responded in two ways. One has been to conduct more refined studies. Some of these studies have indicated that the apparent failures of the modern Keynesian theory may have stemmed from measurement problems and imperfectly constructed tests of the theory's implications. Others, such as a study by Donald Dutkowsky of Syracuse University and H. Sonmez Atesoglu of Clarkson University, have tried to test the broad implications of contracting theories. Indeed, Dutkowsky and Atesoglu have found evidence favoring a one-year contracting model as a good approximation for the U.S. economy.

Another response has been to try to make the basic contracting theory somewhat more realistic. For instance, COLA contracts typically call for wages to rise when the price level increases but hold wages unchanged in the face of unexpected declines in the price level. Recasting the basic contract model to account for asymmetric indexation potentially can help explain why indexation is less frequently utilized than the basic contracting model predicts.

In addition, the basic contracting model drops the classical assumption that the nominal wage adjusts to equate the quantity of labor demanded with the quantity of labor supplied, but it nevertheless maintains the classical presumption that firms are purely competitive. A reformulation of the contracting model that allows for imperfect competition among firms indicates that greater competition among firms makes employment and real output at each firm less sensitive to aggregate demand variability. Consequently, increased competition would lead to less indexation. Figure 12–11 indicates that greater competition could help explain the decline in the use of COLA contracts since the mid-1970s. The same period has seen a steady increase in competition in U.S. product markets, arising both from greater competition among U.S. firms and from increased competition from foreign sources.

The Decline of Wage Contracts: Are Contract-Based Theories Relevant in Today's World?

Although proponents of the modern Keynesian theory have provided a number of responses to critics of their contract-based theories, even some of the proponents themselves have reason to question their theories' ability to explain business cycles and to predict the effects of policies. The reason is that the world has become a much more competitive place. In addition, technological change, increased information flows, and greater labor-force mobility have undermined key rationales for wage contracts.

On the Web

How do firms compensate employees via employee stock ownership plans (ESOPs)? To learn more about this form of profit sharing, visit the ESOP Association at http://www. the-esop-emplowner.org, and click on "What Is an ESOP?"

Figure 12–11   The Share of U.S. Labor Contracts with Indexation Clauses and a Measure of Overall Competition among U.S. Firms

The use of COLA clauses in the United States has declined at the same time that a measure of aggregate U.S. competition has increased..

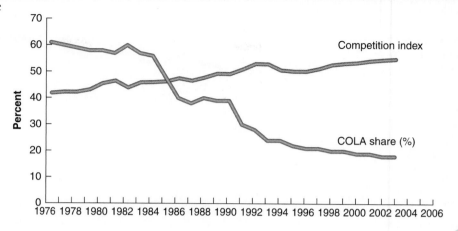

SOURCES: John Duca and David VanHoose, "The Rise of Goods-Market Competition and the Decline in Wage Indexation," *Journal of Macroeconomics* 20 (Summer 1998): 579–598; authors' estimates.

THE DECLINE OF UNIONIZATION   The bulk of long-term wage contracts in the United States typically have been union contracts. As Figure 12–12 on the next page shows, however, unionization of the workforce has been in steady decline since the middle of the twentieth century. A similar trend is occurring in other countries.

This decline has occurred for a number of reasons. For one thing, workers traditionally formed unions and negotiated with employers over many other terms of employment besides wages. Job safety, pension arrangements, health-care coverage, and other fringe benefits have often been key items for negotiation. During the past fifty years, however, federal and state governments increasingly have taken on the tasks of regulating safety in the workplace, supervising pension funds, and guaranteeing availability of essential health-care services. This increased government role surely has undercut the perceived need for unions in the minds of many workers.

Second, greater competition among U.S. firms and industries has undermined the economic feasibility of the union movement. Figure 12–12 also shows a measure of the overall extent of competition in U.S. markets for goods and services. The decline in the extent of unionization clearly has coincided with a rise in overall competition in U.S. product markets. One reason for this inverse relationship between unionization and competition is that one rationale for forming a union is to attain sufficient labor market power to bargain for wages above the competitive level, which is more feasible in industries that are not very competitive. For instance, in years past a number of industries consisted of only a few very large firms, so the firms may have earned excess profits that unions could extract from the firms' owners and managers. Greater competition in these industries would reduce the availability of higher-than-competitive profits for firms, thereby eliminating one reason to form a union.

Figure 12–12   Unions' Share of U.S. Private-Sector Employment and a Measure of Overall Competition among U.S. Firms

The portion of U.S. private-sector workers who are unionized has declined at the same time that an index measure of overall U.S. competition has risen.

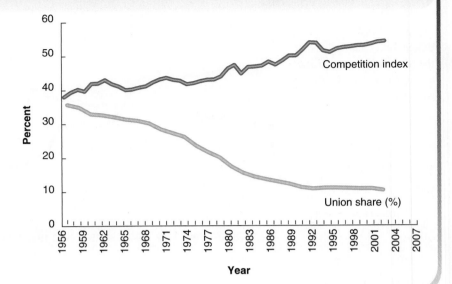

SOURCES: John Duca and David VanHoose, "The Rise of Goods-Market Competition and the Fall of Wage Inflexibility: Endogenous Wage Contracting in a Multisector Economy," *Journal of Macroeconomics* 23 (1, Winter 2001); authors' estimates.

Another reason that greater competition undercuts the rationale for union contracting is that it makes the demand for the products of imperfectly competitive firms more sensitive to price changes by increasing the range of available substitute products and, as a result, raising the elasticity of demand for the goods and services produced by each business. This ultimately makes labor demand more sensitive to fluctuations in aggregate demand and supply. As a result, long-term union contracts become less attractive to both workers and firms, because the contracts lead to greater variability in employment and real output.

THE REEMERGENCE OF THE CLASSICAL LABOR MARKET?   The decline in U.S. unionization is indicative of a broader pattern of change in U.S. labor markets, which casts at least some doubt on the ability of modern Keynesian contract-based theories to explain business cycles or to provide prescriptions for monetary and fiscal policymaking. The advent of computer technology has reduced the scope for informational asymmetries by making more information available to both workers and their employers. Consequently, the incentive to adopt contracts intended to protect against such problems has been reduced.

Indeed, a recent trend has been for individuals to form consulting businesses, selling their labor services to a variety of firms instead of working for a single company for a long period. Although traditional worker-firm relationships of the past remain the predominant form of labor market interactions, the growth of consulting arrangements represents a movement toward a more nearly classical, auction-market structure in a number of U.S. labor markets. This trend is another reason why the contract-based approach of the modern Keynesian theory has arguably become somewhat less relevant as a complete macroeconomic model.

MULTISECTOR MODELS: A CALL FOR HELP?   Many proponents of modern Keynesian theory recognize that the effects of recent trends have been undermining the ability of wage contracting models to explain all the features of the economy. Some modern Keynesians have therefore embedded contracting theories in broader macroeconomic models that admit the existence of a variety of individuals, markets, and industries. Such **multisector models,** they argue, might help to explain why no single macroeconomic theory generally fits all the available evidence.

For example, a multisector framework would predict that real wages would be countercyclical in sectors of the economy where wage contracts are important, but procyclical in other sectors. This could help to explain why the behavior of *aggregate* real wages and price levels for the economy as a whole seems to be both partially consistent and partially inconsistent with predictions of both theories.

Those who work with multisector models also propose that they can help to explain some of the difficult trade-offs that macroeconomic policymakers face. In a multisector macroeconomic model in which some sectors fit the modern Keynesian contracting theory while others do not, policymakers would have difficulty identifying policy actions that would stabilize all parts of the economy simultaneously. For instance, a contracting sector might benefit from a particular monetary policy action, while a classical sector might not gain or might even lose from the same action. A research study of 450 U.S. manufacturing industries by Vivek Ghosal of Miami University and Prakash Loungani of the Federal Reserve has found evidence favoring the applicability of such a multisector approach.

Modern Keynesian theorists are not the only macroeconomists who have begun to explore the possibility that *disaggregated* theories may be an improvement over purely aggregate macroeconomic models. Macroeconomists of both Keynesian and classical persuasions have developed multiple-sector models. Nevertheless, in most respects the differences separating the two groups have, if anything, widened in recent years, as you will learn in the next chapter.

MULTISECTOR MODELS: 365

Macroeconomic models in which the structures of various sectors of the economy correspond to different theories.

CHAPTER 12 Rational Wage Stickiness—Modern Keynesian Theory with Rational Expectations

FUNDAMENTAL ISSUE #5

Are the wage contracting models proposed by the modern Keynesian theorists relevant in today's world?   Critics of the modern Keynesian theory of wage stickiness have questioned the theory's ability to explain the actual behavior of macroeconomic variables. Proponents of the modern Keynesian approach have responded to these criticisms by offering evidence supporting the predictions of their models and by refining their theories. Nevertheless, widespread changes in U.S. labor markets have made it increasingly difficult to apply the theory broadly to the U.S. economy. This has led some proponents of the modern Keynesian approach to consider multisector models in which some portions of the economy fit the classical theory while others adopt wage contracts.

Indexing Employee Compensation to Firm Performance

A number of economists contend that the best wage-setting scheme is *profit sharing,* in which nominal wages vary automatically with employers' profitability. These economists argue that tying workers' earnings to the performance of firms gives workers an incentive to behave more like shareholders. As a result, labor productivity increases, and labor-management strife over wages and benefits subsides. In addition, because reductions in profits lead to automatic wage reductions, companies' wage bills fall whenever profits decline, which helps offset the incentive to lay off workers. Thus, profit sharing can help stabilize employment. Furthermore, some economists suggest that increased profit sharing could actually increase overall employment by effectively reducing the net cost of employing each additional unit of labor.

Profit Sharing on the Rise

Several forms of profit-sharing arrangements are in use in the workplace. A particularly popular example in recent years has been stock options, which are financial contracts giving workers the ability to purchase or sell shares of their employers' stock when share prices reach certain levels.

Figure 12–13 shows that the portion of firms using stock options to reward employees increased considerably in the late 1990s and early 2000s, from less than 20 percent in 1996 to nearly 50 percent in 2002. Overall, the share of companies using stock options, bonus plans, pension profit-sharing schemes, and other forms of profit sharing rose from 65 percent to about 95 percent during this interval.

Is There a Relationship between Lower Wage Indexation and Increased Profit Sharing?

Economists have noted that profit sharing began to increase in the 1980s, which Figure 12–11 on page 363 indicates is the same time when overall competition started to increase in the United States and the portion of U.S. workers covered by COLA clauses began its sustained decline.

A possible rationale for these patterns is that greater competition reduces the pricing power available to individual firms, thereby strengthening the link between labor productivity and firms' profits. This makes employment at each firm more sensitive to variations in productivity—which induce shifts in the economy's aggregate supply schedule—thereby reducing the incentive to index wages to inflation. At the same time, a strengthened relationship between the productivity of workers and firms' profits increases the incentive for firms to agree to profit-sharing arrangements. Hence even as wage indexation has become less widespread, the extent of profit sharing has risen.

Research Project

What factors might make COLA clauses more popular again? Is profit sharing necessarily incompatible with COLA contracts? That is, if the use of COLA contracts were to increase

Figure 12–13   The Share of U.S. Firms Using Profit-Sharing Arrangements

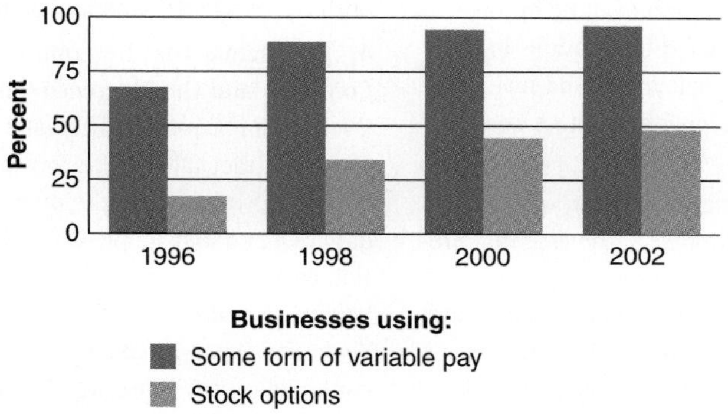

Businesses using:
■ Some form of variable pay
■ Stock options

The portion of companies offering some form of profit-sharing arrangement has increased considerably in recent years.

SOURCES: Board of Governors of the Federal Reserve System; Bureau of Labor Statistics; authors' estimates.

again in future years, would you anticipate that the extent of profit sharing would decline? Explain your reasoning.

Web Resource

What are the latest trends in U.S. worker compensation? To explore how compensation patterns are changing in the United States, go to the home page of the Bureau of Labor Statistics (http://www.bls.gov) and click on "Wages, Earnings, & Benefits."

macroxtra!
Online
Perspective

To learn about how stock options have become an important part of overall employee compensation during the past decade, go to the Chapter 12 reading, entitled "The Effect of Employee Stock Options on the Evolution of Compensation in the 1990s," by Hamid Mehran and Joseph Tracey of the Federal Reserve Bank of New York.
http://macroxtra.swcollege.com

1. The Essential Elements of the Modern Keynesian Theory of Wage Stickiness: The modern Keynesian theory hypothesizes that workers and firms may desire to use wage contracts to avoid the transaction costs entailed in continual wage bargaining, to reduce risks associated with wage variability, or to deal with problems arising from asymmetric information. The theory predicts that workers and firms must make rational forecasts of the price level to set the appropriate wage for the interval that the contract will be in force. During the contract term, unanticipated fluctuations in the price level can induce changes in employment and real output. Consequently, the aggregate supply schedule is upward sloping.

2. How the Modern Keynesian Theory Is Observationally Equivalent to the New Classical Model: The essential predictions of basic versions of both theories are the same. Both approaches indicate that unexpected policy actions are more likely to have effects on employment and real output, whereas completely anticipated policy actions should have no real effects. Therefore, the two theories are observationally equivalent in their fundamental implications even though they are based on very different views about the functioning of the labor market.

3. How the Degree of Wage Indexation Affects the Elasticity of the Aggregate Supply Schedule, and How That Matters for the Optimal Degree of Indexation: Under full wage indexation, the contract wage is adjusted equiproportionately to changes in the price level. Hence, as in the classical model, the aggregate supply schedule is completely inelastic. Under a nonindexed wage contract, however, the nominal wage does not adjust at all to price-level variations,

so the aggregate supply schedule is relatively elastic around a particular price level. Full wage indexation protects real output and employment from the effects of aggregate demand volatility, but enlarges the effects on output and employment caused by fluctuations in aggregate supply. Therefore, neither fully indexed nor nonindexed wage contracts are necessarily better for minimizing variability of employment and real output when there is variability in both aggregate demand and aggregate supply.

4. The Factors That Determine the Duration of Wage Contracts and the Macroeconomic Implications of Overlapping Contract Intervals: The optimal duration of a wage contract falls as the contract negotiation costs decline and as the volatility in the price level resulting from aggregate demand and supply variability rises. Contract negotiation costs differ across firms and industries, so contract beginning and ending dates are staggered. The modern Keynesian theory predicts that the resulting overlapping of contracts causes aggregate demand fluctuations to have persistent effects on employment and real output.

5. The Relevance of Wage Contracting Models Proposed by the Modern Keynesian Theorists in Today's World: Recent changes in the structure of U.S. labor markets have caused some to question the modern Keynesian theory's ability to explain the actual behavior of macroeconomic variables. Proponents of this approach have responded by offering evidence supporting the predictions of their models, by refining their theories, and by proposing multisector models in which some portions of the economy fit the classical theory while others adopt wage contracts.

Self-Test Questions

(Answers to odd-numbered questions may be found on the Web at **http://macro. swcollege.com** under "Student Resources.")

1. Explain, in your own words, why modern Keynesian economists theorize that fixed-wage contracts may be "rational."

2. Suppose that the price level during a contract interval turns out to be lower than what workers and firms anticipated when they negotiated the contract. Will workers end up working more or fewer hours than they had expected to work? Explain your reasoning.

3. Suppose that labor-force participation by teenage workers suddenly increases during a period in which wage contracts are in force for all firms and workers in an economy. According to the modern Keynesian model, what would be the effects, if any, on employment, unemployment, and real output? Explain your reasoning.

4. Explain, in your own words, the concept of observational equivalence as it applies to the basic one-period modern Keynesian contracting model and the new classical theory.

5. Would significant contract staggering and overlap in the general Keynesian wage contracting model make the implications of contracting theory observationally *inequivalent* to the new classical theory? Support your answer.

6. Should governments require all wage contracts to be negotiated on the same dates each year? Justify your stand on this issue.

7. Suppose that all workers and firms agree to COLA clauses in wage contracts that call for complete indexation of nominal wages to changes in the price level. In such a setting, could unanticipated increases in the nominal money stock affect employment and real output? Explain.

8. If real GDP variability and employment volatility over business cycles become significantly less pronounced, this would tend to indicate that aggregate demand and supply variability have declined. What would be the likely effect on the average duration of wage contracts among the portions of the labor market that typically use such contracts? Explain your reasoning.

9. Use diagrams of the market for real output and of the labor market with fixed-money-wage contracts to explain how the *real* wage should respond to a decline in aggregate demand in the basic Keynesian one-period contracting model. In light of the model's prediction, explain why evidence indicating procyclical real wage variations might cast doubt on the validity of the model.

10. Suppose that the economy is composed of two sectors. Sector 1 is made up of workers and firms whose behavior is best described by the classical theory, while sector 2 is composed of workers and firms who use nonindexed wage contracts that are staggered and overlapping. Would the real wage be counter- or pro-cyclical in sector 1? In sector 2? If sector 1 is significantly larger than sector 2, would the aggregate real wage for the economy as a whole be significantly counter- or pro-cyclical? Explain.

Problems

1. Suppose that the equation $N^d = \bar{N} - [a \times (W/P)]$ is a nation's labor demand schedule. Its labor supply schedule is given by the equation $N^s = b \times (W/P)$. Its aggregate production function is $y = c \times N$. (This straight-line function does not satisfy the law of diminishing marginal returns, but it helps to simplify things considerably).

(Answers to odd-numbered problems may be found on the Web at **http://macro. swcollege.com** under "Student Resources.")

a. What is the equilibrium real wage? What is the equilibrium employment level? What is the equilibrium level of real output?

b. According to the rational contracting theory discussed in this chapter, if the expected price level at the time workers establish a contract is equal to P^e, then what *nominal* wage will be established in the contract agreement? At this contract wage, calculate expressions for the actual real wage and employment level during the contract interval in terms of the actual price level, P, and the expected price level, P^e.

c. Calculate an expression for actual output during the contract interval in terms of the actual price level, P, and the expected price level, P^e. This is the aggregate supply schedule for this simple model. Does it slope upward?

d. Verify that if people have complete information, the full-information output level when wages are set by contracts is equal to the equilibrium output level in the absence of contracts (from part a).

2. Again, consider a country with the labor demand equation $N^d = \bar{N} - [a \times (W/P)]$, the labor supply equation $N^s = b \times (W/P)$, and the simple aggregate production function $y = c \times N$. Suppose that nominal wages are fully indexed to changes in the price level. What is the equation for this nation's aggregate supply schedule? Draw a rough diagram of the aggregate supply schedule. How is it shaped? (Hint: With full wage indexation, the nominal wage, W, always doubles when P doubles or falls by one-half when P falls by one-half, so the real wage in the labor market will always turn out to be the same, irrespective of the value of the price level.)

Before the Test

Test your understanding of the material covered in this chapter by taking the Chapter 12 interactive quiz at **http://macro.swcollege.com**.

Online Application

As discussed in this chapter, some economists in recent years have advocated a multisector approach to macroeconomics. Although this approach typically emphasizes differences across structures of the industrial goods market and the labor market, it also could allow for differences in macroeconomic structures across geographic regions of an economy. This application permits you to evaluate whether such an approach might have any merit.

Internet URL: **http://www.dol.gov**

Title: *Department of Labor*

Navigation: Begin at the home page of the Labor Department, which is the above address. Then click on *Statistics, Research, and Publications.* Next, click on *Bureau of Labor Statistics.*

Application: Perform the indicated operations, and answer the following questions:

1. Choose "Local Area Unemployment Statistics. Most Requested Statistics." From this list, you can select unemployment statistics for different states and cities. Choose a local city. Scan the data for the past two or three years. Does the unemployment rate fluctuate?

2. Take a look at the unemployment rates for two or three individual states for the past two or three years. Compare the data for the states that you have chosen with the overall U.S. unemployment rate data. Are there significant differences, either in the magnitudes of the unemployment rates or in the extent to which they vary over time?

For Group Study and Analysis: Divide the class into groups to examine unemployment rates in states located in specific regions of the United States, such as the Midwest, Southeast, and so on. Are there any regional patterns in the unemployment statistics? If so, what current events might account for them?

Card, David. "Unexpected Inflation, Real Wages, and Employment Determination in Union Contracts." *American Economic Review* 80 (September 1990): 669–688.

Duca, John, and David VanHoose. "The Rise of Goods-Market Competition and the Decline in Wage Indexation." *Journal of Macroeconomics* 20 (Summer 1998): 579–598.

———— "Goods-Market Competition and Profit Sharing: A Multisector Macro Approach." *Journal of Economics and Business* 50 (November 1998): 525–534.

———— "The Rise of Goods-Market Competition and the Fall of Wage Contracting: Endogenous Wage Contracting in a Multisector Economy." *Journal of Macroeconomics* 23 (Winter 2001): 1–21.

Dutkowsky, Donald, and H. Sonmez Atesoglu. "Wage Contracting in the Macroeconomy." *Journal of Money, Credit, and Banking* 25 (February 1993): 62–78.

Fischer, Stanley. *Indexing, Inflation, and Economic Policy.* Cambridge, Mass.: MIT Press, 1986.

Fischer, Stanley, ed. *Rational Expectations and Economic Policy.* Chicago: University of Chicago Press, 1980.

Ghosal, Vivek, and Prakash Loungani. "Evidence on Nominal Wage Rigidity from a Panel of U.S. Manufacturing Industries." *Journal of Money, Credit, and Banking* 28 (November 1996): 650–668.

Gray, Jo Anna. "Wage Indexation: A Macroeconomic Approach." *Journal of Monetary Economics* 2 (April 1976): 221–235.

Gray, Jo Anna, and David Spencer. "Price Prediction Errors and Real Activity: A Reassessment." *Economic Inquiry* 28 (October 1990): 658–681.

Gray, Jo Anna, Magda Kandil, and David Spencer. "Does Contractual Wage Rigidity Play a Role in Determining Real Activity?" *Southern Economic Journal* 58 (1992): 1042–1057.

Taylor, John. "Aggregate Dynamics and Staggered Contracts." *Journal of Political Economy* 88 (February 1980): 1–23.

VanHoose, David, and Christopher J. Waller. "Discretion, Wage Indexation, and Inflation." *Southern Economic Journal* 58 (October 1991): 356–367.

macro**xtra!**

Log on to the MacroXtra Web site at
http://macroxtra.swcollege.com for
additional learning resources such as
practice quizzes, Interactive Key
Graphs, readings, and additional
economic applications.

13

Market Failures versus Perfect Markets—

New Keynesians versus Real-Business-Cycle Theorists

FUNDAMENTAL ISSUES

1. What has motivated macroeconomists to propose additional theories of how the economy functions?

2. What are the key features of new Keynesian theories?

3. What are coordination failures, and why do new Keynesians believe that they may be important?

4. How do real-business-cycle theorists explain short-term fluctuations in real output?

5. What is quantitative theory, and why is it so controversial?

The unemployment rate in France has hovered close to or even above 10 percent for several years. In 2000, the French government decided to attack the problem directly: it cut the legal workweek from 39 hours to 35 hours for both hourly and salaried workers; only senior managers and company executives were exempted. The government enforced the law by issuing thousands of citations to senior managers of companies alleging that they were working their employees too many hours and threatening them with fines of up to $1 million and prison terms of up to two years.

In response, French corporations began installing electronic time clocks in factory and office hallways. When workers arrived at their jobs, took coffee and lunch breaks, and departed at the end of the day, they had to swipe their ID cards through the clocks to formally record the time. To grant companies some flexibility, the government allowed employees to work more than 35 hours in some weeks, as long as they worked fewer than 35 hours in others.

Workers could accumulate up to 15 hourly "work credits" in weeks when they exceeded the 35-hour threshold. When workers accumulated 15 credits, managers had to contact them and help them draw up a plan to reduce the backlog. Any workaholics who persistently exceeded the 15-hour limit received special counseling intended to help them cut back on hours spent at work.

This French law, which was recently scaled back somewhat, was intended to tackle the nation's unemployment problem directly. The logic was that if companies had to cut back on hours for current employees, they would have an incentive to hire additional workers. Some economists, however, suspect that a key factor contributing to relatively high unemployment rates in France and several other European nations is not a lack of rules and regulations but rather *too many* laws governing the conditions under which firms can hire and employ workers. Such regulations, they contend, help to perpetuate labor markets in which some have an inside track at employment while others are relegated to the status of outsiders. This may reinforce one approach to understanding unemployment, known as the *insider-outsider theory*.

In this chapter, you will encounter some of the most recent theories in macroeconomics. In the process, you will find that there really are some significant divisions among macroeconomists today. Some advance a *real-business-cycle theory,* which indicates that technological changes help drive swings in economic activity within highly competitive markets for goods and services. You also will discover that other macroeconomists, by way of contrast, believe that market failures may offer an explanation for changes in overall business activity. Nevertheless, you also will find that in some ways the different "camps" within macroeconomics have reached some similar conclusions about how to understand the functioning of the aggregate economy.

Why Are There New Theories?

In many respects, the widespread adoption of the rational expectations hypothesis by modern Keynesian and new classical theorists alike has revolutionized macroeconomics. At the same time, however, the gulf separating the Keynesian- and classical-oriented approaches to macroeconomic theory and policy analysis widened during the past decade. On the one hand, incorporating the rational expectations hypothesis into fully articulated theories of the economy has led a number of today's proponents of the Keynesian approach to develop business cycle models with considerable stickiness of wages and prices. These new theories constitute *new Keynesian macroeconomics.* On the other hand, many proponents of the new classical approach have reached the conclusion that business cycles arise naturally in an economy with fully flexible wages and prices. The macroeconomic models that they have developed comprise the *real-business-cycle* approach to macroeconomics. Our goal in this chapter is to help you to understand why there is such a gap between these two schools of thought, so that you will be able to judge for yourself in the coming years which approach has the greater practical relevance.

You might wonder why macroeconomists have developed yet more theories. Aren't the classical, traditional Keynesian, monetarist, new classical, and modern Keynesian theories enough? The answer is that even though the rational expectations hypothesis helped to resolve long-standing issues about how to include information and expectations in macroeconomic models, by itself it did not provide macroeconomists with a better explanation of the actual performances of real-world economies. Indeed, incorporating rational expectations into previously existing models, which essentially is what the modern Keynesian and new classical theorists have done, opened a Pandora's box of new problems for macroeconomists. Even though the rational expectations hypothesis is intuitively appealing and makes macroeconomic models internally consistent, the modern Keynesian and new classical theories that resulted have had trouble explaining observed *persistence* in employment and real output movements.

The Great Puzzle Posed by the Great Depression

The extreme example of this failure is the Great Depression that gripped the United Kingdom, the United States, and many other nations during the 1930s. A common explanation for the Great Depression, originally proposed by Milton Friedman and other monetarists, is that it was set off by a large decline in the nominal money stock between 1929 and 1933. In fact, the quantity of money in the United States fell by over one-third during that interval, inducing a sizable decline in aggregate demand.

Other competing explanations for the onset of the Great Depression have been offered, but like this monetarist explanation, they focus on the decline in aggregate demand. Both new classical and modern Keynesian theories face a problem, though, in explaining why the Great Depression lasted for such a long time. After all, the policy actions that permitted a continual fall in the money stock and induced the decline in aggregate demand were repeated until they became systematic and, thus, predictable. As you learned in Chapter 11, the new classical theory's central tenet is that predictable policy actions should have no effects on employment and real output. Nonetheless, the Great Depression persisted until the outbreak of World War II in Europe in 1939.

As we discussed in Chapter 12, the modern Keynesian theory with staggered and overlapping contracts might help to explain why the large fall in aggregate demand of the early 1930s had such persistent effects. Nevertheless, this contract-based theory also falters when confronted with both the extreme severity and the significant persistence of the Great Depression. Unions and explicit wage contracts existed in the 1930s, but they actually became more prevalent as the Great Depression progressed. During the early years of the depression, they were not widespread in U.S. labor markets. Even if they had been, it would be difficult for the modern Keynesian theory to explain the persistent declines in real output that occurred in the 1930s. Like the new classical theory, the contract-based model predicts that systematic declines in the quantity of money and the price level will be anticipated, so that within a few years employment and real output will tend to return to their long-run, "natural" levels. The modern Keynesian theory has trouble explaining why this failed to happen over the course of an entire decade.

Modern GDP Persistence

The Great Depression is an extreme example of persistence in employment and real output movements. In the 1980s macroeconomists developed new techniques for examining **time series,** or data recorded over successive periods of time. They discovered that temporary changes in economic conditions often have long-lasting effects on real GDP. Nevertheless, macroeconomic theories, such as those we have discussed up to this point, indicated that such temporary changes should simply result in "blips," or short-term GDP fluctuations that ultimately peter out. In fact, however, many variations in economic conditions seem to have long-lasting effects on GDP.

To a large extent, the development of the new Keynesian and real-business-cycle theories stems from efforts by macroeconomists to understand what could cause temporary changes in economic conditions to persist for months and years. Although these theories are offshoots of the modern Keynesian and new classical approaches that we discussed in the previous two chapters, their emphasis on the persistence issue is what classifies them, at least for the present, as "new" macroeconomic theories.

New theories can be useful, but they also can turn out to be dead ends. You should keep this in mind as you read this chapter. A decade or two from now, some of the approaches discussed in this chapter will have been debunked. Others, however, likely will provide the basis for policy analysis by the coming generation of economists and policymakers. This is why it is important for you to study these new theoretical approaches: In the not-so-distant future, at least one of these theories may guide macroeconomic forecasting and policymaking.

> ### FUNDAMENTAL ISSUE #1
> **What has motivated macroeconomists to propose additional theories of how the economy functions?** Earlier theories have not been successful in explaining why real GDP seems to exhibit persistent responses to otherwise short-lived changes in economic activity. Hence, macroeconomists have developed new theories that potentially can explain this phenomenon.

In the classical and new classical theories, the key to rapid adjustments of real output to the level consistent with an economy's long-run growth potential is flexibility of wages and prices. Inflexible wages and prices are one possible reason why real output might vary from its long-run level. As we discussed in Chapter 12, the modern Keynesian theory has focused its attention on wage inflexibilities. New Keynesian theories, however, concentrate

TIME SERIES: Observed values of macroeconomic variables over successive time intervals.

375

CHAPTER 13 Market Failure versus Perfect Markets—New Keynesians versus Real-Business-Cycle Theorists

Sticky-Price Theories: New Keynesian Macroeconomics

on possible *sources* of stickiness in the price level. Inflexible prices of goods and services could help to explain why real output might be variable in the short run. Price stickiness might also be part of a rationale for persistence in output changes in response to temporary changes in economic conditions. Together with wage stickiness, price stickiness can also lead to real wage rigidities that could help to explain unemployment.

Why Would Prices Be Sticky, and Why Does It Matter if They Are?

Until the early 1970s, traditional Keynesian theorists often worked with models in which the price level was fixed. Just as we assumed in Chapters 6 through 9 that the price level was "given," macroeconomists used to envision a world with inflexible prices, so that real output adjusted to changes in desired autonomous spending. Thus, autonomous changes in household consumption spending, investment spending by firms, exports, or imports could account for business cycles.

Clearly though, some prices change every week and every month. Indeed, since the end of World War II the United States has consistently experienced inflation. By definition, therefore, the price level has risen over time. How then can new Keynesian theorists feel comfortable developing models in which prices are sticky? Let's consider this question before we explore the new Keynesian theories any further.

IS THERE INERTIA IN THE PRICE LEVEL?   New Keynesians argue that persistent inflation does not necessarily mean that the prices of goods and services adjust quickly and fully to changes in current market conditions. For instance, the average inflation rate might be significantly higher, they contend, if prices adjusted as flexibly as possible to changes in demand or in firms' production costs.

For reasons that we shall discuss later in the chapter, sluggishness in price adjustments, or **price inertia,** is a central feature of most new Keynesian theories. Figure 13–1 displays estimates of an index measure of price inertia for five industrialized nations spanning the period from the end of the 1950s through the late 1980s. The higher the value of this index, the more inertia there is in prices of goods and services in a nation. As you can see, according to this measure the United States experienced the greatest sluggishness in price adjustment, as compared with Germany, France, the United Kingdom, and Japan.

TRYING TO EXPLAIN PRICE RIGIDITY: NEW KEYNESIAN MACROECONOMICS   In light of Figure 13–1 and other evidence of price stickiness, the new Keynesian theorists believe that the assumption of complete price-level flexibility in the United States and other nations is unwarranted. In their view, any complete macroeconomic theory should account for the existence of such rigidities and for their potential to explain key features of business cycles, including output persistence.

Although the new Keynesian approach began to attract many adherents during the 1980s, it actually began in the 1960s and early 1970s. During this earlier period, a number of macroeconomists tried to construct more sophisticated Keynesian models. As in the earlier model that we summa-

PRICE INERTIA: A tendency for the price level to resist change over time.

Figure 13–1   Measures of Price Inertia for Five Industrialized Nations

Countries with higher values of the price inertia index tend to exhibit greater sluggishness in price-level movements.

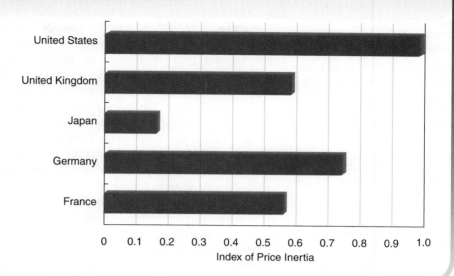

SOURCE: Robert Gordon, "What Is New-Keynesian Economics?" *Journal of Economic Literature* 28 (1990): 1151–1171.

rized in Chapters 6 through 9, these models had fixed prices. In contrast to the basic Keynesian framework, however, these models had "microeconomic foundations." In the macroeconomic frameworks that emerged from this approach, real output was *demand determined,* rather than supply determined as in the classical model. As a result, real output adjusted to market conditions. Short-term business cycles therefore could be explained by variations in aggregate demand.

This approach was largely abandoned by the late 1970s, however. The theory lacked an explanation for price rigidity, and the development of the rational expectations hypothesis seemed to explain why short-run and long-run price-level and output adjustments might differ. Moreover, experience with the Arab oil embargo in 1973 and the sharp effects on real GDP after the run-up in oil prices in the mid-1970s indicated that supply-side factors clearly were important determinants of real output, so a purely demand-based macroeconomic theory made little sense.

Later on, proponents of the new Keynesian approach brought the theories of price rigidities back to life by developing sticky-price models in which the reasons for price rigidities are fully explained and prices respond at least partially to changes in supply-side factors. This is where the idea of price inertia comes in. Theories that predict price inertia indicate that prices can still change with variations in factors affecting business production costs. Nevertheless, sluggishness in price adjustments can lead to considerable short-term variability of real output as a result of variations in aggregate demand, as in the earlier fixed-price theories.

IMPERFECT COMPETITION AND MARKET FAILURES   During the past twenty years, new Keynesian theorists have proposed a number of explanations for price inertia and its implications for business cycles. Although these theories

On the Web

How does the U.S. government seek to limit the extent of imperfect competition? Learn about U.S. antitrust policy at the home page of the U.S. Justice Department at http://www.usdoj.gov/atr.

IMPERFECT COMPETITION: A market environment that may have a limited number of buyers or sellers, barriers to market entry or exit, or differentiated firm products or factor services.

MARKET FAILURE: The potential failure of a private market equilibrium to reflect all costs and benefits relating to production of a good or service.

EXTERNALITY: A spillover effect that arises when market exchanges affect the well-being of an individual or firm that is not a party to the exchanges.

MACROECONOMIC EXTERNALITIES: Situations in which aggregate equilibrium in all, or at least many, markets fails to account for spillovers across markets, so that equilibrium aggregate real output, employment, and the price level all differ from their long-run, natural levels.

differ in many respects, they typically share two features. First, most new Keynesian theories depart from the classical assumption of purely competitive markets for goods and services or for factors of production. Recall that in purely competitive markets, there are many buyers and sellers, there is free entry into and exit from markets, and the products that firms produce and the services of factors of production are indistinguishable. New Keynesian theories, in contrast, are based on the assumption of **imperfect competition.** In these market environments, the number of buyers or sellers may be limited, there may be barriers to market entry or exit, or firm products or factor services may be differentiated.

The other feature common to many new Keynesian models is **market failure,** or the failure of a private market to reach an equilibrium that reflects all the costs and benefits entailed in producing a good or providing a factor service. An example of a market failure is an **externality,** or a situation in which a private cost or benefit differs from a social cost or benefit because of spillover effects stemming from the production or consumption of a good or service. Consider, for instance, noise pollution in the form of classical, country and western, rap, or rock music that booms from car stereos on city streets. Such pollution is made possible by the production and sale of car speakers capable of amplifying sound. The firms that produce car speakers receive private benefits from their sale, and enthusiasts of classical, country and western, rap, and rock music benefit from the ability to listen to the music at high-decibel levels. Meanwhile other people incur costs because they must listen to music when they would prefer peace and quiet. These spillover costs that nonenthusiasts incur are not reflected in the equilibrium price and quantity in the market for car stereo speakers.

The noise pollution produced by booming car speakers is a *microeconomic* externality, or an externality that arises in a single market. New Keynesian proponents contend that there also are **macroeconomic externalities.** In these situations, equilibrium in all, or at least many, markets fails to account for spillovers across markets, so that equilibrium aggregate real output, employment, and the price level all differ from their long-run, natural levels.

The nature of proposed new Keynesian macroeconomic externalities varies across the diverse range of new Keynesian theories. Nonetheless, as we shall discuss in more detail shortly, the proposed macroeconomic externalities arise from the inability of individuals and firms to coordinate their actions. The alleged existence of such *coordination failures* is the cornerstone of the new Keynesian approach to macroeconomics. Before we try to understand the nature of coordination failures, however, let's first survey the main new Keynesian theories.

Small-Menu-Cost Models

What might account for price inertia? After all, profit-maximizing firms adjust their output to the point at which marginal revenue is equal to marginal cost. Furthermore, as firms adjust their output to profit-maximizing levels, market prices should adjust as well.

If prices somehow are relatively rigid even as market conditions change, then profit-maximizing firms must have a *reason* not to vary prices. This is an example of how imperfect competition and market failures might play a role. According to one new Keynesian approach, known as the *small-menu-cost theory,* the absence of pure competition and macroeconomic externalities together could help to account for price inertia and ultimately could help to explain business cycles and the persistent response of real output to temporary changes in economic conditions.

THE ADMINISTERED PRICING HYPOTHESIS The idea that imperfect competition could help to explain price rigidities was first suggested in the 1930s by an economist named Gardiner Means. His theory, which became known as the **administered pricing hypothesis,** proposed that firms that are not purely competitive are able to *set* prices and to maintain relatively *inflexible* pricing policies over lengthy intervals.

Initially, a number of economists were attracted to Means's hypothesis, because they thought that it could assist in explaining the observed stickiness of prices in several U.S. industries during the Great Depression. For instance, as Table 13–1 shows, product prices of agricultural implements and motor vehicles fell by only 6 percent and 16 percent, respectively, although output declined significantly—by 80 percent—in both industries. In other industries, however, such as petroleum and agricultural products, price declines were much more pronounced. Thus, proportionate output reductions were much smaller in these industries. Ultimately, however, the administered pricing hypothesis was abandoned, because it was difficult to understand why even imperfectly competitive firms would fail to change their prices in response to variations in the demand for their products or in the face of changes in their costs of production.

RESURRECTING AN OLD IDEA The small-menu-cost theory, which was first proposed by N. Gregory Mankiw of Harvard University and subsequently was refined in the 1980s and 1990s, has brought the administered pricing hypothesis back to life, albeit in a new form. As the theory's name indicates, the basis of the theory is the proposal that firms incur small but measurable costs, called **small menu costs,** when they change the prices that they

ADMINISTERED PRICING HYPOTHESIS: The view that imperfectly competitive firms set prices of their products at relatively unchanging levels for lengthy intervals.

SMALL MENU COSTS: The costs firms incur when they make price changes, including both the costs of changing prices in menus or catalogues and the costs of renegotiating agreements with customers.

Table 13–1	Declines in Prices and Production for Selected U.S. Industries, 1929–1933	
Industry	Percentage Decline in Price	Percentage Decline in Production
Agricultural implements	6	80
Motor vehicles	16	80
Textile products	45	30
Petroleum	56	20
Agricultural products	63	6

SOURCE: Robert Gordon, "What Is New-Keynesian Economics?" *Journal of Economic Literature* 28 (1990): 1151–1171.

charge their customers. These costs could take the form of expenses entailed in printing new price tags, menus, and catalogues. They also could include costs incurred in bringing together firm managers for meetings on price changes or in renegotiating business deals with customers.

A FIRM'S PRICE DETERMINATION   Figure 13–2 illustrates the small-menu-cost theory as applied to an individual, imperfectly competitive firm whose product differs slightly from those of rival producers. Consequently, the firm faces a downward-sloping demand schedule, labeled D. We assume that the demand schedule is a straight line, which means that the marginal revenue schedule is also a straight line. In addition, we simplify by assuming that the firm's marginal cost (MC) is constant and equal to its average cost (AC), and we consider only a single production period to which these demand and cost schedules apply. When the demand schedule is in the position denoted by D_1, the marginal revenue schedule is located at MR_1. If the firm faces this level of demand and marginal revenue, it maximizes its profit by producing output up to the point at which marginal revenue is equal to marginal cost. The profit-maximizing output level therefore is equal to y_1. The firm then charges a price, P_1, that its customers are willing to pay, which we can determine by reading off the demand schedule at the output level y_1. The profit earned by the firm then is equal to total revenue minus total cost, or $(P_1 \times y_1) - (AC \times y_1)$. This is equal to $(P_1 - AC) \times y_1$, which is the maximum profit at the level of demand given by D_1.

Now think about what will happen if the demand schedule shifts inward, to D_2. Because the marginal revenue schedule is derived from the demand schedule, the marginal revenue schedule will shift inward as well, to MR_2. You learned in your microeconomics principles course that the firm should then adjust its output level to the new point at which marginal revenue equals marginal cost, which is at the output level y_2. The firm will reduce

---

Figure 13–2   Profit Gains and Losses from a Firm's Failure to Change Its Price When Demand for Its Product Declines

If the demand and marginal revenue schedules faced by an imperfectly competitive firm shift downward, and the firm fails to reduce its price, its profit gain is the area B. If the firm cuts its price to P_2, its profit gain is the area A. Consequently, a firm interested in maximizing its profit normally would reduce its price from P_1 to P_2, because $A - B$ is greater than zero, implying that a price cut will result in a net profit gain. If the cost of adjusting its price is greater than the amount $A - B$, however, the firm will leave its price unchanged at P_1.

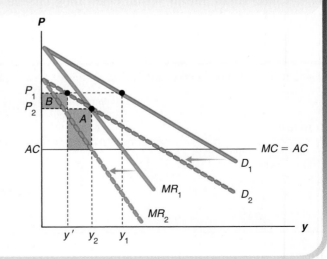

the price of its product to P_2, and its new maximum profit will be equal to $(P_2 \times y_2) - (AC \times y_2)$, or $(P_2 - AC) \times y_2$.

A THEORY OF PRICE STICKINESS   Normally, we assume that a firm faces no costs in changing its price. Suppose that in the face of small menu costs such as those we discussed earlier, the firm contemplates leaving its price unchanged when demand declines from D_1 to D_2. If the firm follows this course by holding its product price steady at P_1, then at the reduced level of demand D_2 the firm will be able to sell only the level of output y', and its profit will be equal to $(P_1 \times y') - (AC \times y')$, or $(P_1 - AC) \times y'$. This profit level is lower than the profit the firm could have earned by reducing its price to P_2, which we just noted would equal $(P_2 - AC) \times y_2$. If the firm keeps its price unchanged, its profit loss is the difference between the two profit levels that the firm could earn.

We can calculate this difference by examining Figure 13–2. If the firm produces the output level y', and keeps its price at P_1 instead of cutting its price to P_2 when demand falls, the firm will obtain a profit increase equal to the area labeled B. At the profit-maximizing price P_2 at the lower level of demand, however, producing y' units of output instead of the actual profit-maximizing output level y_2 will yield a profit reduction equal to area A. Hence, the net profit reduction that the firm will experience by keeping its price fixed at P_1 when demand declines from D_1 to D_2 is equal to the amount $A - B$.

This means that the firm's decision on whether to change its price will depend on a simple comparison of the size of the profit reduction from keeping its price fixed, $A - B$, with the small menu cost it would incur if it changes its price. If the profit loss from keeping the price unchanged is greater than the cost of changing its price, then the firm will choose to change its price as basic microeconomics principles suggest it should. If the profit loss from leaving its price fixed is smaller than the cost of cutting its price, then the firm will leave its price unchanged. The price of its product will be "sticky."

THE APPLICABILITY OF THE SMALL–MENU–COST MODEL   It turns out that the size of the profit loss $A - B$ depends on the elasticity of the demand schedule at the original price. A more elastic schedule would reduce the size of the profit loss $A - B$. One determinant of the elasticity of demand is the availability of close substitutes for the good. We would expect the demand for goods with several available substitutes, including automobiles or agricultural implements, to be more elastic than the demand for such goods as energy-producing petroleum products or food-related agricultural products, for which short-run substitutes may be more limited. Hence, firms producing goods such as motor vehicles, new tractors, or agricultural implements would tend to be more likely to leave their prices fixed in the face of a fall in demand. As Figure 13–2 indicates, a firm that leaves its price unchanged will then reduce its production by a larger amount when demand declines, from y_1 to y', rather than from y_1 to y_2.

If you refer back to Table 13–1, you will see that this story appears to fit the facts that Gardiner Means documented in the 1930s. Essentially, the small-menu-cost model provides the basic theoretical explanation for the administered pricing hypothesis that was lacking at the time Means proposed the hypothesis.

FROM MENU COSTS TO MACROECONOMIC EXTERNALITIES   Figure 13–2 on page 380 depicts the behavior of a single firm. Firms throughout the economy face their own specific demand schedules and have their own marginal and average cost schedules. According to the theory, some firms will reduce their prices in the face of declining product demand. Others will leave their prices fixed.

Laurence Ball of Johns Hopkins University and David Romer of Harvard University have shown how this mix of responses by firms can have macroeconomic implications. The foundation of their argument is that the products of firms are substitutable in consumption, albeit imperfectly. When one set of firms chooses to cut their prices in the face of an overall decline in demand for goods throughout the economy, consumers allocate more of their spending to consumption of the output of those firms, although on net the firms' production levels still will fall. As a result, though, fewer consumer funds are available for spending on the goods produced by firms that keep their prices fixed. Demand at each of the fixed-price firms then declines further, thereby reinforcing the output declines at those firms. Consequently, the decisions by some firms to cut their prices have spillover effects onto firms that do not change their prices, and vice versa. As we shall discuss in more detail later, this could be a source of macroeconomic externalities that could cause business cycles to occur and to persist.

PROBLEMS WITH THE SMALL-MENU-COST MODEL   Critics of the small-menu-cost model point out that the theory assumes that firms attempt to maximize profits only for a single period. More realistically, however, firms earn flows of profits over time. To see why this poses a problem for the small-menu-cost analysis, look at Figure 13–2 once again, and consider the profit loss that a firm will experience if it leaves its price unchanged in the face of a long-lasting decline in demand as illustrated in the figure. The firm will incur the profit loss $A - B$ *every period* from now into the future. Hence, from today's perspective, the firm's total profit loss actually will be the discounted sum of all future values of $A - B$, which is a significantly larger amount than the one-period loss equal to $A - B$. In contrast, the small menu cost that the firm will incur in changing its price is a once-and-for-all cost. Therefore, a firm that wishes to maximize the discounted value of current and future profits in the face of a long-lasting decline in demand will leave its price unchanged only if $A - B$ is *very* small or if the small menu costs are not *too* small.

Another difficulty that critics have with the theory is that it focuses only on the costs of price changes. Arguably, however, changing production levels of real output could also entail significant costs. If such output adjustment costs exist, then an imperfectly competitive firm would be less willing to keep its price the same, because doing so would require a greater change in its output.

Furthermore, ongoing developments in electronic commerce may reduce the applicability of the small-menu-cost model in many settings. The reason is that the model relies on the assumption that firms "post" retail prices, even though a small but growing portion of transactions for goods and services already are conducted via Internet auctions, in which market prices tend to adjust quickly to changes in demand or supply. Current estimates are that Internet auctions will be the means of arranging more than half, and possibly even more than three-fourths, of business-to-business sales and purchases by 2010. Internet auctions are also becoming a more popular means of accomplishing business-to-consumer and consumer-to-consumer transactions.

EFFICIENCY WAGE THEORY: An approach to explaining unemployment that is based on the hypothesis that the productivity of workers depends on the real wage rate.

383

CHAPTER 13   Market Failure versus Perfect Markets—New Keynesians versus Real-Business-Cycle Theorists

New Keynesian Explanations for Unemployment

Firms that are not pure competitors in the markets for their output also behave differently in the market for labor. Recall that the value of labor's marginal product is equal to $P \times MP_N$, or the product price times the marginal product of labor. For a purely competitive firm, the value of labor's marginal product determines the firm's demand for labor. From the perspective of profit maximization, however, what a firm cares about most is the *marginal revenue product of labor,* which is equal to marginal revenue times labor's marginal product, or $MR \times MP_N$. As Figure 13–2 on page 380 indicates, marginal revenue is less than the product price for an imperfectly competitive firm. Therefore, an imperfectly competitive firm's demand for labor is below the demand for labor by a purely competitive firm.

EFFICIENCY WAGE THEORY   This is the starting point for a key new Keynesian theory of unemployment known as the **efficiency wage theory.** This hypothesis proposes that the productivity of workers depends on the real wage rate and that imperfectly competitive firms respond to this relationship by employing fewer workers.

The idea that workers' productivity may depend on the real wage rate developed from the observation that higher real wage payments in developing countries led to better nutrition and education for workers. As a result, workers' productivity improved. New Keynesian theorists have built on this idea by arguing that higher real wage payments by firms increase employees' morale and loyalty, thereby inducing them to work harder and more efficiently. Thus, in contrast to standard labor market theory in which the marginal product of labor is unrelated to the real wage, higher real wages could raise the marginal product of labor.

When the Nobel Prize–winning economist Robert Solow of the Massachusetts Institute of Technology considered the implication of a positive relationship between the real wage and labor's marginal product, he found that it gives imperfectly competitive firms an incentive to hold the real wage fixed. The reason is that paying a real wage below the fixed value reduces a firm's wage costs but raises costs on net because of lost worker productivity caused by diminished morale and reduced loyalty to the firm. Paying a real wage above this value would yield efficiency gains, but they would be more than offset by the resulting rise in the firm's wage costs. Therefore, the imperfectly competitive firm maximizes its profits at a fixed *efficiency wage.*

If the real wage is fixed, then it cannot adjust to the point at which the quantity of labor demanded is equal to the quantity of labor supplied.

INSIDER-OUTSIDER THEORY: The notion that because a firm views its current, "insider" employees as an investment that would be costly to replace, the insiders are able to inhibit the hiring of unemployed "outsiders" at real wages below those earned by the insiders.

Consequently, the amount of labor supplied at the efficiency wage paid by an imperfectly competitive firm could easily exceed the quantity of labor that the firm actually will employ at that real wage. The result would be an excess quantity of labor supplied, or unemployment.

Of course, one obvious problem with the efficiency wage theory is that it ignores the fact that firms compensate their employees in other ways besides direct wage payments. A firm can try to improve its workers' morale and increase their loyalty by rewarding them with special bonuses, quality pension plans, sales commissions, shares of the firm's profits, or perhaps even ownership shares. If these various additional forms of labor compensation are considered, the efficiency wage is no longer necessarily inflexible. This reduces the strength of the efficiency wage theory as a possible explanation for unemployment. (Nevertheless, it is possible that firms facing declining demand for their products will choose to lay off workers rather than cut wages; see *Management Notebook: Taking into Account Morale Effects When Weighing Whether to Eliminate Jobs or Cut Workers' Pay*.)

INSIDER-OUTSIDER MODELS   The other new Keynesian theory that focuses on labor market behavior is known as the **insider-outsider theory.** Proponents of this theory contend that a firm's current employees (insiders) may have an advantage in maintaining their jobs and wages, which imposes barriers on the firm's ability to hire others (outsiders) who would be willing to work at a lower real wage.

According to the insider-outsider theory, firms regard the training of their employees as a type of *capital investment*. Hiring new employees would force a firm to incur additional training expenses, so replacing exist-

Management NOTEBOOK

Taking into Account Morale Effects When Weighing Whether to Eliminate Jobs or Cut Workers' Pay

Suppose that you are the manager of an imperfectly competitive firm, which means that you have influence over both how many workers to employ and how much to pay them. A recent downturn in economic activity has reduced the demand for your firm's product. Should you respond by laying off some workers while maintaining the wages of the workers you continue to employ, or should you cut wages for all your employees to avoid laying off some workers?

Truman Bewley of Yale University surveyed managers to find out how they would respond to this situation and why. Based on the managers' answers, he concluded that firms prefer layoffs. The reason is that pay cuts hurt all employees and reduce morale throughout a company. Layoffs can reduce morale somewhat among workers who retain their jobs by increasing their uncertainty about continued employment, but managers perceive that this morale effect is less dramatic and lasts for a shorter time.

Thus, Bewley argues, in bad economic times real-world managers often behave just the way that efficiency wage theory predicts. They lay off workers instead of reducing wages.

For Critical Analysis
If firms behave the way that the efficiency wage theory predicts, should real wages rise or fall during a recession that takes place because of a fall in aggregate demand?

ing employees would entail a cost that might not be offset by lower wage costs for new employees who are less fully trained. As a result, current employees are able to exercise some control over the terms under which the firm hires new employees.

Although this theory is most clearly applicable to settings with employee unions, some new Keynesian theorists contend that it applies to many nonunionized settings. Terminating a current employee often requires a firm to pay termination wages and perhaps offer retraining programs if it wishes to avoid a court fight with a disgruntled employee and his or her attorney. Hiring a new employee often entails incurring sizable advertising and search costs. Together, these costs, new Keynesians argue, could contribute to the development of insider-dominated labor markets that impose high barriers to entry by outsiders. Hence, these outsiders will be unemployed even though they are willing to work for lower real wages than firms pay current insiders.

A THEORY OF INVOLUNTARY UNEMPLOYMENT An attractive feature of the insider-outsider theory is that it provides a potential explanation for both *involuntary* unemployment and *persistent* unemployment. The wage contracting models discussed in Chapter 12 predict that unemployment could arise if the price level during a contract interval turns out to be lower than workers and firms expected when they negotiated the contract wages. In a sense, however, this unemployment is voluntary, because it results from a voluntary contract agreement. In addition, unless price-level reductions unexpectedly persist, the contract-based modern Keynesian models can at best explain short-term unemployment. The insider-outsider theory also provides potential explanations for observed differences in wages and unemployment within and across industries and countries.

A key weakness of the theory, however, is that it often takes the existence of insiders for granted. It also fails to explain why entrepreneurial outsiders would remain unemployed when they could work together and establish a firm that competes with the firms that employ current insiders. Implicitly, the theory seems to rely on the existence of legal restrictions that inhibit such activities, rather than on behavioral relationships that make them a natural outcome. For this reason, some economists contend that the insider-outsider theory best applies to nations such as France, Spain, and Germany, where rigid labor laws govern interactions between workers and firms. (The insider-outsider theory may also help to explain the existence of such laws; see on the following page *Global Notebook: Voting to Keep the Insider-Outsider Model Relevant to Europe.*)

Are average weekly hours workers are employed in the United States currently rising or falling? Find out via EconData Online.
http://macroxtra.swcollege.com

FUNDAMENTAL ISSUE #2

What are the key features of new Keynesian theories? New Keynesian theories share two key features. One is the view that imperfect competition is widespread. The other is the view that market failures are commonplace and lead to macroeconomic externalities. Small-menu-cost models combine these features to explain why prices might be sticky and real output might fluctuate. In addition, efficiency wage theory and insider-outsider models use these features as a basis for explaining involuntary unemployment.

Voting to Keep the Insider-Outsider Model Relevant to Europe

It is easy to explain why democratic nations such as those in Europe might have laws that perpetuate an environment of employed insiders and unemployed outsiders. Insiders benefit from laws that make it harder to close plants and offices and lay off workers. Hence, they tend to vote for such laws even though the rules make it harder for firms to employ people who currently do not have jobs but might otherwise be willing to work for lower wages. As long as insiders who vote outnumber unemployed outsiders, legal structures perpetuating an insider-outsider environment with relatively high unemployment rates are likely to remain in place.

Some economists suggest that Europe might be able to break out of its insider-outsider mode of behavior by taking advantage of another incentive that insiders face. Because they already have jobs, insiders are likely to favor reduced contributions to unemployment insurance programs, which push up employers' costs and thereby reduce the insiders' wages. In fact, surveys of citizens of European nations bear out this prediction.

As a step toward curbing insider-outsider structures, these economists suggest that European governments provide more generous unemployment benefits to people who were employed for relatively short periods before losing their jobs and cut back on benefits for the unemployed who

had jobs for a long time before being laid off. Thus, the overall net cost of unemployment insurance to society would remain about the same. At the same time, governments might be able to gain overall voter support for cutting back on employment-protection laws that perpetuate insider-outsider structures. Because long-employed insiders possess firm-specific skills that make them less likely to be laid off, they might be willing to support such a mix of changes in unemployment compensation and labor laws. Insiders who have only recently made the transition from being unemployed outsiders might also go along with these changes, because they would receive higher unemployment compensation if they were laid off.

Such a carefully crafted program might obtain sufficient voter support to enable governments to dismantle the insider-outsider structures so prevalent in Europe. Without such a careful mix of changes in the legal environment, however, majority rule is likely to keep insider-outsider behavior in place indefinitely.

For Critical Analysis
Other things being equal, how much would European unemployment rates have to rise to produce a voting bloc sufficiently large to induce governments to scale back employment-protection laws?

Coordination

Failure

COORDINATION FAILURES:
Spillover effects between workers and firms that arise from movements in macroeconomic variables that hinder efforts by individual households and firms to plan and implement their consumption, production, and pricing decisions.

The small-menu-cost, efficiency wage, and insider-outsider theories are the three dominant new Keynesian frameworks. Together, these models potentially explain sticky prices and variable output as well as rigid real wages and unemployment.

As noted above, the rigidity in real wages predicted by the efficiency wage theory potentially could help to explain persistent unemployment, as could institutional rigidities that implicitly lie behind the insider-outsider framework. Nevertheless, the key new Keynesian explanation for persistent responses of real output to temporary changes in economic conditions lies in the idea of **coordination failure.** This refers to the inability of workers and firms to plan and implement labor supply, production, and pricing decisions because of macroeconomic externalities that affect workers and firms in different ways. New Keynesians argue that the failure of workers and firms to share information and to make decisions jointly makes them particularly susceptible to such externalities and can lead to levels of real output that persistently differ from the economy's natural, long-run level.

Coordination Problems with Heterogeneous Workers and Firms

The key to the potential for coordination failures is *heterogeneity*. Workers and firms will be interested in coordinating their actions only if they otherwise might respond differently to events such as variations in the quantity of money, fiscal policy actions, or changes in autonomous exports.

SOURCES OF HETEROGENEITY   Several types of heterogeneity could exist:

1. *Differences in relative size.* The most obvious source of heterogeneity is *size*. Firms vary in size from small businesses to regional firms, national companies, and multinational corporations. Many workers bargain individually with their employers, others participate in professional associations that establish certification standards for their members, and still others belong to unions that engage in collective bargaining on behalf of their members.

2. *Cost differences.* One reason that firms vary in size is that there are cost differences across firms. Even businesses of similar size can have heterogeneous costs, however, because they adopt slightly different technologies. Consequently, *cost differences* across firms are another potential source of heterogeneity.

3. *Product differentiation.* As noted earlier, a key justification for imperfect competition is that firms may produce differentiated products. Because new Keynesian theorists typically rely on imperfect competition as a motivation for their theories, *product differentiation* is a natural type of heterogeneity for them to consider in their models.

4. *Differing tastes and preferences.* Workers and consumers can also have *varying tastes and preferences*. Differences in workers could lead to heterogeneities in worker training and abilities and to different degrees of responsiveness of the labor supply when real wages change. Because consumers' tastes vary, their responses to changes in tax policy, for instance, are likely to differ.

5. *Differing information.* Finally, workers, consumers, and firms may be *differentially informed* about the economy. For example, they may have different views about how the economy functions. Even if they agree on this issue, some may have a better idea of the actual state of the economy than others. Consequently, they are likely to respond differently to actual changes in economic conditions.

MACROECONOMIC EXTERNALITIES AND COORDINATION PROBLEMS   Heterogeneity among workers, consumers, and firms is the key rationale for macroeconomic externalities that new Keynesians argue are central to understanding business cycles and real output persistence. If various groups of workers, consumers, or firms respond differently to changing economic conditions, then spillover effects across groups can take place.

For example, the onset of a recession reduces the real incomes of nearly all households, including those that had planned to save by purchasing stocks and bonds of growing firms planning to expand their operations. This decline in real income reduces the sales revenues of all firms, including the expansion-oriented firms that had planned to use a portion of their revenues to finance sizable capital investments in the near future. Hence, a recession forces growing firms to issue more stocks and bonds at exactly the time that households have less real income available to purchase additional financial assets. Cutbacks in planned investment by these firms then further reduce the sales revenues of established firms and small businesses, leading them to reduce their employment of members of households that allocate most of their income to consumption spending. Such spending cuts may hit small businesses particularly hard, contributing further to the general business downturn.

This example is similar to the traditional Keynesian multiplier analysis, but it adds to the story by including heterogeneous households and firms. It also emphasizes the potential for spillover effects across different groups of households and firms. In the aggregate, such spillover effects constitute macroeconomic externalities.

Coordination Failures and Persistence in Business Cycles

What can household and firm heterogeneity contribute aside from an elaboration of the standard multiplier analysis? New Keynesian proponents argue that it potentially can explain why seemingly temporary changes in economic conditions can cause the aggregate economy to get "stuck" in a recession. It might also explain why a temporary policy action might be able to get the economy back onto a longer-term expansion path.

STRATEGIC INTERACTIONS AND MORE THAN ONE MACROECONOMIC EQUILIBRIUM An important by-product of the presence of heterogeneous groups in an economy is the potential for **strategic interactions,** or the *inter*dependence of economic choices that people make either as individuals or together with others. Economists use *game theory,* or the theory of how people make decisions in light of strategic interactions, to analyze the equilibrium choices that emerge in such settings.

In general, game theory allows for groups to interact strategically in a number of ways. There are two primary forms of interaction, however. One is **noncooperative behavior.** As the term implies, this refers to an environment in which each household or firm looks out for its own interests irrespective of the interests of other households or firms. The other behavioral mode is **cooperative behavior.** This describes a setting in which households and firms work together to achieve their common good.

It turns out that noncooperative behavior often leads to more than one possible equilibrium. Biologists observe this in the behavior of insect populations. For example, consider fire ants, which began to spread through the southern tier of the United States some years ago. These ants construct mounds in clay or sandy soil and swarm against any invaders. Each colony of fire ants tends to look out for its own interests. This noncooperative

STRATEGIC INTERACTIONS: The interdependence of economic decisions that people make individually or as part of groups.

NONCOOPERATIVE BEHAVIOR: An economic setting in which people look out for their own well-being without regard for the well-being of others.

COOPERATIVE BEHAVIOR: An economic setting in which people work together to maximize their joint well-being.

behavior typically leads to two types of outcomes. One, sometimes called a *high-level equilibrium,* occurs when the fire ant colonies spread relatively uniformly over an area, and the individual colonies achieve success in the form of sufficient nourishment for each generation of ants. The result is relatively stable ant populations. Another outcome of the noncooperative behavior, however, can be "turf wars," in which the fire ant colonies fight over space and food following external events such as droughts. The result in this case is sharp variations in fire ant populations in the affected locales. This sometimes is called a *low-level equilibrium.*

EXPLAINING RECESSIONS AND EXPANSIONS: HIGH-LEVEL VERSUS LOW-LEVEL EQUILIBRIA
Although we like to think that human beings are considerably more advanced than fire ants and other insects, like fire ants we are social animals who seek to interact with others of our species. At the same time, we all also value our individual independence from others, which naturally can engender noncooperative behavior.

New Keynesian proponents contend that when combined with heterogeneities that naturally exist across households and firms, noncooperative behavior in human societies can lead to multiple outcomes for human *economies* that are not unlike those experienced by fire ant populations. When economic conditions are relatively stable and predictable, new Keynesians argue, noncooperative behavior can yield a high-level equilibrium of relatively stable employment, real output, and prices. When some kind of outside "shock" occurs, however, such as a change in government or central bank policy or a fall in autonomous spending, noncooperative behavior can push the economy into a low-level equilibrium that can persist until another external shock pushes the economy back into the high-level state.

Noncooperative behavior among heterogeneous households and firms could therefore help to explain persistent recessions or steady economic expansions. In the new Keynesian theory, such variations in economic activity, which we call business cycles, stem from the human propensity to behave noncooperatively. Failure to coordinate can thus cause busts and booms for human economies just as it can lead to busts and booms in fire ant populations.

COORDINATION FAILURE AS A JUSTIFICATION FOR ACTIVIST POLICIES Imagine what would happen if fire ants could coordinate their activities. If queen fire ants centralized their egg production and various colonies of fire ants worked together, fire ant populations would remain as stable as the environment would permit, and fire ants could spread even more rapidly. Indeed, biologists have found some evidence that natural selection may have begun to favor fire ants that behave this way: giant, cooperative fire ant colonies have been found in some locations in the South (not good news for those allergic to fire ant stings!).

Although new Keynesian arguments are not typically based on biological analogies, they point to the same basic implication for human economies. Given the potential for noncooperative behavior and for the resulting coordination failures to produce alternating high- and low-level outcomes, perhaps government can perform the role of "economic coordinator." Taken to an extreme, this could be perceived as an argument for central planning of the type that the old Soviet Union abandoned and that even China has relaxed in recent years.

More generally, however, new Keynesians view the potential for economies to get stuck in low-level noncooperative states as a key rationale for active monetary and fiscal policy responses to sudden changes in economic conditions. In this sense, the new Keynesian theory can be regarded as a more "high-tech" version of the traditional Keynesian argument favoring an activist role for governmental policies.

FUNDAMENTAL ISSUE #3

What are coordination failures, and why do new Keynesians believe that they may be important?   Coordination failures are situations in which individual households and firms are unable to follow through on intended spending and production plans because of macroeconomic externalities. New Keynesians argue that noncooperative decision making by heterogeneous households and firms leads to more than one possible equilibrium state for the economy. If the economy sinks into a low-level equilibrium, the result could be a persistent recession that would require activist macroeconomic policy responses to push the economy into a higher-level equilibrium.

The Real-Business-Cycle Challenge

Even as new Keynesian theorists have emphasized the potential importance of household and firm heterogeneities and provided rationales for activist monetary and fiscal policies, another group of macroeconomists has followed a sharply different course. These macroeconomists have developed models that generally are based on the assumption of *homogeneous,* or identical, households and firms. Such models typically indicate that little, if any, stabilizing role exists for policymakers in modern economies.

This alternative approach is called **real-business-cycle theory.** As its name implies, this approach to macroeconomics hinges on the idea that *real* factors, such as technological or productivity changes, induce cyclical fluctuations in economic activity. Real-business-cycle theorists believe that the key to identifying the determinants of employment, real output, and inflation is to develop a more complete understanding of the processes that govern labor supply and firms' output production and capital investment. According to these theorists, these are the factors that ultimately matter in determining employment and real output.

REAL-BUSINESS-CYCLE THEORY:
An approach to macroeconomic theory in which variations in technology and productivity are the key factors accounting for cyclical fluctuations in real output.

The Essential Features of Real-Business-Cycle Models

Real-business-cycle models share two key elements. First, as in the new classical model from which they have been developed, they are *equilibrium* models. Wages always adjust to equate the quantity of labor demanded with the quantity of labor supplied, and prices always move to equilibrate the desired purchases of goods and services with the amount of goods and services supplied.

Second, real-business-cycle models are **dynamic models,** meaning that they are intended to describe how macroeconomic variables such as real output, employment, and the price level move over time. Although adherents of other macroeconomic schools of thought have also developed dynamic versions of their basic theoretical frameworks, the basic elements of the frameworks could always be captured on two-dimensional diagrams relating one macroeconomic variable to another. Real-business-cycle theorists cannot do this, because one axis on a diagram must always measure time.

DYNAMIC MODELS: Economic models intended to explain how variables such as real output, employment, and the price level vary over time.

391

TECHNOLOGY SHOCKS AND REAL GDP   Following the classical theory that we discussed in Chapters 3 and 4, real-business-cycle theorists argue that real output ultimately is determined by supply-side factors such as the productive capabilities of firms, population and labor-force participation, and the willingness of workers in the labor force to supply their skills. For this reason, real-business-cycle models focus on such real factors as the key sources of macroeconomic fluctuations.

Figure 13–3 on the following page illustrates one key source of macroeconomic fluctuations in the real-business-cycle model: technology shocks, or sudden variations in the technological capabilities of firms. Such sudden changes in technology cause a change in the shape and position of the aggregate production function, $F(N, K)$. For instance, a spurt of new techniques for producing high-speed computer processing chips, as occurred in the 1990s, will cause a jump in the productive capacity of firms that make computers and will improve the efficiency of the computers that they build. This will raise the productivity both of computer manufacturers and of all companies that use computers. For the economy as a whole, this improved productivity will yield an increase in the marginal product of labor, which translates into an increase in the slope of the aggregate production function, as shown in Figure 13–3. The production function will rotate upward, so for any given capital stock, such as K_1, real output will rise, from y_1 to a higher level y_2. Real output will increase, and an economic expansion will ensue.

Some technological innovations turn out to be disappointments, however. Implementation of a more inefficient technology will, for a time, make existing capital less productive than it was in the past. For example, some computer makers switch to a new just-in-time inventory system that ultimately fails to speed deliveries and, for a time, actually slows them down. This will reduce aggregate productivity, causing the production function to rotate downward. Real output then will fall from y_2 to a lower level y_3, as shown in Figure 13–3.

REAL BUSINESS CYCLES   The technological shocks illustrated in Figure 13–3 will end up producing cyclical behavior in real GDP. If we interpret the subscripts 1, 2, and 3 in Figure 13–3 as referring to points in time, then we can plot the behavior of real GDP over time in Figure 13–4 on page 393. To do this, we assume that the intervals between the two shocks that we have envisioned are of equal length.

392

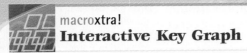

Interactive Key Graph

The graph below shows how real output can vary over time according to the real-business-cycle theory. What happens if the capital stock changes? What occurs if there is a change in technology? You can discover the answers to these questions by interacting with this graph on the Web.
Go to http://macroxtra.swcollege.com

Figure 13–3   Technology Shocks and Real Output Variations

In real-business-cycle models, variations in real output stem primarily from technology shocks, or factors that cause the aggregate production function to rotate. At any given quantity of labor, such as N_1, such rotations in the production function will lead to variations in real output over time.

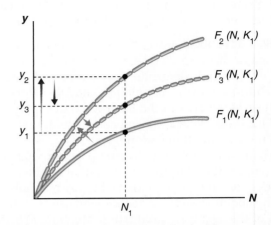

Figure 13–4 displays a sample real business cycle that corresponds to our example. It has a short-run expansion followed by a short-run downturn. As we discussed in Chapter 6, such upward and downward movements in real GDP typically characterize real-world business cycles.

POLICY IMPLICATIONS OF REAL-BUSINESS-CYCLE MODELS   In many respects, the real-business-cycle models have the same basic policy implications as the classical model of Chapters 3 and 4. Tax rate changes can influence the amount of real output produced, although Ricardian equivalence (see Chapter 7) tempers that conclusion. Lump-sum tax changes and variations in government spending typically act only to redistribute real output between the private sector and the government, because real output is supply-side determined.

Real-business-cycle theory differs from the classical model in its treatment of money and the effects of monetary policy. Recall from Chapter 3 that the classical model assumes that the nominal money stock is fully controlled by a central bank. In contrast, in the real-business-cycle theory the nominal quantity of money supply is determined largely by interactions between the depository financial institutions and the public. Real-business-cycle proponents contend that when people's real income rises, so does their demand for transactions services from banks (as in the Keynesian transactions motive for holding money). Banks respond by increasing their

Figure 13–4   A Sample Real Business Cycle

This figure traces the movements in real output owing to the technology shocks illustrated in Figure 13–3. As you can see, such shocks can produce cyclical movements in real output that we observe in actual business cycles.

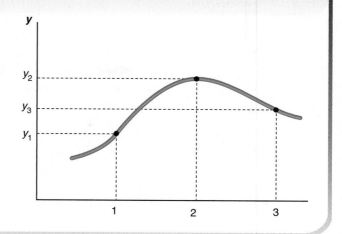

production of transactions services and, hence, deposits that are included in the nominal money stock. The total amount of bank deposit money, called **inside money** because its quantity depends on conditions within the banking system, depends on real income and is outside the control of a central bank. Indeed, the quantity of inside money adjusts automatically to changing economic conditions and performs no separate causal role with respect to any macroeconomic variables.

Consequently, in the real-business-cycle model inside money does not affect the price level. Only **outside money** can do that. Outside money is composed of currency and bank reserves, which a central bank *can* control because they are determined by the central bank's policies. The amount of outside money determines the level of aggregate demand. Because the real-business-cycle theory's aggregate supply schedule is vertical, the amount of outside money effectively *determines* the price level.

A number of economists have found the real-business-cycle theory attractive, largely because it is so clearly based on microeconomic principles. Following the classical model, all households and firms pursue their self-interest, and pure competition prevails with complete price and wage flexibility. In addition, households and firms put any new information to its best possible use. Many economists find these assumptions much more palatable than assumptions of fixed prices, contracted nominal wages, or rigid real wages.

FUNDAMENTAL ISSUE #4

How do real-business-cycle theorists explain short-term fluctuations in real output? According to real-business-cycle theory, short-term output variations stem almost solely from temporary changes in technology and productivity. Furthermore, such output variations take place in equilibrium without the need for price or wage rigidities.

INSIDE MONEY: Bank deposit money.

OUTSIDE MONEY: Money in the form of currency and bank reserves.

INDUCTION: The process of drawing conclusions about real-world behavior from observation of real-world data.

DEDUCTION: The process of making testable predictions about real-world behavior based on a theoretical framework.

Induction versus Deduction: Calibration or Hypothesis Testing?

One of the most controversial aspects of real-business-cycle theory has been the approach that many of its advocates have used in evaluating the theory's relevance. This approach has led to considerable philosophical debate among economists concerning the merits of inductive versus deductive approaches to macroeconomics.

INDUCTION VERSUS DEDUCTION   Economists have prided themselves on their use of the *scientific method*. This refers to a manner in which scientists try to formulate and evaluate their theories. To develop a theory, scientists look at the world around them and attempt to classify their observations based on regularities in the data that they collect. Then they look for relationships in the data and develop theories of causation that could potentially account for these relationships. Traditionally, scientists have then used statistical methods to determine whether the observed data support their theories.

The scientific method entails both *induction* and *deduction*. **Induction** refers to the process of drawing a general conclusion from reference to observed data, whereas **deduction** refers to the act of making a prediction about real-world outcomes based on a theoretical model. Major advances in the science of astronomy, for instance, have resulted from both induction and deduction. For example, the sixteenth-century Danish observational astronomer Tycho Brahe accumulated large volumes of data of planetary observations. Based upon these observations, the German astronomer and mathematician Johannes Kepler was able to infer certain regularities in planetary motion that he realized could be explained if planets followed elliptical orbits. This inductive process led Kepler to develop an initial theory of planetary motion. Later in the seventeenth century, the English physicist Isaac Newton used Kepler's theory to develop a deductive theory for accurately predicting the positions of planets, moons, stars, and other astronomical objects.

The inductive and deductive approaches have produced notable failures in astronomy as well. The second-century astronomer Claudius Ptolemy, for instance, used inductive principles to develop a purely geometrical representation of planetary motions. He envisioned the planets moving along a great system of circles with the earth at the center. Ptolemy's system worked, but it did not describe the universe that we inhabit. More recently, observations of changing brightness in a revolving neutron star led astronomers to propose a complicated deductive theory for what could cause an otherwise inexplicable phenomenon. It later turned out that the observatory where data had been collected had been built on sandy soil and that the observed wobble in the neutron star stemmed from a wobble in the telescope itself.

These examples from astronomy illustrate the potential gains and pitfalls from the use of induction and deduction in macroeconomics. Just as the economy experiences cycles, so does the study of the economy. At times macroeconomists favor deductive techniques, and at other times they seem to become enamored of more purely inductive approaches. In macroeconomics today, part of the struggle between competing groups stems from philosophical differences about the merits of induction versus deduction.

DEDUCTION AND HYPOTHESIS TESTING IN MACROECONOMICS   Until the advent of real-business-cycle theory, the deductive approach dominated the study of macroeconomics. Economists would develop theories and then assess their relevance by applying statistical techniques to real-world data. If the data appeared to "fit" the theory, then the theory would be judged to have received sufficient support to be retained and improved.

To implement this approach, economists traditionally develop *testable hypotheses,* or predictions that stem from their theories. Then they try to evaluate how well their theories fit real-world observations. Before the advent of real-business-cycle theory, macroeconomists of various schools of thought commonly used actual time-series observations of macroeconomic variables in statistical models to test hypotheses implied by their deductively formulated theories.

INDUCTION, CALIBRATION, AND QUANTITATIVE THEORY   Real-business-cycle theorists, however, have developed an alternative technique for evaluating their models. This approach, which is called **calibration,** involves several steps. First, real-business-cycle theorists use estimates of elasticities developed in statistical studies *in their own theoretical models.* They also utilize real-world data for variables such as employment or real output from some point in time. Second, they use computers to calculate how these variables would change over time in the models that they construct. As discussed above, real-business-cycle models typically yield equilibrium outcomes that are cyclical. Finally, the researchers compare the cyclical properties of their *artificially created data*—measures of business cycle duration and variation—with the properties of real-world data. If their artificially generated data exhibit cycles that nearly match those in actual economies, then real-business-cycle theorists judge their models to be successful. If not, they modify the models in an effort to achieve a better fit with real-world data.

Real-business-cycle theorists call their approach **quantitative theory,** or the use of numerical calculations to develop theoretical models that fit observed business cycle facts. Some critics of real-business-cycle theory argue that quantitative theory really amounts to inductive "curve-fitting," a process that mathematicians developed long ago to approximate the actual shape of complicated curves by splicing together equations of many different curved functions. Indeed, some critics liken the quantitative theory approach to Ptolemy's earth-centered system of planetary motion. Just as Ptolemy's system could predict, yet turned out to be dead wrong, such critics argue, quantitative theory could lead to the development of elaborate mathematical models of the economy that predict well for a short while but ultimately will prove to be far off the mark.

Proponents of quantitative theory counter that as a social science, economics does not have the luxury of looking for physical laws such as those that planets must follow. According to Martin Eichenbaum of Northwestern University, for instance, every macroeconomic model is likely to make incorrect predictions along at least one dimension, so there is no *true* model of the aggregate economy. The goal of quantitative theory, he contends, is

CALIBRATION: The use of estimated elasticities and real-world data to create artificial data with theoretical models for the purpose of evaluating the extent to which one's theory appears to match real-world observations.

QUANTITATIVE THEORY: An approach to macroeconomic theorizing in which a model is evaluated by comparing the movements in artificial data generated by the model itself with the behavior of real-world macroeconomic data.

to identify the dimensions along which various theories fail to fit the facts, thereby helping researchers to improve their models so that they ultimately can come very *close* to describing the true behavior of workers and firms in the economy.

FUNDAMENTAL ISSUE #5

What is quantitative theory, and why is it so controversial?   Quantitative theory is the use of calibration techniques to evaluate theoretical models. Calibration entails incorporating estimates of elasticities and initial values from real-world data in theoretical models and then using the models to calculate artificial data. Comparisons of the artificially produced data with real-world data then permit the researcher to evaluate how well the theory fits the facts. This approach to evaluating macroeconomic theories is controversial because it relies heavily on inductive reasoning instead of the deductive reasoning that has guided macroeconomics in the past.

What Have the New Theories Taught Us?

As we indicated at the beginning of this chapter, only time will tell if either new Keynesian theories or real-business-cycle models will help us better predict the macroeconomy. A generation from now, one or both attempts to better understand the economy may be a fading memory. Nevertheless, both approaches have important messages that macroeconomists have been exploring in ongoing research.

Key Messages of the New Keynesian Theory

Real-business-cycle theorists and many other macroeconomists who think of themselves as monetarists or as traditional or modern Keynesians have not been entirely willing to accept all aspects of new Keynesian models. Some disagree with the view that imperfect competition could be so widespread, especially in a U.S. economy that has witnessed two decades of significant deregulation of a number of industries. Others have trouble accepting the idea that price or wage rigidities are so widespread that they could fully explain business cycles and their persistence.

HETEROGENEITY MAY BE IMPORTANT   Nonetheless, the new Keynesians have shown that household and firm heterogeneities could prove helpful in understanding features of business cycles. To the extent that such heterogeneities induce spillover effects that create macroeconomic externalities, they could cause real output to deviate from the natural level it would attain in the absence of such effects.

GAME THEORY MAY PROVIDE SOME ANSWERS   Another key message of new Keynesian theory is that macroeconomists may be able to gain insights from applying game theory in their models. As we discussed earlier in this chapter, new Keynesian theory proposes that noncooperative behavior can lead to more than one equilibrium for the economy, which then potentially could alternate between equilibrium states from time to time. To the new Keynesians, this provides a justification for using governmental or central bank policy actions to "bump" the economy into a better equilibrium whenever it slips into a less desirable equilibrium.

Although real-business-cycle theorists and others generally are not persuaded by this argument, macroeconomists of all stripes have recognized that theories of strategic interactions among individuals and firms—the subjects of game theory—could prove useful in understanding important issues. As you will learn in Chapter 15, this has been particularly true in the area of macroeconomic policy. Considerable research has been devoted to the analysis of games between policymakers and the public, and the findings have caused both economists and government officials to rethink the structures of policymaking institutions.

Consider the similarities and differences between the policy implications of new Keynesian and real-business-cycle theories by going to the Chapter 13 reading, entitled "On Business Cycles and Countercyclical Policies," by Marco Espinosa-Vega and Jang-Ting Guo from the Federal Reserve Bank of Atlanta.
http://macroxtra.swcollege.com

Key Messages of the Real-Business-Cycle Theory

Despite the considerable research that real-business-cycle theorists have conducted during the past two decades, many macroeconomists have doubts about the ultimate usefulness of most of these models for macroeconomic forecasting and policymaking. Even so, most macroeconomists have been persuaded that real-business-cycle theorists have made some very important points.

SUPPLY-SIDE FACTORS ARE IMPORTANT In the 1960s, traditional Keynesians and monetarists argued about whether monetary or fiscal policy had the greater effect on aggregate demand and real output. Then, in the 1970s, new classical and modern Keynesian proponents debated whether monetary or fiscal policy could have *any* systematic impacts on real output via their effects on aggregate demand. In the midst of their arguments about the aggregate demand channel for monetary and fiscal policies, many macroeconomists lost sight of the importance of productivity and technology as determinants of real output.

The real-business-cycle theory's renewed emphasis on these factors has altered the landscape in macroeconomics. Real-business-cycle proponents have proved that technology and productivity can influence the course of business cycles, even if they have not convinced all macroeconomists that these are the *only* factors that cause real output to deviate from its long-run growth path.

BUSINESS CYCLES MAY BE FUNDAMENTALLY RELATED TO ECONOMIC GROWTH Another message of the real-business-cycle theory is that it may be misleading to study business cycles and economic growth as separate topics. As we noted in Chapter 5, the ultimate determinants of economic growth are real factors such as technological progress and growth in population and labor-force participation rates. Short-term variations in these factors can cause cyclical fluctuations in real output that in turn may feed back to affect the economy's longer-term growth rate.

In this respect, real-business-cycle models and the new growth theory that we discussed in Chapter 5 share considerable common ground.

Indeed, one reason that both approaches have attracted so many adherents is that developments in the real-business-cycle models have related so closely to new approaches to the theory of economic growth. Some observers of the real-business-cycle theory have concluded that its ultimate achievement could be a merging of the theory of short-run business cycles with a broader theory of an economy's long-term growth.

Future Prospects

The deep philosophical divisions over the quantitative theory approach of real-business-cycle proponents are likely to continue until either the new Keynesian theory or the real-business-cycle approach does a much better job of making predictions that businesspersons and policymakers can rely on to guide their decisions. At present, both approaches show some promise of bearing fruit. On the one hand, new Keynesian macroeconomics potentially can explain price stickiness, unemployment, and persistent states of recession or expansion. On the other hand, real-business-cycle theorists can provide quantitative theories that mimic real-world business cycles and offer hope of combining business cycle theory with the theory of economic growth.

In their current forms, however, both approaches cannot simultaneously be correct, because they are based on fundamentally different views of the economy. Whereas the new Keynesian theory relies on imperfect competition, heterogeneities, macroeconomic externalities, and coordination failures, the real-business-cycle approach depends on pure competition, homogeneity, perfect markets, and rational, self-interested individuals and firms. Ultimately, some combination of the two approaches may be the wave of the future in macroeconomics. Already some new Keynesian theorists have begun to use techniques borrowed from real-business-cycle enthusiasts. At the same time, some proponents of real-business-cycle theory have begun to experiment with models that include sticky wages and prices. It remains to be seen if the two approaches will ever find a common ground.

Is Labor Market "Flexibility" a Key to Lower Unemployment?

tatutory minimum wages, rights to parental leave, mandated compensation for fired employees, plant-closing notification requirements, legal limits on hours spent on the job—all these are examples of legal restrictions that make labor markets less flexible in some nations than in others. Although the new Keynesian approach emphasizes the possibility that market factors alone can create an economy populated with employed insiders and unemployed outsiders, externally imposed rules can contribute to such an environment and boost the economy's unemployment rate.

Labor Market Flexibility and Unemployment

For some time, a number of economists have argued that countries with inflexible labor markets are likely to experience higher unemployment than nations with relatively more flexible labor markets. Their hypothesis is that when firms face mandates governing how much they pay workers or limiting the scope of layoffs or dismissals, they have less incentive to hire workers in the first place.

Figure 13–5 provides survey evidence about companies' perceptions of their ability to adjust job-security and compensation standards of their employees, measured vertically along a scale from zero (no flexibility) to one hundred (full flexibility). Some European nations, such as France and Spain, have extensive labor market rules that limit business flexibility. Other nations, such as Denmark and Switzerland, have fewer of these kinds of rules.

As Figure 13–5 indicates low-flexibility countries such as France and Spain have had higher average annual unemployment rates than high-flexibility nations such as Denmark and Switzerland. Thus, the figure tends to support the hypothesis that reduced labor market flexibility contributes to higher unemployment.

Lessons from the Irish and Dutch Experiences?

Both Ireland and the Netherlands have recently succeeded in reducing their unemployment rates. As shown in Figure 13–6 (p. 400), the unemployment rates in both nations fell sharply beginning in the mid-1990s. The unemployment rate in the Netherlands has been below the European Union (EU) average for some time and is now about one-third of the average

Figure 13–5   Labor Market Flexibility and Unemployment Rates in Selected Nations

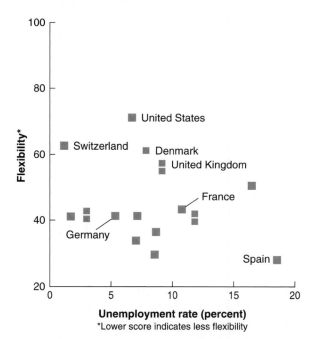

There appears to be an inverse relationship between the degree of labor market flexibility and the unemployment rate. That is, more inflexible labor markets are associated with higher rates of unemployment.

SOURCE: Rafael Di Tella and Robert MacCulloch, "The Consequences of Labor Market Flexibility: Panel Evidence Based on Survey Data," Harvard Business School, November 1998.

Continued on next page

UNIT IV Rational Expectations and Modern Macroeconomic Theory

Link to The Global Economy, continued

unemployment rate in the EU. Ireland's unemployment rate once was more than 8 percentage points higher than the EU average, but now is about half the average EU rate.

In the Netherlands, reforms that were first implemented in the early 1980s have allowed both wages and employment to adjust more flexibly to changes in economic conditions. Since the reforms were instituted, the real value of Dutch minimum wages has declined by more than 25 percent, tax rates firms pay on workers they hired have declined from 30 percent of workers' earnings to about 14 percent, and unemployment benefits have dropped from about 80 percent of a worker's wages to close to 60 percent. These changes, which have given firms greater incentives to hire and have encouraged workers to seek employment, undoubtedly help to explain why the Dutch unemployment experience is better than that of the EU as a whole. Ireland implemented similar reforms beginning in the late 1980s and has experienced similar outcomes since the late 1980s.

For these two countries, policies that reduce firms' costs of employing workers have led to relatively large drops in their national unemployment rates. Many economists regard them as useful case studies for understanding how increased labor market flexibility and pro-employment policies together can contribute to lower unemployment rates.

Research Project

List the factors that influence national rates of unemployment in the short run and in the long run. Which of these do you conclude is likely to be most important in causing near-term and longer-

term variations in the unemployment rate? Explain your reasoning.

Web Resources

1. Where is the best Web site to obtain the most up-to-date inflation and unemployment data for European nations and other industrialized countries? The Organization for Economic Cooperation and Development (http://www.oecd.org) provides monthly updates; after going to its home page, click on "Statistics" at the top of the page, and then click on "Frequently Requested Statistics" for CPI inflation rates and unemployment rates.

2. What Web-based source of inflation-unemployment data is available for less-developed nations? Go the home page of the International Monetary Fund (http://www.imf.org) for annual data for many nonindustrialized countries. Click on "Publications," type "World Economic Outlook," next to "Title" in the "Search by" box, and click on "Search." Then select the most recent issue.

Figure 13–6 Unemployment Rates in Ireland and the Netherlands

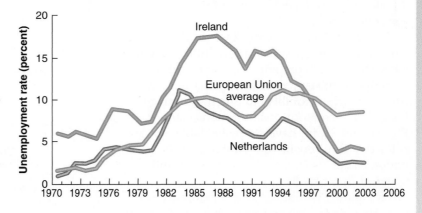

After Ireland and the Netherlands implemented reforms making their labor markets more flexible, their unemployment rates declined below the average for the European Union.

SOURCE: Cedric Tille and Kei-Mu Yi, "Curbing Unemployment in Europe: Are There Lessons from Ireland and the Netherlands?" Federal Reserve Bank of New York *Current Issues in Economics and Finance* 7 (5, May 2001); Organization for Economic Cooperation and Development; authors' estimates.

1. The Motivation for New Macroeconomic Theories: Most existing theories have difficulty explaining why real GDP shows persistent reactions to relatively short-term changes in economic conditions. The development of new macroeconomic theories represents an effort to deal with this failure of the existing theories.

2. The Key Features of New Keynesian Theories: The two main features of new Keynesian theories are the assumption of imperfect competition and the perception that wide-spread market failures cause macroeconomic externalities. These features are used in small-menu-cost models to propose explanations for why prices might be relatively inflexible and for why real output can vary considerably in the short run. Efficiency wage theory and insider-outsider models use the two features as a foundation for proposing models to explain involuntary unemployment.

3. Coordination Failures and New Keynesians' Contentions That They May Be Important: Coordination failures occur when households and firms cannot implement planned expenditures and production as a result of macroeconomic externalities. New Keynesians contend that noncooperative interactions among heterogeneous households and firms can cause more than one equilibrium state to exist for the economy. In a low-level equilibrium, a persistent recession could result. In that case, macroeconomic policy actions might be required to move the economy to a higher-level equilibrium.

4. How Real-Business-Cycle Theorists Explain Short-Term Fluctuations in Real Output: Real-business-cycle models indicate that short-run output variability arises because of temporary variations in technology and productivity. These macroeconomic models predict that short-term business cycles take place in the absence of any stickiness in wages or prices.

5. Quantitative Theory and Why It Is Controversial: Quantitative theory involves the use of calibration, which is a technique for using estimated elasticities and some real-world data to calculate artificial data using theoretical models. Real-business-cycle theorists compare such artificially produced data with real-world observations to evaluate the extent to which their models fit real-world facts. This approach is controversial because it relies on inductive reasoning, rather than on deductive reasoning, which macroeconomists have generally used in the past.

Self-Test Questions

1. Use an aggregate demand–aggregate supply diagram to explain why the existence of widespread price stickiness would be extremely important in judging the potential effectiveness of monetary and fiscal policies.

2. In question 1, you used an aggregate demand–aggregate supply diagram to evaluate the essential policy implications of price stickiness. According to the new Keynesian small-menu-cost theory, is there really an aggregate supply schedule for the economy as a whole? Why or why not? (Hint: Note that in microeconomics, there is no industry supply schedule in the theories of monopoly, oligopoly, or monopolistic competition.)

3. Suppose that the marginal product of labor depends positively upon the real wage that workers earn. What happens to the production function if the real wage rises? Explain.

4. Government regulation of labor market function is more prevalent in a number of European nations than in the United States. Discuss how this difference might be related to many economists' belief that the insider-outsider model explains European unemployment better than it explains U.S. unemployment.

5. In your own words, explain why some new Keynesian theorists believe that coordination failures may be important for understanding business cycles.

6. Suppose that a new firm devises a strategy for significant long-term growth, but a major economy-wide recession makes it impossible for the firm to

(Answers to odd-numbered questions may be found on the Web at **http://macro. swcollege.com** under "Student Resources.")

implement the plan. In response, the firm cuts back on its expansion plan and lays off some of its employees, who are unable to find other jobs. As a result, these unemployed workers must cut back on their spending. Is this a coordination failure? Support your answer.

7. Explain how real-business-cycle theory is more closely related to the new classical theory of Chapter 11 than it is to the modern Keynesian theory of Chapter 12.

8. Some economists have extended the analogy of real-business-cycle calibration modeling to Ptolemaic astronomy (see the discussion on page 395). They point out that Ptolemaic astronomy merely allowed early astronomers to predict the locations of planets in the heavens. Ptolemaic astronomy could not have assisted modern scientists, who rely on Newton's laws to send rocket-propelled probes to the planets. By analogy, these economists argue, real-business-cycle calibration models will never assist in real-world policy-making. Do you agree with this analogy? Take a stand, and justify your answer.

9. Do you find inductive theorizing more or less convincing than deductive theorizing? Or do you believe that both should play a role in macroeconomic theory? Justify your answer.

10. As far as you can tell from your reading of this chapter, do the new Keynesian and real-business-cycle theories share any common ground? Or are the two approaches so distinct that they could never converge? Explain your position on this issue.

Problems

(Answers to odd-numbered problems may be found on the Web at **http://macro. swcollege.com** under "Student Resources.")

1. Recently, the demand for a firm's product declined. If the firm leaves its price unchanged and responds solely by reducing the quantity it produces, then the profit gain from leaving its price unchanged will be $5,000 per week. If the firm takes no action, however, its failure to adjust its output and reduce its price to levels consistent with re-equating marginal revenue and marginal cost reduces its profit by $10,000 per week.

   a. The firm has determined that if it were to change its price in response to the fall in demand, it would incur a one-time cost of $8,000 because it would have to print new catalogues and price lists, pay for employees' time to attend meetings, and so on. Should the firm change its price?

   b. The firm's owners have determined that the decline in demand is likely to be permanent. If they care about the discounted present value (see Chapter 8) of profits, and if the relevant annual interest rate for calculating discounted present value is 5 percent, then should they change the price of the firm's product?

2. An industry's labor demand schedule is given by $N^d = 50,000 - [2 \times (W/P)]$, where N measures the number of people, and W/P is the quarterly real salary earned by each person employed in the industry. The labor supply schedule, which takes into account all people willing to supply labor to the industry, is $N^s = 3 \times (W/P)$.

   a. What is the equilibrium real annual salary in this industry? What is equilibrium employment?

   b. Suppose that a licensing board elected by all workers employed in the industry determines that of all the people willing to work in this industry, only 20,000 are "qualified" to continue their employment. Only board-licensed individuals may work in the industry. What is the real annual salary earned by qualified "insiders" in this industry?

   c. At the real wage earned by "insiders," and assuming that all individuals not hired by this industry cannot obtain employment elsewhere, how many people are unemployed?

Before the Test

Test your understanding of the material covered in this chapter by taking the Chapter 13 interactive quiz at http://macro.swcollege.com.

Online Application

In general, labor unions exist to bargain for wages and benefits on behalf of their member workers, to protect their members from unsafe working conditions, and to lobby for laws that the unions feel are consistent with their members' interests. Many economists also regard unions as a potentially good application of the insider-outsider theory of unemployment.

Internet URL: http://www.aflcio.org/home.htm

Title: *American Federation of Labor–Congress of Industrial Organizations*

Navigation: Start at the AFL-CIO's home page (http://www.aflcio.org).

Application: Perform the indicated operations, and answer the following questions:

1. Click on *About the AFL-CIO.* Then click on *AFL-CIO's Mission.* Does the AFL-CIO claim to represent the interests of all workers or just workers in specific firms or industries?

2. Click on *Partners and Links* to obtain a list of unions that compose the AFL-CIO. Explore two or three of these Web sites. Do these unions appear to represent the interests of all workers or just workers in specific firms or industries? Is this consistent with the insider-outsider theory? Why or why not?

For Group Study and Analysis: Divide up all the unions affiliated with the AFL-CIO across groups, and have each group explore the Web sites listed under *Partners and Links* at the AFL-CIO Web site. Have each group report on the extent to which the unions' activities appear to correspond to predictions of the insider-outsider theory.

Selected References and Further Reading

Akerlof, George, William Dickens, and George Perry. "The Macroeconomics of Low Inflation." *Brookings Papers on Economic Activity* 1 (1996): 1–77.

Ball, Laurence, and David Romer. "Sticky Prices as Coordination Failures." *American Economic Review* 81 (1991): 539–552.

Chatterjee, Satyajit. "Real Business Cycles: A Legacy of Countercyclical Policies?" Federal Reserve Bank of Philadelphia *Business Review,* January/February 1999, pp. 17–27.

Christiano, Lawrence, and Terry Fitzgerald. "The Business Cycle: It's Still a Puzzle." Federal Reserve Bank of Chicago *Economic Perspectives* 22 (Winter 1998): 56–83.

Eichenbaum, Martin. "Some Comments on the Role of Econometrics in Economic Theory." Federal Reserve Bank of Chicago *Economic Perspectives,* January/February 1996, pp. 22–31.

Espinoza-Vega, Marco, and Jang-Ting Gao. "On Busines Cycles and Counter-cyclical Policies." Federal Reserve Bank of Atlanta *Economic Review,* Fourth Quarter 2001, pp. 1–11.

Gordon, Robert. "What Is New-Keynesian Economics?" *Journal of Economic Literature* 28 (1990): 1151–1171.

Hoover, Keven. "Facts and Artifacts: Calibration and the Empirical Assessment of Real-Business-Cycle Models." *Oxford Economic Papers* 47 (1992): 24–44.

King, Robert. "Quantitative Theory and Econometrics." Federal Reserve Bank of Richmond *Economic Review,* Summer 1995, pp. 53–105.

Mankiw, N. Gregory, and David Romer, eds. *New Keynesian Economics,* vols. 1 and 2. Cambridge, Mass.: MIT Press, 1991.

Selgin, George. *Less than Zero.* London: Institute of Economic Affairs, 1997.

Stadler, George. "Real Business Cycles." *Journal of Economic Literature* 32 (1994): 1750–1783.

macroxtra!

Log on to the MacroXtra Web site at http://macroxtra.swcollege.com for additional learning resources such as practice quizzes, Interactive Key Graphs, readings, and additional economic applications.

Unit V
Macroeconomic Policy

Looking for Common Ground in the Theory of Macroeconomic Policy

From one perspective, economists are very far apart in assessing the implications of their macroeconomic theories for the conduct of monetary and fiscal policies. After all, whereas some theories imply that monetary and fiscal policies can do much to promote economic growth and stabilize output and employment, others imply that the capabilities of macroeconomic policymakers to influence real output and employment are much more limited.

Even when economists agree about the suitable theory to apply in the real world, they often form different views about appropriate policy goals. Similarly, economists who concur about policy objectives may still disagree about the best strategies for conducting monetary or fiscal policies. While some recommend that policymakers conduct actions aimed directly at achieving their broad goals for output, employment, or inflation, others may argue that policy actions should be pointed toward the attainment of *intermediate targets* thought to be consistent with broader macroeconomic objectives. Furthermore, there may be disagreement about which intermediate target variable is appropriate.

More broadly, economists often reach different conclusions about whether policymakers should try to respond to every blip in the economy's performance or maintain commitments to steady and predictable policy actions. All agree that *policy time lags* hinder efforts to engage in policies that contribute to macroeconomic stability, but they disagree as to whether policymakers should use their discretion to respond to events that affect an economy's overall performance.

According to one theory of macroeconomic policy, discretionary policymaking has an undesirable by-product: because of the interplay between price expectations and the policy anticipations of households and firms, a propensity for discretionary policymaking can result in a bias toward persistent inflation. This theory has induced economists to explore issues relating to the *credibility* of macroeconomic policymaking, such as how central banks should be designed, whether constraints should be placed on fiscal policies, and whether nations that wish to maintain fixed exchange rates might have greatest success by taking monetary policy out of the hands of central bank officials.

The growing integration of the world's financial systems and of the global economy also poses important macroeconomic policy issues. In particular, in a world of increased capital mobility, the usefulness of monetary policy or fiscal policy is likely to depend critically on whether exchange rates are fixed or flexible. Greater capital mobility may contribute to either more or less macroeconomic stability. To the extent that increased capital flows across national borders create the potential for financial crises that can destabilize the world economy, there may be a rationale for multinational policymaking institutions such as the International Monetary Fund to attempt to prevent or at least to counter such crises. This, in turn, raises issues about the appropriate role of multinational institutions in the global economy, including how such institutions should be designed, how they should conduct policies, or whether they should even exist.

What Should Policymakers Do?—
Objectives and Targets of Macroeconomic Policy

14

FUNDAMENTAL ISSUES

1. What are the ultimate goals of macroeconomic policy?

2. Why might a central bank use an intermediate monetary policy target?

3. What are the pros and cons of alternative intermediate monetary policy targets?

4. What are the key propositions and fiscal policy prescriptions of supply-side economics?

5. What is the assignment problem faced by monetary and fiscal policymakers of a nation that seeks to attain both domestic and international policy goals?

There are numerous macroeconomic variables that central banks might wish to boost, to suppress, or to stabilize. Real GDP, the price level, the interest rate, the rate of unemployment, the exchange rate, and the trade balance are all examples. Most central banks, including the Federal Reserve and the Bank of Japan, take most or all of these into account when determining their policy strategies.

By way of contrast, the Bank of Canada, the Bank of New Zealand, and the Bank of England aim to achieve only one fundamental goal. Each of these central banks tries to keep its nation's inflation rate close to a publicly announced inflation target. Central banks in Sweden, Australia, and even some developing countries have also adopted inflation targeting as an explicit aim of monetary policy. Now some economists are arguing that this policy approach has proved so successful in these nations that it is time for the United States, Japan, and others to make the switch as well.

Up to now, we have examined several broad theories of how macroeconomic policy actions may influence real output, employment, and prices. We have shown that each of these theoretical approaches—classical, traditional Keynesian, monetarist, new classical, modern Keynesian, new Keynesian, real-business-cycle—has its own special implications for fiscal and monetary policies.

We have not yet asked some very tough questions, however. What should fiscal and monetary policymakers do? What goals should they try to achieve? How should they go about pursuing those goals? In this chapter you will learn that even when there is widespread agreement on the appropriate *objectives* of macroeconomic policy, the best way to *implement* that policy still may not be apparent.

The Goals of Macroeconomic Policy

Let's begin by examining the factors that determine the **ultimate goals,** or final macroeconomic objectives, of fiscal and monetary policymakers. Then we can turn to contemplating how policymakers might go about trying to pursue these goals.

Potential Ultimate Macroeconomic Goals

Most macroeconomists focus on three sets of goals that monetary and fiscal policymakers might pursue.

INFLATION GOALS   As we noted in Chapter 10, a number of costs stem from high and variable inflation (see Table 10–1 on page 290). In light of these inflation costs, policymakers have justification for trying to maintain low inflation. In addition, they have a strong rationale for limiting year-to-year variability in inflation rates.

OUTPUT GOALS   According to the classical, new classical, and real-business-cycle theories, monetary and fiscal policymakers can do little to affect real output over any time horizon, and the monetarist and modern Keynesian theories generally indicate that there is little scope for long-run output effects of monetary and fiscal policies. Nonetheless, several theories indicate that unexpected changes in the growth rate of the money stock can affect real output over short-run intervals. Therefore, another potential ultimate goal of macroeconomic policy might be to prevent sharp swings in real GDP relative to its natural, full-information level. According to some of the macroeconomic theories we have discussed, pursuing this policy goal could mitigate business cycles.

EMPLOYMENT GOALS   Labor is a key factor of production, and in a democratic society, workers also account for the bulk of voters. Consequently, both fiscal and monetary policymakers are likely to feel pressures to pursue policies that aim to prevent significant variability in worker unemployment rates and that might spur greater growth in real output and employment.

Legislated Ultimate Goals

Can macroeconomic policymakers pursue inflation, output, and employment goals simultaneously? Certainly, stabilizing output around its long-run natural level often will be consistent with stable employment and a low unemployment rate. Nevertheless, as you learned in Chapter 10, the possible existence of a short-run Phillips curve trade-off indicates that there may be conflicts among macroeconomic objectives.

For this reason, societies sometimes choose to make macroeconomic goals explicit. In the United States, two laws lay out a course for macroeconomic policymakers. The *Employment Act of 1946* legally commits all agencies of the federal government to the objectives of "maximum employment, production, and purchasing power." Thus, this act officially seeks the highest possible employment and real output levels as well as low inflation. The law is silent, however, as to exactly how the U.S. government should address potential trade-offs among the goals.

In 1978, Congress established more concrete objectives in the *Full Employment and Balanced Growth Act,* more commonly known as the *Humphrey-Hawkins Act.* This law set two goals to be achieved by 1983: an unemployment rate of 3 percent and an inflation rate of 0 percent. As it turned out, the unemployment rate in 1983 exceeded 9 percent, and inflation was about 5 percent, illustrating the problems with trying to legislate explicit objectives. By the early 2000s, however, the unemployment rate had fallen to about 4 percent, and the inflation rate hovered around 2 percent—closer to the 1978 targets. Nevertheless, most macroeconomists are doubtful that the natural rate of unemployment in the United States is as low as 3 percent.

In the face of potentially conflicting ultimate goals and generally vague guidance from legislators, how should central bank and government officials conduct monetary and fiscal policies? What near-term goals should they pursue in an effort to achieve broader, ultimate macroeconomic policy objectives? These are the issues that we shall address in the remainder of this chapter and in the chapters that follow. (Recently, some economists have claimed that it is possible to explain the Federal Reserve's policy choices with very simple statistical models; see on the next page *Policy Notebook: Can the Taylor Rule Sum Up Monetary Policy in a Single Equation?*)

On the Web

What was the substance of the most recent statements to Congress by the chair of the Fed's Board of Governors? You can review the chair's testimony and report, which are required under the Humphrey-Hawkins Act, by going to the Fed's Web site at http://www.federalreserve.gov. Once there, click on "Testimony and Speeches" in the left-hand margin. Then click on "Monetary Policy Report to the Congress" (http://www.federalreserve.gov/boarddocs/hh/).

FUNDAMENTAL ISSUE #1

What are the ultimate goals of macroeconomic policy?   The ultimate goals of a government fiscal authority or central bank are the final objectives of its policy strategies and actions. Under the terms of 1946 and 1978 legislation, the formal goals of the U.S. government and the Federal Reserve System include low and stable inflation rates, high and stable output growth, and a high and stable employment level.

Can the Taylor Rule Sum Up Monetary Policy in a Single Equation?

In 1993, John Taylor of Stanford University proposed a policy rule that purported to explain how the Federal Reserve sets its interest-rate target. According to the rule, the Fed establishes its target based on an estimated long-run real interest rate, any current deviation of the actual inflation rate from the Fed's inflation objective, and the gap between actual real GDP and a measure of "potential" GDP under full employment of all resources. This proposed method of determining the Fed's interest-rate target became known as the "Taylor rule."

The Attraction of the Taylor Rule

Since then a number of economists have conducted detailed statistical studies of data from the United States and elsewhere in an effort to determine if the behavior of the Fed and other central banks can be captured by relatively simple equations. If each central bank has its own Taylor rule for determining how to set interest rates, then in theory economists could predict its policy decisions once they had ascertained the exact form of these equations.

Many economists are wary of attempts to describe complicated behavior of an individual, business, or institution with just one equation. Nevertheless, economists studying Taylor rules have found apparently strong statistical evidence that central banks' interest-rate decisions really do seem to be guided by relatively few economic factors. For instance, Robert Barro of Harvard University concluded that nearly all Federal Reserve policy actions taken under the guidance of Alan Greenspan since 1988 could be explained and predicted based on inflation, the unemployment rate, and changes in real GDP relative to its trend.

Is Simplicity Necessarily a Virtue?

Central bank behavior may not fit quite so neatly into a simple equation, however. Patrick Minford, Francesco Perugini, and Naveen Srinivasan of the Cardiff Business School in London have shown that a statistical equation that looks like a Taylor rule could really describe a relationship that has nothing to do with interest-rate targeting by a central bank. They contend, for instance, that policymaking by a central bank that targets a monetary aggregate can cause market interest rates to adjust in a way that looks a lot like a Taylor rule. This would happen even though the central bank actually does nothing to intentionally smooth interest rates. Economists using an estimated interest-rate equation would thereby fool themselves into believing that they had accurately described central bank efforts to target interest rates.

This argument does not necessarily imply that trying to use Taylor rules to sum up central bank decision making is misguided. Nevertheless, it does mean that economists must be cautious in their study of how central banks actually conduct policy. It may be a mistake to presume that statistical evidence indicating a simple relationship among interest rates and a few other economic variables undeniably supports the conclusion that a central bank intentionally aims to smooth interest rates.

For Critical Analysis

If a Taylor rule does a good job of predicting interest rates, does it matter whether the central bank actually engages in interest-rate targeting?

Finding an
Intermediate
Target for
Monetary Policy

As you have learned in previous chapters, nearly every approach to macroeconomics—with the exception of the real-business-cycle model—indicates that monetary policy actions can potentially have short-term or even longer-term effects on real output and employment. All macroeconomic theories imply that monetary policy actions influence the price level.

Hence, central banks clearly perform important tasks. Indeed, some observers have called the chair of the board that directs the operations of the Federal Reserve System, the U.S. version of a central bank, the second-most-important person in the United States, after the president. Before considering the theory of Federal Reserve policymaking in light of its output, employment, and inflation objectives, let's begin with an overview of exactly how the Federal Reserve System works and how the Fed implements monetary policy.

Monetary Policymaking in the United States: The Federal Reserve System

The U.S. Congress established the Federal Reserve System in 1913. Congress created a partly private, partly public institution that it intentionally did not call a "central bank." Private U.S. banks could become members of the Federal Reserve System by purchasing shares in the system. By doing so, they placed themselves under Fed regulation while gaining potential access to Fed loans. These banks had only a minority vote in choosing Fed officials, however. Congress also established a Federal Reserve Board to oversee and coordinate the activities of twelve Federal Reserve district banks around the nation, and it empowered the president to appoint members to this board, subject to Senate approval. One automatic member was the secretary of the Treasury.

One of Congress's key objectives in establishing the Fed was to prevent banking panics, such as those the nation had experienced in 1893 and 1907. After the Fed failed to halt widespread banking panics following the stock market crash of 1929, Congress decided to restructure the institution. In 1935, Congress renamed the top board the "Board of Governors of the Federal Reserve System"; removed the Treasury secretary from the board; and centralized power over the Federal Reserve System, which previously had been shared with the Federal Reserve banks, within this board. These changes ultimately transformed the Fed into a true central banking institution.

The seven members of the Fed's Board of Governors have a number of duties. They authorize any change in the Fed's **discount rate,** which is the interest rate that the twelve Federal Reserve banks charge on loans that they extend to U.S. banking institutions. Under the terms of the Depository Institutions Deregulation and Monetary Control Act of 1980, they also have the authority to determine **reserve requirements,** or rules that require banks to set aside a fraction of each dollar of checking deposits in a cash reserve, either in the banks' vaults or in the form of deposits at Federal Reserve banks. In addition, the Board of Governors has oversight authority over the Fed's district banks.

THE FEDERAL OPEN MARKET COMMITTEE   All seven Board governors serve on the Federal Reserve's twelve-member **Federal Open Market Committee (FOMC).** The remaining five voting members of the FOMC are presidents of the Federal Reserve banks. The president of the Federal Reserve Bank of New York is always a voting member of the FOMC, and the remaining eleven Federal Reserve bank presidents rotate into the other four voting positions on the committee on a regular basis.

macroxtra!
Online
Perspective

To further investigate the evidence concerning Taylor rules, go to the Chapter 14 reading, entitled "How Useful Are Taylor Rules for Monetary Policy?" by Sharon Kozicki of the Federal Reserve Bank of Kansas City.
http://macroextra.swcollege.com

DISCOUNT RATE: The rate of interest that the Federal Reserve charges to lend to a banking institution.

RESERVE REQUIREMENTS: Federal Reserve rules mandating that banks maintain reserve holdings that are proportional to the dollar amounts of transactions accounts.

FEDERAL OPEN MARKET COMMITTEE (FOMC): A group composed of the seven governors and five of the twelve presidents of the Federal Reserve banks that determines how to conduct the Fed's open-market operations.

OPEN-MARKET OPERATIONS: The Federal Reserve's purchases or sales of U.S. government securities.

The FOMC is the Fed's key policymaking body, because it determines policy for the Fed's **open-market operations,** which are the Fed's purchases and sales of U.S. government securities. The Fed conducts daily trading in government securities markets through a department of the Federal Reserve Bank of New York. This department, commonly known as the *Trading Desk,* determines the amount of securities to buy or sell based on instructions from the FOMC.

Because the seven members of the Fed's Board of Governors have numerical superiority relative to the other FOMC members, the governors have considerable authority over the day-to-day conduct of monetary policy. Furthermore, the chair of the Board of Governors automatically serves as chair of the FOMC. Finally, the FOMC oversees Fed foreign exchange market operations, so the governors also have considerable influence over the Fed's international policymaking.

The FOMC meets eight to ten times each year. At these meetings, the voting members of the FOMC determine the wording of the formal instructions for open-market operations and foreign exchange trading at the Federal Reserve Bank of New York. The chief supervisor of this bank's Trading Desk serves as the FOMC's account manager and communicates daily with designated subcommittees of FOMC members.

HOW THE FED INFLUENCES THE QUANTITY OF MONEY IN CIRCULATION   The FOMC is the Fed's key policymaking body because open-market operations are the main mechanism by which the Fed affects the amount of money in circulation in the United States. When the Federal Reserve Bank of New York's Trading Desk executes a purchase of U.S. government securities, it wires

---

On the Web—The Fed on the Net

What is going on at the Fed? Find a wealth of information about the Fed available on the Internet, courtesy of the Fed itself. Following are Internet home page addresses for the Fed's Board of Governors and all twelve Federal Reserve Banks:

Federal Reserve Source	Internet URL:
Board of Governors	http://federalreserve.gov
Federal Reserve Bank of Atlanta	http://www.frbatlanta.org
Federal Reserve Bank of Boston	http://wwwbos.frb.org
Federal Reserve Bank of Chicago	http://www.chicagofed.org
Federal Reserve Bank of Cleveland	http://www.clev.frb.org
Federal Reserve Bank of Dallas	http://www.dallasfed.org
Federal Reserve Bank of Kansas City	http://www.kc.frb.org
Federal Reserve Bank of Minneapolis	http://minneapolisfed.org
Federal Reserve Bank of New York	http://www.ny.frb.org
Federal Reserve Bank of Philadelphia	http://www.phil.frb.org
Federal Reserve Bank of Richmond	http://www.rich.frb.org
Federal Reserve Bank of San Francisco	http://www.frbsf.org
Federal Reserve Bank of St. Louis	http://www.stlouisfed.org

funds to the account of the private bank from which it purchases the securities. In this manner, the Fed begins the process of creating new money.

It is only the start of the process, however. For instance, suppose the Trading Desk purchases $1 million in government securities from a securities dealer that has the Fed wire the funds to its checking deposit account in a private bank based in Chicago. The Fed will respond by applying a $1 million credit to that bank's reserve account at the Federal Reserve Bank of Chicago. The private bank then will earmark these funds for the dealer's checking deposit account. The Fed imposes a 10 percent reserve requirement on most U.S. checking deposits, so the private Chicago bank will be able to lend $900,000 of the funds that it receives via the security dealer's deposit. Suppose further that the Chicago bank makes a loan of $900,000 to a construction company based in Louisville, Kentucky, and that this company places the funds in its checking account at a Louisville bank. Now the Louisville bank has $900,000 in new cash reserves. It can lend as much as 90 percent of these funds, or $810,000. Ultimately, these funds will expand deposits at yet another bank, either in Louisville or elsewhere.

As we discuss in more detail later in the chapter, checking account deposits are part of today's measures of the amount of money in circulation. Consequently, the Fed's $1 million security purchase in our example causes the total quantity of money in circulation to increase by an amount much greater than $1 million. The Chicago security dealer's checking deposits will increase by $1 million, the Louisville construction company's checking deposits rise by $900,000, and some other loan recipient's checking deposits will rise by $810,000. This process continues until the Fed's security purchase has had an ultimate *multiplier effect* on the total quantity of checking deposits included in the nation's money stock.

COMPUTING THE DEPOSIT MULTIPLIER   To determine the size of the multiplier effect in our example, let's denote the amount of checking deposits at private banks as D, and let's call the total amount of cash reserves of these banks R. Finally, let's denote the Fed's ratio for determining required reserve holdings as q. Hence, if banks hold no more cash reserves than the Fed requires them to hold, total reserves in the banking system will be $R = q \times D$, and any change in reserves owing to a change in checking deposits at banks will be equal to $\Delta R = q \times \Delta D$. By rearranging this relationship, we can find the change in checking deposits owing to a change in reserves induced by a Fed purchase of securities. To do so, we simply solve for ΔD by dividing both sides by q, which yields:

$$\Delta D = (1/q) \times \Delta R.$$

Inserting the numbers from our example of a Fed security purchase that causes an initial bank reserve expansion of $1 million with a required reserve ratio of 10 percent, ΔR equals $1 million, and $1/q$ equals $1/(0.1) = 10$. Therefore, ΔD equals $1 million $\times$ 10, or $10 million, so the Fed's $1 million security purchase ultimately will cause the quantity of money in circulation to rise by a multiple amount of $10 million. The ratio $1/q = 10$ is the "money multiplier."

Realistically, the final multiplier effect of a Fed security purchase is smaller than this amount. A key reason is that people hold some money in

INTERMEDIATE TARGET: A macroeconomic variable whose value a central bank seeks to control because it believes that doing so is consistent with its ultimate objectives.

the form of currency. Suppose that the Chicago securities dealer and the Louisville construction company in our example had chosen to convert some of the funds they received into currency rather than depositing all of the funds into checking accounts at their banks. Then their banks would have had fewer funds available to lend. This would have reduced the extent of the deposit multiplier process. Another factor that typically depresses the size of the deposit multiplier effect is bank holdings of reserves over and above those that are required. To the extent that banks hold such *excess reserves,* they have fewer reserves available to lend at each stage of the multiplier process.

THE FED'S POLICY INSTRUMENTS, THE QUANTITY OF MONEY, AND INTERMEDIATE TARGETS
Although the Fed cannot control the total quantity of deposits in the banking system directly, it clearly can influence this amount by conducting open-market operations—buying or selling securities. In addition, by varying reserve requirements the Fed can affect the size of the money multiplier linking a change in reserves caused by its open-market operations to the total amount of money in circulation. Finally, the Fed can influence the total amount of reserves held by private banks by changing the discount rate that it charges these institutions, thereby inducing them to increase or reduce the amounts of reserves that they borrow from the Federal Reserve banks.

As you can see, the Federal Reserve and other central banks of the world cannot directly "control" the quantity of money in circulation. In theory, central banks could use their policy instruments, such as the Fed's open-market operations, discount rate, and reserve requirements, to try to vary the quantity of money in a precise effort to achieve their inflation, output, and employment objectives. Typically, however, most central banks have sought to achieve **intermediate targets** of monetary policy. An intermediate target is a macroeconomic variable whose value a central bank tries to control because it believes that doing so is consistent with its ultimate objectives. Intermediate targets are distinguishable from the central bank's ultimate policy goals but are sufficiently closely related that they can serve as stand-ins or proxies for the ultimate objectives, as indicated in Figure 14–1.

The Rationales for Intermediate Targeting

There are two rationales for using an intermediate target in monetary policy. One is the difficulty that central bank officials have understanding and reaching agreement about the ways in which monetary policy affects infla-

Figure 14–1   The Intermediate Targeting Strategy for Monetary Policy

An intermediate target is a macroeconomic variable that the Federal Reserve seeks to influence as a stand-in for its ultimate goals, which are more difficult to observe or influence in the near term.

tion, real output, and employment in the short and long run. The other rationale is that even if central bank policymakers could unanimously agree on how their policy actions influence economic activity, they typically possess limited information about the economy.

PROBLEMS WITH DIRECTLY PURSUING ULTIMATE POLICY GOALS   As you have learned by now, there is no shortage of theories about how monetary policy actions affect inflation, real output, and employment. Different central bank officials often subscribe to distinctly different theoretical views. These disagreements can complicate the efforts of central bank policymakers to reach a consensus on the best way to attain ultimate policy objectives.

Consequently, seeking to achieve an intermediate monetary policy target might be viewed as a *compromise* approach in the absence of complete agreement among central bank officials about the best way to aim directly at ultimate goals. For example, as we shall discuss in more detail shortly, an intermediate target variable that several central banks have used in the past is the nominal money stock. Not all economic theories agree that changes in the money stock affect real output and employment, but all theories indicate that a given change in some specific measure of the nominal quantity of money should cause the price level to move in the same direction, if not in exactly the same proportion. If they cannot agree on any other aspect of monetary policy, central bank officials might decide to try to achieve a money stock growth rate objective, because that is the only policy approach on which a consensus exists.

CONDUCTING MONETARY POLICY WITH LIMITED INFORMATION   Although an intermediate target is sometimes adopted as a compromise, there also is a strong economic justification for using an intermediate target even when all policymakers agree on what is the "true" macroeconomic theory. The reason is that central bank officials must conduct monetary policy in the absence of perfect information. Some macroeconomic variables, such as interest rates or the quantity of money or credit, can be measured from day to day or week to week. Other variables, such as nominal income, may be estimated on a weekly basis but generally are known only on a monthly basis. Still others, particularly the price level, real GDP, and employment, can be tracked only monthly or quarterly. Even then, central bank and government statisticians often revise their calculations of these variables in the weeks following their initial release.

Consequently, current information about the central bank's ultimate policy goals—inflation, real output, and employment—typically is less readily available. In contrast, interest rates, money, and credit data are more likely to be available for observation and use at any given moment. Nominal income data are not as quickly forthcoming as these financial data, but nominal income estimates generally are available more frequently than information about ultimate policy goal variables.

The notion of using a macroeconomic variable as an intermediate target follows naturally from the fact that information about other variables is more readily available than information about ultimate objectives. By aiming to achieve an intermediate target, a central bank can more directly infer whether it is on the way to achieving the basic intent of its policies.

Otherwise, monetary policymakers might have to wait much longer to make this assessment.

Choosing an Intermediate Target Variable

A central bank that decides to use an intermediate targeting approach to conducting monetary policy must choose the appropriate macroeconomic variable to serve as its intermediate policy objective. In choosing among a number of possible target variables, the central bank considers several criteria.

CHARACTERISTICS OF INTERMEDIATE TARGETS   To be useful, an intermediate target variable should exhibit four key attributes:

1. *Frequently observable.* Because having up-to-date information is a fundamental rationale for using an intermediate targeting approach, an intermediate target variable should be observable more frequently than ultimate goal variables. As we noted, the price level, real GDP, and employment usually are observable at monthly or quarterly intervals. Consequently, a central bank will likely choose an intermediate target variable that can be observed from week to week or, even better, from day to day.

2. *Consistency with ultimate goals.* The target value for an intermediate variable should be consistent with the central bank's ultimate objectives. It would be counterproductive for a central bank to hit its chosen intermediate target successfully, only to discover that it had widely missed its goals for inflation, output, and employment.

3. *Definable and measurable.* Defining and measuring an intermediate target variable should be a straightforward task. If a potential intermediate target variable is susceptible to redefinition because of intermittent regulatory or technological changes, a central bank will have trouble measuring the target variable consistently. Inconsistent measurements would make it more difficult to evaluate the variable's relationship to ultimate policy goals.

4. *Controllable.* An intermediate target variable should be a macroeconomic variable whose value the central bank can readily influence. Otherwise, attaining its intermediate target and achieving its ultimate policy objectives will be difficult even if the intermediate target variable and the ultimate goals are closely related.

THE MENU OF POTENTIAL INTERMEDIATE TARGET VARIABLES   Central banks around the globe have adopted a number of different intermediate targeting procedures over the years. Several alternative categories of macroeconomic variables might qualify as intermediate monetary policy targets:

1. *Monetary or credit aggregates.* Many nations, including the United Kingdom and Japan, have experimented with procedures that use **monetary aggregates,** or alternative measures of the nominal money stock, as intermediate target variables. In the United States,

MONETARY AGGREGATES:
Measures of the quantity of money in circulation.

the Federal Reserve in the past has targeted the monetary aggregates that it calls M1 and M2. M1 is defined as currency (Federal Reserve notes and coins) plus transactions deposits (funds in interest-bearing and non-interest-bearing checking accounts). M2 consists of M1 plus various savings deposits, highly liquid overnight financial instruments, and various money market mutual fund balances.

The basic rationale for targeting a monetary aggregate has been that various macroeconomic theories indicate that the quantity of money should help determine aggregate demand, thereby influencing the price level and, possibly, real output and employment. Thus, central banks have believed that there should be a relationship between monetary aggregates and their inflation, output, and employment objectives. In addition, central banks clearly have the ability to influence monetary aggregates, and their values typically are known weekly.

Nevertheless, central banks have had some difficulties using monetary aggregates as intermediate targets. One problem has been that regulatory and technological changes have blurred the lines among various financial assets that function as money. In the United States, for instance, the Federal Reserve has redefined M1 or M2 every few years as new forms of money-like assets have emerged. The existence of more than one monetary aggregate is itself indicative of the problems defining "money" entails. In the 1980s and early 1990s, a breakdown in the previously consistent relationship between the basic M1 and M2 aggregates and GDP presented another, particularly bothersome problem.

Another quantitative financial target, which central banks in China and Russia have emphasized, is a *credit aggregate* target, which is a measure of the volume of lending. One type of credit aggregate is *total credit,* or the total amount of all lending in an economy. A narrower credit aggregate is *bank credit,* or total lending by banks. Through their monetary policy instruments, central banks can affect such measures of credit. For instance, as we noted earlier, expansion of bank lending accompanies the multiple expansion of bank deposit money. Hence, Fed policy instruments can affect total credit as well as the total quantity of money in circulation. Additionally, credit aggregates usually are straightforward to define and to measure, and credit data usually are observable weekly.

Credit aggregates, however, suffer from problems similar to those associated with monetary aggregates. In particular, relationships between credit measures and ultimate goals generally have been *at least* as tenuous as relationships between monetary aggregates and ultimate goals.

2. *Interest rates.* An alternative credit market variable that can serve as an intermediate monetary policy target is the *price of credit,* or the nominal interest rate. Central banks can observe interest rates daily and often by the minute. In addition, central banks' policy actions can have clear-cut effects on nominal interest rates.

Interest rates and economic activity are not always closely related, however. While lower interest rates can spur capital investment and economic activity, increased income raises the demand for credit and pushes nominal interest rates upward. Hence, the relationship between nominal interest rates and real income is not always predictable. In addition, many interest rates, including interest rates on financial instruments with short and long maturities, could be potential targets.

3. *Nominal GDP.* In recent years many economists have proposed using *nominal gross domestic product (GDP)* as an intermediate target. Even though nominal GDP data are not available more frequently than observations of real GDP and the price level, the essential argument favoring targeting nominal GDP hinges on the fact that nominal GDP by definition is equal to real GDP times the GDP price deflator. There are a number of competing theories about how the money stock relates to the price level and real output and prices, but this definitional relationship indicates that if a central bank wishes to stabilize real output and prices, then minimizing variations in nominal GDP output will help contain volatility in either of these ultimate goal variables. We shall illustrate this argument shortly.

FUNDAMENTAL ISSUE #2

Why might a central bank use an intermediate monetary policy target?

Central banks such as the Federal Reserve sometimes adopt an intermediate target because of limitations on the availability of data on ultimate objectives and different views about how monetary policy actions influence ultimate policy goals. An intermediate target variable should be observable with greater frequency than ultimate goal variables, easy to measure, subject to influence through monetary policy actions, and closely related to ultimate policy objectives. Possible intermediate target variables include money and credit aggregates, interest rates, and nominal GDP.

Choosing an Intermediate Target

No single potential intermediate target variable stands out as the clear best choice. Hence, in choosing the target, a central bank will likely consider various macroeconomic factors. By applying concepts you have already learned, we can examine these factors.

TARGETING THE NOMINAL INTEREST RATE   Figure 14–2 explains the way a central bank can choose and maintain a nominal interest rate target. In panel (b), we assume that the ultimate target for real GDP is equal to y^*. Given the location of the IS schedule, attaining and maintaining this real income target will require achieving the nominal interest rate target r^*. This will require assuring that the LM schedule crosses the IS schedule at point A

Figure 14–2   Targeting the Nominal Interest Rate in the Face of Money Demand Variations

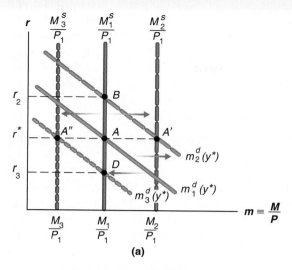

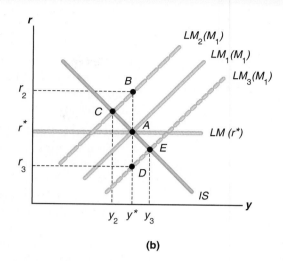

(a)

(b)

If the initial equilibrium quantity of real money balances and real income arises at points A in panels (a) and (b), respectively, then the displayed variations in the demand for real money balances will cause movements between points B and D in panel (a) that will induce the upward and downward shifts of the LM schedule between points B and D in panel (b). As a result, equilibrium real income will vary between points C and E in panel (b). To prevent such vari-

ability in real income at the current price level, the central bank could expand the nominal money stock as money demand rises [point A' in panel (a)] and contract the money stock in the face of a decline in money demand [point A'' in panel (a)]. This policy effectively would make the LM schedule horizontal at the targeted interest rate in panel (b), thereby maintaining an IS-LM equilibrium at point A.

in panel (b). To achieve its nominal interest rate target, the central bank will have to make sure that the supply of real money balances, M_1^s/P_1, crosses the demand schedule for real money balances, $m_1^d(y^*)$, at point A in panel (a).

Suppose, however, that there are variations in the demand for real money balances that arise, say, from changes in the technology by which people make payments, and not from any change in real income. An increase in the demand for real money balances, to $m_2^d(y^*)$, will cause the equilibrium nominal interest rate to start to rise from r^* toward r_2, at point B in panel (a). As a result, the LM schedule in panel (b) will shift upward by the vertical distance between point A and point B. If the central bank does nothing to offset this change, the rise in the interest rate will ultimately lead to a decline in real investment and, consequently, a fall in real income to level y_2 at point C in panel (b), which is below the central bank's target income level y^*. To keep this sequence of events from occurring, the central bank could raise the quantity of money from M_1 to M_2. This will shift the supply schedule for real money balances rightward and return the equilibrium interest rate to r^* at point A' in panel (a) and reattain the initial IS-LM equilibrium at point A in panel (b). This will keep the nominal interest rate at the targeted level and thereby achieve the ultimate real output objective y^*.

If instead money demand falls, from $m_1^d(y^*)$ to $m_3^d(y^*)$, then maintaining the target nominal interest rate r^* will require a reduction in the money stock, from M_1 to M_3. This will keep the equilibrium nominal interest rate from declining toward r_3 at point D in panel (a). Instead, the equilibrium point A'' will be attained, and a downward vertical shift in the LM schedule by the distance from point A to point D in panel (b) will be prohibited. This policy action thus will prevent real income from ultimately moving above the target level y^* to y_3 at point E in panel (b).

INTEREST-RATE TARGETING AND THE *LM* SCHEDULE Note that by targeting the nominal interest rate, the central bank does not allow the LM schedule to shift. It always reacts to changes in the demand for real money balances by raising or reducing the nominal money stock as required to keep the nominal interest rate at its target level. Under this targeting procedure, the central bank effectively makes the LM schedule *horizontal*. As real income varies, the nominal interest rate remains unchanged at an equilibrium that the central bank targets. Hence, $LM(r^*)$ in panel (b) is the *effective LM schedule* if the central bank targets the nominal interest rate.

Clearly, adopting the nominal interest rate as an intermediate target is the best monetary policy procedure in the face of variations in money demand. Unfortunately for a central bank, however, other factors in the economy also can change unexpectedly. Figure 14–3 illustrates the effects of variations in autonomous expenditures. Recall from Chapter 8 that a decline in autonomous consumption, investment, government spending, or exports or a rise in net taxes or autonomous import spending will cause a multiple reduction in equilibrium real income. This translates into a leftward shift of the IS schedule that is equal to the total decline in real income, shown by the movement from point A to point B in the figure, as the IS

Figure 14–3 Targeting the Nominal Interest Rate in the Face of Variations in Autonomous Expenditures

Changes in autonomous saving, imports, net taxes, exports, or government spending will cause fluctuations in the position of the *IS* schedule, causing movements along a typical, upward-sloping *LM* schedule from point *A* to point *C* or from point *A* to point *E*. If the central bank targets the nominal interest rate, however, the result will be an effectively horizontal *LM* schedule. Changes in autonomous expenditures will then cause even greater variability in equilibrium real income, between points *B* and *D*. Consequently, targeting the nominal interest rate is a less desirable policy in the presence of variations in autonomous expenditures.

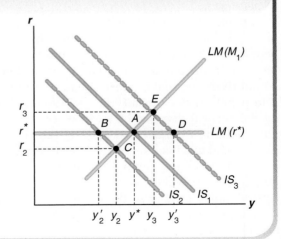

schedule shifts from IS_1 to IS_2. Because the effective LM schedule is horizontal if the central bank targets the nominal interest rate, equilibrium real income will decline by the full distance of the shift in the IS schedule, from y^* to y_2'. In contrast, if the central bank instead allows the equilibrium nominal interest rate to vary normally with changing money market conditions and thus to fall to r_2, then the resulting IS-LM equilibrium will be point C, and equilibrium real income will only decline to y_2. *Not* targeting the nominal interest rate actually will allow the central bank to come closer to achieving its real income target y^* in the face of a variation in autonomous expenditures that reduces real income.

Likewise, *not* targeting the interest rate will result in a smaller increase in equilibrium real income if autonomous consumption, investment, government spending, or exports rise or if net taxes or autonomous imports decline. Any one of these changes in autonomous spending will shift the IS schedule to the right, from IS_1 to IS_3 in Figure 14–3. If the central bank targets the nominal interest rate, the result will be the largest possible rise in equilibrium real income, from the target level y^* at point A to the level y_3' at point D. In contrast, if the central bank forgoes targeting the interest rate, then the new IS-LM equilibrium will be point E, at the interest rate r_3 and the real income level y_3. Again, *not* targeting the nominal interest rate is the more desirable policy in the presence of autonomous spending variations that cause a change in the location of the IS schedule.

TARGETING A MONETARY AGGREGATE   What should a central bank do if variations in autonomous expenditures are significant, making the nominal interest rate less attractive as an intermediate monetary policy target? Figure 14–4 gives one possible answer, which is to target the nominal quantity of money instead. Under this intermediate targeting procedure, the central bank selects a target quantity of money, M^*. By choosing this target, the central bank places the LM schedule, $LM(M^*)$, in the location that

Figure 14–4   Targeting the Money Stock in the Face of Variations in Autonomous Expenditures

If a central bank establishes a target for the quantity of money in circulation, the LM schedule will slope upward. Thus, changes in autonomous saving, imports, net taxes, exports, or government spending that cause shifts in the IS schedule will result in movements along the LM schedule between points B and C. Volatility in real income will be less than the variations between points D and E that would take place if the central bank targeted the nominal interest rate instead.

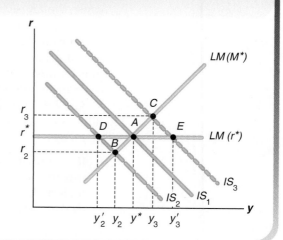

it anticipates will lead to its ultimate real income objective y^*, given the expected location of the IS schedule, shown by IS_1. As in Figure 14–3, variations in autonomous expenditures could cause the IS schedule to be at IS_2 or at IS_3, below or above the position that the central bank anticipated. Then equilibrium real income will fall somewhat below or rise somewhat above the real income target level, as the resulting IS-LM equilibrium points will lie between points B and C, causing equilibrium real income to vary between y_2 and y_3. Although equilibrium real income will deviate somewhat from the target level y^*, using the money stock as an intermediate target is preferable to targeting the nominal interest rate, which will permit much wider variations in real income between y_2' at point D and y_3' at point E.

Interest Elasticity of Money Demand Note that the amount of variability in real income with a money stock target depends on the elasticity of the LM schedule around the intersection with the IS schedule. If the LM schedule in Figure 14–4 were to become less elastic, then the extent of the variability in real income caused by unexpected changes in the position of the IS schedule would decline. Recall from Chapter 8 that the main determinant of the elasticity of the LM schedule is the interest elasticity of the demand for real money balances. A reduction in the interest elasticity of money demand will cause the LM schedule to become less elastic. We can conclude that targeting a monetary aggregate is likely to be a better approach than targeting the nominal interest rate in the face of variability in expenditures if money demand is very interest-inelastic.

Money Demand Volatility As Figure 14–5 shows, however, targeting the quantity of money is less desirable than targeting the nominal interest rate when the demand for real money balances itself is variable. Panel (a) illustrates the effects of an autonomous change in the demand for money that causes variations in money market equilibrium between points B and C, respectively. When the central bank keeps the quantity of money at its target level M^*, these variations in the demand for money will cause the equilibrium nominal interest rate to vary between r_2 and r_3. Because variations in the demand for money that are not caused by changes in real income cause the LM schedule's position to change, the position of the LM schedule will vary between $LM_2(M^*)$ and $LM_3(M^*)$, as shown in panel (b). Therefore, equilibrium real income could ultimately vary between y_2 at point D and y_3 at point E in panel (b) under a money stock target. In contrast, using a nominal interest rate target instead would have kept the nominal interest rate unchanged and maintained the target level of real income y^* at point A.

The fundamental point that the examples in Figures 14–2 through 14–5 illustrate was first made by William Poole of Brown University over thirty years ago:

> **If a central bank must choose between targeting the nominal interest rate or targeting a monetary aggregate, then the key criterion the bank should consider is the main source of variability that it faces.**

If the main source of variability is money demand and, hence, the position of the LM schedule, then the nominal interest rate is the preferable intermediate target. In contrast, if the main source of variability is changes in

Figure 14–5   Targeting the Money Stock in the Face of Money Demand Variations

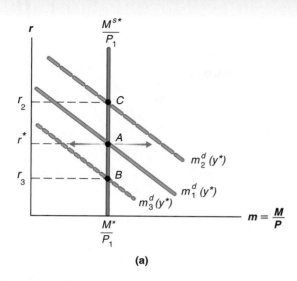

(a)

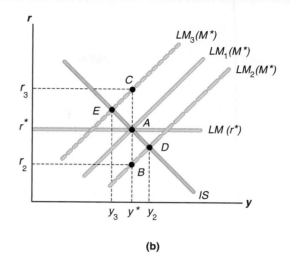

(b)

When a central bank targets the quantity of money in circulation, changes in the demand for real money balances will cause the equilibrium nominal interest rate to vary between points B and C in panel (a), thereby causing the position of

the LM schedule to vary between points B and C in panel (b). As a result, equilibrium real income will vary along the schedule, between points E and D.

autonomous expenditures and, hence, the position of the IS schedule, then targeting a monetary aggregate is a more desirable approach.

A COMPLICATION: AGGREGATE SUPPLY VARIABILITY   Both interest-rate targeting and monetary targeting involve a disadvantage that has been hidden thus far in our discussion by our implicit assumption that the price level is unchanging. Interest-rate targeting or monetary targeting to stabilize real income at a target level in the presence of a fixed price level often amounts to stabilizing aggregate demand. Real-business-cycle theorists, however, have documented that in the real world, at least some real income variability arises as a result of variability in the aggregate supply schedule.

To see this, consider Figure 14–6 on the following page. If a central bank selects the nominal interest rate or the money stock as its intermediate target, then the *best* it can do is to stabilize aggregate demand by ensuring that, for a given level of prices, the economy stays at the same IS-LM equilibrium at its real income target, y^*, at point A. If there is no variability in the aggregate supply schedule, there will be no inflation, and the central bank will attain both its real output and its inflation goals. If there is considerable variation in the position of the aggregate supply schedule, however, as shown by the variation between y_2^s and y_3^s, then the equilibrium level of real income will vary between y_2 at point B and y_3 at point C. In addition, the price level will vary between P_2 and P_3. Thus, the central bank will fail to attain a zero-inflation goal even though it might succeed in perfectly stabilizing aggregate demand.

UNIT V Macroeconomic Policy

Figure 14-6 The Problem of Aggregate Supply Variability

If a central bank uses financial market variables such as the nominal interest rate or the money stock as intermediate targets, then it typically does so to stabilize aggregate demand. Even if successful in this regard, however, such a policy would not necessarily stabilize real output or the price level in the face of variations in the position of the aggregate supply schedule.

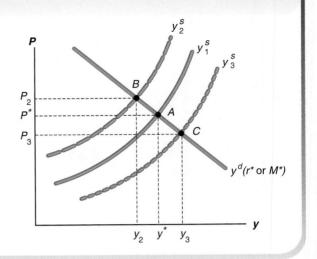

Hence, nominal interest rate targeting and money stock targeting both fail to account for the output and inflation effects of aggregate supply variability. The position of the economy's aggregate supply schedule does vary from time to time. Consequently, a number of economists have proposed nominal GDP as an alternative intermediate target.

NOMINAL GDP TARGETING Figure 14–7 is based on a graphical approach to understanding nominal GDP targeting first proposed by Michael Bradley of George Washington University and Dennis Jansen of Texas A&M University. The figure shows how nominal GDP targeting will work in the face of factors causing a decline in aggregate demand. If a central bank targets nominal GDP, it will treat nominal income, $Y = P \times y$, as its intermediate target. Thus, the central bank will vary the quantity of money as needed to ensure that $P \times y = Y^*$ always holds, where Y^* denotes the central bank's nominal GDP target. In Figure 14–7, we assume that the target level of real GDP is $10,000 billion, or $10 trillion. Obviously, this target can be achieved by many price level–real income combinations, such as $P_1 = 4$, $y_1 = 2,500$; $P_2 = 5$, $y_2 = 2,000$; and $P_3 = 8$, $y_3 = 1,250$. These and all other price level–real income combinations consistent with the nominal GDP target lie along the bowed schedule (called a rectangular hyperbola) labeled $Y^* = 10,000$.

At point A in Figure 14–7, the aggregate demand and aggregate supply schedules intersect at the equilibrium price level $P_1 = 4$ and the equilibrium real output level $y_1 = 2,500$. In addition, the natural, full-information level of output in the figure is equal to $y^* = 2,500$. This is the real output level at which workers and firms have complete information, so the long-run aggregate supply schedule, denoted y_{LR}^s, is vertical. Hence, at point A the market for real output is in equilibrium at the natural output level, and so the central bank's nominal income target achieves this level of real output. In addition, if the central bank can keep the market for real output at point A, it will prevent any rise in the price level, thereby curtailing inflation.

Figure 14-7 Targeting Nominal GDP in the Face of a Decline in Aggregate Demand

Suppose the central bank adopts an intermediate target of $10,000 billion ($10 trillion). Then it will enact monetary policies that achieve an equilibrium price level and equilibrium real output level at a point such as point A, which lies along a set of price level–real output combinations for which $P \times y = Y^* = 10,000$. If there is a fall in aggregate demand that results in a decline in the equilibrium price level and the equilibrium level of output, nominal income will decline. By automatically raising aggregate demand to push nominal income back toward the target level, the central bank will automatically stabilize both real income and the price level.

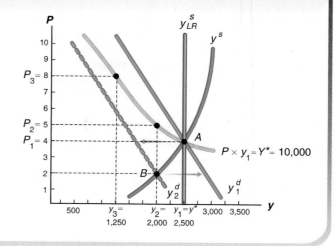

Now consider how the central bank will respond to a decline in aggregate demand from y_1^d to y_2^d in Figure 14–7. The fall in aggregate demand will cause real income and the price level to begin to decline toward levels consistent with point B, so nominal income will also begin to fall. The central bank will respond by increasing the quantity of money to raise nominal GDP back to its target level. Therefore, by conducting monetary policy to maintain nominal income at the intermediate target level of $Y^* = 10,000$ nominal units, the central bank automatically will stabilize aggregate demand and achieve both its real output and its inflation goals.

CONSEQUENCES OF AGGREGATE SUPPLY VARIABILITY   As we noted, stabilizing aggregate demand often is all that nominal interest rate targeting or money stock targeting can achieve. The advantage of nominal GDP targeting is that it potentially can reduce the inflationary consequences of aggregate supply variability, as shown in Figure 14–8 (p. 426). Suppose there is a fall in aggregate supply that is caused by an event such as a worldwide increase in oil prices, a war, or an agricultural famine. As a result, the economy's short-run aggregate supply schedule will shift leftward from y^s to $y^{s'}$ by an amount equal to the unavoidable decline in the natural, full-information output level, from $y^* = 2,500$ to $y^{*'} = 2,000$. Thus, the long-run aggregate supply schedule will also shift to the left by this same amount, from y_{LR}^s to $y_{LR}^{s'}$. In the absence of any response from the central bank, the equilibrium price level will rise from $P_1 = 4$ toward $P' = 7$ at point C, and so nominal income will begin to rise toward $Y^{*'} = P' \times y^{*'} = 7 \times 2,000 = 14,000$. With either an interest-rate or a money stock targeting procedure that would stabilize aggregate demand, these would be the new, much higher values for the price level and nominal GDP. With a nominal GDP target of $Y^* = 10,000$ nominal units, however, the central bank will need to reduce the money stock, thereby lowering aggregate demand. This will yield an actual equilibrium price level equal to $P_2 = 5$ at point B, thereby containing the inflationary effects of the reduction in aggregate supply. Consequently, we can reach the following conclusions:

Figure 14–8   Targeting Nominal GDP in the Face of a Decline in Aggregate Supply

A rise in energy prices, a war, a famine, or another factor causing a reduction in the economy's long-run output level will cause both the long-run and the short-run aggregate supply schedules to shift leftward by the amount of the decline in the long-run output level. If the central bank stabilizes aggregate demand, the long-run result will be a significant rise in the price level shown by a movement from point *A* to point *C*. If instead the central bank maintains a nominal GDP target, it will respond to the decline in the long-run output level by reducing aggregate demand and inducing a final equilibrium at point *B*, thereby automatically limiting the rise in the equilibrium price level.

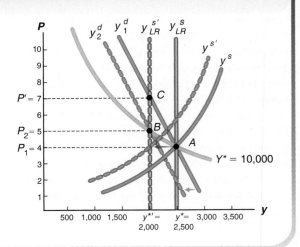

A key advantage of nominal GDP targeting is that it restrains the inflationary consequences of aggregate supply variations. In this respect, nominal GDP targeting is preferable to policy procedures that target monetary aggregates or interest rates.

Of course, central bank policies influence real output and the price level via their effects on aggregate demand. Because monetary policy can affect aggregate supply only indirectly—for instance, by influencing inflation expectations—some economists argue that central banks should directly target inflation (see on pages 442–443 *Link to Policy: Inflation Targeting Gains New Adherents*). Some even promote targeting the price level. We shall return to this issue in Chapter 15, after we explore the role of fiscal policy and the interactions of monetary and fiscal policy in an economy that is open to international trade and flows of funds.

FUNDAMENTAL ISSUE #3

What are the pros and cons of alternative intermediate monetary policy targets?   Using a nominal interest rate as an intermediate target helps to stabilize aggregate demand if money demand is highly volatile while aggregate desired expenditures are relatively stable. In contrast, adopting a money stock target makes aggregate demand more stable if aggregate desired expenditures are variable while money demand is relatively stable. A potential advantage of nominal GDP targeting over targeting either a nominal interest rate or a monetary aggregate is that aiming for a nominal GDP target automatically stabilizes aggregate demand and also minimizes the inflationary effects of variations in aggregate supply. A disadvantage, however, is that accurate nominal GDP data are not available as frequently as data on interest rates and monetary aggregates.

To this point, we have focused on monetary policies aimed at stabilizing the economy. In recent years, however, an area that has received increasing attention from politicians and the media has been the potential role of fiscal policy in contributing to economic growth. Two topics in particular have emerged as important fiscal policy issues. One concerns the long-term implications of the government's budgetary policies—policies regarding deficits or surpluses and their contribution to the government's debt—for economic growth. The other involves growth effects arising from incentives and disincentives generated by federal tax policies.

Deficits, Surpluses, and the Government Debt

From 1969 to 1998, the federal government experienced annual budget deficits. That is, it spent more than it received in tax revenues and user fees. To finance these deficits, the U.S. government borrowed by issuing Treasury bills, notes, and bonds. By so doing, the government accumulated considerable indebtedness to those who purchased its securities. Recent federal budgets have also included deficit spending, so it appears likely that government indebtedness will accumulate further in coming years.

THE NATIONAL DEBT   At any given time, the total accumulation of all outstanding amounts owed to private holders of government-issued securities is the net **national debt.** Therefore, any year that the government runs a deficit, it contributes to the national debt.

The absolute dollar amount of the national debt by itself does not give us much information about its relative importance in the U.S. economy. Figure 14–9 on the following page shows how the net national debt has varied relative to GDP during the past few decades. After reaching a peak during World War II, the net national debt as a percentage of GDP declined to about 25 percent in 1974. Then the ratio turned upward, rising steadily, apart from a brief decline in the late 1980s, until 1992 when it reached about 50 percent. It began to decline thereafter.

Is there anything inherently "bad" about a high ratio of net national debt to GDP? After all, one might reason, running deficits and accumulating debt might allow the government to spend funds on programs intended to assist those in need or to maintain a broad police and military network for internal national security and defense from external threats. Certainly, it is possible that benefits could flow from debt accumulation. Nevertheless, accumulating greater debt in pursuit of such benefits is not costless. Large national debt-to-GDP ratios impose burdens on society, because the debts ultimately must be repaid.

BURDENS OF THE NATIONAL DEBT   Two important social burdens can stem from accumulating a sizable national debt. One is that debts accumulated in current years must be repaid in the future. As we noted in our discussion of the Ricardian equivalence proposition in Chapter 7, deficit spending that adds to today's national debt ultimately must be repaid by future generations.

NATIONAL DEBT: The total accumulation of amounts that the government currently owes to private holders of its debt.

Figure 14–9   The U.S. Net National Debt as a Percentage of Gross Domestic Product

The ratio of net national debt to GDP fell from the end of World War II until the mid-1970s, when it began a steady rise that continued until 1993. Since then, it has trended downward.

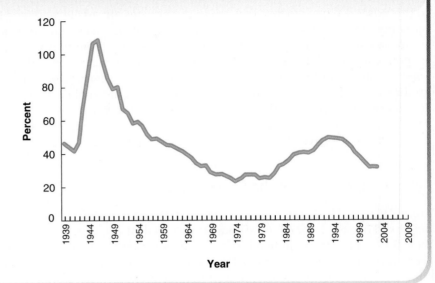

SOURCES: *Economic Report of the President, 2002; Economic Indicators.*

Hence, if we add to the national debt this year to reap the benefits that greater government spending can provide, future generations will have to sacrifice a flow of benefits that they otherwise could receive if they did not have to face the prospect of repaying the higher debt that will result from this year's budgetary decisions.

Not all benefits from government spending are short term, of course. For instance, government expenditures on infrastructure investments—highways, waterways, airports, and the like—constitute longer-term investment that can have payoffs for future generations by increasing their real incomes. To the extent that such future payoffs arise, the social burden of the national debt is reduced.

A second social burden is that some national debt repayments entail flows of U.S. resources to citizens of other nations. As Figure 14–10 indicates, since the mid-1970s between 16 and 37 percent of the net national debt has been issued to individuals who are not U.S. citizens or to organizations located outside the United States. Interest payments to holders of such debt amount to transfers of resources from U.S. citizens to foreign citizens. This can reduce the income potential for future U.S. generations. How much future U.S. citizens may be constrained by these transfers again depends on the way that the U.S. government spends the funds that it raises by issuing debt to foreigners. If it spends the funds on projects that yield only immediate benefits, then future U.S. citizens will face all of the debt that their parents or grandparents accumulated. If, however, the government uses at least some of the funds borrowed from foreigners to finance projects with longer-term benefits, then the size of the potential burden of foreign resource transfers is reduced.

Figure 14-10   The Share of the U.S. Net National Debt Held by Citizens of Other Nations

The portion of the U.S. national debt held by foreign residents declined from the late 1970s until the mid-1980s. Since then, it has trended upward.

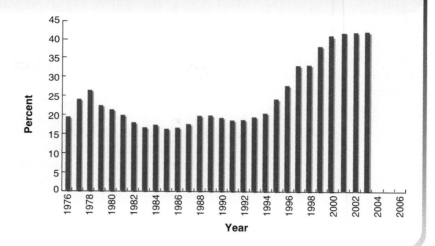

SOURCES: *Economic Report of the President*, 2002; *Treasury Bulletin*.

Do Government Budget Deficits or Surpluses Matter?

For years until 1998, whenever anyone mentioned "fiscal policy," it was nearly always in the context of a perceived "need" to reduce the federal deficit and thereby decrease the rate at which the government accumulated additional debt. Between 1998 and 2001, by way of contrast, a big issue was whether it was desirable for the government to run budget surpluses year after year. Why is an imbalance in the government's budget such an issue irrespective of whether it is positive or negative?

DEFICITS, CROWDING OUT, AND GROWTH   Recall from Chapters 4 and 8 that high government budget deficits can *crowd out* private spending. By inducing a rise in the interest rate, deficit spending by the government reduces private investment. If saving also increases with a rise in the interest rate, then private consumption may decline as well. To some extent, the crowding-out effect is simply a resource transfer from the private sector to the government. Nevertheless, if private investment entails greater capital accumulation as compared with government expenditures, then longer-term economic growth can be slowed by deficit spending.

Although many economists expressed concerns about the burdens of the steadily accumulating debt, this potential negative effect on long-term growth was a key reason that most argued strenuously for reducing the government deficit. On the other side of the debate, however, were those who viewed private investment and government investment as equally productive. For this reason, this aspect of the *macroeconomic* argument about government deficits hinged on the amount of government spending on long-term capital investment and on the relative efficiency of government versus private investment.

On the Web

What is the current outlook for the budget of the U.S. government? Take a look at the most recent testimony before Congress at the home page of the Congressional Budget Office at http://www.cbo.gov.

THE DEBATE OVER BUDGET SURPLUSES   In the past few years, the terms of the debate shifted as the government took in more taxes than it spent. Some forecasts indicated that, in the absence of big tax cuts or increases in the rate of government expenditures, the government might run surpluses for a number of years into the future. During the latter years of the Clinton presidency, the government decided to use a portion of the annual surpluses to begin paying off some of the accumulated debt from years past. Before the 2001–2002 recession and the boost in government spending to wage the war against terrorism, the rosiest forecasts raised the possibility that this debt might be completely paid off by 2015. Doing so, of course, would have been consistent with reducing, or perhaps even eliminating, the potential distributional burdens associated with the national debt.

Nevertheless, a number of economists—many of whom had previously argued against large government deficits—have argued against running big federal surpluses. Their concern, once again, is the possibility of ill effects on economic growth.

To understand why some contend that surpluses might harm economic growth, recall from Chapter 4 that when the government runs a budget surplus, it adds to the total flow of saving in the economy. Look back at panel (b) of Figure 4–3 on page 84, and you will see that in the classical model this results in an interest-rate decline that *stimulates* private investment. At the same time, however, private saving *declines,* so private consumption increases. Thus, in the classical model an increase in government saving in the form of higher budget surpluses induces an equal-sized increase in private spending. (In Self-Test question 8 at the end of the chapter, you are asked to show that in the traditional Keynesian model, an increase in the government's surplus induces a less-than-equal rise in total private spending.)

Naturally, other things being equal, increased private investment tends to spur greater capital accumulation and push up the rate of economic growth. So why do some economists now grumble that government surpluses might *hinder* growth? The argument that they propose hinges on the fact that government surpluses tend to depress private saving. Consequently, by running a surplus the government effectively saves *on behalf* of private individuals: it extracts taxes in excess of the amount required to cover its own expenses and then channels the unspent taxes to financial markets. What critics of government surpluses question is the government's ability to channel this "forced saving" to the most productive uses. They worry that "too much" government saving might be directed to activities with low rates of return. If so, they argue, persistent government surpluses would lead to lower rates of economic growth than the nation could otherwise achieve.

This, of course, is the "flip side" of the argument against government deficits. In the case of deficits, a key issue is whether government investment is as productive as private investment. Likewise, in the case of surpluses a fundamental issue is whether government saving is allocated as efficiently as private saving.

Tax Incentives and Supply-Side Fiscal Policies

Essentially, these debates about the growth implications of government deficits and surpluses revolve in large measure around the issues of government capabilities and private incentives. One set of economists promote a particular approach to macroeconomics, known as *supply-side economics* (see Chapter 5), which is based on two key propositions:

1. The government is inherently less efficient than the private sector at allocating saving and undertaking capital investment.

2. Government tax policies have important effects on private incentives that influence capital accumulation and growth of labor employment and, consequently, economic growth.

Given this starting point, supply-side economists naturally focus their attention on developing and implementing fiscal policies that provide saving, investment, and labor market incentives consistent with the highest feasible rate of economic growth.

THE INCOME TAX SYSTEM AND CAPITAL ACCUMULATION   As you learned in Chapter 7, income tax revenues comprise the bulk of the annual tax receipts of the U.S. government. Both households and corporations pay income taxes. Households, of course, are the main source of saving, most of which is channeled to businesses to fund capital investment. According to supply-side economists, the income tax system provides disincentives for both saving and investment, thereby reducing capital accumulation and economic growth.

To understand this argument, let's apply the classical theory of the loanable funds market from Chapter 4. Take a look at Figure 14–11 on the next page, where we assume that the government's budget is balanced, which allows us to concentrate on the effects of income taxation on private incentives to save and invest. In the figure, we use the symbol τ^s to denote the tax rate on income that households earn from saving. For instance, the U.S. government taxes both interest income and capital gains. Together, these forms of taxation determine the effective tax rate on saving, τ^s. The tax rate on corporate income earned from capital investment projects, which arises from the system of corporate income taxes, is denoted τ^i.

Panel (a) of Figure 14–11 shows the effects of reductions in these tax rates on equilibrium saving and investment. Cutting the effective tax rate on saving, from τ^s_1 to τ^s_2, induces households to increase their saving at any given real interest rate. Likewise, a reduction in the effective tax rate on investment, from τ^i_1 to τ^i_2, gives businesses an incentive to increase their investment at each possible real interest rate. The unambiguous effect of these tax-rate reductions is an increase in equilibrium saving and investment.

Panel (b) illustrates the implications for the growth of real output. At the initial tax rates τ^s_1 and τ^i_1, the capital stock increases from K to $K + i_1$, inducing the aggregate production function to rotate upward from $F(N, K)$ to $F(N, K + i_1)$. Given an employment level equal to N_1, this results in a rise in real output from y_1 to y'. At the lower tax rates, τ^s_2 and τ^i_2, however, the capital stock increases from K to $K + i_2$. As a result, the aggregate production function rotates upward by a larger amount, from $F(N, K)$ to $F(N, K + i_2)$, and real output grows from y_1 to y_2.

Thus, supply-side economists argue that tax rates on income earned from saving and investment should be reduced. Indeed, they conclude that

Figure 14–11   Taxes on Saving and Investment and the Growth of Output

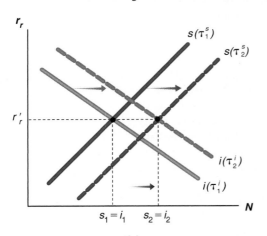

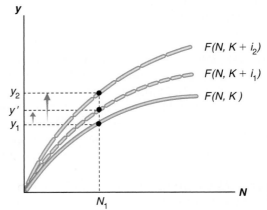

(a)

As shown in panel (a), reductions in the effective tax rates on income earned from saving and investment increase the incentives for households to save and businesses to invest at any given real interest rate. As a result, equilibrium investment increases. Panel (b) illustrates how this

(b)

affects the growth of output. Because the capital stock increases by a larger amount with lower tax rates on saving and investment, the production function rotates upward to a greater extent. At any given quantity of labor, such as N_1, output rises by a larger amount.

in the best of all worlds, income earnings from saving and investment would not be taxed at all.

THE INCOME TAX SYSTEM AND EMPLOYMENT GROWTH   Supply-side economists also contend that the income tax system has employment effects that hinder economic growth. As you learned in Chapter 7, the *marginal income tax rate* is the additional income tax paid on an additional dollar of income. In the United States and most other nations, the government taxes income derived from each additional dollar of wages and salaries that workers earn. Furthermore, the U.S. government has designed a system of income taxes that is intended to be *progressive*. Hence, the marginal income tax rate increases as a worker's total earnings increase. This means that when an individual is contemplating working an additional hour, day, or week, the marginal income tax rate that she faces affects her decision about whether to supply that amount of labor. At a relatively higher marginal income tax rate, the individual naturally will be relatively less inclined to supply additional labor.

Figure 14–12 evaluates the effects on employment and output growth of assessing a lower marginal tax rate on wage income, denoted τ^w. In panel (a), a reduction in the marginal income tax rate, from τ_1^w to τ_2^w, gives households the incentive to supply more labor services at any given real wage. Thus, the labor supply schedule shifts rightward, which generates an increase in equilibrium employment. As shown in panel (b), the result is a rise in real output, from y_1 to y_2. Lower marginal income tax rates applicable to wages and salaries, therefore, are consistent with a higher rate of output growth.

For this reason, supply-side economists also argue in favor of reductions in marginal income tax rates. Many, in fact, contend that the best way to engender economic growth would be to eliminate taxation of labor income altogether.

COULD THE INCOME TAX BE SCRAPPED—OR AT LEAST REDESIGNED? In keeping with their proposition that governments cannot allocate saving and investment as efficiently as the private sector, most supply-side economists tend to favor a limited role for government. Nevertheless, they recognize that there might be collective benefits from funding some functions of government, such as national defense, public safety, and other public-sector activities. If the income tax were eliminated, some new source of taxation would have to take its place.

Figure 14–12   Taxes on Wage Income and Employment and Output Growth

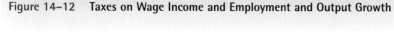
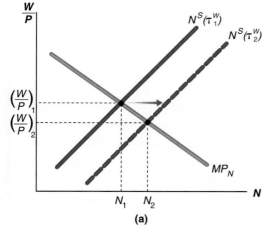
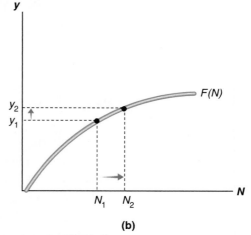

(a)

(b)

Panel (a), depicts the effect of a reduction in the marginal tax rate on wage income earned by workers. This action increases the incentive to supply additional labor, so the labor supply schedule shifts rightward. Equilibrium employment increases, and, as shown in panel (b), that induces an increase in real output.

A number of supply-side economists favor replacing the income tax system with some form of *consumption tax,* such as a national sales tax or a value-added tax. A common argument against sales taxes is that they can be regressive. This can happen if low-income households spend the bulk of their incomes and thereby effectively pay sales taxes on much of their earnings, while high-income households are able to save larger portions of their incomes and earn untaxed income from interest and capital gains. One way that supply-side economists have proposed to avoid a regressive sales tax is to implement a scheme of tax refunds based on households' income levels. Lowest-income households would receive the largest refunds relative to their tax payments, and highest-income households would receive the smallest refunds, or perhaps even none at all.

Supply-side economists have promoted the replacement of income taxes with consumption taxes for many years. So far, however, they have not had much success in convincing governments to implement this change— though many state governments in the United States and a number of national governments around the world have implemented side-by-side income and consumption tax systems. Consequently, some supply-side economists have offered a less drastic proposal for restructuring the current income tax system. Under this scheme, called a *flat tax system,* all income subject to taxation would be taxed at the same rate, as in a proportional income tax system (see Chapter 7). This "flat" rate would be set at a level that would ensure a balanced budget, given the government's rate of spending. The marginal tax rate applied to each dollar of taxed income would be equal to this low rate, consistent with supply-side economists' goal of achieving high growth. To preserve the progressive structure of the income tax system, however, the flat rate of taxation would apply only to earnings above a threshold level. If the threshold were set sufficiently high, for instance, the lowest-income households would pay few income taxes.

It remains to be seen if any of these supply-side proposals will be adopted in future years. They have attracted the attention of a number of politicians, however, and thus are likely to continue to be discussed. (Estimates indicate that marginal tax rates have varied considerably over time; see *Policy Notebook: Meandering Marginal Tax Rates.*)

FUNDAMENTAL ISSUE #4

What are the key propositions and fiscal policy prescriptions of supply-side economics?   One fundamental proposition of supply-side economics is that governments are incapable of allocating saving and investment as efficiently as the private sector. For this reason, supply-side economists are at the forefront of proposals to keep the government's budget in balance with neither persistent deficits nor surpluses. A second key proposition is that assessing tax rates on household and business incomes affects incentives that households and businesses face, thereby influencing economic growth. Supply-side economists advocate reducing or even eliminating tax rates on interest and capital gains income of savers, income that businesses derive from capital investment, and wage incomes of workers.

Meandering Marginal Tax Rates

The U.S. tax laws have been changed numerous times during the past three decades. Figure 14–13 shows how these changes have affected marginal tax rates on wage, interest, and dividend income and on earnings from capital gains on financial assets.

The marginal tax rate on dividend income has fallen since the late 1970s, but the marginal tax rate on capital gains has increased. Marginal tax rates on wage and interest income rose during the 1970s, fell during the 1980s, and trended slightly upward after the early 1990s.

For Critical Analysis
From a supply-side perspective, why is reducing marginal tax rates more important than cutting average tax rates for stimulating employment and output growth?

Figure 14–13   Estimates of U.S. Marginal Tax Rates on Dividends, Interest, Wages, and Capital Gains

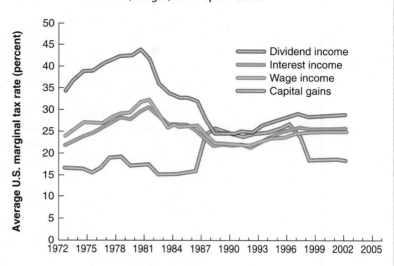

The marginal tax rates faced by a typical U.S. resident converged during the 1990s before beginning to diverge once more in the 2000s.

SOURCE: National Bureau of Economic Research.

Aiming Monetary and Fiscal Policies at Domestic and International Objectives: The Assignment Problem

International linkages among nations can complicate efforts to implement both monetary and fiscal policy. If a nation has an open economy and engages in significant trade with other nations, international considerations may affect policymakers' ability to achieve their ultimate inflation, output, and employment goals. In addition, many citizens may perceive that international variables themselves—such as the nation's merchandise trade balance or its private payments balance—should be ultimate policy goals. Consequently, monetary and fiscal policymakers in open economies typically face pressures to take international objectives into account as they contemplate the appropriate policy strategies to pursue.

Do International Factors Matter for Domestic Well-Being?

Why would individuals and firms in open economies want policymakers to pursue international objectives? One reason is that international factors may play a role in determining domestic goals. Another is that a number

MERCANTILISM: The idea that a primary determinant of a nation's wealth is international trade and commerce. Thus, a nation can gain by enacting policies that spur exports while limiting imports.

of workers and businesses may have a direct stake in the international sector of the economy.

INTERNATIONAL OBJECTIVES AND DOMESTIC GOALS   Recall from Chapter 6 that two determinants of a nation's aggregate desired expenditures are export spending on the nation's output of goods and services by residents of foreign countries and import expenditures on foreign-produced goods and services by the nation's own citizens. A rise in export spending increases aggregate desired expenditures. In contrast, a rise in import spending reduces the portion of disposable income available for domestic consumption. Hence, both of these international factors influence the position of the nation's *IS* schedule, thereby affecting aggregate demand, the equilibrium price level, and, potentially, short-run equilibrium real output and employment.

As a result, macroeconomic policymakers in an open economy must take exports and imports into consideration in their policymaking. If nothing else, policymakers must recognize that trade-related expenditures are likely to have an influence on aggregate demand that is separate from purely domestic influences. More broadly, however, policymakers may conclude that attaining their ultimate domestic objectives may require a "balancing" of international factors. For instance, the policymakers may seek to achieve balanced merchandise trade or a private payments balance equal to zero as a means of achieving their domestic inflation, output, and employment goals.

INTERNATIONAL OBJECTIVES AS ULTIMATE GOALS   In some nations, however, international objectives may be regarded as ultimate goals in and of themselves. For example, workers and firms in industries that rely on foreign purchases of the goods and services they produce may pressure their governments to pursue policies that promote exports. In addition, workers and firms in industries that depend on domestic purchases of their output may push central banks and government officials to enact policies that restrain imports. Such efforts by both types of interest groups could lead a nation's policymakers to seek merchandise trade and private payments *surpluses* as ultimate policy objectives.

Throughout history, nations have aimed for surpluses in their balance of payments accounts. In the seventeenth and eighteenth centuries, for instance, many British citizens advocated a policy of **mercantilism,** which is the idea that a key source of a nation's wealth is international trade and commerce. Key policy goals of the British mercantilists were to promote exports and to hinder imports. Of course, a fundamental problem with mercantilism is that if all nations seek trade and payments surpluses by limiting imports, international trade ultimately may come to a halt. Recognition of this fact led to the decline of mercantilism in the nineteenth century and greater emphasis on free trade among nations. Nevertheless, mercantilist arguments support the goals of various special interest groups, so they often emerge as political party planks or even as features of public policy. At a minimum, groups with international interests commonly exert pressures on policymakers to maintain trade and payments balances, if not surpluses.

Finding the Best Policy Mix for Internal and External Balance

Perhaps because they recognize that international factors influence domestic goals or because they face political pressures from mercantilist advocates, monetary and fiscal policymakers commonly express interest in attaining international objectives. Once they commit themselves to achieving international goals, however, policymakers confront a fundamental problem: domestic and international objectives sometimes conflict. For instance, a cut in the tax rate may be an appropriate fiscal policy action to spur growth in a nation's real income, yet this tax cut could spur import spending and raise the merchandise trade deficit. Increasing money growth may be the best policy for a central bank to pursue to boost output, but the interest-rate reduction that results may cause capital to flow out of the country, thereby contributing to a private payments deficit.

In principle, the solution to this potential conflict seems straightforward. After all, there are two policymakers: a central bank and a governmental fiscal authority. Similarly, there are two basic types of goals that they might pursue: international objectives and domestic objectives. Why not just assign one set of goals to the central bank and the other set to the fiscal policymaker?

Indeed, this division of goals is a possible solution to potential conflicts between international and domestic goals. Nevertheless, a problem remains: Which policymaker should take responsibility for achieving which objectives? Should the central bank concentrate on the nation's real output goals while the government focuses on the private payments balance, or should the assignments be reversed? This question is known as the **assignment problem** in policymaking. Let's consider how the problem might be addressed in various circumstances that a nation with an open economy might face.

THE POLICY ASSIGNMENT PROBLEM WITH LOW CAPITAL MOBILITY   As noted in Chapter 9, a key factor influencing how fiscal policies affect a nation's private payments balance is the mobility of capital. Recall that when barriers such as capital controls inhibit flows of financial resources across a nation's borders, the balance of payments, *BP,* schedule of real income–interest rate combinations that maintain a private payments balance of zero is relatively less elastic in the relevant range as compared with the *LM* schedule, as shown in panels (a) and (b) of Figure 14–14 on the next page. Each panel also displays the same initial *IS-LM* equilibrium point, denoted point *A,* which is below and to the right of the *BP* schedule, so that the nation experiences a private payments deficit. At point *A* in both panels, the interest rate is too low, at r_1, to induce capital inflows sufficient to overcome the sizable barriers to such flows, and real income is sufficiently high, at y_1, that import spending exceeds exports and generates a trade deficit.

Let's suppose that the country's exchange rate is fixed, at least in the near term, so that the *BP* schedule is stationary. In addition, let's consider a situation in which the nation's policymakers have two goals. One is to achieve a zero private payments balance, which will require attaining an *IS-LM* equilibrium point on the *BP* schedule. This goal is the nation's international, or *external balance,* objective. The other goal is to achieve a target real income level, denoted y^*. This is the nation's domestic, or *internal*

ASSIGNMENT PROBLEM: The problem of determining whether monetary or fiscal policymakers should assume responsibility for achieving external balance or internal balance objectives.

Figure 14–14   Achieving Internal and External Balance with Low Capital Mobility

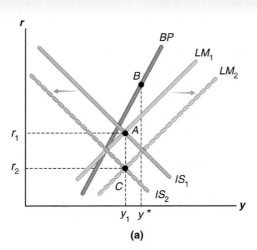

(a)

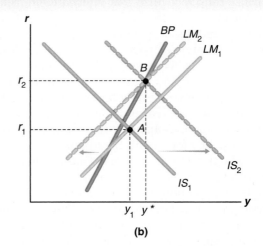

(b)

If capital is relatively immobile, then the *BP* schedule giving real income–interest rate combinations consistent with a private payments balance of zero is relatively steeply sloped. Both panels (a) and (b) illustrate the same initial equilibrium at point *A*, which lies below and to the right of the *BP* schedule, implying a private payments deficit. In panel (a), the central bank tries to attain internal balance by aiming to achieve a target level of real income, *y**, which requires a rightward shift of the *LM* schedule. At the same time, the government's fiscal authority aims to achieve external balance along the *BP* schedule, which requires a leftward shift of the *IS* schedule. The net result illustrated in this figure is a

new equilibrium at point *C* even farther below and to the right of the *BP* schedule, implying a greater private payments deficit. Hence, there is a mismatched assignment of internal and external balance objectives in panel (a). Panel (b) illustrates the result of a correct policy assignment: the central bank aims to achieve external balance at point *A* by shifting the *LM* schedule leftward; at the same time, the government's fiscal authority shifts the *IS* schedule rightward. This assignment achieves point *B*. Here, the policymakers achieve both their internal and external balance objectives.

balance, objective. The issue that the country's policymakers face at point *A* is how to achieve both these objectives simultaneously. Doing so will entail attaining a new *IS-LM* equilibrium at point *B* in each panel.

A POOR ASSIGNMENT   To see why the assignment of domestic and international objectives to the appropriate policymaker is so important, consider the contrasting assignments illustrated in panels (a) and (b). In panel (a), the central bank aims to achieve internal balance by varying the quantity of money as needed to attain the real income objective, while the government conducts fiscal policies that are necessary to pursue the external balance objective of a zero private payments balance. With this policy assignment, the appropriate monetary policy action to aim for the real income target y^* is an increase in the nominal money stock. This action shifts the *LM* schedule rightward, to LM_2. At the same time, however, the appropriate fiscal policy action at point *A* is to reduce government expenditures or raise taxes, thereby causing the *IS* schedule to shift leftward to IS_2. This action reduces equilibrium real income, thereby restraining imports. The resulting *IS-LM* equilibrium is a real income–interest rate combination such as y_1 and r_2 at point C in panel (a). Yet point C could be even farther below the *BP* schedule than point A with no net increase in real income. Thus, the nation's private payments deficit problem will *worsen* even as it experiences no progress toward attaining its internal balance objective.

SWITCHING THE ASSIGNMENT   Clearly, panel (a) of Figure 14–14 illustrates a situation in which the monetary and fiscal policymakers have been assigned the *wrong goals*. As a result, their efforts to pursue their individual objectives push the economy *away* from those goals. Panel (b) shows what happens if the assignment of objectives is reversed, so that the central bank strives to achieve external balance while the government's fiscal authority seeks to attain internal balance. To aim for external balance, the central bank needs to reduce the money stock and shift the *LM* schedule leftward. The fiscal authority needs to increase its spending or cut taxes, thereby shifting the *IS* schedule rightward and raising equilibrium real income toward the target level. This combination of policy objectives and actions enables the policymakers to attain *both* internal balance *and* external balance at point B in panel (b).

THE POLICY ASSIGNMENT PROBLEM WITH HIGHLY MOBILE CAPITAL   It might be tempting to conclude from the previous example that there is a single solution to the assignment problem, namely, that the government should aim its fiscal policies at an internal balance objective while the central bank strives to achieve external balance. Unfortunately, this assignment is likely to be correct only in the situation we considered in Figure 14–14, where the exchange rate is fixed and there is low capital mobility. If we alter either of these background conditions, the nature of the assignment problem will change.

ANOTHER INCORRECT ASSIGNMENT   To see this, consider Figure 14–15 on the following page. In both panel (a) and panel (b), the *BP* schedule is much more elastic in the relevant range than it was in Figure 14–14, indicating that capital is highly mobile across the nation's borders. Again, point A in both panels depicts an initial situation in which there is a private payments deficit and real income is below its target level. Panel (a) shows a possible result of assigning the external balance objective to the central bank and the internal balance objective to the government when capital is highly mobile. The central bank reduces the money stock, which raises the equilibrium interest rate and induces capital inflows that improve the private payments balance. Then the government increases its spending or cuts taxes in an effort to raise equilibrium real income. The resulting *IS-LM* equilibrium will depend on the shapes of the *IS* and *LM* schedules and on the extent to which the policy actions shift those schedules, but a *possible* result is point C in panel (a). At this possible equilibrium point, the nation experiences a private payments surplus, and real income is lower than before. The policymakers did not achieve their objectives. Thus, the correct policy assignment when capital mobility is low could turn out to be the incorrect assignment when capital mobility is high.

Figure 14–15   Achieving Internal and External Balance with High Capital Mobility

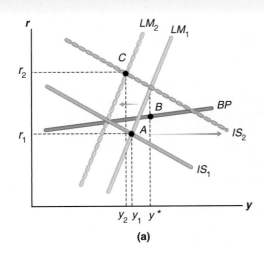

(a)

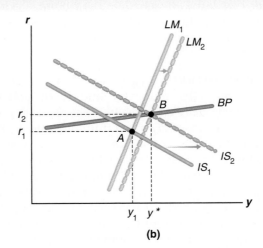

(b)

Both panels (a) and (b) illustrate the same initial equilibrium at point *A*, which lies below and to the right of the *BP* schedule, implying a private payments deficit. In panel (a), the central bank tries to attain external balance, which requires a leftward shift of the *LM* schedule toward the *BP* schedule. At the same time, the government's fiscal authority tries to achieve internal balance by aiming at a target level of real income, *y**. This requires a rightward shift of the *IS* schedule. The net result illustrated in this figure is a new equilibrium at a lower real output level at point *C* above and

to the left of the *BP* schedule, yielding a private payments surplus. Hence, there is a mismatched assignment of internal and external balance objectives in panel (a). Panel (b) illustrates the result of a correct policy assignment. Here, the central bank aims to achieve internal balance by shifting the *LM* schedule rightward toward *y** while the government's fiscal authority shifts the *IS* schedule rightward in pursuit of external balance along the *BP* schedule. This assignment achieves point *B*, at which the policymakers achieve both their internal and external balance objectives.

REVERSING THE ASSIGNMENT, AGAIN   Panel (b) shows what could happen if the policy assignments are reversed, so that the central bank seeks to attain internal balance while the government strives to achieve external balance when there is high capital mobility. To raise equilibrium real income, the central bank increases the money stock and shifts the *LM* schedule rightward. At the same time, the government increases its spending or cuts taxes. This shifts the *IS* schedule rightward, raising the equilibrium interest rate and stimulating more capital inflows that will improve the private payments balance. Thus, after this reassignment of policy goals, the nation's internal and external balance objectives could be attained at point *B*.

The assignment of policy objectives is not a trivial issue, as the examples in Figures 14–14 and 14–15 indicate. These examples illustrate that the degree of capital mobility is an important consideration in assigning goals to policymakers. Nevertheless, in both examples we assumed a fixed exchange rate. As you can imagine, allowing for the possibility of a floating exchange rate would further complicate the policy assignment problem. This is why disagreements are not uncommon between a central bank, such as the Federal Reserve, and a government fiscal agency, such as the

U.S. Treasury (under the direction of the president and Congress), over which policymaker should be focusing on which objectives. Changing macroeconomic circumstances can necessitate changes in the appropriate assignment of policy objectives, and both policymakers may take time to recognize this and agree to an alteration of the goals upon which they should focus their attention.

FUNDAMENTAL ISSUE #5

What is the assignment problem faced by monetary and fiscal policymakers of a nation that seeks to attain both domestic and international policy goals?
The assignment problem refers to the difficulty of ascertaining whether a monetary or fiscal policymaker should pursue an internal balance objective such as a real income target or an external balance objective such as a zero private payments balance. An incorrect assignment of these objectives between a central bank and a government fiscal authority can lead to greater departures from external and internal balance goals. To obtain a correct assignment of objectives that can permit both policymakers to achieve these goals simultaneously, the policymakers must take into account the extent to which capital is mobile and whether the exchange rate is fixed or flexible. Consequently, solving the assignment problem is a potentially complicated undertaking.

Inflation Targeting Gains New Adherents

In most modern approaches to macroeconomics, variations in the price level cannot influence a nation's real output in the long run. Consequently, these theories imply that higher inflation cannot permanently reduce a country's rate of unemployment.

Establishing Inflation Targets

This conclusion has convinced several nations to stop attempting to stabilize output and employment in the short run. Instead, New Zealand, Canada, the United Kingdom, Sweden, and Australia have adopted the policy approach of *inflation targeting*. With this approach, policymakers aim to keep the actual rate of inflation very close to an announced target level.

As you can see in panels (a) and (b) of Figure 14–16, the New Zealand and Canadian inflation-targeting efforts have done much to smooth inflation in those countries. Before New Zealand adopted an inflation-targeting approach to monetary policy in 1990, the inflation rate averaged more than 10 percent per year, but since then the average annual inflation rate has been below 2 percent. Annual inflation in Canada now hovers very close to the same rate, which is noticeably below the rates of inflation the nation experienced prior to implementing inflation targeting in 1991.

The Advantages of Inflation Targeting

A key advantage of inflation targeting is its transparency. It is easy to measure actual inflation rates and see if they fall within target ranges specified by central banks. Furthermore, if people believe that inflation will remain steady, they will be less worried about potential redistribution effects arising from unanticipated inflation. Hence, individuals and businesses will feel more comfortable entering into nominal contracts that assume a stable rate of inflation.

Thus, inflation targeting can provide a foundation for greater constancy in production and investment decisions, which in turn can contribute to greater real output and employment stability. In principle, therefore, inflation targeting is an optimal approach to enable central banks to aim for long-run stability of output and employment as well as greater price stability.

Research Project

What macroeconomic theories indicate that inflation targeting might lead to more volatility of employment and output in the short run, if not in the long run? According to these theories, what factors could lead to greater employment and output variability?

Web Resources

1. How does the New Zealand government set up an inflation-targeting contract with the nation's central bank? Go to the home page of the Bank of New Zealand (http://www.rbnz.govt.nz/), and then click on "Policy Targets Agreement" in the upper-right-hand margin.

2. How does inflation targeting work in Canada? Find out by going to the home page of the Bank of Canada (http://www.bankofcanada.ca), clicking on "Monetary Policy" in the left margin, and then clicking on "Inflation" and "Inflation-Control Target."

Figure 14–16   Inflation Targeting in New Zealand and Canada

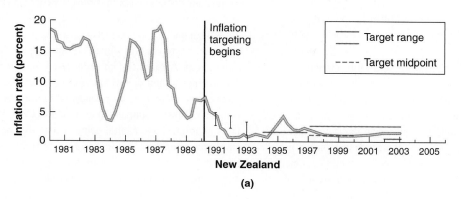

New Zealand

(a)

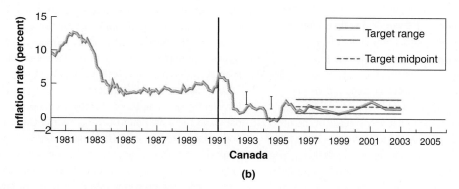

Canada

(b)

Since the central banks of New Zealand and Canada implemented inflation targeting, the two nations' inflation rates have dropped significantly and become less volatile.

SOURCES: Bank of New Zealand and Bank of Canada.

1. **The Ultimate Goals of Macroeconomic Policy:** These are the final aims of the policy strategies and actions conducted by the government fiscal authority or central bank. In the United States, the Employment Act of 1946 and the Humphrey-Hawkins Act of 1978 established low and stable inflation, high and stable output growth, and high and stable employment as formal ultimate objectives of macroeconomic policy.

2. **Why a Central Bank Might Use an Intermediate Monetary Policy Target:** A central bank such as the Federal Reserve typically adopts an intermediate target because it faces limitations on the availability of data on its ultimate objectives and different views about how monetary policy actions influence these ultimate policy goals. Any intermediate target for monetary policy should be a macroeconomic variable that can be observed more frequently than ultimate goal variables. In addition, this variable should be easy to measure, controllable via monetary policy actions, and closely related to ultimate policy objectives. The menu of possible intermediate target variables includes money and credit aggregates, interest rates, and nominal GDP.

3. **The Pros and Cons of Alternative Intermediate Monetary Policy Targets:** On the one hand, adopting a nominal interest-rate target makes aggregate demand more stable when money demand is highly volatile while aggregate desired expenditures are relatively stable. On the other hand, using a monetary aggregate as an intermediate target stabilizes aggregate demand when aggregate desired expenditures are variable while money demand is relatively stable. Nominal GDP targeting automatically stabilizes aggregate demand and also minimizes the inflationary effects of variations in aggregate supply. Nevertheless, accurate nominal GDP data are available less frequently than data on interest rates and monetary aggregates.

4. **Key Propositions and Fiscal Policy Prescriptions of Supply-Side Economics:** One key proposition advanced by supply-side economists is that governments allocate saving and investment less efficiently than the private sector. This has led supply-side economists in particular to argue for governments to operate without running persistent deficits or surpluses. Another fundamental proposition is that taxing the incomes of households and businesses influences their incentives to save, invest, or supply labor, thereby affecting economic growth. Supply-side economists contend that tax rates on interest and capital gains income that households earn from saving, income that firms earn from capital investment, and income workers earn in the form of wages and salaries should be reduced, or perhaps eliminated, to spur economic growth.

5. **The Assignment Problem Faced by Monetary and Fiscal Policymakers of a Nation That Seeks to Attain Both Domestic and International Policy Goals:** The assignment problem is the question of whether a monetary or fiscal policymaker should concentrate on achieving an internal balance objective such as a real income target or an external balance objective such as a zero private payments balance. Incorrectly assigning these objectives between the central bank and the government fiscal authority can cause both policymakers to end up further away from both goals. Achieving a correct assignment of objectives requires that policymakers consider the extent to which capital is mobile and whether the exchange rate is fixed or flexible. As a result, solving the assignment problem is a potentially complex task.

Self-Test Questions

(Answers to odd-numbered questions may be found on the Web at **http://macro. swcollege.com** under "Student Resources.")

1. From a day-to-day perspective, what is the primary way that the Federal Reserve conducts monetary policy? Why is this the case? Explain.

2. Briefly discuss the rationales for a central bank's adoption of an intermediate target. Which do you think is most important? Explain your reasoning.

3. List the key criteria for choosing among alternative intermediate targets of monetary policy. Does any one criterion seem to be more important than the others? Why?

4. Suppose that household consumption spending and investment expenditures by firms are highly volatile, as compared with past years. At the same time, financial market conditions and desired money holdings by households and

firms have been relatively stable. If you were in charge at the Fed and wanted to choose between targeting an interest rate or a monetary aggregate, which would you choose? Why?

5. What are the key advantages of using nominal GDP as an intermediate target of monetary policy? What are the disadvantages? Explain.

6. How can the national debt be a burden on future generations? Is it *necessarily* a burden? Justify your answer.

7. A "stock" is an amount at a point in time, while a "flow" is an addition to a stock that takes place over time. Is the national debt a stock or a flow? What about the federal deficit?

8. Use the *IS-LM* model to trace through the effects of an increase in the government's budget surplus in the traditional Keynesian model. Does total private spending rise by as much as the increase in the government's surplus? Why or why not?

9. In your own words, explain the basic issue associated with the assignment problem. Why is solving this problem important?

Problems

(Answers to odd-numbered problems may be found on the Web at **http://macro. swcollege.com** under "Student Resources.")

1. Suppose that the equation for the *IS* schedule is $r = 5.7 - (0.3 \times y)$, where the nominal interest rate r is expressed as a percentage and real income y is in trillions of real dollars.

   a. To achieve its target level for real income, the Federal Reserve has determined that it should set its target interest rate equal to 3 percent. What is the Fed's target income level?

   b. Simultaneous unexpected declines in autonomous investment and autonomous consumption have shifted the *IS* schedule leftward by 3 trillion real dollars at each possible interest rate. If the Fed leaves its target interest rate unchanged, what is the new equilibrium income level? (Hint: There are two ways to determine the answer. One is much easier than the other, because it involves drawing a diagram and using the answer from part a instead of working out the math. But you can do it both ways to check your answer.)

2. The equation for the *LM* schedule is $r = (2 \times M) + (0.5 \times y)$, where the nominal interest rate r is expressed as a percentage, real income y is in trillions of real dollars, and M is the nominal quantity of money. The equation for the *IS* schedule is $r = 8 - (0.5 \times y)$.

   a. The Federal Reserve has determined that to achieve its target level of real income, it should establish a target for the money stock of $1 trillion. What is the target income level? What is the equilibrium interest rate at this income level?

   b. Suppose that the *IS* schedule shifts leftward by 3 trillion real dollars. What is the new equilibrium level of real income if the Fed maintains its target for the quantity of money?

   c. Now suppose that the Fed had decided to establish a target interest rate at the interest rate you determined in part a. In the face of the leftward shift of the *IS* schedule in part b, what would the new equilibrium level of real income have been under this interest-rate target? Would the Fed have been better off or worse off if it had used the interest rate as an intermediate target?

Test your understanding of the material covered in this chapter by taking the Chapter 14 online quiz at http://macro.swcollege.com.

Online Application

This chapter provided a brief overview of how the Federal Reserve conducts monetary policy. This application allows you to obtain more information about the policy tools and procedures in other countries.

Internet URL: http://www.bis.org

Title: *The Bank for International Settlements*

Navigation: At the above home page of the address, click on *Publications and Statistics.* In the left margin, click on *Economic Papers.* Then go to question 1.

Application: Read the discussion, and answer the following questions:

1. Click on *The implementation of monetary policy in industrialized countries: a survey* (by Claudio Borio). Download the PDF file and skim the article. Are there more similarities or differences in how monetary policy is conducted in these nations? What appears to be the predominant intermediate targeting procedure in these countries?

2. Back up to the previous Web page. Click on *Policy Papers.* Then click on *Monetary policy operating procedures in emerging market economies* (also by Claudio Borio). Download this PDF file and skim the article. Answer the same questions as in question 1. Also, does the conduct of monetary policy in emerging economies appear to differ in any way from how monetary policy is conducted in industrialized countries?

For Group Study and Analysis: Go back to the BIS home page, and click on "Central Banks." This facility provides links to a number of central banks around the world. Distribute countries (perhaps by geographic region) to groups of students to explore for information about the structure and functions of the central banks. Reconvene the entire class, and review the differences and similarities across this large set of central banks.

Selected References

and Further Reading

Cover, James, and David VanHoose. "Political Pressures, Credibility, and the Choice of the Optimal Monetary Policy Instrument." *Journal of Economics and Business* 52 (July/August 2000): 325–341.

Dwyer, Gerald, and R. W. Hafer. "The Federal Government's Budget Surplus: Cause for Celebration?" Federal Reserve Bank of Atlanta *Economics Review* 83 (Third Quarter, 1998): 42–51.

Federal Reserve Bank of Kansas City. *Budget Deficits and Debt: Issues and Options.* Kansas City, Mo.: 1995.

Federal Reserve Bank of New York. *Intermediate Targets and Indicators for Monetary Policy: A Critical Survey.* New York: 1990.

Fischer, Stanley. "Toward an Understanding of the Costs of Inflation: II." In Stanley Fischer, ed., *Indexing, Inflation, and Economic Policy,* pp. 35–69. Cambridge, Mass.: MIT Press, 1986.

Fischer, Stanley, and Franco Modigliani. "Toward an Understanding of the Real Effects and Costs of Inflation." In Stanley Fischer, ed., *Indexing, Inflation, and Economic Policy*, pp. 7–33. Cambridge, Mass.: MIT Press, 1986.

Friedman, Benjamin. "Targets, Instruments, and Indicators of Monetary Policy." *Journal of Monetary Economics* 1 (October 1975): 443–473.

Minford, Patrick, Francesco Perugini, and Naveen Srinivasan. "The Observational Equivalence of the Taylor Rule and Taylor-Type Rules." Warwick University, 2002.

Poole, William. "Optimal Choice of Monetary Policy Instruments in a Simple Stochastic Macro Model." *Quarterly Journal of Economics* 84 (May 1970): 197–216.

Viard, Alan. "The New Budget Outlook: Policymakers Respond to the Surplus." Federal Reserve Bank of Dallas *Economics and Financial Review* 83 (Second Quarter, 1999): 2–15.

macroxtra!

Log on to the MacroXtra Web site at http://macroxtra.swcollege.com for additional learning resources such as practice quizzes, Interactive Key Graphs, readings, and additional economic applications.

15

What Can Policymakers Accomplish?—

Rules versus Discretion in Macroeconomic Policy

FUNDAMENTAL ISSUES

1. What are policy time lags, and how might they cause well-meaning macroeconomic policymakers to destabilize the economy?

2. What are the main arguments favoring discretionary policymaking?

3. Why is policy credibility a crucial factor in maintaining low inflation?

4. How might monetary policy credibility be achieved?

5. How might fiscal policy credibility be achieved?

6. What approaches have some nations with fixed exchange rates followed to make their policies credible?

By and large, European governments have generous unemployment insurance programs. A few nations provide compensation that replaces roughly 100 percent of an individual's lost wages. Several provide benefits for a year or even much longer. In some countries "unemployment" compensation is available even though the recipient still has a job and receives weekly paychecks!

Some economists believe that if all other factors are constant, the relative generosity of national unemployment compensation systems can influence countries' inflation rates. This proposed relationship between unemployment insurance and inflation has nothing to do with potential supply-side effects on firms' labor costs and incentives for firms to produce output. Instead, the idea is that central bank officials' decisions about monetary policy actions may hinge in part on how well protected workers are from the ill effects of economic contractions.

According to this theory, if central bankers know that anti-inflationary poli-cies they implement are less likely to harm workers—and if everyone else also knows that the central bank officials recognize this—then the officials have a greater incentive to adopt such policies to keep inflation low. Consequently, countries with more generous unemployment insurance programs should expe-rience lower inflation, all other things being equal. Nations with relatively stingy unemployment compensation systems should experience higher annual rates of inflation.

Nearly every country on the planet has experienced inflation during the past several decades. Why do central banks, which can do so much to affect aggregate demands for goods and services within their nations, allow infla-tion to occur? Why don't they bind themselves to zero-inflation policies, at least on average? In this chapter you will learn about potential explana-tions for why inflation is such a common experience throughout the world.

Time Lags in Policymaking and the Case for Rules

A fundamental problem faced by any policymaker, be it the president of the United States, the Congress, the Federal Reserve, a public utility, or a college's board of trustees, is the existence of **policy time lags.** A policy time lag is the interval between the need for a policy action and the ulti-mate effects of that action on an economic variable. Any policymaker faces three types of constraints on its ability to make the best policy choices that it can as quickly as these choices should be made:

1. At any given time, policymakers face limited information about cur-rent events, particularly in the presence of time lags.

2. Policymakers are fallible and face constraints on their abilities to rec-ognize and respond appropriately to changing circumstances, particu-larly in light of lags in their recognition of varying circumstances.

3. Policymakers are constrained by their lack of certainty about the actual effects of the policies they may enact and the timing of those effects.

Together, these constraints can slow policymakers' responses even in situ-ations when speedy reactions are needed to attain the policymakers' goals.

Time Lags in Macroeconomic Policy

Macroeconomic policymaking involves three types of time lags: the *recog-nition lag,* the *response lag,* and the *transmission lag.* Let's discuss each in turn before considering their broader consequences.

THE RECOGNITION LAG A key problem that fiscal and monetary policymakers confront as they pursue their ultimate inflation, output, employment, and balance of payments objectives is limited current information. Although

POLICY TIME LAG: The time interval between the need for a countercyclical monetary policy action and the ultimate effects of that action on an economic variable.

RECOGNITION LAG: The interval between the need for a countercyclical policy action and the recognition of this need by a policymaker.

RESPONSE LAG: The interval between the recognition of a need for a countercyclical policy action and the actual implementation of that action.

government statisticians can estimate nominal GDP data weekly, they can compile data on GDP, the unemployment rate, the price level, and international transactions only monthly. Even then, the statisticians often revise these monthly computations when they discover measurement or calculation errors. Although the statisticians try to make their data as reliable as possible, computations of annualized GDP growth rates for certain quarters have had to be revised by more than 50 percent! Hence, policymakers cannot always rely on the accuracy of initial values for these macroeconomic goal variables.

Near-term data uncertainties complicate the lives of policymakers. To see why, suppose that a nation's inflation rate increases substantially owing to an unexpected rise in aggregate demand. Other things unchanged, an appropriate central bank response would be to cut back on the growth rate of the money stock. This action would help to curtail the rise in aggregate demand and alleviate resulting upward price pressures. In light of data limitations, however, central bank officials might not realize that inflation had started to rise until a number of weeks had passed.

The time between the need for a macroeconomic policy action and policymakers' recognition of that need is called the **recognition lag.** Sometimes the recognition lag is only a matter of a few weeks, but it can be longer. For instance, suppose that central bank officials notice the rise in the inflation rate, but are uncertain of its causes. Some officials might speculate that recent but temporary upticks in wage costs of businesses might be responsible, indicating no need for the central bank to take action. Misleading signals such as this might delay central bank action to contain inflation for several additional weeks. Consequently, the recognition lag could easily increase from a few weeks to a few months. This is true for both fiscal and monetary policy.

THE RESPONSE LAG Even after policymakers reach the conclusion that altered macroeconomic circumstances require a policy change, they may not decide on the appropriate action to take for some time. The **response lag** is the time between the recognition of the need for a change in macroeconomic policy and the actual implementation of that change.

In the United States, the response lag for monetary policy should never be more than six to eight weeks, because this is the typical interlude between formal meetings of Federal Reserve policymakers. In fact, the response lag for U.S. monetary policy could be shorter than this, because Federal Reserve officials across the nation communicate daily. The monetary policy response lag could be longer, however, if central bank officials have difficulty reaching a consensus on the best policy to implement. Faced with an observed rise in the inflation rate, for instance, some officials might contend that a swift, significant response is needed. Other officials, in contrast, might argue for a more gradual, measured response. Such disagreements could lead to delays in central bank policy actions, which could lengthen the monetary policy response lag significantly.

The response lag is often even longer for fiscal policy. In the United States, for instance, the executive office of the president and a majority of the 535 representatives and senators in the legislative branch must reach agreement on changes in the federal budget intended to address a given situation. This can be a laborious task that can take many months. Indeed, political gridlock can inhibit fiscal policy actions for years. Consequently, the response lag is typically much longer for fiscal policy than for monetary policy.

THE TRANSMISSION LAG   It takes time for a fiscal or monetary policy action to transmit its effects to overall economic activity. The time that passes before an implemented policy fully exerts its macroeconomic effects is the **transmission lag.** In earlier chapters, we have shifted schedules and envisioned the effects of a particular policy action on real income or the price level without regard to the time that it takes for such effects actually to occur. In fact, months or even years may pass before the effects of policy actions are transmitted to ultimate policy goal variables. Current estimates indicate, for instance, that the average monetary policy transmission lag is just over twelve months. Thus, together the recognition, response, and transmission lags could cause well over a year to elapse between the initial need for a monetary policy action and that action's final effects on the economy. Given the longer response lags that are common in fiscal policy implementation—sometimes several years—time lags of fiscal policy could be even longer.

Time Lags and the Case for Policy Rules

Time lags can pose a real problem for policymakers. To see why, consider Figure 15-1 on the next page. The curve labeled y^a in panel (a) shows the path that real income will follow in the *absence* of any policy actions. For simplicity, we assume that this anticipated path of real income is a relatively smooth business cycle. The curve labeled y^p depicts the path of the policymaker's *planned* contributions to real income in light of its anticipation that real income in the absence of its policy actions will follow the path y^a.

SUCCESSFUL COUNTERCYCLICAL POLICY   We assume that the policymaker's plan is to pursue a *countercyclical* policy strategy by adding to its contributions to real income when the policymaker anticipates that real income will decline. Conversely, the policymaker will reduce its contributions to real income when it expects real income to rise.

At any given time, the actual level of real income in the presence of policy actions, denoted y, will be the sum of y^a and y^p. Note that the figure assumes that macroeconomic policymaking can add permanently to total real income. As we have discussed in earlier chapters, not all economists agree that this can take place. Nevertheless, for purposes of illustration, we shall assume here and in other diagrams in this chapter that policy at least makes some permanent contributions. You should keep in mind, however, that according to the new classical and real-business-cycle theories, policy actions can at best cause short-term variations in real income.

If the policymaker successfully pursues its countercyclical policy strategy, the actual path of real income, y, will be smoother than the anticipated real income path in the absence of policy actions, y^a. In other words, the policymaker will successfully dampen the business cycle.

TRANSMISSION LAG: The interval that elapses between the implementation of an intended countercyclical policy and its ultimate effects on an economic variable.

451

CHAPTER 15   What Can Policymakers Accomplish?—Rules versus Discretion in Macroeconomic Policy

Figure 15–1   How Policy Time Lags Can Make Well-Intentioned Policy Destabilizing

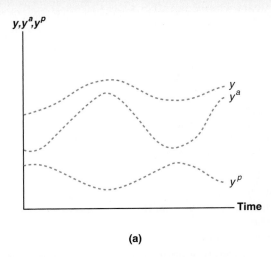

(a)

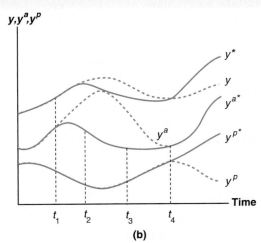

(b)

Panel (a) illustrates a possible situation in which policy actions help to stabilize real income over time. The path labeled y^a illustrates a hypothetical anticipated path for real income in the absence of policy actions. The path labeled y^p shows a planned countercyclical path for contributions to real income based on macroeconomic policy, which causes the path of total real income, y, to be smoother than it would have been otherwise. Panel (b) shows the potential result of policy time lags. Here, the path of actual real income in the absence of policy, y^{a*}, falls below the path anticipated by the policymaker, y^a, beginning at time t_1. Because of the recognition lag, however, the policymaker fails to discover this has occurred until time t_2. The response lag slows the policymaker's response to this change until time t_3, and the transmission lag holds up the actual effects of the policy action until time t_4. By this time, the new policy's contributions to real income are procyclical and destabilizing.

HOW TIME LAGS CAN WORSEN BUSINESS CYCLES   The same curves shown in panel (a) of Figure 15–1 appear as dashed curves in panel (b). The solid curves, however, depict actual movements in real income that potentially could arise in the presence of policy time lags if the policymaker reacts to unexpected departures of real income from the path originally anticipated. In this example, we assume that the path of real income without any policy effects, labeled y^{a*}, drops below the level that the policymaker had anticipated beginning at a point in time denoted t_1. The path of y^{a*} then stays below its anticipated path until the time t_4, when it again returns to the anticipated path.

The time that passes between t_1 and t_2 is the time interval that elapses before the policymaker realizes that the actual path of real income has fallen below the anticipated path, or the *recognition lag.* At time t_2, the policymaker has no way of knowing that without policy actions real income ultimately will return to its anticipated path at time t_4. If the policymaker wishes to adjust its policy plan in an effort to maintain a countercyclical policy, then at time t_3 it may decide to implement a change in policy intended to contribute more to real income. The time that passes between

t_2 and t_3 is the interval between recognition of the need for this policy change and its implementation, or the *response lag*.

Finally, a *transmission lag* occurs between t_3 and t_4 before the policy change begins to have an effect. By time t_4, the policy change finally begins to take effect, and the policy's contribution to real income increases. As a result, the actual path of policy contributions to real income, denoted y^{p*} turns upward, whereas the policymaker's *original* plan called for a reduction in policy contributions to real income beginning at time t_4. At t_4, however, real income in the absence of any policy contribution has already *returned* to its anticipated path. Consequently, the policymaker's well-meaning effort to stabilize actual real income ends up yielding a policy-influenced real income path denoted y^*, which is the sum of the y^{a*} and y^{p*} curves, that is *more variable* than it would have been if the policymaker had not reacted to the temporary fall in real income.

Thus, in this example, even though the policymaker has good intentions to conduct a countercyclical policy:

Time lags in recognition, response, and transmission can end up producing a *procyclical* policy.

The policymaker would have come closer to its original objective of smoothing the business cycle if it had stuck to its original planned policy path, y^p. (As the European Union considers adding new member nations, some economists fret that the structure of the European Central Bank will lengthen the time lags of monetary policymaking; see on the next page *Global Notebook: Will Expansion of the European Union Lengthen Policy Time Lags?*)

POLICY DISCRETION VERSUS A POLICY RULE   Almost fifty years ago, the Nobel Prize–winning economist Milton Friedman argued that situations such as the one illustrated in panel (b) of Figure 15–1 could be common occurrences. The essence of Friedman's argument was that monetary policymakers may have good intentions, but nevertheless their well-meaning attempts to stabilize real income may contribute to cyclical fluctuations in real income. This, Friedman argued, is a fundamental flaw arising from **discretionary policymaking,** or the process of undertaking macroeconomic policy responses on an ad hoc basis rather than staying the course with a fixed policy plan. In the presence of lengthy and variable policy time lags, Friedman contended, discretionary policymaking more often than not can end up destabilizing the economy.

This argument led Friedman to propose that a monetary or fiscal policymaker should adopt a **policy rule.** Under this approach, a central bank or government *binds* or *commits* itself to a strategy and follows it no matter what events take place. In Friedman's view, adhering to a clearly articulated policy rule should, on average, prevent unintentional destabilizing actions by policymakers. The simplest type of policy rule is for a policymaker to neither add nor subtract from its contributions to real income. For instance, the central bank could strive to maintain a constant growth rate for the nominal money stock. Another type of policy rule is a tax system that works as an *automatic* stabilizer, as we discussed in Chapter 7. Such a system somewhat offsets a decline or expansion in equilibrium real income by automatically reducing or raising tax collections, respectively.

DISCRETIONARY POLICYMAKING: The act of responding to economic events as they occur, rather than proceeding as the policymaker might previously have planned in the absence of those events.

POLICY RULE: A commitment to a fixed strategy no matter what happens to other economic variables.

Will Expansion of the European Union Lengthen Policy Time Lags?

Today, the European Union (EU) is a collection of national economies. Nevertheless, its oft-repeated objective is to develop into a single continental economy with ever-more-coordinated monetary and fiscal policies. Currently, the EU is contemplating expanding from 15 members to 20—and possibly to as many as 27—during the next few years. As it grows, however, the potential for significant policy time lags to develop will also increase.

Broadening the Euro's Circulation: A Recipe for Longer Time Lags in Monetary Policy?

The European System of Central Banks is managed by an administrative council composed of a six-member executive board and the governors of the national central banks of members of the European Monetary Union (EMU). Not all EU nations are members of the EMU, but as the EU expands, several existing and new EU members are likely to also seek membership in the EMU. In principle, therefore, if the EU increases to encompass 27 member nations, the council governing the European System of Central Banks ultimately could have 33 members—considerably more than the Federal Reserve Board's 7 governors and 12 FOMC members. Such an expansion would undoubtedly broaden the scope for disagreements in interpreting economic data, thereby increasing the recognition lag of EMU monetary policy. It could also make reaching agreement on appropriate policy actions more problematic, thereby lengthening the monetary policy response lag.

Furthermore, enlarging the EMU could widen the differences among the economies encompassed by the monetary union, thereby complicating the transmission mechanism of monetary policy. This could have the effect of lengthening the EMU monetary policy transmission lag.

Can EU Expansion and Fiscal Coordination Go Together?

The EU has complicated voting rules that give big countries extra votes when decisions are made about such issues as tax coordination and agricultural spending policies. As a result, under most circumstances roughly 70 percent of all votes cast would be required to pass most EU economic initiatives.

The problem is that as the size of the EU increases, so does the number of possible coalitions, from 32,768 for 15 EU members to about 130 million for 27 members. Naturally, this considerably reduces the probability that any economic policy initiative will be passed, thereby lengthening the likely response lag for coordinated EU fiscal policy actions.

For Critical Analysis
As the EMU and EU expand, how might member nations streamline their policymaking procedures to reduce policy time lags?

FUNDAMENTAL ISSUE #1

What are policy time lags, and how might they cause well-meaning macroeconomic policymakers to destabilize the economy? There are three types of policy time lags: (1) the recognition lag, or the time between the need for a macroeconomic policy action and a policymaker's realization of the need; (2) the response lag, or the interval between the recognition of the need for an action and the actual implementation of a policy change; and (3) the transmission lag, or the time from the implementation of a policy action and the action's ultimate effects on the economy. All told, these lags can sum to well over a year in duration. They can also lead a discretionary policymaker that responds to events as they apparently occur to enact a policy change that is procyclical, thereby destabilizing the economy. The existence of these lags is one argument in favor of policy rules, or fixed commitments to specific policy strategies.

Proponents of discretionary monetary and fiscal policies admit that policy time lags can pose serious problems for policymaking. Nevertheless, they contend that the potential social benefits of countercyclical policies are so great that macroeconomic policymakers should have the flexibility to attempt to smooth business cycles, rather than rigidly adhering to fixed rules. They also argue that central banks and governments are uniquely positioned to succeed in such endeavors more often than they fail.

Do Policymakers Have an Information Advantage?

One key argument favoring policy discretion is that situations can arise in which macroeconomic policymakers have more complete information about the economy than households and firms have. Policymakers may also be able to respond more fully to new information about changing market conditions.

As an illustration of the latter point, consider the modern Keynesian theory of wage contracting that we discussed in Chapter 12, in which workers and firms negotiate nominal wages in advance, based on the information that they have at that time. After the wages are set, the parties to the contract become better informed as economic events unfold. Unless wages are indexed to price changes, however, workers and firms cannot make any adjustments, aside from changes in employment that cause real output to fluctuate. Policymakers, in contrast, are not tied down to contracts and can vary their policy instruments in an effort to stabilize economic conditions and limit employment and output variations.

PROPOSED INFORMATION ADVANTAGES IN MONETARY POLICY   The preceding example is specific to a particular theory, however. It is possible that policymakers have other inherent information advantages over the private sector that will make a difference under any theory of how the economy functions.

In the case of monetary policy, a commonly proposed information advantage of a central bank is its constant presence in financial markets. The Federal Reserve, for instance, trades government securities and bonds denominated in foreign currencies nearly every day. It also has considerable ability to influence the nation's nominal money stock. In addition, it regulates a large portion of U.S. banks. Furthermore, Federal Reserve economists tabulate large bodies of macroeconomic data.

The Federal Reserve's various activities give it the opportunity to keep tabs *simultaneously* on the pulse of financial markets, developments in the market for money, changing circumstances in the banking system, and economic fluctuations. As a result, the Federal Reserve arguably has the unique capability to integrate information about all aspects of the national economy, thereby giving it an information advantage over the private sector. Proponents of policy flexibility and discretion argue that this capability also makes the Federal Reserve uniquely qualified to attempt to conduct countercyclical monetary policy.

PROPOSED INFORMATION ADVANTAGES IN FISCAL POLICY   Some observers also argue that fiscal policymakers have advantages in compiling and processing information about the economy that give them the ability to conduct successful countercyclical policies. In the executive branch of the U.S. government, for instance, the Office of Management and Budget collects and collates large volumes of data related to the federal government's budget. In the legislative branch, the Congressional Budget Office performs a similar role. The president's Council of Economic Advisers analyzes these and other sources of information to make economic forecasts and advise the president and cabinet officers.

ARE THE PROPOSED INFORMATION ADVANTAGES REAL OR ILLUSORY? Critics of discretionary policymaking counter that these supposed information advantages are, in fact, minimal or even nonexistent. They point to the sizable economic staffs of banks, other financial firms, and manufacturing corporations and to the elaborate economic consulting networks that give even small businesses access to significant volumes of information. Furthermore, the Internet has made considerable economic information available to anyone willing to invest some time and effort in locating it.

In the modern world, goes this counterargument, central bank or government policymakers are no more sophisticated than any well-trained, private individual. Consequently, there is no reason to believe that policymakers have any special ability to avoid the pitfalls of time lags and conduct countercyclical policies successfully.

As you will recall from Chapter 11, in the new classical theory policy actions can have real effects only if the actions are unanticipated by workers and firms. Otherwise, informed workers and firms will, on their own, alter their behavior in ways that lead to attainment of the economy's full-information, natural output level. New classical critics of discretionary policymaking therefore argue that, given the potential for policymakers to destabilize the economy in the presence of time lags and other impediments to their efforts, society would be better off if central banks and governments simply disseminated any information they have that households and firms do not possess. According to this view, any information advantage for policymakers is a two-edged sword, because it could lead to greater instability just as easily as it could permit policymakers to reduce cyclical fluctuations.

Do Policymakers Face Fewer Constraints?

As we noted in Chapters 11, 12, and 13, the rational expectations hypothesis revolutionized the way that macroeconomists think about the effects of monetary and fiscal policies. If households and firms form expectations rationally and take into account systematic policy actions, then policies cannot have real effects unless there are wage or price rigidities that keep market forces from nudging the economy toward its natural output level. Does this mean that policymakers have no ability to stabilize the economy in a world of rational expectations, even if they could minimize policy time lags and dodge other policy pitfalls?

THE ALTRUISTIC POLICYMAKER Those who promote discretionary policies argue that even in a rational expectations world, policymakers have a key advantage over private individuals and firms: policymakers do not feel obliged to profit from their actions. Suppose, for instance, that the stock market goes into a tailspin and bond prices plummet. Many financial institution managers and stockbrokers recognize that financial asset prices are falling below levels that are consistent with firms' profit potentials. Nevertheless, to protect depositors, clients, and their own institutions from further losses, the managers and brokers feel obliged to continue to sell—instead of starting to buy—shares of stock and bonds from their portfolios. As the values of the portfolios dwindle, all market participants experience a liquidity crunch. As the stock market sell-off becomes a rout, managers at many firms begin to worry that their access to bank loans during the coming weeks may be curtailed, forcing them to halt production and lay off workers. Then, the Federal Reserve announces that it stands ready to lend funds at a low nominal interest rate to any eligible institution. The stock and bond market tailspins suddenly halt as traders realize that liquidity will be easier to come by, requiring fewer sales from their stock and bond portfolios. Asset prices stabilize, and a crisis is averted.

This policy success story is not just a scenario. It actually happened in October 1987. Even though the immediate severity of the 1987 stock market crash paralleled the Great Crash of 1929, no economic depression followed. Indeed, the economy at most felt a tremor from the 1987 crash. The next recession did not occur until nearly four years later.

Proponents of discretionary policymaking see a deep message in this real-life story. The key to the Federal Reserve's 1987 success, they argue, was its willingness to lend funds, even though doing so would reduce the Federal Reserve System's income. After all, lending at low interest rates in the face of falling financial asset prices was not in the Fed's interest. Thus, lending at market rates would have raised the Federal Reserve's profits. Because it does not have a profit motive, the Federal Reserve can be *altruistic* and forgo its own interest in an effort to improve the well-being of the rest of society. The same argument can be offered in support of discretionary fiscal policymaking, because the government is not a profit-maximizing institution.

This argument lies at the heart of the **public interest theory** of policymaking. According to this perspective, central banks and government policymakers are in a unique position to pursue the broad interests of society as a whole. This position, in fact, gives them the capability to respond flexibly to changing circumstances in ways that private households and firms cannot.

ARE THERE LIMITS TO ALTRUISM IN POLICYMAKING?   A more cynical perspective on policymaking is offered by the **public choice theory.** Adherents to this theory argue that we should assume that all individuals, including policymakers, act *as if* they are pursuing their own self-interest. Although central bank or government officials are not trying to maximize profits, according to this theory, they are attempting to maximize their own satisfaction in their chosen occupations. Certainly, for many this effort could entail a measure of altruism. Nevertheless, the pursuit of self-interest could also, at a minimum, induce policymakers to spend public funds unwisely on plush offices, larger staffs than are really needed, and bloated salaries for themselves and their employees. Even as observers have applauded the Federal

PUBLIC INTEREST THEORY: A hypothesis that regards central banks and government policymakers as public servants that pursue the broad interests of society as a whole.

PUBLIC CHOICE THEORY: A hypothesis that views central banks and government policymakers as policymaking bodies composed of individuals who pursue their own self-interest.

Reserve's 1987 performance, they have questioned the 50 percent increase in its expenses that took place over the next few years.

The key macroeconomic issue raised by the public choice theory is whether policymakers' self-interests may stand in the way of the altruistic pursuit of broader economic goals. The president, for example, might justify increased spending on projects that benefit favored constituencies on the grounds that the spending is needed to counter a downturn in the business cycle. Likewise, members of Congress might justify tax cuts for industries that have donated to their campaigns as part of a fiscal policy action intended to stem a recession. Federal Reserve officials might promote interest-rate stability in part because such a policy will benefit banks that are key employers of former Federal Reserve policymakers and, consequently, may some day be *their* prospective employers.

Such concerns lead advocates of the public choice theory to argue that policy rules should be favored over policy discretion. Flexibility in policymaking, they contend, can promote self-interested policy actions just as easily as it can permit altruistic efforts to improve social welfare.

FUNDAMENTAL ISSUE #2

What are the main arguments favoring discretionary policymaking? One justification for discretionary policies is that policymakers may have information advantages because they can tabulate and collate diverse sets of data on macroeconomic activity. Another is that policymakers are not profit-maximizing institutions. Therefore they may be able to act altruistically by pursuing broad social welfare goals.

Discretionary Policy and Inflation

Another argument against discretionary policymaking hinges neither on policy time lags nor on the pursuit of self-interest by policymakers. Indeed, this view is consistent with policymakers having up-to-date information, responding quickly to that information, and influencing the economy immediately. It also allows for the possibility that policymakers may behave altruistically. Nevertheless, its key implication is that society will be worse off under discretionary policymaking than with a policy rule.

This alternative approach was developed by Robert Barro of Harvard University and David Gordon of Clemson University. Its focus is on the likely tendency of a discretionary macroeconomic policymaker to enact policies that are inflationary.

A Macroeconomic Policy Game and a Theory of Inflation

Recall from Chapter 13 that one of the few things that economists of different stripes agree on is that *game theory*—the theory of strategic interactions among individuals or institutions—can be a useful tool for addressing some macroeconomic issues. Barro and Gordon have applied game theory to the problem of rules versus discretion in macroeconomic policymaking. You need not have studied game theory to understand their essential argument, however. All you need are concepts that we have discussed in earlier chapters.

OUTPUT-MARKET EQUILIBRIUM AND ULTIMATE POLICY GOALS   Figure 15–2 illustrates the setting that Barro and Gordon have considered, using the modern Keynesian theory of wage contracting from Chapter 12 as a framework of analysis. Because nominal wages are contracted at the level W_1^c, the short-run aggregate supply schedule, $y^s(W_1^c)$, slopes upward. In the long run, when workers and firms are fully informed, nominal wages will adjust equiproportionately with price changes, so the long-run aggregate supply schedule, y_{LR}^s, is vertical at the economy's current long-run, full-information output level, denoted y_1. Finally, the aggregate demand schedule, y_1^d, slopes downward. A possible output-market equilibrium is point A, where all three schedules cross at the equilibrium price level, P_1. Hence, point A depicts a situation in which the short-run and the long-run equilibrium coincide. Workers and firms have negotiated a contract wage that happens to match the nominal wage that would have arisen if the labor market had equilibrated the demand for labor with the supply of labor, as in the classical model.

In addition, Figure 15–2 includes an output level denoted y^*, which is the ultimate output objective of a macroeconomic policymaker. A key assumption is that this target output level is *greater* than the full-information, natural output level y_1. The reason is that y^* is the **capacity output** for the economy, or the real GDP that firms could produce if labor and other factors of production were employed to their utmost. One reason that the natural, full-information output level typically lies below the capacity output level is the existence of income taxes. By imposing a marginal tax rate on

Figure 15–2   Output-Market Equilibrium and Policy Goals

A full long-run equilibrium in the market for real output takes place at a point where the aggregate demand, short-run aggregate supply, and long-run aggregate supply schedules cross, such as point A. At this equilibrium point, the long-run, full-information output level is equal to y_1, and the equilibrium price level is equal to P_1. The output level y^* is the capacity level of output, which workers and firms could produce but currently do not because other factors, such as income taxes and costs of regulation, reduce the long-run, full-information output level below the capacity level. The basic theory of inflationary policy proposes that policymakers would like to raise the level of output toward the capacity level but also would prefer not to increase the price level.

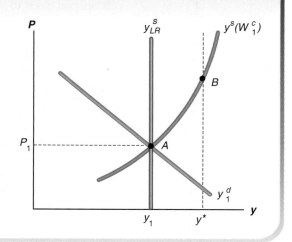

workers' incomes (see Chapter 7), the government induces workers to supply fewer labor services than they otherwise would have desired. As a result, firms produce less real output than they otherwise would have planned to produce in the absence of income taxes.

Another reason that the natural output level usually is below the capacity output level is the presence of government regulations. For instance, governments commonly restrict entry into various industries via licensing requirements, thereby restraining production of goods and services by those industries. Consequently, government regulations can reduce real output relative to what it would have been in the absence of regulations.

In addition to the capacity output goal y^*, the macroeconomic policymaker has one other ultimate objective—to minimize the inflation rate. Because the primary way to influence real output in the short run is through monetary or fiscal policy actions that change the position of the aggregate demand schedule, however, policymakers face a trade-off between their two goals. An increase in aggregate demand from point A in Figure 15–2 will cause a rightward movement along the short-run aggregate supply schedule, thereby raising real output toward the target y^* at point B. A rise in aggregate demand, however, will also cause the price level to rise, resulting in higher inflation. Therefore, remaining at the current equilibrium point A is more desirable from the standpoint of the policymaker's inflation objective. Consequently, a policymaker with both output and inflation goals typically will want aggregate demand to rise somewhat from point A, so as to increase real output. How much expansion of aggregate demand the policymaker will tolerate will depend on the relative weights that it places on its dual objectives of increasing output while keeping inflation as low as possible.

POLICY DISCRETION AND INFLATION   Figure 15–2 depicted a setting with two sets of "players" in the macroeconomic policy game. On the one hand, to determine the contract wage, W^c, workers and firms must make their best rational forecast of the price level given their understanding of the policy goals of the macroeconomic policymaker and the trade-off it confronts. On the other hand, the macroeconomic policymaker must decide what action it should take to alter aggregate demand given its understanding of how workers and firms determine the contract wage.

Figure 15–3 depicts four *potential* outcomes that might arise from the interaction between workers and firm executives, who set the contract wage and thereby determine the position of the aggregate supply schedule, and the policymaker, which chooses a monetary or fiscal policy action that determines the position of the aggregate demand schedule. The four potential outcomes of this interaction are points A, B, C, and D. Let's consider each in turn.

The Incentive to Increase Aggregate Demand   Point A is the same initial equilibrium point that we discussed in Figure 15–2. Because it is a long-run equilibrium point, the contract wage W_1^c reflects a correct expectation by workers and firms that the price level will be equal to P_1. Hence, at this initial point workers and firms produce the full-information output level.

Nevertheless, the macroeconomic policymaker wishes to raise real output above the full-information, natural level y_1 toward the capacity output

Figure 15–3   Potential and Equilibrium Outcomes of a Macroeconomic Policy Game

If the current equilibrium for the economy is point A, and if the policymaker's goals are to raise output toward the capacity output level y^* while keeping inflation low, then the policymaker's temptation will be to split the difference between these conflicting objectives by inducing a rise in aggregate demand, to point B. If workers realize that the policymaker has an incentive to permit prices to rise, however, they will bargain for higher contract wages, thereby shifting the aggregate supply schedule leftward. The result will be higher prices and lower real output at point C. To avoid this outcome, the policymaker will feel pressure to raise aggregate demand as workers expect. The final equilibrium is at point D, with unchanged real output but a higher price level. A noninflationary equilibrium in which the policymaker maintains a commitment to zero inflation at point A can result only if the policymaker's commitment is credible.

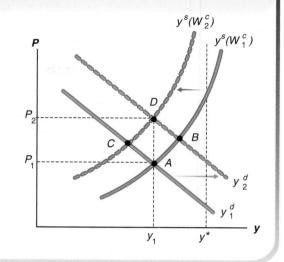

level y^*. Consequently, the policymaker has an incentive to embark on a monetary or fiscal policy action that will raise aggregate demand from y_1^d to y_2^d in an effort to induce a short-run rise in real output, at point B. As noted earlier, a policymaker will not try to cause real output to rise all the way to the capacity level y^*, because this would entail greater inflation. Point B, therefore, represents a compromise outcome for the policymaker in light of the trade-off it faces: Real output will rise *toward* the capacity target at the cost of permitting *some* inflation.

Rational Responses of Workers and Firms   We assume that workers and firms know the policymaker's goals, which implies that they will not let the point B outcome occur. At point B, the price level would be higher than workers and firms anticipated when they set the contract wage W_1^c. Hence, the real wage that workers would earn at point B is lower than they prefer, and real output would exceed the full-information, natural level that firms desire to produce. Therefore, point B cannot be an equilibrium point that could arise in the macroeconomic policy game. It would be inconsistent with the contracting strategy of workers and firms.

Instead, workers and firms will recognize that the policymaker has an incentive to shift the aggregate demand schedule from y_1^d to y_2^d, and they will respond by raising their price expectation and negotiating a higher contract wage, W_2^c. This will cause the aggregate supply schedule to shift leftward, from $y^s(W_1^c)$ to $y^s(W_2^c)$. The result will be point D, which is consistent with the contracting strategy of workers and firms. At this point, they will have chosen the contract wage optimally, taking into account the behavior they expect from the policymaker. In addition, point D is consistent with the policymaker's strategy, which is to raise aggregate demand in an attempt to increase output while keeping inflation low (even though, after the fact, the policymaker will not succeed in its effort). Consequently, unlike point *B,* point *D would* be a possible equilibrium in the monetary policy game.

Given that the policymaker will fail to expand real output toward the capacity goal, one might suppose that the policymaker would recognize its inability to raise output and commit itself to leaving the aggregate demand schedule at the position y_1^d. In other words, the policymaker would follow a policy *rule* instead of responding in a discretionary manner to incentives to try to raise real output in the short run. What if workers and firms do *not* believe that the policymaker will maintain its commitment to a policy rule? In that case, they will still raise their price expectation and negotiate an increase in the contract wage. This will cause the aggregate supply schedule to shift from $y^s(W_1^c)$ to $y^s(W_2^c)$. Then, if the policymaker follows through with its commitment to leave aggregate demand at y_1^d, point *C* will result. Point *C,* however, is inconsistent with the policymaker's strategy, because at this point inflation occurs and real output falls even *further* below the capacity objective. Therefore, point *C* could not be an equilibrium point in the macroeconomic policy game.

Under a special circumstance, one other equilibrium point—point *A*— could arise in the macroeconomic policy game. *If* the macroeconomic policymaker commits itself to maintaining the aggregate demand schedule at y_1^d, and *if* workers and firms believe that the policymaker will honor that commitment, then point *A* will be the final equilibrium point. There will be no inflation, the policymaker will accept its inability to raise real output toward the capacity level, and workers and firms will be satisfied at the long-run, full-information output level.

THE PROBLEM OF POLICY CREDIBILITY   Figure 15–4 is another version of Figure 15–3. It displays only the two possible equilibrium points of the macroeconomic policy game, points *A* and *D,* so that we can focus on these two potential outcomes. Point *A* results from commitment to a monetary policy rule, so it denotes a *commitment policy equilibrium.* Point *D*, in contrast, arises from the policymaker's inability or unwillingness to make such a commitment. In other words, point *D* is a point of *discretionary policy equilibrium.* Thus, these two points constitute the alternative outcomes that result from following a policy rule or pursuing discretionary policymaking.

The key determinant of which equilibrium point actually occurs is **policy credibility,** or the believability of the policymaker's willingness and ability to commit to a monetary rule. If workers and firms believe that the policymaker is willing and able to follow through on its commitment, then the initial point *A* will remain the equilibrium of the macroeconomic policy game, and the economy will remain at its full-information output level without experiencing inflation. If workers and firms doubt the policymaker's willingness or ability to honor its commitment, however, this lack of policy credibility will lead to an equilibrium at point *D.*

THE TIME INCONSISTENCY PROBLEM   Policy credibility is difficult to achieve in the setting that we have described because our example includes a **time inconsistency problem.** This problem arises because although commitment to a policy rule yields zero inflation, as at point *A*, this commitment will be inconsistent with the strategies of workers and firms if the policy-

POLICY CREDIBILITY: The believability of a commitment by a central bank or governmental authority to follow specific policy rules.

TIME INCONSISTENCY PROBLEM: A policy problem that can result if a policymaker has the ability, at a future time, to alter its strategy in a way that is inconsistent both with the desires and strategies of private individuals and with its own initially announced intentions.

Figure 15–4   The Inflation Bias of Discretionary Policymaking

Point A represents a noninflationary equilibrium point of the macroeconomic policy game. It can arise only if the policymaker makes a credible commitment to zero inflation. In the absence of a credible anti-inflation commitment, point D will be the equilibrium point that arises from the macroeconomic policy game, as discussed in Figure 15–3. Hence, the increase in the price level entailed by the movement from point A to point D is an *inflation bias* resulting from discretionary policymaking.

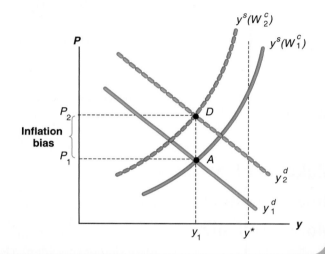

maker is free to alter its policy strategy at a later time. Suppose that after workers and firms have committed themselves to a contract wage, the policymaker attempts to expand aggregate demand, which will help the policymaker achieve its output goal but will not benefit the workers and firms (point B in Figure 15–3 on page 461). Hence, workers and firms protect themselves by raising the contracted wage before the policymaker acts, thereby forcing even a policymaker that might otherwise prefer to stick to a rule to expand aggregate demand to avoid a decline in real output (point C in Figure 15–3). These interactions between workers and firms and the policymaker result in an equilibrium at point D in Figure 15–4.

The result of the time inconsistency problem and the lack of policy credibility in our example is a higher price level at point D as compared with point A. Economists call the difference between the new price level P_2 at point D and the initial price level P_1 at point A the **inflation bias** arising from discretionary macroeconomic policy. This bias toward inflation exists because of the time inconsistency problem and lack of policy credibility that can arise when a macroeconomic policymaker determines its policies in a discretionary manner. The inflation bias of discretionary policy is a third reason—along with the potential for discretionary policy to be destabilizing in the presence of time lags and to serve policymakers' own narrow self-interests if

INFLATION BIAS: The tendency for the economy to experience continuing inflation as a result of discretionary monetary policy that takes place because of the time inconsistency problem of monetary policy.

the public choice perspective is correct—why many economists argue that society should find ways to dissuade policymakers from discretion by making policy rules credible. How society might accomplish this is our next topic.

FUNDAMENTAL ISSUE #3

Why is policy credibility a crucial factor in maintaining low inflation? If people establish nominal wage contracts, then a macroeconomic policymaker has an incentive to enact policies that will raise aggregate demand in an effort to expand real output toward its capacity level. Consequently, workers and firms negotiating wage contracts will be unlikely to believe a policymaker's stated intention to limit inflation, which would reduce the purchasing power of workers' wages. As a result, workers and firms will negotiate higher wages, thereby reducing aggregate supply and causing output to fall in the absence of higher aggregate demand. This pressures the policymaker into raising aggregate demand and thereby creating an inflationary bias. The only way a policymaker can avoid this inflation bias is to make a commitment to low inflation that is credible to workers and firms.

Making Policy Rules Credible: Monetary Policy

It is one thing to argue that there are potential gains from sticking with a macroeconomic policy rule. It is another thing altogether, however, to establish a mechanism for attaining this outcome in the face of a time inconsistency problem. (Even a central bank that is committed to low inflation may have problems deciding just how open it should be about its internal deliberations; see *Policy Notebook: To Avoid Creating Self-Fulfilling Expectations, Should Central Banks Hide Their Forecasts?*)

Three types of macroeconomic policymaking are subject to time inconsistency problems: monetary policy, fiscal policy, and exchange-rate policy. With each type of policymaking, the policymaker can gain from a short-run expansion of aggregate demand after workers and firms have tied themselves to nominal wage contracts. Despite this similarity, the practical approaches to making policy rules credible differ across these various forms of policymaking, so we shall discuss each area in turn, beginning with monetary policy.

As you have learned in earlier chapters, most macroeconomic theories indicate that money growth is a key determinant of the inflation rate. Consequently, this is the natural starting point for most discussions of how to reduce the inflation bias arising from discretionary policy. These discussions focus on finding a way to induce a central bank to follow a policy rule and to make such a rule credible.

Altering Monetary Policy Incentives via Wage Indexation

One approach to eliminating the inflation bias that can result from monetary policy discretion is to take away a central bank's incentive to create inflation. Recall from Chapter 12 that when workers and firms fully *index*

To Avoid Creating Self-Fulfilling Expectations, Should Central Banks Hide Their Forecasts?

To conduct monetary policy effectively, any central bank must develop forecasts of future economic activity. As part of these efforts, a central bank normally develops its own forecasts of inflation during the coming months. In a world where the public is watching the central bank closely to assess the credibility of its commitment to low inflation, these internal inflation forecasts can pose a problem for the central bank.

The problem is that the central bank's inflation expectations affect its own policy choices, and these choices in turn affect the public's inflation expectations. Because the public knows that the central bank's policy decisions also depend on its own forecasts of inflation, ultimately then information about the central bank's inflation forecasts could directly influence the public's expectations of inflation. Of course, the inflation expectations of the public ultimately help determine the position of the economy's aggregate supply curve, thereby affecting the *actual* inflation rate that the central bank wishes to maintain at a low level.

Thus, there is the potential for expectations to be *self-fulfilling:* if the central bank releases a forecast indicating that various events will boost inflation, then the public's inflation expectations will ratchet upward, thereby *causing* higher inflation. To prevent this from happening, central banks may engage in what economists call *cheap talk*. To reduce the inflationary effects of self-fulfilling expectations, central bank officials have an incentive to downgrade their own inflation estimates.

In fact, the inflation rates that central bank officials state that they anticipate achieving at future dates persistently turn out to be lower than the inflation rates that actually occur. Although it is possible that central banks consistently do a poor job of forecasting inflation, it is more likely that their public pronouncements reflect an understanding of the problem of self-fulfilling expectations.

For Critical Analysis
How does the incentive for central bank officials to engage in cheap talk about their inflation forecasts complicate the public's task in assessing the credibility of the officials' anti-inflation stance?

---

nominal wages to unanticipated inflation, the economy's aggregate supply schedule becomes vertical. If wages are fully indexed to inflation, then a rise in the price level automatically causes the nominal wage to rise in equal proportion. As a result, the real wage remains unaltered when the price level changes, so the quantity of real output supplied stays constant at the natural, full-information level.

WAGE INDEXATION AND THE DISCRETIONARY INFLATION BIAS To see the implications of complete wage indexation for discretionary monetary policymaking, consider Figure 15–5 on the next page. Because wages are completely indexed, the aggregate supply schedule is vertical at the natural, full-information output level, y_1. As in Figures 15–3 and 15–4, however, the capacity output level, y^*, is greater than the full-information level of output. Assuming that the economy has initially achieved a short- and long-run output-market equilibrium at point A, then the central bank would, as in our earlier example of the time inconsistency problem, like to raise output toward its capacity output level while keeping inflation as low as possible.

Nevertheless, because full indexation makes the aggregate supply schedule vertical, the central bank cannot, even in the short run, induce a rise in

Figure 15–5   Complete Wage Indexation and Discretionary Monetary Policy

If workers and firms fully index money wages to unanticipated changes in the price level, then the economy's aggregate supply schedule will be vertical, as discussed in Chapter 12. In this case, even if the central bank acts in a discretionary manner, it will have no incentive to increase the quantity of money in circulation in an effort to expand aggregate demand. Even if it did so, the central bank would be unable to induce an increase in real output beyond its long-run, full-information level, y_1, in the direction of the capacity output level, y^*. Hence, the equilibrium point A will be maintained, and there will be no inflation bias.

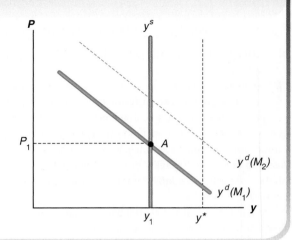

equilibrium real output by increasing money growth and expanding aggregate demand. If the central bank attempts to raise the nominal money stock to shift the aggregate demand schedule from $y^d(M_1)$ to $y^d(M_2)$, the only result will be a higher price level and undesired inflation. Thus, the central bank has no incentive to expand aggregate demand. Point A will remain the equilibrium point, and there will be no discretionary inflation bias.

IS WAGE INDEXATION A SOLUTION?   As we noted in Chapter 12, however, the overall extent of wage indexation in the United States actually has been low in recent years. If full wage indexation could solve the inflation bias problem, why don't more workers and firms index their wages? One reason is that wage indexation is not costless. Workers must negotiate indexed contracts with firms, and they may have to give up something, such as higher base wages, improved health-care coverage, or other nonwage benefits, in exchange for full wage indexation. If the costs of indexing contracts are sufficiently large, many contracts will not have indexation clauses.

Second, as we discussed in Chapter 12, full indexation stabilizes employment and output if fluctuations in aggregate demand are the main source of employment and output variability. If the aggregate supply schedule is variable, however, employment and output volatility is greater with fully indexed wage contracts.

Finally, the slope of the aggregate supply function is influenced by the *aggregate* degree of indexation of all wages. Hence, it is the combined decisions of all workers and firms in the economy that influence the slope of the aggregate supply schedule. To influence the central bank's incentives, all workers and firms would have to coordinate their contract negotiations on indexation. There is no easy way to do this, unless all workers were to join a few large, coordinating unions. To new Keynesians, this is an example of a coordination failure (see Chapter 13). Some new Keynesians, therefore, have advocated government policies requiring indexed contracts as a means of reducing the inflation bias of discretionary monetary policy.

Constitutional Limitations on Monetary Policy

Other economists, such as Milton Friedman of the Hoover Institution at Stanford University, have suggested that it might be better to try to constrain central banks directly, rather than forcing everyone else to determine wages differently than they otherwise would. This might be accomplished in the United States by amending the U.S. Constitution to require a constant annual growth rate for the quantity of money. This approach would seek to tie the hands of the Federal Reserve by legally *requiring* the Federal Reserve, or more broadly the U.S. government, to pursue a monetary policy rule. The legal requirement presumably would establish the credibility of the rule.

One problem with this idea is the difficulty of determining the appropriate numerical rule for money growth. After all, the U.S. economy's real output growth has varied from decade to decade (see Chapter 5).

Achieving Monetary Policy Credibility by Establishing a Reputation

In the absence of such radical institutional changes, how can a central bank make its commitments to low inflation more credible? One approach might be to establish and maintain a reputation as a "tough inflation fighter." To understand how this could enable a central bank to reduce the inflation bias, refer back to Figure 15–3 on page 461. Recall that if the central bank honors its commitment not to raise aggregate demand in pursuit of short-term output gains but is not believed by workers and firms, then the result will be higher inflation and reduced output, shown in the figure by a movement from point *A* to point *C*. If the central bank cares only about today's outcome, it will not want point *C* to occur. If the central bank wants to establish a reputation as an inflation fighter, however, then it might be willing to let the economy experience lower output at point *C*. In that event, henceforth, workers and firms might believe the central bank's promises not to increase aggregate demand.

A number of economists argue that this scenario occurred in 1979 after inflation had risen significantly during the preceding years, as shown in Figure 15–6 on the following page. According to these economists, in 1979 and 1980 the Federal Reserve held firm to a commitment to keep aggregate demand from increasing. At first workers and firms did not find this commitment to be credible. Then, in 1980 and 1981, the United States experienced a sharp recession, as a steady rise in nominal wages pushed up business costs and resulted in a reduction in real output—just as the movement from point *A* to point *C* in Figure 15–3 indicates. As a result, in the years that followed, the Federal Reserve's commitment to lower inflation was credible, and actual inflation rates fell, as shown in Figure 15–6.

Appointing a "Conservative" Central Banker

It is easier for a central bank official to make a credible commitment to low inflation if the official already has a reputation for being "tough" in the fight against inflation. Some observers of the Federal Reserve's fight

macroxtra!
Online
Perspective

To further explore how central bank structure can influence the credibility of monetary policy, go to the Chapter 15 reading, entitled "Policy Credibility and the Design of Central Banks," by Roberto Chang of the Federal Reserve Bank of Atlanta.
http://macroxtra.swcollege.com

Figure 15–6   Annual Inflation Rates in the United States

This figure plots annual rates of change in the consumer price index. Although average inflation fell from the 1980s to the 2000s, as compared with the end of the 1960s and the 1970s, inflation still occurred in every single year.

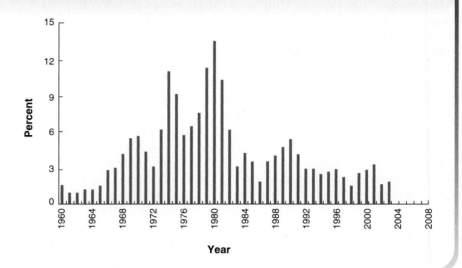

SOURCES: *Economic Report of the President*, 2002; *Economic Indicators* (various issues).

CONSERVATIVE CENTRAL BANKER: A central bank official who dislikes inflation more than the average citizen in society and is therefore less willing to induce discretionary increases in the growth rate of the quantity of money in an effort to achieve short-run increases in real output.

CENTRAL BANKER CONTRACT: A legally binding agreement between a government and a central bank official that holds the official responsible for the nation's inflation performance.

On the Web

Is it possible to keep track of what is going on at most of the world's central banks? In theory, you can do this by going to the home page of the Bank for International Settlements (http://www.bis.org) and clicking on "Links to Central Banks." Here, you will find links to the Web sites of many central banks.

against inflation in the 1980s have concluded that one reason the anti-inflation effort was so successful was President Jimmy Carter's 1979 appointment of Paul Volcker as the chair of the Federal Reserve's Board of Governors. Volcker was a Federal Reserve official who was well known as an opponent of inflation. The Federal Reserve's inflation-fighting reputation then was maintained, these observers argue, when President Ronald Reagan appointed Alan Greenspan, another known hawk on inflation, to that position.

The theory illustrated in Figure 15–4 on page 463 indicates that appointing anti-inflation central bank officials may indeed be a way to reduce the inflation bias of discretionary policymaking. A key factor influencing the size of the inflation bias is how much policymakers dislike inflation relative to how much they wish to try to raise real output toward its capacity level. Thus, appointing a **conservative central banker,** or an individual who dislikes inflation more than the average member of society, is one way to reduce the size of the inflation bias. Such central bankers will choose to expand aggregate demand by a small amount, because a rise in aggregate demand is inflationary.

Central Banker Contracts

In recent years several economists, including Carl Walsh of the University of California at Santa Cruz, have proposed establishing explicit **central banker contracts.** These are legally binding agreements between governments and central bank officials that call for the officials to be punished and/or rewarded based on the central bank's inflation performance. Research by Walsh and others indicates that such contracts could nearly eliminate the inflation bias of discretionary monetary policy.

As an example, New Zealand's Reserve Bank Act of 1989 established a central banker contract, which holds central bank officials directly responsible for any failure to maintain a stable price level in that nation. Under this law, if the top central bank official fails to meet clearly specified inflation targets, then under the terms of the contract, the official is subject to dismissal from the position.

In principle, a central banker contract also could reward officials for maintaining low and stable prices. For instance, central bank officials who eliminate inflation might be rewarded with higher salaries. Although some people argue that the officials would be receiving bonuses for doing the job that they were supposed to be doing in the first place, proponents of such central bank payment schemes argue that this might be a small cost for society to incur in exchange for reduced inflation.

On the Web

What are the current policy responsibilities of the Governor of the Reserve Bank of New Zealand? Go to http://www.rbnz.govt.nz and click on "Policy Targets Agreement."

An Independent Central Bank

The objective of central banker contracts is to make central bank officials more *accountable* for their performances. Using these contracts would not, however, rule out granting the officials considerable *independence* to conduct monetary policy as they see fit, while continuing to hold them responsible if inflation gets out of hand.

Indeed, many economists argue that central bank independence may be the key to maintaining low inflation rates. After all, conservative central bankers cannot establish a reputation as tough inflation fighters if they are hamstrung by legal requirements to try to achieve other objectives as well, such as a low unemployment rate or a high growth rate for real output. Furthermore, even if a central banker contract holds an official accountable for a nation's inflation performance, achieving the required performance may be difficult unless the official has sufficient independence to pursue this objective in the most efficient manner.

DIMENSIONS OF CENTRAL BANK INDEPENDENCE   Central bank independence has two dimensions. One is *political independence,* or the ability to reach decisions without being influenced by the government and other outside individuals or groups. The other is *economic independence,* or the ability to control its own budget or to resist efforts by the government to induce the central bank to make loans to the government or to provide other forms of direct support to government policies. Hence, we can reach the following conclusion:

> **A truly independent central bank is both politically and economically independent. Political independence permits the central bank to conduct the policies that it believes to be best in the long run without being influenced by short-term political pressures. Economic independence gives the central bank the budgetary freedom to conduct these policies.**

EVIDENCE CONCERNING CENTRAL BANK INDEPENDENCE AND INFLATION   Strong evidence that central bank independence is related to good inflation performance has been provided by the Harvard University economists Alberto Alesina and Lawrence Summers. This evidence is summarized in panels

(a) and (b) of Figure 15–7. In each panel, an index of central bank independence is measured along the horizontal axis of the diagram. An increase in this index indicates that a nation's central bank is more politically and/or economically independent. In panel (a), average annual inflation rates between the middle 1950s and the late 1980s are measured along the vertical axis. The diagram shows an *inverse relationship* between central bank independence and average inflation, meaning that countries with more independent central banks tend to experience lower average inflation. Note that the two nations with the most independent central banks, Germany and Switzerland, had average inflation rates of around 3 percent. The two nations with the least independent central banks, New Zealand (before its change in status) and Spain, experienced average inflation rates that were more than twice as high.

Panel (b) measures the variance of inflation along the vertical axis. Again we see an inverse relationship: countries with more independent central banks tend to experience less inflation volatility. Thus, increased central bank independence tends to yield more price stability as well as lower average inflation.

Figure 15–7   Central Bank Independence, Average Inflation, and Inflation Variability

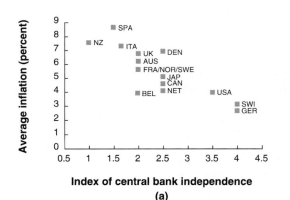

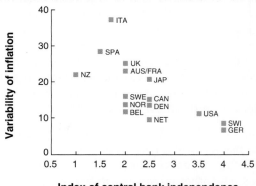

Index of central bank independence
(a)

Index of central bank independence
(b)

Key:

AUS:	Austria	NET:	Netherlands
BEL:	Belgium	NZ:	New Zealand
CAN:	Canada	NOR:	Norway
DEN:	Denmark	SPA:	Spain
FRA:	France	SWE:	Sweden
GER:	Germany	SWI:	Switzerland
ITA:	Italy	UK:	United Kingdom
JAP:	Japan	USA:	United States

As panel (a) shows, nations with more independent central banks, such as Germany, Switzerland, and the United States, have lower average inflation rates as compared with countries with less independent central banks. Panel (b) shows that nations with more independent central banks also have less variable rates of inflation.

SOURCE: Alberto Alesina and Lawrence Summers, "Central Bank Independence and Macroeconomic Performance," *Journal of Money, Credit, and Banking* (May 1993): 151–162.

The strong relationships displayed in Figure 15–7 have convinced a number of countries to grant more independence to their central banks. Recent examples include Japan, Mexico, France, the United Kingdom, and Pakistan. When eleven European nations formed the European Monetary Union and established the European Central Bank, they made it one of the most independent central banking institutions in the world.

On the Web

How is the Bank of England exercising its relatively new-found independence? To find out, click on http://www.bankofengland.co.uk and then click on "Monetary Policy" in the left-hand margin.

FUNDAMENTAL ISSUE #4

How might monetary policy credibility be achieved?   One possible approach is for workers and firms to index their wages completely. Total indexation would make the aggregate supply schedule vertical and eliminate a central bank's incentive to expand aggregate demand. A more direct approach is to make it illegal for central banks to allow inflation to exceed a specified rate. Alternatively, central bank officials could be signed to contracts that condition their employment or salaries on their inflation performance. To help ensure that central banks will be less likely to follow inflationary policies, governments can appoint conservative central bank officials who are known to have a distaste for inflation. Finally, central bankers can gain credibility by permitting output to fall in the near term as a way to convince workers of their commitment to low future inflation. To follow this strategy, the central bank must have sufficient independence.

Making Policy
Rules Credible:
Fiscal Policy

In democratic republics such as the United States, the government is designed to be relatively responsive to the desires of its citizenry. Achieving credible fiscal policies is complicated in a democratic nation, because citizens, either directly at the ballot box or indirectly via votes of their elected representatives, can repudiate fiscal commitments made at some earlier date. Ballooning deficits and national debts can result. Nevertheless, there are two ways in which fiscal policymakers can try to gain greater credibility and overcome the time inconsistency problem that they face.

Establishment of Legal Procedures in Government Budgeting

One way to gain greater fiscal credibility is to develop hard and fast rules for how a legislature can tax and spend. For instance, a legislature could require any representative proposing a tax or spending bill to explain how any necessary funding can be obtained while keeping the government's budget in balance.

The Gramm-Rudman-Hollings Act of 1985, and its amendment, was an example of this procedural approach to attaining greater fiscal credibility for the U.S. government. This law required automatic spending cuts if the U.S. government's deficit failed to stay on a predetermined path. (The law had little effect, though, and was in essence repealed by the Tax Act of 1990.)

DEVALUATION: A policy-induced reduction in the exchange value of a nation's currency relative to the currencies of other countries.

The problem with the procedural approach to greater fiscal credibility, of course, is that a legislature can always vote to suspend its previously established rules. It can collectively "change its mind" about its commitment to greater budgetary discipline. Nevertheless, supporters of procedural constraints on fiscal policy argue that the constraints at least force a legislature to consider the credibility issue, even though they do not prevent all actions that lead to credibility losses.

Extralegislative Budget Balancing: Bipartisan Commissions

Although there are individual exceptions, politicians are notorious for having difficulty maintaining institutional credibility. Indeed, a number of politicians recognize this weakness and have experimented with *bipartisan commissions* as a possible solution. When faced with the necessity for a controversial spending or tax program, a legislature may establish a bipartisan commission and authorize it to examine the situation and make specific recommendations for fiscal actions.

Since the 1980s, for example, the U.S. Congress has recognized that one way to reduce total federal spending and move closer to a balanced budget is to close a number of military bases across the country. The problem, however, is that many local constituencies lose when bases are closed. To distance itself from the difficult decisions of which bases to close and to improve the chances that the decisions will indeed be made, Congress has established base-closing commissions that are authorized to develop lists of military installations that are not crucial to the nation's defense and therefore should be closed. Congress has precommitted itself to adopting or rejecting the entire slate of proposed closures. This move has significantly enhanced the credibility of Congress's general commitment to cutting spending and moving toward a balanced budget.

> FUNDAMENTAL ISSUE #5
>
> **How might fiscal policy credibility be achieved?**   In democratic nations, gaining fiscal credibility often requires that legislatures adopt explicit rules to limit excessive spending. The U.S. Congress also has used bipartisan commissions to help deal with the political problems entailed in reducing government expenditures.

Making Policy Rules Credible: Exchange-Rate Policy

In nations that are smaller than the United States and that traditionally have been more open to international trade, the exchange rate can be a very important instrument of macroeconomic policymaking. Exchange-rate **devaluations**—policy-induced reductions in the value of a nation's currency in terms of the currencies of other nations—make it less costly for foreigners to obtain a nation's currency and buy its goods. This can cause its exports to expand, thereby raising aggregate demand in that nation and causing a short-term rise in real output.

Hence, nations such as Mexico, Hong Kong (when it was a British Crown colony), Italy, and even the United Kingdom have periodically faced time inconsistency problems in their exchange-rate policies. A nation with an open economy always has an incentive to devalue its currency to push real output toward its capacity level, even though devaluations often are associated with upticks in the inflation rate. Hence, discretionary exchange-rate policy can lead to an inflationary bias.

A Fixed Exchange Rate as a Policy Rule

A nation's central bank or government can maintain a fixed exchange rate by standing ready to buy or sell the nation's currency at officially established rates of exchange for other currencies. As we shall discuss in more detail in Chapter 16, there are several justifications for a fixed exchange rate, the foremost being reduced risks of loss in the event of exchange-rate fluctuations.

Because of the potential for short-term output gains from currency devaluations, however, any nation that attempts to fix its exchange rate typically faces credibility problems. Indeed, a commitment to a fixed exchange rate is a type of rule. Attempting to make such a commitment entails a time inconsistency problem similar to those experienced in other forms of macroeconomic policymaking.

Nations have tried to establish their exchange-rate commitments in a variety of ways. In the nineteenth century, many nations established more credible linkages among their exchange rates by using a *gold standard,* in which the values of their currencies were tied to the value of gold. Since the early 1970s, however, very few nations have retained any kind of formal linkage to gold. Consequently, nations that try to fix their exchange rates now rely on alternative approaches to making their commitments to fixed exchange rates credible.

Maintaining Exchange-Rate Credibility

In today's fiat money system, all that "backs" the value of a nation's currency is the credibility of its monetary and exchange-rate policies. If a nation's policies are not credible, those who hold currencies, including *currency speculators* who make their living buying currencies when their values are low and selling them when their values rise, will not be willing to hold the nation's currency at the official exchange rate. Hence, if a nation with a fixed exchange rate is to maintain its commitment, it must persuade currency traders of two points. First, policymakers must convince currency traders that the official exchange rate is consistent with the underlying terms at which their nation trades goods with other countries. The terms of trade for goods exchanges are called the *real exchange rate,* or the rate of exchange for one nation's currency in terms of another currency adjusted for price differences across nations. If the quoted *nominal* rate of exchange unadjusted for price differences that a nation tries to peg in a fixed-exchange-rate system is inconsistent with the real exchange rate, then currency traders will not be willing to hold the nation's currency at the official exchange rate.

Second, policymakers must have sufficient reserves of other nations' currencies so that they can purchase their own nation's currency as necessary to maintain the fixed exchange rate. If foreign currency reserves fall too low to maintain the official exchange rate when changes in the foreign exchange market place downward pressure on the value of the nation's currency, then policymakers' commitment to the official rate will not be credible. They will be forced to abandon the commitment by devaluing.

AN ALTERNATIVE APPROACH: CURRENCY BOARDS   In light of these factors, it can be very difficult for any nation, especially a small one, to "go it alone" with a fixed exchange rate. Consequently, various nations—often smaller, developing nations—have attempted to link or "peg" their currencies to the currency of another nation, usually an important trading partner. Mexico is an example. Until December 1994, Mexico attempted to keep the value of its currency, the peso, within a fixed "trading band," or permitted range of exchange-rate variation, relative to the U.S. dollar. By linking the peso's value to the currency of its key trading partner, the United States, Mexico sought to keep its inflation rate in line with U.S. inflation and to lay a solid foundation for growing trade with the United States and other nations. On November 18, 1994, a headline in the *Wall Street Journal* indicated that the fixed-exchange-rate policy seemed to be successful: it read "Mexico Posts Surprisingly Solid Growth, as Turnaround in Economy Advances." An accompanying figure entitled "On the Move" showed annual Mexican GDP growth at nearly 5 percent.

Nevertheless, from February to December 1994, the peso's value fell by over 10 percent relative to the dollar, to the bottom of the Mexican government's official trading range. Then, in one day, December 21, the peso's exchange value suddenly plummeted by another 12.7 percent following an unexpected devaluation by the Mexican government. Within a week, the peso's value relative to the dollar dropped more than 35 percent in all. In January 1995, the Federal Reserve intervened in foreign exchange markets to boost the peso's value, and in February 1995 the U.S. Treasury made loan guarantees of up to $40 billion to the Mexican government.

The Mexican peso crisis of 1994–1995 occurred for a number of reasons, but the immediate cause was the loss of credibility of Mexico's commitment to its official peso-dollar exchange rate. The official rate was incompatible with the real rate of exchange between U.S. and Mexican goods. Therefore, to maintain the targeted exchange rate, the Mexican government had to buy pesos with dollars. Ultimately, it ran out of dollars and was forced to devalue the peso.

In July 1997, Thailand experienced its own financial crisis and devalued its currency, the *baht.* During the following months, central banks in Indonesia, Malaysia, and South Korea all found themselves running low on dollar reserves and devalued their currencies. Then, in August 1998, waves of uncertainty reappeared when the Russian government defaulted on its debts, Russian financial markets collapsed, and the value of the ruble plunged in foreign exchange markets. By the beginning of 1999, Brazil was in the midst of its own "crisis of confidence," which led it to devalue the *real,* the Brazilian currency.

In light of these currency crises, many observers have argued that a small nation cannot expect to succeed in pegging its exchange rate unless it adopts a **currency board** approach. A currency board is a rule-bound monetary policymaker that issues local currency that is backed 100 percent by the currency of another nation. The first currency boards were established by nations that were members of the British Commonwealth, such as Hong Kong, the Cayman Islands, the Falkland Islands, and Gibraltar, which issued currency based on reserves of the British currency, the pound sterling. Singapore also has a currency board system.

EXPERIENCE WITH CURRENCY BOARDS   A currency board approach to a fixed exchange rate is more credible than the standard approach because the 100 percent backing constraint ensures that a government cannot issue more currency than the amount of foreign exchange reserves it has on hand. Furthermore, this constraint means that a fixed one-to-one exchange rate can be maintained as long as the currency board abides by the rules of the system. Many have credited the solid macroeconomic performances (pre-July 1997) of Hong Kong and Singapore to their currency board arrangements.

Between 1991 and 2001, Argentina used a currency board arrangement in which it backed Argentine pesos 100 percent with U.S. dollars. This arrangement worked well until the late 1990s, when the nation began to struggle to pay off the foreign debt that it had rapidly accumulated. In 2001 the Argentine government abandoned the dollar as a basis for its currency and significantly devalued the peso.

Although Argentina's experience indicates that a currency board is not a panacea for a nation's economic problems, many have proposed the adoption of currency boards in nations that have experienced significant inflation during the 1990s and 2000s, such as Russia and the countries of eastern Europe. Advocates of currency boards argue that adopting currency boards would help these nations cut their inflation rates by giving them the credibility that they need to fix their exchange rates relative to relatively low-inflation nations.

> **CURRENCY BOARD:** A monetary policymaker that is bound to a commitment to issue currency that is backed 100 percent by the currency of another country.

FUNDAMENTAL ISSUE #6

What approaches have some nations with fixed exchange rates followed to make their policies credible?   Committing to a fixed exchange rate is a credible policy only if the targeted rate at which a nation's currency trades for the currency of another country is consistent with the real rate of exchange of those nations' goods. In addition, a nation must have sufficient reserves of foreign currencies that it can use, when needed, to buy its own currency to support its value. It is very difficult for a single, small nation to meet both of these criteria. Consequently, some nations have adopted currency boards that back their currencies with reserves of currencies from other, low-inflation countries.

Central Bank Independence—A "Free Lunch"?

The implications of Figure 15–7 on page 470 are that central bank independence may help produce lower and more stable inflation rates. These implications of the data have convinced a number of countries to grant more independence to their central banks. Recent examples include Japan, the United Kingdom, Mexico, and Pakistan. The evidence also induced nations that have joined the European Monetary Union to grant considerable independence to the European Central Bank.

The (Non)Relationship between Central Bank Independence and the Stability of Real GDP

Some critics of granting central banks considerable independence have argued that the result could be worsened economic performance. If central banks concentrate too much on inflation, the critics argue, they will fail to smooth out business cycles. As a result, real income growth might be reduced.

Panel (a) of Figure 15–8 provides some evidence about this issue. It plots average real GDP growth rates and the variability of these growth rates relative to an index of central bank independence for sixty countries. There is no apparent effect of central bank independence on either average GDP growth or its variability.

Not Quite a "Free Lunch"

One of the first things you learn in an economics principles course is that there is no such

Figure 15-8   Central Bank Independence and Output Volatility and the Inflation–Output Trade-off

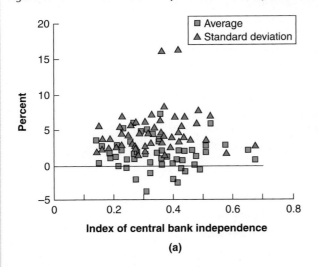

(a)

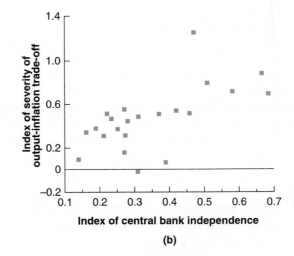

(b)

Panel (a) shows that average GDP growth and the standard deviation of GDP growth for a large number of countries do not appear to be systematically related to an index of central bank independence. Panel (b) depicts estimates of the extent to which real GDP varies with inflation. There appears to be a positive relationship between these estimates and the degree of central bank independence, which implies that a given reduction in the inflation rate may induce a greater proportionate decline in real GDP for a country that has a relatively more independent central bank.

SOURCES: Carl Walsh, "Output-Inflation Tradeoffs and Central Bank Independence," *Federal Reserve Bank of San Francisco Weekly Letter,* No. 95-31, September 22, 1995; Carl Walsh, "Is There a Cost to Having an Independent Central Bank?" *Federal Reserve Bank of San Francisco Weekly Letter,* No. 94-05, February 4, 1994.

thing as a "free lunch." To obtain something, people typically must give up something in exchange.

Panel (b) of Figure 15–8 illustrates that a given reduction in the inflation rate may cause a greater proportionate decline in the real GDP of a country with a relatively more independent central bank. There are two possible reasons for this effect. One is that because the inflation rate tends to be lower in countries with more independent central banks, the general level of prices naturally rises less rapidly in response to an increase in real output. This means that the short-run aggregate supply schedule is likely to be more shallow in a nation with a more independent central bank. As a result, the nation's short-run Phillips curve is also likely to be more shallow, so any given decline in inflation will induce a larger short-run increase in the unemployment rate, holding all other factors unchanged.

In addition, because inflation variability is lower in nations with more independent central banks, people have less incentive to alter the terms of their employment contracts as often. Thus, to the extent that such contracts exist, they will keep nominal wages unchanged for longer periods. They will also call for less wage indexation through cost-of-living adjustments. Again, this means that the short-run aggregate supply schedule and the short-run Phillips curve for a nation with an independent central bank are likely to be more shallow.

Consequently, the positive effects that may result from greater central bank independence—lower and less variable inflation—may have spillover effects. The positive benefits of increased central bank independence can affect the extent to which output and unemployment respond to changes in the inflation rate. A fall in inflation could induce a larger increase in the unemployment rate in a nation that has granted

its central bank greater independence, as compared with a nation with a less independent central bank. As a result, a relatively independent central bank may nonetheless face a problem in trying to reduce inflation: a relatively larger increase in unemployment.

Of course, this potential effect works in reverse as well. With a shallower short-run Phillips curve, higher inflation causes a greater relative reduction in the unemployment rate. For this reason, greater central bank independence has the interesting effect of increasing the short-term benefit of raising inflation. Thus, an independent central bank operated by officials who care about output and employment actually could face a greater temptation to push up the inflation rate in an effort to induce an increase in real income and a reduction in unemployment. This might make households and firms worry about whether even independent central banks will hold inflation down. At least in theory, therefore, central bank independence does not necessarily always make central banks more credible.

Research Project
In what ways can governments grant central banks independence along some dimensions while placing constraints on them along other dimensions? What are the pros and cons associated with granting central banks *complete* independence from government interference?

Web Resources
1. During the course of its history, how did the Bank of England lose and regain its independence? To find out, go to the Bank's home page at http://www.bankofengland.co.uk, click on "About the Bank," and then click on "Bank of England Legislation."

2. Just how independent is the Bank of Mexico? Form your own judgment by going to the Bank's home page at http://www.banxico.org.mx/, where you can click on "English Version," then "About Banco de Mexico," then "Legal Regime," and finally "Banco de Mexico Law."

1. Policy Time Lags and How They Might Cause Well-Meaning Macroeconomic Policymakers to Destabilize the Economy: Policy time lags are the intervals between the need for a policy action and the action's eventual effects on the economy. The recognition lag is the time between the need for a Fed policy action and the Fed's realization of the need, and the response lag is the interval between the recognition of the need for an action and the actual implementation of a policy change. Finally, the transmission lag is the time between the implementation of a policy action and the action's ultimate effects on the economy. Together, these three policy time lags can amount to an interval in excess of a year. They can also cause a discretionary policymaker that reacts to changing circumstances to undertake a policy action that is procyclical, despite the policymaker's intention to enact a countercyclical policy. This potential for policy to destabilize the economy is a key argument favoring the adoption of policy rules, or fixed commitments to specific policy strategies.

2. The Main Arguments Favoring Discretionary Policymaking: One rationale for conducting macroeconomic policymaking in a discretionary manner is that central banks and governments may have information advantages through their abilities to compile and analyze various sources of data on macroeconomic performance. Another justification is that central banks and governments do not seek to maximize their profits. Consequently, they may be able to focus their attention on the well-being of society as a whole.

3. Why Policy Credibility Is a Crucial Factor in Maintaining Low Inflation: When nominal wage contracts exist, a macroeconomic policymaker can push real output toward its capacity level by increasing aggregate demand. Thus, workers and firms that establish wage contracts will doubt the sincerity of the policymaker's commitment to restrain inflation, and they will negotiate higher wages. This will reduce aggregate supply and cause real output to decline in the absence of higher aggregate demand. To avoid this outcome, the policymaker must raise aggregate

demand and create an inflation bias. To mitigate this inflation bias, the policymaker must find a way to make its commitment to low inflation credible.

4. How Monetary Policy Credibility Might Be Achieved: By indexing their wages fully to inflation, workers and firms will make the aggregate supply schedule vertical and eliminate a central bank's incentive to expand aggregate demand. A more direct approach is to make it unlawful for central banks to permit inflation in excess of a certain rate. Another approach is to sign central bank officials to contracts that base their continued employment or their salaries on a nation's inflation outcomes. To reduce the likelihood that central banks will pursue inflationary policies, governments can appoint conservative central banking officials who are known to dislike inflation. Finally, central banks can gain credibility by permitting real output to decline in the short run in the face of people's doubts about the bank's commitments to policy rules. To demonstrate its commitment in this way, however, a central bank must be sufficiently independent from political influences.

5. How Fiscal Policy Credibility Might Be Achieved: Democratic legislatures typically enact explicit budgeting rules to help limit government spending. In the United States, Congress also has entrusted bipartisan commissions with proposing spending cuts so as to avoid political infighting that could limit needed cuts.

6. Approaches Some Nations with Fixed Exchange Rates Have Followed to Make Their Policies Credible: Credible commitment to a policy of maintaining a fixed exchange rate requires selecting a target exchange rate consistent with the real rate of exchange between nations and possessing sufficient reserves of foreign currencies to use in supporting the target exchange rate via exchange market interventions. Because it can be difficult for a small nation alone to satisfy both of these conditions, some countries have established currency boards, which issue home currencies backed 100 percent with reserves of the currency of another, low-inflation country.

Self-Test Questions

(Answers to odd-numbered questions may be found on the Web at **http://macro.swcollege.com** under "Student Resources.")

1. List and define the three types of policy time lags. Which do you think is likely to be *least* problematical for monetary policy? Which do you think is likely to be the *greatest* problem for monetary policy? Explain your reasoning.

2. Which type of policy time lag do you believe is likely to be *least* problematical for fiscal policy? Which do you think is likely to be the *most significant* problem for fiscal policy? Explain your reasoning.

3. Discuss why central banks and governments may be uniquely qualified to conduct discretionary macroeconomic policies. How does the public choice theory create doubts about this notion?

4. Why can the time inconsistency problem lead to an inflation bias in macroeconomic policymaking when workers and firms contract wages?

5. Explain, in your own words, why full wage indexation may not be a viable solution to the time inconsistency problem.

6. Evaluate the following statement: "A real strength of performance contracts for central bankers is that they give central bankers policy discretion while subjecting them to a societal rule."

7. Explain the distinction between political and economic independence of central banks. Are both necessary if a central bank is to be truly free to conduct anti-inflationary monetary policies?

8. Critics of currency boards argue that they are unlikely to enhance a nation's exchange-rate credibility significantly unless preprogrammed computers replace the people on the currency board. Can you think of a reason why critics might make this argument?

Problems

1. In a famous mid-twentieth-century study, Milton Friedman proposed a way to think about just how difficult it might be to stabilize real income in the face of time lags and related impediments. He proposed using the equation $y = y^a + y^p$. As in this chapter, y is real income, y^a is real income in the absence of policy actions, and y^p is the contribution that policy actions make to real income. A common measure of the instability of any variable is its statistical variance. For real income, this is given by $\text{Var}(y) = E[y - E(y)]^2$, where $\text{Var}(y)$ is the variance of real income, and $E(y)$ is the expected value, or average, of real income. By definition, $E(y) = E(y^a) + E(y^p)$; that is, the expected level of real income equals the expected level of real income in the absence of policy actions plus the expected contribution of policy actions to real income.

   a. Subtract the equation $E(y) = E(y^a) + E(y^p)$ from the equation $y = y^a + y^p$.

   b. Square both sides of the answer to part a. Take the expected value of this expression, and prove to yourself that the variance of real income is equal to

   $$\text{Var}(y) = \text{Var}(y^a) + \text{Var}(y^p) + 2 \times E\{[y^a - E(y^a)][y^p - E(y^p)]\}$$

2. Economists often use the notation σ_x^2 to denote the variance of a variable x, so that σ_x^2 is simply another way to write $\text{Var}(x)$.

   a. Rewrite your answer to part b in question 1 in terms of this notation for the variances of y, y^a, and y^p, using the definitions $\text{Var}(y) \equiv \sigma_y^2$, $\text{Var}(y^p) \equiv \sigma_p^2$, and $\text{Var}(y^a) \equiv \sigma_a^2$. Leave the last term as is for now.

   b. The term $E\{[y^a - E(y^a)][y^p - E(y^p)]\}$ is called the "covariance," and it measures cross-variations in y^a and y^p. In terms of the new notation, it turns out that another way to write covariance is in the form $r^{a,p} \times \sigma^a \times \sigma^p$, where σ^a and σ^p are the square roots of the variances of y^a and y^p, which are called the "standard deviations" of these variables. The term $r^{a,p}$ is the "correlation coefficient," which measures the extent to which there are comovements between real income without policy actions and contributions of policy actions to real income. The maximum feasible value for this correlation coefficient is $r^{a,p} = 1$; in this instance, any upward movement in real income without policy actions is accompanied by an increased contribution to real income by policy actions, so there is perfect positive correlation and policy is

(Answers to odd-numbered problems may be found on the Web at **http://macro. swcollege.com** under "Student Resources.")

fully procyclical. The minimum feasible value is $r^{a,p} = -1$; in this instance, any upward movement in real income without policy actions is accompanied by a reduced contribution to real income by policy actions, so there is perfect negative correlation and policy is countercyclical. If $r^{a,p} = 0$, then there is no correlation; the two are unrelated and policy is neither pro- nor countercyclical. Use this definition to rewrite your expression from part a.

c. Let's do just one more bit of algebra. Macroeconomic policy actions will stabilize real income if the variability of income in the presence of policy actions is less than the variability of real income in the absence of policy actions, or if $\sigma_y^2 < \sigma_a^2$. Prove that this implies that the following condition must be satisfied:

$$r^{a,p} < -(1/2)(\sigma^p/\sigma^a) < 0.$$

(Hint: Substitute the expression from part b into the left-hand side of $\sigma_y^2 < \sigma_a^2$. Then rearrange until only the correlation coefficient $r^{a,p}$ appears on the left-hand side.)

d. The expression you came up with in part c tells us the extent to which real income in the absence of policy actions can be correlated with policy contributions to real income if policies will be successful in stabilizing real income. Can policy actions stabilize real income if $r^{a,p}$ is very close to a value of zero?

3. Based on your answer to part c of question 2, suppose that the standard deviation of policy contributions to real income (measured in billions of real dollars) is equal to 2, while the standard deviation of real income in the absence of policy actions is equal to 3. Below what value must the correlation coefficient measuring the comovements of these variables be if policy actions are to successfully stabilize real income?

4. The correlation coefficient relating the movements of real income without policy actions and the effects of policy actions has a value of -0.1. The variance of policy effects on real income (measured in billions of real dollars) equals 1, and the variance of real income in the absence of policy actions equals 4.

a. Is policy countercyclical?

b. Based on your answer to part c of question 2, is policy *sufficiently* countercyclical to stabilize real income? Explain and show your work.

Before the Test

Test your understanding of the material covered in this chapter by taking the Chapter 15 interactive quiz at http://macro.swcollege.com.

Online Application

Internet URL: http://www.ecb.int

Title: *The European Central Bank*

Navigation: Open the above home page of the ECB. In the right-hand margin, click on "Organisation of European System of Central Banks."

Application: Read the discussion, and answer the following questions:

1. Is stabilization of the price level of member nations the only goal of the ECB? Are there other goals? What are they? Explain your basis for making this statement.

2. Based on this discussion, how independent does the ECB appear to be? Compare the degree of independence of the ECB with that of the Fed. Which do you believe is more independent?

For Group Study and Analysis: In the right-hand margin, click on "Links to EU Central Banks." Assign groups to take a look at the Web sites of each member of the European System of Central Banks (keep in mind, however, that Denmark, Sweden, and the United Kingdom are not members of this system). Try to determine the general objectives of each of the central banks within the ESCB. Do any of these central banks appear to have policy goals that conflict with those of the European Central Bank?

Selected References and Further Reading

Barro, Robert J. *Macroeconomic Policy.* Cambridge, Mass.: Harvard University Press, 1990.

Beetsma, Roel, and Henrik Jensen. "Inflation Targets and Contracts with Uncertain Central Banker Preferences." *Journal of Money, Credit, and Banking* 30 (August 1998): 384–403.

Bernanke, Ben, Thomas Laubach, Frederic Mishkin, and Adam Posen. *Inflation Targeting: Lessons from the International Experience.* Princeton, N.J.: Princeton University Press, 1999.

Bryson, Jay, Henrik Jensen, and David VanHoose. "Rules, Discretion, and International Monetary and Fiscal Policy Coordination. *Open Economics Review* 4 (April 1993): 117–132.

Cukierman, Alex. *Central Bank Strategy, Credibility, and Independence.* Cambridge, Mass.: MIT Press, 1992.

Pollard, Patricia. "Central Bank Independence and Economic Performance." Federal Reserve Bank of St. Louis *Review,* July/August 1993, pp. 21–36.

Svensson, Lars. "Price-Level Targeting versus Inflation Targeting: A Free Lunch?" *Journal of Money, Credit, and Banking* 31 (August 1999): 277–295.

Waller, Christopher. "Performance Contracts for Central Bankers." Federal Reserve Bank of St. Louis *Review,* September/October 1995, pp. 3–14.

Waller, Christopher, and David VanHoose. "Discretionary Monetary Policy and Socially Efficient Wage Indexation." *Quarterly Journal of Economics* 107 (November 1992): 451–460.

Walsh, Carl. "Optimal Contracts for Central Bankers." *American Economic Review* 85 (March 1995): 150–167.

macro**xtra!**

Log on to the MacroXtra Web site at http://macroxtra.swcollege.com for additional learning resources such as practice quizzes, Interactive Key Graphs, readings, and additional economic applications.

16

Policymaking in the World Economy—

International Dimensions of Macroeconomic Policy

FUNDAMENTAL ISSUES

1. What are the pros and cons of fixed versus floating exchange rates?

2. How does greater integration of global financial markets affect macroeconomic policymaking?

3. In what ways can greater worldwide capital mobility add to or detract from international macroeconomic stability?

4. What are the key multinational policymaking institutions, and what problems do they face in trying to deal with global instabilities caused by international financial crises?

*I*nflation has been commonplace throughout the world since the end of World War II. Also typical in most nations have been tax systems that are not fully indexed to inflation. Thus, as nominal incomes of individuals and businesses have increased, the portions of income that they pay as taxes have also increased. In most countries, interest payments on debts are tax-deductible, but payments to shareholders are not. Hence, companies around the globe have had an incentive to try to reduce their inflation-boosted tax bills by raising needed funds by borrowing instead of by issuing new equity shares. As a consequence, corporate debt-equity ratios have persistently risen during the past several decades.

During the past decade, however, some nations have broken away from their historical inflationary tendencies. Indeed, a few nations have experienced bursts of deflation. In those nations, corporate debt no longer offers such significant tax advantages. Thus, companies based in those countries have been scrambling to reduce their borrowings in favor of more stock issues.

The current mixed global environment, with inflationary tendencies still present in some regions even as bursts of deflation occur in others, has complicated the financing choices faced by multinational corporations with operations spanning national borders. In many respects, the financial officers of these companies would have an easier time if central banks would coordinate their policies, establishing a common inflationary or deflationary trend for the world as a whole. Then determining the appropriate division between debt and equity would be a less complex endeavor.

Should the world's central banks work together to maintain stable rates of worldwide inflation or deflation, perhaps by fixing exchange rates in an effort to keep the relative purchasing power of each nation's currency the same? Evaluating the pros and cons of fixing exchange rates is one topic you will consider in this chapter, which focuses on the international aspects of macroeconomic policy.

Fixed versus Floating Exchange Rates

As we first noted in Chapter 9, many nations, including the United States, in years past have sought to maintain fixed exchange rates. More recently, a number of nations have permitted their exchange rates to float, or be market determined. At the same time, a large set of European nations fixed exchange rates among their own currencies while allowing their exchange rates vis-à-vis non-European nations to float. Many of these countries have since gone a step further and adopted a single currency, the euro.

What factors should a country take into account when choosing between fixed and floating exchange rates? How is a nation's ability to use monetary and fiscal policies to achieve ultimate macroeconomic objectives affected by its choice? We begin our exploration of the international dimensions of macroeconomics by contemplating these important questions.

Floating Exchange Rates and Foreign Exchange Risks

As you will learn later in the chapter, there are good reasons for a nation to allow the value of its currency to float. Naturally, once this decision is made, variations in the demand for or supply of foreign exchange can cause the exchange rate to fluctuate. Changes in the exchange rate in turn can affect the market value of financial assets that are denominated in foreign currencies. This can increase the risks that a nation's residents face, thereby forcing them to incur costs to avoid these risks.

FOREIGN EXCHANGE RISK   The possibility that market values of assets may vary as a result of changes in the value of a nation's currency is called **foreign exchange risk.** There are three basic types of foreign exchange risk:

1. *Accounting risk.* When exchange rates change, the market value of assets denominated in foreign currencies changes even though the underlying interest returns on those instruments are unaffected. The

FOREIGN EXCHANGE RISK: The possibility that fluctuations in exchange rates can cause variations in the market values of assets.

ACCOUNTING RISK: The possibility that the market value of assets denominated in foreign currencies may vary as a result of changes in exchange rates even when the underlying interest returns on those assets are unaffected.

TRANSACTION RISK: The possibility that the value of a financial asset involved in funding an exchange denominated in a foreign currency could vary with exchange-rate movements, thereby affecting the underlying value of the transaction.

CURRENCY RISK: The possibility that rates of return on financial assets denominated in other currencies can fluctuate as a result of changes in exchange rates that cause variations in the market values of those assets.

risk that a country's residents may experience such variations in the market value of their foreign assets is known as **accounting risk.**

To understand how accounting risk can arise, consider a situation in which a German company has granted trade credit to a U.S. company by sending it German export goods in exchange for a promise to pay for the goods upon their receipt two weeks hence. The U.S. company has agreed to pay the German firm €100,000 (euros) at that time. When the agreement was reached, €1 was equal to $0.91, so the value of the payment that the U.S. firm would owe the German company was equal to $91,000. Further suppose that before the goods are received, the dollar's value falls in the foreign exchange market, so that €1 rises in value to $0.99. Now the dollar value of the U.S. firm's liability is equal to $99,000. Solely as a matter of accounting, the U.S. company's dollar liabilities have risen as a result of the change in the dollar-euro exchange rate.

2. *Transaction risk.* Another type of foreign exchange risk is **transaction risk.** This is the possibility that the value of a financial asset relating to the funding of a transaction denominated in a foreign currency could change due to an exchange-rate movement that affects the underlying value of the transaction.

Suppose for instance, that a U.S. company in the import-export business purchases a large volume of Japanese goods for distribution in the United States and finances the shipment with a loan from a U.S. bank. The bank issues a loan that guarantees payment to the Japanese company selling the goods, and the U.S. company agrees to pay for the goods in yen, the Japanese currency, upon their receipt. The shipment takes several weeks, and in the meantime the dollar's value relative to the yen declines sharply, so the U.S. firm must come up with more dollars to make its yen payment. If the U.S. firm has made many such agreements with Japanese importers, it could end up defaulting on its obligations, leaving the U.S. bank as the responsible party in the transaction. In this manner, changes in exchange rates can increase the risk that banks take on when they issue loans to finance import-export firms.

3. *Currency risk.* In Chapter 11, we saw that when bonds with identical maturities and risk characteristics are issued by two different nations, the difference between the bonds' interest rates should be approximately equal to the expected rate of depreciation of the currency of one of the nations relative to the currency of the other. Because exchange-rate variations can cause expectations of currency depreciation to change, interest rates on bonds and other financial assets issued by different nations can vary relative to one another. Hence, the underlying rates of return on financial assets denominated in other currencies can fluctuate as a result of changes in exchange rates. The possibility of such variations in underlying asset returns due to exchange-rate variability is known as **currency risk.**

HEDGING AGAINST FOREIGN EXCHANGE RISK A country's residents are not defenseless in the face of foreign exchange risk. They can **hedge** against such risks, meaning that they can adopt strategies intended to offset the risk arising from exchange-rate variations.

For instance, as discussed in Chapter 11, individuals and firms can use *forward currency contracts* to ensure that they will receive the current market forward exchange rate on the future delivery of a sum of currency. Forward currency contracts thereby help to shield a firm or an individual from accounting risk and transaction risk. To hedge against currency risk, people can use other types of financial instruments, such as *interest-rate forward contracts*. These financial contracts entail the sale of a financial instrument at a certain interest rate on a specific future date, thereby guaranteeing a predetermined interest return. Companies also use *interest-rate swaps* as hedges. These are contractual agreements under which firms trade the interest returns that they earn on bonds and other assets denominated in different currencies.

A RATIONALE FOR FIXED EXCHANGE RATES Hedging is not costless, however. For one thing, experts in the use of hedging strategies charge fees and commissions to companies and individuals that use them. In addition, hedging strategies themselves can entail taking positions that can be risky if market conditions change unexpectedly. Thus, efforts to hedge against foreign exchange risk sometimes can expose an individual or firm to other kinds of risks.

One common justification for fixed exchange rates is that they could reduce or even eliminate hedging costs. With fixed exchange rates, the potential for exchange-rate variability would be significantly diminished. This would save households and businesses from incurring the costs of hedging against foreign exchange risks.

The Exchange Rate as a Shock Absorber

The argument for fixing exchange rates implies that people worldwide might be better off if their governments agreed to a system of completely rigid exchange rates. Indeed, taken to its logical extreme, the argument indicates that everyone might be better off with a *single world currency*. After all, if we all used the same currency, not only would all foreign exchange risks be eliminated, but we would no longer have to incur the costs of converting one currency into another. For instance, today a U.S. tourist traveling from New York to London must pay a fee to convert dollars to pounds. Such fees would no longer exist if U.S. and British citizens used the same currency.

If a system of rigid exchange rates—or even common currency—is so advantageous, why are there so many separate currencies with floating exchange rates in the world today? The answer must be that there are potential drawbacks to fixing exchange rates or adopting a single currency. Nations must have good reasons for preferring their own currencies and often permitting their exchange rates to float.

HEDGE: The act of adopting strategies to reduce the overall risk resulting from fluctuations in market values of assets caused by such factors as exchange-rate volatility.

THE BENEFIT OF SEPARATE CURRENCIES AND A FLOATING EXCHANGE RATE The theory of *optimal currency areas,* which was developed by Robert Mundell of Columbia University, attempts to explain why different nations might wish to issue separate currencies. It also seeks to determine under what circumstances people in different geographic regions, such as Oregon and New Jersey, might gain from adopting a common currency unit.

A Two-Region Example To understand the basic concept of an optimal currency area, let's consider a fictitious example. Suppose that there is a large island divided into two separate regions with nearly equal areas. In each region, wages and other prices of factors of production are sticky in the short run. Let's call one Region X and the other Region Y. Residents of each region specialize in producing different goods and services. Even though households and firms in the two regions trade goods and services across the border between the regions, there are barriers to movement of people and their possessions across the border. Perhaps the residents of the two regions have political differences, speak different languages, or have different cultures or religions that have induced them to establish obstacles to mobility between the regions. Whatever the reason, these obstacles prevent people in the two regions from offering to exchange labor or other factor services. All they can do is to take their final goods and services to the border to trade.

Each region has its own government, which issues its own currency. Consequently, to trade their goods and services, people in each region must convert their currencies at the prevailing exchange rate between the two currencies.

Adjusting to Changes in the Relative Demands for Regional Products Suppose further that residents of both regions reduce their demand for goods and services produced in Region Y, and increase their demand for those produced in Region X. Consequently, the firms in Region Y cut back on their demands for labor and other factors of production, and real income in Region Y begins to decline. Because wages are sticky, unemployment begins to increase in Region Y. At the same time, to induce firms in Region X to raise production in light of the increased demand for their goods, real income begins to rise in Region X.

If there were no barriers to movement between the regions, residents of Region Y could offer to move to, or commute into, Region X to work, which would help ease both the unemployment problem in Region Y and the inflation problem in Region X. Because obstacles prevent this type of adjustment, however, the burden of adjustment falls on the exchange rate. Because Region Y's residents desire more imports from Region X, the demand for Region X's currency rises. The result is an appreciation of Region X's currency and a depreciation of the currency of Region Y. Thus, Region Y's goods become relatively cheaper, and more of them will be consumed. As a result, firms in that region will begin to increase their production again. Region Y's unemployment rate will begin to fall, and the imbalance between the regions will begin to disappear.

These adjustments will not take place unless the exchange rate is flexible. Consequently, when barriers to movement of labor and other factors of production exist, as in our example, having separate currencies with a floating exchange rate is the right thing to do. If productive factors are immobile between different geographic regions, the exchange rate absorbs the burden of adjusting to changing relative demand and supply conditions. In our island example, therefore, Regions X and Y benefit from having separate currencies. The exchange rate performs the role of "shock absorber" when market conditions on the island change. Though residents of both regions must face currency conversion costs and foreign exchange risks by letting their exchange rate float, they gain from the relative price variations made possible by quick adjustments in the market exchange rate. Such adjustments help speed the relief from rising unemployment caused by changes in the relative demands for the regions' products.

OPTIMAL CURRENCY AREAS Regions X and Y benefit from having separate currencies because of the stickiness of wages and other input prices and the presence of obstacles to movement of labor and other factors of production. To see this, suppose that residents of the two regions eliminate all barriers to island mobility. Now when demand for goods and services produced in Region Y declines, residents of that region can simply move to, or commute into, Region X to supply their labor and other factor services. An exchange rate is not needed to absorb the burden of adjustment to the altered circumstances. The people themselves can adjust by changing the location of their employment.

In this case, the entire island is an **optimal currency area,** or a geographic region in which fixed exchange rates can be maintained without hindering international adjustment. Indeed, Regions X and Y might want to contemplate adopting a single currency, because without any barriers to mobility of goods, services, and productive factors, the entire island, for all intents and purposes, constitutes a single, integrated economy.

PROBLEMS WITH FIXED-EXCHANGE-RATE OR SINGLE-CURRENCY SYSTEMS The theory of optimal currency areas explains why nations might wish to use different currencies and to let their exchange rates float. If nations use immigration restrictions, capital controls, and the like to restrain the flow of people and other productive factors *across* their borders, then it makes sense to use their own currencies *within* their borders. Allowing the exchange rate to adjust to variations in international demand and supply conditions then permits speedier price, output, and employment adjustments to these variations. This explains why Brazil and Argentina, nations with somewhat different languages and cultures and relatively limited mobility of people and productive factors across their borders, prefer to have separate currencies and to let their exchange rate vary.

The theory also helps to explain why residents of Oregon and New Jersey both use dollars, even though they are separated by more than two thousand miles. Because there is such easy mobility of labor and capital in the United States, little social cost is associated with fixing a one-for-one exchange rate and adopting a common currency in these two states, as well as in the other forty-eight. By using a common currency, residents of these states also save the costs of avoiding foreign exchange risks. In addition, when an Oregon resident visits relatives in Newark or when a New Jersey resident buys goods listed in the catalogue of a Portland-based company, neither has to worry about costs of converting currencies.

OPTIMAL CURRENCY AREA: A region in which fixed exchange rates can be maintained without inhibiting prompt internal adjustments of employment and output to changes in international market conditions.

487

CHAPTER 16 Policymaking in the World Economy—International Dimensions of Macroeconomic Policy

Finally, the theory helps to explain why nations within the European Monetary Union (EMU) adopted the euro as a common accounting unit in 1999. These nations are closely linked by trade in goods, services, and financial assets. In addition, in recent years they have somewhat reduced obstacles to flows of people and productive factors. For these reasons, adopting a common currency in EMU nations entailed fewer drawbacks than it would have just a decade or two before.

macroxtra!
Economic Applications

Will the European Monetary Union succeed? To review alternative perspectives on this debate and make your own judgment, go to EconDebate Online.
http://macroxtra.swcollege.com

FUNDAMENTAL ISSUE #1

What are the pros and cons of fixed versus floating exchange rates?   A key drawback of floating exchange rates is the resulting potential for foreign exchange risks stemming from exchange-rate variability. Fixing the exchange rate reduces the extent of foreign exchange risks. A key problem with a fixed exchange rate is that this policy approach eliminates the exchange rate's ability to serve as a shock absorber in the event of changing international market conditions. This is particularly true for nations with barriers to mobility of labor and other real productive factors. Such nations can benefit from adopting their own currencies and permitting their exchange rate to vary with changing market forces.

Macroeconomic Policy in an Integrated World Economy

In many respects, the nations of the world have become more interconnected with each passing decade. Global news networks and the Internet now broadcast up-to-the-second reports of activities in far-flung regions of the globe. The governments of many nations often work together to develop cooperative approaches to smoothing political tensions among pairs or groups of nations. Countries enter into coordinated military projects from time to time.

In the economic sphere, the process by which interrelationships develop among national markets for goods, services, factors of production, and financial assets is called **international economic integration.** In a fully integrated world economy, all national borders would be artificial demarcations indicating only political separations among countries. There would be no "British markets," "Chinese markets," or "Australian markets." Instead there would be a single world marketplace, and products, resources, and funds would flow freely across borders in search of the highest returns available to owners, wherever they might reside. (One thing for certain is that U.S. borders are more open to trade than they were a few decades ago; see *Global Notebook: The Fall and Rise of U.S. Globalization.*)

Integrated International Financial Markets and Macroeconomic Policies

INTERNATIONAL ECONOMIC INTEGRATION: The growth of interconnectedness among the world's markets for goods, services, factors of production, and financial assets.

An important aspect of the growing integration of the world economy has been greater *financial market integration*. Satellite communications and computer technology together have made possible the nearly instanta-

The Fall and Rise of U.S. Globalization

At the beginning of the twentieth century, the world economy was relatively integrated. Then World War I, the Great Depression, and World War II seemed to mark the end of globalization. Figure 16–1 shows how these developments led to significant drop-offs in U.S. trade flows, which then remained at low levels until the mid-1970s.

During the past three decades, world trade has gradually recovered and now is finally close to the total share of world output that it achieved during the first two decades of the twentieth century. U.S. trade flows reflect this recovery of international trade. Relative to GDP, U.S. combined exports and imports are now roughly triple their volumes between 1949 and 1972.

Figure 16–1   Trade Relative to GDP since 1900

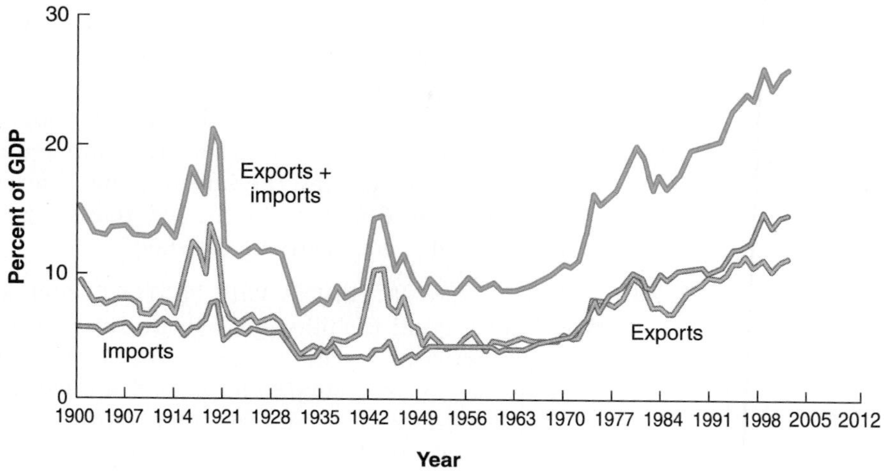

During the 1990s and 2000s, total U.S. trade relative to GDP finally returned to levels experienced in the early part of the twentieth century.

SOURCES: John Fernald and Victoria Greenfield, "The Fall and Rise of the Global Economy," *Chicago Fed Letter*, Federal Reserve Bank of Chicago, No. 164, April 2001; *Economic Report of the President* and *Economic Indicators*, various issues.

For Critical Analysis
What factors do you think accounted for the drop in trade during the early and middle parts of the twentieth century?

neous transfer of billions of dollars, yen, euros, and other currencies. As a result, national financial markets have become increasingly interconnected in a global financial system.

INTERNATIONAL FINANCIAL ARBITRAGE   Recall from Chapter 11 that individual rationality in the formation of expectations leads to the view that financial markets should be *efficient,* meaning that prices of bonds and other financial assets should reflect all available information and traders' understanding of how those prices are determined. The process by which market efficiency is achieved is *international financial arbitrage,* or the purchase and sale of financial assets, such as national currencies, bonds, and stocks, across national boundaries.

A key mechanism linking nations' financial markets is the **Eurocurrency markets,** which are markets for funds denominated in currencies issued by nations other than the nation in which the funds actually are held. These markets are known as Eurocurrency markets because initially most of their trading involved funds held on deposit in European

EUROCURRENCY MARKETS:
Markets for financial assets that are denominated in currencies issued by nations other than the nation in which the financial assets are held.

490 PERFECT CAPITAL MOBILITY: A situation in which financial resources are as mobile across a nation's boundaries as they are within those boundaries.

UNIT V Macroeconomic Policy

banks. Today, however, Eurocurrency trading takes place in Japan, Hong Kong, China, Australia, and other nations around the globe.

Banks and other financial institutions use the Eurocurrency markets to gather deposit funds and redirect them to activities in nations beyond the country of origin. As a result, the Eurocurrency markets are now the focus of global financial arbitrage. For example, suppose that interest yields on dollar-denominated assets held in the United States decline. Many individuals and corporations that hold such assets will respond by shifting their funds to Eurodollar deposits in London, Tokyo, and other locations outside the United States. In addition, many traders will convert their dollar-denominated assets to assets denominated in other nations' currencies. As a result, interest yields on assets denominated in currencies other than the dollar will change, and the international interest parity conditions that we discussed in Chapter 11—*covered interest parity* and *uncovered interest parity*—will more nearly be satisfied.

MACROECONOMIC POLICIES WITH PERFECT CAPITAL MOBILITY AND FIXED EXCHANGE RATES Capital mobility plays a crucial role in determining the effects of monetary and fiscal policy actions. Many observers argue that greater financial market integration around the world is producing a situation in which markets for financial capital in the United States, Western Europe, Japan, and other areas are interlinked. If the world reaches the point at which financial resources are as mobile *across* national borders as they are *within* nations, then we will experience **perfect capital mobility.**

Figure 16–2 illustrates the monetary and fiscal policy implications of perfect capital mobility under fixed exchange rates. In both panels, the *BP* schedule is *perfectly elastic,* because with perfect capital mobility, the smallest change in the nation's interest rate will cause very large movements of funds across its borders.

Panel (a) of Figure 16–2 shows the effects of a central bank's expansion of the money stock when capital is perfectly mobile and the central bank is committed to maintaining a fixed exchange rate. Such a monetary expansion, from M_1 to M_2, would shift the *LM* schedule to the right and cause a movement from an initial *IS-LM* equilibrium at point *A* on the *BP* schedule to a new *IS-LM* equilibrium at point *B* below the *BP* schedule.

The resulting decline in the equilibrium interest rate will cause the nation to experience significant capital outflows, so it will run a private payments deficit. To keep the value of the nation's currency from falling, the central bank will have to respond by selling foreign exchange reserves. If it sterilizes, then for at least some period of time the central bank can maintain equilibrium point *B*. In the absence of sterilization, however, the monetary approach to the balance of payments implies that the loss of foreign exchange reserves eventually will cause the nation's money stock to decline to its original level. Consequently, with perfect capital mobility and a fixed exchange rate, a nonsterilized monetary expansion ultimately will have no effect on real income. Monetary policy will be impotent in such a setting.

In contrast, fiscal policy's ability to affect real income under a fixed exchange rate will, if anything, be enhanced if capital is completely mobile,

Figure 16–2   Monetary and Fiscal Policies with Perfect Capital Mobility and Fixed Exchange Rates

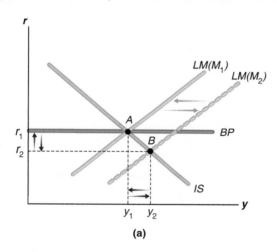

(a)

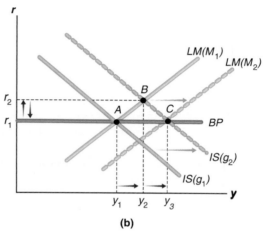

(b)

Panel (a) illustrates the effects of an unsterilized increase in the quantity of money when there is perfect capital mobility, so that the *BP* schedule is perfectly elastic. The expansion of the money stock causes a rightward shift of the *LM* schedule along the *IS* schedule, from point *A* to point *B*, which causes a private payments deficit. To keep the nation's currency from depreciating, the central bank will have to sell foreign exchange reserves, causing the *LM* schedule to shift back to point *A*. Hence, unsterilized

monetary policy actions will have no long-term effects on equilibrium real income. In contrast, as panel (b) shows, an increase in real government expenditures will shift the *IS* schedule rightward along the *LM* schedule, from point *A* to point *B*. To prevent an appreciation, the central bank will purchase foreign exchange reserves, which will cause the money stock to increase, thereby shifting the *LM* schedule rightward to a final equilibrium at point *C*.

as shown in panel (b) of Figure 16–2. A bond-financed increase in government spending from g_1 to g_2 will cause the *IS* schedule to shift rightward, resulting in an equilibrium at point *B* above the *BP* schedule. The nation will experience a private payments surplus because the higher interest rate r_2 will induce capital inflows.

At point *B*, the central bank will begin to accumulate foreign exchange reserves as it acquires foreign-currency-denominated assets in its efforts to maintain a fixed exchange rate. If the central bank sterilizes to keep the money stock from changing, then the economy will remain at point *B* indefinitely. In the absence of sterilization, however, the increase in foreign exchange reserves will lead to a rise in the nation's money stock, and the

LM schedule will shift rightward until the private payments balance again equals zero at a new *IS-LM* equilibrium point *C* on the *BP* schedule. In this circumstance, fiscal policy will have its largest possible effect on equilibrium real income, at least in the short run in which we have abstracted from changes in the price level.

MACROECONOMIC POLICIES WITH PERFECT CAPITAL MOBILITY AND FLOATING EXCHANGE RATES What are the policy implications of *perfect* capital mobility under *floating* exchange rates? To answer this question, consider Figure 16–3, in which perfect capital mobility again is implied by the horizontal *BP* schedules in both panels. Panel (a) illustrates the effects of a monetary expansion with perfectly mobile capital. If the central bank increases the money stock from M_1 to M_2, the *LM* schedule will shift rightward. At point *B*, the induced decline in the equilibrium interest rate will spur considerable capital outflows, so the nation will operate for a time with a private payments deficit. With a floating exchange rate, however, this will result in a depreciation in the nation's currency, which will cause import spending to decline and export spending to rise. Consequently, the *IS* schedule will shift rightward, from IS_1 to IS_2. At the final equilibrium point *C*, the nation's private payments balance again will equal zero. In addition, there will be no further

Figure 16–3   Monetary and Fiscal Policies with Perfect Capital Mobility and Floating Exchange Rates

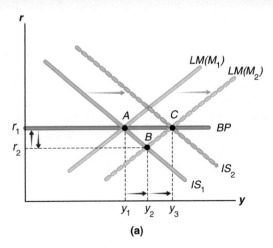

(a)

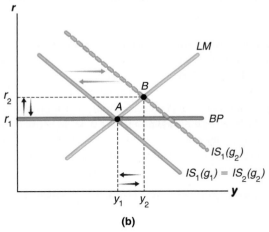

(b)

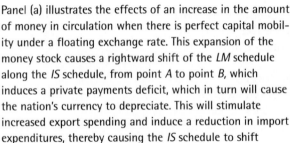

Panel (a) illustrates the effects of an increase in the amount of money in circulation when there is perfect capital mobility under a floating exchange rate. This expansion of the money stock causes a rightward shift of the *LM* schedule along the *IS* schedule, from point *A* to point *B*, which induces a private payments deficit, which in turn will cause the nation's currency to depreciate. This will stimulate increased export spending and induce a reduction in import expenditures, thereby causing the *IS* schedule to shift

rightward to point *C*. In contrast, as shown in panel (b), an increase in real government expenditures will shift the *IS* schedule rightward along the *LM* schedule, from point *A* to point *B*, which leads to a currency appreciation. This in turn will cause autonomous export spending to decline while stimulating a rise in autonomous import expenditures, thereby causing the *IS* schedule to return to its original position at point *A*.

pressure on the value of its currency. Finally, real income will increase as fully as possible, from y_1 to y_3, or by the amount of the horizontal distance that the *LM* schedule shifted to the right. In contrast to the case of fixed exchange rates, monetary policy will have its most *potent* effect on aggregate demand with a floating exchange rate and perfect capital mobility.

Panel (b) illustrates the effects of a bond-financed increase in government spending, from g_1 to g_2. The immediate effect will be a rightward shift in the *IS* schedule, from $IS_1(g_1)$ to $IS_1(g_2)$. At the new equilibrium point *B*, the initial rise in the interest rate will induce significant capital inflows and a private payments surplus. The country's currency will appreciate, causing import spending to rise and export expenditures to fall. As a result, the *IS* schedule will shift back to the left, to $IS_2(g_2)$, which is the same as its original position. Thus, the final equilibrium will be point *A* once again, and real income will be unaffected, on net, by the rise in government spending. Essentially, with perfect capital mobility fiscal policy is subject to *complete crowding out*. A rise in government spending will crowd out an equal amount of net export spending by foreign residents because of the currency appreciation that the fiscal policy action causes. Hence, equilibrium real income will not be affected. In contrast to the fixed-exchange-rate case, with a floating exchange rate fiscal policy actions are *impotent* in affecting aggregate demand when capital is perfectly mobile.

REAL-WORLD POLICY IMPLICATIONS OF PERFECT CAPITAL MOBILITY   These contrasting conclusions about the effects of monetary and fiscal policies under fixed versus floating exchange rates have important implications for a world that may be close to achieving perfect capital mobility among many nations. Recall from Chapter 10 that we can derive the aggregate demand schedule from combinations of *IS-LM* equilibrium. Hence, our conclusion that with a fixed exchange rate, the real income effects of fiscal policy actions will be larger than the effects of monetary policy actions implies that:

> **Fiscal policy is a more important determinant of aggregate demand if the exchange rate is fixed and capital is perfectly mobile. With a flexible exchange rate, however, the reverse conclusion follows. Monetary policy has greater effects on aggregate demand if the exchange rate floats and there is perfect capital mobility.**

Since the early 1970s, many industrialized nations have permitted their exchange rates to float. Although central banks and governments have intervened from time to time to influence their nations' exchange rates, for the most part they have allowed market forces to determine currency values. At the same time, these nations have experienced more nearly perfect capital mobility as their financial markets have become more fully integrated. As a result, in these nations monetary policy has almost certainly become a more important determinant of aggregate demand than fiscal policy is.

A Future Bipolar or Tripolar Monetary System?

Greater international financial integration has complicated macroeconomic policymaking for much of the developing world. In the past, developing countries have tried to rely on fiscal policy as their primary tool for

DOLLARIZATION: A country's adoption of the U.S. dollar as its sole medium of exchange, unit of account, store of value, and standard of deferred payment.

stabilizing economic activity. In a world of increasingly integrated financial markets, fiscal policy is a more potent macroeconomic policy instrument when exchange rates are fixed. Central banks in developing nations have often struggled, however, to keep sufficient foreign exchange reserves on hand to successfully maintain fixed exchange rates. As a result, relatively few of these nations have been able to establish credible commitments to their exchange-rate targets.

THE PROMISE OF DOLLARIZATION   As noted in Chapter 15, some countries have sought to circumvent this problem by establishing currency board arrangements, in which an independent agency substitutes for the central bank and issues currency backed 100 percent by a major international currency such as the U.S. dollar. A few nations have taken an even more drastic step by implementing **dollarization,** in which they abandon their own currencies in favor of the direct use of the U.S. dollar. In 2000, for instance, Ecuador eliminated its own currency and adopted the dollar as its circulating currency.

Other Latin American nations have considered the same idea. For the United States, both pros and cons are associated with the dollarization of part of Latin America. Dollarization would make it easier for U.S. companies to do business with Latin America, which accounts for about a fifth of U.S. trade. In addition, increased use of the dollar outside the United States could also create a financial windfall for the U.S. government. Latin American nations would obtain stocks of U.S. dollars for hand-to-hand trade by their residents by offering interest-bearing securities to the U.S. government, which would earn the interest on those securities but would not pay interest on the U.S. currency. Nearly two-thirds of U.S. currency already circulates outside U.S. borders, generating more than $15 billion per year for the U.S. Treasury. Dollarization by Latin American countries undoubtedly would considerably increase the U.S. gain from overseas use of the dollar.

POLICY IMPLICATIONS OF DOLLARIZATION   Nevertheless, Fed and U.S. Treasury officials have expressed concerns about dollarization. If the Fed were to raise interest rates, say, in an effort to contain U.S. inflation, its action might be inappropriate for a dollarized Latin American economy. Thus, such a Fed action could have negative consequences outside the United States, fostering resentment and encouraging policymakers in dollarized countries to deflect blame for their economic problems onto U.S. policymakers. This could give governments of those countries political cover for dodging tough decisions regarding appropriate economic policies for their countries.

Emerging economies in eastern Europe have extended the idea of dollarization to the European Monetary Union's euro. Bulgaria, for instance, announced in 1999 that it might begin using the euro as its official currency. Other eastern European nations have considered the idea as well.

Some commentators have suggested that Russia should contemplate either "euro-izing" or dollarizing its economy. Dollarization might be easier to implement quickly, given that so many Russians already hold dollars. A key argument favoring Russian adoption of the euro is its relatively large trade flows with western European nations.

macro**xtra!**
Economic
Applications

Does "dollarization" benefit developing countries? To review alternative perspectives on this debate and make your own judgment, go to EconDebate Online.
http://macroxtra.swcollege.com

At present, these proposals are no more than ideas that various nations have explored. Nevertheless, in a world of internationally open financial markets, the idea of dollarization (or "euro-ization") has been one reaction to the reduced scope for relatively small countries to credibly conduct independent monetary policies.

Smaller, developing nations may or may not ultimately follow through with dollarization. Nevertheless, central banks in many of these nations gradually have sought to tie their market interest rates to those of the Fed, the European Central Bank, and, to a lesser extent in recent years, the Bank of Japan. In this way, world monetary policy interactions may become increasingly bipolar, or even tripolar, in the future.

FINANCIAL CRISIS: A situation that arises when financial instability becomes so severe that a nation's financial system is unable to function. A financial crisis typically involves a banking crisis, a currency crisis, and a foreign debt crisis.

FOREIGN DIRECT INVESTMENT: An acquisition of foreign financial assets that results in an ownership share exceeding 10 percent.

PORTFOLIO INVESTMENT: An acquisition of foreign financial assets that results in a less than 10 percent ownership share.

FUNDAMENTAL ISSUE #2

How does greater integration of global financial markets affect macroeconomic policymaking? International economic integration refers to increased mobility of goods, services, factors of production, and financial resources across national borders and markets. The continuing trend toward greater integration of national financial markets could ultimately lead to perfect capital mobility. Under perfect capital mobility and fixed exchange rates, fiscal policy actions have their largest possible short-run effects on real income, whereas monetary policy effects are muted. With perfect capital mobility and a floating exchange rate, monetary policy actions have their greatest short-run effects on real income while fiscal policy actions are impotent.

Assessing the Macroeconomic Implications of International Capital Flows

The late 1990s and early 2000s were marked by a series of **financial crises** that swept through Mexico, East Asia, Central Europe, Russia, and South America. A financial crisis is a breakdown in financial activity that brings about a significant drop-off in economic activity. Some economists have argued that increased worldwide mobility of capital has helped to make developing nations more susceptible to financial crises and their negative macroeconomic spillovers.

The Upsurge in International Capital Flows

Economists often classify international capital flows into three categories. The first two of these relate to shares of ownership of the financial assets (stocks and bonds) issued by foreign firms or organizations. One category is **foreign direct investment,** which involves the ownership of at least 10 percent of the financial assets issued by foreign firms or organizations. The second category is **portfolio investment,** or the ownership of less than 10 percent of the financial obligations of foreign firms or organizations. Because foreign direct investment represents a larger commitment of resources, it tends to be a more stable source of capital inflows than portfolio investment, which tends to include more short-term inflows of funds by international investors in search of the highest returns currently available in world markets. The third category includes loans that banks and other privately owned financial institutions make to foreign firms or organizations.

Since 1990, private capital flows to emerging economies have averaged about $150 billion annually. Figure 16–4 illustrates private capital flows to developing nations in the western hemisphere, such as Argentina, Brazil, and Mexico. As you can see, during the early 1990s, this region experienced significant private capital inflows, of which sizable portions were portfolio investment. Note that private capital inflows to these nations declined precipitously as a result of the Mexican financial crisis of 1994–1995. Although capital inflows recovered by 1996, they involved more foreign direct investment and less portfolio investment.

Figure 16–5 depicts the dramatic increase in private capital flows to the developing nations in Asia that began during the middle 1990s. As the figure shows, banks reduced their lending to Asian nations after the financial crises experienced by several of these nations in 1997 and 1998, but flows of foreign direct investment and portfolio investment into these nations have continued.

Figure 16–4 Net Private Capital Flows to Developing Nations in the Western Hemisphere

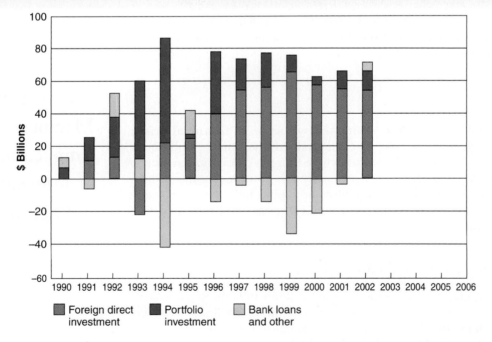

For several years, large portions of the capital inflows into developing nations of the western hemisphere consisted of portfolio investment and bank loans. Financial crises in Latin American nations brought about significant outflows of these forms of private capital after the mid-1990s, and today most capital inflows to these nations are foreign direct investment.

SOURCE: International Monetary Fund.

Figure 16–5   Net Private Capital Flows to Developing Nations in Asia

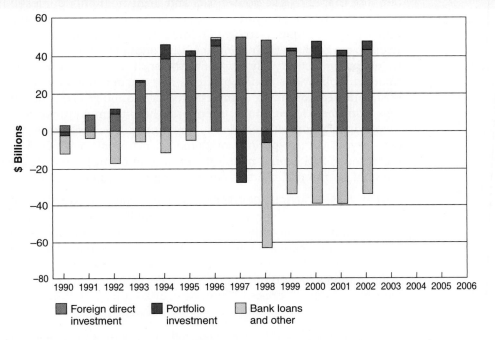

The developing nations in Asia experienced significant out-flows of bank loans during the 1990s, but foreign direct investment has remained relatively stable.

SOURCE: International Monetary Fund.

Capital Mobility and Economic Growth and Stability

Advocates of free mobility of capital across national borders argue that unhindered capital movements allow savings to flow to their most productive use, resulting in a more efficient allocation of scarce resources. In this way, private markets promote productivity enhancements that, as discussed in Chapter 5, contribute to economic growth. Most economists concur that relatively unhindered capital flows are likely to help boost long-term global economic growth. Nevertheless, there is considerable debate about whether freer flows of capital add to or detract from short-term global economic stability.

HOW INCREASED CAPITAL MOBILITY CAN CONTRIBUTE TO GLOBAL ECONOMIC STABILITY
The main reason that households and firms in one country might wish to engage in foreign direct investment, portfolio investment, and lending to residents of another nation is to *diversify risks*. If households and firms were to hold only domestic financial obligations, then when domestic economic downturns occur and cause returns on domestic financial assets to decline, they would miss out on higher returns they could earn in other nations with economies that might be experiencing an upswing.

ECONOMIC FUNDAMENTALS: Basic factors determining a nation's current exchange rate, such as the country's present and likely future economic policies and performance.

SPECULATIVE ATTACK: A concerted effort by financial market speculators to profit from anticipations of the depletion of a nation's official foreign exchange reserves by selling assets denominated in that nation's currency in an attempt to induce the nation to abandon an exchange rate target. If successful, the speculators earn profits in derivative markets.

Efforts by domestic residents to diversify their portfolio risks by holding foreign assets can help to make the domestic economy more stable. Suppose that domestic households and firms hold only domestic financial obligations. In the event of a domestic economic downturn, falling returns on portfolios composed solely of home assets would induce households and firms to cut back on their spending, thus adding to the downturn in domestic economic activity. By way of contrast, if domestic residents also hold financial obligations issued by firms and organizations located in foreign economies experiencing uninterrupted economic growth, then their earnings from their foreign investments can help them continue to spend and invest during domestic economic downturns. They would then repay foreign savers during periods of domestic economic growth. In this way, increased global capital mobility can help to offset business cycles within national economies, thereby contributing to world economic stability.

HOW INCREASED CAPITAL MOBILITY CAN MAKE THE WORLD ECONOMY LESS STABLE   At the same time, however, greater capital mobility can also make it possible for investors to speedily shift funds away from nations. In this way, increased world capital mobility can increase the potential for international financial crises that can contribute to reduced economic stability.

Economists have differing perspectives as to the main causes of international financial crises. They categorize these within three general approaches to understanding the causes of crises:

1. *Economic fundamentals.* The traditional view of financial crises focuses on **economic fundamentals,** which are the underlying factors determining a nation's exchange rate, such as current and likely future monetary and fiscal policies and its future business prospects. According to this view, if foreign exchange traders perceive that the official value of a currency is higher than its true value in private foreign exchange markets based on economic fundamentals, then the traders naturally will tend to sell their holdings of assets denominated in that currency to avoid losses. By unloading these assets, traders who are averse to risk will reduce their losses if the government or central bank runs out of foreign currency reserves used to purchase the currency and maintain the official exchange rate. Furthermore, speculators who anticipate that a central bank may imminently exhaust its official foreign exchange reserves may seek to profit from their expectations by engaging in a **speculative attack** on the nation's official exchange rate. To do this, the speculators sell assets denominated in the nation's currency in an effort to push the government or central bank into giving up its attempt to support the exchange rate at the official target level.

   One example of a misalignment of economic fundamentals that helped trigger a crisis was the situation Argentina faced at the beginning of 2002. Its government had experienced growing budget deficits during the preceding years. Then the economy fell into a recession in 1998, and the government's tax collections plummeted even as many of its debts were coming due. The Argentine peso's value had been equal to 1 U.S. dollar under the nation's currency board arrangement, but the government broke this link to broaden the scope for active monetary policymaking. The Bank of Argentina was ill prepared, however, to limit a decline in the peso's value relative to the dollar. Currency speculators immediately sold off pesos. Within a few weeks, the dollar value of the Argentine currency had declined by more than 50 percent. Then the Argentine government added ammunition for additional speculative attacks on the peso when it limited residents' access to their bank accounts. This only encouraged people who could—mostly people outside Argentine—to sell even more pesos in foreign exchange markets. By the spring of 2002, the peso had lost more than two-thirds of its value relative to the dollar.

2. *Self-fulfilling anticipations.* Another perspective focuses on the potential role of *self-fulfilling anticipations* and contagion effects that, given a slight misalignment of a government's exchange-rate target, can bring about an international financial crisis even when the economic fundamentals are consistent with an officially pegged exchange rate and governments and central banks otherwise have sufficient foreign exchange reserves. According to this view, traders may mount a speculative attack if they merely perceive that a nation's policymakers may find it difficult to maintain the official exchange rate because of the internal costs they would incur; for example, the actions required to defend the exchange rate might be politically unpopular. Thus, the speculative attack takes place simply because the traders expect that it will be successful—not necessarily because the exchange rate is inconsistent with the economic fundamentals. (Some national policymakers have been especially attracted to the self-fulfilling expectations view of financial crises; see on the following page *Management Notebook: Are Currency Speculators Really the "Bad Guys"?*)

3. *Moral-hazard problems.* A final perspective focuses on flaws within the structure of an individual nation's financial system as the major factors that lay the groundwork for a crisis. From this view, crisis conditions exist when governmental policies create rampant *moral-hazard problems* arising from the tendency of unmonitored borrowers to engage in more risky behavior after they receive credit. For instance, suppose that a nation's government requires its banks to make loans to specific firms or industries; because these firms and industries know that they will receive credit no matter how they use the funds, they are more likely to commit the funds to risky undertakings. Many observers of the financial crises in Malaysia and Indonesia during the late 1990s have argued that such moral-hazard problems existed in those nations. Ultimately, these observers conclude, the risks taken on by those who receive government-directed credit generate actual losses and failures, which set off a crisis.

The views of international financial crises that focus on economic fundamentals or self-fulfilling expectations as the impetus for speculative attacks are consistent with the idea that increased global capital mobility

macro**xtra!**
Online
Perspective

One way to try to limit currency speculation is by imposing capital controls, and you can learn much more about their purposes and the experiences countries have had with them by going to the Chapter 16 reading, entitled "An Introduction to Capital Controls," by Christopher Neely of the Federal Reserve Bank of St. Louis. http://macroxtra.swcollege.com

Management NOTEBOOK

Are Currency Speculators Really the "Bad Guys"?

The word *speculator* has never been used to describe someone in a nice way. Particularly in recent years, currency speculators have been the object of especially malicious statements. They have been blamed for not only the downfall of certain economies, but even the supposed near destruction of the world's financial system.

The Head of Malaysia Speaks Up

When the Malaysian government saw its currency, the ringgit, dramatically drop in value a few years ago, Malaysia's leader, Mahathir Bin Mohamad, knew who to blame. The culprits, he concluded, were currency speculators:

> It is said that the value of the currency trade is 20 times that of world traded goods. But apart from the enrichment of the currency traders, what is there to show for this huge trade? On the other hand, we are now witnessing how damaging the trading of money can be to the economies of some countries and their currencies . . . whole regions can be bankrupted by just a few people whose only objective is to enrich themselves and their rich clients.[a]

At an annual meeting of the International Monetary Fund, he declared that currency trading is "unnecessary, unproductive, and immoral."

Are Currency Speculators Really Evil?

If we start with the assumption that currency speculators do not speculate at random, but act only if they think that they can make a profit, then we know one thing for sure. Speculators can make the most profits in the long run by spotting foreign currencies whose values are most clearly out of line with the economic fundamentals of their host coun-

[a]*Wall Street Journal Europe*, September 23, 1997, p. 10.

tries. If currency speculators bet correctly that a currency is improperly priced, then they make a profit. If the speculators are wrong, they incur a loss. In essence, currency trading is no different than buying and selling shares of stocks. Those who bet correctly, win. Those who don't, lose.

According to the International Monetary Fund, some huge currency speculating funds can mobilize between $600 billion and $1 trillion to bet against currencies. One way these funds can place their bets is by selling a currency to be delivered at a future date. They hope that the currency will fall in value before that date so that they can buy it cheaply to satisfy their contracts. These funds do not bet randomly. They spend numerous resources studying economic and political fundamentals in each country. Many of these funds "attack" currencies in countries whose governments have fixed their foreign exchange value. But typically they attack only if they believe this value is out of line with the "real" underlying economy.

Increased Liquidity

A major benefit of currency speculation is that it makes the foreign exchange markets very liquid. Consequently, investors can invest anywhere in the world, knowing that when they want to "get out" there will be a liquid market in the currency in whose value the foreign asset is measured. If speculation were banned, foreign exchange markets would be much less liquid. The result would be much less foreign investment everywhere in the world. There would certainly be less world trade, too.

For Critical Analysis
If you thought that the foreign exchange value of the dollar was going to fall, how could you speculate based on that hunch?

can make the world economy less stable. In addition, even though the moral-hazard perspective emphasizes the importance of financial structures within countries as a proximate cause of financial crises, this view nonetheless indicates that increased capital mobility can expose the fault lines of a weakly structured financial system and contribute to the potential for a crisis.

In what ways can greater worldwide capital mobility add to or detract from international macroeconomic stability?   Households and firms engage in foreign direct investment, portfolio investment, and international lending in an effort to diversify risks. To the extent that they are successful in this endeavor in an environment of increased capital mobility, aggregate household and firm spending is less sensitive to variations in domestic economic activity, and this helps to stabilize the domestic economy. Nevertheless, sudden changes in capital flows can bring about international financial crises that contribute to economic volatility in nations that are recipients of these flows. Although there are alternative views on the causes of such crises, they agree that greater capital mobility can contribute to the likelihood that a crisis will take place and result in negative spillovers on world economic performance.

International Financial Crises and Multinational Policymaking

In spite of years of worldwide effort to develop stable financial systems capable of funneling balanced and diversified sources of funds from domestic and foreign savers to domestic and foreign investors, a number of countries have experienced financial crises. Recognizing that individual countries may be unable to prevent crises and that crises may spread internationally, many of the world's nations have joined together to develop multinational institutions intended to engender multilateral policy cooperation and coordination. These institutions aim both to limit the likelihood of crises and to contain crises when they occur.

The Present Multinational Structure

Two multinational organizations are at the focus of present world efforts to prevent and stem international financial crises: the International Monetary Fund and the World Bank.

THE INTERNATIONAL MONETARY FUND The main multinational institution responsible for addressing international financial crises and their spillovers onto the world economy is the **International Monetary Fund (IMF).** The IMF is a multinational organization with the official task of promoting international monetary cooperation, stable exchange arrangements, and steady economic growth. Panel (a) of Figure 16–6 on the next page charts the growth of the IMF's membership since the organization was founded in 1944. At present the IMF has 182 member nations.

A country that joins the IMF deposits funds to an account called its **quota subscription.** The amount of each nation's quota subscription is based on its real national income. Panel (b) of Figure 16–6 displays current quota subscriptions for selected IMF member nations. Together, the funds contributed by the member nations form a pool from which the IMF can draw to lend to members seeking assistance. A member's quota subscription

INTERNATIONAL MONETARY FUND (IMF): A multinational organization with more than 180 member nations that seeks to encourage global economic growth by promoting international monetary cooperation and effective exchange arrangements and by providing temporary and longer-term financial assistance to nations experiencing balance of payments difficulties.

QUOTA SUBSCRIPTION: The funds deposited by IMF member nations that together form the pool of funds that IMF managers can use for loans to member nations experiencing financial difficulties.

UNIT V Macroeconomic Policy

Figure 16–6   Growth in IMF Membership and IMF Quota Subscriptions

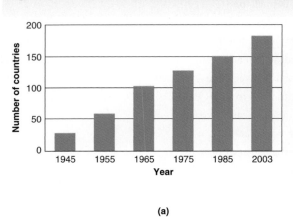

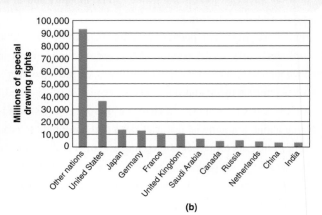

(a)

(b)

As panel (a) shows, the number of member nations in the International Monetary Fund has grown by about six times since the organization was founded. Panel (b) displays the quota subscriptions of the IMF's members, which are denominated in special drawing rights, a unit of account equal to a weighted average of major world currencies. A country's quota subscription determines both its share of voting power within the IMF and the amount it is eligible to borrow under standard IMF credit arrangements.

SOURCE: International Monetary Fund.

CONDITIONALITY: The set of limitations on the range of allowable actions of the government of a country that is a recipient of IMF loans.

EX ANTE CONDITIONALITY: The imposition of IMF lending conditions before the IMF grants the loan.

EX POST CONDITIONALITY: The imposition of IMF lending conditions after a loan has already been granted.

determines how much that member can borrow from the IMF under the organization's standard credit arrangements. It also determines the member's share of voting power within the IMF. The U.S. quota subscription, for instance, is just over 17 percent of the total funds provided by all member nations, so this is the IMF voting share held by the United States.

The IMF provides financial support to a member country under specified rules that place limits on the actions that country's government can take. Under these **conditionality** requirements, the IMF requires the recipient nation's government to cooperate in establishing plans for the nation's financial policies. Often the IMF will not provide assistance to a country unless it implements specific monetary or fiscal policy changes before receiving the loan. This is called *ex ante* **conditionality.** With *ex post* **conditionality,** the IMF imposes conditions after a loan has already been granted. As part of the broader satisfaction of conditionality requirements, the IMF may request only that the country make a general commitment to aim its policies in a certain direction. In this case, known as *low conditionality,* the IMF is said to have a *policy understanding* with the nation. Alternatively, the IMF may impose *high conditionality.* Then it requires a nation to aim for specific, quantifiable monetary or fiscal targets, called *performance criteria.* Failure to meet these targets can lead to suspension of IMF loan disbursements.

Table 16–1 lists the main funding programs offered by the IMF. Originally, the IMF's primary function was to provide so-called stand-by arrangements and short-term credits, and it continues to offer these types

Table 16–1   IMF Financing Facilities

Regular IMF Facilities

- **Stand-by Arrangements (SBA)**   Intended to assist in situations requiring temporary or cyclical adjustments. Arrangements are typically for 12–18 months and are phased in on a quarterly basis, with releases of funds contingent on meeting performance criteria and periodic program reviews.
- **External Fund Facility (EFF)**   Designed to provide assistance in adjusting to problems arising from structural macroeconomic problems for periods of up to 3 years.

Concessional Assistance

- **Poverty Reduction and Growth Facility (PRGF)**   Provides financial assistance via 10-year loans for long-term structural programs intended to foster increased economic growth.
- **Heavily Indebted Poor Countries (HIPC) Initiative**   Provides financial assistance to countries experiencing difficulties in repaying large bilateral and multilateral external debts.

Other Financing Facilities

- **Conpensatory Financing Facility (CFF)**   Intended to assist members experiencing difficulties arising from temporary export declines or increased expenses in importing foodstuffs.
- **Supplemental Reserve Facility (SRF)**   Designed to assist members experiencing sudden and disruptive adjustment problems arising from a loss of market confidence.
- **Contingent Credit Lines (CCL)**   Designed to assist members affected by contagion effects of financial crises originating elsewhere.

SOURCE: International Monetary Fund.

of assistance through *Regular IMF Facilities*. The end of the international gold standard in the early 1970s reduced the need for short-term adjustment credit, however, and the IMF adapted by expanding other lending programs. One of these is *Concessional Assistance,* which the IMF offers to poor and heavily indebted countries, either as long-term loans intended to support growth-promoting projects or as short- or long-term assistance aimed at helping countries experiencing problems in repaying existing debts. The other is *Other Financing Facilities.* Under these funding programs, the IMF seeks to assist any qualifying member experiencing an unusual fluctuation in exports or imports, a loss of confidence in its own financial system, or spillover effects from financial crises originating elsewhere.

THE WORLD BANK   The other multinational institution that provides support to nations experiencing financial problems is the **World Bank.** This institution, which was also created in 1944, is more specialized than the IMF. The World Bank lends specifically to about 100 developing nations with an aim toward reducing poverty and improving living standards. In contrast to the IMF, the World Bank has always specialized in relatively long-term loans used to fund long-term development and growth.

Thus, whereas IMF loans are commonly used to supplement a nation's overall budgetary resources, loans from the World Bank typically fund specific projects, such as improved irrigation systems, better hospitals, and the like. Nevertheless, in recent years some of the World Bank's programs have

WORLD BANK: A multinational institution that specializes in making loans to about 100 developing nations in an effort to promote their long-term development and growth.

overlapped with the IMF's efforts to finance longer-term structural adjustments and debt refinancing activities in heavily indebted nations.

Searching for the Best Mix of Multinational Policies to Promote World Economic Growth and Stability

In recent years, both the IMF and the World Bank have come under two different types of criticisms. One set of critics, while believing that these institutions are correctly designed and structured, contends nevertheless that they could do a much better job of heading off international financial crises and their macroeconomic spillovers before they occur. Another group, however, criticizes the operations of these institutions and, in some cases, even their existence. We will examine some of these criticisms later in this chapter.

INTERNATIONAL CRISIS PREDICTION Like national monetary and fiscal authorities, multinational policymakers face the same types of policy time lags that we discussed in Chapter 15—recognition, response, and transmission lags. In the case of multinational policymaking, however, the recognition lag is likely to be especially problematic. For one thing, multinational policymakers typically lack complete and timely "inside information" about internal economic issues that individual nations face. More broadly, however, anticipating international financial crises is complicated by the existence of several views on their predominant causes, as we discussed above. Consequently, multinational policymakers such as the IMF are currently working to develop better mechanisms for predicting the onset of international financial crises.

Each perspective on the causes of international financial crises points to different factors that might help in predicting them. According to the view that focuses on imbalances in economic fundamentals, variables such as exports, imports, foreign exchange reserves, real income, monetary aggregates, exchange rates, and interest rates might all be useful indicators of the potential for a crisis. In contrast, the perspective emphasizing moral-hazard problems indicates that such changes in economic fundamentals are likely to occur after a crisis is already in progress; hence, variations in economic fundamentals will not necessarily help predict crises far enough in advance to help prevent them. The view that self-fulfilling expectations can induce crises indicates that it may be difficult to find a close relation between fundamentals and crises, because crises may sometimes take place without a previous significant change in fundamentals.

Not only do economists fail to agree on how to predict financial crises, they do not even agree on what constitutes a crisis. For instance, Jeffrey Frankel of Harvard University and Andrew Rose of the University of California propose that a crisis definitely exists when a nation's currency experiences a nominal depreciation of at least 25 percent within a year that follows a depreciation of at least 10 percent the previous year. A number of other economists, however, use more flexible index measures of speculative pressures that take into account exchange-rate changes and variations in foreign exchange reserves. According to this approach, a crisis has occurred when such an index exceeds a threshold that depends on the normal, historical pattern of variation that the index has exhibited in prior years.

Financial Crisis Indicators   In such studies, economists seek to identify economic variables that might serve as **financial crisis indicators,** or factors that typically precede such crises and thereby could aid in predicting them. Morris Goldstein of the Institute for International Economics, Graciela Kaminsky of George Washington University, and Carmen Reinhart of the University of Maryland, for example, considered ratings of countries' debts, such as credit ratings by Moody's and other credit rating bureaus, which might reflect moral-hazard problems. In addition, they evaluated a large set of potential "leading indicators" of financial crises including exchange rates, interest rates, national income levels, quantities of money in circulation, and the like. Such variables, naturally, reflect economic fundamentals that the traditional view of financial crises predicts should play important roles, and these variables also provide important information that traders use to form expectations.

Goldstein, Kaminsky, and Reinhart found that credit ratings do not help predict financial crises. This could be because moral-hazard problems are not a key causal factor in crises, but it is also possible that rating agencies such as Moody's do not have sufficient information to accurately assess the scope of moral hazard and its implications for the true creditworthiness of international borrowers. The authors did find, however, that several economic fundamentals together tend to do a better job of predicting financial crises than any single indicator.

Early Warning Systems   The objective of studies searching for financial crisis indicators is to develop an **early warning system,** or a mechanism for monitoring financial and economic data for signals of trouble that might eventually evolve into a crisis. The idea is that with an effective early warning system, a multinational institution would receive sufficient warning to intervene speedily and head off a crisis before it occurs.

Whether a reliable early warning system can be developed remains problematic, however. Despite some optimism inside and outside the IMF and the World Bank, many economists remain skeptical. Some doubt that any single view of the causes of international financial crises—shifts in economic fundamentals, speculation driven by self-fulfilling expectations, or moral-hazard problems caused by inadequate conditions on domestic or multinational loans—can single-handedly "explain" every crisis. Thus, these skeptics doubt that any early warning system based on a limited set of indicators is likely to improve the capability of multinational institutions to react quickly enough to prevent crises from occurring.

RETHINKING MULTINATIONAL INSTITUTIONS AND POLICIES   The strongest critics of multinational institutions contend that there is little evidence that these institutions have developed the capability to head off financial crises before they occur. Indeed, a number of critics contend that the institutions themselves can contribute to the likelihood of international financial crises by failing to ensure that nations they assist make good use of funds, thereby contributing to moral-hazard problems in international financial markets.

FINANCIAL CRISIS INDICATOR: An economic variable that normally moves in a specific direction and by a certain relative amount in advance of a financial crisis, thereby helping to predict a coming crisis.

EARLY WARNING SYSTEM: A mechanism that multinational institutions might use to track financial crisis indicators to determine that a crisis is on the horizon, thereby permitting a rapid response to head off the crisis.

macro**xtra!**
Economic
Applications

What are the pros and cons of IMF involvement with global economies? To review alternative perspectives on this debate and make your own judgment, go to EconDebate Online.
http://macroxtra.swcollege.com

Accordingly, these critics argue, the world's nations should consider making fundamental reforms in the structure of these institutions.

Most proposals for altering the design of multinational policymaking institutions focus on addressing financial crises. A few of the many proposals relating to this issue are summarized in Table 16–2. They range from making relatively minor changes in existing institutions and procedures to replacing the existing institutions altogether.

Nonetheless, a number of the proposals have several features in common. These include requiring more frequent, in-depth releases of information by

---

Table 16–2   A Sampling of Proposals to Restructure Multinational Policymaking Institutions

National Proposals

- **Canada proposal for emergency standstill clause**   Under this proposal, countries would establish rules for restricting capital outflows that threaten international financial stability.
- **France proposal for an IMF council composed of national finance ministers**   The proposal would upgrade an "Interim Committee" of national finance ministers to the status of the ultimate governing and decision-making body for the IMF.
- **United Kingdom proposal for a standing committee for global financial regulation**   This proposed committee would encompass the IMF, World Bank, and Bank for International Settlements and would establish and implement international standards for financial regulation and economic policymaking.

Private Proposals

- **Calomiris-Meltzer proposals for strict international lending rules**   While these economists' proposals are different in certain respects, they share the idea that current multinational institutions might be replaced with a single institution that makes only short-term loans to illiquid countries.
- **Garten's proposal for a global central bank**   This proposal envisions a new multinational institution overseen by the G-7 and rotating members from emerging economies that would engage in open-market operations using funds raised from members and international taxes.
- **Soros's proposal for an international investor insurance agency**   Under this proposal, nations would create a public corporation that would insure investors against debt defaults up to a specified ceiling level.

International Proposals

- **IMF proposal for internal reforms**   This proposal entails, among other things, requiring borrowers to provide more in-depth financial information, adopting better accounting standards, and releasing more IMF data and information to the public.
- **G-7 proposals for a larger role for private-sector lenders**   This proposal extends the IMF proposal by calling for greater private-sector involvement in providing funds to distressed nations and providing incentives to encourage private lenders to participate.
- **G-22 proposals for greater accountability, stronger financial systems, and crisis containment**   Under this proposal, the IMF would be required to prepare a "Transparency Report" for each nation receiving an IMF loan, nations requesting loans would have to follow common financial and accounting principles, and international loan contracts would contain flexible-payment provisions simplifying loan renegotiations in the event that crises take place.

SOURCE: Barry Eichengreen, *Toward a New International Financial Architecture* (Washington, D.C.: Institute for International Economics, 1999), Appendix A.

both multinational lenders and national borrowers; adopting improved financial and accounting standards for those receiving funds from multinational lenders; making both high and *ex ante* conditionality the norm for IMF lending; and, in several proposals, making increased efforts to induce private lenders to extend credit. Beyond these areas of common ground, however, the proposals typically diverge sharply. Some call for more oversight of the IMF, while others suggest a wholesale change in the IMF's management structure. Still other proposals call for dismantling the IMF and replacing it with new forms of multinational institutions.

So far, few of these proposals have led to actual change. The IMF has adopted some minor changes in its procedures for collecting and releasing information, and it has stiffened some of the financial and accounting standards that borrowers must follow to obtain credit. In addition, a U.S. proposal led to the establishment of Contingent Credit Lines (see Table 16–1), but to this date relatively few nations have made use of this facility.

Naturally, the member nations of the IMF would have to agree to the adoption of the more dramatic proposals for change. To date there has been little movement in this direction. Nevertheless, debate about the desirability of minor changes in the status quo versus potentially significant departures continues. Undoubtedly, proposals for a new direction in multinational policymaking will continue to generate global debate in the years to come.

FUNDAMENTAL ISSUE #4

What are the key multinational policymaking institutions, and what problems do they face in trying to deal with global instabilities caused by international financial crises?   The world's key multinational policymakers are the International Monetary Fund and the World Bank, each of which has more than 180 member nations. A major challenge to multinational policymaking is developing early warning systems to aid in predicting and perhaps even preventing international financial crises. A fundamental problem, however, is that there is not full agreement about why crises occur and, hence, about what indicators should be used to try to predict crises. Proposals for altering multinational policymaking include imposing stronger conditions on the long-term and short-term loans that multinational institutions extend to borrowers, publicizing the internal operations and lending policies of existing institutions, changing the institutions' management structure, supplementing these institutions with additional multinational institutions, or even replacing them with new multinational institutions that would follow different procedures or pursue different objectives.

Inflation, Deflation, and the Choice between Debt and Equity Financing

Around the globe, corporate financial structures appear to depend in part on whether countries experience tendencies for inflation or deflation. This appears to violate a fundamental starting point for the modern theory of finance, called the "Modigliani-Miller theorem," which states that for every additional unit of debt that a company issues, shareholders will simply require a higher rate of return on their equity investment to compensate for the higher risk of bankruptcy. In the simplest of worlds, this basic financial principle should hold whether the price level is rising or falling.

In the real world, however, companies pay taxes, so the choice between debt and equity financing usually does matter, sometimes substantially. The tax structures in many countries give corporate treasurers an incentive to reduce companies' tax bills by taking on more debt. By borrowing instead of issuing new equity shares, companies can reduce their after-tax capital costs and thereby increase their market value.

Another Real-World Complication: A Changing Price Level

Changes in the price level, however, complicate corporate treasurers' calculations of the effects of the differing tax treatments of debt and equity. In most countries, interest payments on debt are tax-deductible, but dividend payments on equity shares are not. Thus, inflation that pushes up nominal profits and stock dividends can also push up a company's tax bill, thereby giving it an incentive to issue more debt instruments instead of additional shares of stock. Higher expected inflation also leads to higher nominal interest rates, which increase the value of debt as a "tax shelter" for a firm that wishes to raise additional funds as cheaply as possible.

Since the late 1940s, corporations around the world have been predisposed to issue debt instead of equity. Tax considerations and inflation together helped to account for this bias in favor of debt.

Recalculating the Debt-Equity Mix in a Deflationary Environment

Since the late 1990s, however, corporate treasurers in a number of countries, especially in parts of Asia, have begun to regard debt as a burden, not a shelter. The reason is that several nations have experienced deflationary episodes in recent years. Deflation, naturally, tends to depress companies' nominal earnings and to reduce nominal interest rates, thereby reducing the "tax-shelter" value of debt relative to equity.

Furthermore, by definition a debt instrument is a promise to repay a nominal sum at a future date. In the early and middle 1990s, many companies around the world continued to issue debt instruments as they had in years past, because they anticipated that continuing inflation would erode the value of their debt repayments. Firms in several locales experienced a rude surprise, therefore, when central banks such as the Bank of Japan and the Bank of Singapore conducted policies that led to bouts of deflation, thereby *increasing* the real value of the firms' nominal debt repayments.

Soon companies in Japan, Singapore, and other nations that experienced deflation were scrambling to try to pay off old debts—in many cases, financing these early debt retirements with funds raised by issuing new equity shares. Of course, a number of factors influence companies' decisions about how to finance their operations. Nevertheless, as Figure 16–7 shows, corporate ratios of debt to equity (also called *leverage ratios*) declined in several nations between the 1980s and 1990s as their average inflation rates decreased.

Research Project

How does deflation complicate a borrower's ability to repay previously accumulated debts? Is it likely to matter whether the deflation is anticipated or unanticipated? How might a multinational corporation's choice between debt and equity financing be influenced by the fact that it may operate in nations with very different central bank policies regarding inflation or deflation?

Web Resources

1. What are debt-equity ratios of various U.S. industries? For these and other financial data for U.S. corporations, go to http://www.stern.nyu.edu/~adamodar/New_Home_Page/data.html. To determine debt-equity ratios, first go to "Capital Structure" and click on "Debt Ratio Trade Off Variables by Industry." The column "MV Debt Ratio" gives the ratio of total debt to the sum of total debt and the market value of equity. To calculate the debt-equity ratio for each industry using market values of equity, divide the ratio in the column by 1 minus that same ratio. (To calculate the ratio of debt to the book value of equity, perform the same calculation using the figures in the "BV Debt Ratio" column.)

2. Where are useful links to sources of corporate financial data? One place to start is http://www.internet-prospector.org/company.html.

Figure 16–7   Falling Inflation Rates and Debt-Equity Ratios in Selected Nations

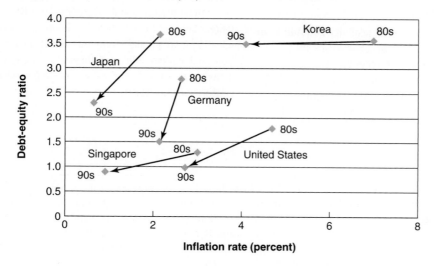

As average inflation rates declined in many nations between the 1980s and 1990s, so did firms' average debt-equity ratios.

SOURCES: Dale Gray and Mark Stone, "Corporate Balance Sheets and Macroeconomic Policy," *Finance and Development*, World Bank, September 1999, pp. 56–59; Stijn Claessens, Simeon Djankov, and Larry Lang, "East Asian Corporates: Growth, Financing, and Risks," World Bank, October 27, 1999; International Monetary Fund, *World Economic Outlook*, various issues.

1. The Pros and Cons of Fixed versus Floating Exchange Rates: The main argument against floating exchange rates is that exchange-rate volatility caused by changing market forces can increase foreign exchange risks. Adopting a fixed exchange rate reduces the potential for such risks to arise, thereby saving people from having to incur costs to hedge against those risks. An important argument against fixed exchange rates is that in nations where workers and other factors of production are relatively immobile, pegging the exchange rate removes a key source of immediate flexibility in relative prices. Thus, a fixed exchange rate eliminates a key means by which the nations' employment and output levels can automatically adjust to changes in international market conditions.

2. How Greater Global Financial Integration Affects Macroeconomic Policymaking: Complete integration of the world's financial markets would permit perfect capital mobility. With perfect capital mobility and a fixed exchange rate, fiscal policy actions have their greatest short-run effects on real income, whereas monetary policy effects on aggregate demand are rendered impotent. Under perfect capital mobility and floating exchange rates, monetary policy actions have their largest possible real income effects, whereas fiscal policy actions have no effects whatsoever.

3. How Greater Worldwide Capital Mobility Can Add to or Detract from International Macroeconomic Stability: Households and firms engage in foreign direct investment, portfolio investment, and international lending in an effort to diversify risks. To the extent they are successful in this endeavor in an environment of increased capital mobility, aggregate household and firm spending is less sensitive to variations in domestic economic activity, and this helps to stabilize the domestic economy. Nevertheless, sudden changes in capital flows can bring about international financial crises that contribute to economic volatility in nations that are recipients of these flows. Although there are alternative views on the causes of such crises, they agree that greater capital mobility can contribute to the likelihood that a crisis will take place and result in negative spillovers on world economic performance.

4. Key Multinational Policymaking Institutions and Problems They Face in Trying to Deal with Global Instabilities Caused by International Financial Crises: The IMF and the World Bank are multinational economic organizations that are owned and operated by more than 180 of the world's nations. These multinational institutions are trying to develop early warning systems that would permit them to predict and more rapidly respond to international financial crises. Nevertheless, it is unclear whether such efforts will bear fruit in light of general disagreement among economists about why crises occur and, therefore, about what indicators multinational policymaking institutions might use to attempt to predict crises. Proposals for redesigning multinational institutions include imposing stricter and more measurable conditions on borrowers, releasing more public information about the internal operations and lending policies of these institutions, creating new management structures for them, or even replacing these multinational institutions.

Self-Test Questions

(Answers to odd-numbered questions may be found on the Web at **http://macro. swcollege.com** under "Student Resources.")

1. Consider a nation whose language is known by few people outside the nation's borders. In addition, legal and natural barriers prevent movements of other factors of production across the nation's borders. The nation's central bank maintains a fixed exchange rate. Recently, demand for the nation's primary products has declined worldwide. Could this nation gain from letting its exchange rate float? Explain your reasoning.

2. Suppose that a nation has perfect capital mobility and a floating exchange rate. Currently, the economy is in a state of recession. Assuming that policy actions leave the price level unchanged, should the nation's fiscal authority or its central bank take the lead in trying to raise real income? Explain your reasoning.

3. In your view, are fixed or flexible exchange rates preferable in a world of increasing financial integration? Take a stand, and justify your position.

4. In a system of fixed exchange rates, does a nation's central bank gain or lose power to induce short-run changes in real income as world financial markets become more fully integrated? Explain.

5. In a system of floating exchange rates, does a nation's fiscal authority gain or lose power to induce short-run changes in real income as world financial markets become more fully integrated? Explain.

6. In the early 1990s, on the heels of a major political restructuring of central and eastern European nations, the IMF granted billions of dollars in loans to Russia. Russia ended up partially defaulting on the loans, rescheduling loan payments, and applying for yet more IMF loans. Then in the late 1990s, in the midst of the fallout from the Asian financial crisis, the IMF granted billions of dollars in additional loans to Russia. Once again, Russia defaulted on loan repayments, postponed many of its payments, and applied for additional IMF funding. Discuss possible reasons for this repetition of IMF-Russian interactions during the 1990s, and offer two proposals for how the IMF and Russia might avoid yet another repetition in the 2000s. Explain why you believe your proposals might be successful.

7. Construct a table with three columns and list each of the views on the causes of international financial crises in the left-hand column. In the second column, list at least one possible financial crisis indicator corresponding to each view that might be tracked in an IMF early warning system for predicting financial crises. In the third column, propose how to evaluate whether each potential indicator you have listed actually helps predict a crisis. Does this exercise help explain why economists have a hard time constructing reliable early warning systems?

8. Table 16–2 on page 506 lists a plan by Jeffrey Garten to establish a global central bank funded by credit lines from national governments and/or revenues from taxes on various international transactions. This central bank would be authorized to conduct open-market purchases and sales of securities issued in the financial markets of member nations. Discuss the strengths and weaknesses that you see in this proposal.

9. Should multinational institutions lend funds at interest rates below, equivalent to, or above private market interest rates? Take a stand, and support your position.

Problems

1. Suppose that a nation has perfect capital mobility, so that the home interest rate, r, equals the world interest rate, r^w, under the assumption of no expected home currency depreciation. The central bank conducts monetary policy to ensure that the exchange rate is fixed. The private payments balance is equal to zero at the current IS-LM equilibrium, and the equations for the IS and LM schedules are given below. Answer the following questions given this information.

$$LM: r = a + (b \times y) - (k \times M). \qquad IS: r = c + (d \times y).$$

   a. What is the value of the interest rate at the current IS-LM-BP equilibrium? (Hint: Recall that capital is completely mobile.)

   b. At the equilibrium interest rate, what is the value of real income? (Hint: You do not have to refer to the LM equation to answer this question.)

(Answers to odd-numbered problems may be found on the Web at **http://macro. swcollege.com** under "Student Resources.")

c. What is the value of the money stock at the current *IS-LM-BP* equilibrium? (Hint: Here you definitely must use the *LM* equation.)

2. This problem is based on your answers to problem 1. The world interest rate rises to a value of $r^{w'}$, which is greater than the initial world interest rate of r^w. The central bank conducts monetary policy to keep the exchange rate unchanged in the face of this interest-rate increase in the rest of the world.

   a. What happens to the equilibrium interest rate for this country?

   b. How does equilibrium income change when the world interest rate rises?

   c. For a new *IS-LM* equilibrium to be attained after the rise in the world interest rate, how must the quantity of money change when the world interest rate rises?

Before the Test

Test your understanding of the material covered in this chapter by taking the Chapter 16 interactive quiz at **http://macro.swcollege.com**.

Online Application

Internet URL: http://www.g7.utoronto.ca

Title: *G8 Information Centre*

Navigation: Go directly to the above URL for the home page of the *G8 Information Centre*. Scroll down to *Summits, Meetings & Documents of the Seven and the Eight* and click on *Summits: Delegations and Documents*. Click on *Köln, Germany*. View the G7 Finance Ministers' report on *Strengthening the International Financial Architecture* by clicking on *Report of G7 Finance Ministers to the Köln Economic Summit*.

Application: Read the report, and answer the following questions:

1. What are the six fundamental reforms recommended by the Finance Ministers?

2. Provide, in your own words, a two- to three-sentence rationale for each of the six reforms.

For Group Study and Analysis: Discuss the reforms and try to identify what steps have been taken since the Köln Summit. Discuss whether national governments, international institutions, private organizations, or some combination of these initiated the reforms you identified. Discuss what remains to be done.

Selected References and Further Reading

Aghion, Philippe, Philippe Bacchetta, and Abhijit Banerjee. "Capital Markets and the Instability of Open Economies." Centre for Economic Policy Research, Discussion Paper No. 2083 (March 1999).

Berg, Andrew, and Catherine Pattillo. "The Challenge of Predicting Economic Crises." *International Monetary Fund Economic Issues* 22 (July 1999).

Choe, Hyuk, Bong-Chan Kho, and René Stulz. "Do Foreign Investors Destabilize Stock Markets? The Korean Experience in 1997." *Journal of Financial Economics* 54 (1999): 227–264.

Council on Foreign Relations Task Force. "The Future of the International Financial Architecture." *Foreign Affairs* 78(6) (1999): 169–184.

Daniels, Joseph, and David VanHoose. "Currency Substitution, Seigniorage, and Currency Crises in Interdependent Economies." *Journal of Economics and Business* 55 (2003), Forthcoming.

Eichengreen, Barry. *Toward a New International Financial Architecture.* Washington, D.C.: Institute for International Economics, 1999.

Frankel, Jeffrey, and Andrew Rose. "Currency Crashes in Emerging Markets: An Empirical Treatment." *Journal of International Economics* 41 (1996): 351–366.

Goldstein, Morris, Graciela Kaminsky, and Carmen Reinhart. *Assessing Financial Vulnerability: An Early Warning System for Emerging Markets.* Washington, D.C.: Institute for International Economics, 2000.

Hutchison, Michael. "A Cure Worse Than the Disease? Currency Crises and the Output Costs of IMF-Supported Stabilization Programs." National Bureau of Economic Research Working Paper No. 8305, May 2001.

International Monetary Fund. *External Evaluation of IMF Assistance: A Report by a Group of Independent Experts.* Washington, D.C., 1999.

Meltzer, Allan. "What's Wrong with the IMF? What Would Be Better?" *Independent Review,* Hoover Institution, Fall 1999.

Neely, Christopher. "An Introduction to Capital Controls." Federal Reserve Bank of St. Louis *Review,* November/December 1999, pp. 13–30.

macro**xtra!**

Log on to the MacroXtra Web site at http://macroxtra.swcollege.com for additional learning resources such as practice quizzes, Interactive Key Graphs, readings, and additional economic applications.

Glossary

ACCOUNTING RISK The possibility that the market value of assets denominated in foreign currencies may vary as a result of changes in exchange rates even when the underlying interest returns on those assets are unaffected.

ADAPTIVE EXPECTATIONS Expectations that are based only on information from the past up to the present.

ADMINISTERED PRICING HYPOTHESIS The view that imperfectly competitive firms set prices of their products at relatively unchanging levels for lengthy intervals.

AGGREGATE DEMAND SCHEDULE (y^d) Combinations of various price levels and levels of real output for which individuals are satisfied with their consumption of output and their holdings of money.

AGGREGATE EXPENDITURES SCHEDULE A schedule that represents total desired expenditures by all the relevant sectors of the economy at any given level of real national income.

AGGREGATE NET AUTONOMOUS EXPENDITURES The sum of autonomous consumption, autonomous investment, autonomous government spending, and autonomous export spending, all of which are independent of the level of national income in the basic Keynesian model.

AGGREGATE SUPPLY SCHEDULE (y^s) Combinations of various price levels and levels of real output that maintain equilibrium in the market for labor services.

AGGREGATION The act of summing up the individual parts of the economy to obtain total measures of economy-wide performance.

APPRECIATION A rise in the value of one nation's currency in terms of the currency of another nation.

ASSIGNMENT PROBLEM The problem of determining whether monetary or fiscal policymakers should assume responsibility for achieving external balance or internal balance objectives.

ASYMMETRIC INFORMATION Information that is possessed by one party to an economic transaction but is unavailable to the other party.

AUTOMATIC FISCAL STABILIZER A mechanism of government policy that automatically reduces volatility in real income caused by changes in autonomous expenditures.

AUTONOMOUS CONSUMPTION Household consumption spending on domestically produced goods and services that is independent of the level of real income.

AUTONOMOUS EXPENDITURES MULTIPLIER A measure of the size of the multiplier effect on equilibrium real income caused by a change in aggregate net autonomous expenditures; in the simple Keynesian model, the multiplier is equal to $1/(MPS + MPIM) = 1/(1 - MPC)$.

AVERAGE PROPENSITY TO CONSUME (APC) Real household consumption of domestically produced goods and services divided by real disposable income; the portion of disposable income allocated to consumption spending.

AVERAGE PROPENSITY TO IMPORT ($APIM$) Real household spending on imports divided by real disposable income; the portion of disposable income allocated to spending on imported goods and services.

AVERAGE PROPENSITY TO SAVE (APS) Real household saving divided by real disposable income; the portion of disposable income allocated to saving.

AVERAGE TAX RATE The ratio of total net taxes to total income.

BALANCE OF PAYMENTS ACCOUNTS A tabulation of all transactions between the residents of a nation and the residents of all other nations in the world.

515

BARTER The direct exchange of goods and services.

BASE YEAR A reference year for price-level comparisons, which is a year in which nominal GDP is equal to real GDP, so that the GDP deflator's value is equal to one.

BEQUEST A sum payable to one's offspring at the time of death.

BP SCHEDULE A set of real income–nominal interest rate combinations that maintains a zero balance for private payments—sometimes called a "balance of payments equilibrium"—in the balance of payments accounts.

BUSINESS CYCLE Fluctuations in aggregate real income above or below its long-run growth path.

CALIBRATION The use of estimated elasticities and real-world data to create artificial data with theoretical models for the purpose of evaluating the extent to which one's theory appears to match real-world observations.

CAMBRIDGE EQUATION An equation developed by economists at Cambridge University, England, which indicates that individuals desire to hold money in proportion to their nominal income.

CAPACITY OUTPUT The real output that the economy could produce if all resources were employed to their utmost.

CAPITAL Goods that people can use to produce other goods and services in the future.

CAPITAL ACCOUNT The balance of payments account that records all nongovernmental international asset transactions.

CAPITAL CONSUMPTION ALLOWANCE The total market value of capital goods that are expended during the process of production.

CAPITAL CONTROLS Legal restrictions on the holdings of foreign currencies or assets by the residents of a nation.

CAPITAL GOOD A good that may be used in the production of other goods and services in the future.

CAPITAL MOBILITY The extent to which funds and financial assets may flow freely across a country's borders.

CENTRAL BANKER CONTRACT A legally binding agreement between a government and a central bank official that holds the official responsible for the nation's inflation performance.

CHAIN-WEIGHT REAL GDP A method of calculating real GDP for a given year that uses prices for both the year in question and the preceding year as weights.

CIRCULAR FLOW DIAGRAM A chart that depicts the economy's flows of income and product.

CLOSED ECONOMY An economy that operates in isolation from the rest of the world.

COMPLEMENTS IN PRODUCTION The term for the situation in which an increased use of capital goods leads to greater use of labor in the production of goods and services.

COMPOUND GROWTH RATE The annual rate at which per capita real GDP accumulates over a given interval.

COMPOUNDED GROWTH Accumulated growth in per capita real GDP over a given interval.

CONDITIONALITY The set of limitations on the range of allowable actions of the government of a country that is a recipient of IMF loans.

CONSERVATIVE CENTRAL BANKER A central bank official who dislikes inflation more than the average citizen in society and is therefore less willing to induce discretionary increases in the growth rate of the quantity of money in an effort to achieve short-run increases in real output.

CONSUMPTION SPENDING Total purchases of goods and services by households.

COOPERATIVE BEHAVIOR An economic setting in which people work together to maximize their joint well-being.

COORDINATION FAILURES Spillover effects between workers and firms that arise from movements in macroeconomic variables that hinder efforts by individual households and firms to plan and implement their consumption, production, and pricing decisions.

COST-OF-LIVING ADJUSTMENT (COLA) A clause in a wage contract that calls for the nominal wage to be adjusted in response to changes in the price level.

COUNTERCYCLICAL FISCAL POLICY A process for managing government spending and taxation so as to smooth out business cycles; the government runs deficits during times of recessions and surpluses during inflationary periods.

COVERED INTEREST PARITY A prediction that the interest rate on one nation's bond will approximately equal the interest rate on another nation's bond plus the forward premium, or the difference between the forward exchange rate and the spot exchange rate divided by the forward exchange rate.

CROWDING-OUT EFFECT The situation when private spending is reduced due to a rise in the real interest rate induced by an increase in the government's deficit.

CURRENCY BOARD A monetary policymaker that is bound to a commitment to issue currency that is backed 100 percent by the currency of another country.

CURRENCY RISK The possibility that rates of return on financial assets denominated in other currencies can fluctuate as a result of changes in exchange rates that cause variations in the market values of those assets.

CURRENT ACCOUNT The balance of payments account that tabulates international trade and transfers of goods and services and flows of income.

CYCLICAL UNEMPLOYMENT The portion of total unemployment resulting from business cycle fluctuations.

DEDUCTION The process of making testable predictions about real-world behavior based on a theoretical framework.

DEPRECIATION A decline in the value of one nation's currency in terms of the currency of another nation.

DEPRESSION An especially severe recession.

DEVALUATION A policy-induced reduction in the exchange value of a nation's currency relative to the currencies of other countries.

DISCOUNT RATE The rate of interest that the Federal Reserve charges to lend to a banking institution.

DISCRETIONARY POLICYMAKING The act of responding to economic events as they occur, rather than proceeding as the policymaker might previously have planned in the absence of those events.

DOLLARIZATION A country's adoption of the U.S. dollar as its sole medium of exchange, unit of account, store of value, and standard of deferred payment.

DOMESTIC VARIABLES Macroeconomic variables that provide information about a nation's economic activity in isolation from the rest of the world.

DYNAMIC MODELS Economic models intended to explain how variables such as real output, employment, and the price level vary over time.

EARLY WARNING SYSTEM A mechanism that multinational institutions might use to track financial crisis indicators to determine that a crisis is on the horizon, thereby permitting a rapid response to head off the crisis.

ECONOMIC FUNDAMENTALS Basic factors determining a nation's current exchange rate, such as the country's present and likely future economic policies and performance.

ECONOMIC GROWTH The annual rate of change in per capita real GDP.

ECONOMIES OF SCALE The realization of reduced average production costs via an increase in the size of a firm's operations through acquisition of new capital.

EFFICIENCY WAGE THEORY An approach to explaining unemployment that is based on the hypothesis that the productivity of workers depends on the real wage rate.

EFFICIENT MARKETS THEORY A theory that stems from applying the rational expectations hypothesis to financial markets; it states that equilibrium bond prices should reflect all past and current information plus bond traders' understanding of how bond prices are determined.

EQUATION OF EXCHANGE An accounting identity that states that the nominal value of all monetary transactions for final goods and services is equal to the nominal value of the output of goods and services purchased.

EQUILIBRIUM REAL INCOME The real income level at which aggregate desired expenditures are equal to the real value of domestic output.

EUROCURRENCY MARKETS Markets for financial assets that are denominated in currencies issued by nations other than the nation in which the financial assets are held.

EX ANTE CONDITIONALITY The imposition of IMF lending conditions before the IMF grants the loan.

EX POST CONDITIONALITY The imposition of IMF lending conditions after a loan has already been granted.

EXCHANGE RATE The value of a nation's currency measured in terms of the currency of another nation.

EXPANSION The period during a business cycle when actual GDP begins to rise, perhaps even above its natural, long-run level.

EXPLICIT CONTRACTS Contractual arrangements in which the terms of relationships between workers and firms, especially about wages, are in writing and legally binding upon both parties.

EXTERNAL BALANCE The attainment of an objective for the composition of a nation's balance of payments.

EXTERNALITY A spillover effect that arises when market exchanges affect the well-being of an individual or firm that is not a party to the exchanges.

FED WATCHING An occupation that involves developing and selling forecasts of Federal Reserve monetary policy actions based on careful examination of the process by which the Fed appears to make its policy decisions.

FEDERAL OPEN MARKET COMMITTEE (FOMC) A group composed of the seven governors and five of the twelve presidents of the Federal Reserve banks that determines how to conduct the Fed's open-market operations.

FINANCIAL CRISIS A situation that arises when financial instability becomes so severe that a nation's financial system is unable to function. A financial crisis typically involves a banking crisis, a currency crisis, and a foreign debt crisis.

FINANCIAL CRISIS INDICATOR An economic variable that normally moves in a specific direction and by a certain relative amount in advance of a financial crisis, thereby helping to predict a coming crisis.

FISCAL POLICY Actions by the government to vary its spending or taxes.

FOREIGN DIRECT INVESTMENT An acquisition of foreign financial assets that results in an ownership share exceeding 10 percent.

FOREIGN EXCHANGE MARKET EFFICIENCY A situation in which the equilibrium spot and forward exchange rates imply a forward premium that is equal to the expected rate of currency depreciation plus any risk premium.

FOREIGN EXCHANGE MARKETS Markets in which currencies of different nations are exchanged.

FOREIGN EXCHANGE RISK The possibility that fluctuations in exchange rates can cause variations in the market values of assets.

45-DEGREE LINE A line that cuts in half the 90-degree angle of the coordinate axes on a diagram relating real income to aggregate desired expenditures; every point on the 45-degree line could, in principle, be a point of equilibrium at which real income equals aggregate desired expenditures.

FORWARD CURRENCY CONTRACTS Agreements to deliver a unit of a nation's currency in exchange for another at a specified price on a given date.

FORWARD EXCHANGE RATE The rate of exchange for currencies specified in forward currency contracts.

FRICTIONAL UNEMPLOYMENT The portion of total unemployment arising from the fact that a number of workers are between jobs at any given time.

GDP PRICE DEFLATOR A flexible-weight measure of the overall price level; equal to nominal GDP divided by real GDP.

GENERAL EQUILIBRIUM ANALYSIS An approach to analyzing the economy by examining the multiple interactions of all individual consumers, workers, and firms.

GOVERNMENT SPENDING Total state, local, and federal government expenditures on goods and services.

GROSS DOMESTIC PRODUCT (GDP) The value of all final goods and services produced during a given period; tabulated using market prices. GDP includes foreign residents' earnings from home production but excludes home residents' earnings abroad.

GROSS INVESTMENT Total spending on capital goods during a year, including depreciation expenditures.

GROSS NATIONAL PRODUCT (GNP) A measure of a nation's total production that includes home residents' earnings abroad but excludes foreign residents' earnings from home production.

HEDGE The act of adopting strategies to reduce the overall risk resulting from fluctuations in market values of assets caused by such factors as exchange-rate volatility.

HUMAN CAPITAL The knowledge and skills possessed by people in a nation's labor force.

IMPERFECT COMPETITION A market environment that may have a limited number of buyers or sellers, barriers to market entry or exit, or differentiated firm products or factor services.

IMPLICIT CONTRACTS Unwritten agreements between workers and firms, concerning terms of employment such as wages; the agreements may or may not be legally binding.

INCOME IDENTITY An identity that states that real national income equals the sum of real household consumption, real household saving, real net taxes, and real imports.

INCOME VELOCITY OF MONEY The average number of times that each unit of money is used to purchase final goods and services in a given interval.

INDUCTION The process of drawing conclusions about real-world behavior from observation of real-world data.

INFLATION BIAS The tendency for the economy to experience continuing inflation as a result of discretionary monetary policy that takes place because of the time inconsistency problem of monetary policy.

INFLATIONARY GAP The amount by which aggregate desired expenditures exceed the level that would cause equilibrium real income to equal its long-run, natural level.

INNOVATION The process by which a new invention is integrated into the economy, where it reduces production costs or provides people with new types of goods and services.

INSIDE MONEY Bank deposit money.

INSIDER-OUTSIDER THEORY The notion that because a firm views its current, "insider" employees as an investment that would be costly to replace, the insiders are able to inhibit the hiring of unemployed "outsiders" at real wages below those earned by the insiders.

INTERGENERATIONAL EXTERNALITIES Spillover effects of economic growth that take years to influence human welfare and therefore have different effects across generations.

INTERGENERATIONAL TRANSFERS Transfers of disposable income, in the form of gifts or bequests, from one generation to another generation.

INTERMEDIATE TARGET A macroeconomic variable whose value a central bank seeks to control because it believes that doing so is consistent with its ultimate objectives.

INTERNAL BALANCE The attainment of the level of real income consistent with the domestic economy's long-run growth path.

INTERNATIONAL ARBITRAGE The act of buying a good in one nation and selling it in another.

INTERNATIONAL MONETARY FUND (IMF) A multinational organization with more than 180 member nations that seeks to encourage global economic growth by promoting international monetary cooperation and effective exchange arrangements and by providing temporary and longer-term financial assistance to nations experiencing balance of payments difficulties.

INVESTMENT SPENDING The sum of purchases of new capital goods, spending on new residential construction, and inventory investment.

LAFFER CURVE A relationship between income tax rates and income tax revenues, which shows that at sufficiently high tax rates, tax rate reductions can increase tax revenues, whereas at lower tax rates, tax rate reductions necessarily reduce tax revenues.

LAW OF DIMINISHING MARGINAL RETURNS The law that states that each successive addition of a unit of a factor of production, such as labor, eventually produces a smaller gain in real output produced, other factors holding constant.

LIQUIDITY CONSTRAINTS Constraints on the availability of cash and credit that people face at points during their lives.

LOANABLE FUNDS The term used by classical economists to refer to the amount of real income that households save, representing claims on real output.

LONG RUN According to the monetarists, an interval long enough that workers can compile full information about aggregate prices and inflation; therefore, expected prices and inflation are equal to actual prices and inflation.

MACROECONOMIC EXTERNALITIES Situations in which aggregate equilibrium in all, or at least many, markets fails to account for spillovers across markets, so that equilibrium aggregate real output, employment, and the price level all differ from their long-run, natural levels.

MACROECONOMIC VARIABLES Aggregate measures of total economic activity.

MACROECONOMICS The branch of economics that focuses on the study of the total economic activity of a nation.

MARGINAL PRODUCT OF CAPITAL (MP_K) The additional output that can be produced following the addition of another unit of capital.

MARGINAL PRODUCT OF LABOR The change in total output resulting from a one-unit increase in the quantity of labor employed in production.

MARGINAL PROPENSITY TO CONSUME (MPC) The additional consumption caused by an increase in disposable income; the change in consumption spending divided by the corresponding change in disposable income; the slope of the consumption function.

MARGINAL PROPENSITY TO IMPORT ($MPIM$) The additional import expenditures stimulated by an increase in disposable income; the change in import spending divided by the corresponding change in disposable income; the slope of the import function.

MARGINAL PROPENSITY TO SAVE (MPS) The additional saving caused by an increase in disposable income; the change in saving divided by the corresponding change in disposable income; the slope of the saving function.

MARGINAL TAX RATE The rate at which tax payments rise when an individual's income increases; the change in taxes divided by the corresponding change in income, $\Delta t/\Delta y$.

MARKET FAILURE The potential failure of a private market equilibrium to reflect all costs and benefits relating to production of a good or service.

MEDIUM OF EXCHANGE Money's role as a means of payment for goods and services.

MERCANTILISM The idea that a primary determinant of a nation's wealth is international trade and commerce. Thus, a nation can gain by enacting policies that spur exports while limiting imports.

MERCHANDISE BALANCE OF TRADE Merchandise exports minus merchandise imports.

MERCHANDISE EXPORTS Domestic firms' sales of physical goods to residents of other nations.

MERCHANDISE IMPORTS Domestic residents' purchases of physical goods manufactured and sold by business firms located abroad.

MICROECONOMIC FOUNDATIONS A basic understanding of the behavior of individual components of the economy that underlies many macroeconomic theories.

MICROECONOMICS The branch of economics that focuses on the study of the allocation of resources and the determination of prices and quantities in individual markets.

MONETARISTS Economists who believe that the main factor influencing aggregate demand is the nominal money stock and that there is not a long-run trade-off between inflation and unemployment.

MONETARY AGGREGATES Measures of the quantity of money in circulation.

MONETARY APPROACH TO THE BALANCE OF PAYMENTS A theory of unsterilized monetary policy under fixed exchange rates; changes in foreign exchange reserves required to maintain a fixed exchange rate cause a nation's money stock to adjust automatically in a direction that leads to attainment of a private payments balance of zero.

MONEY An item that people are willing to accept in exchange for goods and services.

MONEY ILLUSION A situation that exists when economic agents change their behavior in response to changes in nominal values, even though real (adjusted for the price level) values have not changed.

MULTIPLIER EFFECT The ratio of a change in equilibrium real income to an increase in autonomous net aggregate expenditures. When the aggregate expenditures schedule shifts vertically, the equilibrium level of national income changes by a multiple of the amount of the shift.

MULTISECTOR MODELS Macroeconomic models in which the structures of various sectors of the economy correspond to different theories.

NATIONAL DEBT The total accumulation of amounts that the government currently owes to private holders of its debt.

NATIONAL INCOME The sum of all factor earnings, or net domestic product minus indirect business taxes.

NATIONAL INCOME ACCOUNTS Tabulations of the values of a nation's flows of income and product.

NATURAL GDP The level of real GDP that is consistent with the economy's natural rate of growth.

NATURAL RATE OF UNEMPLOYMENT The portion of the unemployment rate that is accounted for by frictional and structural unemployment.

NET EXPORT SPENDING The difference between spending on domestically produced goods and services by residents of other countries and spending on foreign-produced goods and services by residents of the home country.

NET INVESTMENT Gross investment minus depreciation; the result is equal to total expenditures on new capital goods.

NET NATIONAL PRODUCT GNP minus depreciation, or national income plus indirect business taxes.

NEW GROWTH THEORY A theory of economic growth that focuses on productivity growth as a key determinant of technological progress and the rate of growth of an economy.

NOMINAL GROSS DOMESTIC PRODUCT (NOMINAL GDP) The value of final production of goods and services calculated in current dollars with no adjustment for the effects of price changes.

NONCOOPERATIVE BEHAVIOR An economic setting in which people look out for their own well-being without regard for the well-being of others.

OBSERVATIONAL EQUIVALENCE The fact that the basic version of the modern Keynesian theory, which assumes sticky wages, makes some of the same fundamental policy predictions as the new classical model, which is based on pure competition with completely flexible wages.

OFFICIAL SETTLEMENTS BALANCE A balance of payments account that records international asset transactions involving agencies of home and foreign governments.

OPEN ECONOMY An economy that is linked by trade with other economies of the world.

OPEN-MARKET OPERATIONS The Federal Reserve's purchases or sales of U.S. government securities.

OPTIMAL CURRENCY AREA A region in which fixed exchange rates can be maintained without inhibiting prompt internal adjustments of employment and output to changes in international market conditions.

OUTSIDE MONEY Money in the form of currency and bank reserves.

PEAK The point along a business cycle at which real GDP is at its highest level relative to its long-run, natural level.

PERFECT CAPITAL MOBILITY A situation in which financial resources are as mobile across a nation's boundaries as they are within those boundaries.

PHILLIPS CURVE A curve that shows an inverse relationship between inflation and unemployment rates.

POLICY CREDIBILITY The believability of a commitment by a central bank or governmental authority to follow specific policy rules.

POLICY INEFFECTIVENESS PROPOSITION The new classical conclusion that if policy actions are anticipated, they have no real effects in the short run; nor do policy actions have real effects in the long run even if the policy actions are unanticipated.

POLICY RULE A commitment to a fixed strategy no matter what happens to other economic variables.

POLICY TIME LAG The time interval between the need for a countercyclical monetary policy action and the ultimate effects of that action on an economic variable.

PORTFOLIO INVESTMENT An acquisition of foreign financial assets that results in a less than 10 percent ownership share.

PRICE INERTIA A tendency for the price level to resist change over time.

PRIVATE PAYMENTS BALANCE The sum of the current account

balance and the private capital account balance, or the net total of all private exchanges between U.S. individuals and businesses and the rest of the world.

PRODUCT IDENTITY An identity that states that real national product is the sum of real household consumption, real realized investment, real government spending, and real export spending.

PRODUCTION FUNCTION A relationship between possible quantities of factors of production, such as labor services, and the amount of output of goods and services that firms can produce with current technology.

PROGRESSIVE TAX SYSTEM A system of taxation in which the amount of a tax that a person must pay increases as a percentage of the individual's income as that income rises.

PROPORTIONAL TAX SYSTEM A system of taxation in which the amount of a tax that a person must pay remains a constant percentage of the individual's income as that income rises.

PUBLIC CHOICE THEORY A hypothesis that views central banks and government policymakers as policymaking bodies composed of individuals who pursue their own self-interest.

PUBLIC INTEREST THEORY A hypothesis that regards central banks and government policymakers as public servants that pursue the broad interests of society as a whole.

PURCHASING POWER PARITY A condition that states that if international arbitrage is possible, then the price of a good in one nation should be the same as the price of the same good in another nation, adjusted for the exchange rate.

PURE COMPETITION A situation in which there are large numbers of buyers and sellers in a market for a good, service, or factor of production and in which no single buyer or seller can affect the market price.

QUANTITATIVE THEORY An approach to macroeconomic theorizing in which a model is evaluated by comparing the movements in artificial data generated by the model itself with the behavior of real-world macroeconomic data.

QUANTITY THEORY OF MONEY The theory that people hold money for transactions purposes.

QUOTA SUBSCRIPTION The funds deposited by IMF member nations that together form the pool of funds that IMF managers can use for loans to member nations experiencing financial difficulties.

RATIONAL EXPECTATIONS HYPOTHESIS The idea that individuals form expectations based on all available past and current information and on a basic understanding of how the economy works.

REAL CONSUMPTION The real amount of spending by households on domestically produced goods and services.

REAL DISPOSABLE INCOME A household's real after-tax income.

REAL EXPORTS The real value of goods and services produced by domestic firms and exported to other countries.

REAL GROSS DOMESTIC PRODUCT (REAL GDP) A price-adjusted measure of aggregate output, or nominal GDP divided by the GDP price deflator.

REAL IMPORTS The real flow of spending by households on goods and services produced by firms in other countries.

REAL INTEREST RATE The nominal interest rate minus the expected rate of inflation.

REAL NET TAXES The amount of real taxes paid to the government by households, net of transfer payments.

REAL REALIZED INVESTMENT SPENDING Actual real expenditures by firms in the product markets.

REAL SAVING The amount of income that households save through financial markets.

REAL-BUSINESS-CYCLE THEORY An approach to macroeconomic theory in which variations in technology and productivity are the key factors accounting for cyclical fluctuations in real output.

RECESSION A decline in real GDP lasting at least two consecutive quarters, which can cause real GDP to fall below its long-run, natural level.

RECESSIONARY GAP The amount by which aggregate desired expenditures lie below the level that would cause equilibrium real income to equal its long-run, natural level.

RECOGNITION LAG The interval between the need for a counter-cyclical policy action and the recognition of this need by a policymaker.

REGRESSIVE TAX SYSTEM A system of taxation in which the amount of a tax that a person must pay declines as a percentage of the individual's income as that income rises.

REPRESENTATIVE AGENT ASSUMPTION The assumption that all people in an economy have access to the same information and have the same understanding of how the economy works.

RESERVE REQUIREMENTS Federal Reserve rules mandating that banks maintain reserve holdings that are proportional to the dollar amounts of transactions accounts.

RESPONSE LAG The interval between the recognition of a need for a countercyclical policy action and the actual implementation of that action.

RICARDIAN EQUIVALENCE PROPOSITION The proposition that if government spending will be unchanged in the future, people regard a current tax cut as equivalent to a future tax increase and therefore save the proceeds of a tax cut rather than increasing their consumption.

SHORT RUN According to the monetarists, an interval short enough that workers do not have complete information about aggregate prices and inflation; therefore, expected prices and inflation may differ from actual prices and inflation.

SMALL MENU COSTS The costs firms incur when they make price changes, including both the costs

of changing prices in menus or catalogues and the costs of renegotiating agreements with customers.

SPECULATIVE ATTACK A concerted effort by financial market speculators to profit from anticipations of the depletion of a nation's official foreign exchange reserves by selling assets denominated in that nation's currency in an attempt to induce the nation to abandon an exchange rate target. If successful, the speculators earn profits in derivative markets.

SPOT EXCHANGE RATE The rate of exchange for currencies to be traded immediately

STAGFLATION The simultaneous observation of rising inflation rates and declining real output and rising unemployment rates.

STANDARD OF DEFERRED PAYMENT Money's role as a means of valuing future receipts in loan contracts.

STANDARD OF LIVING The capability of an average resident of a nation to consume goods and services.

STERILIZATION A central bank action to prevent variations in its foreign exchange reserves from affecting the total amount of money in circulation.

STORE OF VALUE A function of money in which it is held for future use without loss of value.

STRATEGIC INTERACTIONS The interdependence of economic decisions that people make individually or as part of groups.

STRUCTURAL UNEMPLOYMENT The portion of

total unemployment resulting from a poor match of workers' abilities and skills with current needs of employers.

SUBSTITUTES IN PRODUCTION The term for the situation in which increased use of capital leads to reduced use of labor in the production of real output.

SUPPLY SHOCKS Changes in the position of the aggregate supply schedule caused by significant changes in the costs of factors of production or in technological capabilities.

SUPPLY-SIDE ECONOMICS A school of economic thought that promotes government policies intended to influence real GDP by affecting the position of the economy's aggregate supply schedule.

TIME INCONSISTENCY PROBLEM A policy problem that can result if a policymaker has the ability, at a future time, to alter its strategy in a way that is inconsistent both with the desires and strategies of private individuals and with its own initially announced intentions.

TIME SERIES Observed values of macroeconomic variables over successive time intervals.

TRANSACTION RISK The possibility that the value of a financial asset involved in funding an exchange denominated in a foreign currency could vary with exchange-rate movements, thereby affecting the underlying value of the transaction.

TRANSFER PAYMENTS Governmentally managed income redistributions.

TRANSMISSION LAG The interval that elapses between the implementation of an intended counter-cyclical policy and its ultimate effects on an economic variable.

TROUGH The point along a business cycle at which real GDP is at its lowest level relative to the long-run natural GDP level.

ULTIMATE GOALS The final objectives of macroeconomic policies.

UNCOVERED INTEREST PARITY A prediction that the interest rate on a bond denominated in a currency that is expected to depreciate must exceed another nation's bond rate by the rate at which the currency is expected to depreciate plus a risk premium.

UNEMPLOYMENT The number of people who are interested in finding a job but currently do not have one.

UNEMPLOYMENT RATE The percentage of the civilian labor force that is unemployed.

UNIT OF ACCOUNT A function of money in which it is used as a measure of the value of goods, services, and financial assets.

VALUE OF THE MARGINAL PRODUCT OF LABOR The marginal product of labor times the price of output.

WAGE INDEXATION The automatic adjustment of contract wages to changes in the price level.

WORLD BANK A multinational institution that specializes in making loans to about 100 developing nations in an effort to promote their long-term development and growth.

Index